DICKENS STUDIES ANNUAL
Essays on Victorian Fiction

DICKENS STUDIES ANNUAL

Essays on Victorian Fiction

DICKENS
STUDIES
ANNUAL

Essays on Victorian Fiction

VOLUME
37

Edited by
Stanley Friedman, Edward Guiliano,
Anne Humpherys, and Michael Timko

AMS PRESS
New York

International Standard Book Number
Series ISBN-10: 0-404-18520-7 / Series ISBN-13: 978-0-404-18520-6
Vol. 37 ISBN-10: 0-404-18937-7 / Vol. 37 ISBN-13: 978-0-404-18937-2

Dickens Studies Annual: Essays on Victorian Fiction welcomes essay- and monograph-length contributions on Dickens and other Victorian novelists and on the history of aesthetics of Victorian fiction. All manuscripts should be double-spaced and should follow the documentation format described in the most recent *MLA Style Manual*. The author's name should appear only on a cover-page, not elsewhere in the essay. An editorial decision can usually be reached more quickly if two copies of the article are submitted, since outside readers are asked to evaluate each submission. If a manuscript is accepted for publication, the author will be asked to provide a 100- to 200-word abstract and also a disk containing the final version of the essay. The preferred editions for citations from Dickens's works are the Clarendon and the Norton Critical when available, otherwise the Oxford Illustrated or the Penguin.

Please send submissions to The Editors, *Dickens Studies Annual*, Ph.D. Program in English, The Graduate Center, CUNY, 365 Fifth Avenue, New York, NY 10016–4309. Please send inquiries concerning subscriptions and/or the availability of earlier volumes to AMS Press, Inc., Brooklyn Navy Yard—Unit #221, 63 Flushing Ave., Brooklyn, NY 11205–1054.

Manufactured in the United States of America

All AMS books are printed on acid-free paper that meets the guidelines for performance and durability of the Committee on Production Guidelines for Book Longevity of the Council on Library Resources.

Contents

Illustrations

Preface

The essays in this volume offer stimulating approaches to various novels by Dickens, a new perspective on his family relationships, and a fresh look at Wilkie Collins's best-known book.

We are indebted to all of the scholars and critics who submitted their work, and we have as always greatly, and gratefully, benefited from the recommendations of many generous outside reviewers, readers who assist us with their expertise and their willingness to offer helpful suggestions to our contributors.

This issue also contains a large number of survey essays intended to offer guidance through the increasingly crowded terrain of scholarly studies. Several of these surveys were scheduled for prior issues but were postponed because of their authors' other responsibilities.

We express our gratitude to the following for their valuable survey articles: Kay Li, who discusses distinctive ways in which various Chinese critics view Dickens; Terri A. Hasseler, who offers a thorough consideration of Dickens studies appearing in 2004; Mark Turner, who reviews many new scholarly and critical works on Trollope; Grace Moore, who describes the relevance of recent studies of colonialism in Victorian fiction to such areas as feminism, class relations, and racial concerns; Linda K. Hughes, who describes how recent studies of nineteenth-century women narrative poets point to opportunities for further scholarship; Talia Schaffer, who charts the directions taken by recent work on British non-canonical women novelists writing in the second half of the nineteenth century; and Roger G. Swearingen, who provides a detailed survey of scholarly work done over the last thirty-five years in three areas—editions of the letters of Robert Louis Stevenson, reference books on him, and editions of his literary writings. (In a subsequent volume of *DSA*, this scholar will examine biographical and critical works on Stevenson. We thank Ian Campbell for recruiting Roger Swearingen for us.)

For practical help, we express our gratitude to the following administrators: President William P. Kelly; Acting Provost Linda N. Edwards; Ph. D. Program in English Executive Officer Steven F. Kruger; Marilyn Weber, Assistant Program Officer, Ph. D. Program in English; and Meghan Mehta, Assistant Program Officer, Ph. D. Program in English, all of The Graduate Center,

CUNY; and President James L. Muyskens; Dean of Arts and Humanities Tamara S. Evans; and Department of English Chair Nancy R. Comley, all of Queens College, CUNY.

We also thank John O. Jordan, Director of The Dickens Project at the University of California, Santa Cruz; JoAnna Rottke, Project Coordinator for The Dickens Project; and Jon Michael Varese, the Project's Research Assistant and Web Administrator, for placing on the Project's website the tables of contents for volumes 1–27 of *DSA*, as well as abstracts for subsequent volumes. (These materials are included in the Project's Dickens Electronic Archive.) The Dickens Project can be reached at <http://humwww.ucsc.edu/dickens/index.html>.

We extend thanks to Gabriel Hornstein, President of AMS Press, for his confidence and his enthusiastic support; to Jack Hopper, who, although retired as Editor-in-Chief at AMS Press, continues to give extremely valuable assistance to *DSA*; and to Ashlie K. Sponenberg, now Editor-in-Chief at AMS Press, who has offered sound advice and pleasing encouragement. In addition, we deeply appreciate the conscientious and very skillful work of our editorial assistant for this volume, Alyssa Pelish.

—The Editors

The Editors are delighted to announce that in preparing future volumes they will be joined by Professor Talia Schaffer, of The Graduate Center, CUNY, and Queens College, CUNY, an outstanding scholar who has made numerous contributions to Victorian Studies.

Notes on Contributors

JOHN BOWEN is Professor of Nineteenth-Century Literature at the University of York. His publications include *Other Dickens: Pickwick to Chuzzlewit* (2000), the Penguin edition of Dickens's *Barnaby Rudge* (2003), and, co-edited with Professor Robert L. Patten, *Palgrave Advances in Charles Dickens Studies* (2005). He has held visiting posts at the University of Warwick and the University of California, Santa Cruz, is a member of the faculty of the University of California Dickens Project, and is a Fellow of the English Association.

SEAN C. GRASS is Associate Professor of Victorian literature at Texas Tech University, where he specializes in fiction, non-fiction prose, and the Victorian literary market. He is the author of *The Self in the Cell: Narrating the Victorian Prisoner*. His ongoing project, "'Portable Property': Theft and the Commodification of Identity in Victorian Narrative," is a book-length study of autobiography, sensation fiction, and anxieties regarding identity and property in the mid-Victorian literary market.

TERRI A. HASSELER is Professor and Chair of the Department of English and Cultural Studies at Bryant University. She is co-editor with Sue Lonoff of the Modern Language Association's *Approaches to Teaching Emily Brontë's* Wuthering Heights (2006). She has published articles on British women and imperial travel and postcolonial literature and theory. Her recent research has been on corporate, commercial, and capitalist practices within the academy.

LINDA K. HUGHES, Addie Levy Professor of Literature at TCU in Fort Worth, works on Victorian writing in the context of gender and publishing history. Recent publications include "Women Poets and Contested Spaces in *The Yellow Book*," in *Studies in English Literature*, and *Graham R.: Rosamund Marriott Watson, Woman of Letters* (2005). Her edition of Elizabeth Gaskell's stories in *Cornhill Magazine* and *All the Year Round*, 1859–1864, is forthcoming from Pickering & Chatto. She is currently completing *The Cambridge Introduction to Victorian Poetry*.

JAMES R. KINCAID is the author of nine or so books, some of which, he assures us, still do good in the world. A recent novel, *A History of the African American People (Proposed) by Strom Thurmond, as told to Percival Everett and James Kincaid*, marks what one can only hope will be a permanent turn away from literary criticism. He is Aerol Arnold Professor of English at the University of Southern California.

LINDA M. LEWIS is the Margaret H. Mountcastle Distinguished Professor of Humanities at Bethany College in Kansas, where she teaches English literature and composition. Lewis's research interest is nineteenth-century British literature; her recent books on Victorian authors are *Elizabeth Barrett Browning's Spiritual Progress* (1998) and *Germaine de Staël, George Sand, and the Victorian Woman Artist* (2003). Her article in this *DSA* issue was written in a 2003 NEH seminar of the Dickens Project at the University of California at Santa Cruz.

KAY LI teaches global studies at Wilfrid Laurier University and is currently doing research at the Asian Institute, Munk Centre for International Studies, University of Toronto. Dr. Li's publications, which include the forthcoming *Bernard Shaw, China: Cultural Encounters*, focus on transnational literary and cultural transmission, as well as on the intersection of arts and technologies in contemporary films. She is a founding member of the International Shaw Society and an executive director of the Canadian Foundation for Asian Culture.

GRACE MOORE teaches at the University of Melbourne, Australia. She is the author of *Dickens and Empire* (2004) and the editor (with Andrew Maunder) of *Victorian Crime, Madness and Sensation* (2004). She is currently editing a collection of essays on Victorian piracy and writing a monograph tentatively entitled *Victorian Metamorphoses*.

LILLIAN NAYDER is Professor of English at Bates College, where she teaches courses on nineteenth-century British fiction. Her books include *Wilkie Collins* (1997) and *Charles Dickens, Wilkie Collins, and Victorian Authorship* (2002). She is currently writing a biography of Catherine Dickens.

SETH RUDY is pursuing a Ph.D. in English and American literature at New York University. His dissertation will examine writing for posterity, literary endurance, and the durability of knowledge in the eighteenth century, as well as the relationship between the individual author and generic development. His other interests include Early Modern politics, satire, and the novel.

TALIA SCHAFFER is an associate professor of English at Queens College and the Graduate Center, CUNY. Her books include *The Forgotten Female Aesthetes: Literary Culture in Late-Victorian England* (2001); *Women and British Aestheticism* (1999), co-edited with Kathy A. Psomiades; and a forthcoming reader, *Literature and Culture at the Fin de Siècle*. She has published widely on late-Victorian non-canonical novels, women's writing, and material culture. Her book in progress analyzes the Victorian domestic handicraft as a model for mid-Victorian realism.

ROGER G. SWEARINGEN is best known for his authoritative guide to the writing and publication of Stevenson's prose works, *The Prose Writings of Robert Louis Stevenson: A Guide* (1980) and for the discovery of RLS's first published work of fiction, *An Old Song* (1877), using manuscript and other sources at Yale (1982). He is currently the website architect for a major electronics firm in Santa Rosa, California, and is at work on a full-length biography, *Robert Louis Stevenson: Spirit of Adventure*.

MARK W. TURNER teaches in the department of English at King's College London. He is the author of *Trollope and the Magazines* (2000), *Backward Glances: Cruising the Queer Streets of New York and London* (2003), and co-editor with Caroline Levine of *From Author to Text: Re-Reading George Eliot's* Romola (1998). He co-edits the journal *Media History* and is currently co-editing the journalism of Oscar Wilde.

DEBORAH WYNNE is the author of *The Sensation Novel and the Victorian Family Magazine* (2001). She has also published essays on Dickens, Gaskell, and Ellen Wood and is currently working on a book, *The Object Lesson: Portable Property and the Victorian Novel*. She currently teaches at the University of Chester, UK.

A Garland for *The Old Curiosity Shop*

*The Old Curiosity Shop is a more significant and sophisticated text
than is often recognized, and one that has a peculiar significance for
Dickens's autobiographical self-understanding. These two qualities are
particularly evident in the sharing of certain figures and tropes between
the novel and the extracts from Dickens's "Autobiographical Fragment" printed in John Forster's Life of Charles Dickens. This article
traces some of the most significant of these—in particular the figure of
the floral garland, which forms a particularly overdetermined framework into which is woven much of the affective force both of Dickens's
autobiographical recollection and his staging of the relation of Truth
and mourning in the novel. It argues that* The Old Curiosity Shop *is as
anthological as it is allegorical and that that the contrasting psychic
and narrative investments—festive and mourning, united and dispersed,
hollow and enclosed—that the garland permits are both fascinating and
moving in themselves and offer the possibility of rethinking the ways in
which we seek to bind together "critical" and "biographical" accounts
of Dickens's life and writing.*

1

In June 1841, Charles Dickens, the acclaimed young author of *The Pickwick
Papers*, *Oliver Twist*, *Nicholas Nickleby,* and the recent great success *The
Old Curiosity Shop*, made a triumphal visit to the city of Edinburgh to meet
the distinguished literary figures of the city. The visit climaxed with a dinner
for men only in honor of the twenty-nine-year-old Boz. After the meal, 150

Dickens Studies Annual, Volume 37, Copyright © 2006 by AMS Press, Inc. All
rights reserved.

ladies were admitted, including Kate Dickens, to hear the speeches, of which Dickens himself made three. It is often thought that Dickens was a rather naive artist who, particularly in his early years, wrote in a rather instinctive and unself-conscious way. Yet it is increasingly clear how often and how interestingly he reflects on his art and fiction in his journalism, letters, and speeches. The speech in Edinburgh is just such an occasion, and Dickens there discusses perhaps the most criticized scene in all his work: the death of Little Nell. The charge that he responds to, though, is not that Nell's death was overly sentimental, as many later readers have felt, but that Nell should not have died at all. This is what he says:

> I am anxious and glad to have an opportunity of saying a word in reference to one incident in which I am happy to know you were interested and still more happy to know, though it may sound paradoxical, that you were disappointed: I mean the death of the little heroine. When I first conceived the idea of conducting that simple story to its termination, I determined rigidly to adhere to it, and never to forsake the end I had in view. Not untried in the school of affliction, in the death of those we love, I thought what a good thing it would be if in my little work of pleasant amusement, I could substitute a garland of fresh flowers for the sculptured horrors which disgrace the tomb.   (10)

There are many interesting things about this scene and passage, including the presentation of the public role of its author, the public defense of his art, and its moral and educative purpose that he makes, and the gender difference so emphasized, both in Dickens's speech and in the organization of public space. The most striking phrase, though, is the one in which Dickens describes his purpose: to "substitute a garland of fresh flowers for the sculptured horrors which disgrace the tomb."

The novel, he says, is a garland and not a monument, a ring of flowers and not a statue. Nell has to die in order to permit a different kind of mourning and writing, that is not inert and monumental, but perennially fresh and new. John Ruskin famously remarked about Dickens that he chose to speak "in a circle of stage fire" (Collins 314). Here, it is a circle not of flames but of flowers, and it is only this frail garland that can take the place of, and thus take us away from, the intense loathing and fear that death and its monuments produce. "Sculptured horrors" is a strong phrase and seems to be related to the simultaneous fascination and repulsion that Dickens's characters often feel towards material icons of the dead: Mrs. Jarley's waxworks seem to Nell "so like living creatures, and yet so unlike in all their grim stillness and silence, that she had a kind of terror of them for their own sakes" (222). *The Old Curiosity Shop*, unlike a statue or a waxwork, is a garland, says Dickens, that can grace and not disgrace the tomb, can make the moribund floribund. If the novel can succeed in this, Dickens tells his Edinburgh audience, it will be something that he "will be glad to look back upon in after life." "After life" means both in later life and after death. Dickens imagines himself, looking back with pleasure on mourning, without horror or sculpture, the death of Nell, when he himself is older, or possibly dead.

The Old Curiosity Shop is full of horrors, sculptured and otherwise, both near and far from tombs. One of the most terrifying of these is when Quilp suddenly appears near the gateway of the town at which Mrs. Jarley and Nell have just arrived "like some monstrous image that had come down from its niche" (212). Against such horrors and sculptures, Dickens tells us he wishes to place a garland. Flower stands against stone. Behind this pairing, of stone and flowers, lies a long tradition of relationship and opposition. Jacques Derrida's great exposition and deconstruction of Hegel's *Phenomenology of Mind* in *Glas* (which, of course, means the tolling or knelling of a bell), for example, takes as one its main texts the moment in Hegel when a religion of flowers yields to and becomes a religion of stones and columns, in which, for Hegel, "the innocence of the flower religion" gives place to "the earnestness of warring life, to the guilt of animal religions" (420). Derrida plays off and entwines together Jean Genet's obscene masterpiece *Our Lady of the Flowers* and Hegel's transition from flower religion to the religion of stone and columns: his text is full of the columns of printed text, the male erection, of statues and temple columns. Similar forces are at work in *The Old Curiosity Shop*, as Dickens entwines together the floral innocence, chastity, and spirituality of Nell with the phallic, Gothic, grotesque, oral, sadistic, obscene sexuality of Quilp, that "dismounted nightmare" (372), that monstrous statue come down from its niche.

The flower, for Hegel, is a determinate moment in the movement of spirit, but it also has a particular significance in the history of writing. Another word for a trope or figure of speech, for example, is "flower," as when we talk about flowers of rhetoric; all the many flowers and garlands of *The Old Curiosity Shop* are also matters of writing and rhetoric. The flower is also important for discourses of the aesthetic and the beautiful. For Immanuel Kant in the *Critique of Judgement*, for example, "Flowers are free beauties of nature . . . designs *à la grecque*, foliage for framework or on wall-papers, etc., have no intrinsic meaning; they represent nothing—no Object under a definite concept—and are free beauties. (72). Behind and alongside these flowers, of spirit, of rhetoric, and of beauty, there is a long tradition of thought that relates death to flowers, as Dickens reminds us in chapter 16, where he alludes to the Book of Isaiah: "All Flesh is grass, and all the goodliness thereof is as the flower of the field; the grass withereth, the flower fadeth, because the spirit of the Lord bloweth upon it" (Isaiah 40:6). In the movement of spirit, in rhetoric and writing, in the aesthetics of the beautiful, and in the thought of death, flowers and the flowers of flowers, seem inescapable, our language and thought constantly treading on, tangled in, or intertwined with them, as in the garland that Dickens sought to place on Nell's tomb.

These flowers, which are neither simply literary nor philosophical, figurative nor real, natural nor theological, are often contrasted with, or seen in opposition to, the monumental or the geological, to stand against or twine across immemorial rocks and memorial stones. In the work of Wordsworth and Ruskin, for example, there are constant interplays between stones and rocks, the monumental or geological, on the one hand, and the floral, on the other. Oscar Wilde said that it would take a heart of stone to read the death of little Nell without laughing; part of the brilliance of that remark is the way that it picks up the deep desire of the book to find readers with hearts not of stone but of flowers (Wyndham 119).

Dickens says in the Edinburgh speech, though, not that the novel is a flower but a garland. We make a garland if we weave or bind flowers together into a band or circle, into a kind of frame, with a hollow or blank at its core. Garlands have been used over many centuries for many purposes: to celebrate a victory, a poetic or military achievement, a wedding or festivity, to decorate a shrine or pay homage to a god, or to commemorate and mourn. There are various synonyms for garland, such as "chaplet," "diadem," and, most commonly, "wreath." Another is "anthology," from the Greek "anthos" meaning "flower," a gathering of short or particularly fine literary pieces or extracts. The novel both appears in an anthology of sorts—*Master Humphrey's Clock*—and is in many ways an anthology itself, full of scenes that seem easily detachable, like a set of turns in a variety show or a circus.

Critics, too, are anthologists, makers of garlands. Any act of criticism entails selecting, by cutting out certain passages, certain rhetorical flowers or beauties of the text in order to weave them together, one with another. Perhaps all readers are anthologists, making garlands as we read. My study *Other Dickens: Pickwick to Chuzzlewit* argued that *The Old Curiosity Shop* was a deeply and self-consciously allegorical work; this article tries to show that it is equally an *anthological* one (134–38). And with any garland or wreath lies the question of what remains in the band, what the band encloses, on the one hand, and on the other, what is abandoned, forsaken, lost, left to wander or be vagabond, to flourish or wither uncut or unwoven.[1] It is also one of the central questions of this novel, and perhaps any novel.

The word "garland" does not appear in Dickens's first two books, *Sketches by Boz* and *Pickwick Papers,* nor in the first two-thirds of *Oliver Twist.* When Oliver is safely at the Maylie household, however, it makes its very first appearance in all of Dickens's work, in a graveyard: for Dickens, the memories conjured up by peaceful country scenes "may teach us to weave fresh garlands for the grave of those we loved" (282). The word appears only once more in all his work before *The Old Curiosity Shop*, in the very final sentence of *Nicholas Nickleby*, where on Smike's grave "garlands of fresh flowers wreathed by infant hands rested upon the stone" (831). *The Old Curiosity Shop*, where the word "garland" appears no less than eighty-three times, is a veritable florist's shop by comparison: *The Old Floriosity Shop*. At probably Nell's happiest and most successful moment in the novel, for example, shortly after she has seen Quilp as a statue come alive, she appears on Mrs. Jarley's cart, "decorated," garlanded in fact, with artificial flowers (220). And when she is dead, her little friend comes "with an offering of dried flowers which he begged to place on her breast" (540). Flowers run through the book, beautiful and mortal, fresh and dried, both scattered and drawn together. This article tries to gather some.

2

As a reader or critic of Dickens, one is constantly taken back to that section in John Forster's *Life of Charles Dickens* called "Hard Experiences in Boyhood" in which Forster tells the world about Dickens's time at Warren's Blacking Warehouse in that decisive and terrible year of 1824 when John Dickens was imprisoned for debt (16–27). These are perhaps the most important months of Dickens's life, but we know very little other than what Forster tells us of this time. And what he tells us is fragmentary and interspersed with strange absences or blanks: "I lose here for a little while the fragment of direct narrative" he writes at one point and, even more mysteriously, "there is here another blank" (19, 21). Much of this part of Forster's biography is based on a document that has come to be known as "the autobiographical fragment," which Dickens wrote some time between 1845 and 1849 and which covered his early years. We do not know for certain when it was written, how long it was, or how much of Dickens's life it treated. Neither its manuscript, nor that of Forster's *Life*, survives, and we do not know how or when they were destroyed or lost (Schlicke 153). Nor do we know where the strange blanks or absences within it come from or how or when the cuts were made. The source or origin of the blanks is a blank. So what we have are a number of texts—of which *David Copperfield* and Forster's *Life* are the two most important—which are anthologies of the lost manuscript, gatherings of flowers from whatever it was that Dickens wrote, garlands built around absences, interwoven and intertwined with other material, such as letters, reminiscences, journalism, speeches, and fiction, by Dickens, Forster, and later biographers, re-cut and re-woven over and over again.

It is often thought that the key biographical clue to *The Old Curiosity Shop* is the death of Dickens's sister-in-law Mary Hogarth in 1837.[2] There is clearly truth in that argument, but Steven Marcus is more accurate when he suggests

that Mary's death worked as a catalyst to trigger memories of his own traumatic childhood. In a sense, writes Marcus, "Mary came partly to be an
image of himself, of that conception of himself which he saw as still existing
in the past" (133). In consequence, one can weave together *The Old Curiosity
Shop* and what remains of the "Autobiographical Fragment," or rather see
how they already are, and have always been, intertwined.[3]

In the opening chapter of *The Old Curiosity Shop*, on its second or third
page, there is a passage describing the flowers for sale in Covent Garden
market. We know that Covent Garden was an important place for the young
Dickens when he was working at Warren's (which moved at some point from
Hungerford Stairs near the Thames to near Covent Garden): "When I had no
money," he writes, "I took a turn in Covent Garden Market, and stared at
the pine-apples" (Forster 20). In *The Old Curiosity Shop*, though, it is not
the lonely and isolated twelve-year-old Dickens but the lonely and isolated
Master Humphrey who walks around London and stares at things in Covent
Garden. Here he is at sunrise, in the spring or summer: "when the fragrance
of sweet flowers is in the air, overpowering even the unwholesome steams
of last night's debauchery, and driving the dusky thrush, whose cage has hung
outside a garret window all night long, half mad with joy!" (8). Flowers here
stand as indices of the possibility of another kind of life, a natural or beautiful
one. In a striking oxymoron, they drive the thrush, a captive like Dickens's
father, "half mad with joy." They are not the only captives, however, and
not simply captives. The passage continues:

> Poor bird! the only neighbouring thing at all akin to the other little captives,
> some of whom, shrinking from the hot hands of drunken purchasers, lie droop-
> ing on the path already, while others, soddened by close contact, await the time
> when they shall be watered and freshened up to please more sober company,
> and make old clerks who pass them on their road to business, wonder what has
> filled their breasts with visions of the country.   (8)

As Elizabeth Brennan puts it in her preface to the Clarendon edition of the
novel: "the other little captives cannot all be birds; some are flowers; others
young girls" (xxviii).[4] The flowers and girls, the captives of Covent Garden,
may be prostitutes; the novel will be about another girl, who is not a prostitute,
but who will sell flowers at the races where there are, no doubt, other drunken
and hot-handed purchasers, all too willing to leave her drooping on the path
or soddened by close contact. This is recognized by the woman at the races
"in a handsome carriage," accompanied by two men, who does not need her
fortune to be told because, she tells us, it has been told long ago, who calls
Nell towards her "and taking her flowers put money into her trembling hand,
and bade her go home and keep at home for God's sake" (19).

If flowers and the selling of flowers in the City, which provide a metaphor
for prostitution and the threat of sexual commodification, suggest one possible

fate for Nell, the flowers in the countryside are, for the most part, very close to graves and death, a fate she does not avoid. The ivy in Nell's first graveyard visit, for example, "crept about the mounds, beneath which slept poor humble men, twining for them the first wreaths they had ever owned, but wreaths less likely to wither and far more lasting in their kind, than some which were graven deep in stone and marble" (127). It is a kind of ideal: a wreath which without human intervention binds itself around stone or marble and endures far longer. In the following chapter, Nell talks to the old woman who plucks daisies from the grave of her young husband who died fifty-five years before. Slightly later, the schoolmaster who lives "among his flowers and beehives" (187) tells his dying pupil Harry that "the very flowers have missed you, and are less gay than they used to be" (197). Nell herself gathers "wild roses and such humble flowers" to sell as nosegays and, shortly before her death, she and her grandfather make the village graveyard into a garden, their garden (409–10). On her deathbed, by contrast, there are no flowers or garlands, only "some winter berries and green leaves" (537), but on her coffin, we are told, "many a young hand dropped its little wreath" (542).

In Forster's account of Dickens's early years, by contrast, only a single flower appears, but it does so with all the force of idealizing summation. Reflecting on the effect of the terrible year in the blacking warehouse on Dickens's psyche, he writes:

> nor was it a small part of this manifest advantage that he should have obtained his experience as a child and not a man; that only the good part, the flower and the fruit of it, was plucked by him; and that nothing of the evil part, none of the earth in which the seed was planted, remained to soil him.   (29)

Dickens himself never directly uses such a figure. His own account is, unsurprisingly, darker and more complex. After his family move to prison and he is, at twelve, working at Warren's but living far away in Camden, he writes: "I felt keenly, however, the being so cut off from my parents, my brothers, and sisters; and when my day's work was done, going home to such a miserable blank" (Forster 21). He is cut off—like a flower; he comes home to a blank. Eventually, in a moment of some significance for this novel, he begged his father to let him move nearer to the prison. "A back attic was found for me at the house of an insolvent-court agent, who lived in Lant Street in the Borough [i. e., much nearer the Marshalsea] . . . . A bed and bedding were sent over for me, and made up on the floor. The little window had a pleasant prospect of a timber yard; and when I took possession of my new abode, I thought it was a Paradise" (Forster 21). There is then one of these strange gaps in the account of these years. Having quoted directly Dickens's words so far, Forster then writes "There is here another blank." He does not say why. Having told us of the blank, he then promptly fills it from, he says, "letters and recollections of my own" (21):

> What was to him of course the great pleasure of his paradise of a lodging was its bringing him again, though after a fashion sorry enough, within the circle of home. From this time he used to breakfast "at home," in other words in the Marshalsea; going to it as early as the gates were open and for the most part much earlier.   (21–22)

And then, in a moment that is easy to miss, *The Old Curiosity Shop* makes an appearance, pops up its little head in the blank around which Forster is weaving his letters and reminiscences. He continues:

> I must not omit what he [Dickens] told me of the landlord of this little lodging. He was a fat, good-natured, kind old gentleman. He was lame, and had a quiet old wife; and he had a very innocent grown-up son, who was lame too . . . . They were all dead when he told me this, but in another form they live still very pleasantly as the Garland family in the *Old Curiosity Shop*.   (21–22)

Here Dickens and Forster stitch together the two texts through a word and a name—Garland—of a dead family who come alive again when they are woven into the novel, three characters (who later turn out to be four), all named Garland.

The Garlands, the main reason why the word occurs so often in the novel, are often neglected or ignored in critical accounts of the book, or seen as one of its weaker sides. Yet they may be more significant than they at first appear. The Garlands are a strange, and strangely floral, family; Mrs. Garland always carries, for reasons that are never entirely clear, a very large nosegay "resembling in shape and dimensions a full size warming-pan with the handle cut short off" (115). They are all extremely sedate: as James Kincaid puts it, "All their energy and rebelliousness seems to have been transferred to the pony" (87). The son is 28 years old, the same age as Dickens when he wrote the novel, and he behaves like a child who will never agree to be separated from his parents. He has only once had a day trip away from his mother—to Margate—and found it entirely distressing. He is a child pious beyond piety: "No son had ever been a greater comfort to his parents than Abel Garland had been to his" (116), so much so that he is almost physically identical to his father. What relation they have to the family of Archibald Campbell Russell and Son, whom Michael Allen in a brilliant bit of detective work has identified as their originals, we will never know, but their significance in Dickens's's psychic economy seems clear (88). The Dickens family was sundered; the Garlands hyperbolically united, inseparably bound together. As Marcus puts it, "Here Dickens seemed altogether without control; it is one of the few instances in his major writing in which his neurosis seems to speak out for itself'' (162).

The Garlands are not simply an ideal of family unity, however, for their story invokes two ancient stories of family rivalry and conflict, two founding narratives, one Hellenic, one Hebraic. The Garlands, father and son, are both lame. Marcus has shown how much *Barnaby Rudge*, this novel's immediate successor, was concerned with hostile father-son relationships and essentially oedipal conflicts (184–204). Lameness is, of course, one of Oedipus's most important physical characteristics; Oedipus means swollen-footed. In *The Old Curiosity Shop* we have a father and son identical in appearance and both swollen-footed, a simultaneous intensification and disavowal of their Oedipal relation. The other story comes from the Hebrew Bible. Mr. and Mrs. Garland do not have Christian names, but their son does. He is called Abel, the name of the younger son murdered by his brother Cain, who is then condemned to wander the earth. It is an odd choice, for this Garland has no siblings, no rivalry, and no murder. The novel itself, though, has a good deal of sibling rivalry in the shape of Fred Trent's hostility to his sister Nell, the good child who is condemned to wander. And Charles Dickens? As his father went to prison and his sister Fanny to a scholarship at the Royal Academy of Music, ''I (small Cain that I was, except that I had never done harm to anyone) was handed over as a lodger to a reduced old lady'' (Forster 19).

Catherine Robson has argued convincingly that what often might appear at first as an erotic fascination with young girls among Victorian men can often better be interpreted as a nostalgia for their own lost childhood innocence: the subtitle of her book is the ''lost girlhood of the Victorian gentleman.'' For Robson ''little girls represent not just the essence of childhood, but an adult male's best opportunity of recovering his own lost self'' (3). The love of little girls is, she argues, ''a form of 'temporally displaced self-love''' (10). There are many things that weave together Dickens's account of his early years and *The Old Curiosity Shop*, which is, with the sole exception of *David Copperfield*, the only novel to be mentioned more than once in the crucial chapter of Forster's *Life*. Certain phrases occur in both, as when Nell leaves London with her grandfather and looks down at the city and sees ''St Paul's looming through the smoke'' (122). These are exactly the same words that we find in Forster's *Life* and nowhere else in his work to describe the young Dickens's view from the almshouses at the top of Bayham Street in Camden, where he lived shortly before the time at Warren's, the sight of which was, writes Forster, ''a treat that served him for hours of vague reflection afterwards'' (12). There are many parallels between Nell and Dickens: like Nell, Dickens was little, ''a very small boy even for his age,'' writes Forster; like her, he ''suffers in secret''; like her, he became ill (Forster 27, 21).[5] A vagabond child, with a father-figure who is criminally negligent, and instantly loses any money that is given him, yet who is benevolently intentioned and promises his child great wealth, but nevertheless has to be parented by his child: this is Nell's story and, in a way, Dickens's story, too.

Above all, though, it is walking that binds together the autobiographical fragment and *The Old Curiosity Shop*. Pickwick, Oliver, Nicholas, Barnaby all travel, but none walk so much or so far as Nell. As Hilary Schor puts it, "the central activity of any reader of *The Old Curiosity Shop* is watching Little Nell walk herself to death" (33). This is a novel full of wanderers, of Nell and her grandfather, Codlin and Short, Mrs. Jarley and many more, a book of the unhoused and vagabond. Dickens was by choice a great walker in adulthood; he was perforce a great walker as a child. When John Dickens went to prison and Elizabeth and the younger siblings moved in too, Charles was left alone, working at Warrens', while living in Camden, from where he walked to work and back alone every day, a distance of some five miles or more. Weekends meant more, much more, walking: "Sundays Fanny and I passed in the prison. I was at the Academy [Royal Academy of Music, in the heart of the West End] at 9 o'clock in the morning to fetch her and walked back there together at night" (Forster 20) after the prison shut at nine o'clock: "a round distance," writes Michael Slater, "of some twelve miles" (*Dickens and Women* 26). These forty or forty-five mile walks each week of a twelve-year-old boy who had "complete charge of my own existence" mark this novel, which begins with both its narrator and protagonist walking alone at night in London, in significant ways. We first see Nell wandering the streets at night, alone, just as young Dickens wandered back over Blackfriars Bridge, the route that made him cry, on errands for his imprisoned father, who could not do them himself.

Like Little Nell, then, Little Charles wandered around the streets of London, "solitary and self-dependent" (Forster 26). And it is striking how tightly he binds his own account of these years to the experience of walking—so much so that certain streets became unbearable to walk down or even see. Of Hungerford Stairs where Warren's was, he writes, "I never saw it. I could not endure to go near it" (Forster 27). Of Chandos Street, to which it moved: "It was a very long time before I liked to go up Chandos Street," a tragic or pathetic equivalent of Dick Swiveller's closing all the routes to the Strand through his debts (Forster 27). However, in time and through a process of walking and re-walking, the trauma is mastered or at least narrated: "My old way home by the Borough made me cry, after my eldest child could speak. In my walks at night I have walked there often since then, and by degrees I have come to write this" (Forster 27). Since his eldest son could speak—from 1838 or 1839 that is, just before he writes *Old Curiosity Shop*, he has often walked there at night, a solitary man thinking about a solitary child, like Humphrey encountering Nell. And by walking, he tells us, he has come to write.

In the most famous passage of the autobiographical fragment, Dickens writes about the humiliation of the years of the Blacking Warehouse:

> No words can express the secret agony of my soul. . . . My whole nature was so penetrated with the grief and humiliation . . . that, even now, famous and caressed and happy,—I often forget in my dreams that I have a dear wife and children—even that I am a man—and wander desolately back to that time of my life.   (Forster 18–19)

Memory itself is here figured as wandering and as walking: "I wander desolately back." For Dickens, that desolate wandering, that memory that is also a forgetting, is a fragmentation and loss of identity, the dream of a man who forgets that he is a man—and thinks he is what? A woman? A boy? A girl?

3

Just as the forty-five miles of city street that the twelve-year-old Dickens walked each week links the two texts, so too the River Thames weaves itself in and through the autobiographical fragment and *The Old Curiosity Shop* alike. Among the most vividly etched memories by Dickens of those years are the view from the window of Warren's Blacking "looking over the coal barges and the river"; the moment he remembers in a pub by the riverside of "a vision of eating something on a bench outside, one fine evening, and looking at some coalheavers dancing"; and remembering "to have played on the coal barges at dinner-time, with Poll Green and Bob Fagin" (Forster 18, 23, 23). Wharves, barges, and the river recur and recur in the novel too, from its opening when Humphrey turns from the streets to the bridges and looks down to the river and the "dull slow sluggish barge" and thinks that "drowning was not a hard death, but of all means of suicide the easiest and best" (8). When Nell is not walking, she journeys by barge. Above all there is Quilp, a wharfinger, who lives on the edge of the Thames (and eventually drowns in it) in a "rugged wooden box, rotten and bare to see, which overhung the river's mud and threatened to slide down into it" (167), a place not unlike Warren's Blacking Warehouse, that "crazy, tumble-down house abutting . . . on the river" (Forster, 18).

On his wharf, Quilp is not alone. He is accompanied by "an amphibious boy in a canvas suit, whose sole change of occupation was from sitting on the head of a pile and throwing stones into the mud when the tide was out to standing with his hands in his pockets gazing listlessly on the motion and on the bustle of the river at high water" (34). "Amphibious" is an interesting word, from the Greek "amphi," meaning "of both kinds, on both sides, about or around" and "bios," "life." In our usual sense it means a being equally at home on land or water, or someone in an ambiguous or double position, as the *OED* puts it, "combining two lives, positions, classes." It is hard not to think of the young Charles Dickens when we think of the amphibious boy on the banks of the Thames, combining two lives, positions, classes, in an ambiguous or double position. We learn more about this boy, Tom Scott, as the novel progresses but his most striking feature is that he has "a natural taste for tumbling" (46); indeed, at the end of the book he becomes a professional tumbler. "Tumble" of course means two quite different things. On the one hand, "tumbler" is the older English word for acrobat, someone who has great physical dexterity. On the other, it means to fall headlong, to tumble down. Dickens was a tumbling boy, who had fallen headlong, whose world seemed turned upside down, and yet who learned to live in two elements, and who learned (in its other sense) to tumble very well. As his friend Douglas Jerrold brilliantly observed, Dickens "had the showman instinct so strongly developed that if you only gave him three square yards of carpet, he would tumble on that (like a street-acrobat)" (Slater, *Douglas Jerrold* 176).

There is one more member of the Garland family, Abel's father's brother, the Bachelor, who lives in the village in which Nell dies. This Garland appears in the company of other garlands, the ones that cover the goddess Truth. Like Nell, who is drawn irresistibly to the church and its tombs, the bachelor, Abel's uncle, we are told, "found in the old church a constant source of interest and amusement" (402). However, writes Dickens,

> he was not one of those rough spirits who would strip fair Truth of every little shadowy vestment in which time and teeming fancies love to array her . . . as, unlike this stern and obdurate class, he loved to see the goddess [i. e., Truth] crowned with those garlands of wild flowers which tradition wreathes for her gentle wearing.   (402)

It's a remarkable passage, an allegory of Truth, time, and history. Truth is a woman here, who proverbially was thought to live at the bottom of a well. She is concealed by the waters, by her vestments, which are myths and legends, and by garlands, beneath which she is naked. The old bachelor, who will not strip her, is a Garland who loves to keep Truth in her garlands.

If we are tempted to see this merely as a piece of more or less successful "fine writing" by Dickens, a rather floridly and unnecessarily elaborated metaphor, inorganic to the story, then we should pause. For Dickens picks up precisely the same metaphor, of Truth and a well, in the following chapter, at the very last moment that we see Nell alive. Here the sexton speaks to Nell and suggests that she and her friend, the child whose brother has died, "have been listening by the old well" (415). Nell replies that she hasn't, whereupon the old man takes her down into the crypt to see it. It is the most famous and shocking illustration in the novel: " 'It looks like a grave, itself' said the old man. 'It does' replied the child'' (416). On the edge of Nell's grave and death, there are no garlands, flowers, or vestments of any sort, only stone, a sexton who digs graves, and naked Truth at the bottom of her well, which is like a grave in a crypt.

There is another figure and another garland, though, around which this essay circles, more even than Humphrey, Tom Scott, the Garlands, or even Nell herself, a shadowy, nameless figure who is perhaps the most important link between the autobiographical fragment and *The Old Curiosity Shop*. At some point when they lived in Chatham, the Dickens family took on a servant girl from the workhouse. She moved with the Dickenses when they went to London and stayed in their service. When John and Elizabeth Dickens, together with their younger children, went to prison in the Marshalsea and Charles was lodging in Lant Street, Forster tell us,

> They were waited on still by the maid-of-all-work from Bayham Street, the orphan girl of the Chatham workhouse, from whose sharp little worldly and also kindly ways he took his first impression of the Marchioness in the *Old Curiosity Shop*. She too had a lodging in the neighborhood that she might be early on the scene of her duties; and when Charles met her, as he would do occasionally, in his lounging-place by London Bridge, he would occupy the time before the gates opened by telling her quite astonishing fictions about the wharves and the Tower. ''But I hoped I believed them myself'' he would say.
> (21–22)

We can, if we choose, imagine the scene, some time in 1824, of two poor children, sitting under the arches of Old London Bridge, where the shops on the bridge used to be, watching the barges and wharves that are so important to this novel, the one telling stories to the other, his story tells us. One, an amphibious boy, who seems to have tumbled far, the other the child of the workhouse, the servant of a debtor.

These two are divided and united in so many ways: one is the servant of a prisoner (as Sam Weller would later be), the other, a prisoner's child (as Little Dorrit would be); both are poor, both are young, both are solitary lodgers; both work hard for little money. We do not know and probably never will what those astonishing fictions were that Dickens told the orphan of the Chatham workhouse. We know so much about the prisoner's son, about his extraordinary tumble and the extraordinary later tumbling, of which this novel is a part, of that amphibious boy and man, Charles Dickens, but almost nothing of the nameless daughter, her past or future. Of her fictional counterpart, the Marchioness, Sophronia Sphynx, we know that she went to school, as the twelve-year old Dickens dreamed that he might do one day. She is also given a love-story, ''the one true romance in the whole of Dickens,'' Chesterton called it, with a man called Dick, who is perpetually in debt (56).

She also, miraculously, has her own garland or wreath in the novel, a festive, celebratory, supplementary one, in the chapter which begins what Michael Slater calls "the extraordinarily effective idyll of Dick Swiveller's enchantment of the little Marchioness by awakening her imagination," which he does by giving her bread and beef and teaching her how to play cribbage (Slater, *Dickens and Women* 430). We find the following exchange in a passage that Dickens deleted in proof:

> "Marchioness" said Mr Swiveller, handing her the tankard with profound solemnity, "if you feel that your thoughts are quite collected—if you have no sensation of giddiness, or vague desires to sing a song without knowing one—if you have undiminished confidence in your legs, and are sensible of no unusual thickness or hurry in your speech—I should feel personally complimented by your taking a little more; and if you will be kind enough, at the same time, to wreathe the bowl with flowers of soul, you will enhance the obligation materially."
>
> The Marchioness who understood, perhaps, of Mr Swiveller's conversation, about one word in forty, grinned, accepted the tankard, grinned once more, and still grinning in modest confusion, returned it to her entertainer.   (565)

It is a gift of food and drink—for which nothing is asked in exchange, except an imaginary wreath, or garland, of flowers of soul. A little exchange, between two of London's poorest, it is also a moment of allegorizing and anthologizing by Swiveller of the power of hospitality and hope, a reciprocal, comic, festive exchange between a poor servant and someone who feels he deserves wealth but who is as poor as she. It is a fabulous, in every sense, moment, the beginning of the Marchioness's liberation and a counter or response to the death's head that is Nell's naked truth.

I have here discussed some of the flowers of *The Old Curiosity Shop* and some of the garlands—or nosegays, or perhaps only scattered leaves and berries—that can be made within and beyond the novel from night-walking, imprisonment, barges, wharves, families, sibling rivalry, Truth in her well, sick or parentless children, tumbling up and down, working for a pittance, and watching the river flow. But I have also tried to register some of those absences and blanks that those garlands encircle: the "miserable blank" that was Dickens's home when his father was in prison, the blanks within the autobiographical fragment, the blanks of the grave and of Truth naked in her well. Let us end with another blank. The records of admissions and discharges of the Chatham workhouse only survive from 1867, and so about "the orphan girl," whose "sharp little worldly but kindly ways" (Forster 22) the young Dickens knew, we know not even her name. Of the True history, ungarlanded, of the girl whom Dickens studied for the Marchioness's portrait, the maid-of-all-work from Bayham Street, the orphan girl of the Chatham workhouse, his companion to whom he told stories of the wharves and Tower, there is here another blank.

NOTES

1. The question of banding and binding is a reiterated motif (and more than motif) in Derrida's *Glas*.
2. For a balanced account of Mary Hogarth's role in the conception of Nell, see Slater, *Dickens and Women* 95–96.
3. "In the Preface [to *Master Humphrey's Clock*] we are told how Master Humphrey and his friends would probably 'trace some faint recollection of their past lives in the varying current of the tale.' I have always thought that in the Life of Little Nell, there is in some way such a reflection of his own life." (Langton 174).
4. The link to prostitution is made explicit in a deleted passage from the manuscript: "(It may be some forgotten thought like this—some momentary recollection of an old home—that moved a wretched girl to draw near and beg a flower, and having it to thank the giver humbly and crawl away)" (Dickens, *The Old Curiosity Shop* 1997, 577). In this deleted passage there is a double reversal— the flower is not sold but given, not by a girl but to one; the flower is not akin to the prostitute, but a sign of her memory and possible redemption.
5. Dickens, or rather Forster, tells us one more thing about the family who become the Garlands. When he was living there, Dickens became ill "with one of his old attacks of spasm one night, and the whole three of them were about his bed until morning." (21–22). In *The Old Curiosity Shop*, two people get significantly ill; one recovers, one does not. Dick Swiveller falls ill in lodgings and when he awakes "became conscious by slow degrees of whispering voices in his room. Looking out between the curtains, he espied Mr Garland, Mr Abel the notary, and the single gentleman, gathered round the Marchioness. . . . Old Mr Garland was the first to stretch out his hand, and inquire how he felt.' (489). It is significant also that when Dick is ill the Marchioness tends to him "as if he were a very little boy and she his grown-up nurse" (490). Nell too falls ill, but she does not recover, unlike Dickens or Dick.

WORKS CITED

Allen, Michael. *Charles Dickens' Childhood*. New York: St. Martin's, 1988.

Bowen, John. *Other Dickens: Pickwick to Chuzzlewit*. Oxford: Oxford UP, 2000.

Chesterton, G. K. *Chesterton on Dickens*. Ed. Michael Slater. London: Everyman, 1992.

Collins, Phillip, ed. *Dickens: The Critical Heritage*. London: Routledge and Kegan Paul, 1971.

Derrida, Jacques. *Glas*. Trans. John B. Leavey, Jr. and Richard Rand. Lincoln: Nebraska UP, 1986.

Dickens, Charles. *The Old Curiosity Shop*. Ed. Elizabeth M. Brennan. Oxford: World's Classics, 1998.

———. *Oliver Twist*. Ed. Philip Horne. Harmondsworth: Penguin, 2002.

———. *Nicholas Nickleby*. Ed. Paul Schlicke. Oxford: World's Classics, 1990.

———. *The Speeches of Charles Dickens*. Ed. K. J. Fielding. Oxford: Clarendon, 1960.

Forster, John. *The Life of Charles Dickens*. London: Chapman and Hall, n.d.

Genet, Jean. *Our Lady of the Flowers*. Trans. Bernard Frechtman. London: Panther, 1966.

Hegel, G. W. F. *Phenomenology of Spirit*. Trans. A.V. Miller. Oxford: Clarendon, 1977.

Kant, Immanuel. *The Critique of Judgement*. Trans. James Creed Meredith. Oxford: Clarendon, 1952.

Kincaid, James. *Dickens and the Rhetoric of Laughter*. Oxford: Clarendon, 1971.

Kitton, F. G. *Charles Dickens by Pen and Pencil*. London, 1890.

Langton, Robert. *The Childhood and Youth of Charles Dickens*. London: Hutchinson, 1912.

Marcus, Steven. *Dickens: from Pickwick to Dombey*. London: Chatto and Windus, 1965.

Robson, Catherine. *Men in Wonderland: the Lost Girlhood of the Victorian Gentleman*. Princeton: Princeton UP, 2001.

Schlicke, Paul, ed. *Oxford Reader's Companion to Dickens*. Oxford: Oxford UP, 1999.

Schor, Hilary M. *Dickens and the Daughter of the House*. Cambridge: Cambridge UP, 1999.

Slater, Michael. *Dickens and Women*. London: Dent, 1983.

———. *Douglas Jerrold 1803–1857*. London: Duckworth, 2002.

Wyndham, Violet. *The Sphinx and Her Circle: A Biographical Sketch of Ada Leverson, 1862–1933*. London: André Deutsch, 1963.

Blessings for the Worthy: Dickens's *Little Dorrit* and the Nature of Rants

James R. Kincaid

Little Dorrit *can be read, I propose, as a smug, reactionary, frightened work of banal protective pathology. In my view, this is a novel protecting a paternal incestuous fantasy, rooted in a vague metaphysics of "blessings," whereby the father-daughter combination is played off against all the rest of us, the poor most especially, about whom Dickens cares nothing. Amy Dorrit, the novel's central jailer, works as Dickens's surrogate (and object of sexual attention) to deny any possibility of change, to keep us all in the jail where we can bask in the thin pleasures available to those whose hearts belong to Daddy: more exactly, the Daddys who can freeze their little girls and collect their hearts.*

I wish to present two quotations as polar opposites. One is from the conclusion of *Little Dorrit*: ''They went quietly down into the roaring streets, inseparable and blessed.'' The other is from *King Lear* (5.3.10–11): ''When thou dost ask me blessing, I'll kneel down/ And ask of thee forgiveness.''

How are they opposites? In Dickens's incomplete and self-satisfied world, the final state is blessedness, especially when the blessed are contrasted (in the novel's famous last sentence) with all others, with ''the noisy and the eager, and the arrogant and the froward and the vain, [who] fretted, and chafed, and made their usual uproar.'' So much for them! The blessed in Dickens are silent, static, tomb-like; and they need these hordes of the unblessed, the noisy and the eager, to assure their elevation into metaphysical marshmallow-land. In *Lear*, blessing is simply a way-station on the road to

---

a much higher state, forgiveness: "When thou dost ask me blessing, I'll kneel down/ And ask of thee forgiveness." The verb "to bless" originates from, among other things, the verb "to kneel," so that in Shakespeare, blessings are not isolated and selective: you ask me to bless and I'll ask you to bless and we fold together inside a higher state of forgiveness, of mercy.

Set-Up

In an April 1857 review in *Blackwood's Magazine,* E. B. Hamley said that, lost in the "wilderness" of *Little Dorrit,* "we sit down and weep when we remember thee, O *Pickwick!*" (*Dickens: Critical Heritage* 360). I honor this sentiment. *Pickwick* was open and curious, generous and naïve; *Little Dorrit* is fenced-in and knowing, fearful and snarling. Mr. Pickwick (as well as the novel about him) wanders around naked; *Little Dorrit* protects its own immense ignorance and covers it with beatific mush. I suggest that were this novel by anyone other than Dickens, we would probably ignore it, leave it to its natural audience, the relatively few people who would read this tedious, lifeless, self-indulgent, self-righteous novel with pleasure. The book may appeal to readers who themselves like to rant, to issue angry attacks on the government, readers who find similar comfort in feeling unjustly unappreciated, middle-class men who also find themselves in the grips of a banal mid-life crisis, such as the one Dickens faced here.

We all know that Dickens was rescued from the modernists sixty-five years ago by a strategy which sacrificed early Dickens to late, "early Dickens" being admittedly sentimental and flabby; "late Dickens" being dark and crafted. This was not entirely a bad tactic, since it gave us the exquisite novel of forgiveness, *Great Expectations,* the powerful novel of mercy and love, *Our Mutual Friend,* and the tragically moving *Bleak House.* It also gave us the preposterous costume drama, *A Tale of Two Cities,* and the equally preposterous *Hard Times,* a stupid person's thinking novel. Both suffer from Dickens's imagining he could venture into analytical thought. But they both have their moments and many of them. *Little Dorrit* has its moments too—but very few of them.

Those who align themselves with Dickens, and that's not a bad place to be, should, in considering *Little Dorrit,* issue apologies to Dickens's daughters, and to all daughters, as well as to all who are forced to serve, to all prisoners, all the poor, and the dispossessed. One of the most telling comments comes from G. B. Shaw, who said "*Little Dorrit* is a more seditious book than *Das Kapital*" (51). Shaw loved saying things like that, asserting the palpably ridiculous and then arguing that he's the only one to see its secret truth. But to find radical politics in this narrow and moralistic rant of a book is absurd.

Summary

My argument is easily summarized: the novel is about blessings, but it is based on an economy of blessing scarcity—whereby getting blessed depends on others not being so lucky, many others. The blessed are played off against the multitudes who are not blessed and who are never going to be blessed because nothing changes, and that's because everything is rooted in the past, which controls everything. We never leave prison, we never leave home, we do not forget—or we better not. We certainly do not forgive, since that might compromise our own being. This frightened novel sets out one condition of being, our past, and stays there, showing how vain it is to imagine we can ever escape those conditions, ever leave prison. The real jailer is the novel's central figure, Amy Dorrit, the dutiful daughter of the eternal patriarch. Amy's heart belongs to Daddy because that's where she lives and moves and has her being. She is terrified of change, wants to serve, do her duty, be with a benighted and feeble papa, a papa she makes certain is benighted and feeble. She keeps him on the shortest of leashes and when he tries to get free she hauls him back. Amy and Miss Wade and Mrs. Clennam are really peas in the same little shriveled pod in this misogynist book. The one woman who tries to get free is, ironically, Flora, who wants to misread the past so as to craft a present. But this good fairy, expansive and promising, is made ridiculous, marginal; so the deterministic three Graces of self-pity, self-justification, and wrath can rule. *Little Dorrit* is a novel so smug, so unforgiving and spiteful, so self-satisfied and static, stewing in its own resentments, rehearsing its own wrongs, that few readers would ever bother with it, except Dickens enthusiasts who, like the insufferable Amy Dorrit, are locked into the most tedious of all Vices, a devotion to duty.

Biographical

Little Dorrit is a novel so devoted to the power of the past that its central character, Arthur Clennam, tells us again and again that he was completely determined by his upbringing, that he is what he was, that he cannot change, that he isn't responsible, that he didn't do it. The narrator reinforces Clennam's belief with additional comments. The past we are concerned with, however, is not Arthur's, which was, even allowing for a grim mother and weak father, better than that of innumerable English children then and not something we can understand trapping for forty years anybody who wanted to get free. The real past that counts here, the past we Do Not Forget, is Dickens's own.

In this novel, Dickens mines his childhood, as he had gloriously in *David Copperfield* and would do later with unmatched power in *Great Expectations*. In *Little Dorrit*, however, he manages only to whine, echoing the famous autobiographical fragment Forster published, cringing as he did so, one hopes. In that fragment, as we know, Dickens looks back on his father's imprisonment and his own employment in the blacking warehouse.

Now, let's make allowances for a society that wasn't exactly encouraging of upward mobility from the lowest classes, and for anyone's tendency to make his childhood into a melodrama. Remember what Dickens actually said about his childhood: the work at Warren's was not demanding; he was well treated and generally well-liked; he did his work effectively, he says, and was proud of doing it. What got his dander up was being shoved in with the lower orders. "No words can express the secret agony of my soul," he says, "as I sunk into this companionship" (1: 2: 26). Not that such unspeakably low and unfit companionship as was offered by Bob Fagin and Poll Green (*David Copperfield*'s Mealy Potatoes) was really leveling to little Charles: he says, "Though perfectly familiar with them, my conduct and manners were different enough from theirs to place a space between us" (29; vol.1, ch.2).

At the base of *Little Dorrit* is this fear of contagion, this detestation of the poor, of the lower orders, this complete lack of interest in or curiosity about the lives of others. The word "common" appears in the fragment: he points to his own special little self being forced among "common" boys. It's a word that occurs in *Little Dorrit*, evoking every time a shudder of revulsion. One wonders what Bob Fagin or Mealy Potatoes felt about sinking into companionship with a small child whose father was a prisoner, not that Charles let them know that. He was, he says, "too proud." Such pride so contains him here and in writing *Little Dorrit* that he can see only a slim and narrow slice of life, dictated by the hysterical needs of the self-protecting, resentful child. This is not a great position for a novelist—rigidly bent on class-based self-justification and on ruling out of court any other viewpoint, any competing experience, any complexity. It's a novel hostile to the imagination.

Making things worse is Dickens's own DO NOT FORGET—his self-pitying rant against his mother, whom he overheard arguing for Charles to continue working in the warehouse. Now, we can imagine a lot of good motives for Dickens's mother, given the perilous state of family finances and her own husband's history of amiable but foolish improvidence. Here is Dickens's own measured response to her: "I never afterwards forgot, I never shall forget, I never can forget, that my mother was warm for my being sent back" (35; bk.1, ch.2). Never, never, never. Do not forget. Do not forgive. Mother has a different story to tell? I don't want to hear it. I never shall hear it. I never can hear it. There's only one story and it's mine! I won't budge from it. I won't imagine anything outside it. As I say, this is not good starting point for a novel; it is irresistible starting point for a rant, and a rant is what we get.

Stark Oppositions

In a melodrama, which is what *Little Dorrit* is, the world is divided into extremes and intensely—one might say, simple-mindedly—moralized. It's absolute evil versus absolute good, Arthur and Amy pitted against everybody and everything, all those who are eager and moving. The novel offers the thin but, to some, satisfying pleasures of feeling isolated, victimized, misunderstood, elevated by some mysterious certainty of one's own mystic difference. In such a world, there is no room for ambiguity, complexity, or change; it's a static world sustained by the pleasures of being misunderstood, frolicking in a lip-quivering, self-pitying playground that is simultaneously smug and snobbish.

Interlude

There are two operative terms in this novel, duty and incest, both of which are blessed, in the strange and hysterical metaphysics Dickens rains down on his long complaint. Or, we may refer to two key terms, duty and daughters, which is a more acceptable word than incest.

Duty

One way to approach the unforgiving nastiness of this book is through its unreflecting endorsement of duty, which might be defined as the unreasoning devotion of one person to another, especially of the poor to the well-off, a woman to a man, a young woman to an old man, a daughter to a father. There are not many scenes in the novel where we can escape from Dickens's notions of moral behavior, but I'll choose one, the deeply moving exemplary scene where Mr. Meagles welcomes back the repentant Tattycoram.

Tattycoram has run away because she objected to being treated as an amusing toy and as something worse than a servant. A perverse reader of the novel might find Tattycoram very justly angry with the foolish patriarch Meagles and his spoiled daughter, properly called Pet.

Why does Tattycoram come back at all? Does she have no grievance? A perverse reader might think that she does; but, instead of begging her pardon, as he should, Mr. Meagles lectures her on her presumed ingratitude and uses

Amy Dorrit as a model for correct behavior. Amy, he says, has not succumbed to resentment. No! Amy has devoted her life to "active resignation, goodness, and noble service" (774; bk.2, ch.2). Not incidentally, such noble service has been directed to her father, one of many honored Patriarchs in a novel that pretends to ridicule them. "Noble service": what exactly is that? Does true nobility resides in wiping papa's nose and cleaning up his room and his clothes and his dribbling? Noble service? Was there ever such a patently self-serving oxymoron? Noble service. Just serve me and that's noble? It's exalted servility. And what is "active resignation"? Isn't that like mobile stagnation?

Meagles goes on, "Shall I tell you what I consider those eyes of hers that were here just now, to have always looked at, to get that expression?" (2: 33: 774). This inept, straggling sentence seemingly suggests that Amy's eyes had come visiting while the rest of her stayed home. In response, Tattycoram says, "Yes, if you please, sir," and Meagles replies, "Duty, Tattycoram. Begin it early, and do it well; and there is no antecedent to it, in any origin or station, that will tell against us with the Almighty, or with ourselves." God himself rewards mindless labor, those who keep the privileged where they are. Tattycoram's duty is to serve and she will get her reward by and by. Work, work, work, and never ask why—keep your eyes on the ground—yes, if you please, sir. This is the essence of mindless adherence to the status quo. Some, like Meagles, are born to do nothing whatever, apart from spreading English ignorance around the globe, and others are born to serve and be active in being inactive, to exercise themselves in noble service.

Meagles then goes on to speak of his son-in-law, so devastatingly abusing the daughter that we are told Meagles loves. Meagles says of Gowan, "he certainly is well connected, and of a very good family" (775; bk.2, ch.33). The narrator comments, "It was the only comfort he had in the loss of his daughter, and if he made the most of it, who could blame him?" This brings us to this novel's second key to all understanding: the duty of daughters.

Interlude 2–Biographical 2

Dickens was in a bad state in 1857. His marriage was falling apart, for his wife Kate had become, unlike him, middle-aged, fat, and no longer lively. Dickens was entertaining the banal fantasy often called the mid-life crisis, which might more honestly be called the Lolita complex, offering the idea of guilt-free intergenerational sex. Dickens's fantasy resembles that of Humbert Humbert, who was, we recall, little Lolita's stepfather. It is the fantasy of the eternally changeless and dutiful daughter, a daughter who has no thought but to serve, to have no being outside the circle of the eternally needy, absolutely deserving Patriarch—in this case, Charles Dickens.

The Duty of Daughters

Let us return to the Meagles episode in which the narrator refers to the idea of consoling him for losing his daughter to her husband. What a strange idea it is that condolences would be handed out for this kind of daughter-loss. Isn't that what's supposed to happen? Aren't daughters expected to leave papa and cleave to another, in the course of nature or at least the nature we are used to in patriarchal cultures? Not here, not inside this static world, this venomous fantasy.

Inside this fantasy, all daughters are what Humbert hopes little Lo will be and what Dickens was so ardently looking for: eternal, selfless, and en-wrapped willingly inside the idea of active resignation, noble service. Dickens proceeds a little further into the realm of the discomforting, however, every time (and there are many) that Amy is said to be a child, to look half her years, every time Arthur calls her a child, every time she urges him to think of her as "the little shabby girl," "always, without change" (454; bk.2, ch.4) every time he urges her to think of him as "a father." It is evident when Amy hears the news of her father's release: "She spoke of nothing but him, thought of nothing but him. Kneeling down and pouring out her thankfulness with uplifted hands, her thanks were for her father" (401; bk.1, ch.35); "I shall see him," she says, " as my poor mother saw him long ago. O my dear, o dear. O father, father!" (403; bk.1, ch.35). Even Dickens seems to be going a little far in demanding this much, in having Amy transplanted into her own mother, more exactly, her father's wife. But we know there were no limits to his demands, the demands of the Patriarch, the demands of Jehovah, of Humbert Humbert. This transformation of fathers into lovers and daughters into willing accomplices (often disguised as nurses) emerges too when the narrator evokes the story of Euphrasia, daughter of the deposed king of Syracuse, who visited her old father in prison and suckled him from her breast. Indeed, this is a novel obsessed with breasts, an obsession screened by Mrs. Merdle, whose bosoms we are told nurture nothing. This remark clears the way for the entrance of little girls with big breasts, like Amy Dorrit. After evoking Euphrasia, the narrator makes an explicit application: "Little Dorrit, though of the unheroic modern stock, and mere English, did much more, in comforting her father's wasted heart upon her innocent breast, and turning to it a fountain of love and fidelity that never ran dry" (227; bk.1, ch.19).

Amy's burbling fountain is still pumping out when she replaces one father with another, William Dorrit with Arthur Clennam: the narrator tells us gloat-ingly that she "nursed him as lovingly, and GOD knows, as innocently, as she had nursed her father" (723; bk.2, ch.29). Is anyone deceived by the shrill insistence on innocence?

The Terrible Meek

But meek people, like Amy and Lolita and many servile daughters, often have a way of gathering up all the power. The meek are going to inherit the earth because, all this time, these yes-sayers have been hoarding power. It's the power of the immoveable. The meek can't be rattled, can't be changed, and they freeze the whole world.

Amy Dorrit is, on one level, what we might call an enabler. We are asked to admire her devotion to shielding her father, but why does she do it? Why does she feed his illusions? Her brother says, bluntly, "I don't see why, myself"(94; bk.1, ch.8); and if it weren't for all commentary from the narrator we wouldn't either. Why is she acting as she does—eclipsing herself or making herself the absolute power center?

Oddly, her initial response to the idea of her father's release from prison is panic: "I have often thought that if such a change could come, it might be anything but a service to him" (105; bk.1, ch.9). What? This sweet daughter, who, we are told, "never thinks of herself," manages, from another point of view, to think of nothing else.

Notice the scene when John Chivery, decent and manly and sweet, approaches her on the bridge with a timid declaration of his love. He hardly gets a word out before this meek little black widow spider swallows him alive. How could he think of such a thing? But why is he so unsuitable? His station is actually higher at the time, but we are supposed to recognize something innate in Amy Dorrit that makes Chivery's approach as unthinkable as, say, Mealy Potatoes's wanting to be friends with young Charles. Angelic little Amy then orders John away, orders him off the bridge, orders him never to use the bridge again. So much for her selflessness.

When her father is freed from prison, through no efforts of hers, she does everything she can to drag him back. A free father, on the move, even trying to develop an erotic life of his own, is unthinkable. Under such conditions, Amy would have no power, no being; so she resists ferociously. She is a force of determinism so unrelenting that she resembles what Foucault says were the purposes of ancient punishment, to imprint the crime on the body, so that it is never effaced. Amy doesn't see her father paying for the crime; he becomes it, an image, down deep, of Dickens's determination to make things consequential according to his own incapacity to forget and forgive, his willingness to justify his own petty hatreds.

When Amy Dorrit becomes a tourist in Europe, she is not seen expanding her mind, or learning new things, or making new friends, or enjoying herself. In Venice, "the family began a gay life, went here and there, and turned night into day; but, she was timid of joining in their gaieties, and only asked leave to be left alone'' (450; bk.2, ch.3). She later tells Arthur directly that ''We are all fond of the life here (except me)'' (532; bk.2, ch.11). Her sister expresses what most people would feel: ''There are times when my dear child is a little wearing, to an active mind'' (667; bk.2, ch.24). Amy would not be a desirable traveling companion, for everything—the Alps, Rome, Florence, a play, a party—looks to her like a prison.

Why does Amy act this way? Because her being depends on her father's weakness. She sees the whole world as ''a superior sort of Marshalsea'' (491; bk.2, ch.7), sees the prison as one of those ''lasting realities that had never changed'' (451; bk.2, ch.3). If her father breaks free, where will she be? She resists with all the fierce power of the terrible meek. ''You—ha—habitually hurt me'' (460; bk.2, ch.5), her father complains on the European trip, as she once more pulls him back to the ''lasting reality'' of the prison. Why is the prison real and the pleasures of Italy not real? Only because she has authority one place and not in another. So, when she can't actually haul him back, she kills him and finds another papa-in-prison, Arthur, whom she can nurse and control. It's as if Dickens, even in the grips of the Lolita fantasy, also considers its backlash.

Arthur

Arthur is in no sense Dickens, except, of course, that he *is*, Dickens heavily disguised. Arthur partly screens and denies the urgency of the Lolita fantasy. Arthur is the pedophile figure always pleading that it's not his fault, that he has no will. Has there ever been a character so eager to tell us he didn't do it, long before he does anything whatever? Indeed, for forty years it seems he has been immobile, hands in pockets, lips sealed. Why? As he tells us repeatedly, because Mama was stern. Did he really have a bad childhood? He's a middle-class person in very easy circumstances, off in China not for a weekend but for twenty years. Why does he still feel chained? What's he denying? Why does he never open his mouth but to plead incapacity, say, ''I didn't do it!''?

Let's look at one of complaints: ''I have no will. . . . Trained by main force; broken, not bent; heavily ironed with an object on which I was never consulted and which was never mine; shipped away to the other end of the world before I was of age, and exiled there until my father's death there, a year ago; always grinding in a mill I always hated; what is to be expected from *me* in middle-life? Will, purpose, hope? All those lights were extinguished before I could sound the words'' (33; bk.1, ch.2).

He evidently regards this rehearsed self-justification as iron-tight, but, if so, why does he repeat it so often? Unless we're inside the same fantasy, this insistence on the permanence of the past seems pathological, and the urgency to deny committing a secret sin inexplicable.

In this novel, nothing changes simply because Dickens wills no change. The prison, the past, the doling out of blessings: all are in service of something beyond conservatism, agents of a static condition.

Pushy Prose

So odd is this insistence on the static and the rooted that Dickens resorts to a prose so strained and bullying it almost justifies the modernist protests against intrusive narrators, telling us what we should think, how we should react. Over and over we get: "said the mild Little Dorrit" (242; bk.1, ch.20),"said Little Dorrit mildly" (365; bk.1, ch.31), as if he can't rest, can't be sure, can't just say, "said Little Dorrit." On and on it goes: "Little Dorrit, always thoughtful of the feelings of the weak" (357; bk.1, ch.31). "Little Dorrit's thoughtful eyes met hers, tenderly and quietly" (580; bk.2, ch.15). And it's not just with Amy. Dickens is always distrusting his readers, becoming shrill: Mrs. Meagles "who was always on the good and sensible side" (505; bk.2, ch.9); John Chivery, "highly respectable at bottom, though absurd enough on the surface" (699; bk.2, ch.27). I suppose it's to Dickens's credit that a small part of him recognized the nastiness of his central fantasy and felt the need to scream in hopes that we wouldn't look too closely.

Politics

The friend of the poor, Dickens's proud title in his day and often, perhaps, fitting him, here is a mockery. In his urge to isolate the blessed, Arthur and Amy, there is no room for anyone else, no one. The poor here, despite the pathos we think ought to attend Bleeding Heart Yard, are simply part of the rabble, Merdle-worshipping, Barnacle-caught, and not worth worrying about. After all, nothing changes, nothing can change, and so forget them. There is even less sympathy for the imprisoned, who are noticed only to be reviled. When Arthur lands there, he immediately dissociates himself from, holds himself above, "the herd in the yard" (703; bk. 2, ch.28). The reactionary politics here run so deep that the central catalyst of disaster, Merdle, is condemned by terms even snobs would hesitate using: Merdle is common, has mean, common features. The real problem is that, instead of worshipping "the leaders of the Arts and Sciences," the herd cheers for Merdle, for financial wizards and politicians, instead of leaders of arts and sciences—say arts, say literature, say Dickens.

Inside this resentful politics, either one worships or one doesn't. There is no middle ground, no ambiguity, and nothing ever changes. Pet Meagles's hope that her husband will grow and change is ridiculed by the narrator, as is William Dorrit's idea that it might be more pleasant out of prison than in. So, we rely on those bedrocks of knowledge, intuition and bigotry. Are you for me or against me? Are you among the blessed or, almost certainly, the lost? Are you angelic or devilish?

Evil here is just that. Rigaud is not just evil but a caution against thinking that a human character might be shaded, nuanced, complex. He arouses what the narrator calls "a natural antipathy towards an odious creature of the reptile kind" (490; bk.2, ch.7). The smiling landlady at the Break of Day has the final word on Rigaud and on the politics ruling this novel: "there are people who must be dealt with as enemies of the human race. . . . people who have no human heart, and who must be crushed like savage beasts and cleared out of the way" (131; bk.1, ch.11). But there's no evidence against him, someone protests. "All the world knows it [his guilt]," she replies (132; bk.1, ch.11). Why look for evidence when knowingness and bigotry are so much more efficient? The narrator approves of her words, saying they ought to be taken to heart by "certain amiable white-washers . . . nearer Great Britain" (131; bk.1, ch.11).

The rants against the Circumlocution Office are of the same order. The model for this sort of acute political analysis is Huck Finn's Pap: "Call this a govment! why, just look at it and see what it's like. Here's the law a-standin ready to take a man's son from him—a man's own son, which he has had all the trouble and all the anxiety and all the expense of raising. . . . Oh, yes, this is a wonderful govment" (Clemens 26; 6).

Doyce

Another sign of the hysterical politics here is the curious use of Daniel Doyce, used as an image to represent pathetically what current conditions disallow. Doyce is, presumably, what the fools in the government squeeze out, the true hope for England if only those dolts would wake up and see. And what is he? An engineer. He gets things done. He knows how to do it. What? Never mind. Don't ask. He does it and they don't want it to be done. An engineer. A tinkerer and adjuster, a narrower accomplisher of—never mind what. He does it and that's enough. Were reactionary politics ever more mindless? Where is the imagination, the visionary, the artistic? Oh we weep when we think of thee, Pickwick.

This novel almost justifies all those snobs who said that when Dickens tried himself to think, he became a child. *Little Dorrit* proceeds with a huge, though banal, fantasy, an idea of sorts, and a lot of unreflecting anger.

Blessings

When Arthur and Amy emerge in the novel's final sentence, they emerge not loving, not laughing, not ready for enjoyment, but blessed. Moreover, their being blessed depends evidently on everyone else not being excluded. Why can't everybody be blessed or at least a few more? To bless is rooted in the word for blood, connected both to blood sacrifices, marked by blood, and to a later idea of blood as innate superiority and reputation, spoken well of. To be blessed, then, is to invoke the irrational or, if you prefer, metaphysical notions of sacrifice, station, and sanctification—rather like prunes and prisms. But the blessing economy here is, and has usually been, one of scarcity: it only counts if others are not. And why? Who knows? This justification of mystery goes way back. Why did Jehovah prefer Abel's offering to Cain's? He just did. Don't ask. The quality of the arbitrary, the flighty, the irrational in the preferences of the Almighty has caused endless trouble, starting with Cain's understandable pique. Why not have God say, "You both have good sacrifices there?" Why do blessings so depend on curses? I regard Dickens's evocation of something as vacuous as blessings as all of a piece with this hysterical, forced, ungenerous, incurious novel.

Flora

But Dickens is Dickens, a titanic genius as well as a trivial thinker, and an artist as honest as he was messy. And there's Flora, coming in out of another world and another novel. Moving, resilient, curious, determined, good-hearted Flora. "We do not break but bend" (1: 24: 277), she says, a beautiful sentiment lost in this world of rigid consequence. She is the only character not locked into the past, instead mythologizing it and trying hard to use it to eroticize and enliven the present. She has the ingenuity of all Dickens's great artist figures, the creativity and enthusiasm of Micawber or Dick Swiveller, a flexible Falstaff of the libido.

She parodies what she always brings up, "the dear old days gone forever" (153; bk.1, ch.13), so as to reinvent and release what the rest of the novel and its author want to bottle. Flora is the novel's great artist and its major realist too: "I am not what you expected," she tells Arthur; "I know that very well" (153; bk.1, ch.13). She knows too that he neglects her and she says so, but she does not give up—we do not break but bend—and remains unbroken at the end, a sad reminder of what Dickens had done and a glorious foretaste of what was to come in his career.

In *Little Dorrit* we find not just Flora but, here and there, some other explosions of creative fire, seepings of imaginative juices. There are the

Chiverys and Mrs. Plornish and Miss Wade and some of what Orwell called those little squiggles on the edge of the page. There are so few squiggles, though, that we can sometimes forget them, think that the dominance of the mindless and the unchanging and the unlovely Lolita fantasy were all.

Ending

But that's not all Dickens had to say, nor did he go out on this thin, narrow wail. A mere four years later, after getting *Little Dorrit* out of his system, he penned perhaps the world's greatest novel of mercy and forgiveness, *Great Expectations*, where a mere boy doth offend. An abused and good-hearted boy so understandably wants to join the wealthy that he turns his back on a home that has been for him both a haven and a torture chamber. He is ashamed of home, a shame so lacerating that we think for a time he cannot be forgiven and certainly cannot forgive himself. But unlike the version of Dickens we see in Arthur Clennam, self-pitying and resentful, Pip, on becoming Joe's apprentice, releases his own ego from the past: "once was not now", he says simply and beautifully; "but once was not now" (86; 13). We cannot imagine Arthur or Amy reaching anything like that maturity, simply because Dickens had not. The blessings conferred in *Little Dorrit* are false blessings, the blessings of a selfish preacher. But in *Great Expectations* Dickens reaches Shakespearean heights, conferring blessings on the abusers themselves. Bless them that curse you; do good to them that hurt you. Here the heart swells to include not only all the hurt but those who deal out the pain, simply because they themselves are among the hurt; the two are not distinguishable. Pip's sister is transformed from a resentful, child-beating monster into a fellow creature Pip calls "my poor sister" (213; 35). Shaw says *Great Expectations* is Dickens's "apology to Mealy Potatoes" (46), and it is, but it is more. We know how Dickens felt about his own William Dorrit of an imprisoned father, and we've examined his vow never to forget nor forgive his mother's betrayal. But he did. He just did. Freud says that in forgiving our erring parents, forgiving the William Dorrits and the Mrs. Clennams who hurt us, we are, far more profoundly, forgiving ourselves for all the pain we too deal out. *Great Expectations* is Dickens's apology for *Little Dorrit*, for crafting a work so poisonous, so centered on casting blame and isolating a few victims. But *Great Expectations* is more than an apology; it is Dickens's sublime reach into pity and mercy. As he moves out to forgive his shame-dealing father and the mother he said he could never, would never forgive, he finally is able to forgive himself. In the process, he excludes no one. We ourselves, we who do offend, the fretted and the froward and the vain, are also included. When thou dost ask me blessing, I'll kneel down and ask of thee forgiveness. The blessings are no longer in short supply, doled our so cautiously. Moving beyond the self-pitying narrow economy of blessings ruling *Little Dorrit*, Dickens enters the world beyond guilt and justification, the world of a different father-daughter order, that of Lear and Cordelia, the one Yeats speaks of, at the end of ''A Dialogue of Self and Soul,'' as the uncontrolled, overflowing bounty of blessings: ''When such as I cast out remorse/So great a sweetness flows into the breast,/We must laugh and we must sing,/We are blest by everything,/Everything we look upon is blest'' (232).

WORKS CITED

Collins, Philip, ed. *Dickens: The Critical Heritage*. New York: Barnes & Noble, 1971.

Clemens, Samuel Langhorne. *Adventures of Huckleberry Finn*. Ed. Sculley Bradley, Richard Croom Beatty, and E. Hudson Long. New York: Norton, 1961.

Dickens, Charles. *Great Expectations*. Ed. Edgar Rosenberg. New York: Norton, 1999.

———. *Little Dorrit*. Ed Stephen Wall and Helen Small.. New York: Penguin, 1998.

Forster, John. *The Life of Charles Dickens*. Ed. J. W. T. Ley. London: Cecil Palmer, 1928.

Shakespeare, William. *The Riverside Shakespeare*. 2nd ed. ed. G. Blakemore Evans with J. J. M. Tobin. Boston: Houghton Mifflin, 1997.

Shaw, George Bernard. *Shaw on Dickens*. Ed. Dan H. Laurence and Martin Quinn. New York: Frederick Ungar, 1985.

Yeats, W. B. *The Collected Poems of W. B. Yeats*. New York: Macmillan, 1960.

Madame Defarge as Political Icon in Dickens's *A Tale of Two Cities*

Linda M. Lewis

Dickens's portrait of Madame Defarge alludes to both Furies and Eumenides, as well as to Thomas Carlyle's depiction of political Maenadism in his history of the French Revolution. Further, Dickens revised history to assign undeserved culpability to Madame and her female followers because he imagined bloodthirsty armies of marauding women at the core of the Revolution. As soldier, terrorist, and orator, the goddess/witch of Saint Antoine projects Dickens's horror of women in public and political life. As ersatz mother of the Revolution's children of violence, she is his most chilling perversion of maternity. Using French iconography of public and popular art as evidence of the evolving image of the citoyennes *of the Revolution (Lady Liberty metamorphosed into a monstrous female Terror), this essay traces Madame Defarge's allegorical deterioration from patriot to monster.*

In *A Tale of Two Cities,* Charles Dickens makes allegory of both the abstract qualities that pummel humans and the human characters that represent abstract qualities. The unforgettable Madame Defarge, witch of Saint Antoine, angel of revolution, goddess of retribution, and historian who preserves a text of the Revolution's victims, is a principal allegorical figure of the novel. When she points her knitting needle ''as if it were the finger of Fate'' (328), Dickens associates her with the three fatal sisters who spin, weave, and cut the skein of life. To her dearest disciple she is a ''celestial witness'' and "cherished Chief" (446); to her enemy, the "wife of Lucifer" (452). Although I agree with Michael Slater that Madame Defarge is a "melodramatic creation . . . from Jacobean revenge tragedy" and one of the "spinning hags who personify Fate" (291), she is more than that. Alluding to specific women and to allegorical womanhood from Carlyle's history of the Revolution and capitalizing on the iconography of woman that throughout the Enlightenment and Revolutionary periods had evolved in French art, caricature, and the popular imagination, Dickens creates in Madame Defarge his most memorable allegory for radical feminism. Amazon and virago, Maenad and tigress, she is also the insatiable cannibalistic mother who consumes her own allegorical progeny, and paradoxically—although she has no biological children—she becomes the most malevolent of Dickens's bad mothers, as well as a horrific exemplum of women in civic and military life. Madame Defarge is, in fact, a far more radically political icon than has been previously acknowledged. Not only is she a soldier and terrorist; she is also a would-be politician.

Dickens reported to John Forster, his friend and later his biographer, that during the time he was working on the novel, he read *only* historical texts devoted to this era—mainly Thomas Carlyle's *History of the French Revolution* ("Mr. Carlyle's wonderful book" that he praises in his preface). And Dickens's very source repeatedly employs allegory in his narration of the Revolution; for instance, Carlyle characterizes the rebellion of French mothers agitating for food in the expression "Maternity must forth to the streets . . . " (1: 251–52). Thus Dickens creates a tribe of Revolutionary females to mirror the "Menads" of Carlyle's text—women warriors who organize neighborhood gangs, participate in the bloodiest action of the Revolution, and provide evidence that political womanhood is a force to be feared and rejected. Of Dickens's female patriots Patricia Ingham notes, "Such demons, wandering Grendel-like in the outer darkness beyond England, are the infamous 'other,' the negative that defines that positive, the true Englishwoman" (5). Their chief is Thérèse Defarge, wife of the wine merchant who is the official organizer of the Saint Antoine section of Paris. Madame Defarge herself is a spy, instigator, orator, and renegade soldier who takes control of her marriage, of the Revolution, and of the direction of the narrative—until she is violently and permanently erased from that narrative, thus intimating that the political future should brook neither female revolutionaries nor a revolution favoring female rights. And just as Dickens uses the miserable hunger of Saint Antoine as object lesson that the poverty and distress in his native country, if unrelieved, could well spark an English revolution, he also suggests that the militant and political *citoyennes* of Saint Antoine are a blood-curdling answer to the "Woman's Question" then being debated in England.

Madame Defarge is not only the terrifying power of political womanhood, but also a double to Lucie Manette, the "positive . . . true Englishwoman" of the text (in spite of the fact that she is French born). To her loyal attendant, Miss Pross, Lucie is the "Ladybird" and angel of her house, while to the Vengeance, her faithful lieutenant, Madame Defarge is an inspiring "Angel" of revenge. Perpetually "knitting, knitting, knitting" into "shrouds" the names of those to be "registered" for La Guillotine, she cruelly parodies Lucie, whose "golden thread" binds her extended family in London and on the continent. Both the golden thread and the knitted yarn bind the Past to the Present to the Future. No doubt Dickens discussed this doubling with his illustrator, Hablot K. Browne, because the cover of the monthly installments balances images of Lucie and Madame on the left and right respectively, and the selfsame thread of their handiwork connects them to one another (fig. 1). Elizabeth A. Campbell, in her study of the iconography of Dame Fortune in Dickens's works, points out that in Browne's illustrations (especially for *Nicholas Nickleby* but including other covers as well), a female figure for good fortune appears on the left and another for ill fortune on the right side of the illustration (*Fortune's Wheel* 6).[1] Thus Madame Defarge is the Revolution's bad luck or "Fortune's dangerous attractiveness" (Campbell 19), in addition to being its icon for political woman power.

When Madame "Boldface" (Pross's sobriquet for the angel of Saint Antoine) meets her end at the hands of the grenadier Miss Pross, though, the French murderess becomes a double to the English protectress—hate against love, radical iconoclast versus conservative traditionalist (455). Dickens defends the comic end to Madame Defarge—shot by her own gun in a tussle with Miss Pross—because he wishes to deprive her of the glorious, melodramatic "dignified"death reserved for Sydney Carton. In a letter to Bulwer-Lytton, Dickens writes that in Madame Defarge's case, the "accident is inseparable from the passion and action of the character" and works as "an act of justice" (Forster 3: 324–25). Actually, Dickens needed to murder Madame Defarge both because she threatens to become the star of a novel designed to sensationalize the heroic martyrdom of a male hero *and* because he advocates a future in which woman is denied control of a national narrative. (What kind of New Jerusalem could Sydney Carton imagine for Paris if France were to become a nation in which women legitimately debated, voted, and influenced the republic's destiny?) When he kills Madame Defarge in the comic secondary plot, Dickens also signifies his relief for the burial of the female emancipation that accompanied the revolution for Liberty, Equality, Fraternity. Like his mentor Carlyle, Dickens interprets woman's rule as misrule.

The heroine of Saint Antoine is about thirty years of age, stout and strong, with a gypsy-like style, complete with large earrings and a bright shawl twined around her head. To her admiring husband, Thérèse Defarge is "[a] great woman, a strong woman, a grand woman, a frightfully grand woman!" (224). She is beautiful and graceful, carrying herself about the streets with

Fig. 1. Monthly Wrapper for *A Tale of Two Cities,* No. 1 (June, 1859). Hablot K. Browne.

the freedom of gait of one who in her girlhood had walked "bare foot and bare-legged, on the brown sea-sand" (448). When she discards the colorful shawl for the Phrygian cap of the Revolution, the narrator reports that "her dark hair looked rich under her coarse red cap" (448). Catherine Waters remarks that the text dwells on bodily details that were sites of sexual signification in Victorian middle-class culture: hair, bosom, waist, and legs (137). Madame has that "kind of beauty which not only seems to impart to its possessor firmness and animosity," the narrator says, but also "to strike into others an instinctive recognition of these qualities" (447). Certainly Lucie Manette Darnay recognizes this firmness and animosity when she appeals in vain to her "sister-woman" to spare the lives of those whom Lucie loves. People forget Madame Defarge's youth and beauty, however, because of the horror she inspires—and perhaps because she is the fairy of evil fortune, not lady luck. George Orwell, who considers her as "Dickens's most successful attempt at a *malignant* character," also includes her among the "sinister old women" knitting at the foot of the guillotine (16). As for the 1935 David O. Selznik film, Madame is magnificent, but hardly a beauty. In fact the rose alternately stabbed into and snatched from her headpiece is a very mockery of femininity and flirtation.

Several critics, including Earle Davis (147), Shifra Hochberg (99), and Lisa Robson (325), have identified Dickens's source for Madame Defarge as Anne-Josèphe Théroigne, formerly courtesan and *salonnière*, who joined the woman's march on Versailles in October 1789 wearing a plumed hat, short riding skirt, and red revolutionary sash, saber at her side. Known as the "Amazon of Liberty" because she called for women to arm themselves, Demoiselle Théroigne was also characterized as the "red goddess of death, surging up out of the waves, a new Venus . . . " (Gutwirth 326). In Carlyle, she recalls both Pallas Athena and the Maid of Orléans (1:255), and her slogan as "Sibyl Théroigne" of 1792 is "Vengeance, *Victoire ou la mort!*" (3:299). If Dickens refers directly to Carlyle, he has split or doubled the allegory: Madame Defarge—pistol hidden in her bosom and dagger tucked at her waist—represents the flamboyance of Théroigne with saber at the waist, while the starved grocer's fat wife, known only as the Vengeance, represents simply the quality of revenge that her name labels. In Carlyle's history, in fact, an unnamed young woman seized a drum and shouted to her companions, "Descend, O mothers . . . to food and revenge" (1: 252). When the Vengeance, who is "custodian of the drum" in Dickens's novel (276), flings her arms "like all the forty Furies at once" (272), she recalls the Eumenides as her commander, Thérèse Defarge, does the Fates.

It is likely that, since Dickens wishes to make the women more unnaturally bloodthirsty and more "terrible" than the men (272), he conflates several of the violent female acts (as he does much of the feminist rhetoric) of the

Revolution into the formidable person of Madame Defarge. To intensify the effect, he also assigns to the female participants of the Revolution certain acts that history does not attribute to them. There was not a unified woman's movement during the tense times prior to the outbreak of the Revolution, but women had begun acting out in disorderly ways. Some mobbed storehouses to seize food. Laundresses stole supplies to pursue their trade, thus flouting the laws of private property. Women flooded various neighborhoods, coercing the enlistment of both men and other women. (As dramatized in Dickens's text this is the Vengeance "tearing from house to house, rousing the women" [272]).

In 1789, however, five to six thousand angry women armed with sticks, pitchforks, pikes, muskets, and pistols marched on Versailles demanding bread (Thompson 94), and one of them, Madeline Chabry, placed their demands before Louis XVI. In 1790 women of Marseilles helped eviscerate the citadel commander and danced the farandole while carrying his bodily organs on pikes (Gutwirth 311). In that same year four to five thousand, some with pistols stuffed in belts, confronted municipal officers at Montauban (Sutherland 109). In 1793 Charlotte Corday, a Girondist, assassinated the journalist Marat, for which act she went to the guillotine. Madame Defarge as allegory for female violence is—as W. B. Yeats says of another revolution—"a terrible Beauty."

The allegory of a female body as political icon had existed in French art and the French imagination for quite some time. Indeed, the female body as allegory dates from a far earlier period. In Greek and Roman art the female icon was usually venality, wisdom, or innocence (in the persons of Venus, Athena, or Artemis). In Christian art her extremes are the tender, loving Madonna and the horrifying, decapitating beauty (Judith beheading Holofernes or Salome bearing the head of John the Baptist). The voluptuous French Rococo goddess of an earlier period of the eighteenth century had represented Beauty or Desire, but after 1789 the icon of a beautiful, statuesque, often bare-breasted female (usually armed with spear or sword) was put to use again and again in the service of national chauvinism. According to Marina Warner, the classical tradition was "retrieved and reshaped" for the Revolution, a useful adaptation in that the goddess icon, classical figure for the political state, represents the virtues of Amazonian virginity and independence (273, 280). The female icon was Nike or Victory, Reason, Equality, Truth, Law, but most frequently she was La Liberté and often she leads the charge into battle, as Madame Defarge does. Later Delacroix was to borrow the allegorical icon in his familiar "Liberty Guiding the People," a painting of the 1830 revolution anachronistic in its depiction of Phrygian cap (or *bonnet rouge*), Amazonian body type, shortened skirt, unencumbered legs, and weapon at the ready. This is the iconography that Dickens uses for the armed and dangerous Madame Defarge. Dickens obviously knew this French icon of a female as liberty because when the Parisian mob dances the Carmagnole on the day that Charles Darnay is tried, they place a young woman in a chair and triumphantly carry her as the Goddess of Liberty—a reference to the statue of this very goddess erected at the Place de la Concorde in 1793, where, according to Madelyn Gutwirth, she sat in "relentless immobility above the scaffold" of La Guillotine (301), which is also gendered as female. Indeed Liberty was a terrible Beauty.

As the Revolution continued and as French women became more volatile as activists, protesters, and warriors, the icon of woman evolved from beauty to horror, and the female body as allegory came to represent Discord, License, Disobedience, Malignancy, Wickedness, Calumny, and Vengeance. According to Madelyn Gutwirth, the "most celebrated image of the militant Republican Woman" contemporary to the Revolution is "*Françaises Devenues Libres*" (Frenchwomen Become Free). This particular female soldier holds a spear and stands firmly on a rocky summit, the chains of *her* captivity broken into pieces at her feet. Her caption reads, in part, "And we too, we know how to fight and win. We are able to wield other arms than the needle and the distaff. Oh Bellona! Companion to Mars . . . should not all women walk in ranks and in steps equal to men's?" (295). A similar rhetorical claim to female equality in battle is expressed in Madame Defarge's more blunt "We can kill as well as the men . . . " (263). As previously noted, French women entered the fray and marched as impromptu armies. Carlyle records that both women and men stormed Versailles and forcibly removed the king.[2] (In Carlyle's view, allegorical Menadism joined allegorical Rascality.) Women committed violent acts, resorted to violent rhetoric, and formed societies and political groups. In 1792 they petitioned to bear arms as the men were doing. By that date "it would be the turn of the women of the petty-bourgeoisie and the people to play preponderant roles" in the Revolution (Gutwirth 222). Some iconoclastic women wore the cockade of the revolution and in so doing demonstrated that they too were equal citizens—legally or illegally. Other women counter demonstrated as political societies were formed and the Républicanes attacked Jacobin women. *Sans-culottes* women attended the political rallies of the Jacobins, apparently with more regularity than *sans-culottes* men (Soboul 196). French women, initially demanding bread for their children, eventually demanded political personhood for themselves.

Dickens is writing fiction, not history, and cannot be faulted for simplifying the complexity of the demands and discord among the *citoyennes*; in his allegorical text, all the women at the Bastille are variously armed but "all armed alike in hunger and revenge" (264). For Madame and the other Maenads, though, he taps into the predominant caricature of women who aspire to the manly arts of war and politics. In Carlyle's version women who wielded the cutlass of war were "Amazons" (1:266), "Judiths" (1:252, 253, 254), "Eve's Daughters" (1:256), and "draggled Insurrectionists" (1:261), while the female political assembly was made up of "She-deputies" (1:271) and "squalid women" (1:263)—a "Senate of Menads" (1:272)—and those who eventually turned on Théroigne in 1793 were Gorgons—"serpent-haired Extreme She Patriots" (3:154). Except for the bourgeois woman compelled to join the march on Versailles, the female warriors in figure 2 are harridans who, slightly exaggerated, could be the models for that cackling witch, the Vengeance, in the Selznik movie. Further, some aspects of Chérieux's satiric illustration of a women's political meeting, complete with the tricolors and Phrygian cap (fig. 3), are mirrored in Hablot Browne's illustration of the taking of the Bastille (fig. 4).[3] The ludicrous, unruly, dangerously militant and political woman figure is similar in Chérieux and Browne—especially the plump, gesturing woman on the extreme right—in Browne's work, the Vengeance, identifiable as the keeper of the drum.

Dickens's particular revulsion over woman activists is echoed repeatedly throughout *A Tale of Two Cities*. In the execution of Foulon the "bloody-minded" women "beating their breasts, tearing their hair, and screaming . . ." are "lashed into blind frenzy, whirled about, striking and tearing at their own friends until they dropped into a passionate swoon" (272, 273). They cry, "Give us the head of Foulon, Give us the heart of Foulon, Give us the body and soul of Foulon, Rend Foulon to pieces" (272). As in the shamelessly exhibitionist Carmagnole, their behavior, their sexually-charged frenzy, and their cannibalistic screaming are depicted as unnatural and unwomanly. Yet the scene and the words are not entirely inaccurate. According to Richard Cobb, *sans-culottes* women spoke with bravado of how they would eat the hearts of non-sympathizers, and at village lynchings they boasted in murderous language, such as "It is I who tore out his eyes. . . . It is I who cut off his penis. . . . It is I who severed his head. . . . It is I who chopped his skull" (60). The women's language may not have been more horrifying and bloodthirsty than the men's, but because women are supposed to be tender keepers of the domestic sphere, their ranting *seems* all the more terrible. Waters notes that in Dickens "The Revolution is represented as a kind of Amazonian 'misrule.' It is gendered. . . ." (124–25). In the slaying of Foulon, Dickens recalls the Maenads of Euripides's *Bacchae* who, enraged and inebriated, tore and dismembered the body of Pentheus, or, as Carlyle suggests, those who "hewed off the melodious head of Orpheus" (1:255–56).

It is noteworthy, I suggest, that in Dickens almost every major scene of violence against aristocrats, functionaries of the *ancien régime*, and enemies of the Revolution features frenzied women and Madame Defarge at the center of the action, for example, decapitating Launay or—when the hanging noose

Fig. 2. ''A Versailles, à Versailles, du octobre 1789''; reproduced by permission of the Musée Carnavalet, Photothèque des musées de la ville de Paris.

Fig. 3. Chérieux, ''Women's Political Meeting in a Church''; reproduced by permission of the Bibliothèque nationale de France, Paris.

Fig. 4. "The Sea Still Rises," illustration for *A Tale of Two Cities,* Book II, Chapter 22, by Hablot K. Browne.

breaks—playing with Foulon as a cat does with a mouse. The major exception is the grindstone scene in which males are the central figures, and even in that horrible spectacle the priestesses of the Revolution (in a bizarre doubling of the Mass or parody of nurturing motherhood) hold wine to the mouths of the barbarous savages who sharpen hatchets, knives, bayonets, and swords. Also the feminine is present in that the men are unnaturally and "devilishly" set off with the spoils of women's lace and ribbon (presumably of slain aristocratic women) and some of the savages wear false moustaches made of the pubic hair of massacred female victims.[4] Even in this horrific scene the Revolution is, as Waters says, "gendered." And we recall that the cult of La Guillotine has replaced veneration of the Virgin.

The image of Madame Defarge remains in our memory after we have forgotten most of the plot details and minor characters of the novel. This is because—as Paul De Man says of allegory—metaphors are more tenacious than facts (5). Several brutal images and actions stamp Madame permanently in our minds. For example at the storming of the Bastille she bides her time, waiting near Launay until he is beaten down, then like the tigress she is, she springs into action, placing her foot on her victim's neck and "with her cruel knife—long ready—hewed off his head" (268)—an act not historically attributed to an avenging woman, but to a mob. In his discussion of the Medusa myth, Freud has famously remarked, "To decapitate = to castrate" (212–13). It is a primal fear. The horrific image of Judith sawing off the head of Holofernes or the Maenads' beheading of Orpheus is eerily like Madame Defarge's decapitation of the Bastille's governor, which is also eerily like the cry "It is I who cut off his penis." There is a reason that Carlyle's history obsessively refers to the female revolutionaries as "Menads" and "Judiths." The daggers, pikes, sabers, bayonets, and pistols wielded by men and appropriated by women are phallic imagery, and the arming of women is, symbolically, the *disarming* of men. If Madame Defarge is, as I argue, political womanpower unleashed, the allegory is plain: women, if given the power, will castrate the very civic state that in public art had been personified by the icon of a grand, serene female.

In his study of Dickens and violence, Jeremy Tambling concludes that parricide is the subtext of *A Tale of Two Cities*, with the gallows of Old Bailey as the "national phallus" (132), a male counterpart of La Guillotine. Since the French plot is about the extermination of the patriarchal aristocracy, Tambling equates paralysis to both the Oedipal and the Medusa fear in that both genders perpetrated the violent overthrow of the patriarchy. Nevertheless he relies upon Freud's *The Interpretation of Dreams* in which Juno's promise to "stir up Hell" is interpreted to mean that revolution is chthonic, that the "appeal to hell and to the Medusa-like Allecto suggests the way the woman works when confronted by a patriarchy that blocks her" (134). Despite Tambling's insistence on the Oedipal struggle in Dickens's novel, he admits that "[t]he political-revolutionary and the sexual map onto each other" (139). What Tambling largely ignores, though, is that in Dickens's tale the feminine power is the more frightening, more unnatural, and more insane, just as the guillotine is more blood-curdling (and far more frequently employed) than the gallows. The dark and fearful chthonic of the Medusa figure is in myth written upon (or rather, within) the female body, not the male, and Dickens's Maenads are, the narrator of the novel insists, more chilling than their fellow revolutionaries. In Dickens's text as in Carlyle's history, both male and female lust for blood and decapitation, but in Dickens it is the female icon who dominates the allegory. Dickens selects specific acts that history records as committed by men and attributes them to Madame Defarge because he wishes the actions of the novel to support the narrator's claim that women's violence is the more chilling. Not only is the Revolution gendered, as Waters notes, but Dickens uses the female revolutionaries to undermine female political prerogative; in their indecent and irrational frenzy, the savage *citoyennes* prove themselves incapable of cool-headed political deliberation.

As for the familial allegory, Madame Defarge (now middle-aged) becomes wife and ersatz mother of the Reign of Terror. As "wife of Lucifer" she is also like Lady Macbeth, fearing Defarge to be too full of the milk of human kindness in regard to the kin of his former master, Doctor Manette. Therefore she takes charge of the revenge of the Terror and no longer divulges her evil plots to Ernest Defarge. As mother she perverts her allegorical children, inciting them to bloody vengeance which will in turn destroy them. Except for the little Darnays and a nameless child heedlessly run down by the coach of Monseigneur, the novel is uncharacteristically lacking in children, and the narrator notes that in the village, children are as scarce as are the crops in the surrounding country. In Saint Antoine children suffer as, for example, after the slaying of Foulon, the perpetrators return to their children who are "wailing and breadless" (275). The Vengeance is said to be the mother of two, but we are not informed whether they are as malnourished as the skinny grocer who begat them. Because a curse has been pronounced on the family of Madame Defarge, no patter of little footsteps is heard in the wine shop. Aristocratic women are all tarred with the same brush of "flaring Jezebels" (459), and among their company not one would own to being a mother just because she had brought into the world a "troublesome creature" whom she turned over to a peasant woman to wet nurse (126). In all of France there is apparently no mother to match the gentle Lucie Darnay. But Madame Defarge becomes a stepmother to the children of violence. The mender of roads, upon reporting the execution of Gaspard, is praised as a "good child" and a "good boy" by Defarge (200, 208), and Madame promises the good boy that if he obeys, he will be rewarded in playthings. In gazing at the king, queen, and court today, she says, you have been shown a great heap of dolls or a flock of trapped birds, and you shall have the opportunity to "pluck them to pieces and despoil them for your own advantage" (211).

Madame Defarge's allegorical children are spies, terrorists, and murderers, and like Madame herself, they must be "exterminated" from the future's text. Just as lady Liberty had been an allegorical icon of Revolutionary ideals, the Terror in allegory was characterized as an evil mother slaughtering her young, for example, in a drawing attributed to P.-P. Prud'hon and featuring an enthroned ogress who has replaced the goddess Liberty and whose dying adult children lie in her lap or in a pile at her feet (fig. 5). Indeed, some of the Revolution's great goals (including the desire for female enfranchisement) became casualties, and as Murray Baumgarten notes, the new class of "paper-using notaries and lawyers [and] merchants dealing in Wemmick's celebrated portable property" led the peasantry and emerging proletariat (166). Thus the extremist Defarges leave no progeny. And as allegory for French feminist demands, Madame Defarge causes us to recall that Revolutionary women's agitating for full citizenship and equal rights also produced no legitimate progeny. Legislation did not empower women, and Napoleon exiled Mme de Staël, their most articulate spokeswoman.

It is significant that as allegory, Madame Defarge's final double is Miss Pross, the plain, outspoken British goddess of culinary arts who presides over her death.[5] Pross, "wild, and red, and grim" (116) is physically formidable—a match in size and strength for the cruel Madame. Endowed with stolid qualities and an unimaginative intellect, she is nevertheless "quite a Sorceress, or Cinderella's Godmother" (117) in the kitchen. For her fierce loyalty to Lucie in particular and to middle-class virtues in general, she ranks near to the "lower Angels" (113). In what turns out to be Madame Defarge's death struggle, Pross stresses her Englishness to the "wicked foreign woman" in phrases such as "I am an Englishwoman" (453), "I am a Briton [who does not] care an English Twopence for myself" (454), and "If those eyes of yours were bed-winches, and I was an English four-poster, they shouldn't loose a splinter of me" (453). Elsewhere in the text, though, Pross reveals her English chauvinism as a subject of George the Third in the maxim "Confound their politics, Frustrate their knavish tricks, On him our hopes we fix, God save the King!" (358). Miss Pross, as patriot, royalist, and defender of the English home, doubles and contrasts, as well as eradicates, Madame Defarge—iconoclast, feminist, and king killer.

A Tale of Two Cities does not contain Dickens's only attack on female politicians and activists. A more direct satire is found in *Bleak House* (1852–53) in which the French murderess and "tigress" Hortense is a precursor for the tigress Defarge and English women on "mission" are satirized as ludicrous freaks. Mrs. Jellyby ignores the needs of her own children to save the distant natives of Borrioboola-Gha, and Mrs. Pardiggle involves

Fig. 5. Attributed to P.-P. Prud'hon, ''Allegorical Drawing of the Terror'';
reproduced by permission of the Bibliothèque nationale de France, Paris.

herself in ineffectual canvassing, electing, and the polling of tens of thousands. Evidently the caricatures of Jellyby and Pardiggle satirize individual English women whose names and missions were familiar to the reading public. According to Dennis Walder, however, at the time Dickens was writing *Bleak House*, his own wife, Catherine, was involved in the anti-slavery campaign, helping draft "An Affectionate and Christian Address of Many Thousands of Women" from British female activists to their American sisters urging them onward in the abolitionist cause (164). Certainly Dickens opposed American slavery, and he famously supported charitable causes. But private philanthropy and public campaigns—especially campaigns launched by English wives and mothers—are two different things. Besides, by 1852 the bloom was off the Dickens marriage; Catherine Dickens (her husband was to claim) was given to depression, emotionally disengaged from her many children, and incompatible with her famous husband. If Mrs. Dickens's omissions and commissions had by 1851 begun to rankle, it is likely that Dickens included his wife and her fellow campaigners in the composites of Mrs. Pardiggle and Mrs. Jellyby. (It would not be the only case in which Dickens satirizes a woman he formerly adored, as he does Maria Beadnell in the shallow, garrulous Flora of *Little Dorrit*).

I do not suggest that Madame Defarge is a version of Catherine Dickens, but rather that the involvement of middle-class English women in feminist and political causes prompted the outlandish satire in *Bleak House* and that Dickens chose to raise the stakes in his horrible nightmare of Madame Defarge and her female army. Recall that Dickens often returns to the same human category, sometimes treating individual representatives of that category as buffoons, other times as villains. So it is with feminists. Mrs. Pardiggle and Mrs. Jellyby are misguided, unfeminine, humorless, and ridiculous, while Madame Defarge and the Vengeance are dangerous, calculating, remorseless, and cruel. *A Tale of Two Cities*, among other things, reprises the Dickensian theme of woman's unfitness for political life with the notable difference that the feminists of *Bleak House* are laughable, not malignant. While I agree with Waters that the Revolution is gendered and acknowledge that Madame Defarge was probably inspired by Carlyle's sensational depiction of Anne-Josèphe Théroigne, I also suggest that a likely 1859 reader response would reconsider 1850s English feminism—whether subtle or strident—in light of the murdering Maenads of Revolutionary France and would take the implicit warning of let the nation beware. It is after all an interesting footnote to Mrs. Jellyby's career that, once her mission on behalf of the Africans has failed, she turns to a campaign to seat women in the English Parliament.

Dickens's ideas on feminist politics are not derived from Carlyle, but by happy coincidence both were appalled at the possibility of women's involvement in the civic state; therefore Carlyle's descriptions of disorderly women protesters and revolutionaries prove quite useful for Dickens, who exchanges generic "Menads" for a single grand, albeit terrifying, female terrorist. In *The French Revolution*, Carlyle expresses revulsion at the possibility of firing a musket into a female breast. (No doubt Dickens experienced a similar revulsion, so he awards Miss Pross that privilege.) Carlyle depicts women in warfare as monstrous Bacchanates and women in political debate as ludicrous freaks. Of the French women's political caucus he notes that, like Erasmus's Ape who mimicked Erasmus shaving, "so do these Amazons hold, in mock majesty, some confused parody of National Assembly" (1:272). He imagines the mayhem of a Female Parliament with " 'screams from the Opposition benches' and 'the honourable Member borne out in hysterics' " (2:26). Unlike Carlyle, Dickens does not in his version of the French Revolution depict a political assembly of women in (although he *does* depict their attempts at political organization in *Bleak House*); rather, in the historical novel he illustrates their screeching, scheming, and slaughtering as perverse and unnatural. Their commander, the decapitating/castrating Madame Defarge, serves as his unforgettable iconic warning against woman as leader, soldier, or politician. And as the victorious Miss Pross says on Dickens's behalf, "Confound their politics."

NOTES

1. According to Campbell, Dickens's daughter/mother fates are the "youthful sexually attractive Fortune who attracts the hero's desires" and the "ancient and deadly sorceress who embodies the hero's fears" (xix). They are usually paired, for example, Esther Summerson/Lady Dedlock, Estella/Miss Havisham, or Amy Dorrit/Mrs. Clennam. Perhaps the absence of the crone Fortune in *A Tale of Two Cities* is the reason that some readers mentally transform Madame Defarge into an old witch, although the text describes her as young and attractive.
2. Dickens's depiction of women as playing a major role in the taking of the Bastille is largely invention. It was only months later, however, that they became organized, armed, and militant.
3. Paul Schlicke notes that Browne's composition is undramatic, the plates hastily executed, and the costumes "historically inaccurate" (552). Andrew Sanders, however, comments that the "delineating of eighteenth-century costume" is generally careful (166). I suggest that if "Phiz" did any research, he would likely have perused some of the multitude of visual representations produced during the Revolution.
4. Dickens does not identify in the text the source for the "false eyebrows and false moustaches," but Andrew Sanders believes that Dickens has mistakenly referred to the murder and mutilation of the Princesse de Lamballe, whose body was

desecrated according to both Carlyle and Mercier (in *Nouveau Paris*). See Sanders, 14.

5. Miss Pross is also Madame Defarge's double in the allusion to Lady Macbeth: Madame chastises her reluctant husband as Lady Macbeth does, while Pross holds the candle, as Lady Macbeth does, to assist Lorry in the ''murder''of Manette's shoemaking implements. The allusion to Shakespeare's tragedy is noted by several critics. See, for example, Sanders, 161, 113

WORKS CITED

Baumgarten, Murray. ''Writing the Revolution.'' *Dickens Studies Annual: Essays on Victorian Fiction* 12 (1983): 161–176.

Campbell, Elizabeth, A. *Fortune's Wheel: Dickens and the Iconography of Women's Time.* Athens: Ohio UP, 2003.

Carlyle, Thomas. *The French Revolution.* 3 vols. London: Chapman and Hall, 1896.

Cobb, Richard. *The Police and the People: French Popular Protest, 1789–1820.* Oxford: Clarendon, 1970.

Davis, Earle. *The Flint and the Flame: The Artistry of Charles Dickens.* Columbia: U of Missouri P, 1963.

DeMan, Paul. *Allegories of Reading; Figural Language in Rousseau, Nietzsche, Rilke and Proust.* New Haven: Yale UP, 1979.

Dickens, Charles. *A Tale of Two Cities.* Oxford: Oxford UP, 1982.

Forster, John. *The Life of Charles Dickens.* 3 vols. London: Chapman and Hall, 1872–74.

Freud, Sigmund. *Sexuality and the Psychology of Love.* Ed. Philip Rieff. New York: Macmillan, 1963.

Gutwirth, Madelyn. *The Twilight of the Goddesses: Women and Representation in the French Revolutionary Era.* New Brunswick, NJ: Rutgers UP, 1992.

Ingham, Patricia. *Dickens, Women and Language.* Toronto: U of Toronto P, 1992.

Hochberg, Shifra. ''Madame Defarge and a Possible Carlylean Source.'' Dickensian 91 (1995): 99–101.

Orwell, George. *Dickens, Dali and Others.* New York: Reynal and Hitchcock, 1946.

Nelson, Harland S. ''Substance and Shadow in *A Tale of Two Cities.*'' *Dickensian* 84 (1988): 97–106.

Robson, Lisa. ''The Angels in Dickens's House: Representations of Women in *A Tale of Two Cities.*'' *Dalhousie Review* 72.3 (1992): 311–33.

Sanders, Andrew. *The Companion to* A Tale of Two Cities. London: Unwin Hyman, 1988.

Schlicke, Paul, ed. *Oxford Reader's Companion to Dickens.* Oxford: Oxford UP, 1999.

Slater, Michael. *Dickens and Women.* Stanford: Stanford UP, 1983.

Soboul, Albert. *The Sans-Culottes: The Popular Movement and Revolutionary Government 1793–1794.* Trans. Remy Inglis Hall. Princeton: Princeton UP, 1980.

Sutherland, D. M. G. *France 1789–1815: Revolution and Counterrevolution.* New York: Oxford UP, 1986.

Tambling, Jeremy. *Dickens, Violence and the Modern State: Dreams of the Scaffold.* New York: St. Martin's, 1995.

Thompson, J. M. *The French Revolution.* Oxford: Basil Blackwood, 1985.

Walder, Dennis. *Dickens and Religion.* London: George Allen & Unwin, 1981.

Warner, Marina. *Monuments and Maidens: The Allegory of the Female Form.* London: Weidenfeld and Nicholson, 1985.

Waters, Catherine. *Dickens and the Politics of the Family.* Cambridge: Cambridge UP, 1997.

Scenes of "Incredible Outrage": Dickens, Ireland and *A Tale of Two Cities*

Deborah Wynne

Shortly after visiting Ireland during his first public reading tour in 1858, Dickens set to work to write A Tale of Two Cities. *The novel's depiction of violent crowds, mass hysteria, and spiritual awakening can be related to the religious turmoil which characterized Ireland in 1858 and 1859, when revivalism spread throughout the Protestant community. Many contemporary reports of the revivals in the periodical press likened the public activities of the revivalists to the work of revolutionaries, and there were fears that revivalism would spread to mainland Britain. Indeed, readers of the original serial version of* A Tale of Two Cities *in Dickens's weekly magazine* All The Year Round *were presented with numerous articles emphasizing the links between the Irish revivals and previous examples of revolutionary and religious turmoil. There is evidence to suggest that Dickens, in* A Tale of Two Cities, *engaged with contemporary debates on the social and political situation of Ireland during the late 1850s. This view is strengthened by the fact that he supported the installments of his novel with features based on crowd psychology and the breakdown of social order.*

In a letter to his daughter Mary written from Ireland during his first public reading tour in August 1858, Charles Dickens described the force of the Dublin crowd entering the theater as "so great, that I had difficulty getting in. They had broken all the glass in the pay boxes" (8:640). He went on to recount yet more violent scenes in Belfast:

The people here are much rougher than in Dublin, and there is a very great uproar at the opening of the doors, which, the police in attendance being quite inefficient and only looking on, it was impossible to check. Arthur [his manager] was in the deepest misery because the shillings got into the stalls, and half-crowns got into the shillings, and stalls got nowhere, and there was immense confusion.   (8:641)

This scene of confusion, of "rough" people who, uncontrolled by the police, refused to respect the class divisions signalled by the seating arrangements, was clearly alarming to Dickens. Nevertheless, he felt confident of his powers to subdue the unruly crowd. He added in his letter that the uproar subsided "the moment I showed myself; and all went most brilliantly" (8:641). However, this enthusiastic account of his ability to control the Irish crowd was somewhat contradicted by the *Belfast News-Letter*'s report of "frequent and most unpleasant interruptions" during the first part of Dickens's reading (8:641 n. 3). Shortly after his tour of Ireland, Dickens began to write *A Tale of Two Cities*, another story of "rough" crowds that overturn traditional class barriers; however, unlike the Irish audiences apparently subdued by Dickens's presence, depicted in the novel are crowds that no power can quell.

It is not surprising that Dickens should develop ideas for a novel based on crowd psychology during his first tour, when he read to the huge and enthusiastic audiences filling each theater, and this visit to Ireland stimulated his work on *A Tale of Two Cities*. He had first formulated plans for the novel in 1857 while acting in Wilkie Collins's melodrama *The Frozen Deep*. Inspired by his role as the tormented yet heroic Wardour, who sacrifices his own life to save that of a rival, Dickens envisaged a story based around the themes of self-sacrifice and redemption. In a letter to Angela Burdett Coutts, he remarked that while he was acting the role of Wardour he was "very much excited by the crying of two thousand people" in the audience (8:432). Dickens's sense of fascination and excitement in his ability to manipulate the crowd prompted him to develop his career as a public reader. Indeed, he found his public performances increasingly addictive and, as Helen Small has argued in her discussion of the public readings, the atmosphere at Dickens's performances can be likened to "Chartist rallies and Methodist preaching" (184), where charismatic speakers manipulated the emotions of the crowds.

A link between politics and religion was evident in Ireland during the late 1850s, for Dickens's Irish tour coincided with the emergence of a religious revival which swept through Ulster and isolated areas in the south of the country, a movement that foregrounded the power of the crowd. The revival had its origins in New York in 1858 and swiftly spread to Ireland via visiting preachers who had witnessed events in America.[1] Many areas of Ireland were affected, although it was in Ulster among the Presbyterian community that revivalism was at its most intense. The British press reported numerous instances of "unruly" crowds whose public prayer-meetings were characterized by violent displays of emotion. Many of these were dominated by working-class women who abandoned their work in the factories and mills to display publicly their new-found sense of religious conviction (''Irish Revivals'' 286). Dickens's reports of the crowds breaking the glass in the theater pay—boxes suggests that he was aware of, and stimulated by, the emotional energy latent in the Irish crowds at this period. By tracing the links between Dickens's encounter with the emerging Irish revival and *A Tale of Two Cities*, we may possibly uncover connections between the generic and thematic concerns of the novel—the revolutionary crowd, hysteria, resurrection, spiritual regeneration, and a preoccupation with history—and the Irish Protestant revivals of the late 1850s.

Indeed, revivalism manifested itself as a dramatic upsurge of religious emotion which, as David Hempton and Myrtle Hill have argued, lingered in ''the Ulster Protestant psychology'' as a ''historical event and supernatural encounter invested with almost mythical significance'' (146). An anonymous article, ''The Irish Revivals,'' in the *Saturday Review* in 1859 (when the revival was at its height), reported the events in Ulster in terms of a ''terrible epidemic,'' arguing that the overtly physical displays of emotion on the part of the revivalists constituted an offense against ''public morality, public decency, and public health,'' comparing its effects to that of ''an open sewer or uncovered drain'' (285). Many revival meetings involved outbreaks of hysteria, convulsions, and temporary loss of hearing and sight. In some areas of Ulster the local economy was seriously disrupted by the revivalists' night-long prayer-meetings, where participants were rendered weak and incapable of work by the physical and mental exhaustion attendant on the process of spiritual conversion (Chapman 100).

For many Victorians in mainland Britain, the revivals in Ireland were uncomfortably reminiscent of a revolutionary uprising, and *A Tale of Two Cities*, based on the French Revolution of 1789, can be usefully read as an oblique yet powerful comment on contemporary Ireland. The novel's images of the uprisings of oppressed social groups, unruly crowd behavior, religious excess, spiritual manifestations, resurrection, and prophecy were, as I mentioned earlier, key features of the Ulster revivals. However, this link has not generally been apparent to most twentieth-century critics of Dickens's novel. Philip Collins has argued that while *Barnaby Rudge*, Dickens's previous historical novel, was stimulated by Chartist demonstrations, ''Nothing comparable was happening in England in the middle or late fifties, to give topicality to (or to inspire) the crowd scenes in the *Tale*'' (344). More recently, Hilary Schor has maintained that *A Tale of Two Cities* raises few ''political questions,'' differing from Dickens's other novels of the 1850s in that ''it poses none of the questions of topicality'' associated with his work of this period (73). While *A Tale* is something of an anomaly in the Dickens canon, this is not because of its lack of topicality: indeed, the British media emphatically linked the religious demonstrations in Ireland to the historical precedents of violent mass action in France. Revivals were read as potentially revolutionary because they were characterized by mass public action on the part of the working classes, and the vigor with which the link was made between revolutionary France and Irish revivalism would have made it difficult for readers of 1859 *not* to perceive *A Tale of Two Cities* as topical.

There were, of course, many other factors that undoubtedly fed into Dickens's novel. The influence of Carlyle's *French Revolution* has been well-documented elsewhere.[2] However, recent Irish history was also fresh in the British public's consciousness, an unhealed wound and a register of British guilt and "weariness," as Harriet Martineau suggested in her article, "Conditions and Prospects of Ireland" in the *Westminster Review*: "The world is weary of the subject of Ireland; and, above all the rest, the English reading world is weary of it. The mere name brings up images of men in long coats and women in long cloaks; of mud cabins and potatoes; . . . the faction fight and the funeral howl. The sadness of the subject has of late years increased the weariness" (35). The Famine of the 1840s continued to be brought before the British public throughout the 1850s in articles such as Martineau's, and the prevalence of images of Irish hunger and anger may have acted upon Dickens's imagination during his tour of post-famine Ireland, forging links with another hungry people, the revolutionaries of eighteenth-century France. The poor in *A Tale of Two Cities*, like the Irish poor, are neglected by the powerful, and are represented as pervaded by the "intangible impurities" of "poverty and deprivation" (41). The most readable sign in the Parisian slum district in *A Tale* is hunger:

> It was prevalent everywhere. Hunger was pushed out of the tall houses, in the wretched clothing that hung upon poles and lines; Hunger was patched into them with straw and rag and wood and paper; Hunger was repeated in every fragment of the small modicum of firewood that the man sawed off; Hunger stared down from the smokeless chimneys, and started up from the filthy street that had no offal, among its refuse, of anything to eat.   (34)

There were signs of hunger in Ulster, too, when Dickens read to the "rough" crowds in Belfast. Hunger, according to recent interpreters of the Ulster revivals, provided the catalyst for the most extreme manifestations of unruly behavior at revival meetings (Hempton and Hill 156–57). One Victorian commentator, John Chapman, also emphasized the role played by poverty in the revivals. Writing in the *Westminster Review* in 1860, he argued that the majority of revivalists were working women "whose diet often consists wholly of bread and tea, and who work 13 hours a day"(32). Chapman added that the most vulnerable revivalists were the "mill girls," and he suggested that their public activities constituted a protest against their appalling working conditions. He described how on one morning in 1859 twenty young women in one mill were "struck down—each in an instant—at their work, several becoming insensible at once" (32). This suggestion of a causal link between female hysteria and politics is further reinforced when Chapman describes how one working-class Frenchwoman who suffered for years with "hysterical paralysis" was able to walk freely during the three days of the Paris insurrection in June 1848. Her paralysis returned, however, on the declaration of peace (32).

The heightened tension in Ireland was one of the few things Dickens noted about the social situation in his letters from Ireland during his reading tour. He told an Irish friend, Percy Fitzgerald, that he believed the inhabitants of Belfast to be "A curious people . . . quite in a state of transition" (quoted in Ackroyd 836). This period, when he was establishing himself as a public reader, was also a state of transition for Dickens himself. His marriage had recently ended, and he was disturbed by a turbulent passion for the young actress Ellen Ternan (Ackroyd 808–14). Desiring a second chance, a new beginning, Dickens set about exploring the narrative possibilities of spiritual transformation and social and individual renewal. The Irish revivalists' claims to cross thresholds of experience, to see supernatural visions, experience spiritual rebirth, to be resurrected from spiritual death, and to make prophecies were ideas already haunting Dickens's imagination in the late 1850s, when his performance of Wardour in *The Frozen Deep* galvanized his emotional energies. Revivalists in Ulster claimed that their public activities were outward manifestations of spiritual resurrection, and this coincided with Dickens's own intense desire for a new beginning. While death and revival feature in many of his works, the concept of resurrection is, as numerous critics have suggested, crucially important to an understanding of *A Tale of Two Cities* (see Hutter 1–39). The novel is permeated by the notion of the threshold, its narrative poised on the moment of France's violent break with the *ancien regime* and its forging of a revolutionary future, presenting a range of characters who hover between life and death, imprisonment and freedom, spiritual darkness and enlightenment, burial and revival.

Ireland, then, offered much to fuel Dickens's imagination in the late 1850s, although its contribution to *A Tale of Two Cities* has tended to be overlooked by critics. However, for original readers of the novel (first serialized in Dickens's own weekly magazine, *All the Year Round*) the link between revolutionary France and contemporary Ireland was emphasized. Alongside the novel's installments were numerous features on religious extremism, revivals, and public violence, all of which complicate and enrich any reading of *A Tale*. Original readers of the serialized novel were offered a set of dramatic images in the form of articles and stories depicting crowds, political unrest, and spiritual resurrection, creating a bridge between Dickens's novel and the Ulster revival. *A Tale of Two Cities* was designed to launch *All The Year Round*, the magazine that replaced *Household Words*.[3] The new magazine's subtitle, *The Story of Our Lives From Year to Year*, promised socially relevant features that would be meaningful to contemporary readers. ''The story of our lives,'' however, often turned out to be a story about history, whether in the forms of historical fiction or of articles about the past. This historical focus dominated the magazine's first seven months when *A Tale* appeared. During this period Gaskell's novella *Lois the Witch*, based on the seventeenth-century Salem witch trials, also appeared in three installments alongside later sections of Dickens's novel.

Although most other periodicals did not interweave fiction and journalism as creatively as Dickens did with *All the Year Round* (Wynne 2001, 22–28), many shared his emphasis on a link between violent events in history and the revival in Ireland. Numerous articles on history in Dickens's magazine and other journals reinforced the idea that ''the story of our lives'' was a story of repetition, that the past had a tendency to repeat itself, for the Irish revival was seen as a new outbreak of the traditional mass hysteria which was believed to characterise all popular demonstrations.[4] The historical focus in the press was also pertinent to the revival in Ireland, which was interpreted by many commentators as a return to a superstitious past characterized by religious extremism. Indeed, for many journalists, the events in Ulster were difficult to represent except in terms of history repeating itself. The Dancing Maniacs of the fifteenth century, the French Convulsionnaires and the British Shakers of the eighteenth century, along with the Methodist Camp Meetings of the early nineteenth century, were all seen by various commentators as precedents for Irish revivalism.[5] For many Victorians the phenomenon suggested a form of social rebellion, as those revivalists who claimed to be ''struck'' by the Holy Spirit tended to go on ''strike,'' insisting on their incapacity for work. Indeed, the ground gained by bourgeois capitalism in disciplining the workforce was in danger of being undermined by the strange carnival atmosphere, that sense of release from social restraints and industrial discipline, which characterized Ulster at the height of the revival.

British fascination with the revival in Ulster can be gauged by the plethora of publications that appeared at the time of the outbreak attempting to explain the phenomenon. Revivalists and their sympathizers even established their own journal, *The Revival News: A Weekly Record of Facts and Incidents Connected with the Present Religious Revival*. Whether viewed positively or negatively, the revivals were, according to a number of Irish commentators, an ''important event in our national history'' (Llewellyn Davis 368). Not only did ''experts'' such as clergymen, journalists, and medical specialists see history in the making, but there was a strong belief that the ''problem'' of Irish revivalism was only to be solved by a study of the past. If the lessons of history were learnt, such writers argued, the apparent threat of "contagion" from Ireland could be averted. These arguments attempted to render the revivals harmless by suggesting that the public gatherings were merely symptoms of a mass hysteria which had emerged regularly and irrationally throughout history. If one turned to "the pages of history" (a favorite phrase which attempted to render the past into an easily read text) one could find similar instances of a futile religious mania that afflicted the poor and uneducated before burning itself out ("Hysteria and Devotion" 31–35). This emotional intensity played out in public, along with the huge crowds acting in unison, engendered numerous complaints against revivalism.

Revivals had, of course, occurred before the 1850s. From the early nineteenth century the word "revival" became a derogatory term for religious excess. However, the word itself had other connotations. The *Oxford English Dictionary* defines "revive" as "restore to life; to resuscitate or reanimate; to bring back *from* death or the grave." These aspects of revival are foregrounded in *A Tale of Two Cities*, where Mr. Lorry's message, "Recalled to life" (10), becomes the keynote of the whole novel. Dickens was fascinated with the boundaries between the rational and non-rational, the living and the dead, the material and the spiritual—boundaries which the Irish revivalists' activities brought into public consciousness. Many Irish people, particularly women, claimed to have crossed the threshold between this world and the next, reporting conversations with Christ and knowledge from beyond the grave (Holmes). Yet tracing the ways that Dickens uses the imagery of revivalism in his novel is complex, for while *A Tale* makes overt use of prophecy and works towards the spiritual regeneration of Sydney Carton, it also emphatically denies that the mysteries of spiritual life can be fathomed and pours scorn upon popular spiritualism (2).

Although the narrator of *A Tale of Two Cities* clearly states in the first chapter that there is no access to the world beyond the grave, the novel abounds with characters who hover insecurely between life and death, who are buried and alive, who resurrect corpses and living men, who foretell the future at the moment of death and who are near death yet travel full circle back to the beginning. The notion of revival surfaces in many forms. Defarge tells the Parisian crowd he has "News from the other world" (271), going on to explain that Foulon has been resurrected, not from death, but from hiding after faking his own death. This is one of many deflationary revivals in the novel; others include the English spy Cly's return after *his* fake burial, and Cruncher's semi-comic role as the "resurrection man" who digs up fresh corpses for medical experiments. Yet revival is also treated seriously, both in terms of Manette's resurrection from the spiritual death of his imprisonment in the Bastille and Carton's moral regeneration as he voluntarily sacrifices himself at the guillotine in order to secure the freedom of his rival. Even

Dickens's use of the historical genre is linked to the theme of revival, for history itself, of course, is a way of reviving of the dead.

The Ulster revivals were similarly marked by the ambiguities of the term "revival." Supporters of the revival maintained that the movement had brought about a new spiritual awareness among Irish Protestants; however, critics argued that the phenomenon not only revived memories of a dark past of ignorance and superstition, but was also reminiscent of the French Revolution. Many British journalists sought to demonstrate that the events in Ulster were identical to events that had already taken place, and readers were urged to dismiss the revivals as "the popular hallucinations of darker ages" ("Antecedents of Revivalism" 669). Hysteria (rather than social deprivation, political unrest, colonial rebellion, class resentment, or gender hostility) was, according to many writers, the common thread which united each manifestation of religious fervor. Numerous journals argued that religious mania was an illness to be cured either by increased discipline (according to the more conservative writers in *The Saturday Review*) or by increased political representation (according to writers in the radical press).[6]

Of the many discussions of Irish revivalism in the Victorian press, *The Saturday Review*'s two articles were most virulent in condemning the movement. In "The Irish Revivals," the anonymous author attacked what he termed Irish "hysteria," drawing on the recently published pamphlet by Edward A. Stopford, the archdeacon of Meath, to condemn what was seen as "this ghastly train of disease, disorder, immorality" (286). For Stopford, the fact that the revivals had occurred among the Protestant community was particularly disturbing, and his eyewitness account of a revival meeting is quoted in the article at length:

> I feel bound to give the most solemn warning, and to enter the most solemn protest, against proceedings which fill the streets of Belfast at late hours of the night with hysterical young women, in company with hysterical young men. I dare not enforce my warning, lest I reveal the means [*sic*] of incredible outrage. In the name of all that is sacred in woman, I call for a reform of what every policeman in Belfast sees to be indecent and wrong.   (286)

Such accusations of indecency stemmed from the unrestrained bodily displays of the revivalists and the opportunities this offered for close physical proximity between the sexes. Indeed, Stopford complained that "coarse" men attend revival meetings simply as a pretext for unlicensed sexual contact with women.

Women's roles in the Irish revival were sources of alarm, for their public actions were not only seen as "indecent," but also served to remind observers of the French Revolution. For many Victorians the most significant image of the Revolution was of disruptive Frenchwomen taking to the streets, and this connection between women and revolution may have fuelled fears that the revivals were a harbinger of political trouble in Ireland. However, the Irish press was more cynical and less alarmist than the British media. *The London-derry Standard*, for example, considered the female revivalists of Ulster to be "lazy," using the religious turmoil as an excuse to avoid work, while the *Belfast News-Letter* reiterated this view, casting doubt on the validity of the women's spiritual experiences (Holmes 143). The prominence of women, particularly working women, in the revival activities and their adoption of the role of preachers was a major reason for the attention given to the events in Ireland at this time. Another reason for the wide press coverage of the revivals was a fear that unruliness in Ireland could spread to other Celtic regions in Britain (Elliott-Binns 214). Many periodicals described revivals in terms of a "terrible epidemic" ("The Irish Revivals" 285), a "fever" ("Hysteria and Devotion" 31), having "contagious effects" (Llewelyn Davis 363). There was an awareness that although Ireland was perceived to be on the margins of Britain, it was too close to the main centers of imperial power to make any unrest there seem negligible.

Indeed, the revival in Ireland also entered the literary imagination in significant ways, providing a set of images based on spiritual regeneration and the power of the crowd that was not only captured by Dickens in *A Tale of Two Cities*, but also by its companion in *All The Year Round*, Elizabeth Gaskell's *Lois the Witch*, which also treats the themes of religious extremism and crowd power within an historical context. Both Dickens's and Gaskell's accounts of historical violence were pervaded by religious themes and imagery redolent of events in Ireland. *Lois the Witch* complemented *A Tale of Two Cities* by offering another example from history of the violent consequences of mass action on the part of an oppressed social group. The heroine, Lois, is caught up in the religious hysteria of Salem in the 1690s, and the story ends with her execution when she is accused of witchcraft. However, although Dickens and Gaskell appear to acknowledge in general terms the political motivations of the popular uprisings they represent, both work to neutralize this in their depictions of crowds as hysterical. In *Lois the Witch*, Gaskell depicts the actions of the female community of Salem as a hysterical response to political instability. For her, hysteria is the only form of public action or speech open to powerless women that, despite its apparent irrationality, has a rational basis (Wynne 2005, 90–92). However, the British media's coverage of female political action in Ireland consistently refused to acknowledge the rational basis of women's actions at revival meetings, choosing instead to see the revivalists as emotionally unstable publicity-seekers.

Many periodicals, particularly the conservative *Saturday Review*, went even further, discussing the crowds of Irish revivalists as lacking humanity. Dickens in *A Tale of Two Cities* dramatically captures British anxieties about the politically motivated crowd by emphasizing its non-human qualities. Indeed, denying the humanity of the crowd was a strategy used by Victorian novelists and journalists as a way of signifying the otherness and political extremism of those who took to the streets *en masse* in order to express their disaffection. By suggesting that protestors lacked humanity, commentators implied that their protests were rendered invalid. Such strategies of containment were symptomatic of most bourgeois responses to crowd behavior serving to remove the crowd from the spheres of political action and power into the realms of madness and weakness, thus defusing any perceptions of threat (Plotz). As Hilary Schor has argued, *A Tale of Two Cities* has ''the gothic or nightmare quality of social rage'' (73), the ''nightmare'' quality being centered on Dickens's depiction of the crowd.

Like Carlyle in *The French Revolution*, Dickens was deeply sceptical about the possibility of mass action constituting a rational event. *A Tale* presents a series of crowd scenes in France and Britain, each illustrating Dickens's belief in the irrationality of mass action. All crowds in the novel, whether French revolutionaries, the London mob, or religious fanatics, fail to achieve coherence, and this is because for Dickens the individual members of a crowd simply cease to be human. The London crowd is ''the human stew'' (92), and its behavior at Darnay's trial is ''Ogreish,'' for it desires to see the man accused of treason ''butchered and torn asunder'' (72). On Darnay's acquittal, ''the crowd came pouring out . . . and a loud buzz swept into the street as if the baffled blue-flies were dispersing in search of other carrion'' (91). Later, the mob who follow Cly's funeral in London are depicted as using the event as an excuse for drinking, random window-breaking, and theft (189). Neither crowd is organized around any coherent idea; indeed it is the ''absence of any idea'' which is emphasized when Cruncher asks the British crowd, ''What's it about?'' only to hear choruses of ''*I* don't know'' (187) from the participants.

In the next chapter Dickens continues the image of the irrational crowd with a scene depicting an adoring crowd at Versailles who cheer the French king and queen. The Defarges watch the Road-mender's response as he ''bathed himself'' in the spectacle of royalty, catching the ''temporary intoxication'' of the crowd ''until he absolutely wept with sentiment'' (210). Defarge holds him by the collar ''as if to restrain him from flying at the objects of his brief devotion and tearing them to pieces'' (210). Whether he tears the king and queen to pieces because he loves them or hates them, the Road-mender is depicted as incapable of knowing why he does what he does. A similar confusion characterizes the crowd at Darnay's French trial. When he is acquitted and carried out of court by a ''weeping, embracing, and shouting crowd,'' the narrator states that a few moments before the same crowd would have ''pluck[ed] him out into the streets and kill[ed] him'' (349). For Dickens, then, the political signification of a crowd is impossible because the emotions engendered by people *en masse* preclude rationality. As *A Tale of Two Cities* progresses, the reasons for the French Revolution, stated at the outset of the novel, recede progressively until the crowd is reduced not only to the non-human (such as the "blue-flies" which constitute the London mob), but to things which have never lived, "a vast dusky mass of scarecrows heaving to and fro" (261), a "remorseless sea of turbulently swaying shapes" (268).

It is significant that readers of *A Tale of Two Cities* and *Lois the Witch* in *All the Year Round* encountered such images of violent and irrational crowd behavior at the height of the revivals in Ireland. Dickens's powerfully melo-dramatic images of the London and Paris crowds find echoes in the reports of "incredible outrage" on the streets of Belfast. Such fictional images, however, served to defuse the political message which struggled to emerge from the revivalists' actions. Instead of contemplating a hungry people, ex-ploited by capitalism and colonialism, British readers were prompted to see the Irish revivalists as gullible people manipulated by skilful agitators. Indeed, the revivals in Ulster were blamed on irresponsible preachers who, for rea-sons of their own, encouraged people to abandon their work and take to the streets. Similarly, in *A Tale of Two Cities*, an "excited orator" is shown at work, manipulating a French crowd (310), while elsewhere Madame Defarge is described as "a Missionary—there were many like her—such as the world will do well never to breed again"(224).[7] This representational strategy, whereby mass action is shown as the work of a few cunning individuals rather than a group of like-minded protestors, was repeatedly used by many Victorian writers (both in fiction and journalism) to deflect attention from genuine social problems and inequalities. It is feasible that the protest behavior of the revivalists in Ulster was ineffective for precisely this reason: that it was misrepresented in the British media in terms of an irrational emotional outburst.

Dickens's denigration of "excited orators" who emotionally manipulate crowds is difficult to credit when one takes into account his own career as a public reader. As one contemporary, Charles Kent stated, Dickens's public readings were all characterised by emotional intensity: "Densely packed from floor to ceiling, these audiences were habitually wont to hang in breathless expectation upon every inflection of the author-reader's voice, upon every glance of his eye" (Small 281–82). Small argues that the "[f]ear of an outbreak of crowd hysteria appears repeatedly in all accounts of Dickens's performances," and the organizers were "at times uncertain whether they are producing a glorious public event or provoking a public outbreak of hostilities" (281–82). Yet it is worth asking the question: Did Dickens, in the euphoria of his public readings in Ireland in 1858, find inspiration for his next novel in his apparent power of controlling a crowd which had a danger-ous potential to burst into anarchic action? While Dickens described himself as taming the "rough" Belfast crowd at his public reading, one local woman attending a revival meeting in the city described the mood of the meeting as feeling as though she was "in a house on fire with the doors shut" ("Antecedents of Revivalism" 670). It is possible that the strange energy unleashed in Ireland as the revival spread emerged transformed in *A Tale of Two Cities*. Dr. Manette, in the document he writes in the Bastille, states: "I had never before seen the sense of being oppressed, bursting forth like a fire. I had supposed that it must be latent in the people somewhere; but I had never seen it break out" (401). Dickens himself may have seen it, or something like it, break out in Ireland in 1858.

NOTES

1. For a detailed discussion of the history and development of the Ulster Revival, see Hempton and Hill.
2. See, in particular, Timko 117–19, Gilbert 247–65, and Craig.
3. The first issue of *All The Year Round* appeared in April 1859.
4. *Lois the Witch* appeared in *All The Year Round* on 8, 15, and 22 October 1859. For a discussion of this novella see Wynne 2005, 85–98. Among the historical articles which appeared in *All The Year Round* during this period are "Hysteria and Devotion," "Subterranean Switzerland," "A 'Revival' Under Louis the Fifteenth," and "Drift" (the latter a short feature based on historical anecdotes which appeared irregularly between June and November 1859).
5. See, in particular, "Antecedents of Revivalism" 669 and Llewelyn Davis 368.
6. See "The Irish Revivals" and "Antecedents of Revivalism." For more radical contemporary assessments see Llewelyn Davis.
7. Dickens uses a similar strategy in *Hard Times*, where he blames the strike on the work of cunning agitators, rather than exploited workers. See Craig 80.

WORKS CITED

Ackroyd, Peter. *Dickens*. London: Sinclair-Stevenson, 1990.

"Antecedents of Revivalism." *Saturday Review* 8 (3 December 1859): 669.

"A 'Revival' Under Louis the Fifteenth." *All the Year Round* 2 (19 November 1859): 82–86.

Chapman, John. *Christian Revivals: Their History and Natural History*. London: np., 1860.

Collins, Philip. "A Tale of Two Novels: *Tale of Two Cities* and *Great Expectations* in Dickens's Career." *Dickens Studies Annual* 2 (1972): 336–52.

Craig, David. "The Crowd in Dickens." *The Changing World of Charles Dickens.* Ed. Robert Giddings. London: Vision, 1983. 5–90.

Dickens, Charles. *The Letters of Charles Dickens.* Vol 8: 1856–1858. (The Pilgrim Edition). Ed. Graham Storey and Kathleen Tillotson. Oxford: Clarendon, 1965.

———. *A Tale of Two Cities.* Ed. Andrew Sanders. Oxford: Oxford UP, 1998.

Elliott-Binns, L. E. *Religion in the Victorian Era.* London: Lutterworth Press, 1936.

Gaskell, Elizabeth. *Lois the Witch.* Ed. Laura Kranzler. *Gothic Tales.* London: Penguin, 2000.

Gilbert, Elliot L. " 'To Awake From History': Carlyle, Thackeray, and *A Tale of Two Cities.*" *Dickens Studies Annual* 12 (1983): 247–65.

Hempton, David and Myrtle Hill. *Evangelical Protestantism in Ulster Society, 1740–1890.* London: Routledge, 1992.

Holmes, Janice. "The 'World Turned Upside Down': Women in the Ulster Revival of 1859." Eds. Janice Holmes and Diane Urquhart. *Coming into the Light: The Work, Politics and Religion of Women in Ulster, 1800–1940.* Belfast: Queen's U of Belfast P, 1994. 126–45.

Hutter, Albert D. "The Novelist as Resurrectionist: Dickens and the Dilemma of Death." *Dickens Studies Annual* 12 (1983): 1–39.

———. "Hysteria and Devotion." *All The Year Round* 2 (5 November 1859): 31–35.

———. "The Irish Revivals." *Saturday Review* 8 (3 Sept. 1859): 285–86.

Llewelyn Davis, Rev. J. "The Revivals of 1859." *Macmillan's Magazine* 1 (March 1860): 363–73.

Martineau, Harriet. "Condition and Prospects of Ireland." *Westminster Review* 59 (January 1853): 35–62.

Plotz, John. *The Crowd: British Literature and Public Politics.* Berkeley: U of California P, 2000.

Schor, Hilary. "*Hard Times, Little Dorrit* and *A Tale of Two Cities.*" Ed. John O. Jordan. *The Cambridge Companion to Charles Dickens.* Cambridge: Cambridge UP, 2001: 64–77.

Small, Helen. *Love's Madness: Medicine, the Novel and Female Insanity, 1800–1865.* Oxford: Clarendon Press, 1996.

———. "Subterranean Switzerland." *All the Year Round* 8 (5 November 1859): 31–35.

Timko, Michael. "Splendid Impressions and Picturesque Means: Dickens, Carlyle, and the French Revolution." *Dickens Studies Annual* 12 (1983): 117–95.

Wynne, Deborah. *The Sensation Novel and the Victorian Family Magazine*. Basingstoke and New York: Palgrave, 2001.

———. "Hysteria Repeating Itself: Elizabeth Gaskell's *Lois the Witch*." *Women's Writing* 12:1 (2005): 85–97.

Stage Presence: Performance and Theatricality in Dickens's *Our Mutual Friend*

Seth Rudy

By 1864, Charles Dickens had for more than a generation written within a literary tradition that put staged performances, public readings, and private perusals of novels on equal footing. Dickens's critical awareness and careful deployment of theatrical tropes in Our Mutual Friend *create a novel dependent on multiple layers of performance. The melodramatic romance of Bella Wilfer and John Harmon constitutes the novel's genre piece; set in a world of characteristically Dickensian verisimilitude, its characters are actors in a well-staged and familiar play. That play, however, is being observed by another set of characters within the novel. The Podsnaps, Veneerings, and Buffers are the real targets of Dickens's social commentary. The roles they play outside the context of novelistic melodrama reflect a culture of public performance in the real, living theater of Victorian London. This essay examines that complex interplay of theatricality and reality in contemporary English society.*

Charles Dickens saw London as a stage. He observed the dialects, mannerisms, and values of the highly diverse metropolitan population and redeployed them among the opulent mansions, smoke-filled pubs, and ramshackle houses that constituted the settings of his novels. In *Our Mutual Friend*, his last completed novel, Dickens invites the reader back to the city-stage to hear

Dickens Studies Annual, Volume 37, Copyright © 2006 by AMS Press, Inc. All rights reserved.

another fanciful story of waylaid fortunes, built around the River Thames and founded upon treasures of dust. As the title suggests, though, the reader will have more than a spectator's relationship with the world Dickens presents. Set in "these times of ours," the novel conflates the real and imagined cities; it includes the reader in its complex morality tales and comments on the reader's part in them. The multiple layers of dramatic presentation upon which the novel depends reflect a culture of public performance in the real, living theater of Victorian England. *Our Mutual Friend* both uses and violates the conventions of that culture in order to render its author's critique of contemporary socioeconomic institutions.

Modern readers, separated by nearly a century and a half from the year in which the novel appeared, cannot hope to have the same experience of it as its original audiences. The intervening time has obscured a critical structural layer of *Our Mutual Friend* that contemporary readers, according to Deborah Vlock, would not have overlooked. "Victorian readings of the novel," Vlock writes, "were mediated by the culture of theater—not merely because readings so often took the form of public declamation in the nineteenth century . . . but because novelists like Dickens drew quite freely from the body of sociodramatic possibilities established by the theater" (9). This mediation in many cases precluded the intensely personal interpretative process familiar to the modern reader. Instead of approaching the novel as distinct from other modes of storytelling and in isolation from other readers, Victorians often experienced reading as a performative event in a social context. The theater provided a template for interpreting the novel and in doing so automatically situated any reading in a conceptual, if not actual, social space. As a result, readers participated in a public mode of interpretation bounded by common conceptions of character and story.

Those conceptions circulated through a number of forms, all of which promulgated and validated an author's representation of the world. Murray Baumgarten claims that Dickens "found no difference between theater and fiction" (18). Vlock takes a more conservative position, suggesting that Dickens "demonstrated a reluctance to privilege the literary over the theatrical" (18). At the least, both Baumgarten and she agree that Dickens and the Victorians saw little or no qualitative difference between reading a text and attending a live performance of it. The frame of reference established by theatrical conventions allowed the complete transfer of interpretive value between the genres. In other words, any manifestation of the novel—a recital, a full-stage production, even reading the text in the privacy of one's home—directly or indirectly evoked similar experiences of attending a public performance. When Dickens gave public readings of one of his novels, for example, he performed the various voices of his characters. This model of performance would seem to privilege his interpretation over any other because the intonations and gestures attributed to the various characters came from the author himself; however, because in performing those intonations and gestures the author drew from a set of dramatic conventions shared by other authors and actors, one could be fairly certain of having a similar experience in any other live venue. The collective understanding of character and narrative typologies permitted multiple, simultaneous recreations of a single generalized interpretation in much the same way two orchestras on either side of the world can play a single piece of music and have both performances sound virtually identical to each other. By working within an established set of performative parameters the orchestras will produce essentially similar renditions. A Victorian reader, then, could come away from the Strand with ideas of Fagin, Nickleby, or Copperfield similar to those held by patrons of the Lyceum or visitors at Tavistock House.

Although attending an actual performance was the most direct way to participate in the public aspect of literary interpretation, it was by no means the only way. Readers removed from the physical spaces of performance could indirectly share in the experience and feel confident that their ''private'' interpretations did not differ greatly from the common conception. A performative reading of a specific novel did not require prior experience with it in any form. Novels came with performance notes preinstalled; the reader, fluent in the language of theater and aided by descriptions of characters' physical appearances and facial expressions, as well as textual representations of dialect (Vlock 21), had but to read the notes in order to recreate imaginatively the performances taking place on stages and in drawing rooms across London. To continue the orchestral analogy, the conductor can hold the sheet music in his hands and hear the symphony in his head. The cues remain for modern, uninitiated readers, who can approximate the sounds and mannerisms of the characters, but without the theatrical template they cannot completely decrypt the code.

The similarity of experience allowed by the parity among the forms had significant ramifications beyond literary interpretation. According to Vlock, ''among Victorians . . . theatrical signs were received as genuine and normative—fully legitimate and operative in the social world'' (26). Readers took their collective opinions about characters from theater and novels and brought them back to their daily lives. In this way, novels continued to function even with their curtains or covers closed. Victorians read performance into reality; the practice permanently sewed the theatrical into the social fabric. By 1864, Dickens had for more than a generation written within this recursive structure of expectation, presentation, and confirmation that made the world into what he wrote and what he wrote into the world. When the first installment of *Our Mutual Friend* appeared in May of that year, readers came to it as devotees of an already classic genre. They came to hear a story or to see a show that they partly helped to write, which was ultimately about them (or about whom they imagined Victorian Englishmen and Englishwomen to be), and about which they already knew a great deal. Dickens did not disappoint. In fact, he exceeded expectations.

Our Mutual Friend does function within the dynamics of nineteenth-century readership as Vlock describes them. It has, however, a critical awareness of that dynamic. That awareness is embedded in its structure, which in addition to the performative mode intrinsic to the nineteenth-century novel depends on two other levels of performance within the story to create a balanced representation of Victorian London. Dickens sets a play within the world he represents; the world he represents is in turn based on a further level of quotidian performances that comprise the true subjects of the author's critique. Real life, according to *Our Mutual Friend*, was *not* the stuff of novels, but like the novel, real life did function through a set of collectively agreed upon theatrical conventions.

The reader encounters the disjunction where the edges of the Harmon, Bella, and Boffin plot run into the elaborate dinners staged in the Veneering household. The former constitutes the first layer of performance within the diegesis (the fictional world created by the author); the latter represents a second, supporting layer in which the former unfolds. At once the most "realistic" and the most fantastical, the Harmon inheritance and romance plots occupy a special place in the novel's portrayal of London. The Harmon stories depend for their success, externally and internally, on cleverly deployed theatrical tropes; but because part of Dickens's project in *Our Mutual Friend* is to illustrate the separation of novelistic and real-life theatricality, he repeatedly and conspicuously treats the Harmon story as a dramatic construction. On the one hand, Dickens enriches the scenes and stories connected to Harmony Jail with the verisimilitude characteristic of his novels. He endows the players with complex human motivations such as love, greed, and revenge, and releases them into a convincingly simulated cityscape. On the other hand, in his postscript Dickens affirms the plot's tentative connection to reality. "There is sometimes an odd disposition in this country," he writes, "to dispute as improbable in fiction, what are the commonest experiences in fact. Therefore, I note here, though it may not be at all necessary, that there are hundreds of Will-Cases (as they are called), far more remarkable than that fancied in this book" (798). This defense, which protests too much the likelihood of the events surrounding the Harmon inheritance, does not occur until the postscript; but several characters, in conjunction with the overall structure of the novel, foreground the theatricality of the primary narrative at various points throughout the work.

In the first chapter, Dickens draws back the curtains. The reader sees on stage precisely what one would expect from a Dickensian or indeed almost any opening act of Victorian melodrama: a heroine, a villain, and the seeds of a mystery. Contemporary audiences would have recognized the first figures that appear from a well-established tradition. As Michael Booth observes in *Theatre in the Victorian Age*, "by 1837 all the necessary and familiar elements of melodrama were in place, including the basic character stereotypes of hero, heroine, villain, comic man, comic woman, good old man and good old woman" (153–54). Most of those characters appear as the story progresses, but Dickens wastes no time in presenting a heroine and villain—Lizzie Hexam and Rogue Riderhood, respectively. Booth also notes that "the father-daughter relationship of the stage . . . is a standard feature of Victorian theater" (155).[1] Dickens immediately provides this familiar pairing as well. He states Gaffer and Lizzie Hexam's relationship even before their names, in the novel's second sentence. The words "dread" and "horror" end the second paragraph in an acknowledgment of melodrama's Gothic origins, and before the story has fully gotten underway Dickens has clearly established its grounding in theatrical conventions.[1]

The action of the opening scene continues to emphasize the author's awareness and use of the genre. Gaffer and Lizzie Hexam pull a drowned corpse from the Thames under cover of darkness. The virtuous daughter Lizzie seems too delicate and moral for the work. In the course of their labors they encounter the obviously sinister Rogue Riderhood; the two men exchange insults and threats, and philosophize on the transience of wealth in a corporeal existence. Gaffer reminds Riderhood that he has ended their business arrangement, and that the two are no longer partners. The chapter ends. The third-person, past-tense narration of the scene sets the reader at a remove so slight and conventional that it does not register. The characters in the novel's traditionally crafted beginning perform directly and solely to the reader. In this way the novelist accomplishes the goal of the successful dramatist: "actors" disappear behind their roles and the reader—the Victorian reader, who comes with the mindset of an audience member—momentarily forgets he is watching a "play."

Almost immediately thereafter, Dickens begins to call attention to the proscenium. Several aspects of the Veneering chapters have multiple functions in service to the same project. Their strange mixture of past and present tense, the superficiality of the hosts and many of the guests, and the descriptions of the house itself bear heavily on the novel's examination of the theatrical. Chapter 2, however, has particular significance, as it establishes the Harmon plot as a fictional narrative contained within the novel's larger world. This world, created and occupied by the often unnamed and faceless men of business who perch at the Veneering dinner table, is larger mainly in the sense that those characters' treatment of the Harmon plot makes it appear subordinate to their own. Setting the first half of the chapter aside, the second half sees the narrator stepping aside to share the stage with Mortimer Lightwood. The guests clamor to hear the story of "the man from Somewhere," and after a guileful display of reluctance Lightwood indulges them. His telling proceeds in the style of narration made familiar to the reader through the conventions of novelistic form:

> We must now return, as the novelists say, and as we all wish they wouldn't, to the man from Somewhere. Being a boy of fourteen, cheaply educating at Brussels when his sister's expulsion befell . . . instantly, he absconded, and came over here. He must have been a boy of spirit and resource, to get here on a stopped allowance of five sous a week: but he did it somehow, and he burst in on his father, and pleaded his sister's cause. Venerable parent promptly resorts to anathematization and turns him out. Shocked and terrified boy takes flight, seeks his fortune, gets aboard ship, ultimately turns up on dry land among the Cape wine: small proprietor, farmer, grower—whatever you like to call it.
>
> (25)

This excerpt occurs halfway through a longer tale elucidating the back-story of the elder Harmon, his fortune in dust, and how he desired to settle the money. Throughout it, Lightwood freely attributes mood, motivation, and manners to his "characters." He becomes a third-person, omniscient narrator to the guests.

His direct invocation of the novelist, though, signals an almost postmodern awareness and flaunting of the genre conventions governing his recital. By the end Lightwood abandons the richly detailed depiction of John Harmon's early life for a list of essential plot points. The form has become so familiar that when "the conclusion of the story of the identical man" appears at an "extraordinarily opportune" moment in the form of a note, Lightwood's audience can confidently hazard three guesses as to its contents. The last of them—"a codicil among the dust"—turns out to have merit, but by the time the reader discovers the truth the moment has long been forgotten. "No," Lightwood says. "Remarkable thing, you are all wrong. The story is completer and rather more exciting than I supposed. Man's drowned!" (27). Harmon's apparent death violates the mandates of contemporary narrative formulas his story had followed up to that point. Only this could make the story interesting to the jaded Lightwood and Wrayburn, who find the conventional endings entirely too predictable.

Chapter 2 sets off the Harmon plot from the larger world of the novel by showing to the reader another audience listening to the story. Lightwood's self-consciously theatrical recounting, moreover, warns the reader to look for the machinery of narrative fiction in the fantastic plot Dickens spends the next several hundred pages portraying as "real." Lightwood's excited response to the twist occasioned by Harmon's death foreshadows and renders ironic the eventual revelation of the truth: the story will end precisely as the Buffers and Veneerings might have expected. Baumgarten, quoting Grahame Smith, notes, "those who read the ending back into the beginning have found this [Boffin/Harmon/Bella] plot a 'weakness' that 'seriously undermines the novel's artistic unity' " (19). This part of the novel may indeed fail in its presumed goal of cogent storytelling, but in its designs to highlight and subvert narrative conventions it succeeds spectacularly. The romance plot must not and does not integrate seamlessly into the otherwise realistic world Dickens creates. It remains a spectacle within the larger narrative, observed and commented upon by a representative audience of both the gullible and sophisticated.

Dickens does not rely solely on Wrayburn and Lightwood to call attention to the performative quality of the Harmon plot. The author makes performance an integral and self-evident part of it. John Harmon plays no less than three separate roles over the course of the novel. Leaving his true identity with the drowned corpse plucked from the river, he reemerges in chapter 3 as Julius Handford. A little time and a change of clothes recreate Mr. Julius Handford as Mr. John Rokesmith, who takes a temporary residence to go along with his temporary name in chapter 4. The reader cannot say with certainty that any of these men are the same person for much of the novel, despite Dickens having been "at great pains to suggest . . . that Mr. John Harmon was not slain, and that Mr. John Rokesmith was he" (798). Until the revelation of his true identity, Harmon's performances represent the seductive falseness of the narrative construction. The reader views his performance of the Rokesmith and Handford characters as do the other inhabitants of the "real" world. Harmon disappears; he performs to the Wilfers, Boffins, and readers as an enigmatic figure of Gothic proportions: dark, quiet, and potentially the robber or murderer the Wilfer girls take him for when he first lets a room in their home (47). For several hundred pages, John Harmon performs equally within and across the boundaries of the text. He is in every sense the lead actor in his play.

Dickens might have suspended the revelation of his true identity to coincide with the resolution of the Boffins' part in the play, thereby maintaining the dramatic façade in its entirety until the end of the novel. Instead, he chooses to reposition his audience halfway through by providing privileged information. Chapter 13 of book II, "A Solo and a Duett," once again reminds the reader of the Harmon plot's dependence on performance by calling direct attention to theatrical and novelistic tropes. Dickens actually goes so far as to begin the chapter by having Harmon remove a costume complete with wig and false beard before launching into a long expositional soliloquy. The gesture takes on symbolic value in the context of the chapter, for as he slips the trappings of the "oakum-headed stranger" (his third role, after Handford and Rokesmith) into his pockets, his various identities finally collapse into the single person of John Harmon. He literally and figuratively unmasks himself, and in his chronicle he notes remarkable similarities to what he has "read in narratives of escape from prison . . . where the little track of the fugitives in the night always seems to take the shape of the great round world, on which they wander, as if it were a secret law" (359). The comment is reminiscent of Lightwood's invocation of the novelist in chapter 2 insofar as it identifies familiar, governing narrative principles at work in Harmon's "real" life. Dickens forces the reader to acknowledge the artificiality inherent in the Harmon tale as a conventional narrative. Within the world of the novel, the established reality remains intact, and the play goes on uninterrupted; the reader, though, with the murder, disappearance, and Rokesmith riddles solved, watches the remaining two books from a vantage point closer to the wings than the stalls. Harmon determines to leave his true self dead and carry on a permanent act as Rokesmith; but to the reader he must forever remain Harmon.

The Harmon revelation establishes a permanent unreality in the primary narrative. The Boffin resolution reaffirms it and encloses the plot within a fantastical world of familiar theatrical figures and traditional moral lessons.[2] Boffin's performance of the Miser completes the reifying cycle discussed earlier as it existed in the reader's world: Lightwood presents the Harmon plot as the subject of a novel; Harmon accidentally becomes a stereotypical Lover-in-Disguise in a predictable romance story; Boffin re-presents the be- havior of the stereotypical misers in the books he has Wegg read to him in order to bring that story to a satisfactory close. A "real" story becomes drama and dramatized stories become "real." By containing the cycle within a narrative substructure, however, Dickens identifies the process as properly belonging to a fictive world in which truth wins over deception, virtue over greed, and love over all. The characters become caricatures in service to a conventional story the entire foundation of which is nothing but trash. Chapter 13 of book IV, tellingly subtitled "Showing how the Golden Dustman Helped to Scatter Dust," adds a final instance of strategically foregrounded theatrical- ity that strains the credibility of the narrative to the breaking point. The Harmon plot completely breaks down when Harmon and the Boffins take what amounts to a curtain call before an audience of the readers and Bella Wilfer. Even within a genre of unreality, the story and its characters finally seem too unreal.

Theirs is not the only reality in *Our Mutual Friend*. If Victorian audiences could not find a true London between the outskirts of Holloway and Boffin's Bower, they could locate it in the world of the Veneerings. Dickens may subvert, explode, and parody the narrative conventions governing the Harmon plot, but he reserves satire for the Buffers, Lady Tippins, the Analytical Chemist, the Veneerings, and to a lesser extent Tremlow, Wrayburn,

Lightwood, and the Lammles. Their characters and actions more accurately reflect the operations of daily Victorian life, and Dickens brings a critical scrutiny to bear on them that the Harmon characters do not merit. Performance remains a fundamental component at this level of the novel's structure, but it lacks an explicit moral telos. Whereas the Harmon performances purposefully dramatize a well-known biblical adage—avarice is the root of all evil—in order to test the virtuous and tempt the wicked, the Veneering performances take place outside the context of any self-contained dramatic plot. Their theatricality is a permanent feature of the Victorian socioeconomic system and proceeds from a foundation immediately recognizable to contemporary audiences as disturbingly realistic.

Dickens never explains how heaps of dust might constitute a fortune. As Adrian Poole remarks in an endnote in his edition of the novel, "what exactly these dust-heaps are composed of is a riddle without an answer . . . there have been disputes about what Dickens expected his readers to assume or imagine on this point" (805). The heaps clearly have value as commodities, for Boffin makes his living from them, and Wegg plans to sell them and divide the proceeds with Venus. Any "money, or plate, or jewellery" the mounds might contain do not actually count towards their worth, so the nature of their value must remain as mysterious as their contents (300). The dust therefore easily assumes wholly metaphoric value—appropriate to the plot it supports. It remains a symbolic abstraction and part of the lesson taught by the Harmon plot.

The Veneering fortune is even more abstract and intangible than dust, but it represents reality to a much greater extent. Veneering made his fortune through financial speculation, which in nineteenth-century England "increased at an unprecedented rate until it was checked temporarily by another great financial crisis, brought about by the collapse in May 1866 of the apparent 'cornerstone' of the British financing system, the great discount house Overend, Gurney" (Cotsell 126). The practice of stock speculation attracted huge portions of the public with the promise of high profits to be had for little risk or effort. Many of Dickens's readers would have been participants in stock speculation; all were inhabitants of a strange world in which a whole class of wealthy individuals could spring up seemingly from nowhere and live opulently on nothing more solid than public opinion. Indeed, Dickens published the first installment of *Our Mutual Friend* just under two years before the calamitous correction of 1866, during a peak period of fraudulent business practices that, as Mary Poovey writes in her introduction to *The Financial System in Nineteenth-Century Britain*, "made it virtually impossible for investors to distinguish a legitimate company from one never intended to survive" (18). Poovey describes a litany of nefarious techniques employed by companies to hoodwink unwary investors:

Promoters issued misleading or even blatantly false advertisements for new companies; "rigged" the market by buying up, then reselling, the inflated shares; appointed "guinea-pig" directors (so called because they received a guinea for attending a board meeting); manufactured "dummy" investors to make up the requisite signatories; and decorated the prospectus's cover sheet with the names of "front-sheeters" (prominent men who might—or might not—have agreed to serve as the company's directors).   (18)

A company only needed to appear real in order to generate real profit. Speculators and company promoters—men like Veneering—did not merely engage in unethical practices or tell lies. The methods listed above bespeak a systematized theatrics of finance. Fraudulent companies were elaborate plays staged in order to attract paying audiences. They had directors, paid actors, playbooks, and press reviews, as well as fantastic first runs and disastrous early closings. Cotsell notes that the number of joint-stock companies in England doubled between 1862 and 1865, and that the bankruptcy lists grew ever longer in the years leading up to the failure of Overend, Gurney (128). The pervasiveness of actual theater in the public consciousness as described by Vlock clearly had its match in the institutions of theatrical economy.

Owen Knowles writes in "Veneering and the Age of Veneer: A Source and Background for *Our Mutual Friend*," that "Dickens seems supremely aware in *Our Mutual Friend* of a dangerously new kind of varnished novelty which threatens to transform English social life into a perpetual and self-aggrandising Great Exhibition . . . built upon mere outward show of solidity, and the manufactured illusion of community in elite society" (88). The fly-by-night organizations and opulent lifestyles of the Veneerings and their companions represent that transformation. The society chapters in *Our Mutual Friend* demonstrate how the conventions of fiction production and consumption also operated in the real world. As Victorian authors and audiences recognized the Miser, Lover, and Villain of the Harmon plot as traditional stage figures, so did they recognize the Veneerings and their companions from the literature produced by a culture of rampant stock speculation and social posturing. Dickens did not have a monopoly on literature concerned with what he viewed as society's descent into show, vanity, and institutionalized deception. Many novels, plays, and pamphlets—some still well-known, others less so—written in the time leading up to and following the Overend, Gurney collapse dealt with related subjects in various styles. For the 1848 edition of *Vanity Fair*, for example, Thackeray wrote a preface entitled "Before the Curtain," in which he assigns himself the role of Manager of the Performance for a puppet show. Periodic digressions on the part of the narrator continue to remind the reader that the story remains merely a play, but of course the device may apply equally to the text and to the world it represents. Becky Sharp is an overt and unapologetic performer in a theatrical society; Thackeray calls direct attention to this to effect his satire. A quarter of a century later, in 1873, Trollope reflected his much more desperate view in *The Way We Live Now*. Dauntingly long and generally humorless, the novel and its London are dominated by the Melmotte character—a Veneering exaggerated in grotesqueness and treated without any semblance of Dickens's sense of play. The theatricality affirmed by Thackeray and Dickens through their clever references to genre and stagecraft receives no explicit notice from Trollope; it is as though he found the conditions of artificiality and immorality so deftly satirized by his predecessors too severe to treat with as light a hand.

Trollope, like Dickens and Thackeray, had supporting texts and figures on which to model his commercial rogues and social poseurs. Throughout the period, articles with titles such as "How We Floated the Bank," "How I Discounted My Bill," and "Starting the Rio Grande Railway" enjoyed wide circulation and provided an immediate literary context for their novels. When *Our Mutual Friend* appeared, "the connection was aided by the appearance within the articles of observations, imagery, and character types similar to those in the novel" (Cotsell 128). Dickens recognized the threat represented by the Veneerings in his novel as fully functional in the real world, and the effectiveness of his satire relied upon his audience having a similar awareness. To the Victorian reader, identifying real counterparts to the Veneering set would have proved far less difficult than locating a Golden Dustman or John Harmon. The "Contractor who (it has been calculated) gives employment, directly and indirectly, to five hundred thousand men" and the "Chairman, in such request at so many Boards, so far apart, that he never travels less by railway than three thousand miles a week" who partake in one of the Veneering dinners (610) stood in for well-known Victorian entrepreneurs. Dickens's audiences would have connected such characters with Sir Samuel Peto, " a great contractor . . . ruined by the collapse of Overend, Gurney," or George Hudson, who "had been at the center of the railway share mania of the 1840s." In Veneering himself, Dickens "may have intended to suggest aspects of Albert Gottheimer's unedifying career" (Cotsell 130–34). Once again the incorporation of reality into literature produced a cycle of expectation; but this time the dramatic possibilities came not from the theater but largely from everyday, highly visible figures and events in the financial world.

Though Dickens fictionalizes these men in *Our Mutual Friend*, he does not allow them access to the predictable, safely moral framework of the conventional dramatic narrative. The satire of society arises in part from a reversal created by the divergent stylistic portrayals of *Our Mutual Friend*'s two realities: Dickens treats the theatrical characters as overtly real, and the real characters as overtly theatrical. As stated above, the Harmon characters have recognizable and sympathetic human qualities. The principal players demonstrate a spectrum of emotions and motivations, and by their story's end have moved along fully developed character arcs. Dickens, however, paradoxically prevents the readers' accepting this story as real by deliberately making its resolution unfeasibly fantastic and by calling attention to its dependence on narrative tropes. A series of unmaskings consistently reveals the plot's theatricality from within the diegesis. In contrast, the Veneering characters never display a similar sense of self-awareness. As representatives of a real world based on a largely theatrical economy, they cannot escape their own performativity. The curtain never closes. Dickens uses stylistic devices and details to heighten that reality's apparent falseness and to differentiate it from the fictive constructions operating in the traditionally novelistic Harmon plot.

Dickensian characters' names typically have special significance. *Our Mutual Friend*'s cast list includes such loaded titles as Headstone, Harmon, Rokesmith, and Riah, among others. All of these have metaphorical value or suggest something about their bearers. Headstone appropriately evokes death imagery; Harmon suggests both harm and harmony; "roke" means a mist or fog; and "Riah" could have several connotations based on various Hebrew derivations, each relevant to his character.[3] In each of these examples, the significance does not become apparent until late in the novel, is acknowledged within the story, or remains little more than a clever but non-essential ancillary feature. "Veneering" and "Podsnap," however, stand apart from the others. They sound conspicuously false and out of place, yet the other characters uniformly accept them or at least leave them unacknowledged. The names conform to the rules governing their reality and so escape notice; to the audience, though, they send a clear signal that the society chapters take place in a theatrical context. Dickens calls upon a very well established dramatic convention in choosing such names. They hearken not just to the Pinchwife and Fainall of Restoration theater, but much further back in time to the Conscience and Reason of Langland's *Piers Plowman*. They signify not merely something, but *everything* the reader needs to know about them. "Podsnap" has entered the English language as a word in its own right; the *Oxford English Dictionary* defines a Podsnap as "a person embodying insular complacency and self-satisfaction and refusal to face up to unpleasant facts." In Dickens's time, the name may have derived from the combination of "pod" and "snap," with each word carrying its own set of unflattering connotations. In the mid-nineteenth century "pod" could mean a large protuberant stomach, or to swell up like a pod. Dickens describes the character several times as a "large man" and one point as "prosperously feeding" (21). "Snap" has a larger host of definitions, including one slang term used in 1864 to mean "any articles or circumstances out of which money may be made." "Veneering," more unlikely an actual name than "Podsnap," defines his character to an even greater extent. Veneering, by definition, has only a superficial existence; it puts a valuable looking surface on a worthless foundation. Knowles writes that the name "abolishes the distinction between human and material, reducing both to the high varnish of social furniture'' (88). In fact, it makes Veneering a two-dimensional, functionary whose only purpose is to maintain the appearance of affluence. He has no life beyond his role in the economic play, no wig or whiskers he can peel off to reveal the ''human'' underneath.[4]

Once onstage, the performers have no choice but to maintain their roles. To break character publicly meant risking what to many Victorians was the only force supporting them: reputation. Rumor had long posed a substantial threat to banks and other financial institutions. The dramatic growth of joint-stock companies and the expansion of the credit system throughout the nineteenth century allowed more individuals to participate directly in an economy dependent on sound appearance; this made maintaining such an appearance increasingly a matter of personal interest to speculators and debtors alike. ''An elite habituated to the patronage of shams,'' Knowles observes, ''spawned a whole class of deceivers by compulsion'' (92). No character development can take place in the society chapters of *Our Mutual Friend* because the system represented by them cannot allow change. Any public display of weakness or insecurity invited potentially catastrophic suspicion. Individuals involved with Victorian finance had to perform in accordance with the character typologies expected by collective opinion: the Contractor, Chairman, Buffers, the Analytical Chemist, and so forth. They do not merit names at all, but instead remain known by their socioeconomic functions.

The narrative mode in this novel's society chapters locks these characters in a permanent performative framework symbolic of their real-life condition. The narrator describes them in the same manner Wrayburn adopted for the end of the Harmon story: ''Mrs. Veneering, W.M.P., remarks that these social mysteries make one afraid of leaving Baby. Mr. Veneering, M.P., wishes to be informed whether it is to be conveyed that the vanished person has been spirited away or otherwise harmed'' (406). In addition to creating an irreverent and hence slightly mocking tone, the present-tense description (exclusively used by the narrator in the society chapters) also suggests the conventions of stage directions. For example: ''She puts the book down, takes another book up, turns the leaves, and presents the portrait to Tremlow'' (410). Every gesture and line reads as though it has been carefully staged, resulting in scenes that, despite their realistic grounding, seem highly artificial in comparison to the rest of the novel.

The Veneerings, Podsnaps, and Nameless Rich represent only the theatrical economy's top-billed actors. *Our Mutual Friend* also records the performances of supporting cast members at lower societal levels. Penniless relations of nobles pretend to wealth; matrimonial mercenaries play their part to self-destruction; clientless lawyers ornament new offices in brass; and a benevolent Jew masquerades as a stereotypical usurer. These characters occupy the interstitial area where the fictional and fictionalized realities overlap.

The Lammles, for example, sit in the dining room in the present tense and discover each other's poverty in the past tense. Fledgeby, Twemlow, Lightwood, and Wrayburn similarly receive both societal and novelistic treatment. As long as they remain at the Veneering table, however, they remain two-dimensional. Only when removed from the realist socioeconomic space the Veneerings inhabit can their characters become "real" in a novelistic sense.

Eugene Wrayburn does not return to Society following his marriage to the profoundly moral and sincere Lizzie Hexam. His last words in the novel condemn it and encourage Mortimer Lightwood to "take a look at Society, which he had not seen for a considerable period" (792). Lightwood comes "in among them with a reassumption of his old languid air, founded on Eugene, and belonging to the days when he told the story of the man from Somewhere" (793). He wearily takes up his expected role. The Veneerings' guests express surprise at Wrayburn's departure, and do their best to dismiss him to a world they view as theatrically trite. Lightwood and Tremlow's defending Lizzie and Wrayburn constitutes the completion of Dickens's social criticism. Lightwood does not allow Podsnap and Tippins to reduce Lizzie Hexam's character to her social function. "Was this young woman ever a female waterman?" Podsnap asks. "Never," Lightwood replies. "But she sometimes rowed in a boat with her father, I believe." "And . . . was she ever a factory girl?" Podsnap thrusts. "Never," Lightwood parries. "But she had some employment in a paper mill, I believe" (794). Eugene and Lizzie no longer merely play assigned parts in either world. The veneer is unnecessary; they have the substance of a lady and gentleman.

Dickens's novel ultimately remains cynical. It ends with the curtains closing not on Wrayburn and Lizzie, but on the Veneerings. Their long expected smash symbolizes the collapse of the larger theatrical construct; but truth, virtue, and love, which enjoyed a total victory in the fanciful Harmon plot, here triumph only partially. Veneerings may come and go, but Podsnap and the Buffers endure. The final chapter portends an unfortunate future. *Our Mutual Friend* exposes the presence and power of theatrical conventions beyond the realm of fiction, but cannot tell its audience how safely to escape the theater. Those forced from the theatrical economy, like the Veneerings and Lammles, have to leave the English stage permanently. Those who leave voluntarily, such as Eugene Wrayburn, have nowhere to go but to a world clearly established as fancifully unreal. For Dickens's Victorian audiences, the show must go on.

NOTES

1. Booth lists H. T. Craven's *Milky White* (1864) and George Conquest's *Seven Sins* (1874) as examples of Victorian plays portraying typical theatrical father-daughter

relationships, and Thomas Holcroft's *A Tale of Mystery* (1802) as the earliest English melodrama. Dickens included many other standard features of melodrama in *Our Mutual Friend*. The doll's dressmaker's bizarre relationship with her alcoholic father, for example, simultaneously encompasses the unnatural parent-child relationship and temperance devices common to many Victorian plays and novels alike. Booth cites George Dibdin Pitt's *Simon Lee* (1841) and *The Beggar's Petition* (1841) as examples.

2. Regarding a truthful reflection of Victorian morality, Booth describes the melodramatic form as "essentially unreal: 99 out of 100 melodramas end happily, reward virtue, punish vice, award prosperity and the heroine to the hero, and prove the validity and utility of rigid moral principle" ("Illusion and Reality: The Victorian Stage," 100). The Harmon plot of *Our Mutual Friend* comfortably falls into that overwhelming majority. Harmon and Bella marry and come into a healthy inheritance; the ultimately virtuous Boffins receive rewards for their dramatic efforts; Wegg is unceremoniously thrown into the street; and Riderhood dies gruesomely at the hands of Master Headstone.

3. Whether or not Dickens had one meaning of "Riah" in mind is not immediately apparent; nor indeed that he chose the word for its definition at all. It could simply be a transliterated Hebrew name. Nevertheless, to contemporary Jewish readers it might have suggested the *k'riah*, a mourning tradition of rending one's clothes, or, perhaps more likely, *l'ha-riah*, a joyous shout made upon the abandonment of one's connection to earthly materialism. Dickens's use of Jewish characters has been the subject of much scholarship; his correspondence with Mrs. Eliza Davis, a Jewish woman whose house he bought in 1860, has led some to believe that Dickens intended the benevolent Mr. Riah to atone for his earlier, unflattering portrayals of Jews in such characters as Fagin in *Oliver Twist* (Heller 41). Dickens's having corresponded with Mrs. Davis on the subject of Jews and Judaism starting in 1863 (and therefore most likely during the composition of *Our Mutual Friend*) makes it possible that he would have known some of the potential meanings of Riah's name, but any such result of their communication remains purely conjectural.

4. The last name worth mentioning here is of course that of Lord Snigsworth, whose name constitutes the bulk of his role in the novel. The *Oxford English Dictionary* lists a seventeenth-century definition for "snig" as "a covetous or avaricious person," and an 1862 slang variant meaning "to steal." Both "snap" and "snig" also have business connotations in their contemporary slang usages.

WORKS CITED

Baumgarten, Murray. "Boffin, *Our Mutual Friend*, and the Theatre of Fiction." *Dickens Quarterly* 19.1 (March 2002): 17–22.

Booth, Michael. *Theatre in the Victorian Age*. Cambridge: Cambridge UP, 1991.

————. "Illusion and Reality: The Victorian Stage." *Theatre History Studies* 10 (1990): 183–97.

Cotsell, Michael. "The Book of Insolvent Fates: Financial Speculation in *Our Mutual Friend*." *Dickens Studies Annual* 13 (1984): 125–42.

Dickens, Charles. *Our Mutual Friend*. Ed. Adrian Poole. London: Penguin, 1997.

Heller, Deborah. "The Outcast as Villain and Victim: Jews in Dickens's *Oliver Twist* and *Our Mutual Friend*." *Jewish Presences in English Literature*. Eds. Derek Cohen and Deborah Heller Montreal: McGill-Queen's UP: 1990.

Knowles, Owen. "Veneering and the Age of Veneer: A Source and Background for *Our Mutual Friend*." *The Dickensian* 81.2 (1985 Summer): 88–96.

"Pod." *Oxford English Dictionary*. 2nd ed. 1989.

"Podsnap." *Oxford English Dictionary*. 2nd ed. 1989.

Poovey, Mary. Introduction. *The Financial System in Nineteenth-Century Britain*. New York: Oxford UP, 2003. 1–34.

"Snap." Def. I.2a. *Oxford English Dictionary*. 2nd ed. 1989.

"Snig." *Oxford English Dictionary*. 2nd ed. 1989.

Vlock, Deborah. *Dickens, Novel Reading, and the Victorian Popular Theatre*. Cambridge: Cambridge UP, 1998.

Catherine Dickens and Her Colonial Sons

Lillian Nayder

This essay examines the relationship between Catherine Dickens and her sons in the context of empire-building, emigration, and exile. Most of the Dickens boys were committed to imperial service in the years immediately preceding and following the separation of their parents. Their colonial engagements mark them as agents capable of leaving their motherland and recreating their father's authority in the colonies, while also allying them with their mother as exiled subjects of their father's will. Illuminating the complex needs of their family as well as those of the empire, their experiences complicate our sense of the opposition between colony and home.

> A Shawl brought me by my said son Charles
> from India . . . the Ivory Elephant with Houdah
> sent me by . . . Walter . . . the story card basket
> brought to me by my son Charles from Chi-
> na . . . the photograph of Walter in uni-
> form . . . the photograph of Alfred and Jessie in
> a narrow frame . . . the case of various stuffed
> birds given to me by Sydney.
> (Catherine Dickens, ''Last Will and
> Testament''[1])

Perhaps more eloquently than a traditional narrative could, this catalogue of gifts received by Catherine Dickens and ultimately bequeathed by her in her will suggests the price of empire building to a home-bound mother parted from colonial sons. These objects constitute Catherine Dickens's legacy; but they also register the absences and disconnections that characterized her relationships with most of her boys. Souvenirs of empire, these gifts bear conflicting meanings, as do the imperial experiences they represented for a generation of Dickens sons—young men committed to empire-building and imperial service from the 1850s onward by their famous father.

The making of manhood; the mark of ambition, promise and self-reliance; a chance for superfluous and less-than-brilliant boys; the consequence of inadequacy or failure; exile, banishment—all these meanings resonate in Charles Dickens's plans for Walter, Frank, Alfred, Sydney, and Edward ("Plorn"), destined for India, Australia, and the high seas. The sons' stories point to the needs and dynamics of the British empire during a time of expansion and peril. Yet they also reveal the needs and dynamics of a family in which imperial authority and the authority of the father coincided, as did the "exile" of the sons with that of their mother. In fact, most of the Dickens boys were committed to imperial service in the years immediately preceding and following the separation of their parents and Catherine's banishment from her family and her home. At one and the same time, their colonial engagements mark them as agents capable of leaving their motherland and recreating their father's authority in the colonies, and as the exiled subjects of their father's will, allied with their mother. The colonial destinies of the Dickens sons reveal their identification with their mother as well as their father, and complicate our sense of the opposition between colony and home.

Catherine Hogarth was born on Hart Street in Edinburgh's New Town in May 1815. Her mother Georgina was the daughter of Katherine Miller and George Thomson, the latter a well-known Edinburgh figure who collected and published Scottish ballads and airs. Her father, George Hogarth, was a Writer to the Signet who advised Sir Walter Scott in his financial difficulties and turned from law to journalism in 1831, moving his family to Exeter, then to Halifax, and finally to London in 1834. In April 1836, Catherine married Charles Dickens, who worked with her father at the *Morning Chronicle*. Their marriage, long a happy one by Victorian standards, lasted for twenty-two years, during which time Catherine gave birth to ten children, seven of them boys.

In 1858, Catherine was pressured to leave her home and her children by her "restless" husband, who had become infatuated with the eighteen-year-old actress Ellen Ternan. Having signed a deed of separation, Catherine moved into her own home at 70 Gloucester Crescent, Regent's Park, accompanied by Charley, her eldest son. Her unmarried sister Georgina, who had lived with the Dickenses since 1843, remained with Charles, to the chagrin of her own family members. Battling the scandals that ensued, and that linked him to his sister-in-law as well as to Ellen Ternan, Dickens published statements justifying his separation from his wife. In the most notorious of these, the so-called "violated letter" published in American and English newspapers in

August 1858, he spoke of Catherine as a mentally disordered woman who "has thrown all the children on someone else."[2] After their separation, Charles and Catherine communicated only three times, and then only in writing. Charles died in 1870, twelve years after their separation, and Catherine in 1879.

The separation of Catherine and Charles Dickens created a metaphoric metropole and colony within their family, with the father at its center and the mother at its margins. The deed of separation signed by the Dickenses appeared to create two family centers, since it stipulated that Catherine would have "free access to all or any of her children at all places."[3] But Dickens never honored that clause, and instead did his best to keep mother and children apart. As their daughter Katey told her friend Gladys Storey in later life, for nearly two years following the separation her father "would scarcely speak to [her] because she visited her mother" (Parker 4). If they were to call at Gloucester Crescent, the children would appear to "reproach" their father, Katey explained, and most found it difficult to do so (Storey 219). Whether submitting to or resisting their father's authority, the children recognized it as paramount, and the younger ones understood that they could not stay with their mother, however much they might wish to do so. Recalling a visit from her sons in the summer of 1858, Catherine described to her Aunt Helen "how very happy [she had] been with [her] dear boys": "although they were not allowed to remain with me so long as I wished, yet I think we all thoroughly enjoyed being together. . . . I cannot tell you how good and affectionate they were to me. One of them, little Sydney, was full of solicitude and anxiety about me, always asking what I should do when they were gone, and if I would not be very dull and lonely without them; he should so like to stay."[4]

To convince himself and his children of the dangers of remaining in Catherine's presence, Dickens imagined his wife as a menacing "other" who threatened those who ventured into her domain. "It is her misery to live in some fatal atmosphere which slays every one to whom she should be dearest," he told a skeptical Angela Burdett Coutts in May 1858 (Pilgrim 8:560). In Dickens's production of *The Frozen Deep*, Catherine served as a prototype for the savage Nurse Esther, a Highland woman and maternal surrogate whose power over the young Clara Burnham must be broken over the course of the melodrama and who proves wholly expendable by its end.[5] Catherine was like Medusa, turning her children to stone with a single glance;[6] she was an unstable woman for whom distance and isolation were the best therapies, Dickens alleged, claiming that Catherine herself recognized that fact. As he asserted in the "violated letter," "For some years past Mrs. Dickens has been in the habit of representing to me that it would be better for her to go away and live apart; that her always increasing estrangement made a mental disorder under which she sometimes labours—more, that she felt herself unfit

for the life she had to lead as my wife and that she would be better far away"
(Pilgrim 8:740). The falsehoods of Dickens's claims here have been exposed
by Michael Slater and were contested by Catherine's allies from the start: "I
assure you . . . she had no desire to leave her home or children" and is "perfectly sound in mind," Catherine's aunt told her friend Mrs. Stark in August
1858 (Pilgrim 8:746). But from 1858 onward, Dickens constructed his "own
'plot' for the story of the marriage," as Slater observes, one in which Catherine was reinvented as "unnatural" and other, and relegated to the fringes of
the family (Slater 114).

It might appear that the imperial engagements of the Dickens boys had
little or nothing to do with the family crisis of 1858 or with the exile and
vilification of their mother. Indeed, Dickens's plans to send Walter to India—and his thoughts of sending Alfred and Frank to join him—preceded
his marital troubles, in Walter's case by several years. As early as August
1851, Dickens told Angela Burdett Coutts of his plans "to send Walter . . . to
a Mr. Trimmer at Putney who educates expressly for Addiscombe and India"
(Pilgrim 6:467). And in 1856, Dickens corresponded with W. J. Eastwick of
the East India Company about the possibility of sending Alfred or Frank there
as well (Pilgrim 8:241–42).

Furthermore, Dickens was hardly unique in sending his sons to the reaches
of empire. As the editors of the Pilgrim letters of Dickens note, it was a
"popular practice" to "send . . . sons to India and the Colonies," and Anthony Trollope's son Fred went out to New South Wales shortly before Alfred
Dickens did (Pilgrim 11:xiv).[7] Dickens expressed a widely-held view when
he represented the colonies as an opportune place for his boys to establish
themselves and do credit to their father: as he told G. W. Rusden, Clerk of
Parliaments in Victoria, Australia, and Alfred's mentor there, his sons would
have to "hew out their own paths through the world, by sheer hard work
. . . so, only, can they hope to sustain their name" (Pilgrim 11:127).

But if Dickens's plans to send some of his sons to the colonies preceded
his marital breakdown, his plans to send others there did not, and by the end
of the 1850s, his thinking about what the empire meant for his boys, their
identities, and their manhood clearly intersected with his thinking about himself, his wife, and their differences. As Dickens was sending Walter off to
India in July 1857, he had just concluded his final performances of *The
Frozen Deep*, a work pivotal to the dissolution of his marriage not only
because of its depiction of the maternal "other" but also because it introduced
him to Ellen Ternan, who played Lucy Crayford in the public productions
of the melodrama. And he was complaining to various friends about his
"restlessness" and thinking about his own manhood and lost youth. From
Southampton, Walter's departure point, Dickens wrote to Edmund Yates, the
father of three young sons, telling him:

I have come here on an errand which will grow familiar to you before you know that Time has flapped his wings over your head. Like me, you will find those babies grow to be young men, before you are quite sure they are born. Like me, you will have great teeth drawn with a wrench, and will only then know that you ever cut them. I am here to send Walter away over what they call in Green Bush Melodramas 'the Big Drink' and I dont know this day how he comes to be mine, or I, his. . . . Seeing Charley and he going aboard the Ship before me just now, I suddenly came into possession of a photograph of my own back at 16 and 20, and also into a suspicion that I had doubled the last age. (Pilgrim 8:379–80)

Haunted by a sudden sense of passing time and middle age, with each grown and departing son another tooth to be wrenched from a decaying paternal mouth, Dickens saw himself reflected in the sons he sent off to the colonies and yet distanced from them. His refrain "like me, you" "like me, you" refers to his connection with Yates, ostensibly. But it is his identity with his sons that is at stake, an identity that Dickens wishfully asserted a year later, when publicly justifying his separation from Catherine and his new-found bachelorhood: "All is open and plain among [my children] as though we were brothers," he wrote in the "violated letter" (Pilgrim 8:741). The colonial occupations and youth of Walter and his *real* brothers set them apart from their father. Yet Dickens imagined his sons manfully "authoring" their destinies, as he had. They were heroes in their own "Green Bush Melodramas" or imperial adventure stories. "[Alfred's] object is . . . to make his way in the new world," Dickens told Austen Henry Layard in May 1865. "No arrangements are made for him . . . as he is going out by his own desire—as the story books say, 'to seek his fortune' " (Pilgrim 11:41).

The destinies Dickens imagined for his boys can be understood as imperial romances—as stories of struggle and triumph that would demonstrate their manly strength and their resemblance to their father; in which the son "conduct[s] himself like a Man," as Dickens said of Walter (Pilgrim 8:381). "I have always purposed to send [Alfred] abroad," Dickens told Eastwick, referring to a possible East India cadetship, since he is "a boy of a remarkable character as a combination of self-reliance, steadiness, and adventurous spirit . . . and whom I believe to be particularly qualified for this opportunity" (Pilgrim 8:241–42).

Yet as Dickens constructed the destinies of his "adventurous" boys, his plotlines also read another way: as tales of failure, exile, and banishment. The hero of *The Green Bushes* is, after all, an Irish rebel forced to cross "the Big Drink" because of his transgressions. Alfred was not only self-reliant and steady; he was a boy who had gotten himself into debt and whom Dickens hoped "to dispose of . . . in Australia," as he told Mrs. Lehmann. "I will give you a Patriarchal piece of advice," he continued: "Don't have any more children'' (Pilgrim 11:25–26). When Dickens told his youngest son, in the fall of 1868, that the ''freedom and wildness'' of Australia were ''more suited to [him] than . . . a study or office,'' he might be seen to compliment a rough-and-ready character (Pilgrim 12:187). But when Plorn seemed anxious to return to England in 1870, Dickens made it clear that he was unfit for the demands of a career back home. Plorn ''does not seem to understand that he has qualified for no public examinations in the old country,'' Dickens complained to Rusden, ''and could not possibly hold his own against competition for anything to which I could get him nominated''; ''he seems to have been born without a groove'' (Pilgrim 12:530). In these versions of the boys' stories, Dickens reveals a different truth about them: they are in the colonies because of their weaknesses, not their strengths, and are the sons of their mother rather than his own.

As early as January 1854, Dickens traced what he saw as his eldest son's failings to what he identified as their maternal source: ''he has less fixed purpose and energy than I could have supposed possible in my son,'' Dickens told Miss Coutts. ''He is not aspiring, or imaginative in his own behalf. With all the tenderer and better qualities which he inherits from his mother, he inherits an indescribable lassitude of character—a very serious thing in a man'' (Pilgrim 7:245). By the 1860s, Dickens had reconceived Charley's ''lassitude'' as a ''curse'' that Catherine had placed on his sons as a group—''my boys with a curse of limpness on them,'' as he put it. ''You don't know what it is to look round the table and see reflected from every seat at it . . . some horribly well remembered expression of inadaptability to anything,'' he told W. H. Wills in June 1867, in a letter written on Ellen Ternan's monogrammed stationery and complaining of the financial drain placed on him by his ''wife's income to pay'' (Pilgrim 11:377).

In sending his boys to the colonies, Dickens saw himself as providing a necessary antidote to Catherine's influence; he placed them in situations where they would be forced to overcome their effeminate ''limpness'' and develop the purpose and energy Catherine allegedly lacked. Becoming financially autonomous, they would no longer be economic burdens like their mother. Picturing the ''unfortunate'' Alfred ''up the country at a lonely station'' in the Bush, Dickens thought his son would ''take . . . off his coat in earnest to repair his fortunes'' (Pilgrim 11:236). Referring to the natural ''defect'' of character that Dickens believed Plorn shared with Charley—''his want of application and continuity of purpose''—Dickens claimed that Plorn ''will have more pressing need to make a fight against it in Australia than if he were near home'' and might ''flash up, under such conditions'' (Pilgrim 11:363). If he were to avoid the fate of his brothers, Henry Dickens realized, he would have to prove himself worthy of remaining at home—to define himself, as Henry relentlessly did, as the son of his father, not his mother.[8]

Faced with the prospect of a career in the Indian Civil Service, the destiny Dickens had chosen for his sixth son, Henry asked instead to attend college in England. He was put to the test in 1865, his father asking Henry's headmaster to determine "whether . . . he really will be worth sending to Cambridge . . . if you should not be of this opinion, he should decidedly go up for the Indian Civil Service Examination" (Pilgrim 11:93). For all the talk of the strengths necessary for imperial service, Henry understood that it was more a punishment than a reward in his family's dynamic—at best, a therapeutic treatment for purposeless or incapable sons who, in their father's eyes, took after their mother.

While trying to root out Catherine's traits by sending their boys to the colonies, Dickens also allied them with her in doing so—by treating them as "superfluous" and freeing himself of them at a time when he found their presence particularly irksome.[9] In the 1860s, Dickens devoted himself to Ellen Ternan and led a secret double life as "Charles Tringham." But secrets were difficult to keep with his sons at home, Dickens quickly realized, having been "caught" by Charley when walking with Ellen on Hampstead Heath in the early days of their acquaintance (Tomalin 111). Although Katey was more willing to question her father's behavior than the devoted Mamie proved to be, their brothers seemed most likely to contest and publicly challenge Dickens's authority, as Charley sometimes did in the late 1850s and early 1860s: allying himself and moving in with his mother; marrying Bessie Evans against his father's explicit prohibition; and supporting Thackeray rather than Yates in what came to be known as the "Garrick Club Affair." When Charley criticized his father's ally in *Punch* in December 1858, Dickens had his son's name removed from the club's list of proposed members.[10] Perceiving his sons as obstacles to his relationship with Ellen, as Catherine was, and as opponents to his authority generally, Dickens became "ruthless" in his treatment of them, Claire Tomalin contends, "obsess[ed] with ridding himself" of them (185).[11]

As Dickens's eldest son and the protégé of Miss Coutts, Charley was able to fix on a career in England. When he traveled to Japan, China, and India in 1860, he did so temporarily and by his own volition, hoping to become a tea merchant and "start . . . in London for himself" (Pilgrim 9:246–47). But such was not the case with his younger brothers, who were more easily dispatched by their father—some permanently. As Dickens made clear to Frederick Lehmann, *any* foreign colony would do as a destination for Alfred, so long as it *was* foreign. "If I could get him abroad. . . . I should prefer it much," Dickens told Lehmann, who had hoped to find work for Alfred in London; "I still hanker after India or some such distant field" (Pilgrim 10:191, 208). Dickens justified his "hankering" for far-flung sons by telling Lehmann of his fear that Alfred and Frank, if left together in London, would "spoil . . . one another" (Pilgrim 10:191). Yet Lehmann, evidently unconvinced, was shocked by Dickens's determination to exile his sons—whether to Ceylon, to China, or to Australia, of which Dickens wrote in turn. While Dickens wept over his daughter Katey's marriage to Charles Collins and her apparent desire to leave her home at any cost, "he seems to have been only too anxious to send his sons away to the ends of the earth," Frederick Lehmann's grandson notes in his family memoir. "In 1863 Dickens consulted Frederick, in a series of letters which my father [Rudie] carefully kept from publication during his lifetime, about the possibility of getting . . . Alfred a business post abroad," John Lehmann explains. "In the end these mysterious negotiations, which must have been decidedly uncomfortable for my grandfather, were cut short by . . . Dickens's decision to make Alfred learn the silk trade in order to earn a living in China. The wretched boy was, however, eventually sent to Australia" (Lehmann 165–66).

In Tomalin's analysis, as in Lehmann's, Dickens unfeelingly "banished" most of his boys, their "wretched" fate replicating that of their mother. All were subjects of Dickens's "ruthless" will. Yet not all of those subjects proved as tearfully submissive as Plorn or as eager to please and venerate as Henry. Charley's decision to marry into the proscribed family of Evanses, whom Dickens had prohibited his children from so much as *visiting* because of their support for Catherine, reminds us that the possibilities for defiance were wide-ranging. In fact, the notorious "failures" of Dickens's sons, most of whom "disappointed" their father (Pilgrim 11:150), can be seen as types of resistance to his authority, and suggest their ties to their mother in a sense that Dickens did not intend: as a form of protest against his treatment of Catherine and themselves rather than proof that her "limpness" had cursed them.

Sydney, the fifth son, provides an interesting case in point. He decided on a naval career before his father could decide on one for him, and Dickens identified him as "*the* boy of the lot, and the one who will be heard of hereafter" (Pilgrim 9:247). "If he fails to pass [his examination] with credit," Dickens told Wills in 1860, "I will never believe in anybody again" (Pilgrim 9:303). Instead of bringing credit to his father's name, however, Sydney threatened to disgrace it and in one of the ways most hurtful to his father—by getting into debt. Writing to Dickens from Vancouver Island in March 1869, as second lieutenant aboard the HMS *Zealous*, Sydney warned his father that if he declined to pay his son's debts, "the result of your refusal . . . is not exaggerated—utter ruination" (Pilgrim 12:349–50, n. 1). When Dickens wrote a last letter to Alfred in Australia three weeks before his own death, he expressed his "unbounded faith" in his correspondent while complaining about other sons; Plorn was not "taking to Australia," Dickens feared, and failed to share his father's aspiration that he and Alfred achieve "first positions in the Colony." It was for Sydney, however, that Dickens reserved his final and most scathing remark: "I begin to wish that he were honestly dead" (Pilgrim 12:529–30).

Sydney *did* die at an early age, aboard the steamship *Malta* in 1872—but not before he had countered his father in another way: by identifying *his* home as that of his mother, where he had so wanted to stay in 1858, when he was eleven years old. According to Georgina Hogarth, Dickens's last letter to Sydney informed him "that he would not be received at Gad's Hill on his return to England" (Adrian 123).[12] But if that was, indeed, the case, Sydney could be seen to have achieved his end. Like Catherine and like Charley, Sydney helped redefine the geography of his family, by collapsing the polarity between its margins and its center. In 1870, after Dickens's death, Charley outbid the agent who represented his father's executors to become the new proprietor of Gad's Hill Place, and he often invited his mother to stay at the home from which she had been excluded by her husband. While Henry, too, spent time with Catherine, increasingly so during her widowhood, he allied himself with his Aunt Georgina and stayed with her near Hyde Park during his school vacations. By contrast, Sydney resided with Catherine during his leaves, describing himself as "Mr. Sydney Dickens . . . of 70 Gloucester Crescent, Regent's Park."[13]

As for Catherine, she had no say in the destinations chosen for the boys.[14] In the Dickens household, the right to make such decisions was always her husband's prerogative and by the time Walter died in Calcutta at the end of 1863, while preparing to return to England on sick leave, Dickens had willfully banished his wife from his thoughts. He made this clear to Miss Coutts when she encouraged him to communicate with Catherine in their grief: "a page in my life which once had writing on it, has become absolutely blank, and . . . it is not in my power to pretend that it has a solitary word upon it" (Pilgrim 10:356). Not surprisingly, then, Dickens did not consult Catherine about sending either Alfred or Plorn to the Antipodes, although he could have imagined her objections. As a woman "very happy to have all . . . [her] dear children at home"[15] and convinced that they did best in their "native air,"[16] Catherine was deeply upset by their departures from England. She hoped they would be happy in the colonies but also missed them "most sadly,"[17] telling Plorn she "long[ed] to see [his] face again."[18]

As events proved, Catherine's longing went unfulfilled. Yet she could not be as easily written out of her children's lives as she was written out of her husband's. Deeply "shock[ed]" by the death of her "poor beloved Walter," whom she was "looking forward with so much joy to the prospect of seeing," Catherine "endeavour[ed] with God's help to submit to His will with resignation," she told Miss Coutts;[19] but submission to her *husband's* will was another matter. It was Dickens's prerogative to train their boys for the colonies if he saw fit and to arrange for their passages out of England. However,

Catherine could provide them with a sense of themselves—and herself—that differed from their father's, one in which they would always have value and a home regardless of their successes or failures: because they were the children of an "always . . . loving mother," as she put it.[20] Sent to Australia by his father, who saw him as unfit for a career in England, Plorn found a letter from Catherine awaiting him on his arrival in Melbourne and understood that, to his mother, his experiences were valuable by definition, because they were his own: "I . . . shall expect that long account of [the voyage] you promised me," Catherine wrote in her first letter to Plorn in New South Wales. "The smallest details will of course be greatly interesting to me."[21] Dickens might complain that Plorn "seems to have been born without a groove" but Catherine sounded a very different note. She was "so proud of [her] darling handsome son Plorn," she told him in 1874—not because he had obtained one of those "first positions in the colony" urged on him by his father, but simply because, judging from a photograph he sent to his mother back home, he "seem[ed] to be very tall, and altogether much improved."[22] Catherine hoped he would be "prosperous" as well as "happy" but would not think less of him if he were not.[23]

In her correspondence with Plorn and Alfred, as in her embrace of Sydney, Catherine developed ties that Dickens had hoped to sever and countered his self-justifying claim that "life is half made up of partings," as he told Plorn in sending him away (Pilgrim 12:187). Emphasizing, instead, the theme of reunion, Catherine told Plorn of her longing to see him and wondered if she would "live to have that happiness."[24] "A darling little Australian granddaughter!" she exclaimed in a letter to Alfred's wife: "How I should love to see [the children] and give them a good kiss. . . . Don't let dear Kathleen forget [to] talk about her Grannye."[25] Catherine's last will and testament amplifies on the theme of reunion, though in a less literal sense than her letters do—by using the souvenirs of empire and the relics of her partings from her sons to draw connections among family members, even as she herself was preparing to part from them: "To my daughter Katherine : . . The story card basket brought to me by my son Charles from China [and] . . . the case of various stuffed birds given to me by Sydney . . . to my grandson Charles Walter Dickens . . . the Ivory Elephant with Houdah sent me by his Uncle Walter [from India]." Identifying the origins of the objects she bequeaths and their first givers, Catherine provides her heirs with a sense of interconnection, as if to eclipse the distances so many of those objects represent. Bringing margins to center, she positions herself, her children, and her grandchildren at the heart of a family that was fragmented, and its members dispersed, by the needs of her husband and the empire.

NOTES

I would like to thank Mark Charles Dickens for granting me permission to quote from the unpublished letters of Catherine Dickens and from the Ouvry Papers. I am grateful to the following libraries and archives for allowing me to draw on material in their collections: Beinecke Rare Book and Manuscript Library, Yale University; Dickens House Museum; Huntington Library; National Library of Australia; Pierpont Morgan Library; Rare Book Department, Free Library of Philadelphia.

1. Catherine Dickens, "Last Will and Testament," 31 January 1878; typescript, Dickens House.
2. Although Dickens claimed that he did not intend to publish this letter, which he addressed to Arthur Smith, he told his correspondent: "You have not only my full permission to show this, but I beg you to show, to any one who wishes to do me right, or to any one who may have been misled into doing me wrong" (Pilgrim 8:568).
3. Deed of separation (draft); Ouvry Papers, Dickens House.
4. Catherine Dickens to Helen Thomson; quoted by Miss Thomson in a letter to Mrs. Stark, [30] August 1858 (Pilgrim 8:749). Just come of age in 1858, Charley alone was free to leave his father and take up quarters with his mother, allying himself with her. He was to remain one of her staunchest supporters until her death.
5. See Nayder, chapter 3.
6. As Dickens told Angela Burdett Coutts in May 1858, "Mary and Katey (whose dispositions are of the gentlest and most affectionate conceivable) harden into stone figures of girls when they can be got to go near her, and have their hearts shut up in her presence as if they closed by some horrid spring" (Pilgrim 8:559).
7. Between 1840 and 1873, the Colonial Emigration Committee established by the British government assisted well over six million Britons to find new homes overseas; and in the decade before Alfred and Plorn emigrated to New South Wales, the population of Australia more than doubled, from 400,000 to 1.1 million, largely a result of the 1851 gold discovery (Lloyd 145, 165).
8. Henry described himself as "a son who was entirely devoted" to his father, "and whose great pride it is to bear his name" and he recounts Dickens's tearfully grateful response to the news that he had won a scholarship at Trinity Hall, Cambridge (H. Dickens, *Memories* 30). "During the latter years of my father's life my whole being was engrossed in his," Henry claims, "and since his death I live upon my memory of him, which is a very deep and living thing" (H. Dickens, *Recollections* 3).
9. "If I had no boys holding on to the skirts of my coat, I think I should keep a yacht and go sailing about," Dickens told Thomas Mitton in the 1860s (Pilgrim 11:37).
10. The "Garrick Club affair" was spurred in June 1858, when Edmund Yates insulted Thackeray in *Town Talk*, and an enraged Thackeray successfully moved to have Dickens's protégé expelled from the club, whereupon Dickens resigned from the board. Dickens was furious when, in December, Charley joined the

fray—on what he saw as the wrong side. As Thackeray reported to William Webb Synge, Dickens's "quarrel with his wife has driven him almost frantic. He is now quarrelling with his son; and has just made himself friends of the whole Garrick Club, by withdrawing his lad's name, just as it was coming up for ballot . . . and the poor boy is very much cast down at his father's proceedings" (Thackeray to Synge, winter 1858–59, Gordon N. Ray, *Thackeray: The Age of Wisdom, 1847–1863* [1958]; qtd. Collins 2:69).

11. As Tomalin notes in discussing the fate of Plorn, unwillingly "packed off to Australia" in 1868, "Gad's Hill was now entirely free of boys . . . and Dickens displayed the same blend of callousness and sentimentality as when his other boys were banished; the bewildered and tearful 16–year-old was given a letter at parting in which his father told him he loved him and was sorry to part with him, 'but this life is half made up of partings, and these pains must be borne' [26 Sept. 68] . . . Even when all the circumstances of Victorian family life and economics are taken into account, it seems a harsh way of treating a not very bright boy" (185).

12. Georgina made this claim in a letter to Annie Fields, 18 June 1872, held by the Huntington Library.

13. "Please describe Mr. Sydney Dickens as of 70 Gloucester Crescent, Regent's Park, Lieutenant in the Royal Navy," Catherine's lawyer told Frederic Ouvry, the Dickens family solicitor, when Sydney gained his promotion in 1871 (ALS Frank Richardson to Frederic Ouvry, 23 February 1871; Ouvry Papers [15:33], Dickens House). On his return to England from India for a six-month leave in March 1871, Frank may have resided with Catherine as well, since Georgina Hogarth complained to Annie Fields that she and Mamie "don't see much of him" (Georgina Hogarth to Annie Fields, 1 March 1871, Huntington Library, FI 2698; qtd. Adrian 167).

14. As Tomalin notes, she "was not consulted on the fate of her youngest [Plorn] any more than that of the others" (185).

15. ALS Catherine Dickens to Mrs. Brown [Hannah Meredith], 16 July 1856; Pierpont Morgan Library, New York, MA 1352.

16. ALS Catherine Dickens to Angela Burdett Coutts, 8 March 1864; Pierpont Morgan Library, New York, MA 1352.

17. ALS Catherine Dickens to "Plorn" (Edward Bulwer Lytton Dickens), 9 October 1868; Free Library of Philadelphia, Rare Book Department.

18. Catherine Dickens to "Plorn," 6 May 1873; typescript, Yale University.

19. ALS Catherine Dickens to Angela Burdett Coutts, 8 March 1864; Pierpont Morgan Library, New York, MA 1352.

20. Catherine Dickens to "Plorn," 11 August 1874; typescript, Dickens House. ALS Catherine Dickens to Alfred Dickens, 16 February 1870; National Library of Australia, MS 2563.

21. ALS Catherine Dickens to "Plorn," 9 October 1868; Free Library of Philadelphia, Rare Book Department. Praising her youngest son for being "a most regular correspondent," Catherine told him: "I derive the greatest comfort and happiness from your letters, my own dear Plorn" (Catherine Dickens to "Plorn," 18 November 1873; typescript, Dickens House).

22. Catherine Dickens to "Plorn," 11 August 1874; typescript, Dickens House.
23. Catherine Dickens to "Plorn," 16 December 1873; typescript, Dickens House.
24. Catherine Dickens to "Plorn," 6 May 1873; typescript, Yale University.
25. ALS Catherine Dickens to Jessie Dickens, 17 May 1876; National Library of Australia, MS 2563.

WORKS CITED

Adrian, Arthur A. *Georgina Hogarth and the Dickens Circle*. London: Oxford UP, 1957.

Collins, Philip, ed. *Dickens: Interviews and Recollections*. 2 vols. London: Macmillan, 1981.

Dickens, Catherine. "Last Will and Testament." 31 January 1878. Typescript. Dickens House.

Dickens, Charles. *The Letters of Charles Dickens*, Pilgrim Edition. Eds. Madeline House, Graham Storey, and Kathleen Tillotson. 12 vols. Oxford: Clarendon Press, 1965–2002.

Dickens, Henry. *Memories of My Father*. London: Duffield, 1929.

———. *The Recollections of Sir Henry Dickens, K. C.* London: Heinemann, 1934.

Lehmann, John. *Ancestors and Friends*. London: Eyre & Spottiswoode, 1962.

Lloyd, T. O. *The British Empire: 1558–1983*. Oxford: Oxford UP, 1989.

Nayder, Lillian. *Unequal Partners: Charles Dickens, Wilkie Collins and Victorian Authorship*. Ithaca: Cornell UP, 2002.

Parker, David and Michael Slater. "The Gladys Storey Papers." *Dickensian* 76 (Spring 1980): 3–16.

Slater, Michael. *Dickens and Women*. 1983; rpt., London: J. M. Dent, 1986.

Storey, Gladys. *Dickens and Daughter*. London: Frederick Muller, 1939.

Tomalin, Claire. *The Invisible Woman: The Story of Nelly Ternan and Charles Dickens*. New York: Knopf, 1991.

The Moonstone, Narrative Failure, and the Pathology of the Stare

Sean C. Grass

Beginning with The Moonstone*'s seemingly comical concern for ''detective-fever,'' this essay argues that the novel centers upon the possibility that detective work—and staring more generally—functions much like a disease in the novel, debilitating the investigation and the characters who undertake it instead of producing a definitive account of the crime. Structurally and thematically, the novel makes staring the basis of its claims to hermeneutic power, but staring fails repeatedly to produce knowledge of the Moonstone's theft. The real consequences of the novel's pervasive ocular practices are bigotry, cruelty, and crushing psychological repressions that mean to conceal criminal and sexual desire. In its epidemic proportions and deleterious effects, staring in the novel becomes every bit the disease that the complaint about ''detective-fever'' makes it, and* The Moonstone *comes to account for the complex failure of staring as a detective and narrative practice.*

Considering its longstanding reputation as ''the first, the longest and the best of the modern English detective novel,'' Wilkie Collins's *The Moonstone* (1868) reaches rather unexpected conclusions about the kind of detective work that promises to deliver answers about crime.[1] Early in the novel, Franklin Blake explains to Gabriel Betteredge that the account of the diamond they and the other narrators are writing will depend explicitly upon the power of visible evidence, for it will consist of a series of narrative by characters who may tell only ''as far as [their] own personal experience extends, and no

Dickens Studies Annual, Volume 37, Copyright © 2006 by AMS Press, Inc. All rights reserved.

farther'' (22). But in chapter 15, as Betteredge recounts his first day of snooping with Sergeant Cuff, he confesses, ''If there is such a thing known at the doctor's shop as a *detective-fever*, that disease had now got fast hold of your humble servant'' (131). The remark sounds like Betteredge's way of excusing his sudden and unseemly curiosity, and perhaps too like Collins's way of poking sly fun at the growing (and also unseemly) interest that a ''polite'' reader might be taking in his sensational novel. Though the drollery leaves readers, critics, and other characters free to wink at Betteredge's ''malady,'' his remark suggests something more important than we might first suppose: that detective work, and staring more generally, function much like a disease in the novel, debilitating the investigation and the characters who undertake it instead of producing a definitive account of the crime. *The Moonstone* records not only Cuff's detective work and the novel's plentiful amateur sleuthing but also—amid other staring—the Indians' spying, Drusilla Clack's drapery peeping, Rosanna Spearman's furtive glances at Franklin, and Ezra Jennings's deliberately spectacular attempt to restage the crime. By recording these ocular activities, *The Moonstone* comes partly to resemble other works of its kind, since, as Patrick Brantlinger writes, ''[o]bsessive curiosity and voyeurism characterize all mystery stories'' (25). But there is a sense, too, in which the propensity to stare really does plague Collins's novel, pervading and poisoning the action even as it fails to produce a satisfactory account of the diamond's disappearance.

Since *The Moonstone* reaches its famous climax in Jennings's unorthodox detective experiment, it is no surprise that psychoanalytic critics have argued very often that the novel is really about the failure of conventional detection.[2] Pointing to the novel's interest in psychology and carefully crafted polyvocal structure, Lewis Roberts argues that *The Moonstone* is a ''critique of rationality'' that calls ''the possibility . . . of objective knowledge [and] objective narration into question'' (168), and Jenny Bourne Taylor writes that it is Collins's ''most ambitious exploration of social and psychic identity . . . a study in ambiguity itself'' (176). According to such readings, the novel's conventional investigations reveal mostly the inadequacy of visual evidence and forensic knowledge in a world where the explanation for crime belongs to the hidden story of criminal desire, which can be told much more ably by a proto-psychologist like Ezra Jennings than by the eminently rational agents of the law. But critics who have written particularly of the novel's ocular practices have reached very different conclusions. In his study of domestic surveillance, Brian McCuskey argues that the novel's servants make spying a considerable mechanism of power, becoming ''surrogates of discipline'' in a genteel world defined by the absence of real police (363). For D. A. Miller, the novel's pervasive staring shows that ''policing power inheres in the logic of the world,'' making the novel ''thoroughly *monological*—always speaking a master-voice that corrects, overrides, subordinates, or sublates all other voices it allows to speak'' (50; 54). His argument is persuasive, and especially so because, as he points out, *The Moonstone*'s polyvocality ends in the narrators all reaching a unanimous conclusion about the crime. But Miller also misses a fundamental point: that the several narratives, written by characters who must report only what they have seen, are unanimous in their conclusion mostly because they are first unanimous in their reliance upon the hermeneutic power of the stare—a power that the novel shows is unable to produce a complete account of the theft. If *The Moonstone* like other detective stories has as its basic aim the complete narrative elucidation of the crime, it is the novel's great detective and narrative misfortune that its characters trust so entirely to what they see.

Despite its innumerable detectives and clear preoccupation with ocular practices, *The Moonstone* records above all the disastrous consequences of obsessive staring—the way that rampant spying and prying end in the novel's decisive failure to provide a certain account of the crime. From the start, the novel is troubled by things that escape the stare, from the Moonstone to the paint-stained nightgown, and from the reclusive John Herncastle to Rosanna, who vanishes irretrievably beneath the Shivering Sand. To some extent, as we know from Tzvetan Todorov, this must be the case, for a detective story is the "story of an absence" that the investigation restores gradually to the text (46). But in *The Moonstone* things essential to the crime never come fully into view, so that the novel is characterized by staring but punctuated throughout by the intractable absence of what it must see. Partly, as psychoanalytic critics suggest, the novel's detective failures underscore the insufficiency of the stare—the inadequacy of visual policing in a world of divided subjects and repressed desire. But the novel also tells the story of how staring, whether as detection or voyeurism or gratuitous spying, creates the very conditions that cause this failure, and that ensure that the crime can never enter the novel's narration. Trusting to the stare, *The Moonstone*'s characters ignore the subjectivity of those they see, dealing instead in superficialities that produce bigotry and cruelty. Surrounded by staring eyes that belong to the operation of detective and social power, they engage in unconscious and willful psychological repressions that mean to conceal their illegitimate desires. These cruelties and repressions are not only coincidental with the novel's staring, nor are they, as the causes and consequences of crime, only what the novel must see. They are the psychological and social brutalities that the novel's obsessive staring engenders—a demonstration that the propensity to stare ends in producing the very psychological omissions that confound the novel's efforts at detection and narration. In its epidemic proportions and deleterious effects, staring in the novel becomes every bit the disease that Betteredge's complaint about ''detective-fever'' makes it, and *The Moonstone* comes to account for the complex failure of staring as a detective and narrative practice.

2.

The Moonstone begins already enmeshed in the quandary that defines the novel: though the novel's detection and narration depend upon the hermeneutic power of staring, that power fails repeatedly to produce knowledge about the crime. The novel begins with a ''Prologue'' that, its narrator writes, means to explain ''the motive which has induced [him] to refuse the right hand of fellowship to [his] cousin, John Herncastle'' (5). Apparently that motive is the narrator's moral distaste for the crimes that Herncastle may have committed to get his hands on the diamond. But the story that the narrator tells is only explicitly about these crimes; implicitly, it is about failed surveillance and narrative inadequacy, a story that explains his motive by resorting to a radically incomplete account of Herncastle's rapacity and supposed wrongdoing. Like the narratives that follow, the ''Prologue'' attempts a chronological reckoning of the facts of the Moonstone's story, from the time when Vishnu first commanded three Brahmins to watch the diamond ''night and day, to the end of the generations of men,'' to the time of the British storming of Seringapatam, when the general sets Herncastle and the narrator to watch the troops and ''prevent the plunder and confusion'' he fears will follow the victory in battle (12; 14). Though the Indians and British alike initiate programs of surveillance to protect the diamond, neither prevents its theft, nor can the narrator even write certainly about what Herncastle has done. Instead, he confesses that he cannot accuse Herncastle openly of having stolen the Moonstone, for he ''cannot say that [his] own eyes saw the deed committed'' (15–16). Knowing requires seeing, and what the novel can see is that Herncastle returns to England with the Moonstone and a reputation as a blackguard. It *never* tells us for certain, though, whether he is guilty of murder or just how he has acquired the stone. Trusting to surveillance but recording its limitations, the ''Prologue'' enacts the cycle of staring and hermeneutic failure that the rest of the novel will unfold.

As the novel shifts to England, the staring becomes increasingly pervasive, often in ways that have little to do with the detective plot. The Verinder estate is rife with peeping even before the Moonstone's theft, from Penelope's spying on the Indians to her peeking at Godfrey and Rachel from ''behind the holly,'' and from the Indians' lurking vigilance to Godfrey's ''looking on, in effigy'' from a picture beside Rachel's dressing table (75; 68). Such instances show that the novel's staring functions in many ways—for discovery, voyeurism, discipline, the expression and exhibition of desire—but it still belongs most often to *The Moonstone*'s detective work and the broad exercise of hermeneutic power. As William Marshall writes, the novel presents seeing as "a form of *knowing*" (81), even when Penelope only wants to learn the result of Godfrey's proposal or Rosanna wonders breathlessly "Oh! who is it?" when she first sees Franklin (39). The novel's particular business is to "know" about the diamond, and its detective work is allied invariably to the stare. From the time the Moonstone disappears, and whether the inquiry is in Superintendent Seegrave's hands or Cuff's, the police focus entirely on visible evidence: the smeared paint, the clothing that bears it, and the hidden contents of locked wardrobes and portmanteaus. At Frizinghall, the magistrate holds the Indians on flimsy charges to keep them in view until Cuff is sure of their role, and the narrators often describe the investigation in ocular terms. As Betteredge puts down his pen, he writes, "In the dark, I have brought you thus far. In the dark I am compelled to leave you," and Franklin twice calls the investigation a journey "from the darkness to the light" (197; 335; 360). Throughout the novel, he writes, "the horrible fact of the Theft—[is] the one visible, tangible object . . . in the midst of the impenetrable darkness" (351–52). It is the investigation's and novel's business to shed light on the remainder, so that not just the fact of the theft but also its techniques and motivations can be brought into narrative view.

This is, after all, the stated aim of the novel's odd structure: to tell "the whole story" of the diamond by letting those characters "concerned in the events" describe what they saw (21). As Betteredge explains, "the plan is, not to present reports, but to produce witnesses" (197). Under Franklin's editorship, the novel becomes a compilation of thirteen narratives by eleven writers—not including Rosanna or her letter—all of whom are told to write only what they have seen. Franklin admits the "Prologue" as testimony because it "relates the necessary particulars on the authority of an eye-witness," and elsewhere he reminds Clack to "limit herself to her own individual experience" and leave "[l]ater discoveries . . . [to] those persons who can write in the capacity of actual witnesses" (22; 247). Betteredge, meanwhile, makes two false narrative starts before deciding (with Penelope's help) to work chronologically through *events* instead of tracing the origins and characters of the people involved. Though we still get asides regarding Rachel and Rosanna, the strategy explicitly makes the temporal arrangement of what Betteredge has seen the raison d'être of his narration, now structured according to the principle that "things must be put down in their places, as things actually happened" (33). In important ways, the novel also comes literally to be shaped by seeing in the sense of Franklin's supervision and overwriting of the text. In Betteredge's narrative, Franklin gives writing instructions; in subsequent ones, when he is not narrating, he makes editorial intrusions, from the epistolary exchange in Clack's narrative to the footnotes there, in Rosanna's letter, and in Cuff's Report. According to the first of these, Franklin wants to ensure that the narrators produce "genuine documents . . . endorsed by the attestations of witnesses" (202). In this interplay of "witnessed" testimony validated by rigorous editing, *The Moonstone* returns to what John Sutherland (80) has called the "forensic" structure of *The Woman in White* (1860). It also comes to depend, structurally as thematically, upon the hermeneutic power of the stare.

As we might expect in a detective story, *The Moonstone*'s inability to "see" the crime and its collateral secrets stems, in the first instance, from the ingenuity of characters who want to avoid the stare. Elisabeth Rose Gruner writes that the book is "characterized and perhaps even motivated by secrets," its plot driven by characters who hide what the detectives most wish to see (130). In a way, the novel's real trouble begins partly because Lady Verinder "decline[s] to see" her infamous brother, making his bequest of the Moonstone an indecipherable act of generosity or malice (45). Like other things that will escape the novel's prying eyes, Herncastle is menacing because he is elusive, is central to the plot because he is impossible to "know" for sure. Perhaps because they are so beset with detectives and voyeurs, the novel's other characters also become adept at hiding what they want no one to see. Clack makes herself vanish behind the drawing-room curtains, and artfully enough that she can still "see and hear" Rachel's interview with Godfrey, who hides in turn his own licentious secret life (259). Rachel hides in her bedroom during the theft and investigation, then leaves for London because she knows that her departure "puts an obstacle in the way of . . . recovering [her] Diamond" (159). As architects of the novel's most complex plots, Rosanna and the Indians are exceptional at concealment, eluding detection though they are the primary objects of suspicion. Dogged by Cuff, the other housemaids, and the hapless Joyce, Rosanna makes secret visits to Frizinghall and Cobb's Hole, hides Franklin's stained nightgown under her clothes, makes him another, and leaves the stained nightgown and her letter where only she can find them. As for the Indians, they and their predecessors keep the Moonstone in view for eight centuries, then follow it all over England, kill Godfrey, and return it to India, all without being caught. In a novel that makes visual "knowing" the key to detection and narration, such evasive measures are critical means of attenuating the detective plot.

But it does not necessarily follow that resolving the plot is a simple matter of uncovering what characters choose to hide. Gruner writes that the novel's most important secret is Rachel's since, "[w]hile she is silent, the truth will remain hidden" (137). In *The Moonstone*, though, secrecy is not entirely a matter of choice, for the novel's most important omissions stem from secrets that cannot be helped, and that cannot be confessed to resolve the investigation. Franklin has no wish to keep his guilty secret, and Dr. Candy tries miserably to recall the "joke" he played at the party. When Rachel does confess that she saw Franklin take the diamond, her confession has no impact on the discovery of the crime: the "unanswerable evidence of the paintstain" has already named Franklin the thief, and Godfrey's villainy is detected by the other part of the investigation, which traces the Moonstone to London and waits for someone to redeem it from Septimus Luker (345). In fact, since Cuff's final report includes what Godfrey told Luker of the theft, even the information yielded by Jennings's experiment is superfluous, a doubtful demonstration of what the novel will anyway come to know. As Ross Murfin argues, "the real mystery" of the novel is not the identity of the thief; rather, it is the motive and intention of the crime, the great blank posed by the secret promptings of repressed desire (659). Two years earlier, in *Armadale* (1866), Collins had shown his interest in narrating criminality "from the inside" by writing much of the novel as the diary of its murderess, Lydia Gwilt.[3] *The Moonstone* returns to this interest by drawing from Collins's experiences with opium and writing his fascination with self-division into the text, finally giving us the proto-psychologist Jennings to continue the inquiry that Cuff gives up.[4] The nature of the crime may require this change in detective tactics, but not because Jennings's experiment produces "facts" that Cuff and Franklin cannot. The experiment matters mostly because it confirms what the rest of the novel only implies: that what one can see is not all that one must know in order to account for the Moonstone's theft.

The novel's pivotal absences do not stem, that is, from a failure to detect potentially visible facts; rather, they stem from the impossibility of seeing private desire. Though we cannot know it until we reach the end of the novel, even the beginning suggests this when Franklin says that he wants to tell "the whole story" of the diamond's disappearance in order to protect "the characters of innocent people" (21). But the innocent person whose character most needs saving is Franklin, so the novel's implicit function is, from the start, to clear him of suspicion for the crime. This cannot be done by reporting visible facts, for Rachel *saw* him take the diamond. Clearing him will require the *complete narration* of the crime, including its origins in the hidden workings of desire. This is the problem for Collins's novel, this need to make desire enter the visible world of the text, and the novel shows it from the time that Franklin, Betteredge, and Lady Verinder begin to wonder about "the Colonel's motive" in leaving Rachel the stone (53). Rachel sees Franklin take the diamond but misunderstands his guilt, and Rosanna stays silent about the stained nightgown because she misreads Franklin's coldness and the potentially sexual meaning of the stain.[5] Even Cuff errs because he cannot comprehend Rachel, suspecting her of guilt because of "three suspicious appearances" he notes when he arrives and because of what his "own eyes and ears inform [him]" during the days after (173). Though Cuff insists that

Lady Verinder and Betteredge trust the evidence of their senses, too, the former replies simply, "I know my child," and Betteredge declares himself "constitutionally superior to reason" (172; 174). Their disagreement is, as Miller points out, "explicitly epistemological," characterized on one side by empirical knowledge collected by detection and on the other by subjective knowledge that claims to know private desire (40). The latter proves correct, but it is worth noting that Cuff's failure does not stem from shoddy detection or ratiocination. It stems from the flaw inherent in the novel's broad herme- neutic and structural plan—from the impossibility of seeing what the novel must know.

Meanwhile, what characters *can* see is an increasingly perilous problem. In an aside meant to excuse one of his innumerable digressions, Betteredge writes, "But, there!—Persons and Things do turn up so vexatiously in this life, and will in a manner insist upon being noticed" (34). Harmless as an observation about his distracted storytelling, his words identify a real danger in a world where, as Lonoff writes, "appearances are deceiving" and charac- ters anyway suffer from an irresistible impulse to peep and pry (227). In a detective novel the deliberate spectacle is usually the red herring, a distraction meant simultaneously to lure and confound the stare. This is certainly true of *The Moonstone*, which is rife with spectacles, from the diamond itself (which makes Rachel "more particularly the centre-point" of attention during her birthday party) to the painting with which Rachel and Franklin decorate the door (which belongs to the complications of the love plot but, as it happens, has very little to do with the discovery of the crime) (76). Aware of this propensity to stare, the villains devise stratagems to dupe and manipu- late those looking on. Godfrey and the Indians each manage to steal the Moonstone largely because they exploit the faith in ocular evidence, the former by making himself a "public character" in his philanthropy, and the latter by masquerading as jugglers and pretending to be respectable foreigners in order to get lodgings and a consultation with Matthew Bruff (67). In a novel published just a decade after the Sepoy Rebellion, the Indians would in any case have provoked suspicion in contemporary readers.[6] But these Indians put themselves deliberately on display and even plan their attacks on Godfrey and Luker according to each man's tendency to stare. Attracting each to the display of "an ancient Oriental manuscript, richly illuminated with Indian figures and devices," the Indians ambush them suddenly from behind (205). As we see again when the Indians' accomplice shams drunk at the "Wheel of Fortune," the novel's villains often aim to *at*tract and *dis*tract the stare—to undermine the novel's ocular practices by letting them work a little too well.

To a great extent, then, *The Moonstone* is about the hermeneutic limitations of staring, and the way in which the novel's preoccupation with visible evi- dence hinders its detective work and ability to narrate the crime. But some- thing more insidious is also going on, in the novel's persistent concern with the negative consequences of excessive staring—something that belongs to the novel's complex psychological content and interest in criminal motives and illicit desire. In chapter 7, long before he names his malady "detective-fever," Betteredge issues a telling warning about the propensity to stare:

> Gentlefolks in general have a very awkward rock ahead in life—the rock ahead of their own idleness. Their lives being, for the most part, passed in looking about them for something to do, it is curious . . . how often they drift blindfold into some nasty pursuit. Nine times out of ten they take to torturing something, or to spoiling something—and they firmly believe they are improving their minds, when the plain truth is, they are only making a mess in the house. . . . You see my young master, or my young mistress, poring over one of their spiders' insides . . . or you meet one of their frogs walking downstairs without his head—and when you wonder what this cruel nastiness means, you are told that it means a taste in my young master or my young mistress for natural history. Sometimes, again, you see them . . . spoiling a pretty flower with pointed instruments, out of a stupid curiosity to know what the flower is made of. Is its colour any prettier, or its scent any sweeter, when you *do* know?
>
> (62)

Like much of what Betteredge writes, the remark is funny and irreverent, not to mention entirely apt for a servant who must clean up young master's or young mistress's mess. But in a world characterized by the propensity to "look about," it is a chilling account of the brutality bred by scientific observation, detective work, and other techniques of "knowing" that depend upon the stare. These consequences do not belong only to the novel's detective plot any more than staring belongs only to the detectives; rather, they penetrate to the core of genteel life, turning even the Verinders' idyllic domestic space into a theatre of cruelty where children commit acts of savage violence. However inclined we may be to scoff at "detective-fever," in other words, there really is a sense in which staring infects the novel, and in which Betteredge's complaint regarding the genteel habit of "looking about" begins to identify that malady's most appalling effects.

In a general way *The Moonstone* is deeply concerned with illness, more subtly but no less entirely than its famous predecessor *The Woman in White*. Selina Betteredge, Mr. Blake, John and Lady Verinder, and Ezra Jennings all die of illness, and Rosanna, Rachel, Franklin, and Candy suffer from nervous complaints. Indeed, the complications of the novel's detective plot depend upon not only the effects of Candy's fever but also, in the first place, upon Franklin's insomnia, which prompts Candy to prescribe for him secretly on the night of the party. Under the circumstances, it is fitting that a doctor like Jennings becomes the principle detective, for *The Moonstone* is really more troubled by illness than by crime. As Collins explained in his 1871 preface to the novel, he was "crippled in every limb by the torture of rheumatic gout'' when he wrote it—so ill, the story goes, that he had to employ an amanuensis who could write the novel from his dictation (5).[7] By the time *The Moonstone* began appearing in *All the Year Round* in January 1868, his mother was also failing, and her death in March coincided nearly with his attack of gout and his writing of Lady Verinder's death for an April number. Small wonder, then, that *The Moonstone* treats illness so broadly, and as a cause of more than physical suffering. It is the origin of psychological and social malaise in the novel: the cause of the Moonstone's disappearance, the dissolution of the Verinders' domestic circle, and the broader decay of genteel life that this and other sensation novels seem always to record. The novel's greatest concern with illness is the one that Franklin finally expresses just before leaving England: "When I came here from London with that horrible Diamond . . . I don't believe there was a happier household in England than this. Look at the household now! Scattered, disunited—the very air of the place poisoned with mystery and suspicion!" (188). Upon his return, he resumes the investigation for reasons that have little to do with detecting the crime; rather, he "want[s] to make Rachel come to an understanding" that will restore the novel's love plot and set the household to rights (306). As he and Jennings conduct it, then, the investigation is an antidote to "poison" of a distinctly social kind, a cure for whatever ails *The Moonstone*'s troubled world.

At first, the novel suggests that the Moonstone itself is the infection, a colonial sickness acquired abroad and carried home to an imperiled England. In the "Prologue" we are told that the Moonstone is "cursed," for Vishnu "predict[s] certain disaster to the presumptuous mortal who [lays] hands on the sacred gem" (12–13). In Betteredge's words, the Verinders' "quiet English house" has been suddenly "invaded by a devilish Indian Diamond—bringing after it a conspiracy of living rogues, set loose on us by the vengeance of a dead man" (46). To some extent, as many critics have pointed out, the alleged "curse" belongs to the novel's wider imperialist discourse, in which the jewel and its Indian pursuers are foreign bodies that infest and endanger the domestic state. But it is a prejudice voiced mostly by characters from the lower class—as when Penelope assumes that the Indians are mistreating their ragged boy, or when Betteredge describes the Sand as a treacherous "broad brown face"—so that the novel consistently undercuts it (39). Still, the Moonstone seems at least to sicken Herncastle, who becomes an outcast, untouchable, from the moment he acquires it. At Seringapatam, the narrator will not offer Herncastle his hand, and the colonel returns to England having gotten the "sunstroke" and "a character that had closed all the doors of his family against him"—as if he returns "contaminated" (11; 43; Carens, 249). In the years that follow, Herncastle lives in seclusion, turning up on Rachel's sixteenth birthday bearing signs of illness. He is "wasted, and worn, and old, and shabby,'' dissipated, Betteredge contends, by a life of low associates and opium (44). Though Betteredge suggests that the addiction is just another sign of vice, it is worth remembering that Jennings shares it. Like the doctor, Herncastle seems to require relief from an unrelenting illness: the Moonstone, an exotic something he has picked up abroad, and that infects not only him but also the English social body.

But Carens is correct to point out that the idea of colonial infection is one of the novel's many red herrings, a distraction from the fact that English passions are mostly to blame for the trouble. As he argues, the novel's most ''striking irony is that . . . diabolical forces need not colonize [England], because they are already indigenous inhabitants'' (243). To be more precise, empiricism rather than empire is the problem, for *The Moonstone*'s most dangerous affliction is the propensity to stare. Herncastle is never really in danger from the Moonstone; rather, he is in danger from the Brahmins who are pledged to watch and retake it, and whose vast ''organization'' in England troubles no one until they begin snooping after the stone (289). Even when we first see them, the Brahmins function like an infection by insinuating themselves into the palace of a ''host,'' the Sultan Tippoo, then waiting dormant for their chance to strike. When they arrive later in England to look after the jewel, they touch off a staring epidemic that stretches from London to Yorkshire and includes not only the counter-surveillance that Franklin uses to evade his ''dark-complexioned'' pursuer in London but also the sudden staring impulse that afflicts the Verinders' domestics, prompting them to peep and pry from the time that the Indians appear (252). Penelope and the lodge-keeper's daughter spy on them through the hedge, and Betteredge determines ''to have an eye, that evening, on the plate-basket'' (32). The Moonstone's arrival only magnifies what is already a vexing problem in Collins's England: that its inhabitants are all too ready to stare, and that they may ''all be struck dumb together'' by the ''[p]rying, and peeping'' after the theft of the stone—silenced by staring, as it were, just when the novel and the police need them to speak of the crime (152). Betteredge may regard ''looking about'' as a genteel affliction—a hereditary aristocratic disease, something like Panoptical gout—but staring in the novel is a widespread and socially sanctioned practice, less a colonial infection than an inborn condition of English life.

We should not be surprised, then, that staring spreads so virulently across the novel, nor should we wonder that characters who share the novel's broad obsession with staring share also the novel's tendency to ignore private motive and desire. When the Indians appear in Yorkshire, Betteredge mistrusts them because they have ''mahogany-colored'' skin and manners ''superior'' to his own. Later we learn that Jennings labors under similar suspicions in Yorkshire because his ''gipsy darkness,'' ''piebald hair,'' and other exotic features mean that "his appearance is against him, to begin with" (326–27). Much the same can be said of Rosanna and Limping Lucy, both of whom bear deformities that make them repulsive to the stare. As Cuff remarks, "ugly women have a bad time of it" in *The Moonstone*'s world, for that world asks characters to value each other according to what they see so that visible difference becomes grounds for mistrust and scorn (113). The dark consequence of the novel's staring is, then, that characters routinely justify Betteredge's complaint regarding "looking about" by dealing in superficialities and committing cruelties born of disregard for the subjectivity of others. On one occasion, Franklin apologizes for his "involuntary rudeness" in staring at Jennings, and elsewhere Clack observes, "It is a piece of rudeness to stare at anybody" (326; 357). But staring is not just a matter of social impropriety in *The Moonstone*; often, characters stare to inflict deliberate emotional and psychological harm. Days after Rosanna's suicide, Betteredge provokes Lucy when she speaks of "Murderer Franklin Blake," looking into her face and saying, "Pooh!" to put her "out of temper" (190–91). When Franklin visits Lucy later to get Rosanna's letter, she stares long and hard, making him feel how he "inspire[s] her with the strongest emotions of abhorrence and disgust" (308). Such moments suggest the extent to which staring is a technique of brutality as well as detection, its deleterious effects more than a matter of failed hermeneutic power.

No one endures more of this brutality than Rosanna, perhaps because of all characters she is the least fit to be seen, and the least often seen by others as a legitimate subject or object of desire. She is, Betteredge says, "the plainest woman in the house," an unsuitable object of the male gaze and unable, from a detective standpoint, to bear much looking into because of her criminal past (35). And although Betteredge hints that he is Rosanna's greatest protector in the house, even his treatment of her borders on mental cruelty. When she remarks at the Shivering Sand that she feels her "grave is waiting for her" there, Betteredge ignores the subjective import of her words and blames her empty stomach (38). When Penelope tells him that Rosanna has fallen in love with Franklin, he laughs so lustily at the "absurdity" of the idea that his daughter calls him "cruel" (48). Once, he does write that Rosanna has "a little dash of something . . . that *was* like a lady, about her," but he goes no farther (35). Only just before her death does he begin to see her as anything other than what she appears: a deformed serving girl with ludicrous romantic pretensions, an eminently unsuitable locus of desire. Perfectly aware of the tenor of Betteredge's practical and empirical English mind, Rosanna tries to explain herself to him in ocular terms. He writes:

> The day before, Rosanna had taken out a spot for me on the lappet of my coat, with a new composition, warranted to remove anything. The grease was gone,

but there was a little dull place left on the nap of the cloth . . . The girl pointed to that place, and shook her head.

"The stain is taken off," she said. "But the place shows, Mr. Betteredge—the place shows!" (37)

She cannot make Betteredge understand her in more than visual, superficial terms, and he ends by offering to "take her in to dinner" instead of engaging her as a complex subject (37). It is a fit precursor of things to come in the novel, for it is a tending to the needs of the tangible body rather than the hidden self, an empirical response to a problem rooted in desire.

Franklin is cruelest to Rosanna, which is appropriate since he is the novel's principle thief, detective, and editor—the person who inspires most of its obsessive staring. Indeed, part of what makes Franklin such an unsavory protagonist is that he treats Rosanna and Lucy pitilessly because he sees them as irrelevant and undesirable, yet he should know better than anyone that appearances may deceive. He tells Lucy that he feels "no remorse" when he sees a poor girl in service, and he confesses "unaffected surprise" when he learns from Rosanna's letter that she loved him—this, though even Betteredge notices that she puts herself constantly in Franklin's way, and that he takes "as much notice of her as he [takes] of the cat" (309; 322; 69). Kemp argues that "Rosanna's failure to 'attract' Franklin . . . is a matter of class" (xviii), and Heller writes that Franklin does not " 'notice' Rosanna or her narrative" (156). But Franklin *does* notice Rosanna, at least enough that he can narrate his odd encounters with her after the theft. The problem is that he does not care to know more about her than he sees—especially not the secret of her puzzling behavior, which is bound up with not only the visible evidence of the stained nightgown but also her desire for him and motive for hiding what she knows. Franklin is willing to see Rosanna and her letter insofar as either can shed evidential light upon the crime. What he objects to is having her subjective existence thrust upon his notice, and he grows "bitterer and bitterer against Rosanna" as he reads her confession of love (322). Thrusting it away, Franklin tells Betteredge to read it and show him only what he "*must* look at" (322). He will only "see" Rosanna's letter, then, in a way that reinforces the irrelevance of her private, desiring self.

This is the most important consequence of *The Moonstone*'s staring, this psychological brutality engendered by the novel's detective fever. Aware of the cruelty that awaits visible desire in their world, characters repress and mutilate their desire in order to hide it from the stare. Much of this repression is explicitly self-willed, as when Godfrey disowns his sexual appetites by taking his "lady in the villa" under another name, and when Rachel tries to quash her desire for Franklin by choking down her passion until she "feel[s] as if [she] is stifling for want of breath" (452; 242). Other repressions are

Freudian, emerging in linguistic and psychological displacements of which the characters seem unaware. Clack narrates her desire for Godfrey as if it is Rachel's, and Rosanna belies her repressions when she says that the Shivering Sand looks ''as if it had hundreds of suffocating people under it—all struggling to get to the surface, and all sinking lower and lower in the dreadful deeps!'' (39). In Victorian fiction we expect this response to sexuality, but there is something excessive about the responses in *The Moonstone*—excessive in the way that Penelope calls Rosanna's feelings for Franklin ''monstrous,'' and in the way that images of suffocation and enclosure dominate the novel until they culminate in Rosanna's letter and suicide, which both underscore the repressions to which desire in the novel is subject (153). To write the letter and make her desire into a visible text, Rosanna must escape to the isolation of Lucy's bedroom, seal the letter in a box, and sink the box into the Sand. Such measures reflect not only Victorian prudery but also, as Taylor writes, the transgression implicit in the fact that ''an ugly working-class woman *has* a subjectivity and a sexuality'' (199), both of which must be kept from the prying eyes of the novel. Lucy's solution to her undesirability is to reconstitute desire, turning it into intense hatred of the novel's men and a perverse (by Victorian standards) sexual yearning for Rosanna. Meanwhile, Rosanna's attempts to repress her desire for Franklin amount to a rejection of the core of her subjective self, a psychological death that anticipates her fate at the Sand. The final, terrible spectacle she offers is not her suicide—*that* is only her way of removing herself from view. Rather, it is her appearance as ''a creature moved by machinery,'' a body without desire, a nightmare example of what the novel's ocular practices have always made her (154).

In important ways, Rosanna's fate is also the novel's: repression, yes, but also the death of desire, a profound sexual sterility engendered by the stare. Psychoanalytic critics often argue the reverse, remarking that the Moonstone's theft is transparently sexual, a symbolic rendering of physical and colonial violation.[8] Sneaking into his innocent lover's boudoir in the middle of the night, Franklin returns bearing her ''priceless jewel'' and the stained nightgown that proves he authored the crime, and he does these things amid voyeurism—Rachel's and Godfrey's—that makes the scene a complex triangulation of desire. But it is worth pointing out that the crime is *always and only figuratively sexual*, not sex, but rather a displacement of it into an eroticized but impotent symbolic order. Collins makes the crime sexually symbolic, in other words, by rendering the novel sterile, a prolonged record of repressed rather than satisfied desire. Thus Godfrey's mistress exists in the novel only where she will not be seen, as do Franklin's vaguely hinted sexual indiscretions. At one point, Franklin steals a kiss from Penelope, but this happens off stage even though her own father remarks, ''Mr. Franklin was welcome to *that*'' (42). What Kemp calls the novel's ''pleasure in voyeurism'' ends in unequivocal sexual frustration (xxx). Godfrey may look on in effigy from Rachel's bedside or watch while Franklin plunders her jewel, but he will never culminate a sexual liaison with his pretty cousin, nor will the rampant peeping and furtive glances of Clack, Rosanna, or Lucy ever move them any nearer to the objects they desire. Like Franklin's theft of the jewel, voyeurism stands for but cannot be sex—it reinforces, not remedies, the sterility engendered by staring. Tellingly, the most consequential result of the theft is not the loss of the stone but the fact that it delays Franklin's sexual union with Rachel, and not because she believes Franklin is the thief. His great sin, in Rachel's eyes, is that he sets the novel staring, acting as "the foremost person . . . in fetching the police" (354).

Such instances suggest that *The Moonstone* is not just prudish about sexual matters; rather, it is fundamentally *about* sterility, and the way that the novel's sexual, detective, and narrative failures all begin in the repressions caused by pervasive staring. Even if we read the crime literally and take Franklin at his word, the theft of the diamond is prompted by a desire that *must* be repressed, for it is a desire that cannot be allowed to come before the novel's prying eyes. From the time he becomes the Moonstone's bearer, and before he falls in love with Rachel, Franklin considers keeping it from her to shield her from the danger it poses. But he knows that this is a socially illegitimate desire, one that will make him subject to the novel's policing unless, as he reminds Betteredge, he has "got the value of the stone" in his pocket (55). However we read the scene, then, Franklin steals the jewel at the prompting of a desire that staring has driven underground, into the invisible world of sexual and criminal motives that the novel must narrate if it is to give a complete account of the crime. Often the novel's love and detective plots seem inextricably intertwined, and they are so because both are shaped by the same repressions, or at least by the way in which repression results from the pervasiveness of the stare. The novel's detective and narrative failures are not caused only by the obvious limits to what the novel can "see." They are caused by staring itself, which forces all stories of transgressive desire into secret places that conventional detection cannot find. *The Moonstone* is really the story of the way that detection ensures its own hermeneutic failure, and the way that narration premised upon staring simultaneously causes and records the inevitable inadequacy of the story it can tell. It is no accident that the Moonstone is never recovered, for the novel's detective work has always been its ultimate red herring: a distraction from the fact that the novel's staring has less to do with solving the crime than with diverting sexual and narrative desire from their proper course.

Jennings's experiment becomes the primary technique for solving the crime precisely because it is less a piece of conventional detection than a treatment for the novel's "detective-fever," a measure that means to restore desire to the visible world of the novel and to its rightful place in the story of the crime. From the start, Jennings tells Franklin that the experiment means to show "in the presence of witnesses" that Franklin is "guiltless, morally speaking, of the theft of the Diamond" (389; 391). Jennings's aim is to force practical people like Betteredge and Bruff to "witness" what he already suspects: that Franklin took the diamond in a state of self-division, prompted by his desire to rid Rachel of the stone. Because Jennings explains the scientific bases of his experiment, Roberts calls him "a figure of objectivity, almost a personification of the scientific method" (175). But even a generous appraisal of Jennings's techniques must conclude that they are every bit as dubious as he fears. After days of listening to Candy's feverish wanderings, Jennings claims that he has "penetrated through the obstacle of the disconnected expression, to the thought, which was underlying it connectedly all the time"; more to the point, he has done so by composing a transcript of "[l]iterally and exactly what [he] heard . . . except that the repetitions are not transferred . . . from [his] shorthand notes" (387). His "except" shows emphatically that he has not relied only on empirical evidence, conducting instead an interpretive and editorial process that resembles Franklin's supervision of the novel. First turning the audible text into a legible one—to expose it to the hermeneutic power of the stare—Jennings pares away what he regards as its superfluities to make its real "meaning" apparent. It is not true, as Murfin contends, that Jennings "works arbitrarily" (654), but neither is it true that his aim is literal transcription. Jennings intends to bring desire into view by recording its irruptions and laying it bare to the novel. His experiment can do very well without the burst buzzard and broken Cupid because his aim is not anyway to recreate the objective realities of the crime; it is to make Franklin's repressions into a "public spectacle" (Thomas 240), thus to reveal and restore to the novel the meanings of his hidden desire.[9]

This is why the experiment's success seems sexual rather than detective—why it restores Franklin and Rachel to one another even as it fails to produce anything like certain knowledge of the crime. As Jennings tells us, Rachel's letter giving him permission to try the experiment makes it "plain that she has loved [Franklin], through the estrangement between them," and he exults that he, "of all men in the world, [might be] chosen to be the means of bringing these two young people together again" (399). Though Franklin does not restage the entire crime during the experiment, he reenacts enough of it to show what the rampant staring has made him hide: his sexual longing for Rachel and desire to protect her from the diamond. Jennings's experiment recovers both of these private meanings, reuniting the lovers in a scene that is implicitly risqué. With Franklin sleeping away the effects of the laudanum in Rachel's sitting room, Jennings leaves them alone—an act that seems to justify Mrs. Merridew's concern with the experiment's social impropriety. A

few paragraphs later, when Franklin resumes narrating, he heightens the sense
of impropriety by addressing these lines to the reader:

> . . . I have to report that Rachel and I understood each other, before a single
> word of explanation had passed on either side. I decline to account, and Rachel
> declines to account, for the extraordinary rapidity of our reconciliation. Sir and
> Madam, look back at the time when you were passionately attached to each
> other—and you will know what happened, after Ezra Jennings had shut the
> door of the sitting-room, as well as I know it myself.   (431)

The remark hints that Jennings has set everything to rights, for he has enabled
Franklin and Rachel to reach an understanding—a new phase of emotional
and perhaps even sexual intimacy in a private space reserved from the stare.

But it is worth remembering that Mrs. Merridew interrupts this reconciliation in a scene that is more than just a comic touch. Bustling in to check on
her niece, Mrs. Merridew becomes a final example of the sterility caused by
staring—a last reminder that the novel's unrelenting ocular practices end
finally in sexual, detective, and narrative frustration. Mrs. Merridew worries
from the start that the experiment will end in an "explosion," an apt concern
considering Franklin and Rachel's eager reunion, though the old spinster
seems unaware of the sexual suggestiveness of her fear. Her intrusion—and
the return of staring to the novel—ensures that no "explosion" comes (so
to speak). Despite several narrative gestures that hint otherwise, the novel
ends in moments that mirror this sexual frustration, never delivering a complete account of the crime. Prompted by laudanum to repeat the theft, Franklin
gets no farther than taking the Moonstone from the India-cabinet, so that the
experiment defers answers regarding the diamond's fate. More to the point,
the experiment also fails to establish Franklin's motive, for he expresses it
only ambiguously. As the laudanum takes effect, he says, "I wish I had never
taken it out of the bank," and, "How do I know? The Indians may be hidden
in the house?" (423; 424). These remarks suggest that he acts because of
concern for the Moonstone's safety, but he also says suspicious things like,
"It's not even locked up," and, "How the devil am I to sleep . . . with *this*
on my mind?" (424). We may be inclined to believe that Franklin acts from
no underhand desire to steal the stone, but if we and the other characters
acquit him, we do not do so because of what the experiment "shows." As
Rachel writes in reply to Jennings's description of the experiment, he has
already "satisfied her of Mr. Blake's innocence . . . without the slightest need
. . . of putting [his] assertion to the proof"; the prize witnesses, Betteredge
and Bruff, can attest only that the experiment has made Franklin steal the
Moonstone a second time (399). As Allan writes, "the experiment does not
so much vindicate him as confirm his criminality" (191), for it does not
really let us see or know his private desire. Instead, it asks us to agree

quietly that staring has failed as a hermeneutic practice, and that the novel's resolution depends upon faith in things that will always escape the stare.

This is the lesson of *The Moonstone*'s final narratives, which repeat and elaborate the experiment's failure by inscribing over and over Jennings's inability to account for the crime. The novel may ask us to believe otherwise, but Franklin's carefully edited compilation of eyewitness testimony never delivers on its promise to describe the Moonstone's theft or subsequent peregrinations. Instead, it dissolves into a series of fitfully reliable narratives, each disfigured by the absence of something crucial to its explicit aim. Cuff's narrative seems trustworthy though his earlier theories have been disproved, for he has at least seen firsthand the proof of Godfrey's secret life. When he tries to account for the fate of the Moonstone, however, he must resort to repeating what he learned from Luker, who heard Godfrey tell three different stories about how he got hold of the diamond. Cuff asks us all to trust the third story, and for the simple reason "that Mr. Godfrey Ablewhite was too great a fool to have invented it" (457). But this is hardly reassuring, since the great fool has duped everyone but the Indians for hundreds of pages. In the epilogue, meanwhile, we are asked to believe in accounts that are more unsure: the narrative of Cuff's man, who is supposed to follow the Indians but cannot keep them in view; the narrative of the ship's captain, who does not see the Indians for the designing murderers they are; and Murthwaite's narrative, which sees the Moonstone but cannot explain its return to India. Indeed, perhaps the novel's most fitting moment is its ending, which records Murthwaite's confession of narrative inadequacy instead of any confession regarding the crime. He writes, "How [the Moonstone] has found its way back to its wild native land—by what accident, or by what crime . . . may be in your knowledge, but it is not in mine" (472). Really, as *The Moonstone* takes great pains to show, the story cannot be told, for it exists in the knowledge of no one at all. The novel's final words are a long way from the "plain facts" the opening pages promised, and a long way, too, from celebrating the hermeneutic efficacy of the stare. The first English detective novel thus concludes paradoxically that detection is but a poor way of knowing and accounting for crime, for the new age of detection will require overcoming—not embracing—that modern epidemic, "detective-fever."

3.

Perhaps Collins wrote about ocular practices in this way because, as Sutherland argues, he had reached an apex of frustration regarding the new species of private investigator bred by the 1857 Matrimonial Causes Act—"gimlet-hole" peepers, he had called them in *Armadale* (517)—who obliged him to bury the details of his unconventional sexual life.[10] Or perhaps he despised generally the prurient vigilance of Victorian England, characterized increasingly by tabloid journalism, sensational crimes, Scotland Yard detectives, and disquieting faith in empiricism and scientific observation. Whatever the case, Collins draws in *The Moonstone* a world plagued by a destructive propensity to stare, and he asserts through this portrait that psychological repression is a particular consequence of the modern age—a response to social discipline, new forms of scientific and social materialism, and new technologies of surveillance that were encroaching upon the desiring Victorian subject. Collins's most important innovation in *The Moonstone*, then, is not a new subgenre called detective fiction, nor yet Jennings's proto-Freudian reading of Candy, however suggestive the latter might be as an early moment of psychoanalysis. Rather, Collins's most important innovation is his portrait of a world where psychoanalysis is required—where staring drives desire so deep into the self that nothing short of psychoanalysis can find it. *The Moonstone* does not only anticipate Freud, then; it anticipates the *need* for Freud, tracing repression and self-division to the pressures exerted by an increasingly empirical and vigilant Victorian world. Indeed, though the Brahmins are often pitied for the punishment they receive when they return to India—they are sentenced, after all their trouble, to part ways forever, ''[n]ever more . . . to look on each other's faces'' (471)—the truth is that they are not so much punished as freed. They are cured, one might say, from the thralldom of obsessive staring. Like the failure of the novel's criminal investigation, the Brahmins' fate underscores that the point of *The Moonstone* is not anyway to account for crime. It is to diagnose and treat the debilitating effects of Victorian surveillance.

NOTES

1. T. S. Eliot gave *The Moonstone* this praise in his 1928 ''Introduction'' to the novel (xii). Though there is some reason to doubt whether *The Moonstone* was really the first detective novel, critics have repeated Eliot's claim so often that it has become part of the familiar lore of the text. For a brief but effective discussion regarding the accuracy of Eliot's assessment, see Sandra Kemp's ''Introduction'' to *The Moonstone* (xxx, fn. 1). Future references to Kemp's ''Introduction'' and to the novel are to this edition and appear parenthetically in the text.
2. Lewis Lawson was among the first critics to make such an argument, but many others have followed. See for example Hutter, Roberts, and Taylor (especially 174–206).
3. Sutherland makes this case in his ''Introduction'' to *Armadale* (xvi). For a detailed discussion of Collins's treatment of Lydia Gwilt and her diary in *Armadale*, see also my work in chapter 6 of *The Self in the Cell*, especially 205–06 and 210–17.

4. While writing *The Moonstone* Collins suffered through depression over his mother's death and a painful struggle with "rheumatic gout," the latter of which drove him to large doses of opium as a palliative. Several biographers have described Collins's chronic medical complaints and struggles with opium, including Peters, 249–57 and 312–37; and Clarke, 103 and 163–66.

5. In her letter to Franklin, Rosanna describes her reaction to finding the nightgown by writing:

> Here's the proof that he was in Miss Rachel's sitting-room between twelve last night, and three this morning!
>
> I shall not tell you in plain words what was the first suspicion that crossed my mind, when I had made that discovery. You would only be angry—and, if you were angry, you might tear my letter up and read no more of it. (321)

6. Several critics have written about the novel's imperialist content and implicit engagement with the 1857 Sepoy Rebellion. See for example Duncan, Nayder, and Reed.

7. In a letter to Harper Brothers, his American publisher for *The Moonstone*, Collins wrote in February 1868: "This weekly part [No. 15] . . . [has] been partly dictated, partly written by me, in intervals of severe pain from rheumatic attack—which has tortured my eyes this time as well as the rest of my body." See *The Letters of Wilkie Collins*, v. 2, 306. Collins may have exaggerated the extent of his illness or at least its effect on his writing, for only six pages of the extant manuscript appear in the hand of his amanuensis, Carrie (Elizabeth Hartley) Graves. But there is little doubt that he was in considerable intermittent pain. For a full discussion of Wilkie's illness while writing *The Moonstone*, see Peters, 295–96.

8. For the most recent reading of the novel's psychosexual implications, see Bisla. Critical assessments of the novel's sexual symbolism also include Gruner, 132–36; Hutter, 200–02; and Lawson, 64–66.

9. Heller makes a similar argument in *Dead Secrets* (146).

10. For an excellent discussion of the Matrimonial Causes Act of 1857 and its effect on private investigation, see Sutherland, especially 76.

WORKS CITED

Allan, Janice M. "Scenes of Writing: Detection and Psychoanalysis in Wilkie Collins's *The Moonstone*." *Imprimatur* 1.2/3 (1996): 186–93.

Bisla, Sundeep. "The Return of the Author: Privacy, Publication, Mystery, and *The Moonstone*." *boundary 2* 29.1 (2002): 177–222.

Brantlinger, Patrick. "What is 'Sensational' about the 'Sensation Novel'?" *Nineteenth-Century Fiction* 37.1 (1982): 1–28.

Carens, Timothy. "Outlandish English Subjects in *The Moonstone*." *Reality's Dark Light: The Sensational Wilkie Collins*. Eds. Maria K. Bachman and Don Richard Cox. Knoxville: U of Tennessee P, 2003. 239–65.

Clarke, William M. *The Secret Life of Wilkie Collins*. London: W. H. Allen, 1989.

Collins, Wilkie. *Armadale*. Ed. John Sutherland. New York: Penguin, 1995.

———. *The Letters of Wilkie Collins*. Eds. William Baker and William M. Clarke. 2 vols. New York: St. Martin's, 1999.

———. *The Moonstone*. Ed. Sandra Kemp. New York: Penguin, 1998.

———. *The Moonstone*. Introduction by T. S. Eliot. Oxford: Oxford UP, 1928.

Duncan, Ian. "*The Moonstone*, the Victorian Novel, and Imperialist Panic." *Modern Language Quarterly* 55.3 (1994): 297–319.

Grass, Sean. *The Self in the Cell: Narrating the Victorian Prisoner*. New York; London: Routledge, 2003.

Gruner, Elisabeth Rose. "Family Secrets and the Mysteries of *The Moonstone*." *Victorian Literature and Culture* 21.1 (1993): 127–45.

Heller, Tamar. *Dead Secrets: Wilkie Collins and the Female Gothic*. New Haven; London: Yale UP, 1992.

Hutter, Albert D. "Dreams, Transformations, and Literature: The Implications of Detective Fiction." *Victorian Studies* 19.2 (1975): 181–209.

Lawson, Lewis A. "Wilkie Collins and *The Moonstone*." *American Imago* 20.1 (1963): 61–79.

Lonoff, Sue. *Wilkie Collins and His Victorian Readers: A Study in the Rhetoric of Authorship*. New York: AMS, 1982.

Marshall, William H. *Wilkie Collins*. New York: Twayne, 1970.

McCuskey, Brian W. "The Kitchen Police: Servant Surveillance and Middle-Class Transgression." *Victorian Literature and Culture* 28.2 (2000): 359–75.

Miller, D. A. *The Novel and the Police*. Berkeley: U of California Press, 1988.

Murfin, Ross C. "The Art of Representation: Collins' *The Moonstone* and Dickens' Example." *ELH* 49.3 (1982): 653–72.

Nayder, Lillian. "Robinson Crusoe and Friday in Victorian Britain: 'Discipline,' 'Dialogue,' and Collins's Critique of Empire in *The Moonstone*." *Dickens Studies Annual* 21 (1992): 213–31.

Peters, Catherine. *The King of Inventors: A Life of Wilkie Collins*. Princeton: Princeton UP, 1991.

Reed, John R. "English Imperialism and the Unacknowledged Crime of *The Moonstone.*" *Clio* 2.3 (1973): 281–90.

Roberts, Lewis. "The 'Shivering Sands' of Reality: Narration and Knowledge in Wilkie Collins' *The Moonstone.*" *Victorian Review* 23.2 (1997): 168–83.

Sutherland, John. "Wilkie Collins and the Origins of the Sensation Novel." *Wilkie Collins to the Forefront: Some Reassessments.* Eds. Nelson Smith and R. C. Terry. New York: AMS, 1995. 75–90.

Taylor, Jenny Bourne. *In the Secret Theatre of the Home: Wilkie Collins, Sensation Narrative, and Nineteenth-Century Psychology.* London: Routledge, 1988.

Thomas, Ronald R. "Minding the Body Politic: The Romance of Science and the Revision of History in Victorian Detective Fiction." *Victorian Literature and Culture* 19.2 (1991): 233–54.

Todorov, Tzvetan. *The Poetics of Prose.* Trans. Richard Howard. Ithaca: Cornell UP, 1977

Dickens and China: Contextual Interchanges in Cultural Globalization

Kay Li

A survey of Charles Dickens and China reveals that his works cross to China over contextual bridges in cultural globalization. Since Dickens did not write with either China or the Chinese in mind, the passage of Dickens to China is made possible because of contextual interchanges that enable the Chinese to discover specific, nearly targeted relevance, so that Dickens's works fit the Chinese reading context in limited ways. Dickens is manipulated to justify certain cherished aims of the Chinese, and whenever he does not fit, he is criticized as limited, especially by virtue of his capitalist bourgeois background. However, rather than saying the Chinese critics have misread Dickens, we may observe that their readings are meaningful and relevant in the Chinese context. Dickens's works are universal, and global readings of Dickens are possible, though even when readings by individual cultures and nations may differ.

A survey of Charles Dickens and China reveals that his works cross to China over contextual bridges in cultural globalization. He wrote his novels with a specific time, place, and readership in mind: nineteenth-century Victorian England and the readers of its magazines and newspapers. China, which was then under the imperial Manchu rule of the Qing Dynasty (1644–1911), was a very remote region. Dickens's references to China (The Hyperconcordance of the ''Victorian Literary Studies Archive'') reveal how he regards the country. First, China is a faraway place used in exaggerations, an indication of

---

great distance as found in "cast away in China" or "from your deepest Cornish mine to China." Next, China is nearly an unreal fairy-tale with "Prince of China," "Emperor of China," and "Princess of China." China with its imperial rule and great distance from England fits into the exotic fairy-tales Dickens created in his novels. At other times, China is regarded more realistically within the limited economic globalization the world had developed. The country is part of nineteenth-century mercantile trade and there are "China traders," captains and merchants bringing back silk, tea, and china. Probably Dickens, like George Bernard Shaw, was not aware that he and his works would become part of this exchange of goods and ideas between the East and West. The novels and writings have been taken to China, translated into Chinese, and published in unauthorized Chinese editions. In present-day China, Dickens websites can be found on the Chinese internet. Therefore, Dickens has had a very real presence in China for a long time, though the writer himself never intended such an encounter.

The reading of Dickens in China demands contextual interchanges, prompting the readers to make comparisons and contrasts between the text and the context of reading. Reading changes within the context of consumption. Dickens's works arrived at China more than a century ago. "Cultural globalization," though the term has been used in different ways by different writers, basically means a global multidirectional cultural passage. In the reading of Dickens in China, this passage involved not just the physical transportation of the novels from the West to the East, but the beginning of a series of cultural encounters. For instance, Pearl Buck (1892–1973) recalls in "A Debt to Dickens" (1936) that in about 1899, when she was seven, on a hot August midafternoon, she found a collection of Dickens's novels in her family library and started reading *Oliver Twist*, *Hard Times*, and *David Copperfield*. While many western children might have done similar things when they first came in touch with Dickens's works, Buck's case was special because she read the novels in China, in a remote Chinese village surrounded by rice fields. Taken to China by her parents, who were Presbyterian missionaries to Zhenjiang, China, when she was only three months old, she found the encounter with Dickens a complex cultural experience. Buck begins her essay with these words: "My debt is to an Englishman, who long ago in China rendered an inestimable service to a small American child. That child was myself and that Englishman was Charles Dickens. I know no better way to meet my obligation than to write down what Charles Dickens did in China for an American child" (11).

In Buck's reading of Dickens in the Chinese countryside, there is a coexistence of cultural heterogeneity and homogeneity. On the one hand, there is the intercultural difference between the East and the West, as well as the intracultural difference between British English and American English. On the other hand, Dickens also offers something that crosses cultural barriers and touches common chords, as he presents some universal human qualities and values in the portrayal of a large variety of characters, in the attacks on hypocrisy and in the celebration of human kindness. His caricatures of good and bad people are vivid images showing his passion for life. Above all, Buck was aware of the contextual difference in the production of Dickens's works in Victorian England and the consumption of his writings in rural China, for she draws attention to the juxtaposition between the famine in China in winter and her reading of Dickens's depictions of luxurious Christmas celebrations in England. But human conditions may be universal, and to Buck, the characters in the *Pickwick Papers* are as real as the poor people living on the other side of the wall marking the missionaries' quarters.

Dickens played a role in the literary reforms in modern China, especially in the elevation of the status of novels. This may be common in both the West and the East. In the Western world, Dickens's novels might not be regarded as serious as other philosophical works and other genres. For instance, in Buck's family library in China, Dickens's novels were put on a top shelf, while the more "serious" works of Plutarch and John Foxe, as well as the Bible and poems by Tennyson, were more conveniently located. This comparatively low regard for novels was also shared by the native population of China. Before Dickens and other Western novelists were introduced, novels in China did not enjoy as high a status as poetry and essays. But the novel was an old genre in China, and classical novels included *Dream of the Red Chamber*, *Journey to the West*, *Legend of White Snake*, *Tale of Water Margin*, *Three Kingdoms*, *Strange Tales of Liaozhai*, and others. Qian Li-qun, Wen Yu-min, and Wu Fu-hui show that in the Qing Dynasty (1644–1911), conventional Chinese government officials and scholars refused to make use of vocabulary and sources from novels. It was not until the end of the Qing Dynasty and the beginning of the Chinese Republic in 1911 that novels began to move from the margin to the center.

There were internal and external reasons for the growing importance of novels in modern China. Within China, people preferred the "eight-legged" essays to the Chinese classics, and the novels to the essays. Since the latter were essays with eight parts, and each part had a specified number of characters, it was a very rigid form. The novel, on the contrary, was very flexible and gave the writer much more room to maneuver. At the beginning of the twentieth century, the time was ripe for the rise of the modern novel in the vernacular in China. Supporters of the novel include Liang Qi-chao (1873–1929), a famous Chinese scholar advocating reforms, and Kang You-wei (1858–1927), who started the "novel revolution" in 1902 and linked the novel to his advocacy of reforms. In the short-lived Hundred Day Reforms in 1898, Liang Qi-chao took charge on July 3 of a translation bureau in the government. Liang thought that the novel was the best genre in literature and could be used to fulfill a social function: "To renew the citizens of the nation, the novels in the nation should be renewed first. To better the government, one should begin with the revolution in the novel. To renew the people, the novel should be renewed" (Qian 58). This view raised the position of the novel.

Externally, the rise of the novel in modern China was attributable to the introduction of Western novels, which played a role in the change of the Chinese novel from classical to modern. Although Chinese novelists played a significant role in the 1917 Intellectual Revolution (1917–1923), the movement had started much earlier in the introduction of Western novels through translations. Between the introduction of foreign novels in 1896 in the *Shi Wu Bao* ("Current Affairs") and the commencement of the Intellectual Revolution, about 800 foreign novels were translated and published (Qian 30). One prominent figure was the translator of Dickens, Lin Shu (Lin Qin-nan) (1852–1924).

Dickens was among the earliest foreign writers introduced to China. Beginning in 1897, Lin Shu translated 163 foreign novels and was famous for conveying the meaning and spirit of Western European novels rather than giving literal translations. He introduced novels from the United States, England, France, Russia, Greece, Germany, Japan, Belgium, Switzerland, Norway, and Spain to China. Lin Shu translated such of Dickens's works as *David Copperfield*, *Oliver Twist*, *Hard Times*, *The Old Curiosity Shop*, *Dombey and Son*, and *Nicholas Nickleby* into Chinese, mostly published between 1907 and 1908 at the end of the Qing Dynasty. It is noteworthy that Dickens was just one of the international authors Lin translated. Among his other famous translations are his first one, Alexandre Dumas's *La dame aux camellias*, H. Rider Haggard's *King Solomon's Mines*, *Montezuma's Daughter*, and *Beatrice*, and Sir Walter Scott's *Ivanhoe, The Talisman*, and *The Betrothed* (Hsü 520). These translations of foreign literary works enabled Chinese readers to acquire a global consciousness, a global context in which China could be located. With his prolific translations, Lin was essential in the introduction of world novels to China, creating a new generation of Chinese novelists and readers and enabling them to know the world (Qian 30).

The early translations of Dickens proved the importance of cultural translations. While literal translations give semantic equivalents, cultural translations provide parallels found in the host culture. The former is a one-way translation that does not adapt the cultural work into the context of the host country, while the latter may involve Sinicization or making things Chinese, as well as assimilation, in which the incoming culture is absorbed into the host culture, resulting in a loss of its original characteristics. Lin Shu's translations of Dickens could not readily be literal translations because Lin did not know any foreign language, and his translations were collaborations. While his collaborator translated orally, Lin wrote the words down in classical Chinese. These translations were bound to include inaccuracies, but Lin came close to the essence of the original novels because he was able to grasp the spirit, mood, and humor instinctively (Hsü 521). Lin writes: "People in a book become at once my nearest and dearest relatives. When they are in difficulties, I fall into despair; when they are successful, I am triumphant. I am no longer a human being but a puppet whom the author dangles on his strings" (Hsü 521). A competent judge of Lin's translations of Dickens is Arthur Waley, an authoritative translator of Chinese works. Waley compared Lin's translations and the original Dickens novels, and concluded: "The humor is there, but is transmuted by a precise, economic style; every point that Dickens spoils by uncontrolled exuberance, Lin Shu makes quietly and effectively" (Hsü 521). Thus, Lin's translations are like cultural adaptations conveying the spirit of Dickens's novels, while the cultural specificities which the average Chinese reader might not be able to grasp are conveniently de-emphasized.

Lin's translations not only bridged China and the rest of the world; they also helped to offer China a global perspective. While he was introducing Western literature and literary currents into China, he was also introducing Western society, ranging from customs and social problems to ethical concepts and familial relations, all of which differed from those found in China (Hsü 521). Politically, Lin provided his translations with prologues and introductions promoting not only better human relations and social progress, but also patriotism and nationalism, much needed in China at that time because of the foreign encroachments. For example, in the preface to his translation of *David Copperfield*, he states that Dickens presents the minute details of everyday life, including strange characters and events, and turns the decayed into the miraculous, the fragments into a whole. Dickens's works provide a wonderful amalgamation of the unusual and most absurd (Li Na 29). What was familiar to Western readers may appear strange and absurd to the Chinese. As we have seen, Lin's works emphasized various political points. For example, he also translated with Wei Yi other literary texts, including Harriet Beecher Stowe's *Uncle Tom's Cabin*, in 1901. Ouyang Yu-chien, who played a role in the first dramatic production in Chinese of *Uncle Tom's Cabin*, entitled *Black Slaves Appeal to Heaven*, said that there was an underlying anger towards the ferocity and cruelty of imperialism. The translation was meant to warn the Chinese that they had to be independent and strengthen themselves (Tien, *Zhong* 14). These kinds of political and social suggestions are also found in Lin's translations of Dickens. *A Tale of Two Cities* was introduced into China at the end of the 1930s. According to Gao Jian-hong, the 1930s were a turbulent period in China, and the background of *A Tale of*

Two Cities, the French Revolution, made the novel seem especially relevant in China. Besides depicting a people's revolution, the English Dickens looked at the French Revolution objectively and coolly.

Lin Shu's translations of Dickens deviated from the original, most notably in his use of the classical style as opposed to the original vernacular. This was a central debate in the Chinese Intellectual Revolution (1917–23). While young Chinese intellectuals such as Dr. Hu Shih (1891–1962) advocated the *pai-hua* or plain language vernacular style, Lin Shu's translations were classical and stylized, and in the Intellectual Revolution he remained a firm advocate of the classical tradition. The dichotomy between the formal classical Chinese style used in Lin Shu's translations and the plain vernacular style used by Dickens therefore crystallized into an ongoing debate among Chinese intellectuals at that time. Cai Yuan-pei (1876–1940), chancellor of Peking University, advocated reforms, while Lin Shu and Yen Fu promoted traditionalism. When Lin wrote to Cai ridiculing the vernacular writing style as the work of "roadside peddlers," Cai retorted by saying that the plain language differed from the classical style in form rather than content, and that the fiction of Dickens and other writers translated by Lin and Yen was originally written in plain language. Cai asked them rhetorically whether they considered their translations better than the originals (Hsü 604). The plain language or *pai-hua* was subsequently adopted by the young Chinese intellectuals, and Lin, Dickens's foremost translator was dismissed as conservative. Novels written in plain language flourished, particularly with the emergence of writers such as Lu Xun (1881–1936), who played a significant role in the Chinese Intellectual Revolution.

More recently, modern readings of Dickens were shaped to pursue goals prescribed by the prevailing Communist ideologies in the People's Republic of China, the government established on October 1, 1949. The Cultural Revolution followed, lasting from May 1966 to October 1976, during which time any individuals associated with the old culture were publicly humiliated, most old-fashioned, traditional, or Western art was banned, and all forms of religious practice were virtually suppressed (Mackerras 19). In 1978, China shifted to a policy of reform and tolerance. This included changes in economic policy in the direction of market socialism and free enterprise in the countryside. Mackerras believes that China seemed able to throw out all the Maoist propaganda, which had been deleterious to the Chinese revolution as a whole. As a result, economic and social freedoms of various sorts became permissible (Mackerras 18). The Third Plenum had far-ranging effects and ushered in extensive changes in more or less all major spheres of life, including the legal system, the economy, ideology, education, literature and the arts, the minority nationalities, and religion (Mackerras 18). China entered a "new era" in which the reappearance and renewed study of Dickens became possible.

Dickens has appealed to the Chinese ideologically. When Dickens was first introduced into China, his realism fit into the young Chinese intellectuals' prevailing clamor for realism and pragmatism. Dickens has also been found ideologically suitable to modern China, for he is readily adapted to the rhetoric of socialism, social realism, and critical realism. Modern Chinese readings of Dickens have remained ideological rather than aesthetic. Here are some contextual interchanges.

The first is biographical. Dickens's life is a popular topic, and many critics such as Zhang Peng note parallels between Dickens's life and works. Indeed, Zhang Peng asserts that Dickens's novels reflect nineteenth-century English society. Many critics talked about the three periods of Dickens's writings: the utopianism in 1836–41, the dislike of and disappointment in his society in 1842–50, and the even less hopeful attitude towards English corruption in 1852–70, corresponding to the optimism in Dickens's youth, the anger in his middle age, and the hopelessness in the last period of his life.

The correspondence between Dickens's life and works was used to support Chinese socialism. Pan Qiulin and Peng Xiaoqiang discuss the three stages of Dickens's writing and his artistic achievement. To Pan and Peng, the first stage of Dickens's works from 1837 to 1841 was optimistic, and the social criticism was comparatively mild. The second stage lasted from 1842 to 1858, and his trips to America, Italy, and France deepened his understanding of capitalist society. For instance, *Dombey and Son* shows the moral ugliness of the capitalist class, while *Hard Times* shows the acute class contradictions in England in the 1830s to 1840s. The third stage, running from 1858 to 1870, shows Dickens's increased knowledge of social darkness. Pan and Peng identify three main aspects of Dickens's works: they criticize Victorian British capitalist society; they are moralistic; and they explore human nature. These three aspects are connected by Dickens's humanism, and the social criticism is a result of humanistic observation and evaluation. Pan and Peng conclude that the tone of Dickens's works "changed from naïve optimism to gloom, which shows that Dickens criticized and exposed the evils of capitalist society from the humanist point of view" (85).

Just as in the first introduction of Dickens to China, Dickens is now a cultural bridge positioned midway between China and the world, according to Jiang and Wen's conclusion: "Dickens is a writer the Chinese people like. Many of his works are well known to them. Throughout his life, he reveals deeply the darkness, decadence, and cruelty of capitalist society. His hardworking and brilliant life contributes immensely to English and world literature. He is the greatest English writer of critical realism" (195).

Dickens attracts Chinese readers because of his social realism and his interest in the social function of literature. To Pan and Peng, his novels are examples of popular art using contemporary materials from actual real social life. Dickens reflects and criticizes life in his writing, revealing and condemn-ing social darkness and injustice. Pan and Peng's essay, as well as Tang's, affirms the legitimacy of Dickens in China, since Karl Marx regarded him as one of the outstanding novelists. Gao Jian-hong remarks that Friedrich Engels, while living in England in January 1844, observed that in the preceding decade there had been a complete revolution in the nature of the novel, with the protagonists changing from kings and princes to poor people and the lower classes. The novels are made up of the lives, fates, happiness, and sufferings of these people. Dickens is one of the writers practicing this new trend.

Dickens is also welcomed by the Chinese readers because of his critical realism. Nineteenth-century "critical realists," as defined by Lu Jian-guo, were "strongly critical of the social reality of their time but they had never thought of overthrowing the existing social order so that in this way, they could establish a new one" (39). Critical realist writers like Dickens "had a world of sympathy for the miseries of the poor laboring masses" (39), and we remember that the "laboring masses" have an important place in Communist rhetoric. Tang Yan-ping considers Dickens "the greatest critical realist." Jiang Ping and Wen Qing also explore his artistic techniques and language in this context. Dickens's life is an ideal critique of capitalist society. Having gone through poverty, he understood poor people and knew the defects of capitalist society: the hypocrisy of the charity business, the blemishes of the legal system, and the corruption in politics. To Jiang and Wen, concern with the ideological relevance (content) supersedes artistic matters (style). Thus, *Oliver Twist* is a social novel showing the sad, tortuous, and difficult child-hood of Oliver, and reveals the cruelty in the deceptive human relationships in capitalist society (192). Oliver's "Please, sir, I want some more" is re-garded as revealing of barbaric infringement of the right of human existence, and reflects the people's striving for basic rights in the nineteenth-century British Reform Movement. For Jiang and Wen, Mr. Micawber and Uriah Heep in *David Copperfield* are the sort of vivid literary characters recom-mended by Friedrich Engels, each being both a type and an individual (193).

Despite the topical concerns of Dickens in these novels, he also explores universal social problems that can be understood across cultural barriers. Zhu Jiang looks at Dickens's critical realism by examining the portrayals of children, especially Oliver Twist and David Copperfield. These reveal salient social problems such as the bringing up of children and their welfare and education in Victorian England. Through Dickens's exposure of the ugliness of East London, the poverty and crime in the slums are seen as a revelation of the darkness of the capitalist society. To Zhu Jiang, these features make the works universal, since they depict real life and social criticism. The images, whether they are regarded historically or realistically, have great ideological and aesthetic value.

Although most critics focus on the novels, some Chinese critics study Dickens's speeches. Ding Jian-ping and Yin Qi-ping examine *The Speeches of Charles Dickens* and find that they improve understanding of Dickens's literary works, as well as our comprehension of other Victorian novels, literature, society, politics, economics, education, and public health. The speeches give the motivations of characterizations and reveal Dickens's romanticism and what he thinks about the function of literature. Ding and Yin conclude that more attention should be paid to these speeches.

Dickens is often linked with the socialist rhetoric of class struggle. Zhang Jing-feng studies the polarizations of the rich and poor in the novels, and finds the poor characters mostly suffering in capitalist society. Gao Jian-hong, in his study of *A Tale of Two Cities*, shows how Dickens is sympathetic towards the masses. Dickens revealed that the main cause of the French Revolution was the rulers' oppression and exploitation of the masses. His sympathy for the common people and his humanism are shown in this novel, and these qualities developed from Dickens's own early experience of poverty.

While there is no reason to assume that all of the social problems Dickens explored in the novels—those found in nineteenth-century capitalist England—can be found in twentieth-century socialist China, certain universal concerns are still relevant. Since one of the social problems Dickens explored is children's education, a commentary on his treatment of this appeared in the *Journal of Chenzhou Teachers College*. Chen Qing-lan begins the article by telling why Dickens is relevant: his depictions of children suffering under unhealthy conditions in society, especially in schools and families, as well as his enticing accounts expressing his consciousness and experience of life, his emotions, and his moral standards. Therefore, Chen thinks that Dickens is a classic writer who should be presented to primary and secondary school students in different kinds of social systems. Chen examines the education problem Dickens explored from three perspectives: social education, school education, and family education. The defects of social education in a selfish, money-worshipping society are shown in *Oliver Twist*, which exposes the supposedly philanthropical workhouse's maltreatment of poor children and also reveals how the London gangsters misled innocent children. Malpractice in the schools for poor children is shown in *Nicholas Nickleby*, while the mistreatment of the pupils in better schools is explored in *David Copperfield*. The importance of family education is examined in the depictions of the poor and lonely children in *Oliver Twist*, or the toils of young Amy Dorrit in *Little Dorrit*. Dickens shows how the social system and the social structure are responsible for these adversities. Thus, through these novels, Dickens explores the problem of childhood education from various perspectives and guides children in learning how to distinguish between the true and the false, and how to cultivate different virtues. Chen concludes that Dickens is relevant to China: ''The business of children's education concerns the nation's fate and future. In the past, present and future, and whether it is under capitalism or socialism, the society, schools and the family should pay attention to how to educate children correctly and healthily'' (63).

Another issue is law and the legal system depicted in Dickens's novels. While the twenty-first-century Chinese readers may not comprehend nineteenth-century capitalist British laws, Sun Jian-fang explores the conflicts between emotions and law depicted in the novels. Thus, what is socially and historically specific—law—becomes generalized in Sun's investigation of Dickens's humanism. To Sun, Dickens's mild humanism is shown in his advocacy of the ''final victory of philanthropy over evil, beauty over ugliness, and love over the law.''

When critics appreciate Dickens's writing techniques, the social topic is never far away. Zhang Yan-hong and Sit Hong think that Dickens's use of labeling in the portrayal of characters managed to produce many vivid and memorable characters, even though the plot and the titles of the novels may be forgotten. On the one hand, they cover technical details: Dickens's use of local dialects, of names, and of borrowings from eighteenth-century novels about wanderers and eighteenth-century dramas with vivid villains and exaggerated plots. On the other hand, the authors also attribute the novels to English social history: how the country changed from rural, agricultural merry Old England, with inns, carriages, and gentlemen who liked hunting, to an industrialized, urban nation with railways, factories, slums, and the proletariat class in the cities. Dickens's novels reveal these social problems and criticize society's weaknesses.

The focus on Dickens's writing techniques accompanies interest in the social use of these techniques. Li Jun examines the artistic features in *A Tale of Two Cities*. There are two distances: the distance from the setting of the French Revolution to Dickens's England, and the distance from Dickens's England to present-day China. In the first instance, Li recognizes Dickens's attempt to make use of the French Revolution to warn British rulers to reform their country. In the second case, the French aristocracy's exploitation and oppression of the people may find resonance in China which favors mass movement against feudalism. Li appreciates Dickens's ''siding with the labouring people'' and his opposing the nobles' oppression (9). Above all, the article appears in the *English Corner*, a journal for the exploration of the English language. Not surprisingly, Li draws attention to Dickens's depiction of mass scenes contrasting the rich nobility and the poor, employing contrast, symbol, exaggeration, and other techniques. The critic draws attention to the use of hyperbole and vivid and lively language, parallelism and contradictory antithesis, and metaphor and symbol to highlight the class struggle and portray the antagonism between aristocrats and working people.

Some of Dickens's writing techniques are culture specific. Li Na examines the popular dissemination of Dickens's fiction, particularly the publication of several of the novels as serials in Dickens's periodicals *Household Words* and *All the Year Round*. Li Na also considers the theatricality of Dickens's works, made evident in Dickens's own public readings. The detective elements, the happy endings, the depiction of details of everyday life, the sympathy towards the common people, the expression of common ideals, tastes, and needs, and the use of paradox and exaggeration all contribute to the popularity of Dickens's works. While these can cross cultural barriers and be intelligible to Chinese readers, some of Dickens's caricatures are language specific when the description of physical features involves wordplay.

The above shows that Dickens's passage to China is only through contextual interchanges, limited bridges supported by targeted issues such as socialism, critical realism, mass movements, the social use of literature, and writing techniques. These are valid concerns given the reading context: China in transformation from tradition to modernity at the beginning of the twentieth century, and China in transformation after 1978 from the Cultural Revolution to a country under the policy of reform and opening up, resulting in rapid economic development. It is noteworthy to study as well how Chinese critics treat those areas when Dickens was found not so suitable to China.

When Dickens falls short of the Chinese context, Chinese critics think that he has limitations. Reading Dickens in China involves the interplay of two contexts: the context of cultural production in Dickens's Victorian England and the context of cultural consumption in modern socialist China. Gao Jianhong notes that Dickens is limited by history and class. Although Dickens is conscious of the common people, it does not mean that he is one of the common people. Gao draws attention to the contrast between the rapid development of colonialism and capitalism in Victorian Era, and the extreme poverty of the proletariat and the common people. While Dickens is sympathetic towards people at the grass roots level, he is also attracted to the gentry and the British upper classes. Gao thinks that despite England's expansionist actions in India and China, the British remained gentlemanly on some occasions, and Dickens demonstrates this gentlemanliness in characters like Sydney Carton and Jarvis Lorry in *A Tale of Two Cities*. On the other hand, Gao senses a clear conflict and double standard in the treatment of revolution, revolutionary violence, and the masses' revolutionary behavior. While Dickens was sympathetic towards the people's sufferings, he was clearly against revolutionary violence, thinking that the revolution was mad, cruel, barbaric, and irrational as shown in Ernest Defarge and Madame Defarge. Be they common people or aristocrats, Dickens's sympathy was with the exploited, for he advocated harmony of classes, moral amelioration, forgiveness, and control. Gao thinks that Dickens's ideal society is that of the gentlemanly, polite, accommodating British salon.

Dickens's petit bourgeois background becomes a salient concern in a nation supporting proletarian and agrarian revolution. Li Jun recognizes Dickens's "class limitation" (9). Tang Yan-ping, who links Dickens's life history to his contempt for bourgeois politics and state institutions (65), finds Dickens inadequate. In the first period of writing, which includes *Sketches by Boz*, *Pickwick Papers*, *Oliver Twist*, *Nicholas Nickleby*, *The Old Curiosity Shop* and *Barnaby Rudge*, Dickens showed a "naïve optimism . . . characteristic of the petitbourgeois humanitarians of his time" (66), as he "believed that all the evils of the capitalist world would be remedied if only men treated each other with kindliness, justice, and sympathetic understanding" (65). Works written in the second period, including *American Notes* and *Martin Chuzzlewit*, show that the social evils at that time were less a result of individual will or action, than of "the inhumanity and social injustice innate in bourgeois rule," indicating Dickens's loss of the old naïve optimism about bourgeois society (66). In the novels written in the 1850s and 1860s, including *Bleak House* and *Hard Times*, capitalism was criticized bitterly. While Dickens "saw the contradictions of capitalist society and felt the class antagonism between the bourgeoisie and the proletariat," he "was himself a petitbourgeois who could not overstep the limits of his class" (68).

Gao Jian-hong, in a study of *A Tale of Two Cities*, also notices Dickens's duality and double standard. While Dickens had strong sympathies towards the lower classes, he also appreciated the way of thought and behavior of the upper classes, and his works exhibit an idealistic plan of social amelioration with tender feelings.

Dickens's humanism is a major controversial issue in China. Critics such as Li Qing-hua note the change from Dickens's early optimism to mature satire and sentiment. However, the emphasis in Chinese criticism is less on humanism than on class. Li remarks on Dickens's attack on bourgeois society and his sympathy with the benevolent, the innocent, the poor, and the oppressed. Dickens's efforts to "relieve people from the exploitation exerted by the bourgeoisie" are noted, together with his exposure of the "cruelty of the members of the upper classes and the wrongs they did to the people at the bottom of society" (30). Dickens's humanitarianism is conveniently reduced to a polarization: "In one word, the soul of Charles Dickens's humanitarianism is to love the innocent poor, but to curse hypocritical rich" (30). To those Chinese critics, Dickens's early belief in the kind-hearted gentleman that can end the misery of the poor and deprived reflects naïve optimism, such as in the trust in Mr. Brownlow in *Oliver Twist*. Dickens's disillusionment after his trip to America is clear in *American Notes, Martin Chuzzlewit, The Chimes*, and *Dombey and Son*. Dickens has become more realistic, placing his hopes on a young man such as David Copperfield, who faces life courageously and relies on himself. Novels such as *David Copperfield* feature the struggle of the individual. Li thinks that works written at the climax of Dickens's career, such as *Bleak House, Hard Times, Little Dorrit,* and *Great Expectations* expose the greed and hypocrisy of the bourgeoisie and the corruption of the English judicial and executive institutions. While Chinese critics appreciate the focus on intense class contradiction and the struggle of the revolutionaries, Dickens's preference for mild social reform and abstract unrestrained universal love and tolerance are regarded as limited. As Li Qinghua notes, this shows Dickens's "historical limitation" as a "great writer of critical realism in the Victorian Age" (32).

So Dickens's humanism is regarded as bourgeois humanism by the Chinese critics. Yin Ai-ping talks about Dickens's bourgeois humanism and English critical realism, criticizing his contemporary British society and its hypocrisy. To Yin, Dickens's humanism is shown in two aspects. As a novelist, he reflects the suffering and poverty of the working people while showing the criminality of the ruling class. As a social practitioner, Dickens tried to provide a good remedy for society. However, his humanism is seen as more a liability than an asset, because in *A Tale of Two Cities* Yin thinks that Dickens regards human love as greater than hate, class harmony more desirable than class struggle, and that social life with peaceful coexistence is preferable to violent revolution (15). Dickens is found inadequate because as a social pragmatist trying to change society he tries to rely solely on moral power for the development of human society.

This does not mean that Dickens's humanism is not appreciated. Zhang Jing-feng acknowledges Dickens's humanism. Likewise, Li Jun recognizes Dickens's "humanitarianist ideals" and the use of "revolutionary savage acts" to highlight the themes (10). However, Zhang Jing-feng finds Dickens's attempts to reconcile the poor and the rich through sentimental descriptions of the poor characters rather unsuccessful, for these characters seem pale and weak. Nor does Zhang find Dickens's use of coincidences to get the poor characters out of trouble convincing, though he recognizes Dickens's moralistic notion of rewards for virtue and retribution of wrongdoing. The problem, to these critics, is Dickens's cherishing of a specific type of class-oriented humanism: bourgeois humanism.

To Chinese critics, Dickens's bourgeois humanism results in a preferential treatment of the middle class. Many critics spend substantial parts of their essay describing Dickens's biography and how it influences his works. This does not mean that Dickens neglected the poor. Critics such as Yin Ai-ping show how Dickens's experience of poverty in childhood gets into his novels, as it does *Little Dorrit*. His advocacy of kindness towards the "little people" originates from this experience of poverty. Dickens's work experience, such as his time in a lawyer's office and as a recorder in Parliament, enabled him to know society and have insider knowledge of the upper echelons of the capitalist class. As a writer of critical realism, Dickens was concerned with big social problems and described disturbing social phenomena. He was sympathetic towards the "little people" in the lower social strata, as seen in *Oliver Twist* and *Old Curiosity Shop*. In *Our Mutual Friend*, all the positive characters are working people, such as Jenny Wren, with her beautiful mind and spirit exemplifying Dickens's strong humanism.

Bai Shu-jie acknowledges Dickens's humanitarian thinking and advocacy of the Christian spirit: stressing humanity, forgiveness, and conciliation rather than class antagonism. However, Bai thinks that Dickens's progressiveness cannot overcome his limitations. For example, in the 1820s to 1830s, the Reform Movement was active and the British capitalist class carried out reforms in the Parliamentary system. Although Dickens satirizes delays in legal matters, the dark educational institutions, the farcical elections, the evil Poor Law, and the hypocrisy of religious frauds, he is criticized as aiming only at individual members of Parliament, individual loan sharks, and individual social structures. Bai thinks that Dickens's criticism at this time was mild and mixed with humor. In the 1830s, Dickens's kind capitalists were replaced by unkind ones, and his optimistic imaginings were displaced by disappointment, but he remained intent on using emotions to educate and change the individual capitalists and society, resulting in the reform of Martin Chuzzlewit, Scrooge, and Dombey. In the 1840s to 1850s, *David Copperfield* shows a decadent legal system and a suffocating kind of child education. The hypocrite Heep is chastised, and David is sympathetic towards lower-class working people. Humanism was the way to solve society's problems. To Bai, *Hard Times* shows the fundamental controversy in capitalist society between the proletariat and the capitalists. The exploitation by capitalists is shown, countered by kindness that leads to a humanistic, harmonious society. *A Tale of Two Cities* reveals the inhuman rule of the French aristocrats. To Bai, Dickens has correctly shown the reason for the people's revolution. This is the highest level that can be reached by a writer belonging to the capitalist class and advocating humanism and democracy but writing about violent revolution. For Bai, Dickens's shortcoming is that all humanists could not stand violent revolution, since they assumed that it would lead to sacrifices and an unstable society. Therefore, once Dickens wrote about the cruelty of the revolution and the suppression of anti-revolutionaries, he grew afraid and denied their worth, which was also his limitation.

The issue of moral improvement is also very important to Chinese critics. Bai Shu-jie thinks that *A Tale of Two Cities* shows that social disaster results from inhuman and immoral rulers. To Dickens, change was achieved through moral improvement. People should use forgiveness and kindness to eliminate hatred, return to humanity, and improve society. On the one hand, Bai affirms Dickens's starting from capitalist thinking, revealing the dark side of capitalism, and being sympathetic to the people's sufferings. On the other hand, again Bai notes Dickens's limitation. The novelist opposes all antagonistic forces and all forms of suppression: he opposes the aristocrats' oppressing the peasants, as well as the people's control over the aristocrats after the revolution. To Bai, Dickens did not understand, or was even afraid of, violent revolution, and was limited by his wish to use kindness and humanitarianism to resolve struggles, to use morality to uproot the defects of capitalist society and construct a rational society.

For Chinese critics, in Dickens's depiction of the struggle between the capitalist and the socialist, the defects of capitalism are revealed. They think that Dickens's humanism is characterized by a strong idealism regarding human relationships, so that evil members of the middle class are reprimanded. Gradually, this idealism developed into an open criticism of the capitalists. For example, discussing *Pickwick Papers*, Yin Ai-ping draws attention to Pickwick's selflessness and kindness and the moralistic world where people are naturally kind and evil is punished. This optimistic tone and light-heartedness show that the young Dickens was simple and naïve, not knowing much about English society at that time. In *A Christmas Carol*, the middle-class capitalist Scrooge, who is cruel, evil, stingy, and suspicious, learns the need to express his inherent kindness. In *Dombey and Son*, the fatal flaw of capitalist society, the obsessive pursuit of money, is attacked. The image of the capitalist has changed from that of a savior to one showing the negative nature of his class. For Yin Ai-ping, Dickens's humanism is an obstacle limiting his creativity, as Dombey is redeemed by his abandoned daughter who transforms him and makes him regret his past wrongdoings. After Dickens's trip to America, he became disillusioned. In *Hard Times*, Josiah Bounderby's anti-humanistic nature is shown, whereas the good nature and kind spirit of the proletariat are shown in Sissy Jupe and Stephen Blackpool. Although *A Tale of Two Cities* shows Dickens's anger towards the extravagant and cruel aristocrats, and his disapproval of the people's incensed riots, Yin Ai-ping thinks that Dickens's views are limited. Dickens thought that love is greater than hate, class harmony more desirable than class struggle, and social life should be marked by peaceful coexistence rather than violent revolution.

Thus, Dickens's bourgeois humanism and his support of the middle class became popular targets of attack for the socialist Chinese critics. Tang Yan-ping thinks that his bourgeois humanism and wish to improve social conditions by means of reforms in the direction of reducing aristocratic privilege was balanced by a reservation towards extending middle-class privileges to the lower classes. To Yin Ai-ping, Dickens advocates bourgeois humanism, as he hopes people can understand and respect one another. While the poor people should not lose their dignity and character, the rich should treat the ''little people'' at the bottom of the social strata with kindness (13).

Dickens's racial discrimination is also noted. Qiao Guoqiang shows the prejudice in Dickens's critical realism. Instead of presenting objective social reality, Dickens depicts in *Oliver Twist* social crimes that reflect his own anti-Semitism, which is revealed in his derogatory portrayals of Jewish characters. In the novel, Fagin represents the evil force in society corrupting children. Tracing the history of anti-Semitism in Europe, Qiao explains that anti-Semitism in the characterization of Fagin is intentional, for it reflects the racism prevalent in society, supported at that time by believers in social Darwinism.

All these criticisms of Dickens's "limitations" are less attacks on Dickens's than they are attempts to restrict his passage to China to contextual interchanges. On the one hand, these contextual interchanges further cultural globalization, enabling Dickens's works to reach the general public in modern China. On the other hand, the conditioned interpretations also make sure Dickens will fit into the Chinese context. The limited readings are less misreadings or partial interpretations than they are cultural adaptations necessitated by the reading context.

Finally, the Chinese are actively seeking connections to Dickens by studying his relationships to other writers. The novelist is less considered alone than within a network of global writers. Just as Dickens was first introduced together with other writers around the world, so the modern Dickens is also studied together with other writers. While Dickens has not written extensively on China and the Chinese, Pearl Buck has linked him to the country. Zhang Chun-lei and Zhu Cheng look at how Buck's works are self-consciously influenced by both Chinese and Western cultures, especially in the choice of social topics, humanistic themes, portrayal of characters, and the design of plot structures. Buck wrote about China using Dickens's writing techniques. For instance, Dickens examines society and social development and gives a panoramic view of mid-nineteenth-century British parliamentary politics, law, education, orphanages, debtors' prison, and different social classes. Similarly, Pearl Buck gives an epic of early twentieth-century Chinese society, such as showing Chinese people, especially peasants, suffering from conscription, imperialism, warlords and local looting in *The Good Earth*. Dickens is concerned with the poor: orphans, debtors, and washing women. Similarly, Pearl Buck depicts and celebrates the Chinese peasants making up the majority population. Like Dickens, Buck is a humanist, reflecting a kind of Christian secularism, sympathizing with the lower class and showing their good morals. Both writers oppose the evil forces and expose various immoral acts, trying to produce different ways to reform society. Dickens and Buck use similar techniques: broad and multifarious subjects, traditional ways of writing. While the two writers share common defects, such as using marginal or even light topics, and shallow depiction of characters, to Zhang Chun-lei and Zhu Cheng, Buck uses a more rational characterization, giving more objective, real, and rounded characters as a result of her long-term observation of Chinese peasants and Chinese working women, and her deep feelings towards the lower-class people in China. Buck shares Dickens's tendency to substitute idealism and romanticism with realism and objective analysis, and she, too, tends to simplify complex problems. For Zhang Chun-lei and Zhu Cheng, Buck and Dickens have a common theme: humanism, expressed in their works as a sympathy towards the suffering of the poor, the celebration of their morality and intelligence, the contemplation of the good morals and intelligence in these people, and the contemplation of violence.

Besides leading to the use of similar writing techniques, contextual interchanges also work through *guanxi* or "relations,"—through personalized networks of influence. The study of Dickens was encouraged by Pearl Buck, who had a close connection to Zhenjiang, a province in central China where her translation of "A Debt to Dickens" was published in the *Zhenjiang Teacher's College Newspaper*'s Social Science Section in 2003. Buck was an "old friend" of China, for her missionary parents took her to Zhenjiang in 1892 when she was only three months old. She was raised in China and knew the Chinese language and customs. Although Buck earned her academic degrees in America, she worked in China for a long time. Her novel *The Good Earth* (1931), about a peasant family in China, shows how the protagonists Wang Lung and O Lan try to overcome rural difficulties such as famine and flood, as well as urban challenges such as poverty and alienation. Just as Buck's novels like *East Wind: West Wind* (1930) are about cultural bridging and showcase China to the Western world, Dickens is also introduced through the study of Buck in China. Zhang Zhiqiang, the translator of Buck's "A Debt to Dickens," came from the Hunan Teacher's College Foreign Languages Department in Hunan province. He writes in the translator's note: "The study of the influence of other writers on Pearl Buck is an indispensable part of Buck studies, but so far not enough attention has been paid to it. In this article, Pearl S. Buck traces Charles Dickens's influence on her literary productions, which justifies a Chinese version" (61).

While it may be premature to predict what the future of Dickens studies in China will be, an interesting phenomenon is that most of the articles written on Dickens are found in journals of teachers' colleges and journals of universities of science and technology, rather than in journals specializing in literature or foreign literature. The study of Dickens is utilitarian and pragmatic, going beyond literary studies to indicate how the novels can be adapted to the Chinese political, social, and ideological contexts. However, rather than saying that the Chinese critics have misread Dickens, we may observe that their readings are meaningful and relevant in the Chinese context. Dickens's works are universal, and global readings of Dickens are possible even when readings by individual cultures and nations may differ. The Chinese are looking for contextual interchanges, ways of bringing the world to the country without compromising its national and social characteristics.

NOTES

I would like to thank Professor Melba Cuddy-Keane for her advice and for reading drafts of this paper. Sincere gratitude is also owed to Professor Michael Timko for encouraging me in this project.

WORKS CITED

[I have provided my own translations of Chinese titles of essays, and I have Anglicized the titles of Chinese periodicals. Translations into English from Chinese commentators on Dickens are also my own.]

Bai Shu-jie. "Realistic Affinity to the People—Analysis of Humanitarian Thinking in Dickens' Works." *Journal of Qinghai Junior Teachers' College* (Social Science Edition) 2 (2001): 35–37.

Buck, Pearl S. "*Wo qian Di Geng Si yibi zhai.*" ("A Debt to Dickens.") Trans. [into Chinese] Zhang Zhiqiang. *Zhenjiang Teacher's College Newspaper Social Science Section* 3 (2003): 59–61.

———. "A Debt to Dickens." *Saturday Review of Literature* XIII No. 23 (1936): 11, 20, 25.

Chen, Qing-lan. "*Di Geng Si bixia de ertong jiaoyu wunti.*" ("Child's Education Problems in Dickens's Novels.") *Journal of Chenzhou Teachers College* 23.6 (2002): 62–63.

Ding Jian-ping and Yin Qi-ping. "*Di Geng Si yuanlin zhong de qipa.*" ("Wonderful Flowers in Dickens's Gardens—A Tentative Approach to the Value of *The Speeches of Charles Dickens.*") *Journal of Zhejiang University (Humanities and Social Sciences)* 29.3 (1999): 60–63.

Gao Jian-hong. "*Pingmin yishi he shenshi qingjie di shangchong bianzou.*" ("An Analysis of Dickens's *A Tale of Two Cities.*") *Wuhan University of Technology (Social Science Edition)* 16.4 (2003): 462–65.

Hsü, Immanuel C. Y. *The Rise of Modern China.* Hong Kong: Oxford UP, 1975.

Jiang Ping and Wen Qing. *"Di Geng Si zuopin yishu teshi pingxi."* ("An Ironic Exposure: On Dickens's Artistic Creation.") *Journal of Lanzhou University (Social Sciences)* 27.2 (1999): 191–95.

Li Jun. "On the Artistic Features of *A Tale of Two Cities* by Dickens." *English Corner* n.d.: 8–10, 16.

Li Na. *"Cha Yi Si. Di Geng Si Xiaoshuo de tongsuxing."* ("The Popular Content of Charles Dickens's Fiction.") *Journal of Xianning Teachers College* 20.2 (2000): 28–31.

Li, Qing-hua. "The Evolution of Charles Dickens's Humanitarian Outlook." *Journal of Kaifeng Institute of Education* 21.2 (2001): 30–32.

Lu Jian-guo. "Charles Dickens and His Oliver Twist." *Journal of Yuxi Teachers College* 20.7 (2004): 39–40.

Mackerras, Colin, Pradeep Taneja, and Graham Young. *China since 1978: Reform, Modernisation and Socialism with Chinese Characteristics.* Melbourne: Longman Cheshire, 1994.

Pan Qiulin and Peng Xiaoqiang. *"Qianxi pipan xianshi zhuyi zuojia Di Geng Si."* ("An Analysis of the Realistic Writer—Charles Dickens.") *Journal of Jiangxi Science and Technology Teachers' College* 4 (2003): 83–85.

Qian Li-qun, Wen Yu-min, and Wu Fu-hui. *Zhong Guo xiandai wenxue sahshi nian.* (*Thirty Years of Modern Chinese Literature.*) Beijing: Peking UP, 1998.

Qiao Guoquang. *"Cong Wu du gu er kan Di Geng Si de fan You Tai zhuyi qingxiang."* ("The Anti-Semitism in Charles Dickens's *Oliver Twist*.") *Foreign Literature Research* 2: (2004): 63–67.

Sun Jian-fang. *"Di Geng Si xiaoshuo de qinggan secai he falu yinsu."* ("Emotional and Legal Elements in Dickens Novels.") *Journal of Anshun Teachers College* 5.4 (2003): 6–7.

Tang Yan-ping. "Dickens the Greatest Critical Realist." *Journal of Ling Ling Teachers' College* 2:3 (1995): 65–68.

Tien Han, Ouyang Yu-qian, et al., ed. *Zhong Quo Hua Ju Yun Dong Wu Shi Nian Shi Liao Ji* (*Fifty Years of the Chinese Drama Movement*) Beijing: Zhong Guo Xi Ju Chu Ban She, 1958.

"The Victorian Literary Studies Archive." <http://victorian.lang.nagoya-u.ac.jp/concordance/dickens/>

Yin Ai-ping. *"Di Geng Si de renai sixiang chutan."* ("Preliminary Studies on Humanitarianism of Charles Dickens.") *Journal of Zhenjiang College* 14. 4 (2002): 13–15.

Zhang Chun-lei and Zhu Cheng. *"Tsai Chun-zhu dui Di Geng Si xiaoshuo de jiejian."* ("Pearl S. Buck's Drawing From Dickens's Novel Writing—Also a Discussion on

Western Culture in the Study of Pearl S. Buck.'') *Journal of Jiangsu University* (Social Sciences) 5.1 (2003): 74–79.

Zhang Jing-feng. ''Charles Dickens's Portraits and Arrangements for the Poor and the Rich.'' *Journal of San Ming Teachers' College* (Social Science Edition) 1 (1994): 65–67, 83.

Zhang Peng. ''*Di Geng Si shenghuo xiezhao.*'' (''A Portrait of Dickens's Life.'') *Journal of Shengyang College of Education* 3.3 (2001): 61–63.

Zhang Yan-hong and Sit Hong. ''*Cong 'Jiannan Shishi' kan Di Geng Si xiaoshuo de renmu kehua.*'' (''Looking at the characterization in Dickens's novels through *Hard Times.*'' *Journal of Hebei Institute of Architectural Science and Technology* (Social Science Edition) 20.4 (2003): 53–54.

Zhu Jiang. ''*Di Geng Si bi xia de liangge ertong xingxiang.*'' (''Two Children Images Described by Charles Dickens: Oliver Twist and David Copperfield.'') *Journal of Huaiyin Institute of Technology* 9.3 (2000): 62–64.

Recent Dickens Studies: 2004

Terri A. Hasseler

This survey focuses on the year 2004's essays and books on Dickens's work. The texts reviewed are grouped into the following categories: postcolonial criticism; the post-Victorian; political and individual agency; social class analysis; gender studies; Dickensian linguistic style; public performances; Dickensian forays into secular and spiritual scripture; textual studies; influence studies; and, finally, bibliographic and resource materials. The boundaries among these categories are permeable, and articles and monographs can easily appear in several sections. When that is of particular significance, this review draws attention to cross-listed items. This survey considers the changing relationship of scholars to Dickens's work, commenting upon a critical backlash towards certain theoretical fields, as well as the critical ennui scholars feel regarding theoretical trends that have lost their appeal due to overuse. It also considers a palpable nostalgia among some scholars, who wish to return critical attention to the ethical position of the author.

Introduction

Faced with the task of reviewing everything written on Dickens within a given year, I turned to my predecessors for guidance. I found that they have seen several interesting patterns emerging over the course of the last few years: critical backlash, critical ennui, and critical nostalgia. In any given year, all three are alive and well, and I see this to be, to some degree, the case in 2004. The critical backlash position includes a lamentation for a

Dickens Studies Annual, Volume 37, Copyright © 2006 by AMS Press, Inc. All rights reserved.

literary critical past somehow despoiled by theoretical schools of thought such as deconstructionism, postmodernism, and postcolonialism. Attacks on these "new" theoretical positions can be scathing. David Garlock draws attention to this perspective in his 2000 review essay when he refers to one author who wishes to "lead a retro revolution" and to reject what this scholar calls "aerobic criticism" (333). A handful of years later, I can say that Garlock was prescient to note that such a backlash would be slow in the making. In Dickens studies, the predicted anti-theory backlash has been not so much a backlash as a more qualified alliance that allows for both critique and theory. There were in 2004 none of the extreme anti-theory essays that are prone to make their way into publication, but there were the periodic anti-theory comments. What tended to be more interesting were those texts that deconstructed theoretical positions and postulated new ways of seeing those positions—several essays in a section I have called post-Victorianism and in a section on agency offer this reinterpretation of critical theory. Molly Anne Rothenberg and Roger D. Sell, in particular, offer differing ways to think about this issue.

Although there was no backlash this year, there was more than a little bit of critical ennui. Over the years Michel Foucault has been trotted out for all sorts of reasons in all sorts of occasions and that has not changed this year. Barry V. Qualls in his 1993 review notes the "thinness and derivativeness" of writings on Foucault and D. A. Miller, with Goldie Morgentaler in her 2003 review remarking upon the continued dominance of Foucault. I believe Robert R. Garnett captured the feeling of critical ennui the best when he commented upon the danger of applying the same critical patterns over and over again: "At some point, once-fresh critical models become exhausted, and rather than stimulating thinking, become instead a substitute for thinking" (336). The frustration that I felt when faced with reading another essay using Foucault as its critical starting point is hard to express. I saved those essays for waiting rooms at the doctor's or the dentist's when I was trapped and the essay was the better option. And this comes from someone who really likes Foucault. However, I can happily state that there are a number of cases where Foucault was carefully reapplied in interesting ways. In this case, I would draw attention to Caroline Reitz's arguments on the detective and empire.

Finally, a reminiscent look "backwards" towards more ethical approaches to literature emerges in the critical nostalgia category. This nostalgia is marked by a less depreciatory response than the backlash approach, and it is prone to be more of a commentary on the shifting nature of literary critical traditions. Michael Lund in his 1999 review identifies this sentiment when he comments upon the shift in focus from the writer providing illumination for the reader through his or her text, to an understanding of the text as an artifact that readers illuminate. In my readings in 2004, there is a sense of a return to this notion of the artist as illuminator. Several essays near the end of the section on postmodernism and agency consider the return of ethics in response to narratives, and they use Dickens as their exemplum. However, there are solid examples of the text and artist as artifact, and those can be found throughout this review. Many of these readings are very useful because they allow for a critical distance from the text and its author. Some studies in this review provide a careful balance of the two approaches, such as that adopted by Vincent Newey in his book on Dickensian secular scriptures.

In this survey, I focus on critical interpretive books and essays written in 2004; this includes four monographs and over 65 articles. Also, I look briefly at several texts that serve as resource guides for the student, the teacher, and the scholar. I provide, in most cases, a fairly thorough review of each text, enabling the reader to make choices about the usefulness of the article to his or her own research; however, the venue of a review does not allow for elaboration on some of the more interesting and nuanced points that each author considers, so I often found myself cutting and cutting and cutting again. In the process, I hope that I continue to capture the value of much of the work on Dickens this year. I apologize for neglecting some texts, and I also send my apologies in advance for any misinterpretations of argument. The vast array of critical work which drew from such disparate fields of analysis (from disability studies to corpus analysis) at times exceeded my areas of comfort; however, I engaged in a very careful reading and became student to these texts. I learned a great deal in the process. I have offered mostly descriptive reviews without judging too extensively the texts being considered. I believe the descriptions are likely to reveal the quality of the argument.

In *Investigating Dickens' Style,* Masahiro Hori states that there are approximately 4.6 million words in the Dickens corpus—a staggering number, no doubt. However, after spending an entire year on this 2004 review, I certainly feel *as if* I have read, if not written, 4.6 million words myself. I would note that, as a number of previous reviewers have stated, this is a big task. However, surprisingly, it was fun, and this, I believe, is due to the very useful and well-written materials available on Dickens this year. Of course, some are uninspired and others are just "odd," but much is worth the effort of locating and reading. I have divided the review into several sections, covering the fields of postcolonial criticism; the post-Victorian; political and individual agency; social class analysis; gender studies; Dickensian linguistic style; public performances; Dickensian forays into secular and spiritual scripture; textual studies; influence studies; and finally, bibliographic and resource materials. Of course, the boundaries among these categories are permeable, and articles can easily appear in several sections. When that is of particular note, I draw attention to these cross-listed sources.

Postcolonial Criticism

In her 1997 review of critical studies on Dickens, Elisabeth G. Gitter notes that, " 'Empire' appears, unaccountably, to have declined as a topic of critical interest'' (199). I was surprised to note the early demise of postcolonial criticism on Dickens, considering that Patrick Brantlinger's text, *Rule of Darkness*, had only been released in paperback in 1990. Brantlinger's text and others like it paved the way for a more thorough critique of colonial practices in Victorian literature. However, 2004 does not follow this pattern; rather, it yields a solid collection of essays with a postcolonial bent, including Grace Moore's full-length study, *Dickens and Empire*. It is also clear that postcolonial criticism has worked its way into other critical foci; for instance, essays in the post-Victorian section are decidedly postcolonial in focus, with most of the articles attending to Peter Carey's rewriting of *Great Expectations* in *Jack Maggs*. Similarly, Eric G. Lorentzen's essay on contamination in *Bleak House*, though placed in the section on agency, considers the impact of telescopic philanthropy, revolution, and colonialism.

Alicia Carroll, in her 2002 review essay, observed that some critics are still "rankle[d]" by those critiques that call Dickens's political position into question, or, in other words, the critical backlash approach (365). Over the years, there has been a shift in the application of postcolonial criticism to Dickens's texts. And perhaps this is a result of the ways that emerging fields of inquiry are tested and then brought into the mainstream of discussion. The beginning is marked by strong espousal of the critical approach, a hard-hitting critique of Victorian systems provided through postcolonial theoretical lenses, followed by an equally intense rejection of that critical perspective, the angered response that contemporary ethical and moral standards are unfairly used "against" Dickens. This is then followed by a search for the middle ground; however, how that middle ground defines itself is of particular importance. Is it apologetic? Does it search for ways to understand the complexity of Dickens's response to colonialism and his representation of it? Does it mediate contemporary critical standards in light of those operating in Dickens's time? The age-old position that we cannot apply contemporary ethical/ critical standards to someone like Dickens, for instance, strikes me as a particularly unhelpful stance since it limits critical inquiry. Fortunately, we do not encounter such thinking in any of the articles for 2004. What we do see is a more nuanced reading that not only carefully analyzes Dickens in light of his times, but also looks at his shifting and changing opinions in response to imperialism.

In a two-part article appearing in *Dickens Quarterly*, Jeremy Tambling takes an approach more consistent with a critical postcolonial perspective, demonstrating the connections among imperial history, culture, and the context of Dickens's work. Although arguing that contradictions inform Dickens's approach to China, Tambling concludes that China is representative of an Other, which Dickens understood through its perceived stagnation. Through analysis of Dickens's articles "The Chinese Junk" and "The Great Exhibition and the Little One," Tambling reads Dickens's need "to make China an oppositional model of lack of change because it wishes to set Britain in opposition to the European revolutions of 1848. Britain stands between Chinese stasis and European haste" (33). The article responds to the pointed question of why it was so deeply significant for Dickens that China does not underwrite a doctrine of British advancement. Though Tambling argues that this is never adequately addressed by Dickens, he proceeds to look at the subtle references to the China trade within Dickens's texts, hinting at what Arthur Clennam was possibly doing during his time in China. This may suggest that his guilt extends beyond the domestic and may be a colonial form of guilt for participation in the opium trade. Tambling also argues that China is poised as a feminized figure against British masculinity, which is an argument that has been made elsewhere, but he adds the discussion of asexuality of British men in China, which seems a more interesting assertion in light of the policies that did not allow European women in the settlements: After all, Clennam comes home alone.

Sir John Bowring, Hong Kong Governor from 1854 to 1859, is a focal point for Tambling's argument. Bowring's contradictory response towards policies in Hong Kong, Tambling argues, mirrors Dickens's similar response: "radical liberalism with coercion, of Utilitarianism with religion, and membership of the Peace society with imperialism towards China points up the split within British nineteenth century ideology of one attitude at home, another abroad" (41). Bowring's part in the second Opium War sets the stage for legalized opium and further expansion of British control in China. Bowring wrote for *All the Year Round* in his retirement. With Charles Dickens, Jr. in the mix, Tambling suggests that the hostile tone towards China continued, but the prevalence of articles on China in *All the Year Round*, nevertheless, indicates Dickens's enduring fascination with China. When China arrives in London in *The Mystery of Edwin Drood*, Dickens presents a multicultural London of dangerous forces that have brought the city "under the power of the Orient" (108). Tambling's conclusion is interesting, noting that the splitting of Jasper's character mimics the "splitting of the subject in Dickens. His tendencies are also Bowring-like . . . manifest[ing] similar contradictions, including the double standard whereby opium is a fact of life in China but a threat in London" (110).

Like Tambling, Joachim Stanley, in "Opium and *Edwin Drood*," explores the impact of opium on Dickens's unfinished text. Though he points out the

"Oriental" aspects of the texts, Stanley provides a compelling analysis of the ways in which the Orient functions less centrally than one might think. Moreover, he argues that it is not the addictive features of the drug that Dickens's was concerned with, but its hallucinogenic properties. Dickens, in a letter to John Forster, indicated that he felt the account of a "schism of self" caused by the drug was something original he would be contributing, and, in this way, Stanley argues that Dickens prefigures Sigmund Freud (13). Stanley notes that opiate consumption was extremely high at the time of Dickens's writing of *Edwin Drood*: concern about recreational use in the working class community, its connection with crime as a doping agent, and its use by children brought the problem to the attention of the medical establishment and the general public. Stanley's focus on the drug's Oriental influence and its habit-forming properties are interestingly deconstructed. He suggests that habituation to the drug was of concern to Dickens, since certainly the characters that use the drug are presented as weak and feel guilt for their use, but it was not his primary focus. Similarly, Stanley concedes that it is clear that the Orient plays a role in the text. Dickens' Eastern characters, such as Neville Landless, are more susceptible to the violent aspects of the drug, and the drug symbolizes an Eastern invasion of sorts; however, the complexity of addiction and the hallucinogenic effect of the drug suggest that opium operates on several levels. Opium helps to split Jasper's psyche, bringing to consciousness what was unknown of his desires, and then it provides him with the ability to fulfill those desires. Instead of being solely consumed by the East, Jasper engages in a "civil war, both between [the] macrocosm (Cloisterham) and microcosm (Jasper)" (22). Arguing that Dickens prefigures Freud on this topic, Stanley concludes, however, that Dickens's approach to the hidden psyche made visible differs ultimately from Freud since the text suggests that it makes little sense to have one's secret desires made evident.

Using Edward Said's observation that exile is "'fundamentally a discontinuous state of being,'" Kristy Reid, in "Exile, Empire and the Convict Diaspora," explores this discontinuous state through an examination of transportation and the returned convict (qtd. in Reid 66). Reid argues that the structure of Empire needed "the maintenance of rigid divisions and fixed hierarchies between imperial and imperialised populations. Convicts, straddling the fault-lines between metropolis and colony, undermined such spatial and cultural boundaries" (66). In the narrative forms they used to express themselves, transported criminals continued to tell their stories throughout the Victorian Era. This article is helpful because it identifies the voice of transported criminals in Victorian popular culture and in the creation of the image of Empire. As Reid notes, the order that Empire sought to establish was upset by the haunting of the imperial convict who "threatened to unsettle and subvert hierarchies of metropolitan power and systems of imperial accumulation'' (57). Magwitch, Reid argues, functions as an "alien other" and, at the same time, as "Everyman" (58). Debates current to the time demonized the transported criminal as racially and criminally other. Reid argues that despite Dickens's shrill response to the Indian Rebellion and the Morant Bay Rebellion, *Great Expectations* can be read in a way that confuses the "fixed hierarchies of difference" (59). Though the Frankenstein connection is often drawn in Magwitch's creation of Pip, Reid argues that Magwitch was created by a Frankenstein-like system, which suggests that Magwitch-as-monster was made and not born. What is most interesting about Reid's argument is her discussion of the sustained and intimate connections transported criminals maintained with family in England—through letters that continued to be sent decades after transportation, through cultural memories, through elaborate tattoos of names, through folklore, and particularly through ballads sung on the streets. This, of course, subverts the purpose of transportation, which was horrifying, because it made the convict, as Reid argues, unknowable. Reid also looks at the political work of two returned convicts, George Loveless and William Ashton, who strikingly enough, go so far as to use "the symbol of the transported convict to link the oppression of working people within the British Isles with the experiences of indigenous peoples under colonial rule'' (66).

Caroline Reitz's monograph *Detecting the Nation* is the inaugural text in a series edited by Donald E. Hall. The Victorian Critical Interventions series agenda is to provide "diverse, theory-based contributions to the broadly defined field of Victorian cultural studies . . . [focusing] on brief, accessibly written manuscripts that make brash and revisionary claims'' (ix). Hall writes that the "series volumes work to redefine what we know and do as 'Victorian studies' in the twenty-first century'' (ix). Such a series is very welcome: the book is reasonable in length, accessibly written, and theoretically rich. The text has pedagogical strengths as well, since the theory is presented in a challenging yet intelligible way. It could be used effectively in an undergraduate advanced course in detective fiction or Victorian studies. The books itself explores a range of contributors to the development of "detective fiction,'' starting with Godwin and Mill, moving through Thuggee narratives and Dickens and Collins, and ending with Doyle and Kipling. Such a reading list would indicate, even if one did not know from the title, that Reitz's agenda is to illustrate how depictions of the detective are mediated by notions of Empire.

In the introductory chapter, "Imperial Detection,'' Reitz maps out the major agenda for the text, focusing on two issues of Victorian national identity that remain unsatisfactorily explained: "(1) a shift over the course of the century from suspicion of to identification with the detective, and (2) a shift

from insular lack of interest in to identification with the imperial project''
(xiii). Her contention is that traditional scholarship on the detective only
considers the gradual incorporation of the detective into Englishness without
investigating fully enough why the detective becomes more English as what
he patrols becomes more alien and foreign. She speaks, to borrow from Mary
Louise Pratt, of the Victorian ''contact zone,'' in which ''mutual dependency
of domestic and imperial narratives'' inhere (Reitz xvii).

These arguments that move beyond merely reading the Empire as a separate
location or simplistic applications of postcolonial criticism to Victorian literature are valuable because they focus on the more ambiguous and ambivalent
relationship Victorian culture had with its imperial peripheries. I find her
reading of the reciprocal relationship between Empire and Victorian society
to be a strength of this text and an important direction in postcolonial criticism
in Victorian studies. By focusing on the ubiquitous presence of Empire in
detection, Reitz provides an important problematization of recent detective
fiction criticism, which has always looked to imperial concerns, but has done
so more often as backdrop, catalyst for events, or justification for authority.
In this study, Reitz turns to Empire as a concept that helped to define the
''Englishness'' of the detective.

To do this, Reitz, like others working in postcolonial criticism, rethinks
the purpose of Foucault's Panopticon, building on the work of D. A. Miller
and others. Traditional criticism, she argues, provides ''a too-tidy explanation
of the rise of the detective figure in which both imperial and police power
are almost effortlessly panoptical, and the detective the embodiment of this
power'' (xxii). Challenging the us-them model of panopticism, which locates
the detective as an invisible arm of surveillance, Reitz argues convincingly
that this model ''replays the Victorian hope that the detective will do the
work of England and not the work of Empire, so that the two—England and
her Empire—can remain separate and distinct. But even as these detective
narratives at times gratify our taxonomic fantasy, they never fail to reveal
the murky relation between island nation and sprawling empire that such a
fantasy presupposes'' (xxv).

In her chapter ''Making an English Virtue of Necessity,'' Reitz argues that
Dickens and Collins were central players in introducing imperialism into the
genre of detective fiction and in merging the role of the police with the
English nation. The messiness of Empire, Reitz argues, makes the detective
necessary. She writes, ''reconciling the detective with English virtues[,] Dickens finds the English public within the detective, where Collins works to
place the detective within the English public . . . accepting the detective means
understanding imperialism to be a central part of English identity'' (46).
Through a discussion of the rise of the New Police, Inspector Field, and
Dickens's detectives, she argues that Dickens rejects the notion of the police

as ''invisible'' and focuses on their ''visibility.'' In order to manage the
imperial expansion, the police are called upon to be visible. Dickens's insistence on the Englishness of the New Police is necessary because it combats
the growing foreignness within England. Detectives, such as Charles Field,
are posed as benevolent imperial/explorers. In contrast with Dickens, who
stamps the detective with the English seal of approval, Collins, Reitz argues,
brings the isolated English family in contact with the larger world. The detective must be knowledgeable about the Empire as well as being receptive to
local knowledge: ''As the detective needs the common man to understand a
new mystery, Collins argues, the common man needs the detective to understand the mysterious new world in which he already lives'' (60–61). Both
Collins and Dickens merge the detective with the imperial explorer, thus
concluding that the definition of Englishness comes from outside of England.

The only extended study of imperialism in 2004 is Grace Moore's *Dickens
and Empire*. Her text, appearing in the Nineteenth Century Series, edited by
Vincent Newey and Joanne Shattock, includes sections on Dickens's thoughts
on emigration, national identity, abolitionism and slavery, the Crimean War,
the Indian Rebellion of 1857, the Morant Bay Rebellion of 1865, and the
Irish Question. In her introduction, Moore considers the social and personal
forces at work on Dickens's thoughts on Empire—namely, his concern about
the working poor and emigration's failure to ameliorate that situation, the
connections between urban poor and the colonized, and his growing unhappiness with ''imperial and domestic mismanagement'' found in both the Crimean War and the Indian Mutiny. She also devotes consistent attention to
national symbols, such as the Crystal Palace's impact on Dickens's thinking.
What is a running concern in Moore's text is the need to contextualize Dickens's vitriolic racist response to the Mutiny in light of a shifting Dickensian
approach to race, imperialism, and social class. She states that ''this book
does not seek to exonerate Dickens from charges of racism, but rather to
examine his changing imaginative engagement with the empire and his complex attitude toward the racial other at key stages of personal, national and
global significance'' (5).

Because Moore offers an extended study, I cannot do justice to the full
extent of her argument; however, I will point to a number of key issues and
examine her consideration of Dickens's response to the Indian Mutiny as a
pivotal moment in his development. Her text is clearly written and relies on
both Dickensian narratives and his journalistic pieces to flesh out his position.
Her attention to the journalistic pieces is very helpful, and they do support
her comments about Dickens's often wide-ranging swings of thought and
tone. This is a particular strength of the text. Most arguments tend to pigeon-
hole Dickens; however, Moore is much more interested in the difficulty of
pinning Dickens down. She notes that he tends to vacillate among positions,

but those positions do remain within the particular trajectory of racial superiority. In her thoughts on emigration, Moore comments that Dickens lost interest in the narrative device of emigration as a redemptive process. His concern about the Condition of England and his rejection of simple techniques for narrative closure made him "reluctant to resort to what he regarded as an evasive form of closure, which obscured the need for urgent social reform" (11). Tip Dorrit's failed emigration becomes a comedic reflection on this point, and in the process also undermines emigration as a reasonable solution to the problems at home. In the case of Magwitch, she sees Dickens's "middle-class radical[ism] . . . encapsulated," his sympathy with Magwitch's condition counterbalanced with his concern for law and order (18).

In her discussion of slavery and abolitionism, she further delineates Dickens's support for abolition (though this would shift and become lukewarm, at times) and, in contrast, his belief in the inferiority of the Other: "Dickens's stance on racial matters may have oscillated between contempt and pity by 1853, but by no means did he hold the extreme and reactionary views that he manifested for a time during the Indian Mutiny" (70). Noting that abolitionism became an important place to voice concerns for disenfranchised groups, such as women, she also comments that it distracted those people from addressing untenable conditions in England and it validated a feeling of superiority over Americans. What also resulted is that abolition became the acceptable cause to work on; if one turned one's energies closer to home, that person was characterized as " 'Not English' " (49). Dickens's response to slavery moved between "a revulsion that made him so uncomfortable on entering a slave state that he wished for an immediate end to the system, and a more cautious belief that the dismantling process should be a gradual one" (54). We can see the complexity of these stances in practice in characters such as Cicero in *Martin Chuzzlewit*, the Native in *Dombey and Son*, and the ambiguous Neville Landless in *The Mystery of Edwin Drood*. Moore presents Sam Weller as the Native who takes on subjectivity, or in Gayatri Spivak's terminology, as the speaking subaltern, who is, therefore, no longer a subaltern.

Moore notes that Dickens was not Thomas Carlyle in his racism, but then Carlyle did practice a particularly loathsome brand of racism; however, Dickens did shift decidedly towards Carlyle, especially with his polemical "The Noble Savage." Part of this may be personal, Moore notes, since Dickens was irritated by abolitionist critiques of his telescopic philanthropy presentation in *Bleak House* (despite the fact that the text was well received in America. See Hollis Robbins's article reviewed in the section on Textual Studies). "The tone of the piece," as Moore notes, was "completely at odds with anything he had written in the past, and indeed, anything he was writing at the time" (66). Moore argues that the first part of the essay, which is more vitriolic in nature, was done to play along with the "allegations" from abolitionists, such as Lord Thomas Denman, that his writing was for slaveholders: "After the introductory paragraphs, the tone becomes much more moderate and is more akin to Dickens's own voice" (67). However, Moore notes that this text, as well as Dickens's interests in evolution, which she explores in this essay, must be seen as a part of a shift in Dickens, a "transitional work," that denotes a change in thinking between 1848 and 1853 (69).

The debacle of the Crimean War and the Condition of England set the stage for Dickens's public explosion over the Indian Rebellion of 1857, to which Moore devotes three chapters of her book. Though Brantlinger argues that the writing of "The Perils of Certain English Prisoners" is a "logical consequence of an ingrained racism" illustrated in "The Noble Savage," Moore argues that Dickens's response is not so easy to define (95). For instance, *Household Words* produced numerous hard-hitting journalistic pieces that exposed the corruption of the East India Company, its use of torture, and its misrule. Dickens, however, was "totally unprepared for the insurrection when it occurred" (108). For Dickens, it was a "betrayal" (108). The English stereotypical understanding of India as an indolent, static country caught in the past was shattered with the Indian Mutiny. Though Moore provides a discussion of the historical context of events at Cawnpore and several readings of pertinent texts, it is her discussion of Dickens's psychological projections that make for an interesting read. Dickens's reaction to the press's depictions of slaughtered English women at Cawnpore, Moore states, symbolize his extreme discomfort with a number of issues—issues that had been building in his mind. Moore suggests that Dickens could "discharge his fury [against the sepoys], without any fear of being labelled either a reactionary or a subversive" (126). To demand retribution and to lash out with such rage at the sepoys gave vent to his contained anger and rage at the government's "domestic maladministration and nepotism" (126). With William Howard Russell's reports back on British extreme "retaliation," Dickens began to modify his calls for revenge.

Moore discusses the impact such thinking had on the writing of *A Tale of Two Cities*. She concludes that, "the Indian revolt was significant in reformulating and complicating his racial views, but not in the totalizing manner that previous studies have suggested, and certainly not for any sustained period of time" (132). Indeed, *All the Year Round* dropped its "anti-India stance" fairly swiftly and moved back to "normal" (142). Nevertheless, Dickens participated in "the re-assembly of the British sense of identity, which is a key reason behind the endless need to reinvent the revolt as a tale of military triumph" (149). Though Dickens had no need to do this and does appear, to Moore, to be more inclined to set "the record straight," these revisions make clear his "ongoing attempts to make sense of the British national identity and imperial identity'' (154). Her interpretation of *A Tale of Two Cities*, as well as her exploration of William Howard Russell's writings are very helpful for contextualizing and complicating Dickens's response. The impact of this moment on Dickens, as Moore sees it, is that he, in the 1860s, ''separate[d] class and race issues'' despite their conflation elsewhere, and he dealt with domestic and imperial cases individually, not ''allowing his anger to accumulate and finally erupt,'' thereby becoming more moderate in his stance (177).

Moore's last chapters look at the Irish Question and the Morant Bay Rebellion of 1865, in which Dickens's response is seen as surprisingly moderate, though her reading conflicts with most critics who see this as a continuation of Dickens's racist stance. By 1865, she argues, Dickens was far removed from someone like Carlyle. In *The Mystery of Edwin Drood*, Moore concludes that one can see that Dickens had ''unravelled his discussions of class and race,'' and ''he evidently wished to make clear the dangers inherent in the process of subconsciously conflating the two'' (184).

The Post-Victorian

Great Expectations was of particular interest this year since several articles looked to Peter Carey's *Jack Maggs* 1997 revision of Abel Magwitch's story for inspiration on reframing Dickens. In addition, a very smart article by Susan Johnston looks at Alfonso Cuarón's 1998 film, *Great Expectations*. Regardless of what one thinks of the film, I would recommend reading Johnston's article for her intelligent assessment of questions of authenticity.

Through an analysis of several revisions of Dickens's texts, Georges Letissier proposes a theoretical interpretation of the ''Post-Victorian'' novel and its presence in contemporary culture. This article appears in a collection, *Refracting the Canon in Contemporary British Literature and Film*, which uses the metaphor of light refraction to consider the relationship between postmodernist critical perspectives and the canon of British literature. Considering different critical positions on post-Victorianism, Letissier places at odds critics who ''see in post-Victorianism a monolithic, static 19th century that would be complacently revisited by late postmodernist writers, ready to pander to the dictates of polite correctness, and to the taste of a large readership'' versus those who ''claim that the representation of the past can aim at 'disturb[ing] what was previously considered immobile' '' (112). This first group, relying upon the work of Frederic Jameson, ''tend[s] to view post-Victorianism as a retrogressive movement, fostered by late capitalism and propounding a collective misrepresentation of the past'' (112). The second group, based more on Foucault, ''open[s] up the Victorian past by making it the locus of an intertextual, dialogic, historicised self-understanding, going far beyond mere nostalgia, voyeurism or epistemological popularisation'' (112). Using the concept of ''refraction'' of light, Letissier states that when applied to the post-Victorian text, the Victorian body of works have been filtered through contemporary lenses, which provide a ''mediated'' production of the originary text, furthering the complexity of reading as an isolated and, at the same time, collective process (112). The ''polyphony'' of a Bakhtinian narrative analysis is useful in Letissier's argument since it helps in his process of debunking ''the notion of a fixed, normative canon'' (127).

In the case of Dickens, Letissier asks whether the process of refracting a canonized text ''decanonizes'' said text, or does the contemporary relevance of the text, in the revision, bring the entire concept of canon under scrutiny? Letissier provides several texts for discussion: Charles Palliser's *The Quincunx* as an example of out-Dickensing Dickens (121), and Peter Ackroyd's *The Great Fire of London* in connection with *Little Dorrit*, as well as his *English Music* in connection with *The Mystery of Edwin Drood* and *Great Expectations*. However, since *Jack Maggs* has held such critical interest this year in intertextual analysis, I will turn to his discussion of Peter Carey's text as a representative post-Victorian revision of *Great Expectations*. Putting *Jack Maggs* in the tradition of other postcolonial texts which have written back to the center—such as Jean Rhys's *Wide Sargasso Sea*—Letissier argues that Carey's text provides a ''specular reflection'' of the original text since it essentially provides a reverse image of everything in Pip's narrative (124). This reversal is concretely illustrated in the letter that Maggs himself writes, which is written backwards and must be read with a mirror. Magwitch's gaps in narrative are given presence in *Jack Maggs* through Maggs's personal narration. Tobias Oates, ''Dickens' intradiegetic *alter ego*,'' illustrates the rampant greed of Victorian England, the writer who would pilfer the mind of the convict and thus the Empire in order to make his name and to fill his purse (125). In this way, Letissier argues that Jack Maggs is the avenger in this text.

Collette Selles's argument in ''Heritage in Peter Carey's *Jack Maggs*'' differs from Letissier's in that she looks at the position of the Victorian gentleman and Empire in order to refocus a discussion of canon. Carey rewrites the position of the English gentleman, and in the process, revises the position of the colonial center against its ''periphery'' in New South Wales. Pip's ''Great Expectations'' becomes the returned convict Jack Magg's ''High Hopes'' or, more ironically in Percy Buckle's case, ''Great Good Fortune'' (qtd. in Selles 64, 68). Referring to Samuel Smiles's discussion of the Victorian gentleman, Selles argues that the gentleman's moral position is completely annihilated by Carey. Henry Phipps, Maggs's Pip, is unredeemable and posed as a ''degenerate,'' carrying with that, however, homophobic implications (65). This is unlike Dickens's Pip, who, she suggests, undergoes some redemption. In contrast, Carey and Dickens, Selles points out, "invest" their convicts with liberality and gratefulness "for the boys who have saved them, endowing them with a moral worth which is found lacking in so-called gentlemen" (65). Selles traces the inspirations for the characters in the text—for example, Percy Buckle's relation to H. T. Buckle, whose argument about evolutionary progress is contradicted in Percy Buckle, who appears to be the backward slide of an evolutionary process based on "material obsession" (68). Selles argues that "both Phipps and Buckle are emblems of a degeneracy which dismantles, explodes, the notion of the gentleman and intimates that, instead of evolving towards improvement, English society is being undermined and threatened by decay, a subversive view of nineteenth-century England which glorified its march towards progress" (67).

Carey's deconstruction of the gentleman is also a part of his dismantling of the English social system, which to my mind puts him more in line with Dickens than Selles suggests. Of course, Carey's creation of Tobias Oates as a parody of Dickens is a frequently referenced point for Dickens studies. Oates's mesmerism creates the Phantom which haunts Maggs and also creates the tale of *The Death of Jack Maggs*, which, ironically, becomes an Australian canonical text. Also, Selles argues that Maggs's personal narrative, which interrupts the text repeatedly, is a rewriting of Pip's personal narrative—though this time written backwards and rendered with invisible ink. Ultimately, Selles believes that Carey's text attacks Britain itself, symbolized in the character Ma Britten, who illustrates the deconstruction of basic English national myths—"the ideal of the gentleman, of filial and motherly love, of an English home, the idealized view of a country" (74). Maggs escapes the hegemony of England to return to Australia and forges a new life, constructing a new national myth in Australia. In this way, Selles's argument uses the story of Maggs to reconsider both postcolonial critical impulses in post-Victorian texts and thus serves to reframe, or in Letissier's terminology, refract, the initial text. The new canon is Australian this time, *The Death of Jack Maggs*, Oates's fictional text within Carey's fictional revision.

In "A Ghost Story in Two Parts," Alice Brittan provides a deeply layered intertextual analysis of the relationship among texts such as *Great Expectations*, *Jack Maggs*, and Shakespeare's *Hamlet* and *Macbeth*, with Shakespeare providing the basis for the return of "the outraged dead . . . to reveal the fraudulence of a social imposter" (40). Socially dead, the transported criminals in both Carey's and Dickens's stories do not accept their death; rather, they return like ghosts coming to name, as in Shakespeare's texts, the wrong done to them. However, Brittan notes that this revenge is a complicated one because both do not come to seek revenge but to witness the results of their generous actions to the orphaned boys. Though for Pip, Magwitch functions as a ghostly figure, it is Henry Phipp who becomes the Phantom for Maggs.

For Dickens, Brittan notes that critics have always been interested in his disinherited heroes and how that relates to the formation of the self. Pip himself is haunted throughout the text by the "father," much as Hamlet's father's ghost haunts his text, and, of course, Hamlet directly figures in the text in Wopsle's performance. Brittan suggests that Magwitch's return illustrates that material possessions are ghostly, as are the illusions of wealth. Like the questions asked and unsatisfactorily answered by the ghost in *Hamlet*, questions are prompted by Magwitch's presence—namely, where do Pip's wealth and possessions come from? Brittan states that "Magwitch's return provoked a crisis of origins, revising the paternity of all of Pip's property, including Estella, and unsettling the social hierarchies in which Pip had such faith. If Magwitch shows his 'son' that portable objects, like orphans, are haunted by invisible histories, Pip attempts an exorcism through his colonial career" (48). Carey's text, too, deals with the discomfort of property and its lack—perhaps most forcefully, she argues—in the character of Tobias Oates, who "both incarnates the ambivalence of Dickens's need to censure as well as profit by capitalism" (49). Maggs, who has had his memories stolen by Oates through animal magnetism, stresses that this property has much more value than anything in the house. Oates also replaces the memories he has stolen with the image of the Phantom, which he creates to explain Maggs's pain—harkening back to Dickens's own experimentations with treating people through mesmerism. However, in this text, Phipps, ambivalent, but nevertheless armed with a gun, returns to kill, rather than help the ghostly father. He does so in the form of the Phantom created by Oates in Maggs's mind. However, this, too, functions as an exorcism, for this time Maggs is freed of the ghostly son. Like Selles, Brittan concludes that this is ultimately a comment upon England, and it is England that is haunted by the phantoms of pain, not colonial Australia.

In her article, "Historical Picturesque," Susan Johnston, through reference to a range of adeptly chosen cultural theorists, argues a case for questioning claims of authenticity in two film adaptations, Ang Lee's *Sense and Sensibility* and Alfonso Cuarón's *Great Expectations*. Elevating *Great Expectations* over *Sense and Sensibility*, Johnston argues that "the film's willingness to grapple with the paradoxes of adaptation that the historical distance may be traversed, if not overcome" makes for a very interesting theoretical idea, even if one does not like the film (180). Through Jean Baudrillard's world of simulations, Lyotard's comments on a postmodernist nostalgia, and Frederic Jameson's observations on *anomie* of the centered subject, Johnston comes to her thesis: "While both films clearly signal their status as adaptations, Lee's fairly straight version and Cuarón's 'free' adaptation provide instructively distinct responses to the problem of authentic relations with the source text" (168). Adaptation theory provides language for this discussion with its focus on "issues of fidelity" (168). Cuarón takes on the question of authenticity through an engagement with simulacrum and commodification. Through a discussion of Estella's nude scene in the film paired against her later posing of herself within the same position, Johnston argues that in this moment, "Finn's desire is finally realized, Estella herself becomes even less real than those earlier versions he has painted. In this way, the depthlessness of the paintings themselves reflects Estella's own rendering as image" (170).

Through a presentation of current thoughts on the post-Victorian, Johnston discusses the role of nostalgia within the context of these films—seen particularly in Lyotard's reification of "the already-reified past" (172). Fixation on fidelity to the text/context, critics have argued, becomes another claim on authenticity. Ang Lee's film of *Sense and Sensibility*, Johnston argues, embraces the historical picturesque, which relies on the "cultivated eye" or "connoisseurship" approach and "depends not on its objects but on the traditions they recall"; in other words, it is another "mode of inauthenticity" (173). The text becomes an elite object for the cultivated, who are in the know and can discern in the accuracy of the texts multiple layers of attempts at authenticity. Johnston maintains that the text's faithfulness can only be understood now in terms of a love story because the passage of time and changes in gender, class, and economy cannot be rendered: "Surface fidelity becomes, in this film, an end in itself; the consequence is a rupture of matter and form" (176). In contrast, Cuarón's "licentious adaptation" suggests that the new text is "no longer powerfully linked" to the "original form" (178). She questions what Pip's struggle with his gentleman status can mean to a time such as ours when the gentleman is a "functionally empty" category (178). She argues that it is the emphasis on commodification and essentialism that makes the text interesting. Acting as tourists to this past, she states that we cannot know this "foreign country" with its "foreign tongue," and it is only in the films' playful struggle with these questions of authenticity that we can at least partially cross the historical distance.

Political and Individual Agency and Ethics

The essays in this section reconsider the understanding of political and individual agency through a discussion of tactical and rebellious forms of speech and narrative. This might be seen as an agency exerted by a disabled character or through Stephen Blackpool's muddle, in Wat Tyler's rebellion or in radical ideology. The section ends with observations on narratives and ethics.

Julia Miele Rodas's essay "Tiny Tim, Blind Bertha, and the Resistance of Miss Mowcher" discusses Dickens's disabled characters in relation to current trends in disability studies. Offering the concept of the "satellite," Rodas argues that his views on disability shifted as he considered his own sense of himself in relation to a disabled character's agency. The "satellite," defined by Rodas, is "a nondisabled person who appears to construct his or her personal identity around a central nexus of disability, which is perceived as requiring mediation. The category of satellite may include any one of the array of individuals who work or live in orbit around the disabled/celebrated body . . . " (93). Rodas's thesis is that disability becomes a more complex concept for Dickens as he understands that he cannot summarize it with simplistic stereotypes.

Victorians shifted in their understanding of disability as the "freak" was understood less and less as a spectacle and understood more and more in terms of pathology (59). Dickens's own understanding shifted, too. Rodas starts her analysis with the case of Laura Bridgman, the blind-deaf girl at Boston's Perkins Institution who is mentioned in *American Notes.* Dickens provides a stereotypical description of her and attempts to be her narrator, Rodas argues, thereby becoming the classic satellite bringing her story to the larger world and measuring his "normalcy" against her disability (62). He later shifts from the active stereotype to a more complicated notion of the disabled characters' conscious manipulation of their disabilities as spectacles. Probably the most well-known cliché for the disabled is Tiny Tim; however, Rodas's notes that critics have emphasized his knowledge of himself as "cultural text" or a "sympathetic spectacle," but she adds that he "invites the public gaze and shapes its meaning instead of submitting unwillingly or unwittingly to public scrutiny while secondary or satellite figures describe his allegorical function" (67–68). He associates himself with Christ when he invites the congregation to look and remember what Christ did for the lame and the beggars. Blind Bertha in *The Cricket on the Hearth* also asserts agency, moving from a woman defined through her father's fiction and entirely controlled by the world he creates, to the woman who can now "see" and becomes the care-giving figure to her father. Asserting that she is no longer blind, she struggles for agency that cannot be contained by the father.

Rodas argues that Dickens seems less certain of what to do with disabled figures who attempt to claim their agency over the nondisabled. In *David Copperfield,* disability becomes a "continuum with other ostensibly nondisabled characters depicted in the text" (80). Rodas states, "illness and disability are a part of the ordinary course of life; despite any freakish idiosyncrasies, the disabled here are not explicitly partitioned off from the 'normal,' nor are these characters symbolically set apart in their narrative roles" (80). Miss Mowcher stands as a potentially villainous figure that is later moderated, but this was due to the agency of Mrs. Jane Seymour Hill. Hill was offended by Dickens's characterization of her as Miss Mowcher. Threatened with legal recourse by Mrs. Hill, Dickens revised Miss Mowcher's character, and though that revision is still problematic, it nevertheless illustrates the agency Hill was able to exert, albeit through a solicitor. This article provides an interesting study of Dickens's complex relationship with agency and disability.

In "*Hard Times*: Fancy as Practice," Christopher Barnes revisits the Dickensian concept of fancy to illustrate its connection to hegemonic disciplinary powers, arguing that the willful naiveté of characters such as Sissy Jupe and Stephen Blackpool is a form of resistance that Dickens labeled "fancy." Such fancy becomes a political practice with which characters exercise limited forms of power in response to Utilitarianism and industrial capitalism. Using the postcolonial terminology of the "subaltern" and referring to Michel de Certeau's notions of "strategy" and "tactic," Barnes suggests that the subaltern characters practice everyday acts "to shape, modify, and deform the alienating environment in which they live" (234–35). Unable to use direct forms of resistance characterized by de Certeau's notion of strategic action—for example, strikes—the characters engage in tactical practices that misleadingly appear as "nonresistance" but whose composite effects function as an ongoing critique. This use of de Certeau is particularly interesting, for it helps to politicize the text in light of de Certeau's understanding of everyday practices. Theorizing power in this light allows for a broader identification of forms of resistance that are accessible to those not immediately implicated in power structures. In this way, Sissy and Blackpool are not, as other critics have argued, ineffective in their resistance: "When tactical (hidden, non-confrontational) resistance is added to our definition of fancy, a more cogent and coherent opposition to authority of the world symbolized by 'fact' emerges" (235). Though fancy is understood in Dickensian studies as "a distraction and as amusement," its political role in resistance comes forward in several concrete ways (241). One such way is in Sissy's "denseness," in her "reluctance to alter her perception of the world to suit the Gradgrindian system" (242). While refusing to become one with this system of knowledge, she criticizes "the system without directly confronting it" and thereby forces Gradgrind "to doubt the comprehensiveness of his system" (242). Blackpool's muddle functions in a similar way. Rather than seeing him as the Uncle Tom or martyr figure, we can read his actions as tactical. Such reading of everyday practices allows the critics to see the impact of seemingly meaningless action. Barnes reveals that the disenfranchised tactically act within systems that they cannot entirely dismantle through strategic insurgence. By chipping away at the structure, they illustrate Foucault's point that power, though far-reaching and seemingly stable, is subject to change.

In contrast with Barnes, Cynthia Dereli in "Stephen Blackpool's 'muddle' in *Hard Times*," returns to a discussion of Blackpool's limited agency in relation to middle-class intervention. To begin, Dereli reconsiders several critical interpretations of Dickens's Blackpool, particularly those that say he is "too good to be true" versus those that see him, in his failure to join the union, as weak and contradictory. Considering Dickens's intended reader, she notes middle-class fear of working-class violence. Dereli suggests that the intended middle-class reader was unlikely to be soft on crime. This discussion runs in accord with Blackpool's passive participation in the near murder of his wife. Though sympathetic to the poor and to the problem of the chains of marriage, Dickens, Dereli argues, would not have condoned the attempts of the poor "to rectify the situation by taking the law into their own hands through theft or violence" (104–05). Though Dickens did argue against capital punishment, by the 1850s his position had changed so that he supported it, and did so particularly in reference to wife-murder. Therefore, she argues that Blackpool, who is nearly guilt of murdering his wife, is not "too good to be true." In terms of discussing his failure to join the union, critics have highlighted that his motivations are unclear. Referring to Joseph Butwin's discussion of the deleted text in which Rachael speaks of her sister who was killed by factory machinery, Dereli argues that, in this deleted passage, when Stephen becomes angry, Rachael asks him to calm himself, and he promises to follow her wishes. Dickens's deletion of this scene, Butwin argues, removes Stephen's motivation for failing to join the union; however, Dereli agues that Dickens could have deleted the scene since the justification had already been provided in the previous scene: "Such uncontrolled anger was an aspect of working-class mentality which had already been explored by Dickens in an article in *Household Words* where he had argued that the working men, understanding their predicament and the problems they face, should appeal to the middle classes to right their wrongs" (106). Blackpool emerges as a "flawed hero" whose anger could explode without the guidance of Rachael (106). In the death scene, then, which emphasizes the issue of "aw a muddle," Stephen speaks of the injustices, and the "muddle" is not his understanding of these things, but his failure to know a resolution to them. Unlike the tactical Blackpool in Barnes's argument, Dereli's Blackpool must rely on "middle-class intervention" (108).

Direct references to agency and revolt occur in two articles that look at *Bleak House.* Eric G. Lorentzen brings *Bleak House* into the center of a discussion of Dickens's social criticism of the Victorian response to Empire in the 1850s, this time not solely through a discussion of telescopic philanthropy, but through a study of the metaphor of contamination as political revolt. In " 'Obligations of Home,' " Lorentzen notes that at a critical point in *Bleak House,* the text has been altered in many recent editions, removing a "clever reference to Wat Tyler that represents how thoroughly [Dickens's] text becomes infected with the disease of revolution" (156). Contamination in *Bleak House* is not from the Empire outside of England but from within and originates in the "neglect of English natives" (157). Dickens, of course, was frustrated with expansion overseas and its accompanying neglect at home and with fears that neglect at home might lead to domestic revolt. The danger of telescopic philanthropy is noted in many critical approaches as is Dickens's arguably racist perspective on imperial natives. Lorentzen, however, argues that the "only sympathetic philanthropist" is John Jarndyce, whose focus is domestic (163). Lorentzen further argues that Woodcourt's colonial exploit is driven by ambition, not need, and therefore sets the stage for Dickens's critique of contamination in Esther and Jo. Due to his absence, Woodcourt cannot provide any solace or assistance to Esther in her illness. However, he "reveals heroism through his eventual willingness to stay at home" (167).

In the famous section about "Tom-all-Alone's," Lorentzen notes, the languages of contamination, colonialism, and revolt coalesce. This illustrates that revolt infuses the text and spreads like a contamination. Though critics such as Arnold Kettle have observed that *Bleak House* is " 'a revolutionary novel without revolutionaries' " (qtd. in 171), Lorentzen differs, seeing resistance present in the brickmakers' "absolute revolt against the class system and its machinations" (172), and in Jo, who, as the victim of colonial neglect, "becomes the primary memento mori in a contaminated text full of revolutionary danger" (173). Sir Leicester and the Dedlock clan exhibit the "sleeping through a revolution" element with Sir Leicester representing obsession with revolt—and Rouncewell and his son, Watt, the causes of his discomfort. Though associated with James Watt, father of the Industrial Revolution, there is also reference to Wat Tyler, leader of the 1381 Peasant Revolt, a revolt that Lorentzen argues is infecting all parts of the text: "Significantly, the Peasant Revolt of 1381 was the result of focusing too much on overseas matters and neglecting the poor at home as well" (175). In *A Child's History of England,* written while working on *Bleak House,* Dickens is "sympathetic in his portrait of Wat" (175). Dickens used the spelling of "Wat" when speaking of "Watt," and recent editions have changed this "misspelling"; however, Lorentzen argues that in removing this, the text omits Dickens's reference to Wat Tyler and to the linking of colonial contamination and the ensuing revolution at home, arguing the absence of the revolutionary in the text is due to incorrect copying of the novel.

Chris R. Vanden Bossche's "Class Discourse and Popular Agency in *Bleak House*" looks at the impact of popular radicalism and the extension of the franchise on Dickens's construction of *Bleak House.* Vanden Bossche argues that popular radicalism was less concerned with "economic transformation" and more interested in the "extension of the franchise to the people" (8). Radical discourse spoke of the people as divided between the included and the excluded. Looking at the constitutional narratives of class (a discourse based on historical and constitutional changes which sought to legitimize

political agency of the middle class while affirming the agency of the aristocracy and the exclusion of the people) and the narrative of the national marriage plot (a marriage of the best features of the middle class and aristocracy),
Bleak House, Vanden Bossche argues, attempts to present popular agency
through a revision of the marriage plot, ''but it stops short of envisioning
that agency in terms of the electoral franchise sought by the Chartists''
(9–10). Instead, Vanden Bossche argues that *Bleak House* makes the issue of
exclusion ''a problem of discourse and seeks to reform the discursive terms
in which public discourse is framed, making resistant discourse the preliminary to the achievement of popular agency'' (10). Class identities are not
shaped solely by economic interests; they can also be shaped by a desire
for enfranchisement. Vanden Bossche suggests that the narratives developed
matched the interests of the class, with those in favor of reform embracing a
narrative that established the Glorious Revolution as a restoration of a middle
class displaced by the Norman Conquest, and those opposed to reform tracing
the aristocratic line back to the conquest, with the Glorious Revolution seen
as a disruption of the ''traditional hierarchical order'' (10–11). Chartists similarly employed constitutional narratives arguing that their labor produces
property, thereby speaking in the language of parliamentary rather than economic reform.

Dickens, Vanden Bossche argues, used radical and middle class discourse
strategically, not consistently (12). Though the text ''favors the abolition of
aristocratic privilege,'' it similarly reaffirms ''the narrative of the rise of the
middle class'' (13). Presenting middle class and aristocratic discourse in the
text embodied by Mrs. Jellyby and Mrs. Pardiggle, and Turveydrop and
Skimpole respectively, Vanden Bossche demonstrates that Esther rejects both
languages, suggesting that ''the claims of each class to social and moral
superiority mask self-interested motives'' (15). Esther and later Woodcourt
remain outsiders to this discourse, as characters that refuse to ''perform''
class roles (24). Nevertheless, though outside, Esther refuses to be excluded,
a position especially made evident by her refusal to accept the ''identity of
the excluded, unmarriageable woman'' (17). Through an interesting discussion on Rouncewell and Sir Leicester Dedlock, Vanden Bossche further illustrates how the constitutional narratives are played out, turning to the Peasant's
Revolt, as Lorentzen does, to illustrate Dickens's interest in the working
''man'' and the exclusion of people from political agency. Popular action is
understood in a system that still denies them enfranchisement, and Dickens
does not reconcile this problem. In this way, class identities in the novel and
for its author are not stable categories.

Molly Anne Rothenberg's ''Articulating Social Agency in *Our Mutual
Friend*'' engages in a rather complicated and densely written discussion of
political agency. Through the critical lenses of Judith Butler and Michel de

Certeau, in particular, Rothenberg illustrates that Dickens's *Our Mutual Friend* "emphasizes the impossibility of distinguishing between self—and social determination when it comes to agency" (720). Various characters enact differing relationships with agency, but, Rothenberg argues, that Dickens demonstrates that agency is hard to use to measure character since it is difficult to determine intentions, and it is equally hard to locate the impact of social conditioning. What results is a device "blurring the difference between autonomy and heteronomy" (720). J. S. Mill's work is helpful to Rothenberg, who argues that volitional activity must be understood within the social framework that conditions such activity; therefore, intention becomes a mix of both internal and external motivations, which "calls into question the modes for claiming agency and assigning responsibility expounded from Victorian times to our own" (721); therefore, the text examines the manner in which agency can occur within the "social arena" (722). Victorian approaches to agency are constructed upon the dichotomous polarities of "free or determined, essential or constructed, unencumbered or situated," whereas postmodern and other contemporary theorists tend to see these antitheses as unhelpful (723). Rothenberg turns to theorists who complicate concepts of political agency as individualized or intentional—Judith Butler's performative theory and Michel de Certeau's and Pierre Bourdieu's French cultural studies. In the end, Rothenberg suggests that agency is an "effect rather than as a cause of socially-generated meaning" (723).

Through an in-depth analysis of Pleasant Riderhood, Rothenberg evaluates the ways in which this minor character negotiated her agency in her controlled refusal of Venus (in terms of performance theory) and her habitual hair winding (emblematic of habit in which choices are made "among behaviors to which one is already predisposed") (731). Perhaps most interesting in Rothenberg's essay is her extended discussion and critique of theoretical positions on agency, especially her comments on the difficulty of unpacking the discussion of agency within a context of social conditioning and the prescription of political agency for change. As she notes, these theoretical approaches avoid the "individualistic, intentionalist account of agency, but their political thrust—their avowed purpose of transforming social systems—requires that they present agency in terms of individual actions that not only escape systemic dictates but also are able to govern outcomes" (738). In this way, she pinpoints a key dilemma in discussions of agency in contemporary cultural theory, which is the repudiation, as Rothenberg discusses it, of the "transindividual or social sphere in which all political action must transpire" (738). Indeed, Rothenberg argues that Butler's and de Certeau's discussions are "unethical" because they approach agency in a manner that does not account for the "ethical force" of the "social dimension of agency" (742). Individuals, then, are a part of the "collective" and are "distinct" as well; however, individuals negotiate the boundaries by insisting on that distinctness without completely removing one's self from the collective. In acknowledging the collective, we understand the fallacy of intentionalism. But we cannot entirely reject the "fantasies of control" as long as we exist within the social arena (743).

Since Rothenberg ends with a discussion of ethics, I briefly turn to two other articles that consider this subject, Marshall Gregory's "Ethical Engagements over Time" and Roger D. Sell's "Blessings, Benefactions, Bear's Services." Gregory establishes a case for continued attention to ethical dimensions in narrative analysis, noting the ethical impact of stories upon us due to our continual engagement with them. Gregory provides several readings of Emily Brontë's *Wuthering Heights* and *David Copperfield,* which appealed to him at different moments in his life. Suggesting that stories fill in the gaps left in our lives, Gregory reveals how his own ethical engagement with these two texts has changed through numerous readings across time. He prefers stories that have "theories, so to speak, over those that merely have objections," with *Wuthering Heights* falling in the latter category for him (298). He elevates those stories that, for him, are both inspired and inspiring, those that connect with human consciousness more than those that merely entertain. This makes stories useful, he argues, as readers attempt to understand choices about their own lives: "As Dickens's novels show and as Brontë's *Wuthering Heights* does not, we really can live better lives if we shape them in accordance to an ethical vision that encourages us to meet everyday standards of decency, honesty, justice, and compassion" (299). Though his discussion of the impact of stories might be found in any standard introduction to literature syllabus—the material we all use to seduce our unsuspecting undergraduates into a love fest with literature—Gregory's article, I think, misses his own point. His foreclosure of *Wuthering Heights* doesn't mean the text is without the concepts he searches for. He just doesn't see them in it, whereas others might. And others might also construct an entirely different ethical universe.

In a rather lengthy article on the connections among narratological analysis, communication theory, and Dickens's *Great Expectations,* Roger D. Sell argues that many literary texts are understood and discussed within frameworks that do not necessarily "suit them" (50). His essay, on some levels, revolves around considerations of how modernism functions within narratological studies: "The de-ethicalizing masochism of much twentieth-century culture left its mark, not only on some strands of deconstructionist criticism, but also on other scholarship in the humanities, including narratology" (54). Through an exploration of classical and post-classical narratology, he notes a "dehumanisation . . . for reasons that were ultimately ideological. In a nutshell, its analyses tended to play down the scope for human decision-making, as regards both the story-teller and the story-internal characters'' (57). The danger, he notes, is that ''if narratology is to consolidate its twentieth century achievements, then that same century's de-humanisation and anti-hedonism must be firmly qualified'' (58). If not, the text stands in danger of being misunderstood and distorted and will ''risk anachronistic misrepresentations. . . . And the entire narratological project will come to seem increasingly outmoded, in its insensitivity to the many ways in which pre-Modernist attitudes, perceptions and values are already being re-recycled'' (58–59).

To resolve this dilemma, Sell brings communication pragmatics into a discussion of narratology to discuss the impossibility of sharing an identical context and to search for empathy despite this. In communication theory, the unitary contextual fallacy demonstrates the ''unconscious assumption that a context, even at the outset of communication, can be identical for two or more people involved'' (63). Sell points out the danger of unitary scripts being forced on texts like Dickens's *Great Expectations*, whether that script is by Freud or Bakhtin. Sell posits the concepts of primary tellability (the material that hooks the reader) and secondary tellability (interpretation of moral) as ways to negotiate this dilemma. And he argues that we are only now starting to be able again to be ''re-sensitised'' to the secondary relating, the moral of the story (69). Providing several instances of unmotivated generosity in *Great Expectations*, Sell then looks at Pip's motivated forms of generosity or bear's services as Sell calls them: his help of the convict qualified by fear, his forgiveness of Miss Havisham qualified by the force with which he holds her down after the fire, his failure to reveal Estella's parentage, his subtle lie to Magwitch on his deathbed about Estella's love. As Sell points out, *Great Expectations* was not a favorite among Dickens's contemporaries because his ''selectional politeness,'' those moments dealing with anthropological elements such as taboo and fashion that marked Dickens's earlier texts, is transformed into a ''presentational politeness,'' found in the manner of presentation, and he thus violates his selectional politeness with his readers. The text was off-putting to his contemporaries, functioning as a pre-Modernist text, which made later Modernist texts possible. Sell argues, then, that Modernists, by embracing ''the gloomy and darker elements which had not pleased Victorian taste . . . were downplaying the primary tellability's more cheerful aspects, and ignoring the extent to which its secondary tellability involves a moral axis'' (78).

Social Class Analysis

This year's articles on social class analysis raise important questions about Dickens's thoughts on his own social mobility, on the role of inheritance, on the debate between the gentleman and the developing professional class, and on the larger questions of society.

In "Drink in *David Copperfield*," Gareth Cordery places Dickens's treatment of alcohol within a historical and autobiographic context, arguing convincingly that Dickens's thoughts on drink highlighted his anxieties about class mobility. Cordery discusses how *David Copperfield*, Dickens's most autobiographical novel, "betrays his own anxieties about his origins and his class, as David-Dickens looks back from the security of middle-class respectability to the trauma in the 1820s of the bottling-blacking warehouse" (29). Though not a drinker himself, Dickens was also no prude, Cordery argues, and was opposed to Cruikshank's teetotalism, advocating moderation instead. In *David Copperfield*, "drink . . . is the site where class issues are played out and where the seemingly seamless ideology of moderation as publicly expressed and personally practiced becomes fractured" (61). Looking at two particular textual moments, the scene at the Red Lion and David's binge with Steerforth, Cordery argues that each illustrates Dickens's negotiation with class. In the first, young David attempts to assert a higher social class position by ordering Genuine Stunning ale. The landlord reads through this performance, and the kindly landlady returns his money, further revealing the transparency of David's social climbing. Phiz's illustration of this scene presents a homey and non-threatening space. This image is countered with Cruikshank's more overtly negative images of gin-shops. In contrast, while drinking with Steerforth, David becomes drunk, and it is his drunkenness that makes this moment important. Cordery refers to the *Old Curiosity Shop*, in which Kit Nubble's intoxication, for which he feels moderately repentant, is understood within a class context; Kit-as-servant is allowed this moment and is forgiven, but David appears not to be forgiven. With Steerforth, the middle-class values of Doctor Strong and Aunt Betsey are suspended, and David steps into the role of dissolute aristocrat. Agnes is the one who brings him back to middle-class values. But, like Kit, Cordery argues that this is also an escape from middle-class values, if but a momentary one: "Drink in the novel, then, is not only a forum for interrogating shifting attitudes and social relationships during a crucial period of nineteenth-century history, but also the site where Dickens's radical unease with his own place in society is displayed" (72).

John B. Lamb's "Faces in the Window, Stains on the Rose" refers to the moment when Oliver Twist sees the faces of Monks and Fagin peering in at him, piercing the safety of the Maylie's cottage. This is, according to Lamb, the "quilting or anchoring point, and the moment, according to Slavoj Žižek, when a perfectly natural and familiar situation is denatured, becomes uncanny, loaded with horror and threatening possibilities (1–2). In this moment, Lamb reads the the traumatic kernel of the Dickensian real where the domain of sexuality, of economics, of the modern city itself'' come together (2). Lamb's essay considers the negotiation of and incompatibilities between the innocent pastoral and economic urban locations. Dickens, Lamb argues, confronts disorder not with a discussion of social science, which is the language of reformers, but with pastoral myth. However, ''Fagin's face at the window points to elements of sexual and economic excess that resist the pastoral mode of symbolization'' (3). Innocence is fetishized in *Oliver Twist,* but it is Oliver's innocence that makes him potentially corruptible, thereby blurring the urban and pastoral worlds. Fagin is discussed as both capitalist and alien, but Monks offers the more compelling reading as providing a ''perverse economic logic, the logic of inheritance'' (6). Oliver ''twists'' this throughout the text in his ''failure to stabilize identity'' and his final presentation as a gentleman's son is ''haunted by the traces of his earlier nominations and the 'stain' of his blood inheritance'' (7). Monks, however, demonstrates that he is undeserving of inheritance. Referring to Julia Kristeva's work on abjection, the ultimate abjection of the novel is ''that the urban world fails to respect the borders and subject positions erected by the pastoral and its concomitant myths'' (9). This is seen in Nancy's analogous presence in Rose's stain, which functions as symbolic ''feminine contagion'' of ''uncertain parentage and familial shame'' (10). The text is haunted by the repressed characters, and there is no home for any of the problematic characters, such as Fagin, Monks, Nancy, and Agnes: ''Dickens's interrelated and interdependent pastoral and domestic myths promise to rub out, to make invisible the 'stains' that mark the sexuality, violence, and betrayal that haunt middle-class conceptions of the family and family ties, just as those myths promise to gentrify the indeterminate and terrifying urban world'' (12). However, the repressed always returns and the text is marked by disfigurement: the pastoral/domestic attempt to erase the urban unrest and the family's shame is continually disrupted and disfigured by the return of the ''dead.''

Inheritance and class mobility are also discussed in Patrick Parrinder's '''Turn Again, Dick Whittington!''' Parrinder considers the influence of the mythic representations of Richard Whittington on the Dickensian oeuvre. The article begins with an important distinction between London and other cities that consistently combine the secular and the sacred seats within the confines of the city. The ancient city's outer boundary encased the servile population, with the inner boundaries inclosing the sacred seat of the king and the church. London, however, placed its secular government in Westminster outside the ''boundaries'' of the walled city of London, and the sacred seat was located in Canterbury, thus setting in motion the secularization process. The boundaries of the city become indistinct; in the male bildungsroman the crossing of the outer boundary of the city promises the penetration of the inner boundary where his hopes and desires may be fulfilled, but the uncertainty of

London city boundaries sets the stage for, as myth has it, poor, ragged, little Dick Whittington to be the mayor of London. (This is despite the fact that Whittington was probably the son, though the younger son, of a lord.) Traveling to London to seek his wealth, Dick Whittington becomes disillusioned in the outer city and turns to go home, stopping at Highgate Hill only being called to "turn again" by the sound of the bells of the inner city. The poor boy returns, marries the master's daughter, and gains his wealth.

For Wordsworth, the Dick Whittington story is associated with a more immature or childish stage of mental development, whereas Dickens's associations, Parrinder states, are more "facetious" (410). Almost every Dickensian novel refers to the myth, though *David Copperfield,* Parrinder argues, does not do so until later, after David's success has been determined. In *Barnaby Rudge,* Joe Willet, sitting near Highgate, hears no message in the bells, and the silence, Parrinder suggests, signals the "moral corruption of capitalism" (412): the "mercantile ambitions symbolized by the Whittington legend" is "tarnished for Dickens . . . " (412). However, it is the inheritance plot of the Dick Whittington tale, the marrying the master's daughter, which resonates for Dickens, whose inheritance plots rest on male characters achieving an adequate amount of wealth but not creating new forms of wealth. Marrying the master's daughter is seen in Pip and in Walter Gay. Returning to his discussion of the boundaries of the city, Parrinder notes that Dickens's texts often present the city as cannibalistic and labyrinthine, especially as seen in Bill Sikes's failed attempt to leave the city at the end of *Oliver Twist.* In *Our Mutual Friend,* Parrinder argues, that there is nothing at the center of the city but a phantom, and the master's daughter portion of the tale is further problematized in the relationship of John Harmon and Bella Wilfer: Parrinder maintains that "what has vanished at the end of *Our Mutual Friend* is the heavy, unintelligible weight of a city where the bells have 'grown worldly' and the noble merchant of the Whittington legend has given place to a phantom" (418).

David Hennessee's "Gentlemanly Guilt and Masochistic Fantasy in *Great Expectations*" continues this discussion of inheritance and social position, though this time through the discussion of the social class position of the gentleman. Hennessee argues that many critics have focused on the prevalence of guilt and its paralyzing aspects for Pip in *Great Expectations.* Most have seen this as an "immature stage of development" that Pip must outgrow in order to embrace home. Hennessee, however, believes that such reading is too optimistic and does not emphasize the elements of Pip's masochistic approach to his guilt. Hennessee notes an element of self-flagellation in this guilt, one that takes an almost "intrapsychic, autoerotic pleasure" in beating one's self up (319). Guilt fantasies begin to take precedence over the actual world Pip inhabits. This approach to his guilt, and the masochistic pleasure he gains from maintaining a position as the guilty gentleman, make him unable to bridge the moral and social differences present in the text.

This perspective, for Hennessee, "represents a pessimistic shift in Dickens's views on the ability of moral sympathy to enable social fellowship" (318). Rather, it "lays bare the idea that gentlemanly status involves exclusion, even in the quasi-democratic middle-class form in which it is equated more with moral attributes than economic or social distinction" (318). The setting of the text in the Regency is not lost, then, on the reader, nor is the fact that contemporary debates from Ruskin, Arnold, Newman, and Smiles all indicated that the gentleman was less an economic position and more a moral one, though a moral one still governed by elitism. Pip, who attempts to "reconcile his private world with the world of society," repeatedly fails (308). Though a snob, Pip feels guilt, and a true snob would not feel guilt; therefore, he is failing on this level as well: "Pip's story represents the consequences of this failure: to be a truly moral gentleman is to feel guilt about one's status in the social hierarchy, and to be guilty means to replace real-world connections to social inferiors with connections that exist only in fantasy" (310–11). The text offers no way to reconcile this dilemma, hence the inadequacy of both endings, which do not confront the "ideological contradictions the novel has all along explored" (311). Hennessee's reading of these guilty fantasies is very helpful for understanding Pip's actions and the unresolved bildungsroman. His guilt gives rise to fantasies which "distort his real connections with the world" (314). In this way, Pip-as-gentleman does not produce the sympathy that marks "ethical conduct"; in fact, "his bonding with others as 'fellow sufferers" only goes so far. Rather, Pip is sensible of social inequities, feels painfully responsible for them, and substitutes this fantasy world of guilty connection for real-world relationships" (318–19). In this way, Pip does not dismantle the hierarchical elements of the gentleman but keeps them firmly in place.

In "The Self-Sacrificing Professional," Jennifer Ruth provides a discussion of the professional in contrast with the gentleman. In her examination of the development of the professional class in Victorian England, Ruth illustrates Dickens's thoughts on the authority of the professional class over the private sphere—taking on particularly the private's sphere's valorization of self-sacrifice. Her text looks at the connections between *A Tale of Two Cities* and Dickens's short story, "Hunted Down," written for an American magazine, the *New York Ledger*. Ruth provides a useful discussion of critical responses to the creation of the professional class, such as its rejection of industrial capitalist market/money issues and the rejection of aristocratic gentlemanly excess. The professional, in contrast, is focused on service; following his calling, he must set aside his own personal interests, and in the process, he also commands authority over women within the private sphere. By convincing the private sphere that "he knows their interests better than they do," domesticity is rewritten so that education, health, and other welfare services are removed from the responsibility of family and taken on by the state, and the professional becomes the necessary intervention into this resultant vacuum (285). Ruth argues that "in order to convince us that the family is unsustainable alone, the professional must do more than appropriate the moral authority of the wife and mother; he must also demonstrate that the capitalist father is unable to succeed in the business world *and* protect his family" (287).

However, this knowledge and action must be without self-motivation. In "Hunted Down," Meltham, the actuarial insurance man and hero, helps the evil uncle Slinkton to take a policy out on his niece. When she dies, Meltham investigates, but he must sacrifice his own life rather than win the lovely remaining niece at the end of the tale. He cannot profit in the domestic sphere for his work. The paradox, as Ruth points out, is that if there were no insurance, he would not need to intervene in the home and sacrifice himself in the first place. Thus, the professional creates the problem he must step in to resolve. Ruth suggests, "It is not, or rather not only, that the professional must reinforce a wall that will then exclude him; he must reinforce a wall that operates in the opposite direction as well by excluding the home from any share in professional knowledge" (293). Ruth argues that this perspective illustrates Dickens's thinking at the time he was working on the character of Sydney Carton. She writes, "Only disinterested love, however romantic in nature, can distinguish the professional's version of 'disinterest' from the more calculated variety exercised by the businessman," and Carton illustrates that disinterest in his sacrificial act, emblematically functioning as the disinterested professional rather than the cold businessman or the excessive aristocrat (296).

David Paroissien in "Ideology, Pedagogy, and Demonology" contends that the context of education present in *Hard Times* and *Our Mutual Friend* illustrates Dickens's "indebtedness to the writings of midcentury educational reformers" whose work critics of Dickens's texts tend to overlook (260). Seeing a "threat" in their theoretical approaches to education "added further intensity to his mission as a writer" (261). Exploring the context of educational issues between 1815 and 1846, Paroissien concludes that the battle over secular and sectarian forms of education gave rise to two approaches in education: "nonconformists, who insisted on teaching their doctrines, and . . . the radicals, who advocated secular schooling free from any sectarian instruction" (263). The government intervention into education between 1832 and 1846 happened due to changes following the First Reform Bill, the founding of Utilitarian belief systems, and a consciousness of trouble among the disaffected in urban centers. Citing numerous educational theorists of the time, Paroissien argues that several, such as James Kay-Shuttleworth, conclude that a secular education was a means to prevent revolution, Dickens

himself concurring by arguing that a secular education was to help deal with
the dangerous members of society (265). However, educational reformers of
the time, though sharing Dickens's interest in secular schools, were driven
more by classist notions of how to educate the disaffected—based on drilling
and indoctrination to one's place in society. In writing to Kay-Shuttleworth,
Dickens proposed a system of education different than the one growing within
the country; this one would be founded on "a curriculum designed to amuse
and instruct by encouraging 'much greater hopefulness' among the young
charges" (265–66). The schools produced their own teachers, thus reinforcing
these same principles: "England's Normal Schools operated on the same
principle as factories, mechanically producing teachers like so many lathes
busily shaping piano legs from pieces of wood. Yet the comparison is historically accurate, true to the replacement of the foot treadle by steam-power in
the mid-century as inventors developed techniques compatible with mass
production" (272–73). Johann Heinrich Pestalozzi's notion of fact-based
teaching, endorsed by Kay-Shuttleworth, influenced numerous educators of
the time, including Charles Mayo, Richard Dawes, and William Ellis. Fitting
the person to his social position in life became the goal: "an emphasis on
common things would bear usefully on the industrial pursuits of the middle
and lower classes and simultaneously help promote unity between the
classes" (275–76). The purpose of such education, then, was to keep the poor
from destitution and to teach them to inhabit comfortably their social class
position. Dickens rejected such notions, creating characters such as Charlie
Hexam and Bitzer to illustrate this rejection.

Narain Prasad Shukla's "Macrocosm v. Microcosm" surmises that Dickens's *Little Dorrit* makes clear that "the reach of society is inescapable"
(123). This Dickensian truism is used to set the ground for an exploration of
the ways in which will and imagination are socially connected categories and
to express the view that "to be less than fully social requires finally that one
be less than fully human" (123). The "good" characters, such as Amy and
Arthur, are "failures, social and usually psychological misfits" (123). Shukla
suggests that it is this misfit status which allows them in part to escape society,
unlike other characters: "One must be handicapped—by birth, character,
misfortune or, most significantly in this novel, a failure of will or imagination—to be excluded from the mainstream of society and so from its worst
contaminations" (123). Though no one is allowed to choose to live outside
of society, some may be barred entrance and as such they achieve some
independence and a "higher degree of decency" (123). In contrast to Little
Dorrit, who is outside of society, Fanny and William Dorrit are examples of
always being within society even within the Mashalsea. Moreover, contrary
to our discussions of imagination in relation to education and *Hard Times,*
imagination in *Little Dorrit* appears as a form of corruption in the text, with

Rigaud as an example. Shukla states that it is Clennam's sins of society—speculating on Merdle and his fantasy of marrying Pet—that need to be expiated in order for him to win Amy. Thus, only when Clennam has lost the rewards of wealth and love in Victorian society can he see Amy Dorrit as his reward. As Shukla argues, Clennam and Amy are rather "colourless" and lack "humor," but this is because imagination and will, wit and charm are only vehicles into society, and the text argues for escape, though partial, from society as the only saving grace (130).

Carol Colatrella, in "The Innocent Convict," argues that *Little Dorrit* is where Dickens's argument about the nature of society is brought to bear on the symbol of the prison. Dickens "sketches the figure of the innocent convict as a means of understanding criminality, particularly representing cultural anxieties about who ought to be judged criminal and how criminals ought to be punished" (185). Colatrella suggests that in *Little Dorrit,* Dickens suggests that the prison might be a comfortable home and also that the home might be like a prison, revealing that "social status, money, family connections, and gentility are transient states rather than reliable indicators of innocence or criminality" (186). The text illustrates that crime and punishment are strange terms where small crimes are "cruelly punished" and large ones can escape notice (186). In doing so, Dickens suggests that the conventional understanding of criminality and its relationship to poverty is "faulty" and does not "explain social inequalities" (186). Dickens asks readers to sympathize with the criminal because of the "human propensity to transgress" (187).

Fascination with the innocent criminal was a contemporary interest of Dickens and his colleagues. The prison functioned as a source of corruption and contagion, and the "taint" or Little Dorrit's "speck" is evident in all the characters who have been incarcerated (189). However, the Mashalsea and high society are shown to be very similar. Colatrella argues that virtuous characters are often blamed or made invisible, and the innocent are trampled by the most selfish of characters. In the text, the metaphor of imprisonment is rife, as all characters endure some form of imprisonment, from Mrs. Clennam's wheelchair, to Merdle's cuffing of himself, to Flintwich's tie. And all characters are marked by the propensity for corruption. Even Amy and Arthur do not escape, with, for instance, Amy's excessive devotion and love for her father serving as a symptom of her potential corruption evidenced in her infamous "speck." Her excessively forgiving nature is seen as transgressive, and Arthur's response is one from the more conventional world that feels the criminal must pay for his crime, whereas Amy, in this case, represents the ideal world. Nevertheless, though Amy continually refuses to participate in the Dorrit's world of morality and propriety, she ends up being scapegoated. The argument includes an interesting discussion of Arthur's absent mother, in which Colatrella concludes that Amy "continues to pay for crimes she did not commit; her story like that of Arthur's mother, proposes that existing social values are hypocritical and cruel and that the criminal justice system, which causes needless suffering for those who do not deserve to be punished, ought to be reformed" (202).

Gender Studies

As with many of the subjects addressed this year, Gender Studies crosses the artificial boundaries I have created. I would draw particular attention to Vincent Newey's text reviewed in the section on Dickensian scriptures, as well as David Hennessee's article on the gentleman reviewed in the section on social class analysis. In this section, I have included articles that look at male friendship and heterosexual marriage. I have also included a full-length study on gender and madness and an essay on women and contamination.

Carolyn Oulton's " 'My Undisciplined Heart' " places David and Steerforth's relationship in the context of nineteenth-century male romantic friendship. Romantic same-sex friendship was demonstrated through intense feelings and intimacy, "startling rhetorical expression," "intense, sometimes exclusive, focus," and the "pattern in which passion for friends of the same sex gives way to the marriage plot" (157–58). Referring to Gesa Stedman, Oulton argues that Victorians understood the physical aspect of emotion only within the framework of its social relevance, and as such the expression of romantic friendship must be understood within that context; therefore, "a superficial reading of romantic friendship might . . . suggest that it depends for its free expression on an ironic oblivion to the possibilities of sexual attraction, which it might, in theory, serve to regulate. This view must be modified if we are to appreciate the complexity of the ideal and the delicate balance it was obliged to maintain if it was to preserve its status as an acceptable form of passion" (158). Though later in the century such friendships would become suspect, in the mid nineteenth-century, romantic friendships were also bound by rules that kept it within heterosexual norms; this balance between the expression and control of emotions is important to the careful establishment of boundaries. One such boundary is that male friendships are reserved for the extreme youth, where one in the pair is presented as naïve and, ironically, "safe" from the advances of the more "lascivious" friend. Steerforth, Oulton argues, tries to feminize David, but David in time exerts control over the narration. Though the younger may be exploited, as she argues is the case with Tattycoram and Miss Wade, David, though adoring, later withdraws from this role into heterosexual marriage. He reveals his "maturity" by leaving behind this youthful passion for marriage. As Oulton argues, it is telling that Steerforth's and Dora's deaths coalesce in David's thoughts so that by "overcoming these losses, David is finally able to redefine himself with a fully integrated masculine identity" (167). In such ways, the text makes "subversive sexuality" acceptable by keeping it within the safe boundaries of heterosexual marriage, and, further, through Steerforth's death, the dangerous figure of the pair is destroyed.

However, heterosexual marriage, according to Shuli Barzilai's "The Bluebeard Barometer," is not an entirely safe location either. Barzilai considers Dickens's personal anxieties about marriage in her reading of Dickens's tale of Captain Murderer, which appears in *The Uncommerical Traveller* (chapter 15, though cited as 18 in the article). The nurse's story of the infamous Captain Murderer, who in Bluebeard style kills his wives, is disrupting in a surprising and humorous manner. Barzilai queries why this tale of Bluebeard held such sway over Dickens's creative works, noting that more than a dozen references to Bluebeard appear. Barzilai considers a Dickensian autobiographical interest due to the emotional intensity surrounding the tale and its repetition. She similarly adds the Freudian notion of the "tendentious joke," whose intention was never innocent humor but instead a "satiric, hostile, aggressive, or self-defensive" purpose (506). The target of such jokes in Dickens's case appears to be the institution of marriage. Building upon the Charles Perrault version of Bluebeard in which the last lucky bride escapes the wrath of the murderous bridegroom, and the Grimm Brothers' tales of "The Robber Bridegroom" or "Mr. Fox" in England, in which the last lucky bride escapes the cannibalistic impulses of the bridegroom, Dickens's tale of Captain Murderer centers on a bridegroom, who similarly weds tender young brides for dining purposes; however, in his tale the second beautiful sister of the married-and-eaten-sister tricks the Captain into marriage, but, instead of escaping, she poisons the pie crust in which she is baked and thereby kills the Captain who turns blue and explodes. Nobody survives, and the joke is on the listener who is fooled into believing he will receive a classic fairy tale in the same fashion as the other tales mentioned. Disturbing the generic expectations of the fairy tale, this version leaves the reader shocked and in laughter. Establishing a carnivalesque laughter suggests that the tale is meant to be shared in performance to bring others into the joke.

Barzilai concludes that such a tale resonated for Dickens because of his own feelings about the institution of marriage; indeed, in *Pickwick Papers*, Sam Weller laments poor Bluebeard as a victim of connubiality over which his chaplain shed a tear. The "palimpsest" that Barzilai finds within this story is the questionable relationship Dickens shared with his two sisters-in-law—Mary Hogarth, whose death at a young age contributed to Dickens's fascination with her and her ghostly presence in the home, and Georgina, who stayed on after Dickens's separation from Catherine. Barzilai argues that Dickens furnishes the concept of the "happy triangulated family" as the ideal, and suggests that such arguments appear in other Dickensian texts such as *Barnaby Rudge*, *Bleak House*, and *Hard Times* (513). One sees this comparison perhaps most convincingly in *Bleak House* with Esther and her keys. However, it is in the Esther-Woodcourt-Jarndyce triangle that Barzilai finds the blurring of kinship boundaries and the movement of Jarndyce from a quasi-Bluebeard figure to a fairy godmother. Barzilai also contends that in addition to being a mask of Dickens's autobiographical impulses and a tendentious joke, Bluebeard serves as a "barometer" functioning in a way that "both conceals and reveals, both masks and exposes, the pressures weighing upon the writer who introduces the Bluebeard motif into varied textual situations that involve sexual relations and the institution of marriage" (518).

If Oulton and Barzilai read Dickens as both policing and blurring the boundaries of mid-nineteenth-century homosexual and heterosexual relationships, Marianne Camus in her extended study *Gender and Madness in the Novels of Charles Dickens* explores the manner in which Dickens's madwomen push the boundaries of acceptable femininity. Sylvère Monod, in his preface to the book, argues that this "terse study of Dickens' madwomen bids fair to occupy a distinguished position among the studies of Dickens produced by French scholars" (xi). Monod, noting that Camus applies the diagnosis of "madness" to many characters that others might not normally think of as mad, suggests that this is possibly a sticking point in the text, though he graciously dismisses that concern. Acknowledging Dickens's understanding of cruelness as a quality possessed by humans, Monod argues that Camus's application of madness to characters that might be thought of as cruel may be appropriate, for it indicates that sadism is a form of madness. However, the text does not always fully respond to this concern, and it may stand that many of Dickens's female characters could be understood as mad based on Camus's application of the term.

In her introduction, Camus states that "the artist's use of mental derangement, in its ambivalence and contradictions as far as gender is concerned, is what is under scrutiny here" (1). She states that she is not applying psychoanalytic criticism because it has been used so often in other studies and fails to meet expectations. But her primary reason, paradoxically, is that she is focused on the gendered aspect of madness, and nineteenth-century representations of female insanity do not match Dickens's presentations. Rather, she looks to the "non-directly sexual, representation of the gendering of madness" in order to "uncover the impact of social and ideological forces and pressures on the definition of the self [and] the damage they can inflict on the very notion of self," as well as to consider the "strategies" women use to resist and "circumvent" these forces (5). I might have been inclined to include this text, as well, in the section on agency since the texts in that section focus on agency for those in a compromised relationship with power, and that is decidedly Camus's argument.

Camus argues that Dickens did not use the Ophelia stereotype to define his madwomen, and in this discussion she sets the standard for her inclusion of some marginally mad characters. Drawing a distinction between "literary madness" and "clinical madness," Camus looks at a "continuum of mental unbalance. . . . This continuum, which goes from eccentricity to downright loss of one's mind, is slowly built by Dickens in his fiction through his many portraits of people who suffer mental derangement, whether temporarily or permanently" (7). Pain is important in her analysis as signifying suffering and madness. Referring to Foucault's observations that madness shifted from being a personal responsibility to a sense that the person was not responsible for his or her madness, Camus argues that Dickens was born in the midst of this shift and would apply both definitions in his writing. How this affects women, in particular, is that madness is seen when women transgress the rules of patriarchal society. She argues that the position of madness gave Dickens more freedom to negotiate the humanity of his female characters. In her short chapter, "Patterns of Madness," she continues in her positioning of Dickens's treatment of madness. He looked at a breadth of patterns, from senility to violence, but Camus tends to emphasize aspects such as "moral, emotional or mental stress" and its connection with madness (13). Indeed, Dickens's depiction of madness suggests that madness may have more than one origin and "the threat lies in each of us as much as it comes from the uncaring or even brutalising world around us" (13). Though she draws some distinctions between male madness (in violence and alcoholism) and female madness, she does argue that the boundaries are perhaps more blurry than one might think. This is perhaps her most compelling point, this and the argument that madness is understood as a continuum that we all traverse.

In "Public and Private Spheres," Camus looks at the frequently discussed separation of spheres doctrine and its application to Dickensian representations of madness. Madness for men is connected with the wider world, whereas madness for women is bounded by the domestic. Since women exist outside the power structure, "they do not have anything at stake and therefore cannot suffer to that extent from its demise. They are, moreover, traditionally supposed to suffer from a deficiency of reason which, again, prevents them from being as utterly destroyed" (19). She goes on to argue a trajectory for madness in women: that since "social norms" are applied differently, the result is that mental illness is "naturally gendered" (23). It follows then that excessive freedom makes men mad and too much restriction makes women mad, with Dorrit being gendered feminine in his madness. A second point she makes is that "eccentricity leads more quickly to mental derangement in a woman, or that it is more quickly perceived as such'' (25), citing Mrs. Jellyby and Mrs. Clennam as examples of this.

In ''Madness Visible,'' she argues ''that it is the women themselves who elaborate, if not their own madness, at least its forms and rituals,'' referring to Foucault's notion that the mad person, abandoning herself to madness, chooses her manner of performing that madness (35). Contrary to the previous chapter which looks to external factors to understand madness, this chapter considers the ways in which women choose to invent their madness. Again citing Foucault, she argues that Dickens's madwomen are exemplary of Foucault's notion of death in life—all of them living in buried or imprisoned states, with Miss Wade living in homes that reflect her mental state, Mrs. Clennam letting her house go to reflect her mental collapse, and Miss Havisham creating her home. Ironically, the gendered role of preserving and creating the home is attacked by these women. Camus argues that because they are ''negated as persons because they are women,'' these characters undermine the roles they are asked to perform and choose to perform roles outside their expected status as women (39). Dickens's radical perspective, as Camus sees it, is that his madwomen inhabit ''alternative versions of womanhood which they construct to survive and to withdraw more completely from the accepted models'' (41). The alternative womanhood is performed in several ways—namely dress, ghostlike appearances, and food rituals. Mrs. Clennam's and Sarah Gamp's food rituals are ''comforts and compensatory measures in a situation of exclusion so unbearable that it has unhinged them,'' with Willian Dorrit again feminized because of his food rituals (45). This is in contrast to Miss Havisham's anorexic response to her solitariness. In accepting their social isolation, these women may enact a subtle liberating effect, though that is mediated by their exclusion from society and their inhabitation of their madness.

In ''Women, Power and Punishment,'' Camus argues that women's madness is related to their lack of power in contrast with their desire for power. Most of the madwomen she studies, Camus argues, are that way in part due to being ''hooked on power'' (76). Though many of Dickens's women do exercise a form of power that is accepted, this power is not necessarily understood within a masculine framework. Such feminine power often relies upon female ''weapons . . . tears, fainting or hysterical fits, convulsions,'' though these actions are never associated with madness (72). This dominance becomes pathological in the case of Miss Wade, who has an ''obsessive and perverse desire to rule over other people's hearts'' (74). Attraction to power is ''fundamentally destablising'' (76). Camus's major argument is that Dickens's texts are interested in the newer language of madness that focuses on societal or private trauma explanations and psychological imprisonment. Noting Jeremey Tambling's point that madness may be an ''allegorical way of thinking'' (90), she also suggests that there is a subtle sympathy with this madness found in the space Dickens gives to the characters to work through their madness. Concurrent with this, however, is a more disapproving tone which is witnessed in the ''fierce punishments that are meted out'' to these women, punishments that ''give the impression that their creator is an active supporter and defender of the idea of women's natural subordination'' (92). She argues, however, that though Dickens punishes these women, he also seems to be questioning relationships of power.

From a gendered study of madness, we turn to a discussion of women's relationship with contamination. Contamination is a continuing theme in relation to Dickensian and other major Victorian texts. In ''Little Dorrit's 'speck' and Florence's 'daily blight,' '' Karl Smith considers the female heroine's interceding on questions of contamination. In *Bleak House*, he suggests that Dickens illustrates ''the religious inadequacy of merely discarding the stained'' and contaminated (150). Through a discussion of Little Dorrit's ''speck,'' he concludes that the ''environment and inherited blurred values can indeed contaminate character. Finding an effective means of transcending the stain becomes imperative'' (150). Little Dorrit, however, transcends the prison atmosphere, so that ''the need for forgiveness is even more important to Dickens than the (essential) willingness to restore what has been lost'' (128). She understands the ''transformed, *re*formed city'' (150). In *Dombey and Son*, Smith concludes that ''what is significant to Dickens in the work of Christ is his ability to deal with and purify that which is stained and not merely to sweep it out of sight'' (150). Smith's thesis is that the heroines of the texts uncover the ''goodness'' hidden within the contamination, thereby arguing that ''one's place in an interdependent universe does indeed have value, contradicting the message written in the surrounding dirt'' (150). Smith relies on much of the previous criticism on the environmental connection to a character's morals, especially the idea that filth ''create[s] social, as well as physical harm'' and that ''polluted air poisons minds as well as bodies'' (119). The question he discusses is whether the female heroines can be contaminated by their environment, and he points out that there are strong implications that dirt sticks; however, he concludes that Florence remains unsullied and Little Dorrit transcends her ''speck.'' The role of the daughter within the family hierarchy explains this conclusion: ''Yet in the Dickensian narrative, as in other Victorian stories, the daughter embraces this dirtiness on the father's behalf in order to restore a clearly defined network of relationships denied by paternal isolationism'' (134). By taking on the ''redemptive task of assuming responsibility,'' Amy and Florence assure that reconciliation is achieved, the ''inadequacies of the self-contained father's house'' are exposed, and the connections among all members of society are acknowledged (134).

Dickensian Style

In 2004, studies of Dickensian linguistic style have covered some familiar ground, including Pickwickian language, as well as possible connections between Dickensian and Joycean language. Pilar Orero, providing another foray into Wellerisms, and Peter Wilson, with his discussion of Jinglese, look at the more specific character speech patterns of two Pickwick characters, with Peter Wilson's discussion of James Joyce's Leopold Bloom setting the stage for Ira B. Nadel's emphasis on Dickens's influence on Joyce's style. Of particular interest, however, is the helpful monograph provided by Masahiro Hori, entitled, *Investigating Dickens' Style*, which provides a wonderfully thorough exploration of Dickens's creative use of collocations or word-groups.

Starting with "Edward Lear's Wellerisms," Pilar Orero explores the connections between Dickensian creation of "Wellerisms" and their influence on Edward Lear. While noting that they never met, Orero observes that Edward Lear and Dickens reveal many biographical similarities, and he remarks that they also shared an interest in presentation of speech. Lear, who is still in print, is considered the "best representative of Nonsense Literature" (287). This sets the stage for Orero's discussion of the possible shared influence between Dickens and Lear. Wellerisms, as Wolfgang Mieder and Stewart A. Kingsbury propose, are a type of proverb based on a three-part structure: the statement (often a moral or proverb), followed by the identification of the speaker, and ending with the ironic or humorous shift that illustrates the context of the situation: "Prevention is better than cure, said the pig, when it ran away from the butcher" (290). What Wellerisms ultimately did was upset the moral of the story through humor. The moral part could also be broken down into three effects—challenging the initial moral, providing a social context, and then also a pun. Orero notes that Lear's nonsense literature was influenced by *Pickwick Papers* and that Dickens was likely in turn influenced by Lear. The subversive potential of the Wellerisms is the most interesting part of this article, though this has been discussed. The possibility of Dickens's and Lear's shared influence is not directly illustrated, though it is interesting to think of ways in which each shades the work of the other.

More interesting, perhaps, is Peter Wilson's exploration of the influence Dickens might have exerted over James Joyce's language. In "The Corpus of Jinglese," Wilson complements Orero's discussion by considering the language of another Pickwickian character, this time Alfred Jingle. Wilson's paper looks at the "nature of . . . brokenness [in Jinglese language], its distribution and discernible categories" (78). Stating that Jingle's speech is unique—not marked with orthographic indicators of dialect—critics have argued that the brokenness of his speech has been considered to be disjointed but intelligible. Wilson builds upon this by noting Jingle's telegraphic ellipsis, which is "characterized by paratactic strings of single noun phrases usually not part of any subject-predicate structure, widespread omission of so-called function words and fragmentation not recoverable from the linguistic context" (79). What Wilson concludes about telegraphic ellipsis is that understanding is "dependent upon the situation context" (79). After studying the Jinglese corpus, Wilson concludes that 88% of the time, Jingle engages in syntactically incomplete expression. Though most often context can help fill in the gaps, there are times when the context cannot recover the text, but, as Wilson observes, Dickens never allows Jingle to go entirely misunderstood; indeed, the other characters in *Pickwick Papers* seem to understand him well. Some critics have argued that the text is understandable when read and not so much when spoken; Dickens, Wilson argues, did not let this cloud understanding in the text itself for characters.

Wilson goes on to argue that Jingle prefigures Joycean language. Leopold Bloom and Jingle engage in the same manner of ellipsis, though more aspects of the text remain unrecoverable from the linguistic context for Bloom than Jingle. Moreover, the interiority of Bloom's narrative does not match Jingle's. However, "Jingle can be seen to prefigure Bloom in the syntax of what is expressed, in the formal residual structures of speech and thought representations" (91). Wilson asks if there is an intermediary between Jingle and Bloom, another text that furthers the possible linguistic connections between these two characters.

Ira B. Nadel seems to be responding in " 'Nightplots.' " Nadel presents Dickens's *Our Mutual Friend*'s as an anticipation of Joyce's *Finnegans Wake*—perhaps not a prefiguring of Bloom, then, but certainly a link between Joyce and Dickens. Recounting Joyce's admiration of Dickens and stating that direct references to *Our Mutual Friend* are frequent in *Finnegans Wake*, Nadel turns his most useful critical attention to Dickens's conception of language as the important link. Wilson, citing the "complex power of words" and the "heteroglossia of books and documents" as elements that set the stage for Joyce's later work, describes a number of linguistic similarities: both Dickens and Joyce thematically address the textualized self and illustrate the "decomposition and recombination of language" (79). What language reveals is its inability to convey meaning. We see this in ways that Dickens and Joyce manipulate language—the frequent name changes, the inability of characters to read, the oral sense of language, and particularly the structural element of riddles. Observing that Joyce's use of riddles has been examined, Nadel argues that riddles have not been applied as thoroughly to a study of *Our Mutual Friend*. In *All the Year Round*, Dickens published riddles by contributors, and he also used riddles in his personal correspondence. As

Nadel points out, *Our Mutual Friend* begins with a riddle in the serial and first editions. Moreover, the reader must work to understand the riddles in the text: "For Dickens as well as Joyce, riddles interrogate language," and some characters serve as "articulators" who work to solve the riddles (82). Other linguistic devices Nadel attributes to Dickens that prefigure Joyce's techniques are the "fragmented rendition of words and . . . [the] use of initials" (82), misspellings, and insertions of visual texts. Nadel argues that it is the linguistic "fragmentation of the body" that links the two texts the most (85).

Though critics have argued that Dickens's prose illustrates his great authorial control over the language of his characters, George Goodin, in "Margins of Conversation in the Dialogue of Dickens," suggests that such rhetoric calls attention to the characters as well. Goodin argues that the speech becomes a "way of doing" for the characters and a "way of getting on with the narrative" for Dickens (171), a point perhaps proven more substantially by some of the results in Masahiro Hori's collocational analysis. Like Wilson, Goodin observes that Dickens's characters speak in "glitches and breakdowns much more often than do other novelists.' 'False starts, self-corrections, uptake problems, and infelicitous speech acts occur commonly in real conversation but uncommonly in most novels" (171). Goodin relies upon several theorists to forward a thesis on the rules of logical conversation and to discuss Dickens's appropriation and transformation of those rules: Paul Grice, who argues that conversation is based on cooperative rules and conversational maxims, such things as "truthfulness, informativeness, economy, relevance, and perspicuity" (172); Herbert Clark and Susan Haviland, who see Grice's discussion of cooperative principle as a social contract, governed by the "maxim of antecedence," in which one constructs one's speech in relation to a direct antecedent (173); and Robin Lakoff's understanding of politeness, which requires that speech is clear and polite without imposition, is open to options, and makes the other party comfortable and happy. Goodin claims that in all cases such speech is open to "flouting"—where gaps are left in speech and other missteps occur so that speech is momentarily left in doubt (173). Goodin asserts that Dickens "relied on these three sets of conversational rules to develop three of his most common character types. Bullies seek conversational dominance by minimizing their cooperation. . . . Muddlers use various forms of incoherence. Con artists offer pseudo familiarity, hoping to receive real intimacy from their victims" (174–75). Goodin's bullies, with Eugene Wrayburn as an example, use stage-based language, such as echoing the person they wish to bully, as a means of providing an "antithetic reinterpretation of others" but also to disguise "a deeper self" (176). His muddlers, like Mrs. Nickleby, may muddle for defensive purposes or for more sinister effect.

And his con artists, exemplified in Carker, use "self-depreciation and flattery" to build trust and intimacy (178). In this way, Goodin provides a rubric for understanding the fits and starts that characterize Dickensian style.

Masahiro Hori's *Investigating Dickens' Style* is an important addition to studies of Dickensian stylistic devices and particularly to the discussion of collocations within Dickens's oeuvre. Because of the development of projects such as COBUILD (the Bank of English), Hori is able to provide an analysis of Dickens's collocation style in relation to other authors of the eighteenth and nineteenth centuries. John E. Joseph's foreword to the book highlights three major contributions to stylistic study that Hori offers: (1) the focus on collocations (word-groups that are a part of a closely connected unit) rather than on word or sentence analysis; (2) the methodological development of studying "corpus data, linguistic analysis and stylistic interpretation" (xiii); and (3) the focus on specific character stylistic elements, or the "voice" of the speaker. Joseph's foreword emphasizes some of the most interesting and useful portions of Hori's text.

Starting with an overview of the history of collocational research, a developing field of analysis in linguistics, Hori provides a study of some of the familiar and creative collocations that Dickens uses in his texts, followed by an in-depth analysis of collocations in *Bleak House*. Hori gives particular attention to the individualization of characters on the basis of collocations (for instance, "blue" and "eye," when associated with each other, generally identify a positive characteristic); the "typification" of characters by profession, region, social position, and other elements (for instance, Joe's "smith's eye" in *Great Expectations* or Mr. Lorry's "business eye" in *A Tale of Two Cities*); the structural use of language or the manner in which the collocations compare across characters (for instance, the use of eye in relation to Dora versus Agnes, which reveals comparisons between characters and indicates David's personal growth); and finally, the experimental use of collocation (for instance, animals used in relation to eyes to describe characters, such as Rob the Grinder's "ferret eyes" in *Dombey and Son* or Miss Murdstone's "Dragon's eye" in *David Copperfield*). When analyzing these materials, Hori relied on two methods to measure the commonness or uniqueness of the collocation: the use of native informants and comparisons to the database of electronic texts of the eighteenth and nineteenth centuries. The first method, Hori notes, is unreliable since contemporary native informants do not exist in the some contextual moment as the Dickensian constructions; however, the electronic databases can serve as a control for this problem.

The Dickens corpus that Hori worked with contains 4.6 million words. In this, Hori found that Dickens used the word "gentleman" much more often than his contemporaries; moreover, he has a higher frequency of referring to body parts. Interestingly enough, the word "love" had a "much lower frequency'' for Dickens than for his contemporaries (38). Hori then studies the nature of these collocations, looking at nouns, adjectives, and adverbs in collocation with other parts of speech—the noun ''gentleman,'' for instance, is most often collocated with ''old'' or ''young'' (39). Some of the collocations indicate gendered readings, such as ''great'' often collocated with a man but only once with woman in the case of Madame DeFarge (42). Hori looks also at semantic ''prosodies,'' the indication that ''some words not only have particular collocates but also that these connect more broadly across certain semantic groups'' (53). An example of a Dickensian semantic prosody can be found in his use of ''heartily'' with terms such as ''laugh'' or ''thank.'' This is a positive collocation, whereas Dickens's contemporaries were more inclined to create negative collocations of ''heartily''—with ''hate'' or ''despise'' (53). He also refers to colligations, which are defined as ''grammatical company a word keeps and the positions it prefers'' (qtd. in Hori 54). For instance, Dickens tended to connect ''heartily'' with intensive adverbs, such as ''very'' and ''so'' (55).

Dickensian creative collocations are varied and many. Metaphorical collocations are found in Dickens's frequent and unusual use of ''business-like'' with a noun or his well-known use of ''fog'' plus behavioral terms such as ''creeping'' (61, 67). Transferred collocations occur when a term's modification is misplaced: in the reference to Peggotty's ''honest forehead,'' for example, the word ''honest'' modifies ''forehead'' grammatically but Peggotty literally. Dickens used this style readily with body parts (69). Oxymoronic collocations refer to the collocation of two terms understood to be antonyms, such as William Dorrit's ''amiably distraught'' state in *Little Dorrit* (81). Modified idiomatic collocations are a unique stylistic device to Dickens. This includes creatively modifying idioms through substitution, expansion, abbreviation, or rephrasing. Hori also considers disparate, unconventional, parodic, and relexicalized collocations. After this, he describes a number of Dickensian neologisms and discusses the impact Dickens had on the spread of slang.

The final part of Hori's text turns to *Bleak House* to pinpoint the particular use of collocations within the text in relation to the first-person narration of Esther Summerson and the omniscient, third-person narrator. There are a few of Hori's discoveries especially worthy of note. First, critics have suggested that the third-person narrator's portions are more linguistically creative; however, Hori's collocation study reveals that the use of creative collocations occurs only slightly more often with the third-person narrator than with Esther, demonstrating that Esther is a ''linguistically experimental'' narrator as well (170). One noted difference is that Esther tends to modify her comments of characters less frequently, thereby behaving in a noninvasive manner, whereas the third-person narrator controls his narration more fully. When comparing Esther to Dickens's other first-person narrators, Pip and David Copperfield, Hori finds that Esther tends to allow her characters to speak more on their own, and Pip does so the least. He also presents some interesting comparisons among their uses of collocations: "My own" tends to be collated with words like "room" for Esther, "room" or "heart" for David, and negative terms for Pip, such as "ingratitude" (191). Hori ends with a discussion of new compound words presented in *Bleak House*, estimating that there are 201 new terms with first citations in Dickens.

Public Readings

Public performances attracted great interest this year in *Dickens Quarterly*, with one article considering Dickens's "set" and two others unearthing public performances that used Dickens as their subject. The first, by Malcolm Andrews, "The 'Set' for Charles Dickens's Public Readings," traces the development of Dickens's presentation of self and his set as he attempts to balance the more domestic coziness of a private reading with the public performances that would be a major part of his career. As Andrews argues, "to trace the evolution of that 'set' is to sense this tension between the two milieux as well as to understand the nature of the relationship Dickens tried to fashion with his audience" (211). Dickens's public readings amounted to a third career for him, in which he earned over 45,000, the equivalent of 2 million today. Andrews observes that Dickens wanted to master the art of public Reading, and excel in it (212). He stood rather than sat, he insisted that no one stand behind him or at his sides, and he wanted to be seen clearly from all points in the hall. All of these factors contributed to concerns about how to arrange the desk, the platform, the acoustics, and the lighting. Determined to be separated from his audience spatially, he manipulated the theatrical device of the stage to bring the audience closer to him, relying not solely on his skills as a storyteller and performer. Dickens was known to be fussy about his stage. As Andrews argues, "the whole arrangement testifies to the fastidiousness and iron control exercised by Dickens in maximizing the effect of these performances" (222). In time, the color he worked with was a rich maroon, so that "the back-screen, rug, and Reading Desk . . . increased the distinctiveness of the Reader" (222–23). Andrews argues that this color must have "kindled a warmth of response . . . he was the fire. The lustrous glow of the set, the warmth of his personality as narrator, the iridescent virtuosity of his impersonations, the sheer blaze of energy throughout the performance raised the temperature of a Dickens Reading" (223).

The use of public reading extended to those who selected Dickens as their subject, with the American Kate Field presenting lectures on her view of

Dickens's public readings in the United States, and with Harry Furniss employing Dickens's public performances, as well as the revival of interest in Dickens, to define Englishness. Gary Scharnhorst, in "Kate Field's 'An Evening with Charles Dickens,' " notes that "in her heyday, Field was the most prominent American woman journalist of the period" (84). A contributor to the *Atlantic Monthly*, she was, as Scharnhorst comments, "also a popular lecturer and prolific travel writer for a number of newspapers during the 1860s and '70s" (84). Field edited and published her own paper, *Kate Field's Washington*, and she wrote "an estimated three thousand newspaper and magazine articles during her career" (84). She was an avid fan of Dickens and attended the majority of his performances given in Boston, New York, and Philadelphia, from December 1867 through January 1868. Her fame as a Dickensian was established when she set out on the lecture circuit with her performance, "An Evening with Charles Dickens." Between 1870 and 1871, she presented talks on Dickens over a hundred times. No manuscript of this lecture survives; however, Scharnhorst provides a reconstructed version of the speech drawn from eyewitness accounts made available in texts such as the *Boston Daily Advertiser*, *New York Times*, *Missouri Republican*, and *Kate Field's Washington*.

Scharnhorst's recreation of Field's speech reveals a great fan memorializing Dickens and responding to critics who question his characters' use of alcohol (an issue Gareth Cordery addresses in an article on *David Copperfield* and drink) and his representations of the church (an issue that Natalie Bell Cole discusses in an article on the Dickensian material church). However, it is Field's discussion of Dickens's women that is the most interesting. She states that critics argue that "Dickens never yet drew a woman" (81). Drawing comparisons with similar complaints made against Shakespeare, she states, "If Shakespeare's and Dickens's men play the more prominent part, is there no reason for it? Drama and novel demand action, and the sphere of man up to this year, being broader, gives to him the greater variety of character. Neither writer dreamed of the 'coming woman,' but shall they be reviled for this?" (81–82). In many ways, she prefigures the critical debates I mentioned earlier about the degree to which one can criticize a writer for accepting the common values of his or her time. What is interesting to see, of course, is that Dickens's contemporaries make these similar arguments. The comparison to Shakespeare runs throughout, as is expected in a speech that seeks to establish Dickens as the national representation of England. Field's talk ends with a reference to Dickens's love of truth, which she argues is greater than Shakespeare's.

Gareth Cordery's two-part article "Harry Furniss and the 'Boom in Boz' " considers Furniss's role in helping to shape the Dickensian revival at the turn of the nineteenth century. As Pierre Coustillas has noted, the 1890s marked the lowest point in Dickens's reception among critics, some of whom saw him as "gutterly," "merely fantastic," and "merely antique" (qtd. in Cordery 91). Despite this, popular feeling was in Dickens's camp, with formations of the Boz Club in 1900 and the Dickens Fellowship in 1902, and with the wide circulation of his books from public libraries. Furniss becomes a part of this debate with his 1910 limited edition of Dickens's works, which was "tailored to middle class preoccupations with book collecting and sold as much to look impressive on the shelf as to be read" (92). The books were an investment and signal the commodification of Dickens, who "was produced, packaged, and marketed as a particular brand of Englishness . . . " (92). Ultimately, Cordery argues that Furniss's text does not add much to our knowledge or interpretation of Dickens: "There is considerable repetition of conventional wisdom" (99), but his significance is in his role as a Dickensian revivalist. Why, Cordery asks, did this revival take place at the turn of the century? The answer, he asserts, is that the revival served as a compensation for the Empire's decline, made evident in events like the Boer War. But it also helped to create a brand new Englishness built upon the revised Dickens. Chesterton's Dickensian Christmas, with its references to cozy domesticity, as well as J. Cuming Walter's comments in his address "Dickens's Influence on National Character" set the stage for this political, propagandistic revival of the "humane, moral and cosily domestic Dickens" as a "rallying call" during a time of national crisis (144). Cordery argues that Furniss's agenda was even more nationalistic and was marked by a decided embracing of everything understood to be mid-Victorian, at the same time as it was being denounced elsewhere. Cordery further asserts that "what Dickens provided for the pro-Victorians at the turn of the century was a confirmation of nationhood through a vast stock of instantly recognizable characters" (147). The merging of Dickensian types with Shakespearean types illustrates the degree to which Dickens was equated with Englishness: "In a little known and short-lived weekly magazine founded and edited by Furniss called *Lika Joko* after his *Punch* sobriquet, Fred Barnard drew for a series called 'The Shakespeare-Dickens Combination Company' twenty 'Shakespearean characters as played by well-known Dickens Stars,' " which appeared between November 1894 and February 1895 (149). Illustrations are provided in the article. These images add force to Cordery's argument and indicate the extent to which Dickens's conflation with Shakespeare sets the stage for the co-opting of Dickens's nationalist agendas, a trend that went well into the twentieth century.

Dickensian Scriptures: Secular, Spiritual, and Scientific

The title of this section is drawn from Vincent Newey's study *The Scriptures of Charles Dickens,* which is not a book about Dickens and canonical scripture. Indeed, Newey's text provides a broad range of definitions of scripture through the merging of spiritual and secular philosophical approaches. In his introduction, Newey describes his basic theories: namely, Dickens's ambivalent responses to both orthodox and humanist principles; his search for "order and value in individuals rather than in any overarching institution"; his use of characters to negotiate the existential struggle and the struggle with society; and his development of an "experiential reader engagement," in which the reader participates in the performance of the moral and ethical questions of the texts (2–3). The "Dickensian epiphany," as Newey calls it, is the recognition of literature's role in building the canon of secular scripture: " 'the Novel made Word' " (3). Newey's text presents a range of Dickensian scriptures that mutually support but also simultaneously conflict with each other. Newey also calls upon Louis Althusser's concept of "interpellation," the instillation of ideology within an individual and his or her accompanying performance of that ideology. As Newey notes, Dickens's provided great insight into the individual as a function of the system, and Dickens himself was interpellated into ideological systems; however, Newey argues that there is "never a single ideology in play but a plurality" (9). Newey offers "extrapellation," a process of sitting on the outside, establishing an external critical perspective on the ideology under question. Newey rejects, however, Althusser's ordered individuals who are robotic in their following of the system, and he places that pattern in contrast to Dickens's "dysfunctional field," in which individuals are never fully interpellated into any system (11).

To establish Dickens's position within this dysfunctional field, Newey states a number of Dickensian critical truisms. He notes that Dickens had radical tendencies but, as we know, was not a revolutionary. Though orthodox religion was displaced in his texts, he still retained in his ethical views "the structure of subordination and layered mutuality" (6). He may have "democratized the cast list of the novel," but he ultimately expected his poor characters to be poor and happy within that state (7). Newey also states that Dickens was focused on connection—the empathy and sympathy that embraces even the most outcast—which is "a quintessential benison of the Dickensian secular scripture" (12), and that Dickens struggled with his fascination with social ascendancy and with the under classes. Indeed, these are standard assertions in Dickensian analysis, and yet what Newey does with these assertions is complicated, thorough, and full of rich approaches to the text. He provides lengthy close readings of *A Christmas Carol*, *Oliver Twist*, *David Copperfield*, *Great Expectations*, and *Our Mutual Friend*. He refers to John Milton and John Bunyan perhaps the most in the text, though he also mentions Thomas Hughes and a host of Dickens's other contemporaries. Newey relies on theoretical positions offered by Michel Foucault, Louis Althusser, Edward Said, and others, but most of all, the text is a nuanced character analysis that places the characters in relationship with each other, with the systems they are interpellated into, and with the "epiphanies" of extrapellation that they practice.

The space here does not allow me time to explore thoroughly his argument; however, I will mention a number of points that I found very interesting. I will begin where Newey begins, with Scrooge. Despite rejecting the overarching power of a God, Dickens retains the idea of a structured universe built upon a naturally occurring hierarchy. In this case, Scrooge is still the master, but this time a kinder one. Dickens's commitment to reforms in education does not contradict his continued support of this hierarchy. In his rehabilitation, "Scrooge not only enacts the appropriate roles and relationships of a flourishing and orderly society, he mutates at last into a composite image of them, an icon within a larger bourgeois iconography" (47). This is seen in John Leech's illustration of Scrooge entertaining Bob Cratchit, who sits meek and mild, like a good schoolboy. Christmas itself, with its charity, becomes also the "exception that proves the rule of customary rift and bleak indifference" (49). Scrooge's reclamation, then, can also be understood within the framework of falling from grace and the perpetual struggle to regain it. For Bunyan, as Newey notes, conversion was never complete. Like a recovered addict, Scrooge must bring himself under restraint and practice an abstinence, which encourages us to reread Newey's earlier suggestions that Scrooge's unhappiness and isolation may also be a product of his possible homosexuality. This practiced restraint brings new meaning to the urge to live Christmas every day—less as a calling to do good acts than as a condemnation to perform them. After all, as Newey observes, we remember the miserly Scrooge more fully than we ever remember his redeemed self. And though we might "rejoice in his rescue from the brink," we may "yet have an interest in his brinkmanship" (55).

Throughout the text, we are more frequently introduced to Newey's discussion of the humanizing features of hated characters: Bumble's tear for Oliver and Murdstone's bereavement. This is a "bedrock of the Dickensian 'secular scripture.' A counterpart of biblical exhortation, it functions to humanize perception through a recall to feeling and is one of the main reasons why we should still read Dickens" (68). This sympathy extends to even the most reviled characters; in Bill Sikes's flight and isolation, we feel sympathy for him, evidenced in the actions of his dog. But, of course, this is not extended to Fagin. His Jewishness excludes him, whereas the bull dog Englishness of Sikes evokes some sympathy. Dickens only attempts to redeem Fagin later in life in his writing of Mr. Riah. A more complicated analysis of these reversals of character is presented in relation to Uriah Heep, who Newey argues, functions as a double of David. Heep is the externalization of David's desires—his desire for Agnes and class advancement. Orlick functions in this way for Pip in *Great Expectations*, especially in the desire to harm his sister.

Even Orlick claims that Pip has done it. The ambivalent restraint of goodness finds expression for darker sides in these doppelgangers. Bradley Headstone, Newey argues, like Mr. Riah for Fagin, is Dickens's attempt at moderating the representations of Heep and Orlick. He is treated seriously and with respect, but the social climber is not yielded an inch. Nevertheless, Newey still elevates Sikes over even Headstone. Sikes remains the figure that fulfills to a limited degree the desire to "define and transgress cultural limits. Headstone simply unsettles presuppositions" (259). Newey also suggests that Eugene Wrayburn provides a reconsidered Steerforth in *David Copperfield* and James Harthouse in *Hard Times*. In this way, Newey's argument illustrates that the characters are rarely stable and are often in conversation with each other cross-textually. What results is the Dickensian scripture of uncovering sympathy where none might be thought to exist.

Newey's discussion of *Great Expectations* is also worthy of extended attention. Newey sees this text as Dickens's "richest and most complex . . . Puritan spiritual autobiography" (183). Starting with *Tom Brown's Schooldays,* Newey argues that Pip is a Tom Brown character—evident in his first fight with Herbert—and he, too, must struggle towards " 'manfulness and thoughtfulness' " (qtd. in Newey 177). If fighting is a condition of the world, as Hughes suggestions, then Pip, in Dickens, must also learn to fight honorably, but his position as an outsider complicates this. Pip must also learn sympathy, as exemplified by Joe. In Joe we see the qualities of the gentleman; however, in doing this, Dickens places the rules of social hierarchy under some strain. Yet Joe is decidedly constructed as someone who would never question those rules. Pip's journey is also theorized through Freud's notion of "abreacting" or working through the material that is brought to attention (190). This is paired with " 'acting out,' where the patient compulsively repeats repressed material in displaced or symbolic form" (195). See Orlick's attack mentioned above. Because of this, we can never fully trust Pip in his narrative—what is a symbolic "acting out" and what is not? And because Pip does not work through his material, "Pip is looking for an easy ride" (201). Newey argues that Pip's embracing of a work ethic in exile brings him back, but not as completely as David Copperfield's return. Running concurrent with this discussion is Newey's observations on the masochistic sexual frustration between Orlick and Mrs. Joe, the fiery punishment reserved for Miss Havisham and not imposed on Scrooge, the reformation of Estella through a "good" beating, and the implication that young Pip may be Pip's child. Newey ends with a discussion of *Our Mutual Friend.*

These secular scriptures that Newey discusses emerge in different shapes and forms in other critical studies this year. In " 'Amen in a Wrong Place,' " Natalie Bell Cole begins with a provocative question, "How, Dickens asks, can we apply Christian ethics to social practices within and beyond the material church, even as most churches cease to be vital locations for practices of faith and worship?'' (205). With special attention to the essays in *The Uncommercial Traveller,* Cole looks at Dickens's interpretation of religion through a discussion of representations of the material church, the primary dilemma being the ''compulsion to visit the church site coupled with a confusion about what is sought there'' (205). Cole writes that at this time the meaning of the church was undergoing dramatic transformation. In the church, Dickens uncovers a ''rich trope for the paradoxes of Victorian life: vitality persisting in the face of decay, permanence altered by change, theatricality contesting with earnestness, the wonder and threat of urban spaces that dislocate tradition, yet yearn for the transcendent'' (205). Despite Dickens's reluctance to place overtly religious elements in his texts, Cole notes that his representations of church and faith illuminate his struggle with these issues. Contemporary reviews, particularly those in the evangelical and the Catholic press, were highly critical of Dickens's perceived failure to use ''doctrinal language,'' his absence of church attendance in his texts, and his emphasis on ''benevolence without religion'' (207).

''Amen in a wrong place'' refers to Dickens's 1860 ''City of London Churches'' essay, in which he provides a ''parabolic reading of the interplay of decaying churches, vitiated faith, and persistent human vitality'' (207). An exhausted congregation is energized by the play of children, sparking the distracted clergyman to interpret the children's playful interruption as an ''amen in a wrong place'' (207). Cole argues, that ''a metaphoric 'amen in a wrong place' pervades Dickens's canon, as he reiterates a fatigued practice of faith and laments the scarcity of 'true, practical Christianity' within the institutional church'' (207). Dickens's representation of the urban church, depicted as caught up in debates about ''doctrinal differences'' and drawn to ''vanity and wealth,'' is placed in contrast with his vision of the village church, which he valorized for its connection with the natural world; however, as Cole notes, even the village church is spoken of in elegiac tones (210). In contrast, an ''amen in the right place'' is illustrated in *Dombey and Son.* Florence's wedding ceremony serves as the ''necessary corrective to the previous wedding of commodity-driven exchange,'' represented in her father's wedding. Cole argues that this is Dickens's illustration of ''*Amens* in the right place,'' which come from ''human goodwill and genuine practices of faith that make up in strong feeling what they lack in shallow form'' (213).

Dickens's ''amen in the right place'' is performed by Stephen Roose Hughes in ''The Shipwreck'' from *The Uncommerical Traveller.* In Hughes, who takes care of the survivors and of the bodies of the drowned victims of the *Royal Charter* shipwreck, Dickens describes a clergyman focused on a reverence for humankind in life and in death, and he depicts a church literally transformed to honor those lives—the pulpit itself removed to make room for the dead. Hughes, Cole argues, is Dickens's example of the ''Christian

man as worker, detective, survivor, and consoler, with no concomitant feminization'' (227). Cole's reading of this issue is much subtler than this, however,
and she looks at several interesting interpretations of St. Paul's Cathedral
and a discussion of the church as "always becoming," in line with Julian
Wolfrey's observations on the city as becoming. She reflects on Dickens's
satirization of hypocritical evangelical speakers and a number of other subjects, but it is her mapping of the metaphor of the "amen in a wrong place"
transformed into an "amen in the right pace" that makes her essay an interesting addition to discussions of Dickensian scriptures in 2004.

Another potential Dickensian scripture is offered by Jennifer Gribble in
"Why the Good Samaritan was a Bad Economist." Gribble argues that imaginatively inhabiting the place of another, or the moral of the Good Samaritan
parable, becomes a central trope in Dickens's *Hard Times*. It is interesting to
see a Dickensian scripture of sorts emerging in his use of the Good Samaritan
and also the Mary and Martha parables; however, I am not sure this reading
provides a new point of entry into the basic analysis of the text. Furthermore,
her observation that Dickens's interest in the Good Samaritan has not been
fully explored due to postmodernism's "repression" of the Bible is just an
unsubstantiated assertion in spite of the footnote reference she provides (428).
While writing *Hard Times*, Dickens, according to Gribble, had these thoughts
of empathy on his mind, particularly in relation to questions of education.
She notes that "what Dickens finds in the Good Samaritan parable is a story
in which the outgoing and self-transcending impulses in human nature have
the power to confront the stereotyping assumptions that derive from class,
gender, and ideology" (433). She posits Bounderby as a "perverse Samaritan" (434) and Mrs. Sparsit as "a malign Samaritan" (435). Against this,
Blackpool is positioned as the fallen victim that the Samaritan stops to help.
Bitzer, on the other hand, is situated as the good economist who makes a bad
Samaritan. In this parable, Gribble feels that the moral actions of the individual are brought to the fore, since "the Samaritan acts counter-culturally,
effecting a decision about the meaning of self, other and moral action [that]
the novel affirms as the proper ground of all moral action and communal
well-being" (439).

Helen Small's "The Bounded Life: Adorno, Dickens, and Metaphysics,"
provides an interesting analysis of metaphysical concerns in *The Old Curiosity Shop* through a study of Theodor Adorno's early and later reflections on
the boundedness of life. This Dickensian scripture focuses on the difficulty
of thinking about the limitations of existence. Small presents Adorno's struggle with the "temporal, biological limit on lives" (547). She explores those
boundaries—between life and death and between the physical and metaphysical. Reading the older Adorno, found in his *Metaphysics: Concepts and Problem,* which emphasizes the power of age against his younger counterpart,

found in his writing on *The Old Curiosity Shop*, Small looks at how attention to aging and impending death provides a critical approach to life. Small similarly considers Adorno's thoughts on the failure of modern culture to incorporate death, which pushes us towards the temptation of metaphysics as a "mere survivalist need" (550). She concludes that Adorno's agenda presses metaphysics further: "The wish to think the possibility of transcendence, of immortality, of something beyond the physical, becomes at that point no longer merely a panicked reflex of modernity, but the means to imaging the potential freedom of thought" (550).

Small then turns to Adorno's earlier discussion of *The Old Curiosity Shop* and the relationship between the grandfather and Little Nell. Because of editing decisions which removed a Lear-like moment for the grandfather, Dickens establishes an impossible separation of old age from youth with the old man associated with objects and Nell seeming to promise "something beyond this bounded existence" (554). The "spirituality of children" comes to the fore, and Small notes that this might even be seen in the dropping of Old Master Humphrey as the narrator, though Elizabeth Palmberg, in an essay to be noted later, suggests market factors. Small maintains that we might read the killing of children in light of their service and guardianship as an indication of what might follow. Dickens's anxiety at the death of Mary Hogarth is referenced, and Small concludes that Dickens in his letters "confronted his own mortality, and the boundedness of his own life and thought, in the dialectical opposition between the old age toward which he felt himself to be slowly growing, and the young girl he would like to have believed might rescue him from the promised end" (557). The paradox is in the hope of a future and the proof of the boundedness of existence. Against these readings, Small posits comic alternatives and resistances present in "Pickwickian" elements in which children are protected by the comic. Noting Adorno's comments on the limitations of comedy, however, Small writes that, "comedy, in the single work of art, is only a way of shoring up our boundaries, not a way of putting them seriously to the test of thought" (561). By taking mortality away from the old and by giving it to the young who are not immediately pressed by the boundaries of life, Dickens suggests a hope limited by its circular movement back to children. This reading, then, embraces Adorno's "definitive predicament of metaphysics: trying to save what at the same time it destroys" (561).

Robert J. Heaman, in "Hebraism and Hellenism in *Our Mutual Friend*," applies Matthew Arnold's theories discussed in *Culture and Anarchy* to *Our Mutual Friend*. The secular scripture is promised in Arnold's Hellenism. Beginning with an examination of Riah as a "positive" Jewish character created in response to concerns about his negative representation of Fagin, Heaman suggests that critics have been mixed in their interpretation of Mr.

Riah's character. Using Jonathan H. Grossman's observations, Heaman sees "the representation of Riah as Dickens's *successful* 'attempt not to depict a Jew, but rather to represent the impossibility of doing so' '' (3). Heaman also states that the marriage of Eugene and Lizzie "represents, for Dickens, an emblem of what Matthew Arnold believes must be done to correct the misdirection of culture in Britain at this time" (4). Thus, the analysis of Riah's Jewishness needs to be understood within a framework that places Hebraism against Hellenism. For Heaman, Riah is *"intentionally"* stereotyped in order to "make a larger point than correcting an impression made by the representation of Fagin in *Oliver Twist*, important as that may be" (4). The rivalry that Arnold identifies between the impulses of "spontaneity of consciousness" in Hellenism and the "strictness of consciousness" found in Hebraism is evident in Dickens's embracing of the need for a "return to Hellenism as the answer to England's cultural crisis" (5–6). Riah is identified with the "stereotypically Hebraic past," which leads some critics, like Goldie Morgentaler, to see him as a "collective stereotyped whole" (6). Eugene is a stereotype as well, this time of indolent Hellenism. Heaman sees Eugene as "immobilized," but later finding clarity through Lizzie's beauty, which saves him (9). Heaman claims that for Dickens, the time is not right for Mr. Riah, but that it is the time for England to embrace an awakened Hellenism found in the reformed Eugene.

Moving from a discussion of Dickensian scriptures, we turn to spiritualism proper in two articles by Louise Henson. Her "Investigations and Fictions" analyzes Dickens's role in the Victorian supernatural debate by looking at his journalistic responses to the scientific, medical, and theoretical conversations surrounding ghosts. As she notes, Dickens liked a ghost story and also played a primary role in its development in Victorian narrative; however, it is the skeptical Dickens that offers an interesting point of entry into "wide-ranging and sometimes fierce debates about the nature and authenticity of ghostly phenomena" (44). Through an analysis of varying responses to ghosts—from Catherine Crowe, Samuel Hibbert, David Brewster, to John Elliotson—Henson positions Dickens within the critical debates surrounding supernatural representation. Dickens was also known for his fascination with mesmerism, animal magnetism, and psychic sympathy. Henson observes that it is this element of the mind that is important to Dickens, and she illustrates that Dickens's interpretation of the subject, though naturalistic, is fairly nuanced. It is mainly her focus on the journalistic pieces more so than the narratives that makes for useful analysis. She notes that with the development of *Household Words*, Dickens showed interest in the authenticated ghost story but was more concerned with the role of mental phenomena. This agenda to "normalise the extraordinary powers of the mind continued in *ATYR* with a new theory of ghostly presentiment which was attributed to physiological impressions on the brain'' (53). Henson concludes that Dickens's ''position in the ghost controversy can thus be identified as a naturalistic one, although the explanations he endorsed relied on occult as well as known physical forces. Dickens's writings, those of his associates, and his adversaries, moreover, reveal how complex ideas and debates about the nature and origins of ghosts were before 1860'' (61).

Another version of similar arguments posed by Henson appears in her article, '' 'In the Natural Course of Physical Things,' '' which borrows heavily with complete repetitions of passages from the previous essay. One point of interest she adds, however, is the battle Dickens conducted with William Howitt and his Christian *Spiritual Magazine*. Howitt felt that Dickens's skeptical treatment failed to allow for supernatural explanations for ghosts. Dickens claimed that he himself was not prejudiced on the matter but had yet to have a ghost story proven to him. Howitt's theological explanation of such matters did not sit well with Dickens, and in his review of Howitt's *History of Spirituality*, he argues that ''Howitt's strong desire to believe in the supernatural caused him to accept the authenticity of the most suspicious incidents'' (120), which, of course, upset Howitt. And yet Dickens was cleverly claimed by the spiritualists as one of their own. His attendance at Hayden's séance and his printing a report of the ghostly encounter of Thomas Heaphy were used against Dickens, and he had to grapple with the fallout. The *Spiritual Magazine* noted that Dickens's skepticism was ''offset by the perpetual claim that he was in fact a secret sympathizer'' (122). Thus, Dickens's cautionary approach to ghost stories was subverted by Howitt, and Dickens's name was claimed by the spiritual press to further Howitt's agenda.

From spiritualism, we move to science in A. J. Larner's ''Dickens and Monboddo,'' a short article that looks at the Monboddo connection to Dickens's thinking on science and evolution. Larner argues that, contrary to George Orwell's opinion that Dickens did not possess a scientific mind, Dickens could have been interested in evolution as early as 1842, predating his review of Robert Hunt's *The Poetry of Science* where he begins ''to trace such influences'' (39). Dickens refers to Monboddo in chapter 1 of his novel, *Martin Chuzzlewit*. ''Monboddo's doctrine'' of language for apes suggests that they fail to speak not because they are incapable, but because they have not been taught to. Though Monboddo was labeled an evolutionist, Larner argues that Monboddo did not believe in evolution; rather, he believed in a ''divinely-ordained chain of being'' (37). By focusing on the potential for speech, Monboddo was arguing that humans and apes share similarities. Larner explores how Dickens came to know Monboddo's work through Boswell's *Life of Johnson*; moreover, there was a renewal of interest in Monboddo following Charles Darwin's publications, but, of course, this is after Dickens's *Chuzzlewit*, though it does precede *Our Mutual Friend*, which, informed by evolution, does not refer to Monboddo.

Herbert Sussman and Gerhard Joseph, in "Prefiguring the Posthuman," illustrate Dickens's ambivalence about the reconstruction of the human and the machine. Arguing that Dickens's novels reflect this ambivalence and uncertainty on the issues of ethical will and the human automaton, Sussman and Joseph turn to *Dombey and Son* for their evidence. Dickens's fiction offers an important view of the posthuman, particularly in relation to prosthesis, "as a trope for the hybridity of the modern world" (618). Victorians approach "prosthesis as material artifact and as metaphor" (618). Captain Cuttle is a frequently cited example of the posthuman, whose "combination of flesh, hard wood, and metal functions conjointly, like the wood and iron components of a power loom" (619). However, he is associated with benefi- cence in the text. The underlying contradiction in Dickens—that the mechani- cal as demonstrated in *Hard Times* has a human cost—is offset in his representation of this fused, posthuman subject in Cuttle. It appears that moral will is still exercised by Cuttle, Sussman and Joseph argue. There are other useful connections that Sussman and Joseph draw, including Major Bag- stock's cane utilized as a prosthetic extension with which he can torture his servant, or Toodle's brain functioning like a train engine in line with Bab- bage's Engine. It is in Cuttle and Toodle, however, that the "mechanical, fleshly, and mental parts of the self remain under the firm control of a free, autonomous individual subjectivity, the bourgeois liberal humanist subject. But if that is sometimes the case in Dickens, he also evokes the fear that within such a body the self-acting, self-governing component part may take over, may move beyond central control" (622). This is demonstrated in Cark- er's smile, which enacts a separate agency and independent will, thereby demonstrating "the fear of prosthesis or subsystem taking over control from the liberal subject or will" (623). Through an analysis of synecdoche and metonymy, Sussman and Joseph argue that in Carker's independent and con- comitantly managed teeth, one sees that "Dickensian prosthesis can move now in the direction of articulating a kind of carceral condition for nineteenth- century man, now in an articulation of his total freedom" (626). In their argument, Sussman and Joseph conclude that Dickens prefigures Freud's observation on the prosthetic man/god: " . . . a Dickensian prefiguration of precisely the Janus-faced condition recent theorists have attributed to that newest of fictions, the prosthetic man/god of *Civilization and Its Discontents* and of posthuman cyborg theory" (626).

Textual Studies

In this section, I use a rather loose definition of textual studies in order to include anything directly related to the production, destruction, and consump- tion of Dickensian texts. Therefore, this section will include essays on Dick- ens's relationship with plagiarism and copyright infringement, as well as an article on the burning of his letters. There are four essays which explore narration, one through Esther's first-person narrative perspective and another through Baktinian analysis, another through Hannah Crafts's borrowing of Dickensian narrative style, and yet another through the relationship between illustration and narration in *A Tale of Two Cities.* This section also includes an essay on texts as dangerous or, more specifically, literacy as dangerous. It turns to two essays that consider the commodification of textual practices within a consumer framework. Finally, it ends with an extratextual focus on the potentiality of narrative. Dickens's death left a rather significant hole in Edwin Drood's tale, and the final essay looks to critical responses as one way to stop that hole or at least organize all of the pieces slipping through it.

Paul Schlicke's "Dickens and the Pirates" considers Dickens's concern about international copyright laws. Schlicke's focuses on the pirate Henry Hetherington, who felt entirely justified in his raiding of Dickens's *Sketches by Boz,* which he reprinted in *The Odd Fellow,* a four-page weekly newspaper. After reprinting no. 37 of the sketches, the printing stopped, and Hetherington issued an apology. Appending a justification to the published apology, Hetherington notes that he feels his actions have actually increased the publicity for the piece due to his circulation, and that he, through his editorial comment, was grateful not to be facing legal charges, but appeared in some respects not particularly apologetic for his actions either. In Robert Hanna's two-part article on plagiarism, it is Dickens who stands accused in the popular press of being a plagiarist. When Dickens's comic opera *The Village Coquettes* was performed in 1836, a reviewer for the London *Sunday Times* suggested that it was a copy, and a bad one at that, of several other operas. Reviewers for others, such as *The Champion and Weekly Herald,* leveled similar charges. This issue surfaces again in *The Champion* and *The Magnet,* this time against Dickens's comic burletta, *Is She His Wife?* Hanna, through careful reading of the original texts, demonstrates that the charges were without merit. I would be interested to learn Dickens's reactions to these charges, but they are not discussed in the pieces.

Paul Lewis, in "Burning: The Evidence," explores the context surrounding Dickens's burning of his letters, first at Gad Hill Place on September 3, 1860, and periodically afterwards. Lewis observes that the "eyewitness" accounts of the burning were false and offers a discussion of who really must have witnessed the burning and what might have motivated Dickens's action. The account of the bonfire entered public discourse not with Forster's *Life,* but, ironically, with the publication of the first edition of Dickens's letters in 1880. For 70 years, only this correspondence provided information on the burning. However, Gladys Storey's 1939 book, *Dickens and Daughter,* discusses Dickens's daughter Kate's recollections of the fire—but these memories come from a Kate who was well advanced in years and were recorded by an author who did not publish the work until ten years after Kate died. Kate's recollections are of roasting onions on the ashes of the great bonfire; however, Lewis notes that it would have been impossible for Kate to have been there because at the same time she was on her honeymoon. Peter Ackroyd's biography places Mamie and not Kate there, but Lewis maintains that Mamie could not have been there either because one of Dickens's letters, which discusses the bonfire, notes that she was in Scotland. Accounting for the whereabouts of all of the children, Lewis concludes that only Frank and Plorn could have been present. Lewis argues that after-the-fact-pleading on the part of the older children probably inspired the tales of others being there to witness the conflagration. Causes for the letter-burning are numerous, but Lewis notes two in particular. One is that Dickens was full of self-reproach for leaving his wife and the effect this had on the children, and the second is that Wilkie Collins's plots often relied on the discovery and destruction of letters, with this recurring in his *Household Words* pieces several times. In this way, Lewis argues that Collins's literary discussions of burning letters motivated Dickens to do the same.

Questions of narration as a textual activity surface in Robert Tracy's article "Time in *Bleak House*," in which he investigates the centrality of the month of November to the narrative. Looking closely at the role Esther plays in keeping the narrative together, he argues that "she must establish 'Esther Summerson' both as a character with admirable traits and as a reliable narrator, as well as a kind of stage manager or master of ceremonies, who brings on the performances of the other, unnamed narrator" (225). Esther has "an excellent sense of time. She remembers when things happened, and in what sequence, so that she is able to order her complex tale into a coherent chronology" (225). Despite a few inconsistencies in time, inconsistencies that Esther herself acknowledges with her comments on the irregularity of her tale, she remains a solid narrator. Dickens also worked to place within his tale contemporary events, such as the unexpected general election. November is, however, the guiding time of the text and the guiding metaphor that Dickens uses, as Tracy observes, to establish the traditional "bleak and gloomy month, [and] to give his novel a kind of symmetry" (234).

Keith Easley's extended discussion of Bakhtinian narrative analysis in relation to Esther Summerson's character and *Bleak House* in general is a very thorough consideration of the concept of "self-consummation." A lengthy article that is difficult to summarize concisely, "Dickens and Bakhtin: Authoring in *Bleak House*" considers the narrative aspect of authoring the hero through discussions of love: "For Bakhtin, love is an actively contemplated, intelligent self-forgetting in the service of another, not something to be produced at will for oneself" (196). In this way, to love the self is an impossibility, "while self-consummation is silly at best and fatal at worst.

Dickens resembles Bakhtin in identifying self-consummation as no consummation at all. With a slightly different emphasis, however, he also directly presents it as a moving force within society, the aesthetic means of procuring power for egoism and an ambiguous agent for change'' (196). Easley presents the untenable nature of self-consummation in several examples, including the death of Esther's mother and Esther's disfigurement. He concludes by discussing the prevention of sliding into self-consummation.

Hollis Robbins's article ''Blackening *Bleak House*'' considers the influence Esther Summerson's narration and Dickensian style had on the narration of Hannah Crafts. In addition, this essay considers the impact of Dickens's *Bleak House* on American abolitionist discourse. Beginning with a striking scene which occurs two-thirds of the way through Crafts's narrative, Robbins describes a moment where Hannah, a house slave in Washington D.C., watches as her mistress, Mrs. Wheeler, dons some beautifying powder that only serves to blacken her face. We learn that Mrs. Wheeler, on an errand to advance her husband's employment, uses the powder to enhance her beauty, only to find that she has been pleading her husband's case ''in the guise of a colored woman. . . . The Wheelers, mortified, return to North Carolina to avoid the scandal'' (72). Hannah, after telling her mistress that the powder must have done it, provides a chemical explanation, revealing that she has knowledge of the powder's blackening properties, Mrs. Wheeler is furious, and Hannah decides to escape. This scene, as Robbins notes, ''comes out of nowhere and serves as the pivot of the novel's plot; it is the reason for Hannah's fall from favor and flight to freedom'' (72).

How Hannah knows of the properties of the powder is in itself an interesting investigation in the essay; however, it is the text's connection to *Bleak House* that makes this article of particular importance to this study. The rain which accompanies this opening scene, Robbins argues, is central to a discussion of the impact of Charles Dickens's *Bleak House* on the text. The book was ''extraordinarily popular in American [sic] after 1852 among both white and black readers. *Frederick Douglass's Paper* (originally known as the *North Star*) serialized the novel in its entirety from April 1852 through December 1853'' (73).The vast popularity of the text is evident in Douglass's comments that ''We wish we could induce everyone to read *Bleak House* . . . Charles Dickens has ever been the faithful friend of the poor—God bless him for that!—and in portraitures that he, ever and anon, weaves into his books of fiction, we see the touch of a master hand'' (73). *Bleak House* serves as a ''rich source of comic and ironic allusions for the community of antislavery readers, columnists, and letter-writers'' (74).

Robbins argues that Crafts uses the language of various writers, but mostly that of Dickens, when she seeks ''to limit the verisimilitude of her own words—that is, when she has not quite seen something firsthand, when she is embellishing, when she is admonishing, or when she would rather not be blamed for what happens in her narrative'' (74). Hannah Crafts herself is similar to Esther: "Hannah and Esther are neat, modest, good orphans to whom much happens and around whom events revolve'' (75). Comparisons with Jo, Lady Dedlock, Esther, Mr. Tulkinghorn, Mr. Jarndyce, and Tom-all-Alone's occur throughout the text. The "borrowings," as Robbins demonstrates, are numerous and varied—from description to dialogue to character traits. Robbins does not place this copying within the framework of plagiarism but instead views it from Hannah's perspective as a slave woman struggling to write within a "tradition of writing movingly about the poor and powerless'' (74). As a slave, her status as "property," Robbins argues, "perhaps mitigates her act of violating intellectual property rights'' (78). More importantly, Robbins indicates that it is a strategic use of discourse manipulated on her part in order to engage in what Henry Louis Gates, Jr. calls "double-voiced discourse," and particularly the mode he calls "the Speakerly Text'' (78). This "complicates the idea of a speaking subject. It is not necessarily Hannah's voice who is telling her story'' (78). This authorial uncertainty in both her personage as a slave and in her creative borrowing from Dickens de-centers the narrative position of the text. However, all aspects of Dickens's *Bleak House* cannot translate fully into her text. For instance, Robbins argues that domestic contentment cannot be the ending of the narrative—unlike Esther, who finds this, Hannah is a slave, and therefore the result must be escape not contentment. This device functions as a "conspicuous borrowing from Dickens. Or, put another away, it is a controlled yielding of the pen to another writer. This is fiction, Hannah seems to be shouting'' (77). Analysis of this sort is helpful not only for revealing this connection but also for providing a unique look into the ways in which others have made use of Dickens as a platform for speaking.

In Crafts's case, borrowing from Dickens gave voice to what might have been a textual silence. In Mitsuharu Matsuoka's "Slips of Memory and Strategies of Silence in *A Tale of Two Cities*,'' textual gaps and silences are the important critical focus. Matsuoka states that slips of memory occur in the writing and illustration of Dickensian texts—misplaced allusions to other works and lapses in illustration, such as Captain Cuttle's switched hook. However, Matsuoka draws attention to one glaring "error." In the frontispiece illustration to a *Tale of Two Cities*, Phiz and Dickens place Sydney Carton in the background underneath the plane tree looking down on the party and watching Lucie. Matsuoka writes, "Dickens and Phiz, working together, may have liked the idea of Carton silently and secretly giving love and protection to Lucie. The illustration depicts Carton as keeping himself away from the family scene before him. He appears to be gazing upon Lucie'' (112–13). This is presented despite the text's statement that Carton had not been outside with the family but had "lounged in" (113). Matsuoka reads the plane tree as symbolic of protection and emblematic of Carton's protective care for Lucie. Matsuoka also argues that there are two reasons to explain Dickens's interest in silences and gaps in narration at this time in his life. The first is Dickens's interest in self-reflection, which is incompletely supported in the argument, but the second is his engagement in public readings and performances that profit by well-placed moments of silence. Matsuoka argues that Dickens uses textual silence more fully in this text than in any that proceed it—silences in which he "invites his readers to refer to their own life experiences, ideas, wishes and fantasies to understand what Carton is experiencing" (114). Lucie and Carton share a "silent communication," in which "she can interpret his metaphysical silence, transcending time and space, with the secret code she shares with him" (118–19). Dickens's message, Matsuoka argues, is revealed less in Carton's famous final speech than in the fact that this monologue is silent.

Ruth Tross's article "Dickens and the Crime of Literacy" provides a theoretically rich approach to questions of literacy in Dickens's texts—particularly *Hard Times* and *Our Mutual Friend*. Though Dickens was complicit in the act of comparing illiteracy with the potentially criminal, the danger of the illiterate, Tross argues, needs to be understood in light of the greater threat of literacy. Because the illiterate, in *Hard Times,* are in awe of texts, they are bound to "submission to a mysterious and dominant written order, but this is not necessarily for the good" (235). The passage she starts with, the posting of Stephen Blackpool's guilt by Josiah Bounderby, is the case in point because Bounderby is "a master of distorting fictions" (235). It appears, she argues, that Dickens is more worried about the danger posed by the literate than the problem posed by illiteracy. This fear, she observes, is illustrated in *Our Mutual Friend*. Though Dickens himself was deeply concerned about education, it is rarely portrayed in positive ways and is consistently paired with domination. Referring to Foucault's notion that educational systems serve to " 'capture and fix' " (238), Tross reveals the carceral nature of educational systems. Indeed, we learn that literacy itself, in forms such as blackmail, can be criminal. Tross questions how Dickens "can justify his own writing, when such acts are constantly inscribed as almost criminally dangerous. The ambivalent relation Dickens has towards his readership makes this a rather complicated issue to explore" (241). Though reading and writing are posed as dangerous, Dickens also seems to suggest that reading can be for good and "even for liberation" (241). Tross notes that Dickens's view that reading and writing can both dominate and liberate was not new to Victorians, referencing Derrida's *pharmakon* as a medicine that is both poison and the cure. This dual and opposing approach is found in Dickens's relationship with his reading public, Tross argues, that although he wishes to mold the minds of his receptive, passive readers, at the same time the active readers are offered the potential for a criminal freedom.

In an interesting and complicated argument, Elizabeth Palmberg's essay "Clockwork and Grinding in *Master Humphrey's Clock* and *Dombey and Son*" discusses two critical movements in Dickens's approach to literary serialism and consumerism. The first is a Dickensian search for a serial format and presentation of the authorial perspective that will give him a chance to maximize profits without succumbing to the device of nostalgia to encourage purchasing by readers. The second is an awareness of the novel "as an industrial-age consumer commodity" that must be balanced by a sympathetic critique of nineteenth-century economic selfishness in light of the novel's equally selfish "consumerist appeal" (18–19). Worried that readers would tire of the serialized form, Dickens presented *Master Humphrey's Clock* as a periodical, which helped Dickens to avoid "the tension between novelhood and novelty" (21). The clock metaphor central to the text was built upon the Victorian knowledge of what was already becoming a "quaint" concept: William Paley's natural theological understanding of an ordering God. Both Paley and Dickens, Palmberg argues, share admiration for the craftsmanship element of the discussion; however, the clock metaphor did not work for readers, and Dickens was compelled to move back to the novel form in order to respond to the desire for a "continuous tale" (24). Palmberg argues that Dickens continues in novel form with the image of the clock as a form of "saleable nostalgia" (25).

Dickens would further displace Paley's natural theology with the vision of the novelist as the one who makes "visible not only . . . stories, but also the natural and social worlds, in a way that natural theology no longer could" (29). Palmberg notes that Dickens's goal in writing is to point out the impossibility of the world being read clearly like a clock. Of even greater import is the critique of people's blindness to the world that surrounds them: "Unlike the natural theologians, Dickens's moral is not rational admiration, but sympathy" (30). In *Dombey and Son*, Palmberg suggests that "clockwork 'science' has been replaced by tactile mass"—large watches being forced into small pockets (32). Those characters focused on clocks become obsolete and quaint because the consuming material world, especially of the body, takes precedence. Oddly enough, Dickens finds support for this in Paley's later appeal to the body rather than intelligence. Owning property becomes a part of physical pleasure. Captain Cuttle demonstrates this adherence to "clockwork 'science' " and "childlike delight in material manifestations of monetary value" (33), which renders him even more antiquated since the shift in the nineteenth century was to money, not objects. Why, Palmberg asks, would Dickens wish to render materialism as outdated as clockwork science? She answers by presenting Carker as the representation of a rapacious materialism; his teeth are emblematic of his consuming "material appetite" (35). To separate Cuttle from Carker, Dickens must delineate a difference between the two experiences of pleasure of commodities. Another question she poses is how can Dickens's interest in sympathy be understood in what seems to be a contradictory fascination with commodities? One way is to locate pleasurable experience with commodities in safe characters such as Captain Cuttle. Palmberg ends with an extended discussion of Rob the Grinder: we find in "the Grinder's and Carker's capitalism a dishonorable—as the clockwork model is a charmingly obsolete—foil to the genial, saleable materialism of Dickens's commodity-text" (40).

Commodification of the text is further demonstrated in "The Haunted House of Victorian Advertising," by Sarah Thornton. Thornton argues for the connection between Gothicism and advertising made clear in the fact that "advertising recognizes the Gothic for what it has often been—a money-spinner—for Gothic helps evoke the fear and destabilization which sells products" (59). By looking at the advertisement supplements that accompanied two of Dickens's major texts, *Bleak House* and *Our Mutual Friend*, Thornton explores how Gothic elements are echoed and translated within the Gothic-oriented advertisements. She considers how readers' attention must have been influenced by the presence of so many advertisements, as many as 12 to 16, pages with occasional inserts offering as many as 6 to 15 additional pages. The advertisers were named after the text—"Bleak House Advertiser," for instance—which demonstrates that there must have been a reading process that necessitated the "flow between advert and novel" (59). The ads, like the Gothic labyrinthine narratives and homes of the texts, were full of secrets and surprises. Reading was "palimpsestuous" in nature, with a three-dimensional space that relied on both a "linear trajectory" and a "physical depth" (60). The ads themselves were full of disembodied parts—hearts, trunks, and heads—and they also addressed potential threats and horrors—"contaminated water and its threat to health, the body suffering from unknown diseases all cured by the same pill" (62). The echoes this text would have in a book like *Our Mutual Friend* are obvious.

Thornton provides several compelling (and rather repugnant) examples of the Gothic ad narrative found particularly in testimonials. The effectiveness of these advertising tales comes from the first-person narrative perspective. Thornton touches on the Freudian hysteria and paranoia evident in, for instance, the rather revolting testimonial of George Holden, who pregnant with his corruption, literally explodes with bodily fluids after taking his cure. The ad describes a magical cure that is for sale; however, these cures are often mightily destabilizing: "The body in this testimonial seems to lose its rigid gender marking and to navigate or melt between the sexes. . . . This is part of a making-strange of the self which is evident in Gothic constructions of character" (67). Paranoia is evident, as well, in the fear of the surgeon and his knife, which is alleviated when taking the magical pills. Doctors are the Gothic villains hoping to cut open their victims. The Gothic in these advertisements tempts us with horror and danger, and we are disturbed and attracted, but these fears are palliated by the ad itself, which promises commerce. The ad's connection to Dickens is made very well in the "anti-Bleak House ad" posted near the end of her argument; however, it would have been helpful to have a more extended discussion of the connections or interconnected readings between the books and the ads. Nevertheless, this is an instructive, as well as entertaining, article.

Ray Dubberke's "*Edwin Drood* by the Numbers" details the various critical responses towards the text's two unsolved questions: is Drood dead, and who is Dick Datchery? What is particularly interesting in this essay is the account of how different critical traditions shift in response to these questions. Applying statistical analysis to the critical essays on the subject, Dubberke considers three different critical moments: John Cuming Walters's conclusions in *The Complete Mystery of Edwin Drood*, which draw from critical responses between 1870 and 1912: Philip Hobsbaum's survey in 1972; and the more recent studies of Carlo Fruttero and Franco Lucentini. Dubberke concludes that most critics believe that Drood is dead. Surprising Dubberke is the fact that the "Undertakers" gained even more ground recently over the "Resurrectionists" (134). The opinion of four Dickensian confidantes (John Forster, Charles Allston Collins, Charles Dickens, Jr., and Luke Fields) was that Dickens intended for Drood to be dead, and this is probably the basis for this enduring position—with Forster's *Life* swinging the tide firmly to the Undertakers. The Datchery issue becomes cloudier and more convoluted, depending upon the moment, but most often Bazzard remains the choice, with Helena Landless running a close second, at one point, and with the idea that Datchery is an entirely new person beginning to gain ground of late. Because of this narrative gap, the "mystery" of Edwin Drood continues to provide for creative and interpretive possibilities and also frustration.

Influence Studies

How does one define and determine influence? This question seems to undergird much of Dickensian discussion this year, as critics attempt to locate his theoretical and historical antecedents, and as they try to place him in conversation with his contemporaries and those that follow. In this section, I look at those features that influenced Dickens's literary texts—historical, philosophical, or psychological perspectives. I will also turn to Dickens's influence on D. W. Griffith. Hollis Robbins's essay on Hannah Crafts, in the section on textual studies, may have fit here quite well, too, as would all of the essays in the post-Victorian section.

Elisabeth Gitter's article, "Dickens's *Dombey and Son* and the Anatomy of Coldness," provides a unique explanation of Paul Dombey's character. Not looking to contemporary psychological discussions, nor relying on therapeutic notions of character development (family of origin explanations), Gitter reaches back to the pre-industrial concept of "humors" to explain Dombey's coldness. Dickens thus deploys a remnant of the "vestigial baroque in the service of a new kind of social criticism" (113). How, she asks, does one explain Dombey's coldness? He does not fit the literary tradition of comic misers, such as Scrooge, whose psychological history help to explain their coldness. For Dombey, "his coldness is the dominant metaphor of the novel, yet we never understand it" (101). Gitter notes that Edith hints at one point that she may understand him because of his history, but the narrative does not bear that out, and what remains is the glaring "absence" of a history that explains Dombey (103). Unlike other characters in the novel, who are provided with psychological and historical explanations for their behaviors, Dombey exhibits a coldness that exists in "narrative isolation," and it appears to come to him "naturally" (104). In other words, Dombey is melancholic. Gitter ultimately concludes that Dickens turns away from the "language of psychology" and looks towards the "language of humoralism—a theory of human nature based on a systematic explanation of the body's composition and functioning" (104). Though Dickens, she argues, did not believe in humoralism as literal explanation, it did fit his belief in "the material basis in the body for human temperament" (106), with Dickens's understanding of material psychology coming from his connections with phrenologist and mesmerist John Elliotson. Dombey, then, is a stock character, emblematic of something larger than himself, and in this case, Gitter argues that for Dickens, Dombey functions as "a mournful and frightening synecdoche for the desolate world he inhabits" (113).

In "The Making of the Old Bailey Trial Scene in *A Tale of Two Cities*," Harvey Peter Sucksmith and Paul Davies explore the historical antecedents to the Old Bailey trial scene in Dickens's *A Tale of Two Cities*. Arguing that many critics have seen the trial as pure creative invention, Sucksmith and Davies convincingly demonstrate that the torturous punishment promised is not mere "dramatic device," but existed on the statute-book until the 1780s (23). Hanging, drawing, and quartering, or what Foucault might call elements of "sovereign torture," figure prominently in a case brought before the Old Bailey in 1781 when a Frenchman, Francis Henry De la Motte, was tried and horribly executed for treason. Drawing comparisons between De la Motte's social position, his trial, his appearance, and the indictments brought against him, Sucksmith and Davies illustrate that Dickens, familiar with the sources in *Howell's State Trials* and *The Gentleman's Magazine*, would have known of this trial and had probably used De la Motte as a model for his presentation of Darnay.

Similarly, in their discussion of Sir James Fitzjames Stephen's highly critical contemporary review of *A Tale of Two Cities*, Sucksmith and Davies refer
to further interesting primary sources. Stephen, a lawyer and reviewer, takes
Dickens to task for his representations of De la Motte, arguing that "it is
difficult to doubt that the one trial is merely a fictitious 'rendering' of the
other" (24). Stephen "was an enemy of Dickens, both of his fiction and his
opinions," and he "had also come to believe that Dickens had lampooned
his father, Sir James Stephen, as one of the Barnacles in *Little Dorrit*"
(28). Stephen argued for "strictly realistic" representations in fiction, and
Sucksmith and Davis argue that it is "a classic case of the clash between
conservative and radical points of view; and thus Stephen fails to perceive
what Dickens is doing. To the literal-minded, matter-of-fact lawyer, Dickens
is presenting a distorted version of the De la Motte trial" (29). Though
Stephen sees the trial as justified, he appears appalled by Dickens's failure
to render this event in terms of its factual import. Sucksmith and Davies
argue that Dickens uses satire to speak of injustice, a fact which Stephen
seems unable to grasp. What is particularly interesting in this article is the
examination of historical references to the trial, as well as the references to
the Stephen review. What is less useful is the discussion of verisimilitude in
relation to authorial choice. Aside from their off-hand comments about creative writing programs, they provide an interesting insight into the influence
of an historical event on Dickens's writing and Stephen's review.

"Realities of the Prison" is Harry E. Shaw's contribution to the study
of influence. Shaw begins by revealing another anxiety of influence—after
Foucault, discussion of the prison is almost a critical cliché. Nevertheless, he
argues that the eighteenth-century texts of *Tom Jones* and *Clarissa* set the
stage for depictions of incarceration in the nineteenth century. The prison
provides a "heightened access to reality" (170–71), for it both "concentrates
the mind" and functions as a "place of guilt" (171). Shaw argues that
Richardson and Fielding provide two different ways to understand the prison
in later British realist texts: the first is the guilt/everyday life axis and the
second is the guilt/transcendence axis, represented in Effie Dean's refusal to
leave the prison in *The Heart of Mid-Lothian*. These arguments are tied to
representations of female debasement in relation to imprisonment: "The
prison is a place of guilt, and women often serve in Western literature as
crystallizations of guilt, actual or imputed" (174). To illustrate the application
of these two approaches in the nineteenth century, Shaw turns to *Little Dorrit*.
This novel calls upon the "failed pastoral" in Arthur's imprisonment and
"the figure of the debased woman" in Little Dorrit's night roaming with
Maggie: "Contact with the prostitute draws her back into the real world; at
the same time, the prostitute's recoil prevents Amy from being pulled too far
into the direction of the mundane, and thus preserves Amy's ability to hover

between that world and transcendence'' (177). Amy Dorrit's infamous ''speck'' reveals her ability to be drawn into the world, but she also transcends it. However, growing secularization is a part of the formula. Therefore, one might think the everyday axis might be weighted more heavily due to the growing secularization of the period, but Shaw argues that the transcendence axis is very important. The prison in *Little Dorrit* has a timelessness even when it is most clearly a part of the social world.

Two articles pertinent to our review appear in the edited anthology, *The Victorians and the Eighteenth Century*: one, by Helen Small on Fielding's influence on Dickens, and the second, by Nick Groom, on the impact of Chatterton and Wainewright on Dickensian texts. Drawing attention to the relative absence of Nietzsche in discussions of literary influence, Small turns to his concept of guilt and its relations with debt. In ''The Debt to Society,'' Small highlights her focus on literary indebtedness—particularly Dickens's ambivalent relationship with Fielding. Nietzsche's concepts of debt and guilt illustrate the indebtedness one generation feels to the generations which preceded it: ''Over millennia the 'sacrifices and deeds' through which indebtedness is acknowledged become internalized or 'moralized' into guilt, duty, and religious precept—forms of obligation that inhere in our notion of the self, and that we know can never be discharged'' (14). Her thesis is applied in two particular ways: the first is Dickens's ambivalent relationship to Fielding, and the second is Dickens's critique of the eighteenth-century patronage system for writers. Dickens's ''chariness'' of the metaphor of debt should, of course, not be surprising due to biographical reasons; however, Small provides a very interesting look at Dickens's manipulation of Fielding's influence on his work and Dickens's statements of indebtedness: ''When expressing his relation to his literary predecessors, Dickens preferred a more intimate vocabulary, to do less with literary exemplarity and more with registering old affections. The metaphor of debt thus remains Nietzschean rather than Dickensian in its source, here. Dickens's avoidance of it, even as he strove to be seen as Fielding's inheritor, underlines the strength of the desire for writerly self-determination'' (16). Small argues that Dickens seeks to diminish his admiration for Fielding by couching that admiration in the language of the childish amusement found in Fielding's texts. For Victorians, Fielding's work, as Thackeray notes, was harmful for two reasons: ''Sexual incontinence and financial incompetence'' (19). Dickens's connections to Fielding, in terms of sex, wealth, and work, are seen in this light—that he attempts to lessen the impact of these themes. Small sees connections to Fielding's sexual escapades in comparing the bed-switching scenes in *Joseph Andrews* with a similar scene in *Pickwick Papers*. Dickens's scene is marked with less disorder and sexual innuendo than Fielding's; therefore, he restored the order in his text, denying his debt to Fielding even as he ''retains strong traces of a social or class logic of sex characteristic of Fielding, whereby the erotic (or, in Dickens, narrative agents who mark the place where the erotic might have been) is, among other things, a decoy from the possibility of downward social mobility'' (21). Small notes that Dickens's anxieties about losing his social position is "a concern which again involves both debt to Fielding and moralizing resistance to that debt'' (21). Small's discussion of the flexibility of money is particularly useful as she looks at Fielding's more superficial response to the disposability of money in *Tom Jones* versus Dickens's greater anxiety about misplaced money in *David Copperfield*. Fielding's failure to take money and work seriously or his more "elastic" approach, as Small discusses it, is "ostensibly alien to David, whose distress and shame at the experience of impoverishment are continually impressed upon the reader'' (29).

In the second part of her essay, Small considers Dickens's attacks on the eighteenth-century practice of patronage: Fielding, in this system, was especially skilled at praising his benefactors in his dedications. For Dickens, these comments "reeked of indignity" (33), for he, rather than being beholden to a patron, spoke of being beholden to the public. In his actions on the Royal Literary Fund and later in his development of the Guild of Literature and Art, Dickens tried to develop a system to help writers. Small argues, however, that Dickens did not entirely throw out patronage, indicating his "immersion in an eighteenth-century vision of his profession," although he moved "toward imagining a future in which writers will no longer be debtors'' (35).

Nick Groom's discussion of the eighteenth-century legacy of forgery and its impact on literature and on Dickens and Wilde, in particular, is another foray into literary and historical antecedents of Dickensian types. In " 'I am Nothing,' " Groom speaks of the haunting of the self by the self, and how Victorian responses to literary forgeries "are haunted by such an anxiety of personal authenticity, by the problems generated when different versions of the self compete with and contradict each other, by what constitutes authentic and legible character'' (203). Establishing Thomas Chatterton and Thomas Griffiths Wainewright as two central figures for discussion of forgery, Groom considers how the presentation of the self is never stable, both for the forgers themselves, and for the audience that co-opted their images and re-created them afterwards. Dickens reputedly saw Wainewright, accused of forgery and also likely guilty of murder, in Newgate as he was about to be transported to Van Diemen's Land. "Pathetically proud and unrepentant of both his supposed murders and of his committal for forgery," Wainewright, Groom argues, is a model for Jonas Chuzzlewit, Rigaud, and also to some degree for Abel Magwitch (205). Dickens also published Walter Thornbury's biography of Wainewright in *All the Year Round*. In the Victorian cultural imagination, Wainewright was transformed into a monstrous type—the poisoning forger—and he functions in Dickens's work as "a theatrical baddie, as a shorthand for wickedness" (206).

Wainewright is a crucial figure, Groom argues, in presenting the shift in response to forgery from the Romantic notion of inspiration to the Victorian legal understanding of forgery as fraud and crime. By exploring the charges against Wainewright, which are full of conflicting rumors, Groom shows how the characterization of Wainewright's evil is tied to his forgery, his supposed murders, and his unrepentant villain celebrity status. Groom sees this theme of forgeries haunting texts such as *Great Expectations* (Pip using the metaphor of counterfeiting when he lies to himself) and *Little Dorrit* (Rigaud, who looks like Wainewright, and Merdle, who is guilty of forgery and thievery). *Bleak House* is the text in which he sees the greatest comparisons with Nemo's death inspired by Chatterton's apparent suicide and Wainewright's opium use. Groom turns to a discussion of Wilde that is very useful for considering how Wilde became a victim of his attempt to redirect the discussion of the forger in late Victorian England.

Dickens's attendance in 1842 at the home of William Hone at the request of his friend George Cruikshank is the starting point for Sally Ledger's "From Queen Caroline to Lady Dedlock." Ledger builds a convincing case for the radical antecedents in Dickens's narratives: "William Hone, a radical pamphleteer and bookseller, had for a brief spell wreaked political havoc with his satirical attacks on George the Fourth, his government, the clerisy, and the corrupt legislature that he saw all around him in Regency England" (575). Though many note "Dickens's classical and middle-class novelistic satirical antecedents," little attention, Ledger asserts, has been given to the "popular radical culture" and its influence on Dickens (575–76). Pointing out that Humphry House's "evaluation" of Dickens "as an essentially middle-class writer committed to middle-class values" has become the critical standard, Ledger focuses instead on the popular radical tradition: "Dickens acted as a cultural bridge between, on the one hand, an older, eighteenth-century political conception of the People; and, on the other hand, a distinctly mid-nineteenth century, modern conception of a mass-market 'populace' that had been created by the rise of the commercial newspaper press during Dickens's formative years as a journalist and a novelist" (576). Ledger draws attention to the importance of radical satire and the melodramatic tradition in the works of William Hone and George Cruikshank, with specific attention to the two Regency cultural texts of Queen Caroline and the massacre in Manchester's St. Peter's Fields. During that time, Hone and Cruikshank produced a great deal of work together.

Ledger argues that during the Regency differences between high and low culture were not set, and satire and parody were tools manipulated by both. Satire, mock trials, and melodrama were prevalent, especially melodrama in the Queen Caroline affair, where she is depicted as a "heroine, wrongly accused of adultery and bravely crossing the English Channel to face her accusers and prove her innocence in a show trial" (577). This type of radical melodrama had a direct impact on Dickens, since Hone's widely popular mock trials of Queen Caroline were used as a model for the Bardell versus Pickwick trial in *Pickwick Papers*. Moreover, the actual trial of Hone for his three biblical parodies "that vicariously and hilariously attacked what he regarded as a corrupt and heartless government and its church" is also an influence (579). Initially accused of sedition, Hone was later charged with blasphemy, for fear the first would not stick. In Hone's text, the jury laughs with him at the ridiculousness of the accusations, and he is acquitted. Dickens had Hone's work in his library, and Ledger also points out that Robert Seymour, the initial illustrator for *Pickwick* who killed himself, was a part of a radical popular cultural tradition, producing an important piece for the anti-poor law propaganda.

Similarly, Ledger proposes that works by C. J. Grant and George Cruikshank provide the context for Dickens's anti-poor law satire in *Oliver Twist*. She makes a convincing case for this in relation to the parish beadle and his representation in the popular radical press and Dickens's caricatures—merging radical satire and political melodrama. Political melodrama was considered a force to be reckoned with by the dominant structures and was "coded" as a "disruptive genre" (590). Dickens, like the radical popular press before him, paired "commercial populism" with the "popular radical cultural traditions," and Dickens's debt to these radical traditions and to Hone, in particular, is more extensive than noted (588). Where they differ is that Hone focused on individuals within the system, whereas Dickens focused on systems themselves—such as the Chancery. With the decline of the radical press, the novel became even more important in imparting radical ideological elements. Popular and radical, however, become increasingly more distinct categories as time passed. Dickens's "genius," as Ledger sees it, is that he built upon and "promote[d] popular radical cultural traditions at the same time as commercially exploiting them and becoming a very rich man" (589).

Greg Hecimovich's "Rehearsing *Nicholas Nickleby*" looks at the influence of the actor to whom Dickens dedicated *Nicholas Nickleby*. Describing the famous battle Macready had with theatrical manager, Alfred Bunn, Hecimovich argues that such off-stage theatricals influenced Dickens's understanding of the link between the public and the private as stages. Macready is known to have attacked Bunn because of his outrage at having to perform a truncated version of *Richard the Third*. Hecimovich refers to Macready's readings of *Sketches by Boz* as inspiration for Macready's actions, where Dickens's text suggests "that the real pantomime is not the staged one, but, rather, the 'primitive, unreserved, and unstudied' pantomime of the audience" (16).

Shortly after the actor's assault on Bunn, Macready acted in *Macbeth* at Covent Garden, a performance attended by Dickens. The audience cheered Macready, despite the spectacle discussed in the press. This performance made a significant impression on Dickens.

Hecimovich further notes that Dickens's work on the life of Joseph Grimaldi helped to establish his fascination in the interplay between the public and the private as stage—using a variant on Shakespeare's comments on life and stage in *Macbeth* as culminating comments in his article "The Pantomime of Life." Hecimovich also foregrounds the importance of the clown figure, the significance of dramatic gestures which Dickens gathered from observing Macready, and the importance of the "bacon principle"—the dramatic effect of placing side by side as in the stripes of red and white in bacon "the tragic and the comic scenes" (19). Noting that Dickens very nearly pursued a career as an actor, Hecimovich turns to a discussion of *Nicholas Nickleby* as a stage performance: "Significantly, the main plot of *Nicholas Nickleby* . . . is a melodrama of heroes and villains, in which innocence is threatened, wickedness defeated and virtue rewarded. It is the plot of pantomime" (22).

In "Dickens and Dogs," Beryl Gray considers the influence on Dickens's work of his friendship with Sir Edward Landseer, the renowned animal painter and modeler of the lions in Trafalgar Square—particularly his Alpine Scenes in *Little Dorrit* and his dramatic text, "No Thoroughfare," written with Wilkie Collins. Landseer and Dickens were both particularly fascinated with dogs. In 1845, Gray notes, "Dickens invited the painter to provide an illustration of the dog Boxer for 'Chirp the Second' of that year's Christmas book, *The Cricket on the Hearth*" (7). Landseer's representation, which is more of a "dog portrait," does not correspond to the actual narrative representation of Boxer, unlike John Leech's illustration, which remains more "faithful" to the story (7). However, Gray argues that Landseer was no more "subservient" to Dickens's text than Dickens himself allowed his "text to be subservient to the productions of illustrators" (8). The primary thrust of Gray's argument is that Landseer exerted a subtle influence over Dickens's texts.

In Raphaëlle Costa de Beauregard's "Screening the Gothic Genre in *Broken Blossoms* (1919) by D. W. Griffith," we turn to a Dickensian influence on an early American film. Costa de Beauregard comments upon the frequent allusions to Dickensian texts, as well as to *The Castle of Otranto*, in Griffith's film *Broken Blossoms*. Numerous Gothic elements that appear in *Little Dorrit* and in *Bleak House* appear in the film—the "haunted" house, which Mrs. Flintwich renders humorous and "casts doubt on its verisimilitude," as well as the world of stone or the Gothic urban context found in Dickens's texts (229). These Gothic elements, Costa de Beauregard suggests, undergo a "metamorphosis or a grotesque displacement . . . which Griffith also uses as a subtext to give his American viewer a 'truthful,' or 'authentic,' representation of London'' (230). Dickensian Gothic remnants are turned into melodrama seen in the perversion of family life and ''uncontrolled sexual fantasms of the father'' (231). Dickens's texts naturalize these perversions and turn them into devotion between the young daughter (Amy Dorrit or Little Nell) and the father, ''to the point of destroying the 'child' by filial egotism'' (231). *Broken Blossoms* presents, instead, a rather disturbing narrative of the father who kills his child: ''there is nothing left of the burlesque fanciful descriptions in Dickens's novels which often cast a humorous spell on the 'gothic remains' which are woven into the textual fabric. In *Broken Blossoms*, the gothic fragments rather contribute to creating a chilling account of a London slum tragedy'' (232).

In ''Dickens and Digitation,'' John Bowen provides some titillating information on a possible influence on Dickens. Only eight or nine of Dickens's requests in the 1830s for books from the British Museum survive, and one of these is for Francis Foster's *Thoughts on the Times,* a sexual polemic from the previous century. The chief threat described is men-midwives who arouse sexual appetites of women. Doctors are presented as ''digitating'' the woman's genitals and preying upon the weak female character (122). No connection is drawn to Dickens's work to see if this claim had an effect on his literary treatment of women.

Bibliographical and Resource Materials

There are a handful of resources to direct attention to this year. Two books in the Routledge Literary Sourcebook series are helpful for students: Janice M. Allan's *Charles Dickens's* Bleak House, and Richard J. Dunn's *Charles Dickens's* David Copperfield. Each text provides an introduction and a contextual overview of the novel considered. Contemporary materials are included: for instance, Samuel Smiles's *Self Help* (1859) in Dunn's book, and Dickens's ''On Duty with Inspector Field'' in Allan's. Both include contemporary reviews as well as recent critical essays. Dunn also provides discussions of dramatic adaptations. Both editors choose essays that remain relevant to the text, cross a number of literary critical boundaries, and provide good introductory access. Each text includes a reprinting of approximately 20 primary scenes—such as Tom-all-Alone's. Both books include selected illustrations, although it would be useful to have more of these.

Another book of interest is Pierre Coustillas's first volume of the *Collected Works of George Gissing on Charles Dickens*, which includes Gissing's essays ''Dickens in Memory'' and ''The Homes and Haunts of Dickens.'' Coustillas provides the introductions to the Rochester edition, as well as the *David*

Copperfield introduction from the Autograph Edition. We also find reviews (Swinburne and Kitton), an afterword by Alan S. Watts, and appendices, which include Temple Scott's introduction to Gissing's *Critical Studies of the Works of Charles Dickens*, B. W. Matz's introduction to Gissing's *The Immortal Dickens*, three books reviews, and Pierre Coustillas's article, "Gissing's Two Introductions to *David Copperfield:* Veracity in the *Bildungsroman.*" Volume 2 will contain Gissing's *Charles Dickens: A Critical Study* and Volume 3 Gissing's *An Abridgement of Forster's Life of Dickens.* The preface notes that with the exception of the missing Rochester Edition introduction to the *Christmas Books*, all works of Gissing on Dickens will be in these volumes. Coustillas observes, "For too long, Gissing's writings on Dickens have been unfairly overshadowed by those of G. K. Chesterton, despite the fact that Chesterton described [Gissing] as 'the soundest of the Dickens critics, a man of genius.' They are now due a fresh reassessment" (vii). Coustillas's introduction thoroughly maps Gissing's relationship with Dickensian texts: "To Gissing, Dickens was to remain much more than a prominent fellow writer of a former generation, and anyone who browses among his writings, correspondence or personal papers is sure to come across many mentions of Dickens's name or works or allusions to some of his most memorable characters before long" (3).

Coustillas presents us with a Gissing who balances his feelings of indebtedness to Dickens and his desire to establish himself as well. When Gissing was asked to write a monograph on Dickens for a series to be published by Neville Biemen, critics noted this choice with some irony: "So when it was rumoured about in paragraphs that Gissing was writing a book on Dickens, the news was felt as something of a paradox and the volume was awaited in some quarters with knitted brows. C. K. Shorter, for instance, a prosperous man who edited no less than three magazines simultaneously, remarked in his *Illustrated London News* 'Literary Letter' that it was 'a curious irony to have given Mr. Gissing the task of appreciating Dickens. The one writer makes poverty so much more depressing that it really is, the other so much more joyous than it is' " (10). Gissing's book was published in 1898, when Dickens's reputation was at its lowest. Coustillas notes that the book was well received, and Gissing received a fair share of the praise: "For instance the *Saturday Review*, while praising Gissing, complained that he was too generous to Dickens" (18).

In 1899 Gissing began work on the introductions to the Rochester Edition with Methuen. The project failed, but the introductions are reprinted here with the added mystery of the *David Copperfield* introduction explored: "the quest for and revival of the introductions to the defunct Rochester Edition rested for over fifty years, but research being endless and its results unpredictable, the Dickensian scholar Richard J. Dunn chanced upon an overlooked set of proofs of Gissing's introduction to *David Copperfield* during a research campaign at Dickens House in the early 1980s,'' which was later published by Dunn in *The Dickensian* (24). The Autograph Edition met a similar fate: ''Kitton wrote to Gissing in August 1901, proposing that he should write a new introduction to *David Copperfield*—a choice which was ratified with particular gratitude. Gissing promised to have his piece ready by the end of the year'' (26). The edition was not available until Gissing had died, and the publisher went bankrupt.

Alan S. Watts, in his afterword, examines Gissing's reverence for Dickens. Although contemporaries showed disappointment with Dickens's later works and loved his earlier tales, Gissing ''ushered in a more serious treatment . . . [and] was among the first to examine the [later] books coolly and critically,'' providing a space for modernist considerations of these novels (213). As Watts notes, people were surprised that Gissing would write these introductions because they thought he would not see Dickens's lighter side: ''It has been said that Chesterton gave the world 'the fat man's Dickens' while Gissing gave 'the thin man's.' . . . In fact Gissing presented a 'fat man's Dickens' just as surely as Chesteron. He was as much concerned with the bonhomie and good fellowship displayed in the novels as Chesteron. He may not have declared this with quite the same gusto, but his enjoyment of the fun was no whit less'' (215). Watts provides a useful discussion of the Gissing/ Chesterton debate on Dickens's later works.

Finally, we end with a mammoth bibliographical reference text edited by Duane DeVries. The first of four volumes, one does not know where to begin to review such an impressive undertaking. As DeVries notes in his preface, he began work on this project in 1978, and certainly these impressive materials that will be an aid to any Dickens scholar are a testament to over twenty-five solid years of effort and devotion to the subject. The text includes 2,500 annotations, some more extended than others, but all of those I examined are helpful in briefly summarizing items reviwed. The first part includes bibliographies and bibliographical materials on the Dickensian canon, including some anonymous texts and their attribution to Dickens. The second part discusses bibliographies and bibliographical studies of Dickensian adaptations—from translations to Dickens's public reading versions to plagiarisms to stage to film adaptations. DeVries also considers later illustrations of other Dickens related items, such as stamps of Dickens made worldwide on the one hundredth anniversary of his death. The third part covers Dickens studies in general: general and serial bibliographies, bibliographies of studies of individual works, and bibliographies of specialized studies of Dickens and his works, including listings of the more consistent Dickensian websites. This section concludes with a discussion of comments upon bibliographies and bibliographical studies, including the discovery of the missing Gissing introduction to *David Copperfield*. Part 4 includes library catalogues and catalogues of Dickens collections, guides to collections (which are always helpful), scrapbooks, Dickens museum guides, and reports on collections and library accessions. The fifth part focuses on exhibitions, and part 6 reviews work on collecting Dickens (auction sale catalogues, booksellers' catalogues, and materials related to the collecting of Dickens materials). This area is relatively unknown, as DeVries notes, and is also entertaining to examine. The final part looks at manuscripts and textual changes, calling attention to individual works.

Conclusion

I end with one final piece that looks at the nature of Dickensian popularity. In "Trotty and Etty," Shu-Fang Lai examines the association between one obscure needlework design for a kettle-holder that appears in the 1 March 1845 edition of *Punch* and Charles Dickens's ubiquitous presence as a cultural reference. The pattern of Trotty Veck was based on a sketch by John Leech in *The Chimes*; however, the pattern entitled "Poetry of the Worsted" reminds Lai of William Etty's work. The text accompanying the pattern is a "parody of Fine Art criticism," and its humor comes more from the application to William Etty's paintings, not for its reference to Trotty Veck. Etty had been commissioned to paint a fresco (one of a series of eight) for Buckingham Palace. However, his work was considered unsatisfactory and was later replaced with a work by William Dyce. *Punch* commented on this decision with a poem reflecting on the crown's disrespect for the artist. Thackeray thought that the affair was a "slap in the face to every artist in England" (141), for he himself, although not a fan of Etty, was nevertheless roused to artistic solidarity at this moment. Lai concludes that "it confirms how popular Dickens was, and how easy it was to make allusions to his work," even when the allusion has absolutely no connection to the source (143). In some ways, Dickens may function in our own popular culture much as he did in this instance in *Punch*, as a type of simulacrum. He is found in film, in other adaptations, and even in a Paul McCartney song on Jenny Wren. In the works reviewed, we see the enduring "popularity" and presence of Dickens and his writings—in literary and cinematic adaptations, in his position within contemporary critical debates, and in his role in awakening new fields of analysis.

WORKS CITED

Allan, Janice M., ed. *Charles Dickens's* Bleak House: *A Sourcebook.* New York: Routledge, 2004.

Andrews, Malcolm. "The 'Set' for Charles Dickens's Public Readings." *Dickens Quarterly* 21.4 (December 2004): 211–24.

Barnes, Christopher. "*Hard Times*: Fancy as Practice." *Dickens Studies Annual* 34 (2004): 233–58.

Barzilai, Shuli. "The Bluebeard Barometer: Charles Dickens and Captain Murderer." *Victorian Literature and Culture* 32.2 (2004): 505–24.

Bowen, John. "Dickens and Digitation." *The Dickensian* 100 (Spring 2004): 121–22.

Brittan, Alice. "A Ghost Story in Two Parts: Charles Dickens, Peter Carey, and Avenging Phantoms." *Australian Literary Studies* 21.4 (2004): 40–55.

Camus, Marianne. *Gender and Madness in the Novels of Charles Dickens.* Sylvère Monod, Preface. Lewiston: Edwin Mellon P, 2004.

Carroll, Alicia. "Post-Millennial Dickens: A Review Essay 2002." *Dickens Studies Annual* 34 (2004): 351–73.

Colatrella, Carol. "The Innocent Convict: Character, Reader Sympathy, and the Nineteenth-Century Prison in *Little Dorrit*." *In the Grip of the Law: Trials, Prisons and the Space Between.* Eds. Monika Fludernik and Greta Olson. Frankfurt: Peter Lang, 2004. 185–204.

Cole, Natalie Bell. " 'Amen in a Wrong Place': Charles Dickens Imagines the Victorian Church." *Victorian Religious Discourse: New Directions in Criticism.* Ed. Jude V. Nixon. New York: Palgrave, 2004. 205–34.

Cordery, Gareth. "Drink in *David Copperfield*." *Redefining the Modern: Essays on Literature and Society in Honor of Joseph Wiesenfarth.* Eds. William Baker and Ira B. Nadel. Madison, NJ: Fairleigh Dickinson UP, 2004. 59–74.

———. "Harry Furniss and the 'Boom in Boz' (Part One)" *Dickens Quarterly* 21.2 (June 2004): 90–103.

———. "Harry Furniss and the 'Boom in Boz' (Part Two)" *Dickens Quarterly*. 21.3 (September 2004): 143–56.

Costa de Beauregard, Raphaëlle. "Screening the Gothic Genre in *Broken Blossoms* (1919) by D.W. Griffith." *Anglophonia: French Journal of English Studies* 15 (January 2004): 227–32.

Coustillas, Pierre. Ed. and Introduction. *Collected Works of George Gissing on Charles Dickens. Vol. 1: Essays, Introductions and Reviews.* Alan S. Watts, Afterword. Grayswood, England: Grayswood, 2004.

Dereli, Cynthia. "Stephen Blackpool's 'muddle' in *Hard Times*: Some Critical Issues Revisited." *The Dickensian* 100 (Spring 2004): 101–09.

DeVries, Duane. *Bibliographies, Catalogues, Collections, and Bibliographical and Textual Studies.* Vol. 1. of *General Studies of Charles Dickens and His Writings and Collected Editions of His Works: An Annotated Bibliography.* New York: AMS, 2004.

Dubberke, Ray. "*Edwin Drood* by the Numbers." *The Dickensian* 100 (Spring 2004): 132–37.

Dunn, Richard J., ed. *A Routledge Literary Sourcebook on Charles Dickens's* David Copperfield. New York: Routledge, 2004.

Easley, Keith. "Dickens and Bakhtin: Authoring *Bleak House.*" *Dickens Studies Annual* 34 (2004): 185–232.

Garlock, David. "Recent Dickens Studies: 2000." *Dickens Studies Annual* 31 (2002): 305–36.

Garnett, Robert R. "Recent Dickens Studies—2003." *Dickens Studies Annual* 35 (2005): 335–95.

Gitter, Elisabeth. "Dickens's *Dombey and Son* and the Anatomy of Coldness." *Dickens Studies Annual* 34 (2004): 99–116.

———. "Recent Dickens Studies: 1997." *Dickens Studies Annual* 28 (1999): 197–224.

Goodin, George. "Margins of Conversation in the Dialogue of Dickens." *Dickens Quarterly* 21.3. (September 2004): 170–82.

Gray, Beryl. "Dickens and Dogs: 'No Thoroughfare' and the Landseer Connection." *The Dickensian* 100 (Spring 2004): 5–22.

Gregory, Marshall. "Ethical Engagements over Time: Reading and Rereading *David Copperfield* and *Wuthering Heights.*" *Narrative* 12.4 (October 2004): 281–301.

Gribble, Jennifer. "Why the Good Samaritan was a Bad Economist: Dickens' Parable for *Hard Times.*" *Literature and Theology Today: An International Journal of Religion, Theory, and Culture* 18.4 (December 2004): 427–41.

Groom, Nick. " 'I am Nothing': A Typology of the Forger from Chatterton to Wilde." *The Victorians and the Eighteenth Century: Reassessing the Tradition.* Eds. Francis O'Gorman and Katherine Turner. Aldershot, England: Ashgate, 2004. 203–22.

Hall, Donald E. "Series Editor's Preface." *Detecting the Nation: Fictions of Detection and the Imperial Venture.* By Caroline Reitz. Columbus: Ohio State UP, 2004. ix.

Hanna, Robert C. "Dickens and Plagiarism: Part I" *The Dickensian* 100 (Spring 2004): 144–52.

——. "Dickens and Plagiarism: Part II." *The Dickensian* 100 (Winter 2004): 209–14.

Heaman, Robert. "Hebraism and Hellenism in *Our Mutual Friend.*" *Dickens Quarterly* 21.1 (2004): 3–11.

Hecimovich, Greg. "Rehearsing *Nicholas Nickleby*: Dickens, Macready, and the Pantomime of Life." *The Victorian Newsletter* 105 (Spring 2004): 16–24.

Hennessee, David. "Gentlemanly Guilt and Masochistic Fantasy in *Great Expectations.*" *Dickens Studies Annual* 34 (2004): 301–28.

Henson, Louise. " 'In the Natural Course of Physical Things': Ghosts and Science in Charles Dickens's *All the Year Round.*" *Culture and Science in the Nineteenth-Century Media.* Eds. Louise Henson, et al. Aldershot, England: Ashgate, 2004: 113–23.

———. "Investigations and Fictions: Charles Dickens and Ghosts." *The Victorian Supernatural.* Eds. Nicola Bown, Carolyn Burdett, and Pamela Thurschwell. Cambridge, England: Cambridge UP, 2004. 44–63.

Hori, Masahiro. *Investigating Dickens' Style: A Collocational Analysis.* New York: Palgrave, 2004.

Johnston, Susan. "Historical Picturesque: Adapting *Great Expectations* and *Sense and Sensibility.*" *Mosaic: A Journal for the Interdisciplinary Study of Literature* 37.1 (March 2004): 167–83.

Lai, Shu-Fang. "Trotty and Etty: Unlikely Partners in *Punch.*" *The Dickensian* 100 (Spring 2004): 139–44.

Lamb, John B. "Faces in the Window, Stains on the Rose: Grimaces of the Real in *Oliver Twist.*" *Dickens Studies Annual* 34 (2004): 1–16.

Larner, A. J. "Dickens and Monboddo." *Dickensian* 100 (Spring 2004): 36–41.

Ledger, Sally. "From Queen Caroline to Lady Dedlock: Dickens and the Popular Radical Imagination." *Victorian Literature and Culture* 32.2 (2004): 575–600.

Letissier, Georges. "Dickens and Post-Victorian Fiction." *Refracting the Canon in Contemporary British Literature and Film.* Eds. Susana Onega and Christian Gutleben. Amsterdam: Rodopi, 2004. 111–28.

Lewis, Paul. "Burning: The Evidence." *The Dickensian* 100 (Winter 2004): 197–208.

Lorentzen, Eric G. " 'Obligations of Home': Colonialism, Contamination, and Revolt in *Bleak House.*" *Dickens Studies Annual* 34 (2004): 155–84.

Lund, Michael. "Seeing Dickens: Dickens Studies 1999." *Dickens Studies Annual* 30 (2001): 343–72.

Matsuoka, Mitsuharu. "Slips of Memory and Strategies of Silence in *A Tale of Two Cities*." *The Dickensian* 100 (Spring 2004): 111–20.

Moore, Grace. *Dickens and Empire: Discourses of Class, Race and Colonialism in the Works of Charles Dickens*. Hampshire, England: Ashgate, 2004.

Morgentaler, Goldie. "Recent Dickens Studies—2001." *Dickens Studies Annual* 33 (2003): 367–424.

Nadel, Ira B. " 'Nightplots': *Our Mutual Friend* and *Finnegan's Wake*." *Redefining the Modern: Essays on Literature and Society in Honor of Joseph Wiesenfarth*. Eds. William Baker and Ira B. Nadel. Madison, NJ: Fairleigh Dickinson UP, 2004. 75–88.

Newey, Vincent. *The Scriptures of Charles Dickens: Novels of Ideology, Novels of Self*. Aldershot, England: Ashgate, 2004.

Orero, Pilar. "Edward Lear's Wellerisms." *Proverbium: Yearbook of International Proverb Scholarship* 21 (2004): 287–97.

Oulton, Carolyn. " 'My Undisciplined Heart': Romantic Friendship in *David Copperfield*." *Dickens Quarterly* 21.3 (September 2004): 157–69.

Palmberg, Elizabeth. "Clockwork and Grinding in *Master Humphrey's Clock* and *Dombey and Son*." *Dickens Studies Annual* 34 (2004): 17–50.

Paroissien, David. "Ideology, Pedagogy, and Demonology: The Case against Industrialized Education in Dickens's Fiction." *Dickens Studies Annual* 34 (2004): 259–82.

Parrinder, Patrick. " 'Turn Again, Dick Whittington!': Dickens, Wordsworth, and the Boundaries of the City." *Victorian Literature and Culture* 32.2 (2004): 407–19.

Qualls, Barry V. "Recent Dickens Criticism: 1993." *Dickens Studies Annual* 24 (1996): 275–91.

Reid, Kristy. "Exile, Empire and the Convict Diaspora: The Return of Magwitch." *Creativity in Exile*. Ed. Michael Hanne. Amsterdam: Rodopi, 2004. 57–70.

Reitz, Caroline. *Detecting the Nation: Fictions of Detection and the Imperial Venture*. Columbus: Ohio State UP, 2004.

Robbins, Hollis. "Blackening *Bleak House*: Hannah Crafts's *The Bondwoman's Narrative*." *In Search of Hannah Crafts: Critical Essays on* The Bondwoman's Narrative. Eds. Henry Louis Gates, Jr. and Hollis Robbins. New York: Basic Civitas, 2004. 71–86.

Rodas, Julia Miele. "Tiny Tim, Blind Bertha, and the Resistance of Miss Mowcher: Charles Dickens and the Uses of Disability." *Dickens Studies Annual* 34 (2004): 51–97.

Rothenberg, Molly Anne. "Articulating Social Agency in *Our Mutual Friend*: Problems with Performances, Practices, and Political Efficacy." *ELH* 71.3 (Fall 2004): 719–49.

Ruth, Jennifer. "The Self-Sacrificing Professional: Charles Dickens's 'Hunted Down' and *A Tale of Two Cities*." *Dickens Studies Annual* 34 (2004): 283–99.

Scharnhorst, Gary. "Kate Field's 'An Evening with Charles Dickens'; A Reconstructed Lecture." *Dickens Quarterly* 21.2 (June 2004): 71–89.

Schlicke, Paul. "Dickens and the Pirates: The Case of *The Odd Fellow*." *The Dickensian* 100 (Winter 2004): 224–25.

Sell, Roger D. "Blessings, Benefactions, Bear's Services: *Great Expectations* and Communicational Narratology." *European Journal of English Studies* 8.1 (2004): 49–80.

Selles, Collette. "Heritage in Peter Carey's *Jack Maggs*." *Commonwealth Essays and Studies* 27.1 (September 2004): 63–75.

Shaw, Harry E. "Realities of the Prison: Dickens, Scott, and the Secularization of their Eighteenth-century Inheritance." *In the Grip of the Law: Trials, Prisons and the Space Between*. Eds. Monika Fludernik and Greta Olson. Frankfurt: Peter Lang: 2004. 169–84.

Shukla, Narain Prasad. "Macrocosm v. Microcosm: Society and the Individual in *Little Dorrit*." *The Dickensian* 100 (Spring 2004): 123–31.

Small, Helen. "The Bounded Life: Adorno, Dickens and Metaphysics." *Victorian Literature and Culture* 32.2 (2004): 547–63.

———. "The Debt to Society: Dickens, Fielding, and the Genealogy of Independence." *The Victorians and the Eighteenth Century: Reassessing the Tradition*. Ed. Francis O'Gorman and Katherine Turner. Aldershot, England: Ashgate, 2004. 14–40.

Smith, Karl. "Little Dorrit's 'speck' and Florence's 'daily blight': Urban Contamination and the Dickensian Heroine." *Dickens Studies Annual* 34 (2004): 117–54.

Stanley, Joachim. "Opium and *Edwin Drood*: Fantasy, Reality, and What the Doctors Ordered." *Dickens Quarterly* 21.1 (March 2004): 12–27.

Sucksmith, Harvey Peter, and Paul Davies. "The Making of the Old Bailey Trial Scene in *A Tale of Two Cities*." *The Dickensian* 100 (Spring 2004): 23–35.

Sussman, Herbert, and Gerhard Joseph. "Prefiguring the Posthuman: Dickens and Prosthesis." *Victorian Literature and Culture* 32.2 (2004); 617–28.

Tambling, Jeremy. "Opium, Wholesale, Resale, and for Export: On Dickens and China (Part One)." *Dickens Quarterly* 21.1 (March 2004): 28–43.

————. ''Opium, Wholesale, Resale, and for Export: On Dickens and China (Part Two).'' *Dickens Quarterly.* 21.2 (June 2004): 104–13.

Thornton, Sarah. ''The Haunted House of Victorian Advertising: Hysteria, Paranoia, Perversion'' *Anglophonia: French Journal of English Studies* 15 (2004): 59–73.

Tracy, Robert. ''Time in *Bleak House.''* *Dickens Quarterly* 21.4 (December 2004): 225–34.

Tross, Ruth. ''Dickens and the Crime of Literacy.'' *Dickens Quarterly* 21.4 (December 2004): 235–45.

Vanden Bossche, Chris R. ''Class Discourse and Popular Agency in *Bleak House.''* *Victorian Studies* 47.1 (Autumn 2004): 7–31.

Wilson, Peter. ''The Corpus of Jinglese: A Syntactic Profile of an Idiolectal 'System of Stenography.' '' *Critical Survey* 16.3 (2004): 78–93.

Trollope Studies: 1987–2004

Mark W. Turner

This survey of Trollope criticism picks up where Nancy Metz left off in her overview of Trollope studies in Dickens Studies Annual *published in 1992. All of the major full-length studies and a large number of shorter works (in English) are considered. The survey is divided into sections that seek to provide a useful map of the field of study: Trollope's Lives; Bibliographical and Reference Works; Full-length Studies; Articles and Chapters in Books. The article-length studies are organized according to topic/area of research, to provide an immediate snapshot of the major critical concerns (gender; politics, commerce, and the middle classes; law; form and language; comparative studies).*

Attempting to review a seventeen-year period of criticism for any major author is a daunting task. Doing so for Trollope during this period is perhaps particularly so, given that his critical stock has risen gradually (and substantially) since the mid-1980s and that he is no longer consigned to the second tier of Victorian novelists as he was a generation or so ago. During the past decade, all of his novels, stories, and travel-writing were brought into print, most with critical introductions and notes, some in multiple editions. The only cache of writing remaining to be collected is his journalism, which publishers have yet to be convinced to offer. If the period from the late-1960s through the mid-1980s was about arguing for and defining the field of Trollope studies, then the period since has been about consolidating Trollope as a subject of serious sustained critical inquiry.

One striking thing to note, in recent Trollope criticism especially, is a shift in tone: critics feel less inclined to have to explain exactly *why* they are writing about Trollope and less inclined to apologize for doing it. Still, as recently as 1993, Louise Weinberg, writing in *The American Scholar*, admitted to feeling defensive about her love of reading Trollope and asked, "is it all right to read Trollope?" Trollope, of course, did himself no favors as a literary artist in *An Autobiography* by frankly discussing his writing methods, but as Weinberg hopes, "surely these days we have got over the Victorians' romantic delusion that the true mark of a life in the arts is a feckless bohemianism" (447). The first wave of Trollope critics in the 1970s and early 1980s in part wrote their books in order to make the case for Trollope studies, and a generation later, we are reaping the rewards of their valiant efforts.

In an interesting panel discussion published in *Lit: Literature, Interpretation, Theory* in 1992, some of the pioneers who led the way—James Kincaid, Juliet McMaster, Robert Tracy, Ruth apRoberts, Robert Polhemus, and John Halperin—were asked to revisit their own work in light of critical developments in the intervening years (the rise of theory, most notably) and comment on what they would do differently if they were writing about Trollope in the early 90s. Most of the critics said they would embrace feminism in some way, but new historicism and poststructuralism were also felt to offer significant ways of interpreting Trollope. Although none of these critics has written full-length studies of Trollope since 1987, many others have, and in the overview of criticism that follows, we see not only the critical legacy of that earlier generation of Trollope critics, but also the particular impact of feminism, poststructuralism, and new historicism. These discussions sit alongside others informed by critical legal studies, post-colonial theory, body criticism, critical disability studies, and gender and queer criticism, to name only some of the ways critics have come to interpret Trollope. Writing some twelve years after Weinberg, there is no longer the need to be defensive about taking Trollope seriously. To that extent, the field of Trollope studies is confident, even robust.

While this article cannot comment on every individual piece of scholarship published during the period under review (more than a dozen full-length studies, hundreds of articles, dozens of chapters in books, in several languages), it will cover a significant and representative proportion of that work (in English). What I hope to offer is a map of Trollope studies in the past seventeen years, indicating in particular those topics and areas of research where Trollope scholars have consolidated their work. I have organized the survey in a slightly uneven way, but in a way that I hope will still be helpful: Trollope's Lives; Bibliographical and Reference Works; Full-length Studies; Articles and Chapters in Books (organized by area of research). I hope this gives due attention to the many books published on Trollope, while also helping to shape the critical conversations appearing in journals and elsewhere.

Trollope's Lives

If the single most important event in Trollope studies in the 1980s was the publication of the collected *Letters*, edited by N. John Hall, then it was the four major biographies published in as many years, from 1988 to 1992, that make this period of study particularly rich: R. H. Super, *The Chronicler of Barsetshire* (1988); Richard Mullen, *Anthony Trollope: A Victorian in His World* (1990); N. John Hall, *Trollope: A Biography* (1991); and Victoria Glendenning, *Trollope* (1992). I can think of no other author to be honored with such a biography deluge after such a longstanding drought. Certainly, the fact that there was no major, modern scholarly biography at all meant that the demand was great by academic readers, and as Trollope continues to be among the most popular of Victorian novelists, the desire by general readers for a weighty life of the author was keen. Trollope scholars and readers now face an embarrassment of riches when it comes to biographies, and are lucky to have four hefty tomes from which to choose, each with its own rewards.

Hall's life has become the standard reference work, while Glendenning's is the people's choice. Hall's is a drier work to read, whereas Glendenning's (the only woman biographer, and the only one to warmly call her subject "Anthony" throughout) is engagingly and vividly written. What separates all four is less a matter of substance, and more a matter of emphasis and tone. All of the biographers were working with more or less the same material, and since the publication of the letters, there was little more to be revealed. Trollope's life seems not to have had any great, sensational moments; there were no mistresses (that we know of), no major details that weren't already known. Yet his life is extraordinary, at least for us: consider the amount of writing in different genres, the day job at the civil service, his life in Ireland, his bid for public office, his editing a magazine, and all that riding to hounds. It may not have been a sensational life, but it was certainly an energetic and full one.

The text that looms over each biographer is *An Autobiography*. This is where Trollope creates the version of himself that he wants to circulate—a very public figure, a self-made and prosperous gentleman, and a tireless, hard worker. Perhaps no passages in the *Autobiography* are more poignant than the early ones when Trollope describes his childhood. Here, we learn of his flight of fancy and imaginative life as he builds castles out of the clouds; we also learn of the bullying he endured at public school and of his difficult family circumstances. Whether this version of the self is accurate is another question. For Super, Trollope overstates, and, on the contrary, his childhood was happy and he very much enjoyed his time at both Harrow and Winchester.

The other biographers tend to go along with Trollope and use the childhood as a way of explaining the ambition, hunger for acceptance by peers, and sheer energy of the man in later life. What I think this suggests is that the different versions of Trollope you get in the biographies is really a question of degree, rather than of major disputes.

None of the biographers takes any liberties with his or her subject; they resist speculation and they avoid psychologizing, and in Super, the most cautious of all, the reader sometimes wishes for a bit more recklessness, a little less common sense. On the cultural contexts and sense of the period, Glendenning has a novelist's engaging tone, and Mullen is especially strong and often extremely detailed. None of the biographers spends much time analyzing the fiction. Unlike other recent biographies of Victorian novelists that highlight the writing more obviously—Jennifer Uglow's life of Elizabeth Gaskell, say—there is little by way of literary criticism here. With forty-seven novels published, you can see why a biographer would resist trying to discuss them all, but sometimes I wished for that method of biography that integrates the fiction more fully into the life.

One short work worth mentioning is Andrew Sanders's *Anthony Trollope*, published as part of the "Writers and Their Work" series. He offers a brief account of the life and writings in four sections: on Trollope's life; his critics and contemporaries; on class; on politics. There is a useful select bibliography, and Sanders is particularly strong on comparisons with Trollope's contemporaries, notably Dickens. In fewer than 100 pages (small pages at that), this is a compact version of Trollope, but a helpful first stop for a reader new to Trollope, and there are useful lists of the novels and selected criticism.

An Autobiography has been seen as one of Trollope's more curious texts since its posthumous publication. Its plain-speaking honesty, its frank discussion of his writing method and his earnings, and its refusal to discuss private matters (his wife Rose barely figures) make this is an unusual account of his life and one that has intrigued critics. R. H. Super's article on *An Autobiography* points out its unreliability as a strict account of Trollope's life. Super argues that Trollope didn't actually count every word he'd written every day; rather, he had a good idea how many words would fit on a page, and he likely just counted pages. He discusses the way Trollope "refashions one of the early reviews of his novels" and generally reminds us that Trollope is a novelist and "teller of tales." Reader, beware. Donald D. Stone's study of *An Autobiography* argues that Trollope was particularly inspired by the competing power relations of father and son—think of Plantagenet Palliser and his son, or Mr. Scarborough and his offspring. Stone links this fascination to Trollope's account of his own father in *An Autobiography*, a figure who reappears in some ways in the moody, unhappy Mr. Crawley in *The Last Chronicle of Barset*. Stone is good at discussing a range of fathers and sons across Trollope's fiction, although this study is not particularly analytical and much of what he says remains descriptive, if well observed. Richard Della-mora turns in an article to *An Autobiography* to discuss how male homosocial-ity in Trollope's schoolboy years "later shaped his politics" (22). Dellamora focuses on events like Trollope's being branded a troublemaker at Harrow, with its whiff of sexual misconduct, and links this to the writer's anxieties later in life. Trollope sought "substitutes for the sexual desire, fear, and violence impressed upon him as a schoolboy," and he did so "in the endless series of foxes he pursued" and "in novelistic surrogates." This is a some-what speculative article, but certainly an interesting one that tries to relate Trollope's formative homosocial years to his later fiction. Peter Allen's study of the *Autobiography* focuses on Trollope's narrating voice, which sounds a lot like that of his fiction. He seeks to understand the different versions of Trollope that get constructed—both "vulgar materialist" and "gentlemanly man" (13)—and reads the text as Trollope's "revelation of self to the circle of his readers" (14), but a self that is contradictory and confused, showing a kind of desperation to be understood.

Bibliographical and Reference Works

Two bibliographical studies add to the considerable work that already exists on Trollope, stretching back to Michael Sadleir's work in the early twentieth century. Walter E. Smith's bibliography of American first editions is, as Smith notes, "a supplement" to Sadleir's. He offers a bibliographical catalogue with detailed descriptions of the American first editions between 1858 and 1884, which is a useful resource. Included are a number of photographs of covers and bindings and, more unusually, the wrappers of several publications that are seldom seen or available in most libraries. Elizabeth R. Epperly's mono-graph, *Anthony Trollope's Notes on the Old Drama*, reproduces the annota-tions and end notes that Trollope wrote in his copies of Elizabethan and Jacobean plays, drawing on the Folger Library's collection of 96 of Trollope's annotated volumes. Trollope was an avid reader of drama, reading over 270 Elizabethan and Jacobean plays between 1866 and 1882, including Shake-speare (his favorite, unsurprisingly), Beaumont and Fletcher (of whom he reads more than anyone else), Dekker, Jonson, Marston, Marlowe, Massinger, and many others. What Trollope has to say is tantalizing, and Epperly's introduction illuminating. Shakespeare is praised above all others—*Macbeth* is his finest, *Hamlet* the "greatest work of man," and certain passages in *King Lear* never bettered—but fascinatingly, Trollope pays a great deal of attention to the women characters, which Epperly believes is "the single most revealing element implicit and explicit in the drama notes" (29). One other work worth mentioning is Lance O. Tingay's *The Trollope Student*, which provides an annotated list of full-length studies of Trollope from 1883 to 1990. This is extremely useful for scholars (perhaps even more useful if circulated in electronic form). He also includes a checklist of writings by Trollope and other members of the family, from 1743 to 1909, which reveals the extent of literary undertakings by Trollope's relations.

Three reference works for the Trollope scholar provide extensive information about the writer's fiction, his life, and a number of contexts. Richard Mullen's *The Penguin Guide to Trollope* offers encyclopedia-style, cross-referenced listings of all the novels, shorter works, characters, family members, contemporaries, and topics. It was compiled almost entirely by Mullen himself, with the aid of the historian James Munson, and is a useful companion. More wide-ranging and with more in-depth analyses is R. C. Terry's *Oxford Reader's Companion to Trollope*. Terry, general editor of the volume, enlisted thirty-six others to write specific entries according to their expertise, and many of the names featured below in this survey contributed to that volume. Essentially, it aims for the same reader as Mullen's volume, but this one—part of Oxford's fine "reader's companion" series—has become the first port of call for most scholars. These two volumes will certainly replace Winifred and James Gerould's *A Guide To Trollope*, first published in 1948. George Newlin's four-volume labor of love, *Everyone and Everything in Trollope*, delivers what the title promises, including full listings of all characters (classified by nationality, occupation, nicknames, and aliases) and a "Topicon," which offers passages by Trollope relating to a range of topics (from "Spirit and Moral Qualities" to "Transportation and Travel"). The volumes are hefty and cumbersome, and this is the sort of reference work that would be more useful on a CD ROM, but they make for surprisingly good browsing, which is what Newlin suggests the reader do with them anyway.

Three general evaluations of Trollope are worth mentioning here. In his *Oxford English Literary History* for the period 1830–1880, Philip Davis discusses Trollope alongside his friend George Eliot in a chapter on "High Realism." This is an elegant introduction to the author that covers a small range of the fiction, making a number of suggestive ideas worth pondering. Trollope gets his own chapter in Alan Horsman's *The Victorian Novel*, part of the Oxford History of English Literature series. This is a fast, fluent overview of Trollope's oeuvre, but not one that offers much by way of new critical insight. K. M. Newton's account of Trollope appears in the "Major Authors" section of *A Companion to the Victorian Novel*, edited by William Baker and Kenneth Womack. Newton, who calls Trollope the most "realistic" of Victorian novelists, focuses on *Barchester Towers* and its narrator, in order to complicate our understanding of realism and how realist narratives work. This is a more focused study than those above, but a useful introduction for new readers.

Full-length Studies

In advance of the major biographies published shortly after her study, Susan Peck MacDonald's *Anthony Trollope* for the Twayne single author series provided a useful overview of the author's work. The major novels are discussed, although none in great detail, and there are regrettable omissions, including no extended discussion of the Irish fiction. However, the Twayne series is intended less as a place for new and innovative critical readings than as a brief account of an author that obviously cannot examine all the novels. It is successful in its own terms, and, in particular, short sections on topics such as "realism" and "Trollope's narrator" are helpful introductions for the undergraduate reader, as are the short sections on the novels. The conclusion provides a useful survey of Trollope's critical reception, from his own day up to 1987, indicating the renewed critical interest since the late 1960s.

Most other books on Trollope attempt to cover less ground, and focus on specific parts of the *oeuvre*, organized by topic. Christopher Herbert's *Trollope and Comic Pleasure* begins with a discussion of the "Trollope problem": "Trollope's unique ability to baffle critical analysis, to foster conflicting opinions, and by so doing, as we are bound to feel, to throw our methods of scrutiny and our standards of judgment into question" (1). Understanding Trollope's "gravitation" towards the outmoded genre of comedy, Herbert suggests, will help us understand how we are to read and interpret his work. Comedy enabled Trollope "to focus in particular on a phenomenon of which he was almost obsessively aware: the appearance of a rapidly deepening split in the field of literature between the popular and the serious, a development that introduced a new dimension of ambiguity in a writer's vocation" (5). Herbert's insightful study argues that Trollope is indebted to the structures of stage comedy—*The Way We Live Now* resembles Jacobean comedy, for example—and this "most anarchronistic-seeming element of his fiction turns out to be basic to its most riskily modern lines of thought and its most inventive artistic experimentation" (9). Stephen Wall's *Trollope and Character* (1988), perhaps the longest single study published, divides into four sections: Living with Characters; Reappearing Characters; Recurring Situations; Character and Authorial Purpose. Wall argues that "Trollope was able to write so much so quickly because he lived with his characters so closely," a notion, he admits, that "may now look almost quaint, and often seems to be disregarded by modern critics—or at best tolerated as an inevitable embarrassment" (7). Wall takes a novel-by-novel approach which gets a bit wearying over the course of nearly 400 pages, but he makes a number of suggestive points along the way. In discussing Trollope's narrator—part of the "Trollope problem" of a meddling, interventionist narrative voice—Wall argues that critics too often look for unity where there may be none. Unlike a writer like Balzac, with a more unified, "inherently imperialist" view of the world, "Trollope characteristically leans toward devolution" (238). Wall clearly engages with Trollope, but *Trollope and Character* suffers from a lack of critical engagement with others. There are only 22 endnotes to the whole book, so the critical conversation is limited, and if you want to know where James Kincaid says something that Wall quotes, you likely won't find it. Like many Faber and Faber books, this one has one eye on the general reader market, and isn't fully satisfying for the scholar.

One of Wall's primary interests is Trollope's use of repetition, which he notes was "a fundamental part of his authorial practice, and was therefore inextricably bound up with his desire to live with his characters" (7). Elizabeth R. Epperly covers similar ground in her study *Patterns of Repetition in Trollope*, which focuses on repeated allusions and cliches, arguing that "Trollope learned to use repetitions ingeniously; through repetition he shared with his readers an accessible and sophisticated shorthand" (1). The most interesting and repetitious character turns out to be the narrator, who echoes characters directly, or "uses expressions we can easily imagine the characters using. . . . Trollope's control of tonal register enables him to sustain the separate voices of the characters and the narrator making a whole novel resonate with multiple-level repetitions. He masters pitch, volume, and echo" (206–07). Epperly's study is somewhat limited, addressing only six novels as case-studies—*Barchester Towers*, *The Last Chronicle of Barsetshire*, *He Knew He was Right*, *Phineas Redux*, *The Prime Minister*, and *The Way We Live Now*—but it usefully highlights a formal aspect of Trollope's writing that critics in the past have often overlooked or denigrated. However, there may be more to say about repetition and echoes, in particular given that serialization was so significant to Trollope, both as a publishing form and as an organizing principle for his writing. It would be interesting, for example, to think about those echoes across the extended reading time of some of those novels.

Trollope's serial form is the subject of two full-length works that bring his writing methods and the dynamics of reading serials to the fore. Mary Hamer's excellent *Writing by Numbers: Trollope's Serial Fiction* looks closely at Trollope's serial method, arguing that "the need to produce serials was in the end a paradoxically liberating experience for Trollope, from which he made rich imaginative gains" (ix). The first half of Hamer's study examines how publishing conditions and serial publication impacted on and, indeed, "determined," his fiction. She concludes that "the subliminal effect of serial form helped Trollope to write with greater psychological penetration and with bolder insights" (x). The second half of the book examines novels published after *Framley Parsonage*, when he breaks into the serials market, and before 1868, when he gives up his civil service work. According to Hamer, these six years are crucial for Trollope who became both more confident in writing serial novels and more adept at managing the large, multiplot novels for which he is best known. Hamer's study helped to open up a vital field of inquiry for Trollope studies by taking his writing method seriously. Rather than apologize for Trollope's "writing by numbers" method described in *An Autobiography*, she seeks to understand the dynamics of writing, and to a lesser extent reading, in parts. Two useful appendices that I still often turn to—"Trollope and Millais," on the relationship between author and serial illustrator, and "The initial publication of Trollope's novels in England"—make this a book that I keep close to hand.

My own study of Trollope's serialization, *Trollope and the Magazines* is indebted to Hamer, but where Hamer focuses on Trollope's writing methods, I focus on how Trollope's fiction might have been read in the context of a range of cultural debates taking place in the magazines where that fiction appeared. This is a series of case studies of texts published in the 1860s, including *The Small House at Allington* in *Cornhill Magazine*, *The Belton Estate* in the *Fortnightly Review*, and *Phineas Finn* and *An Editor's Tales* in *St. Paul's Magazine*, which Trollope also edited. I highlight the ways debates about gender—for example, the Woman Question and discussions of bachelorhood—circulate in the serial novel, the magazines, and in cultural production broadly, and I approach this material through a range of critical methods, including reading a single instalment in the context of a single issue. There are also discussions of key aspects of magazine culture in the period, including the role of anonymity and the ways magazines positioned themselves in the literary marketplace. My book closes with a chapter discussing theoretical approaches to studying periodicals, borrowing eclectically from a range of (mostly) poststructural thinkers. Both Hamer's and my work can be seen as part of a flourishing interest in serialization and print culture, and might helpfully be read alongside other studies such as Peter L. Shillingsburg's study of Thackeray, *Pegasus in Harness*, or Linda K. Hughes and Michael Lund's study of Elizabeth Gaskell.

My study is only one of a number of books focusing on aspects of gender in interpreting Trollope. Most studies interrogate Trollope's representation of women, including Deborah Denenholz Morse's *Women in Trollope's Palliser Novels* (1987). For her, reading Trollope requires us to understand a fundamental tension in his work, between affirming the status quo and subverting it, which "manifests itself in a variety of ways: disruption of traditional narrative structure, ambiguous characterization, tension between narrative intent and resolution, between characterization and narrator's commentary, or between text and illustration" (2). The kind of ambivalence we see in Trollope's response to Victorian womanhood and the Woman Question is "the characteristic Trollopian form" (137), and his representations of women embody the cultural anxieties and express the tensions of his time about women's role in society. Morse's account obviously owes a great deal to feminist criticism of the 1980s, but, seventeen years after its publication, it continues to be a thoughtful study about a topic that is clearly among the most significant in Trollope's work. Published two years after Morse, Jane Nardin's *He Knew She Was Right* looks at the way Trollope's view of women changes across his career. "Trollope began his career as an unreconstructed believer in the doctrine of separate natures and separate spheres," Nardin argues, "but by the time he completed *The Belton Estate* . . . he had decided that this doctrine and the code of behavior based upon it were making life difficult for women" (210). That is, between 1855 and 1865, Trollope moves from a position of simply accepting women's position in society to one of dissenting from it, and later novels, such as *The Claverings*, simply fail to resolve the tensions. Nardin spends most of the book on the early period, and her novel-by-novel approach allows her to show how each novel introduces a new difficulty in depicting women. It is a little schematic, however, and by addressing the later novels in only a single chapter, she leaves a number of unanswered questions about some of the more difficult novels of the 1870s. However, Morse covers some of this ground in her study of the Pallisers, as did Juliet McMaster in her *Trollope's Palliser Novels* in 1978. Taken together, Morse's and Nardin's books represent a particularly important moment for feminist readings of Trollope, which make his fiction complex and nuanced texts in which the role of women can never be taken for granted.

Margaret Marwick's *Trollope and Women*, a master's thesis developed into a book-length study, also considers the range of Trollope's women. While aimed more at the Trollope enthusiast than the scholar as such (there are no footnotes, for example), there is useful material here. In particular, the discussion of "sex" in chapter five argues that while "there is no graphic description of sexual intercourse" in Trollope's fiction, "there is an open acknowledgement that being in love and desiring to marry is about wanting to touch someone in an intimate way, and about enjoying being touched" (80). Marwick helpfully reminds us that in between the lines of Trollope's courtship-and-marriage plots is a great deal of physical desire, and that gender issues in Trollope are often predicated on moments of sexual tension. Desire is interrogated more theoretically in Priscilla L. Walton's *Patriarchal Desire and Victorian Discourse*, the title of which indicates clearly the overall framework. She argues that in the opening pages of *An Autobiography*, when Trollope describes his childhood, a paradigm is formed: "The pattern of weak father and strong mother established in these pages provides for a paradigmatic displacement of blame that will come into play in the Palliser Novels, wherein strong women are quelled and suppressed to ensure masculine dominance. In *An Autobiography*, Trollope's identificatory process is disrupted through the shift in gender roles he witnesses when his mother, as family provider, performs a 'man's' job and so abrogates Victorian codes of feminine behavior'' (13). The ''man's job'' that Walton is talking about is novel-writing, but I am not convinced that novel-writing *was* a man's job, certainly at the period of Trollope's boyhood (see, for example, Gaye Tuchman's *Edging Women Out*, which argues rather differently), and so the paradigm Walton sets up at the beginning never carries weight. She concludes that ''Trollope's Palliser Novels work to establish patriarchy as a natural order, at the same time that they reveal its reliance upon the subjugation of women'' (9) and that ''the Palliser Novels serve as pleas to women to accept their objectification in the system'' (19). Walton's study can be provocative and suggestive, but it may be more interesting to the Lacan scholar than the Trollope scholar, and there seems little room for nuanced complexity once the paradigm takes over.

A number of studies sit more happily by themselves than as part of a critical school or grouping. L. J. Swingle's *Romanticism and Anthony Trollope* is a unique take on the author, which argues against the prevailing notion that Trollope was an anti-Romantic (as suggested by Trollope critics including Juliet McMaster, Ruth apRoberts, and Robert Tracy). For Swingle, Trollope's concern ''with the individual's freedom from or obligation to the world of other human beings'' is deeply indebted to the ''preoccupations of early nineteenth-century Romantic writers'' (20). Taking issue with the noted Trollope critic Christopher Herbert, Swingle believes that ''Trollope's art is directed toward making us conceive of human beings in terms of possibility rather than of fixed nature.'' For Trollope, people change, particularly when under pressure, so that ''the essence of a human being. . . . is the apparent absence of any fixed essence'' (159). Swingle discusses Madame Max's decision about whether to marry the Duke of Omnium in chapters 60–62 of *Phineas Finn* as central to this point, and it is a genuinely enlightening way of interpreting the role of uncertainty in Trollope's characters. Swingle asks us to do two things: firstly, rethink what we think we know about Trollope, in light of the history of ideas, and of Romaniticism in particular, and, secondly, to blur the boundary between Victorianism and Romanticism, to find ''a continuum, not a contrariety'' (22).

Jane Nardin's *Trollope and Victorian Moral Philosophy* can similarly be thought of in relation to the history of ideas, though she is concerned with the way Victorian moral philosophy (that is, the work of the utilitarians, intuitionists, and idealists) impacts on Trollope's writing. While Trollope was not a student of philosophy, Nardin argues that he certainly would have been aware of the major debates, and he knew personally many of the important figures. In part, her work extends Ruth apRoberts's *The Moral Trollope*, although Nardin finds in Trollope the moralist more theoretical options. According to Nardin, ''morality for Trollope is largely a matter of action. By learning how to behave in a variety of situations, people come to grasp (though perhaps not very clearly) the principles that guide their conduct'' (112). His morality is "traditional, yet skeptical," and at heart his fiction adheres to common morality. We see this common morality in Trollope's moral center, in a character like Mr. Harding, for example, for whom restraint is more important than great acts. As Nardin tells us, "common morality does not require heroic displays of generosity or self-supression" (16).

Ellen Moody's *Trollope and the Net* is a book about two revolutions that took place in the 1990s—the return of the book group, or reading group, and the emergence of the internet. She brings those two phenomena together, in a study that charts her experiences on two different internet discussion lists dedicated to Trollope. Written by a passionate reader of Trollope and a fine close reader, this is a quirky study, full of enthusiasm and insights into how different people read Trollope. There are some unexpected and illuminating moments, in particular a good discussion of Trollope's illustrations and how they relate to the reading experience. There is still relatively little work on the relationship between serial text/image in the period, and so Moody's thoughts, even from the perspective of so different a communal reading context, are welcome. By combining scholarship and wide critical reading with her own passion for Trollope (and the passion of other readers), this is a book that speaks both to the scholar and the general reader.

Trollope and the Church of England, by Jill Felicity Durey offers a "preliminary examination of the people and ecclesiastical issues behind Trollope's work,'' and as she states, there is no "close textual analysis of Trollope's fictional world of clerics," nor is there any in-depth discussion of the historical context. The book is, she says, an "entry-point to illuminate the depth of strong feeling on Church matters exemplified by many of Trollope's characters'' (9). It is true that a full-length study of Trollope and the Church needed to be written, but Durey's study doesn't fulfill the need as I see it. This is a largely descriptive study that lacks sufficient analysis; no sustained, strong argument emerges here, apart from the suggestion that even in his late, more pessimistic novels, his belief in the Church as a force for good never wavered. Without in-depth historical/contextual discussion and without close analysis, it is difficult to prove that. Furthermore, sometimes the book doesn't particularly strike me as about the Church at all. In a chapter on women, Durey seems most interested in discussing the influence of clerical wives and daughters on the men around them, but she never argues that this is unique to women connected to the Church. What about Trollope's political women, who may exert a similar influence? How do these church women differ from women in other institutions? By limiting the intellectual reach of the study so much, Durey ends up merely describing a range of women, without a sufficiently sophisticated grasp of, say, gender relations or ecclesiastical power dynamics.

A book that contextualizes Trollope's fiction in light of contemporary Church debates—Sabbath day reading, sensationalism and the evangelicals, popular versus religious reading—would not only tell us more about Trollope in relation to his own time, but also about the interface between religion and popular literature. That book remains to be written.

Articles and Chapters in Books

The titles to several of the books discussed above gesture towards some of the primary areas of interest in Trollope studies, perhaps in particular on issues of feminism and gender, where research has tended to cluster. This section surveys shorter studies of Trollope and organizes them by area of research: Gender; Politics, Commerce and the Middle-Classes; Questions of Identity; The Law; Form and Language; Comparative Studies; Others. What becomes apparent quickly is that the areas of research I have designated are porous—to write about Irishness in the Phineas novels requires an understanding of gender; to write about femininity may similarly necessitate a discussion of the political sphere. The overly neat way that I have organized what follows belies the richness of much of the criticism. However, these broad categories do reflect the primary foci of Trollope studies over the past couple of decades, and to that extent, I hope they provide a useful way of shaping the field of study.

Gender

As the monographs by Morse, Nardin, and Turner suggest, no single area of research has been more considered in Trollope studies in recent years than explorations of gender and sexuality. While critics are increasingly discussing men and masculinity in his fiction, most of the criticism addresses his women and questions related to femininity and female sexuality. The critical frameworks used to discuss gender draw on a range of critical practices, including traditional modes of feminism (representations of women), body criticism, Foucauldian understandings of sexuality, Freudian and psychoanalytic analysis, and reader-reception. The grounds for the gender debate in Trollope are still rooted in considering his feminism, or the extent of radical understandings of gender in his work. Critics have long been divided on whether Trollope is more traditional or more forward-thinking in his representations of masculinity and femininity, but in the conclusion to his book *Fixing Patriarchy*, Donald E. Hall draws on poststructuralist accounts of subjectivity and identity (Judith Butler's notion of "gender trouble," for example) to suggest that Trollope's attempt to make the discourse of gender seem "natural" and therefore less threatening "never succeeds in erasing the diverse gender transgressions that he shows to be pervasive and proliferating" (201). Hall singles out Lady Glencora for discussion—as so many critics do when considering Trollope's feminist credentials—and argues that the conclusion to many of the novels "seem designed to provide a balm for frazzled male nerves," so we are offered "temporary restabilizations of gender definitions and reinscriptions of male hegemony" but on a lesser scale (206).

Popularly, Trollope may continue to be thought of as the novelist who best captured English women in the drawing room and on the lawn, to paraphrase John Blackwood, but he was also the novelist who repeatedly sought to represent the tyrannies of domesticity, and, in particular, domestic violence. Kate Lawson interprets the "marked," continually exhibited body of Signora Neroni, "an abused wife, irremediably crippled by an unspecified act of domestic violence," as a "pollutant" that must be removed from Barchester society. She draws on the work of Julia Kristeva in *The Powers of Horror* to suggest that *Barchester Towers* "defines" and "inscribes" the female body as abject. "The resolution of the novel," she argues, "is achieved through a facile separation of the female body into the clean and the unclean," with Signora Neroni's "marked body" coming to act as the "other" and Eleanor Bold's as "pliable, submissive and pure" (66–67). Cindy LaCom reads Madeline's body in relation to discourses about illness and female disability in the period. Writers like Trollope, she suggests, "(re)inscribed a negative attitude by associating female disability with diseased female sexuality and suspect morality" (190). Madeline must be eradicated from Barchester society because she can never be a "whole" woman, can never be a mother or have a lasting union with a man. Both Lawson and LaCom are suggestive and have a truly interesting line of inquiry, although one fantasized female body that critics continue to overlook, and that might complicate matters and would be fascinating to consider alongside Madeline's, is Josephine de Montmorenci, the eponymous heroine of Trollope's neglected short story, whose crippled body is not so much exhibited as hidden away, before being revealed.

The violence we find in *Barchester Towers* is perhaps less expected than in Trollope's late fiction, and Monika Rydygier Smith's article on *The Way We Live Now* argues that that novel's darkness arises from its pervasive physical and psychological violence by men against women. She believes that the novel "can be used to demonstrate how masculinist structures, which rely on the oppression of women, are facilitated not only by epistemic violence as feminists have cogently argued, but also by means of battery and assault" (16–17). To that extent, the novel exposes "male privilege" and the "sexual dynamics that can and do lead to physical assault" as a result of it (17). While not an article expressly about gender, Christine S. Wiesenthal's study of Louis Trevelyan's melancholic body in *He Knew He Was Right* shifts attention to male bodies and suggests that rather than viewing him strictly as a monomaniac as critics have tended to do, Trevelyan needs to be understood in relation to the longer historical context of the "anatomy of melancholy." Wiesenthal is less interested in diagnosing Trevelyan than in "exploring the forms and dimensions of the body that is melancholy" (230), and she concludes that, like Freud, "Trollope stresses the nature of self-tormenting ambivalence as a native element of the human condition" (244). Wiesenthal's long view of the melancholic body is not only informative but genuinely makes the reader think about Trevelyan in new ways.

Mr. Harding remains one of Trollope's most captivating characters, and Jim McDermott, in an article on the "New Womanly Man," argues that the character is a heroic, feminized man who becomes an "exemplary citizen" because "he symbolizes the functional dialogue of the center, where work gets done" in *The Warden* (86). Mr. Harding represents the best case for compromise in troubled Barchester society, and the novel suggests that "a politics of androgyny uses reformist impulse and reactionary obligation to create a fertile center that . . . offers a polarized society the greatest hope for peace and justice" (87). Kevin Floyd's article, however, takes issue with the assumption of Mr. Harding's ethical heroism. According to Floyd, Trollope makes Mr. Harding so likeable that readers want to find redeeming qualities in him, and to make him out to be better than he is, when in fact, "he is an inert old man who is torn between sophists, until he sees the chance to give his son-in-law the slip and escape in the only way possible" (94). Floyd's argument is tough on the received wisdom concerning Mr. Harding, but his emphasis on the character's age is significant and worth pursuing further. From Mr. Harding to Mr. Scarborough, Trollope was a keen observer of the aging man, and a thorough study of the politics of old age in his work remains to written.

William A. Cohen's "Trollope's Trollop," an article which reappeared in his book, *Sex Scandal*, focuses on *The Eustace Diamonds* and Lizzie Eustace, a character who, like the sensation novel genre generally, has become more interesting to critics through feminist and gender criticism. Cohen argues that the novel marks a shift in the representation of sexuality in the Victorian literary imagination. For him, Lady Eustace's jewels are both obvious and ambiguous: they both "stand in for sexual meanings" and resist those meanings; "they make use of opportunities availed by unspeakability and lend their own status as objects of monetary value back to sexuality. The gems at once metaphorize sexuality and literalize the economics of sexual difference" (236). After a discussion of the sexual economy of Lizzie's jewels as property, Cohen shifts our attention to questions of narrative, and concludes that

> the pose that narrators such as Trollope's strike ("of course . . . everybody knows . . . so why bother saying so?") allows them to have it both ways with

sexual meanings, and it marks a paradigmatic moment in the discourse of
sexuality. For we can finally understand that the mutually reinforcing oppositions, which apply not only to property but to narrative language as well,
constitute a principal means of defining sexuality as the unspeakable subject in
nineteenth-century England.   (255)

When first published in book form, Cohen's arguments received widespread
attention, and some years later, I continue to believe that this is significant
work, but less for its outré suggestions than for the way it requires an important rethinking of Trollope and gender. Cohen is both a playful and clever
reader, whose readings of sexuality in Trollope (and others) are helpfully provocative.

   Cultural materialist/historicist readings of Trollope have shed new light on
the ways various cultural contexts inform gender in his novels. Andrew Maunder reads *Miss Mackenzie* alongside mid-Victorian etiquette manuals and
demonstrates the way the "ideological and narrative devices" in both inform
each other. For example, he discusses "Conduct and Carriage," a series of
fictional dialogues appearing in the *Ladies' Treasury* between 1858 and 1862
and shows the way these texts, like Trollope's novel, participated in "constructing a social world" and evoked "a common (middle-class) ideology"
(67). Nicola Thompson's case study of the critical reception of *Barchester
Towers* also helpfully focuses our attention on Trollope's cultural, critical
context. From the 1860s to the end of the century, she argues, "the criteria
used by Victorian reviewers to judge novels became increasingly polarized
according to gender, with 'masculine' qualities in writing more strongly valorized, and 'feminine' qualities denigrated accordingly" (152). Appreciation
of *Barchester Towers* backs up that assertion, for as the *Westminster Review*
put it, it was "a novel that men can enjoy" (157). Trollope's critical status
declines from the mid-1860s, by which time he is firmly associated with
circulating libraries, which led to him being taken less seriously. He was
thought of as someone who "reproduces rather than creates" (160)—which
stems from the assumption that "high art should not rely too much on everyday life" (161)—and implicit in this assumption is a gendered binary: mascu-
line/"high" and feminine/popular. Both Thompson's and Maunder's work
can usefully be read alongside my own study of Trollope and gender in the
magazines of the 1860s, all of which in their different ways seek to embed
interpretations of Trollope in the literary culture of his day.

Politics, Commerce, and the Middle-Classes

In his article, "Transgression in Trollope: Dishonesty and the Antibourgeois
Elite," John Kucich begins with the assumption that Trollope is an "antisepti-
cally conservative writer" (595) but rather than conclude from that that

Trollope's writing is also inherently conservative, he argues that "we tend to overlook the role of transgression in middle-class culture" and to overstate cultural normativity (593). Reading Trollope's fiction, we can see the way he "projects illicit energies outside the middle class, stigmatizing them as the moral defects of the enemies of the bourgeois culture, only to reappropriate these same antibourgeois energies for his protagonists" (595). In other words, there is often a tension between normative morality and other desires in Trollope's treatment of the middle classes. Kucich focuses on the early novels—*Barchester Towers* and *Framley Parsonage*, in particular—and discusses the way Trollope's fiction both dismisses dishonesty from his communities while simultaneously making it a center of attention. Elsie B. Michie also examines Barsetshire—comparing *The Last Chronicle of Barset* to Margaret Oliphant's *Phoebe Junior*—in order to explore the "anxieties about the expansiveness of late-Victorian commerce" (78). For Michie, "both novels function in a quasi-anthropological sense, evoking, through the drama of individual characters' financial problems, an entire culture's response to dramatic changes in ecomonic practice and theory taking place in the last third of the nineteenth century" (78). In Mr. Crawley, Trollope creates a character whose lack of worldliness is his virtue, whereas in *Phoebe Junior*, "Oliphant insists that money allows us to gratify our tastes" (87). The honorable, ascetic gentleman in Trollope gets deconstructed in Oliphant.

Most discussions of middle-class politics and commerce tend to look to Trollope's later novels, especially the Pallisers, where the definition of the gentleman continues to hold interest. Audrey Jaffe's fascinating article "Trollope in the Stock Market" begins by questioning the meaning of the jagged line of the stock market graph. What narrative does this line reveal? How are we to interpret this sign, which, swinging between optimism and pessimism, represents narratives of emotion, of the "national (or global) mood" (45)? She moves from this musing to *The Prime Minister*, in which "one can read a man's character" through "the way he manages his money." However, such a reading does not do justice to the complexity and scope of the novel:

> *The Prime Minister* also offers other ways of understanding our own assimilations of feeling and the market and the lines we continue to draw in their name, perhaps most strikingly in its status as a precursor of today's stock market dramas: those episodes, played out in the daily newspapers and the nightly news, in which a violation of financial rules . . . registers as a general social violation, an offense against middle-class culture and feeling.   (46)

The novel may be one man's story, but the implications of the narrative are far-reaching. Our emotional selves are bound up with our finances, with our own "fluctuating numbers," and it is this "transfer of identity into numbers that is the market's lifeblood" (60). For Jaffe, part of Trollope's interest in the novel is in delineating the distinctions between gentleman and non-gentleman; for Courtney C. Berger, *The Prime Minister* highlights the need for bipartisan politics, since "without a formal system of differentiation . . . people will no longer be distinguishable from one another" (331). Berger's discussion begins by trying to get at the heart of contemporary reviewers' charges of "vulgarity" in late Trollope novels, which emphasizes the crucial critical problem: is Trollope's "common-ness" his gift or his failing? Berger argues that reviewers objected to *The Prime Minister* because social and political realms "become interchangeable" in the novel: "The eradication of formal distinctions both within the political arena as well as separating politics from the social world precipitates a crisis of identity within the novel" (317). The very notion of a coalition government at the beginning suggests that in this world boundaries have collapsed, that "otherwise divided parties have mingled, and otherwise separate spheres, such as economics and politics, have become indistinguishable" (318). The cries of vulgarity by reviewers express contemporary anxieties about uncertain, and, arguably, collapsing economic, social, national, gender, political, and religious distinctions. Richard Dellamora's suggestive reading of the novel in his book *Friendship's Bonds* puts it in its post-Reform Bill context, and notes that in this still-gendered political world the novel

> registers the existence of individuals and groups demanding entry into public life: namely, women, Jews, immigrants, and upper-working-class male voters. In terms of the novel, the contemporary crisis of democracy in England is created by the demands for participation made by these players. The result, in terms of the novel, is a demonstration of the failure of the existing consensus. This outcome leaves the country in a state of stasis.					(103)

Lopez's suicide suggests the "total destruction of an alien interloper" who "fails to fulfill the terms of the code of gentleman" (119).

Jeffrey Franklin, in "The Victorian Discourse of Gambling," reads *The Duke's Children* alongside *Middlemarch* and begins with the premise that "the discourse of money" is "a primary vehicle for the progressive or liberal ideologies of the ascending middle class" (899). By examining the discourse of money, we are forced to examine the discourses of marriage and work: "Gambling is analyzed as that which binds together and problematizes this central trinity of Victorian concerns" (900). Ultimately, the trouble with gambling in *The Duke's Children* is that it mixes high and low (high is made low, and low becomes high) and such speedy social mobility is a threat to social boundaries. It also raises questions about what constitutes value in contemporary society—is it land, labor, or exchange?

Virtually all of the critics who write about Trollope's middle classes, whether in relation to politics, commerce, or both, have to grapple with his vision of the English gentleman. Lauren M. E. Goodlad, in a chapter in her book *Victorian Literature and the Victorian State*, looks at two neglected texts, Trollope's condition-of-England essays, *The New Zealander*, and his novel *The Three Clerks*. Whereas in the Barchester novels Trollope "affirms the aegis of well-bred men" (137), in *The Three Clerks*, he writes "a disturbing allegory in which wrongheaded civil service reforms exacerbate destructive modern tendencies" (120). In the different treatment of middle-class men and aspirations in the series as opposed to *The Three Clerks*, we see a tension between "the upper-class myth of the born-and-bred gentleman, and the entrepreneurial myth of the self-made man," and what is at stake, as Goodlad sees it, is the balance between the two.

Questions of Identity: Irish, Jewish, Colonial

The resurgence of interest in Trollope and the Irish that Nancy Metz identified in her survey of Trollope criticism from 1982 to 1986 gathers even more force in recent years. Many of the questions raised by critics interrogating politics and commerce are also crucial to those interested in Ireland and Irishness, in particular in connection with land and power, the figure of the outsider, and the way identity is formed in mid-Victorian Britain. As a recent special issue of *Victorian Literature and Culture* on "Victorian Ireland" (2004) suggests, Trollope's work is clearly significant to Irish questions in the period. Laura M. Berol's article for that special issue suggests that Trollope's Irish novels in the 1840s "enter a broader conversation and engage with popular English fears regarding the Anglo-Irish. The novels construct relationships among Anglo-Irish, native Irish, and English characters that implicitly critique the interactions of all three" (104). Furthermore, the role of gender is central to the novels' critique "since it marks power differentials among the groups and shapes readers' expectations of their behavior to one another," and through the gendered representations of the different groups, Trollope, like Thackeray, raises "issues of inequality and exploitation, especially as perpetrated by the Ascendancy" (104). Bridget Matthews-Kane's article on romantic allegory in *Castle Richmond* argues that "Trollope assigns distinctive traits to his characters so that they can allegorically represent components of the debate regarding Irish independence, particularly the issues raised by the cultural nationalists" (119). Matthews-Kane suggests that part of the difficulty with the novel is its genre—romance—which promises love. The "emotional register of Trollope's novel" is sometimes at odds with ideological arguments; however, "the friction between the emotional and ideological responses to the text does not mar the novel on its own but does highlight the rationalizations that justify the British approach to Ireland, thus raising uncomfortable associations for a British audience" (117). In an article in the *Irish University Review* on *Castle Richmond*, Margaret Kelleher argues that the novel offers a "representation of famine's effects, through the construction of a female spectacle, more extensive and disturbing than any of its predecessors" (262). Rather than reading the famine as incidental to the novel as critics have tended to do, she locates the novel in the context of famine writing—in particular, Trollope's seven letters to the *Examiner* published between 1849 and 1850 and the earl of Dufferin's *Narrative of a Journey from Oxford to Skibbereen during the Year of the Irish Famine*, 1847.

Sooner or later, discussions of Irishness in Trollope lead to one of his great characters, Phineas Finn. Roy Foster puts Trollope at the center of his discussion of Parliamentary novels, arguing that Phineas's "Irishness remains a vital dimension of his politics, particularly regarding the tenant right and the moral test imposed by giving a correct vote on the issue" (145). As an historian of Ireland, Foster interestingly suggests that there is value in the historian studying Trollope's novels, since Trollope so clearly understood how politics operates, the "rhetoric" and "shadowboxing" of the political arena. He suggests that historians need to learn to interpret political novels, to analyze the genre's "implicit internal assumptions, as well as the reasons why they were read," and in reading *Phineas Finn*, Foster offers us an argument for doing so.

How we read Phineas has been a vexed question ever since Trollope famously admitted in his *Autobiography* that he regretted making Phineas an Irishman, and readers have been wrestling with the significance of Phineas's national/racial identity ever since. Jane Elizabeth Dougherty argues that making Phineas Irish was both a help and hindrance, both "crucial and incidental" (133). For her, the contradiction rings true "because of the self-contradictory status of Ireland after the Union, a union which is explicitly defined in *Phineas Finn* as a marriage contract and which rendered Ireland an anomalous entity within the contractarian society of the United Kingdom prior to and during the time that Trollope was writing the Palliser novels" (133–34). At a time of Fenian antagonisms, Trollope appears to advocate "the mid-Victorian policy of seeking to establish a 'union of hearts' between the two countries," but such a policy was fraught with tensions. Patrick Lonegran argues that Phineas was a sympathetic representation at a time when there were few other such depictions. For Lonegran, Phineas is a feminized man, and this "characteriziation of Ireland as wife to England's husband . . . allowed both countries to fit into a metaphor for the Act of Union whereby the feminine Irish would be united with—though inferior to—the English" (155).

Julian Wolfreys's article "An Other Trollope: Questions of Englishness, or Towards Politicized Readings," has a dual purpose. On the one hand, it seeks to make an argument about *Phineas Finn* and national identity; on the other, it hopes to make an argument about how to read, about critical interpretation, more generally. Writing at the time that Trollope had been declared the literary favorite of Conservative Prime Minister John Major in the early 1990s, Wolfreys sets out to provide a politically dissident reading of the text that works against dominant ideologies. In other words, he wants to reclaim Trollope from the conversatives, and he does this through a skillful and intelligent deconstructivist interpretation of the novel. In Wolfreys's view, "the decenterd center is the pretext of Trollope's writing" (305) and his novels reveal that "there is no heart at the heart of the British Empire, and Englishness has nothing solid, its identity being a simulacrum" (306). Phineas is significant in this regard because of his disruptive tendencies; his name "exists on borderlines, socially, culturally, politically" and it "refuses to be settled in one place" (307). As in all deconstructive practice, the text is something of a moving target, refusing to be pinned down and settled, and Wolfreys makes a compelling case for attending to the instabilities in a novel like *Phineas Finn*. There is an urgency in doing so, he argues, since the "ideological chicanery underneath the speculative concepts such as 'family,' 'nation,' and 'gentleman,' . . . are still the stock in trade of the New Right's polemic" (327). Wolfreys offers his own polemic in response, but it is one that is energetic, thoughtful, and genuinely requires the reader to think about the cultural status of a novelist like Trollope, then and now.

Identity and social distinction are at the center of Paul Delany's reading of *The Way We Live Now* in his study *Literature, Money and the Market*. He argues that Trollope "deplores" "Melmotte's eagerness to consolidate his position in Britain by buying an estate," and that he "can accept the commercial classes so long as they remain 'in their place,' deferring politically and socially to the landed aristocracy" (22). *The Way We Live Now* offers a vision of "miscegenation in the widest sense: not just the entry of new races or types into the traditional ruling class, but the calling into question the whole basis of social differentiation within a known hierarchy." The question of Melmotte's Jewishness "corresponds to the opacity of his speculations and the slippery anonymity of finance capital itself" (26–27). In the world they live in now, ambiguity and vagueness are seemingly the only certainties. While Trollope may be "an evident enemy of the emerging 'Open Society,' " he also has to admit "that there is now no consensus about how classes are constituted, or where the boundaries between them should be fixed" (28). Like Delany, Derek Cohen examines the representation of Melmotte's Jewishness, and notes the way Trollope draws on stereotypes of the Jew (also seen in the character of Lopez in *The Prime Minister*). As Cohen reads him, Melmotte "follows the tradition of Jewish villainy that is embedded in the accepted canon of English literature" (65). The problem with perpetuating a stereotyped character such as Melmotte is that it "contributes to the tradition by which the notion becomes a received truth and augments the hold which the notion exerts over recipients of its 'truth'—Trollope's public" (75).

Work on Trollope's travel writing has made some critical impact in recent years, although the fiction remains the focus on interest for most. Simon Gikandi's article on "writing the West Indies" provides a welcome focus on issues of colonial identity and English identity. This study, later published as part of his full-length study, *Maps of Englishness*, is interested in the politics of identity and the way writing about the colonies challenged forms of writing, and considers English writers such as Kingsley and Froude alongside Trollope. Gikandi's work can be read alongside Catherine Hall's excellent study *Civilising Subjects: Metropole and Colony in the English Imagination*, which also discusses Trollope's engagement with the West Indies at length. Hall reads the distinction between Trollope's novels and his book on the West Indies as analogous to that between home and colonies, with an obviously gendered dimension. According to Hall, "Trollope's manhood was constantly at risk on the feminised site of the novel, particularly since so much of his writing was focused on romance and domestic life. In his travel writing that interest in manners, in dress, and in emotionality could be offset with a commentary on economic and political life—of a sort which women were not supposed, in his view, to be able to make" (219). Rooted in close reading and historical investigation, and theoretically informed, Gikandi's and Hall's work is intelligent and challenging and requires us to think about the politics of texts in splendid ways. Two other pieces complement Gikandi's and Hall's studies. Nicholas Birns offers a good introduction to the subject of Trollope's colonialism in his article, "The Empire Turned Upside Down," and Trollope's vision of the Orient in *Tales of All Countries* is taken up by Thomas L. Cooksey, who finds in that work a pervasive sense of what he calls "romantic disillusionment" with the region.

The Law

While discussions of politics, commerce, and Jewishness cluster around *The Prime Minister* and *The Way We Live Now*, and discussions of Irishness around *Phineas Finn*, critics engaged with Trollope's view of the law almost always settle on *Orley Farm*. This is for good reason, since this is the novel in which Lady Mason, the forger, is acquitted of a crime the reader (and most of society in the novel) knows she committed. It naturally raises the questions, what is truth and what is justice? Trollope critics have frequently engaged with Trollope's representation of lawyers and legal issues, but there was a renewed interest in these matters with the rise of Critical Legal studies in the late 1980s and 1990s. What legal cases and novels have in common is narrative. Paula Jean Reiter examines the relationship between male barrister and female client in a study of *Orley Farm* alongside the "real" case of Adelaide Bartlett, a woman accused of poisoning who is acquitted, in order to show the "overlapping cultural dynamics shared by law and literature" (248). Reiter argues that "the stories barristers tell and the dynamics of the attorney-client relationship articulate and mimic the lines of conventional Victorian gender roles, particularly those within heterosexual marriage" (247). The client is the quiet, dependent wife, while the barrister is the vocal, public-speaking husband. In both Trollope's novel and the case of Adelaide Bartlett, the women "play the role of a wife as part of their legal defense and, one suspects, as part of their rehabilitation. They buy their acquittals, but the price is embracing the very stereotypes and roles that would continue to cripple them and that would perpetuate the very conditions against which their crimes rebelled" (267).

Jan-Melissa Schramm's discussion of *Orley Farm* raises the question, how should a lawyer act when he knows his client is guilty? She notes that Trollope's novel is the exception to the law that the guilty are always found guilty by the law. For her, the novel "explores the legal profession's move towards 'testing the prosecution' theory of the criminal trial and it is premised on an inversion of the literary models espoused by Dickens, Eliot, and Gaskell" (127). Kieran Dolin's chapter on the novel, in his book *Fiction and the Law*, argues that it "challenges us by its championship of the individual and its attack on conventional advocacy in the name of truth" (100). What is at stake here is the nature of truthful representation, a keen concern to Trollope the realist novelist. Glynn-Ellen Fisichelli's article "The Language of Law and Love" suggests that the connections between language and law are central to *Orley Farm*. By focusing on a legal case, Trollope is able to explore "the subtleties of language and the ways in which it may reveal and conceal the truth" (635). Fisichelli makes a compelling case of her own for focusing closely on Trollope's language (which most critics have tended not to do, Juliet McMaster being the primary exception). For Trollope, words "have an almost talismanic power to damage or vindicate, and he defines conduct through each character's judgement about the ways in which he will speak" (638). Ultimately, although sometimes in perverse ways, Trollope's novel is about the ability of words to communicate truth. Two other pieces of work are worth mentioning, not least because they examine different texts. Karen Odden considers white collar crime in *The Way We Live Now* and Cathrine O. Frank considers questions of legitimacy in Forster's *Howard's End* and *Ralph the Heir*, a novel that it is good to see scholars working on, despite Trollope's condemnation of it. Both Odden's and Frank's work make interesting interventions in our understanding of Trollope and the law.

Valentine Cunningham's article on Trollope and legal issues widely defined does not provide a single sustained argumentative line, but its ruminations may be suggestive nonetheless. He notes the plethora of lawyers in Victorian fiction, that many of these are in Trollope, that lawyers have always been

keen readers of his novels, and that considerations of the "law," broadly
defined (Christian vs. Old Testament law, for example, or more specifically
the 1839 Infant Custody Act) find their way into Trollope's fiction in a variety
of ways. This article sometimes reads like a sweeping lecture that has been
written down, and there is no critical analysis of any texts in particular. Still,
its wide range raises issues and questions that other scholars may pursue
more closely.

Form and Language

Increasingly, serious attention is being paid to the series/serial forms in which
most of Trollope's writing after 1860s appeared. Hamer's book pioneered
this work, and my own study also indicates continued interest. Shortly after
Hamer's book appeared, Andrew Blake's *Reading Victorian Fiction* explored
the ways print culture and the magazines provide significant cultural and
interpretive contexts for readings Victorian fiction. While there is no single
chapter devoted to Trollope, discussion of his work extends throughout the
study and he considers understudied novels, including *Lady Anna*.

   Laurie Langbauer's excellent book *Novels of Everyday Life* devotes a chapter to Trollope's series fiction. She reads the Barchester novels (in particular,
Framley Parsonage) together with Trollope's travel books, "to see how these
politics of cultural performance work, to see what the everyday and the series
tell us about our attempts at reading the web of cultural interconnectedness."
Langbauer argues that there is a "limitlessness of context" in Trollope's
fiction that "forecloses the possibility of thinking everything at once politically." She attends to the "intricate mesh of endlessly interwoven relations"
at the level of the cultural object, and her interpretation of this complexity is
both challenging and rewarding. Her work is informed by poststructuralist
thinking—including Derrida on speech acts, and Homi Bhaba and Kobena
Mercer on hybridity—and she argues that attempts to "fix" Trollope are
misguided because the messy series form shows us not an endpoint, but an
ongoing process. So, for example, J. Hillis Miller's arguments about Trollope's subversion and D. A. Miller's arguments about his conservatism both
neglect to consider the way form complicates matters. Readers interested in
sequence novels will also want to take a look at Lynette Felber's reading of
the Phineas novels as a "diptych."

   Graham Law's article on "Trollope and the Newspapers" examines a
mostly unknown area of research, the novel serialized in a newspaper. By
focusing on the publication of Trollope's novels in weekly papers, Law provides a corrective to Hamer, myself, and others who focus on the 1860s
and almost exclusively on serial publication in magazines. He argues that

serialization of Trollope's later fiction in a range of newspapers, from "metro-politan illustrated to Society papers and groups of provincial news miscellan-ies," offers evidence of "the growing importance of the newspaper press in the market-place for later Victorian fiction" (47). He provides sections on the context of newspaper serialization and on Trollope as a newspaper novel-ist, and provides a case study of the publication of *Ayala's Angel*, a novel which has hitherto not been thought to have been serialized. In fact, it was published (and republished) in several different types of newspapers. While not quite a first foray into the field (see also Law's earlier book, *Serializing Fiction in the Victorian Press*), he is correct in his conclusion that we still have a lot to learn about publication in newspapers and how readers con-sumed and interpret that fiction differently.

Randall Craig's study of Trollope's language in "Rhetoric and Courtship in *Can You Forgive Her?*" explores the formal aspects of Trollope's writing, and complements work by critics such as Elizabeth R. Epperly on other aspects of Trollope's language. Craig argues that Trollope's "direct and self-effacing style . . . tends to obscure his subtle insinuation of questions of rheto-ric into the conduct of romance" (218). Trollope's use of two strategies, oxymoron and rhetorical questions, helps him explore contradiction in the novel.

Comparative Studies

Trollope has always been a novelist who gets compared to others, and Henry James's work has often figured prominently, not least because of James's lengthy essay on Trollope, published in the *Century* in July 1883. Sara B. Blair takes James's critical reading of Trollope as her point of departure for a discussion of James's positioning of himself in relation to the Anglo-Ameri-can reading public. She suggests that "James takes up the case of Trollope in order to link himself with and distance himself from particular national traditions, thereby to invent an Anglo-American reading public and the novel that will represent it: a vehicle for coherent moral discourse, distinct from the commodity culture it scrutinizes, embodying the stable values of a reified English tradition." For Blair, what is at stake in James's reading of Trollope is a powerful statement about the significance of the novelist and the "role of cultural guardianship" (42). This is a serious and interesting study of an essay well known in both Trollope and James studies, and Blair makes this critical encounter with Trollope a vital part of a wider cultural project to define the parameters of a new kind of fiction. Far less illuminating is Adeline R. Tintner's comparison of James's "The Patagonia" with Trollope's "The Journey to Panama," arguing fairly simply that James rewrites and betters Trollope, in his similar tale of a woman on a sea voyage who is traveling out to marry her fiancé. James's heroine is "unusual and neurotic" while Trollope's is "practical" (65), and the different treatments of the young women show that "James considered Trollope's version inadequate to the tragic possibilities" (66), a conclusion I don't think warranted by the level of discussion. Another account of "The Journey to Panama" also fails to make much of an impact. Denise Kohn's article suggests that the story shows a "brave, Feminist Trollope" and notes that the story was first published by Emily Faithfull's Victoria Press, which links it with a particular feminist history (an interesting enough point), but there is little by way of extended, sophisticated analysis here. In fact, there have been relatively few extended discussions of Trollope's stories in recent years (my discussion of *An Editor's Tales* is a rare exception), which is regrettable, particularly given that the stories are now more easily accessible than ever before in John Sutherland's two-volume (early and later stories) edition for World's Classics.

Margaret Oliphant is another contemporary often compared with Trollope (see, for example, Elsie B. Michie's article discussed above), often for the way her Chronicles of Carlingford can be read suggestively alongside the Barchester novels. Joseph H. O'Mealy's argues that in *Phoebe Junior*, Oliphant is directly attacking Trollope's version of clerical life. Oliphant's 1876 novel was a last chance to weigh in on the "realism wars," and "she knew that her versions of family and clerical life and her attitudes toward love and marriage were grounded more firmly in the actual than Trollope's or Yonge's romances, and she was not shy about saying so" (137). Tess O'Toole is interested in the ways adoption is represented in fiction, and she reads Dinah Craik's 1886 novel *King Arthur: Not a Love Story* in relation to Trollope's *Doctor Thorne*. Craik's novel is about the "advantages of wise adoption" (63), while Trollope's intertwines "the idea of adoption as a civilizing process and of the female as a civilizing agent" (67). Comparisons with continental literature in the period are relatively scarce in Trollope studies, and so Helmut Kuzmics's study of Theodor Fontane's *Effi Briest* in relation to *Can You Forgive Her?* stands out, although it may not be all that enlightening about either text. As he states, his article "aims at a sociological description via fiction and not at a deeper understanding of the novels themselves" (153), and the result of his comparison of Effi with Alice Vavasor is merely speculative as a result. He is too insistent on his sociological approach and overly uses the novels to explain "real" elements of Prussian and English culture in the period.

Other Studies

Some work on Trollope resists being categorized too easily, and the criticism of J. Hillis Miller is frequently a case in point. He has long been an admirer of Trollope, as his important chapter on Trollope in *The Ethics of Reading* suggests. Miller's study explores what he calls the "ethical moment" in literature, when "there is a claim made on the author writing the work, on the narrator telling the story within the fiction of the novel, on the characters within the story at decisive moments of their lives, and on the reader, teacher, or critic responding to the work" (8). He reads closely Trollope's *An Autobiography* as an example of "self-reading." Early in the text, Trollope reveals how he came to write novels, essentially through daydreaming as a youth, but Miller's argument is that his daydreaming tale is "incoherent," that "Trollope wants above all to say one thing, but in spite of himself he says another thing which subverts the claim he wishes to make for the nature and function of his novels" (84–85). Miller's deconstructed Trollope is a subversive one; Trollope "wants to show that his novels are moral in the sense of affirming the values of that society" (96), while, in fact, he does the opposite.

Miller's work in whatever field is always challenging and thoughtful, and his return to Trollope in the joint text, *J. Hillis Miller; Or, Boustropedonic Reading/Black Holes*, combines a critical study of Miller by Manuel Asensi with Miller's own study of what he calls "black holes" in literature. The two texts are printed on facing pages, as if in dialogue, so Alensi's discussion of Miller's way of reading appears opposite Miller's actual reading. The first half of Miller's text seeks to understand the "unusually rapid changes in literary study" in American research universities, in particular through new electronic media; the second half of the text focuses primarily on two texts, Trollope's *Ayala's Angel* and Proust's *A la recherche du temps perdu*, and Miller seeks to "understand, to 'read' in the sense of seeing through, the strangeness of particular literary works" (xi). For Miller, reading literature is full of strange encounters with "others" and with things we don't necessarily understand. Drawing on the internet as a metaphor, he posits literary study as encountering uncertainty, "confronting something radically alien, something that interrupts the continuity of all those wonderfully rational information highways the university, with help from governments, along with communications and technology corporations is building" (186). Reading is disruption, then, and, unlike D. A. Miller, whom he critiques, Hillis Miller believes that "what is interesting in a writer like Trollope is the revelation, perhaps inadvertently, of cracks, fissures, and contradictions in the ideological construct he apparently endorses." These are tensions that "led in later stages of British cultural history to this ideology's self-destruction." The particular ideology that Miller pursues in his case study of Trollope is that of love, which he says becomes something unpredictable in *Ayala's Angel*. This is truly original, innovative work by a fiercely intelligent Trollope reader.

Conclusion

As this survey indicates, the field of Trollope studies is rich and continues to draw scholarship from a range of conceptual approaches and disciplines. In a way, perhaps, that other Victorian novelists do not (the Brontës, Thackeray, George Eliot), Trollope lures readers and students of law, politics, and economics, besides devotees of literature and culture. This interdisciplinarity is one of the features that continues to distinguish Trollope scholarship. Another sign of the buoyancy of Trollope studies is the large number of doctoral dissertations that have been written on his work in recent years. This, of course, points to the scholarship of the future, one good indication of where interests may be heading. Topics covered by younger scholars in recent years include criminality, flirtation, imperialism, insanity, gender and law, the short fiction, and, unsurprisingly, more on representations of Trollope's women. All of this suggests that the next survey of Trollope studies promises to be even more wide-ranging and critically eclectic than this one.

WORKS CITED

Allen, Peter. "Trollope to His Readers: The Unrealistic Narrator of *An Autobiography.*" *Biography: An Interdisciplinary Journal* 19:1 (Winter 1996): 1–18.

apRoberts, Ruth. *Trollope: Artist and Moralist.* London: Chatto and Windus, 1971.

Asensi, Manuel and J. Hillis Miller. *J. Hillis Miller; Or, Boustropedonic Reading/ Black Holes.* Stanford: Stanford UP, 1999.

Berger, Courtney C. "Partying with the Opposition: Social Politics in *The Prime Minister.*" *Texas Studies in Literature and Language* 45:3 (Fall 2003): 315–36.

Berol, Laura M. "The Anglo-Irish Threat in Thackeray's and Trollope's Writings of the 1840s." *Victorian Literature and Culture* 32:1 (2004): 103–16.

Birns, Nicholas. "The Empire Turned Upside Down: The Colonial Fictions of Anthony Trollope." *ARIEL: A Review of International English* 27:3 (July 1996): 7–23.

Blair, Sara B. "Changing the Subject: Henry James, *Dred Scott*, and Fictions of Identity." *American Literary History* 4:1 (Spring 1992): 28–55.

Cohen, Derek. "Constructing the Contradiction: Anthony Trollope's *The Way We Live Now.*" *Jewish Presences in English Literature.* Eds. Derek Cohen and Deborah Heller. Montreal: McGill-Queen's UP, 1990. 61–75.

Cohen, William A. *Sex Scandal: The Private Parts of Victorian Fiction*. Durham: Duke UP, 1996.

———. "Trollope's Trollop." *Novel: A Forum* 28:3 (Spring 1995): 235–56.

Cooksey, Thomas L. "Trollope and the Mysterious Orient: The Romanticism of Disillusionment in *Tales of All Countries*." *International Perspectives on English and American Language and Literature* (1999): 29–40.

Craig, Randall. "Rhetoric and Courtship in *Can You Forgive Her?*" *ELH* 62:1 (1995): 217–35.

Cunningham, Valentine. "Anthony Trollope and Law, Laws, Legalisms and Assorted Legislations," *REAL: Yearbook of Research in English and American Literature* 18 (2002): 89–107.

Davis, Philip. *The Oxford English Literary History Volume 8. 1830–1880: The Victorians*. Oxford: Oxford UP, 2002.

Delany, Paul. *Literature, Money and the Market: From Trollope to Amis*. Houndsmills: Palgrave, 2002.

Dellamora, Richard. *Friendship's Bonds: Democracy and the Novel in Victorian England*. Philadelphia: U of Pennsylvania P, 2004.

———. "Stupid Trollope," *Victorian Newsletter* 100 (Fall 2001): 22–26.

Dolin, Kieran. *Fiction and the Law: Legal Discourse in Victorian and Modernist Literature*. Cambridge: Cambridge UP, 1999.

Dougherty, Jane Elizabeth. "An Angel in the House: The Act of Union and Anthony Trollope's Irish Hero," *Victorian Literature and Culture* 32:1 (2004), 133–45.

Durey, Jill Felicity. *Trollope and the Church of England*. Houndsmills: Palgrave, 2002.

Epperly, Elizabeth R. *Anthony Trollope's Notes on the Old Drama*. Victoria, BC: U of Victoria P, 1988.

———. *Patterns of Repetition in Trollope*. Washington, DC: Catholic UP, 1989.

Felber, Lynette. "Trollope's Phineas Diptych as Sequel and Sequence Novel." *Part Two: Reflections on the Sequel*. Eds. Paul Budra and Betty A. Schellenberg. Toronto: U of Toronto P, 1998.

Fisichelli, Glynn-Ellen. "The Language of Law and Love: Anthony Trollope's *Orley Farm*." *ELH* 61:3 (1994): 635–53.

Floyd, Kevin. "Discerning Motive: Another Look at Trollope's *The Warden*." *The University of Mississippi Studies in English* 11–12 (1993–1995): 88–96.

Foster, R. F. *Paddy and Mr Punch: Connections in Irish and English History*. London: Allen Lane, 1993.

Frank, Cathrine O. "Fictions of Justice: Testamentary Intention and the (Il)Legitimate Heir in Trollope's *Ralph the Heir* and Forster's *Howard's End*." *English Literature in Transition, 1880–1920* 47:3 (2004): 311–30.

Franklin, Jeffrey. "The Victorian Discourse of Gambling: Speculations on *Middlemarch* and *The Duke's Children*." *ELH* 61:4 (1994): 899–921.

Gikandi, Simon. "Englishness, Travel, and Theory: Writing the West Indies in the Nineteenth Century." *Nineteenth-Century Contexts* 18:1 (1994): 49–70.

———. *Maps of Englishness: Writing Identity in the Culture of Colonialism*. New York: Columbia UP, 1996.

Goodlad, Lauren M. E. *Victorian Literature and the Victorian State: Character and Governance in a Liberal Society*. Baltimore: Johns Hopkins UP, 2003.

Hall, Catherine. *Civilising Subjects: Metropole and Colony in the English Imagination, 1830–1867*. Chicago: U of Chicago P, 2000.

Hall, Donald E. *Fixing Patriarchy: Feminism and Mid-Victorian Male Novelists*. Houndsmills: Macmillan, 1996.

Hall, N. John, James R. Kincaid, Ruth apRoberts, Juliet McMaster, Robert Tracy, Robert M. Polhemus, and John Halperin. "Trollopians *Reduces*." *Lit: Literature, Interpretation, Theory* 3:3 (1992): 175–87.

Hamer, Mary. *Writing by Numbers: Trollope's Serial Fiction*. Cambridge: Cambridge UP, 1987.

Herbert, Christopher. *Trollope and Comic Pleasure*. Chicago: U of Chicago P, 1987.

Horsman, Alan. *The Victorian Novel*. Oxford: Clarendon, 1990.

Hughes, Linda K. and Michael Lund. *Victorian Publishing and Mrs. Gaskell's Work*. Charlottesville, VA: UP of Virginia, 1999.

Jaffe, Audrey. "Trollope in the Stock Market: Irrational Exuberance and *The Prime Minister*." *Victorian Studies* 45:1 (Autumn 2002): 43–64.

Kelleher, Margaret. "Anthony Trollope's *Castle Richmond*: Famine Narrative and Horrid Novel?" *Irish University Review* 25:2 (Autumn/Winter 1995): 242–62.

Kohn, Denise. " 'The Journey to Panama': One of Trollope's Best 'Tarts'—or, Why You Should Read 'The Journey to Panama' to Develop Your Taste for Trollope." *Studies in Short Fiction* 30:1 (Winter 1993): 15–22.

Kristeva, Julia. *Powers of Horror: An Essay on Abjection*. Len S. Roudiez, trans. New York: Columbia UP, 1982.

Kucich, John. "Transgression in Trollope: Dishonesty and the Antibourgeois Elite." *ELH* 56:3 (1989): 593–618.

Kuzmics, Helmut. "Aristocracy and Bourgeoisie in Late Nineteenth-Century Prussia and England: Comparing Processes of Individualisation in Fontane and Trollope." *Theodor Fontane and the European Context*. Eds. Patricia Howe and Helen Chambers. Amsterdam: Rodopi, 1999. 153–66.

LaCom, Cindy. " 'It is More than Lame': Female Disability, Sexuality, and the Maternal in the Nineteenth-Century Novel." *The Body and Physical Difference: Discourses of Disability*. Eds. David T. Mitchell and Sharon L. Snyder. Ann Arbor: U of Michigan P, 1997. 189–201.

Langbauer, Laurie. *Novels of Everyday Life: The Series in English Fiction, 1850–1930*. Ithaca: Cornell U P, 1999.

Law, Graham. *Serializing Fiction in the Victorian Press*. Houndmills: Palgrave, 2000.

———. "Trollope and the Newspapers." *Media History* 9:1 (April 2003): 47–62.

Lawson, Kate. "Violated and Defiled: Signora Neroni's Body in *Barchester Towers*." *Victorian Review* 21:1 (Summer 1995): 53–68.

Lonegran, Patrick. "The Representation of Phineas Finn: Anthony Trollope's Palliser Series and Victorian Ireland." *Victorian Literature and Culture* 32:1 (2004): 147–58.

MacDonald, Susan Peck. *Anthony Trollope*. Boston: Twayne, 1987.

Marwick, Margaret. *Trollope and Women*. London: Hambledon, 1997.

Matthews-Kane, Bridget. "Love's Labour's Lost: Romantic Allegory in Trollope's *Castle Richmond*." *Victorian Literature and Culture* 32:1 (2004): 117–31.

Maunder, Andrew. " 'Alone into the wide, wide world': Trollope's *Miss Mackenzie* and the Mid-Victorian Etiquette Manual." *Victorian Review* 26:2 (2000): 48–74.

McDermott, Jim. "New Womanly Man: Feminized Heroism and the Politics of Compromise in *The Warden*." *Victorians Institute Journal* 27 (1999): 71–90.

McMaster, Juliet. *Trollope's Palliser Novels: Theme and Pattern*. London: Macmillan, 1978.

Metz, Nancy. "Trollope Studies, 1982–1986." *Dickens Studies Annual* 21 (1992): 281–312.

Michie, Elsie B. "Buying Brains: Trollope, Oliphant, and Vulgar Victorian Commerce." *Victorian Studies* 44:1 (Autumn 2001): 77–97.

Miller, D. A. *The Novel and the Police*. Berkeley: U of California P, 1988.

Miller, J. Hillis. *The Ethics of Reading: Kant, deMan, Eliot, Trollope, James and Benjamin*. New York: Columbia UP, 1987.

Moody, Ellen. *Trollope on the Net*. London: Hambledon, 1999.

Morse, Deborah Denenholz. *Women in Trollope's Palliser Novels*. Ann Arbor: UMI Research, 1987.

Mullen, Richard, with James Munson, *The Penguin Companion to Trollope*. London: Penguin, 1996.

Nardin, Jane. *He Knew She Was Right: The Independent Woman in the Novels of Anthony Trollope*. Carbondale: Southern Illinois UP, 1989.

———. *Trollope and Victorian Moral Philosophy*. Athens: Ohio UP, 1996.

Newlin, George, ed. *Everyone and Everything in Trollope*. 4 vols. Armonk, NY: M. E. Sharpe, 2005.

Newton, K. M. "Anthony Trollope and 'Classic Realism'." *A Companion to the Victorian Novel*. Eds. William Baker and Kenneth Womack. Westport, CT: Greenwood, 2002. 329–39.

Odden, Karen. "Puffed Papers and Broken Promises: White-Collar Crime and Literary Justice in *The Way We Live Now*." *Victorian Crime, Madness and Sensation*. Eds. Andrew Maunder and Grace Moore. Aldershot, UK: Ashgate, 2004. 135–45.

O'Mealy, Joseph H. "Rewriting Trollope and Yonge: Mrs. Oliphant's *Phoebe Junior* and the Realism Wars." *Texas Studies in Literature and Language* 39:2 (Summer 1997): 125–38.

O'Toole, Tess. "Adoption and the 'Improvement of the Estate' in Trollope and Craik." *Nineteenth-Century Literature* 52:1 (June 1997): 58–79.

Reiter, Paula Jean. "Husbands, Wives, and Lawyers: Gender Roles and Professional Representations in Trollope and the Adelaide Bartlett Case." *Un-Disciplining Literature: Literature, Law and Culture*. Eds. Kostas Myrsiades and Linda Myrsiades. New York: Peter Lang, 1998. 246–70.

Sanders, Andrew. *Anthony Trollope*. Plymouth, UK: Northcote House, 1998.

Schramm, Jan-Melissa. *Testimony and Advocacy in Victorian Law, Literature, and Theology*. Cambridge: Cambridge UP, 2000.

Shillingsburg, Peter L. *Pegasus in Harness: Victorian Publishing and W. M. Thackeray*. Charlottesville, VA: UP of Virginia, 1992.

Smith, Monika Rydygier. "Trollope's Dark Vision: Domestic Violence in *The Way We Live Now*." *Victorian Review* 22:1 (Summer 1996): 13–31.

Smith, Walter E. *Anthony Trollope: A Bibliography of his first American editions 1858–1884 with photographic reproductions of bindings and titlepages. A supplement to Michael Sadleir's T: A Bibliography*. Los Angeles: Heritage Book Shop, 2002.

Stone, Donald D. ''Prodigals and Prodigies: Trollope's Notes as a Son and Father.'' *Victorian Perspectives: Six Essays.* Eds. John Clubbe and Jerome Meckier. Houndmills: Macmillan, 1989. 42–67.

Super, R. H. ''Truth and Fiction in Trollope's *Autobiography.*'' *Nineteenth-Century Literature* 48:1 (June 1993): 74–88.

Swingle, L. J. *Romanticism and Anthony Trollope: A Study in the Continuities of Nineteenth-Century Literary Thought.* Ann Arbor: U of Michigan P, 1990.

Terry, R. C., ed. *Oxford Reader's Companion to Trollope.* Oxford: Oxford UP, 1999.

Thompson, Nicola. '' 'Something Both More and Less than Manliness': Gender and the Literary Reception of Anthony Trollope.'' *Victorian Literature and Culture* 22 (1994): 151–71.

Tingay, Lance O. *The Trollope Student: An Annotated List of Full Length Studies (1883–1990) and A Check List of Writings of Anthony Trollope and other members of the Trollopw Family (1743–1909).* London: Silverbridge, 1990.

Tintner, Adeline R. ''James's 'The Patagonia': A Critique of Trollope's 'The Journey to Panama.' '' *Studies in Short Fiction* 32:1 (Winter 1995): 59–66.

Tuchman, Gaye, with Nina E. Fortin. *Edging Women Out: Victorian Novelists, Publishers and Social Change.* London: Routledge, 1989.

Turner, Mark W. *Trollope and the Magazines: Gendered Issues in Mid-Victorian Britain.* Houndsmills: Macmillan, 2000.

Wall, Stephen. *Trollope and Character.* London: Faber and Faber, 1988.

Walton, Priscilla L. *Patriarchal Desire and Victorian Discourse: A Lacanian Reading of Anthony Trollope's Palliser Novels.* Toronto: U of Toronto P, 1995.

Weinberg, Louise. ''Is It All Right to Read Trollope?'' *The American Scholar* 62 (Summer 1993): 447–51.

Wiesenthal, Christine S. ''The Body Melancholic: Trollope's *He Knew He Was Right.*'' *Dickens Studies Annual* 23 (1994): 227–58.

Wolfreys, Julian. ''An Other Trollope: Questions of Englishness, or Towards Politicized Readings.'' *Dickens Studies Annual* 22 (1993): 303–29.

Colonialism in Victorian Fiction:
Recent Studies

Grace Moore

*This essay examines a range of the numerous publications dealing with
literature and imperialism in the Victorian period to have appeared
over the last fifteen years, many of which have been influenced by the
theoretical works of Edward Said, Homi K. Bhabha and Gayatri Spivak.
The piece begins with a survey of recent essays and monographs on
Dickens and colonialism, before broadening its scope to discuss a sample of more general book-length studies. The essay is arranged thematically and consideration is given to areas of interest to Victorian
scholars including emigration, the representation of India, and policing
the empire.*

The publication of Edward Said's magisterial *Orientalism* in 1978 signaled
a new direction for Victorian scholars with its examination of how the West
has misrepresented the East and how, as a consequence, the East has been
marginalized. Nearly thirty years on, the field has been enriched by developments in postcolonial theory, stemming from Said's work on the symbiosis
between the rise of the novel and the growth of empire, and from that of
other influential critics, including Homi K. Bhabha and Gayatri Spivak. Victo-
rianists have recognized the need to reclaim colonized others from the margins to which they were too frequently consigned both in fiction and in fact.
The quantity of articles, chapters, and books engaging with issues of race and
colonialism is quite overwhelming, and any survey must be almost ruthlessly
selective. This overview begins with a discussion of recent studies of Dickens

Dickens Studies Annual, Volume 37, Copyright © 2006 by AMS Press, Inc. All
rights reserved.

and imperialism, before broadening its scope to consider a sample of book-length studies and essay collections.

Dickens and the Colonies

While he spent little time in the empire outside Great Britain, visiting only Ireland and the dominion of Canada, Charles Dickens exiled a number of his sons to far-flung destinations, including Australia and India. Britain's overseas territories played an important role in Dickens's imagination throughout his career, just as they did in his real life, and in recent years increasing attention has been paid to the role of the empire in his novels and journalism. Both William Oddie's ''Dickens and the Indian Mutiny'' and Patrick Brantlinger's *Rule of Darkness*, although beyond the chronological scope of this essay, have heavily influenced a large number of studies of Dickens and imperialism. Between them, these two works have stimulated critical interest in Dickens's stance on race and the ways in which he frequently uses the empire to comment upon domestic matters. Having recently completed my own book on Dickens and imperialism, I have benefited enormously from the growing body of work dealing with his complicated and, at times, dramatic engagements with the world beyond Britain's shores.

Laura Peters's *Orphan Texts: Victorian Orphans, Culture and Empire* builds upon her earlier work, ''Perilous Adventures.'' Peters extends her examination of Dickens and Collins's controversial short story, ''The Perils of Certain English Prisoners'' to a broader range of texts, including *Oliver Twist*, *Bleak House*, and *Great Expectations,* as well as Emily Brontë's *Wuthering Heights*, George Eliot's *Silas Marner* and *Daniel Deronda*, and Rose Macauley's *Orphan Island*. Driven by the omnipresence of the orphan in nineteenth-century writing, Peters seeks to understand connections between the orphan state and imperialism. She offers an interesting examination of migration schemes aimed at removing parentless children from British shores and explores the benefits and pitfalls of the marginalized orphan state. Interestingly, Peters perceives orphan as having a ''pharmaceutical function'' in Victorian society (27), presenting the body politic as suffering from a sickness which can only be cured through the disruptive, but ultimately restorative, presence of the orphan. Peters's study is by no means restricted to the saintly Dickensian orphan, but rather extends her discussion to encompass foundlings, foreigners, and criminal orphans, along with the policing of empire. Peters considers the empire as a space where the exiled orphan could prosper, focusing particularly on the space for adventure offered by distant territories. Peters's prose is clear and engaging, and this short book carefully interweaves the experiences of orphan characters with what she terms ''orphan texts.''

She writes with modesty, drawing attention to ideas yet to be developed and leaving the reader with the pleasing sense that she has yet more to say on the matter. Interestingly, Peters is at work on a study of Dickens and race in which she will, no doubt, return to some of her compelling discussions of the 1857 Indian Mutiny, which are a particularly strong feature of *Orphan Texts*.

Dickens's initial reactions to the uprising in India, particularly his call to exterminate the sepoy rebels, are the most notorious aspect of his colonial engagement and are often cited as representative of his views on non-European races throughout his career. In fact, Dickens's attitudes towards both India and the imperial other were in a constant state of flux throughout his lifetime. An essay by Peters, entitled " 'Double-dyed Traitors and Infernal Villains': *Illustrated London News, Household Words*, Charles Dickens and the Indian Rebellion,'' appears in David Finkelstein and Douglas M. Peers's important collection *Negotiating India in the Nineteenth-Century Media*, along with another interesting piece by Hyungi Park, " 'The Story of Our Lives': *The Moonstone* and the Indian Mutiny in *All the Year Round*.'' Both chapters examine the role of the periodical press, particularly *Household Words*, in generating or circulating "hysteria" in the wake of the Indian uprising and in influencing Dickens's responses to the event. Park looks at the interplay between fiction and news and demonstrates the degree to which the media ran wild in reporting, and at times fabricating, incidents on the subcontinent. Park addresses *All the Year Round*'s curious silence on the mutiny and suggests that fiction became a space in which gruesome international news could be mediated. Arguing for a series of "Indias" in the Victorian press, Park moves smoothly to an analysis of *The Moonstone* as a mutiny master-narrative, before examining the more factual articles that framed it in *All the Year Round*. The collection by Finkelstein and Peers is excellent as a whole and offers a series of important contributions to our understanding of the ways in which India was presented to those Victorians who remained in the mother country.

As a glance at *The Moonstone* reveals, Dickens's good friend Wilkie Collins responded much more evenly to events in India, and his admission of British culpability in the rebellion is at odds with Dickens's most extreme pronouncements of September 1857. Lillian Nayder's study of the at times difficult collaborations between Dickens and Wilkie Collins incorporates a wealth of material on the ways in which both authors engaged with the empire. Nayder builds upon a number of her earlier articles to produce a sustained examination of both novelists' fascination with the British empire, whilst also seeking to recover Collins from Dickens's shadow. As always, Nayder's scholarship is meticulous, and her work here incorporates a much needed analysis of articles and essays from *Household Words* and *All the Year Round*, alongside close readings of novels by both writers. *Unequal*

Partners complicates the idea of a rift between Collins and Dickens in the final years of Dickens's life, stemming from Dickens's jealousy at the success of *The Moonstone*. Nayder goes back to examine the trajectory of Collins's and Dickens's differing reactions to the Indian uprising, asserting that Dickens had difficulty in accepting Collins's more lenient approach to the Indian "rebels" as played out in his section of "Perils of Certain English Prisoners," his article "A Sermon for Sepoys," and his clear sympathy for the plundered Indian nation in *The Moonstone*. Nayder returns to a large number of Collins's sources for *The Moonstone*, pointing out that he "seem[ed] more interested in excusing than indicting Indian violence in *The Moonstone*" (170). She then goes on to read *The Mystery of Edwin Drood* as forming a dialogue with Collins's novel, asserting that *Drood* anticipates the great critiques of colonialism of the 1880s and 1890s. While for many readers *Drood*'s incompleteness has rendered it a stumbling block, Nayder reads it in context and presents a convincing case for regarding the work as Dickens's great anti-imperial text.

According to Goldie Morgentaler, Dickens was far more attuned to issues of race and origins than some of his heated public statements might suggest. Morgentaler's *Dickens and Heredity* offers a breathtaking survey of Dickens's interest in inherited traits. As a young man who had firsthand experience of humiliating social descent during his brief spell at Warren's Blacking Factory, Dickens was, according to Morgentaler, acutely attuned to issues of deracination throughout his adult life. Central to Morgentaler's argument is the need to jettison modern day understandings of genetics in an attempt to recapture the nineteenth-century mind-set. The book begins with a helpful survey of the history of inherited characteristics, from the ancient Greeks through to the Darwinian revolution, in a bid to provide readers with an anchor. Morgentaler skillfully registers the interplay between politics and speculation about human origins and does an excellent job of situating Dickens within the debate.

Ranging from an analysis of the racialization of class in early novels like *Oliver Twist*, to a collation of parenthood with the imperial venture in *Dombey and Son*, Morgentaler outlines "Dickens's faith in hereditary endowment as a force for the propagation of good" (59) in his early works. She then continues to look at the increasing complexity of Dickens's treatment of heredity in his later works. Morgentaler re-evaluates the opening scenes of *Great Expectations*, reading Pip's experiences in the graveyard, when his solitary musings are interrupted by Magwitch's appearance from behind a tombstone, through a Darwinian lens. Morgentaler suggests that *Great Expectations* saw a rupture from Dickens's previous belief in inherited personality, which she explains by suggesting that for Pip, whose orphan status leaves him isolated from his genetic history, experience and encounters with other people are the factors that shape him. Morgentaler reads this shift from heredity to environment as evidence of Dickens's post-Darwinian revision of his understanding of human nature. She goes on to suggest that by the end of his career Dickens had fully assimilated Darwinian theory into his writing, as is evidenced by his growing interest in both sexual conflict and atavism. Dickens experienced what Morgentaler regards as a crisis of faith in heredity in the wake of the Darwinian revolution, so that by the final novels, heredity is displaced by images of disintegration. *Dickens and Heredity* is a major contribution to the growing body of work on Dickens and race, and Morgentaler is an able and enthusiastic guide through the complexities of Dickens's ever-changing involvement with inherited traits.

Although not uniquely concerned with imperialism, the late Anny Sadrin's collection *Dickens, Europe and the New Worlds* contains a number of essays addressing Dickens's fascination with the empire. Brian Cheadle's "Despatched to the Periphery" addresses the oppositions between the center and the margins in a broad range of Dickens's novels, including *Oliver Twist, Dombey and Son, David Copperfield,* and *Our Mutual Friend.* Cheadle rightly argues for the "periphery as a receptacle for the unwanted" (102), going on to consider the importance of exporting undesirable elements overseas to maintaining a "pure" center. Cheadle concludes with a brief discussion of the dissolution of distinct boundaries between margins and the center by the publication of *The Mystery of Edwin Drood*, leaving us with the ever-tantalizing question of how Dickens would have represented the great age of empire had he only lived longer. Both Jennifer Gribble and James Buzard offer interesting considerations of *Bleak House* in an imperial context, Gribble examining domestic slavery in the novel, and Buzard reading it in the context of 1850s nation-building. The final essay dealing explicitly with the empire is Patricia Plummer's "From Agnes Fleming to Helena Landless," which draws attention to "silences, gaps, darkness and invisibility" (268) in *Oliver Twist, David Copperfield,* and *The Mystery of Edwin Drood.* Plummer is particularly concerned with issues of alienation, and her contribution includes a compelling re-visitation of Dickensian outcasts, ending with a detailed analysis of *Drood*, which seems to directly answer some of Brian Cheadle's earlier questions and which focuses on the character Helena Landless as an embodiment of the chaos which ensues when the marginalized return to the center.

Wendy S. Jacobson's anthology *Dickens and the Children of Empire* brings together an equally important series of essays, covering a diverse range of imperial issues and interlacing many of them with studies of childhood. In a chapter on "Dickens and the Native American," Kate Flint revisits George Catlin, the theatrical impresario who gained notoriety for dressing up working-class men and attempting to pass them off as Ojibbeway Indians. Flint rereads Catlin as a figure committed to preserving Native American culture, rather than exploiting it, and reminds us of Catlin's early influence on Dickens's stance towards the Native American. Refusing to read Dickens's encounters with Native Americans through the lens of his later, unpleasant comments on other races, Flint conveys the respect and admiration that Dickens felt for the culture. She goes on to examine the controversial ''Noble Savage'' piece of 1853 by which time Catlin's deception had been exposed. Flint argues that Dickens's understanding of other races had regressed by this point and that he was becoming increasingly prone to homogenize the other. Flint charts a gradual decline in his empathy and sympathy for the Native American, but resists making a case for a continuum of racism. She points to later, more sophisticated pieces from *All the Year Round* to conclude that the Native American became a site of ''cultural contestation . . . on which a range of connotations could be deployed, serving a variety of ends.'' In short, the Native American is ''put to work'' in order to shed light on elements of the Condition of England Question, while at other times, such as in *Little Dorrit* s/he is deployed for humorous ends.

Grahame Smith's chapter ''Suppressing Narratives: Childhood and Empire in *The Uncommercial Traveller* and *Great Expectations*'' is a thoughtful study which considers the range of emotions that Dickens was forced to suppress from himself in the 1860s, drawing attention to his wholesale export of his sons to the empire as a consequence of his inability to cope with their failings. Smith considers Dickens's personal sorrows as informing his portrait of Magwitch, arguing that his brief experiences of childhood ''slavery'' at Warren's Blacking Factory were vividly recalled to him during the late 1850s and 1860s. According to Smith, Dickens poured these traumas, past and present, into his portraits of abused and neglected children, enslaved as part of the British workforce. Smith moves elegantly between biographical material and analysis of both fiction and journalism, extending the colonial metaphor to suggest that Dickens ''opted for a form of inner migration,'' retreating from trauma, or channeling it into his writing, before concluding with a compelling parallel between Magwitch and his creator.

Personal anxieties may also have been at the heart of Dickens's stance on India, and in his important article ''The Short Career of Walter Dickens in India,'' Dick Kooiman looks to Dickens's domestic life for insights into his reactions to the Mutiny. As is well known, Dickens's second son Walter departed for life in India as a military cadet in 1857, having been destined for imperial service from a very early age. Dickens's enormous bonfire of September 1860, in which he burned all of his correspondence, means that we will never know what Walter may have told him of events on the subcontinent. However, Kooiman has scoured an impressive array of primary sources in order to piece together as much of Walter's history as possible. Kooiman's style is both scholarly and charming, as he details the thrill of reading Walter's cadet papers. He is not afraid to speculate when facts are not available, and he offers some important insights into the struggles faced by soldiers after the dissolution of the East India Company. Kooiman suggests that "Dickens never showed any undue interest in India" (21), an assertion that is somewhat at odds with the numerous references to India which appear in a novel like *Dombey and Son*, or the many articles Dickens published on the need for administrative reform in the country, both before and after the Mutiny. Notwithstanding, Kooiman's piece provides valuable information about Walter Dickens's tragically short life.

Suvendrini Perera's *Reaches of Empire* is rich in the attention given to Dickens's novels, whilst also broadening out to consider works by Edgeworth, Austen, Thackeray, Gaskell, and Charlotte Brontë, not as part of a meta-argument, but as a series of individual, self-contained readings. Perera's work is one of the pivotal studies that argued for the need to pay attention to the mid-Victorian novel's more peripheral concern with the empire, rather than simply examining overtly imperial texts from the post-1870 period. Perera makes this peripheral concern her focus, re-reading classic novels that either criticized imperial expansionism, or seemed to ignore it altogether. As she asserts in the introduction, "if to go to India is to fall off a cliff, the absence over the other side is itself telling; not blank but a space accessible to reading" (3). Perera probes silences and margins in order to understand how the ever-expanding mid-Victorian novel was complicit in the dissemination and upholding of imperial values, honing her attention on descriptions of telling minutiae and artifacts that represent the silent trappings of colonial power. She examines the interplay between discourses of class and race, as well as the overlaps between the management of gender and that of the empire. Perera's oft-anthologized chapter on empire and the family in *Dombey and Son* appears in this volume; the piece is complex in its reading of the novel as "a parable of mercantile capitalism" (61). Perera rejects a polarized, oppositional reading of gender and imperialism, arguing instead for a much more subtle interchange between the two and citing the romance attached to colonial expansion like the adventure story of Walter Gay as evidence for her conclusions. She also addresses Dickens's somewhat ambivalent portrait of the East India Company, contrasting it with more damning indictments such as Harriet Martineau's in "Cinnamon and Pearls" and cleverly interspersing her discussion with close readings of Dickens's "Review of the Niger Expedition." The book ends with a brief discussion of race in *The Mystery of Edwin Drood* in which De Quincey's influence is outlined and opium is put forward as a signifier for "a whole spectrum of 'oriental' vices, among them effeminacy, homosexuality, and 'thuggee' " (112). Perera revisits the issue of Thuggee, initially raised by Edmund Wilson and Howard Duffield, in some depth and offers an intriguing analysis of the novel's tone in the wake of the 1865 Governor Eyre controversy. Ultimately, she concludes that Drood has been strangled and that his death, at Jasper's hand, is symptomatic of the empire striking back to the center, interpreting the novel as a transitional text between the allusive mid-Victorian novels, which elided the imperial issue, and the more overt post-1870 adventure narratives. Any work on *Drood* is by its very nature speculative, but Perara puts forward an engrossing series of arguments, which have opened up the novel for further critical analysis.

In addition to ranging from Macaulay to H. Rider Haggard, Deirdre David's *Rule Britannia* includes an excellent chapter on Dickens and imperialism. David's focus is on how British writing, especially—but not exclusively—writing by women, was complicit in producing the British empire. Closely informed by Edward Said's work, David charts the participation of women in the imperial venture, while also considering reverse colonization. She examines how everyday consumerism was affected by the arrival of items like exotic fruit from far-flung corners of the world and chooses to read these articles as signifiers of the colonial invading the center, rather than as the spoils of international trade. David draws upon a wealth of novels, essays, reports, speeches, and parliamentary reports in this work, juxtaposing figures as unlikely as Macaulay and Emily Eden in order to reveal what appears at times to be a conspiracy of power and privilege on the part of the governing race. David astutely recognizes that while upper and middle-class female travel writers might align themselves with the colonized and show particular sympathy towards indigenous people, the leisure that enabled them to produce their musings was usually indirectly funded by the exploitation of native peoples. Nevertheless, David maps a number of important parallels between women and the colonized, most notably in her final chapter where she examines the crossover between rebellious women of the fin de siècle and the rebellious ''native'' body, arguing for a ''conjoining'' of gender and race in subordinating diverse social groups.

David's chapter on Dickens is especially interesting in that she examines *The Old Curiosity Shop* as an imperial novel, electing to consider it alongside a more obvious imperial text, *Dombey and Son*. For David, the ghastly dwarf Daniel Quilp becomes a representative of savage, dark maleness at odds with Little Nell's civilized female pallor. Unlikely though this assertion may initially appear to be, David assembles a convincing case, arguing that Quilp's grotesqueness taps into early Victorian myths of the savage. David reminds us of the numerous parallels within the novel between Quilp and an African chief, arguing that he should be viewed as a ''symbolic cannibal'' (60) and reading him alongside some of the Bushmen Dickens encountered at exhibitions in London in the 1850s. Indeed, if there is a flaw in David's argument it is that she seems too ready to look forward to the 1850s in order to define

Dickens's stance on race in the early 1840s. Her observation that "In *The Old Curiosity Shop*, eradication of male barbarism is accompanied by the forfeiture of female life, or, to suggest how Victorian ideas of gender get affiliated with Victorian ideas of race, native savagery can be tamed only by the sacrifice of Englishwomen" (63) seems to read the text back through the later Indian Mutiny and the anxieties that the event generated surrounding the vulnerability of the Englishwoman abroad. Nevertheless, David offers some engaging close readings of the otherwise neglected colonial imagery in Dickens's earlier works.

The number of articles dedicated to Dickens and imperialism has also increased steadily in recent years. In " 'Two Spheres of Action and Suffering,' " Darin E. Fields addresses the globalism of *Little Dorrit*, picking up on Dickens's concern with internationalism and decadence, and interpreting the port of Marseilles as a kind of "gateway to the East." In this brief but stimulating article Field considers tropes of sickness and infection, suggesting that Arthur Clennam's remark that the East is "the country of the plague" expresses Dickens's deeper fears about the spread of colonial bureaucracy and the dangers of trading in the East. He goes on to suggest that William Dorrit's final journey to Rome anticipates Dickens's more overt engagement with decadence and progressive decline in *Our Mutual Friend*. Field asserts that the lethargy pervading the novel represents a "progressive slide into the decadence which plagued previous great empires" (383), extending his argument to consider the ways in which empires have, historically, enslaved themselves.

Novels like *Dombey and Son*, along with the many articles that Dickens published on the Indian cotton trade in *All the Year Round* demonstrate that he was well aware of the empire's role in British trade. Imperial commodities are at the heart of Eitan Bar-Yosef's essay " 'An Ocean of Soap and Water.' " The essay registers Dickens's complex and shifting views upon the empire and links his thoughts on Britain's overseas territories to more pressing domestic concerns. Bar-Yosef posits the idea of an "empire within" Britain, pointing to similarities between representations of Major Bagstock's shadowy "native" and the Toodles children (226). As Bar-Yosef puts it, Dickens is complicit in the system of imperial appropriation, plundering the empire for literary spoils, and almost blurring with the bashaw-like Dombey:

> Dickens, in this respect, might be said to treat the world as if it was made for Dickens to trade in, and the sun and moon were made to give his stories light, and rainbows to give him promise of fair reviews in the periodicals, to preserve inviolate a system of which he is the center.   (229)

While the mysterious "Native" is of peripheral concern to Bar-Yosef, he forms the focus of Rajeswari Sunder Rajan's article, " 'The Shadow of that Expatriated Prince.' " Rajan reclaims the "Native" from the margins and attempts to piece together an identity for him, based on the rumors and gossip offloaded onto him by a host of other, minor characters. Rajan examines the animal imagery surrounding the "Native" and the "social limbo" into which the character is placed through his paradoxical status as both "native" and "exile" (93). Given the careful readings that Rajan offers, it is curious that she accepts the "Native's" purported royal identity as a fact. Notwithstanding, her article presents interesting insights into the ways in which imperial imagery is deployed to highlight the plight of English women in *Dombey and Son*.

The cross-over between female identity, commodities, and the empire is a major concern for Jeff Nunokawa in his essay, "For Your Eyes Only." Nunokawa complicates the Victorian equation of sexuality and capital by suggesting that they merge in the novel and become endangered through public display. The East is presented as one long exhibition in *Dombey and Son* and Nunokawa argues, referring to displays of "savagery" in London and the daily orientalized spectacle of Edith Dombey's mother, Cleopatra, that female sexuality must be "privatized" and detached from the imperial discourse. Stability can only be restored to the world of the novel if displays, either of wealth or of self, are spurned, as Nunokawa states, "for property to be secret and therefore secure, it must be cleansed of both capital and sexuality" (144). Indeed, according to this reading, *Dombey and Son* anticipates the more overt emphasis on the domestic in *Bleak House*, seeming to advocate the process of private world-building that is such a hallmark of the later novel.

Shows of native peoples like those mentioned in Nunokawa's essay were extraordinarily popular in London during the 1850s, and they have formed a significant backdrop to a number of recent essays on Dickens and imperialism. In "Charles Dickens and the Zulus" Bernth Lindfors focuses on Caldecott's exhibition of a troupe of thirteen Zulus, which is believed to have been one of the catalysts for Dickens's controversial essay "The Noble Savage." Lindfors ably demonstrates Dickens's dependence upon a pamphlet by Caldecott's son, which was published to coincide with the tour. Caldecott, Jr.'s pamphlet, from which Lindfors quotes liberally, is filled with scurrilous generalizations and misrepresentations of Zulu culture, which Dickens drew upon in his account of Zulu marriage ceremonies. This short chapter is refreshing for its unwillingness to pass judgment on one of Dickens's least palatable essays, remarking that those of us who condemn Victorian ethnocentricity may be guilty of a similar process if we expect audiences of the 1850s "to react with a more modern sensibility and to come away from such a performance with a richer understanding and appreciation of Zulu culture" (79).

The Mystery of Edwin Drood has continued to perplex Dickens scholars, many of whom regard it as Dickens's most overt engagement with the British empire. Joachim Stanley, taking his cue from Barry Milligan's excellent study, *Pleasures and Pains*, considers Dickens's innovative representations of drug use and abuse in both *Drood* and *Our Mutual Friend* in his essay "Opium and *Edwin Drood*." Stanley displays an impressive combination of both medical and literary knowledge, reading the novels alongside articles on opium dens that appeared in *All the Year Round*. Unlike De Quincey's representations of opium-inspired hallucinations, Dickens's trances, according to Stanley, created and sustained an inner logic of their own, with a level of reality that existed independently of the user's experiences and concerns. Stanley repudiates arguments that *The Mystery of Edwin Drood* is caught up with fears of Eastern invasion and suggests that instead we are privy to a civil war between the macrocosm of Cloisterham and the microcosm that is John Jasper. Finally, the article moves gracefully toward a psychoanalytic reading of Jasper, suggesting that not only did Dickens anticipate Freud's work on the unconscious, but that he also anticipated flaws in his treatment of patients. For Dickens it is unhealthy for men to confront their repressed impulses and ultimately the fantasy world brought about through opium addiction leaves Jasper completely unable to cope with reality.

Jeremy Tambling takes a very different, but nonetheless compelling approach to opium and the East in his two-part article "Opium, Wholesale, Resale, and for Export," in which he considers Dickens's eldest son Charley's time as a tea merchant in China and Hong Kong and the ways in which Charley's travels shaped Dickens's representations of the East. Tambling contends that "China was never a matters of indifference to Dickens. As an entity it is represented, misrepresented and repressed within his fiction and journalism . . . " (30). Beginning with a discussion of the Victorian representation of China and its lack of modernity through displays of Chinese cultural artifacts, including the spectacle at the 1851 Great Exhibition, Tambling explores early influences upon Dickens's impressions of China. The *Household Words* article that Dickens penned with R. H. Horne, "The Great Exhibition and the Little One," is particularly illuminating in that it sets up a vision of a backward China as a means of setting Britain apart from the revolutionary Europe of 1848. As Tambling puts it, "Britain stands between Chinese stasis and European haste" (33).

Tambling's article continues by highlighting a number of Dickens's Eastern travelers, including Arthur Clennam, Walter Gay, and Pip, before moving on to draw a compelling comparison between the feckless Charley Dickens and the gentle, languid Herbert Pocket. Other interesting discussions in this marvelously rich piece include Flora Finching's breathless accounts of her impressions of Chinese culture, examining Flora herself as a figure of stagnation, who ultimately becomes a "figure for China." (37) Tambling concludes with a short discussion of opium in *The Mystery of Edwin Drood*, commenting upon the dual standard applied to the drug, which, for Dickens, was a commodity to be traded in the East, but a threat on its arrival in London.

Some of the ground for Tambling's fascinating article seems to have been prepared by Susan Schoenbauer Thurin in an earlier piece, "China in Dickens," which asks whether "Dickens's utterances on China make him 'worthy' of the regard shown him by Chinese readers" (99). Like Tambling, Thurin examines the presentation of Chinese "weakness" in sources like the *Illustrated London News*, and she also pays attention to a number of London shows and exhibitions dealing with China. Thurin charts a number of examples of Dickens's 'Chinoiserie' in works that include *American Notes* and *Bleak House*. She remarks that for Dickens Chinese culture is often a source of the absurd, citing Dora Spenlow's acquisition of a pagoda for her little dog Jip as an example, before aligning it with the "Pagoda Department of the great Circumlocution Office" that appears in "The Great Tasmania's Cargo" in *The Uncommercial Traveller*. While Thurin also concludes that Dickens perceives the East as contaminating the West through the spread of opium and its abilities to transform British users into likenesses of the Chinese, her article closes with a convincing case for reading *The Mystery of Edwin Drood* as a kind of Dickensian volte-face. According to Thurin, the final, unfinished novel offers an indictment of English imperial expansion, suggesting that John Jasper becomes an 'emblem' of a blight stemming from overseas involvement, and arguing that through his exploits the East is at last vindicated. Thurin has widened her discussion to consider less well-known figures in her more recent monograph, *Victorian Travelers and the Opening of China, 1842–1907*, in which she discusses a series of travelogues by a small, but diverse, selection of tourists.

Miriam O'Kane Mara argues in "Sucking the Empire Dry" that Dickens uses his final novel to present a critique of imperial consumerism. Mara's essay addresses opium use, but it also looks at how the peculiar characters in this final novel are engaged in a conspicuous consumption of which their creator disapproves. Hyungi Park has also noted the puppet-like nature of the characters in "Going to Wake Up Egypt," reading them as flimsy caricatures, who are propped up by the rather more spectacular empire. However, examining Rosa Bud's lumps of delight, the gorgeous orientalized excess of the Cloisterham shops, and the ring Edwin Drood gives to Rosa, Mara reveals how English cultural identity is in danger of being overrun by Eastern products. Characters like Rosa, who devour the spoils of the Orient, are shown to be completely uninterested in any of the true wonders of the East. Mara astutely points out that the novel's primary consumers are women (Princess Puffer offering the other prominent example) and that their voracious appetites threaten to overwhelm their femininity and their understanding of the world around them. John Jasper stands out as the novel's exemplar of Eastern danger; his consumerist impulses have run wild, and he has been reduced to the three functions, "pursuit, possession and destruction" (240). His obsession with Rosa has turned her into a commodity that, like the East, can be desired and consumed. Yet, the nature of these desires is unhealthy and un-English, and, as Mara cleverly contends in her conclusion to this most inconclusive of novels, *The Mystery of Edwin Drood* "creates, but refuses to solve, a *mystery* about Dickens's stance on colonialism" (244).

While *Drood* presents the overwhelming dangers of the East, Britain is frequently positioned as a point of stability in Dickens's world, albeit one that is constantly endangered by misplaced priorities like telescopic philanthropy. Focusing on the domestic and the draw of home, Eric G. Lorentzen's thought-provoking " 'Obligations of Home' " argues that *Bleak House* is Dickens's "most sustained polemic against colonialism," pointing out that the disease that pervades the novel emanates from England and spreads out to the colonies, rather than vice versa. Beginning with the novel's most obvious colonial reference points, Mrs. Jellyby and Mrs. Pardiggle (discussed more extensively in Timothy Carens's earlier, valuable essay "Empire, Gender, and National Reform in *Bleak House*," Lorentzen then shifts his attention to minor figures like the Bagnets, who always gravitate back to their home. He cleverly points out that the empire seems to have killed off Mrs. Bayham Badger's previous husbands, while Alan Woodcourt nearly loses his wife-to-be when he neglects his domestic responsibilities to pursue imperial distractions. Connecting colonialism, contamination, and revolt, Lorentzen ends his riveting essay with an examination of a typo, suggesting that the text itself has become infected, when Wat Tyler and Watt Rouncewell are blurred together through an editorial oversight.

Leon Litvack has produced a brace of two-part articles, the first on the convict Magwitch, and the second addressing Dickens's attitudes towards Ireland. "Dickens, Australia and Magwitch" gives a detailed summary of the historical context behind *Great Expectations* and charts Dickens's changing perceptions of Australia, as influenced by his involvement with the Urania Cottage project in the 1840s and by contributors to *Household Words* from the 1850s onwards. Litvack sheds light on Dickens's views on transportation in the 1840s, reminding us that he even wrote to the Home Secretary volunteering to pen an article warning prisoners of the hardships to be endured in a colony he had never visited! This rigorous article goes on to address the problematic figure of the returnee from Australia, astutely commenting that in *David Copperfield* only Daniel Peggotty, an exemplar of working-class diligence who has never committed a crime, is permitted to return to England. Dickens's depictions of Australia were always somewhat hazy, given that he lacked first-hand experience of the colony. Litvack is too responsible a scholar not to observe that details of Magwitch's time in Australia are extremely sketchy and that therefore a degree of conjecture is inevitable. As a consequence, Litvack refers both to articles published by Dickens and historical figures like Samuel Terry, the "Rothschild of Botany Bay" in a bid to trace Magwitch's "off-stage" Australian life, both as a convict and later as an entrepreneur.

Litvack's extended essay "Dickens, Ireland and the Irish" is equally detailed and provides a similar historical outline of the novelist's relationship with Britain's closest colony. Offering what seems to be an exhaustive list of Irish influences upon Dickens and Irish figures in his works, Litvack does more than any critic to date to chart Dickens's slippery stance on the Irish question. Once again, he examines *Household Words* and reads articles that Dickens published, like Harriet Martineau's "The Irish Union" of 1852, alongside more reactionary pronouncements from sources including the letters. The article makes the important distinction between Dickens's attitudes toward the Irish in Ireland and his opinions on the Irish in London; the latter were usually desperately poor and were frequently represented in a stereotyped manner. Finally, Litvack turns his attention to Dickens's Irish reading tours of 1858 and 1867, and looks at *All the Year Round*'s growing interest in the troubled Irish political climate of the 1860s.

Emigration

Emigration, for many, seemed to offer an immediate solution to the "Condition of England Question," and it was advocated in fiction and in fact as an opportunity for the thrifty poor to begin their lives anew. While British emigration policies revolved largely around what Charlotte Erikson has termed the "shovelling out of paupers" (14), Rita S. Kranidis examines the exportation of surplus women in *The Victorian Spinster and Colonial Emigration: Contested Subjects*. Kranidis draws attention to the gender imbalance of nineteenth-century assisted emigration schemes, highlighting the possibilities that Britain's dominions seemed to offer for the woman who had exhausted her opportunities for marriage in England. The colonial environment, like the voyage out, was a deeply hostile one for the would-be female settler. Unmarried women were viewed as an encumbrance since they were rarely sufficiently robust to be able to partake in the hard labor required of imperial pioneers. Kranidis points to the disjunction between the needs of the colony and the policies of assisted emigration schemes, asking, "In what sense could these philanthropic societies be said to be serving the needs or interests of women?" (28). Concentrating particularly on the middle-class woman, Kranidis focuses her arguments around "the unmarried Victorian woman's cultural place and hegemonic function'' (170), exploring constructions of female identity, sexuality and cultural agency. Interwoven with examinations of pamphlets, articles, and memoirs by eminent figures like Florence Nightingale and Caroline Chisholm are discussions of women in novels like Collins's *No Name*, Eliot's *The Mill on the Floss*, and Dickens's *Great Expectations.* Kranidis draws interesting parallels between the body of the middle-class spinster and the invisibility of the British working classes, suggesting an analogy between the transplantation of unmarried women and the displacement of the very poor.

Of course, those who left for the colonies as emigrants were unlikely to return home again, and migrant culture was often characterized by a yearning for the mother country. Diana C. Archibald's *Domesticity, Imperialism and Emigration in the Victorian Novel* is a lovingly written study of the export of women and homes from Britain to a number of new worlds. Archibald begins her study with an account of her great-great grandmother's journey from Scotland to the American West and writes throughout with an engaging sensitivity and empathy for her subjects. The study spans several continents, including work on emigration to Australia, Canada, New Zealand, and the U.S.A. Archibald moves deftly between fact and fiction in her interdisciplinary study, quite rightly regarding the novel as only one site where new worlds were invented and re-shaped. At the heart of this project is an attempt to draw out the tensions between the domestic ideology of ''home'' and advocates of immigration; as Archibald expresses it, ''as millions of British citizens left England for the New Worlds, hearth and home were physically moved from the heart of the empire to its very outskirts'' (6). The study examines attempts to cling to hearth and home in vastly different and often hostile climates. While for some commentators the harsh living conditions of the colonies were antithetical to constructions of appropriate feminine behavior, Archibald is drawn to those women who pitted themselves against convention and sought to adapt the home fires to their new environments. Archibald offers a range of discussions of novels by Samuel Butler, Dickens, Elizabeth Gaskell, Trollope, and Thackeray to name but a few, and she carefully identifies emigration's central paradox, that for many it was necessary to leave their homes in order to gain a home.

Janet Myers has produced a complementary study in her doctoral dissertation, entitled ''*Antipodal England*,'' which is in the process of being revised into book form. Myers examines how ''portable domesticity'' allowed British emigrants to preserve their cultures overseas. Myers's focus is primarily with middle-class emigrants and she examines the transplantation of the domestic from the home to the more public sphere of the emigrant ship, casting the vessel in a mediating role between England and the colonies. Myers's study offers an in-depth exploration of the Australian experience, suggesting that the colony was the most "home-like" settlement in its mimicry of life back home. Myers examines the work of novelists including Mary Elizabeth Braddon, Dickens, Trollope, and Catherine Helen Spence, alongside primary sources, which include letters, memoirs, emigration guidebooks and visual artifacts. *Antipodal England* also includes an extended study of those who returned from Australia to Britain and the chaos that could ensue when the margins came back to the center. Myers's work is a valuable contribution to studies of emigration.

India

Developments in shipping technology, a growing connection between the East India Company and the British government, and a rise in missionary activity from the 1830s onwards made India an increasingly acceptable destination for British women. While traditionally British men in India had married Indian women, or kept native mistresses, the arrival of British women overturned this mixing of cultures and did an enormous amount of damage to race relations. British men lost the understanding of Indian customs and religions that they had gained through mixing with the locals, and racism also began to rise. In *Allegories of Empire*, Jenny Sharpe produces a fascinating study of womanhood in colonial India. Her main focus is on the parallels between the imperial "mission" and the violation of female bodies. Sharpe points to a relationship of guilt and anxiety between colonizer and colonized, leading to a plethora of rape narratives circulating around and about India. These fears stemmed from Edmund Burke's analogy between the Indian subcontinent and a repeatedly violated woman, but then metamorphosed into anxieties about the vulnerable European woman's body in the wake of the 1857 Indian 'mutiny' and the numerous (and mostly false) allegations of rape to emerge after the discovery of the massacre at Cawnpore. Sharpe's research is meticulous, and her combination of feminist and postcolonial theories makes for a riveting read. She examines a number of twentieth-century texts, including Forster's *A Passage to India* and Paul Scott's *The Raj Quartet*, concentrating particularly upon their dialogue with mid-Victorian crises of both masculinity and colonial rule.

More directly relevant for Victorian scholars, however, is the excellent chapter on *Jane Eyre*, in which Sharpe considers narratives of mastery and slavery in the novel, before progressing to an examination of sati and female sacrifice, which appears to have been heavily influenced by the work of her mentor, Gayatri Spivak. Equally useful is Sharpe's reassessment of a mutiny "myth," the story of Miss Ulrika Wheeler. Originally celebrated for her spirited defense of her chastity when faced by libidinous sepoy rebels, mutiny legend asserted that the pure, English Miss Wheeler shot several would-be assailants before drowning herself. It later emerged—after she had been depicted in a number of mutiny narratives, including Charles Ball's monumental *History of the Indian Mutiny* (1858)—that far from sacrificing herself to defend her virtue, Miss Wheeler seemed to have willingly absconded with one of the rebels, with whom she was later found to be living. Interestingly, when this co-habitation was uncovered, representations of Miss Wheeler's racial identity became unfixed, and historians, including George Trevelyan, recast her as Eurasian. As Sharpe points out, "what determine[d] her membership to the English race is less her class or racial origin than her 'choice' of death over dishonor; female moral fortitude is the sign of racial purity" (73). Sharpe's work is, however, not restricted to representations of English womanhood; she also includes a lively analysis of the life of the notorious female bandit or freedom fighter, the Rani of Jhansi who refused to surrender to the British when her city was captured. Sharpe's scholarship is remarkable for its combination of theoretical rigor and archival research, and *Allegories of Empire* remains an essential contribution to the consideration of women and imperialism.

Also concerned with women and violation, Nancy L. Paxton's *Writing Under the Raj* is rich in the wide range of texts it considers. Paxton's powerful study builds upon Sharpe's work on rape anxieties, revisiting figures like Miss Wheeler and also looking at lesser-known chroniclers of life in the Raj, including the Canadian writer Sara Jeanette Duncan. Paxton complicates the debate by pointing out that rape narratives disappeared from English novels towards the end of the eighteenth century and argues that anxieties surrounding violation were displaced onto the colony. Paxton agrees with Sharpe that the Mutiny brought about a crisis in gender relations between colonizers and colonized, but for her the issue remains tangled up with unarticulated domestic concerns.

Sara Suleri's *The Rhetoric of English India* has become another keystone text for scholars working on nineteenth-century India, providing as it does a wealth of background material on the tensions which combined to generate the sepoy rebellion. Examining a series of defining moments in the sequence of cultural clashes that marked Britain's involvement in India, Suleri moves from Edmund Burke's commitment to the "India Question" and his uncanny predictions of the results of continued exploitation of the subcontinent, to a consideration of the state of postcolonial Indian writing. Suleri's study moves seamlessly from early considerations of Macaulay and James Mill, through to an extended discussion of Salman Rushdie's controversial novel, *The Satanic Verses*. Suleri considers the position of the Englishwoman in India both before and after the Mutiny, commenting upon the ways in which life in the Raj fractured the English family unit. She asks how Anglo-Indian female authors negotiated what she terms "the veiled realities of colonial panic" (82) in their writings, examining depictions of an alien landscape and a completely other culture in novels, travelogues, and diaries. Texts under discussion include Fanny Parks's pre-Mutiny journal and Harriet Tytler's memoir of life in post-Mutiny India. Suleri provides an interesting discussion of women's attempts to understand and convey the aesthetics of the Indian landscape, often by offloading colonial tensions onto the terrain or by mapping it through an English aesthetic framework. She probes the origins of the post-Mutiny perception of a landscape which is hostile to women, arguing for a uniquely "feminine picturesque" (87). Suleri also includes an important analysis of Rudyard Kipling's *Kim* as a text responding to a climate of colonial terror and a questioning of the imperial venture as a whole. Significantly, she seeks to redress Edward Said's claim that *Kim* is a text devoid of imperial conflict, suggesting that "Kim's collaboration [in the Great Game] is . . . emblematic of not so much an absence of conflict as the terrifying absence of choice in the operations of colonialism" (116). Suleri concludes by reading Kim as an analogy for imperial casualty, arguing for the inevitability of his death in a world where he is torn between cultures and cannot be completely assimilated. Ultimately, it is the British colonial education that is held responsible for the silencing and death of the imperial hybrid.

It wasn't simply womanhood and race that were reconfigured in nineteenth-century Anglo-Indian relations, and British representations and misrepresentations of the Indian insurrection are at the forefront of Gautam Chakravarty's wonderful *The Indian Mutiny and the British Imagination*. Drawing some compelling parallels between present-day global conflicts and Victorian imperial strife, Chakravarty looks at depictions of the Mutiny in novels written prior to Indian independence in 1947. He asserts that the novels are engaged in enacting a fantasy of mastery, but that they also chart fluctuations in Britain's relationship with India. In the present day, the uprising is regarded as the first Indian war of independence and an example of British misrule. However, Chakravarty suggests that the Victorians shifted from a state of traumatized outrage to a position wherein they could reimagine the revolt as "a site of heroic imperial adventure, and an occasion for conspicuous demonstrations of racial superiority" (6). Interestingly, Chakravarty attempts to reclaim the rebellion from feminist scholars like Paxton, Sharpe, and Suleri, contending that their respective emphases on gender have downplayed political and ethnographic concerns. He also represents the diversity of reactions to the uprising, both in England and India, avoiding the tempting propensity to polarize each nation's responses and presenting a more complicated picture of one of the most traumatic events for the mid-Victorians.

Don Randall's *Kipling's Imperial Boy* presents a sustained analysis of the education of adolescent boys, picking up on Sara Suleri's connection between adolescence and cultural hybridity to suggest that during this transitional period of their lives young men shared a fleeting understanding with the colonized. In addition to a sustained analysis of Kim's hybridity, Randall devotes a significant portion of his study to examining Kipling's school stories and the parallels between the disciplining of the boy and the ordering of British overseas subjects. Randall explores Kipling's imaginary empire, suggesting that the schoolboy Stalky may most usefully be considered as a "fetish-image of imperial representation," who "embodies and stages the contradictions that inhere in Kipling's imperial imagination" (108). Viewing Kipling's boys as both "Imaginary heroes" and "mediator[s] of a Symbolic ordering of 'the Empire' " (61), Randall productively reads the ultimate colonial adventurer, Kim, as the archetypal imperial boy. The Irish orphan as hybrid is, Randall contends, a potentially disruptive figure who defies containment and who evades imperial disciplining structures. This is a thought-provoking study of young empire-builders in the aftermath of the Indian Mutiny, which reads Kipling's eager young adventurers as reflecting a moment of adolescent-like crisis and self-scrutiny in the imperial mission.

While the majority of studies of Anglo-Indian relations at this time concentrate upon British reactions to India, in the provocatively titled *Home and Harem*, Inderpal Grewal looks at travel and cultural tourism from both Indian and English perspectives. Positioning herself within transnational feminist studies and critiquing the white, Western appropriation of the discipline, Grewal helpfully problematizes the ways in which feminism has perpetuated Western ideals of democracy and moves beyond the binary of Western women versus women of color to look at a wide array of feminisms. Grewal probes silences surrounding migration, immigration, deportation, indenture, and slavery, seeking to promote an awareness of what she aptly labels "the dark side of travel" (1) and to demonstrate the far-reaching effects of imperialism upon everyday culture. This study draws upon a diverse range of sources, including museum guidebooks and essays by English suffrage campaigners. The work is divided into two sections, section one addressing class and gender in an English context, positing "home" as a space to return to or yearn for. The second section concerns itself with the conditions of Indian women, and "harem" becomes a kind of shorthand for the incarcerated Eastern woman and debates surrounding the body of the female "other." Grewal argues that home is always mediated through notions of the harem and reads home as the site of women's struggles, both nationalist and feminist. She examines a multiplicity of imperial race and gender discourses, arguing that they shaped the contexts in which "feminist subjects became possible in both England and India" (11). Grewal engages in case studies of Indian women visiting England and America, examining the relations among class, caste, and mobility and contrasting Indian female travelers with the likes of Harriet Martineau,

who frequently ignored the female population of countries she visited, prefer-
ring to focus her attention upon monuments and the past (84). Grewal's
Indian travelers re-shaped Western structures of travel to reconfigure themselves, and the study points out that their journeys were "complicated both
by imperial notions of travel within which Indians were seen as being liber-
ated by European modernity constructed through notions of education and
progress, and by the Indian travelers' desire to take advantage of these discourses but for various ends that reconstituted and sometimes, though not
always, subverted European cultural superiority" (137). Grewal's theoretical
approach involves a synthesis of postcolonial and feminist theories in a bid
to show how "nationalism narrates gendered, classed and racialized bodies"
(230). Her discussion is complex and highly readable, closing with a plea for
more work on travel, nationalism, and narratives of nation and empire within
Victorian culture.

The Mid-Victorians, Class, and Race

Looking at the broader Victorian picture, Shearer West engages in an exploration of the politics of postcolonial theory in the introduction to her wonderfully eclectic interdisciplinary collection *The Victorians and Race* (1996). The
book's range is broad, and West has taken the bold decision to order the
collection thematically, rather than chronologically. The result is a stimulating
series of insights into a wide range of Victorian perceptions of race, moving
from studies of the Caribbean and analyses of gender in Olive Schreiner
to neglected areas of study, including Joseph A. Kestner's examinations of
colonized Celtic peoples and Inga Bryden's compelling essay on the connections between Victorian constructions of King Arthur and the mid-Victorian
valorization of Anglo-Saxonism. Many of these fascinating essays draw connections between art history and literature, and particularly noteworthy are
Tim Barringer's interesting examination of the interplay of class and race in
Victorian visual, sociological and literary texts and Reina Lewis's lavishly
illustrated chapter on women and orientalism, which includes an extended
discussion of Lucy Snowe's visual Orientalism in *Villette*. Although it is
nearly a decade since *The Victorians and Race* first appeared, it remains, in
my opinion, one of the most useful contributions to the debate.

Ethnicity is also a central concern in Sophie Gilmartin's *Ancestry and
Narrative in Nineteenth-Century British Literature*, which develops a number
of the discussions of race and origins that are addressed in West's collection.
Gilmartin probes the nineteenth-century fascination with issues of bloodline
and pedigree, examining the ways in which the two became entangled with
individual identity and national politics. She considers the stories the Victorians told themselves about their origins, looking not just at blood and heredity

but also at blood-line narratives. She examines how writers like Disraeli engaged with the invention of pedigree and considers the mutability of English myths of origins at a time of dynamic social change and profound instability, focusing particularly on the connections between the written word and the "authentic" bloodline. She also examines links between Jewish identity and the marginalized existence of Celts, who were popularly believed to be direct descendants of Noah.

Gilmartin's survey is lively and entertaining, beginning with Maria Edgeworth's novel *The Absentee* and ending with two provocative chapters on Hardy, whose fascination with both human and geological origins pervades novels like *Tess of the d'Urbervilles* and *The Well-Beloved*. Other chapters deal with Disraeli's "Young England" novels and George Meredith's writing. Gilmartin also incorporates a gripping extended section on Mary Queen of Scots, a figure who became prominent in the Victorian imagination after the publication of Agnes Strickland's edition of her letters in 1844. Scott, Martineau, Burns, Wordsworth, Swinburne, and Charlotte M. Yonge all engaged with Mary in their writing, and while parallels between Victoria and Elizabeth I have become a commonplace, Gilmartin reminds us of the imaginative appeal of the executed monarch, and the pity she inspired in the young Queen Victoria. Gilmartin looks at the genealogical chaos which ensued in the aftermath of Mary's execution, with Elizabeth I displacing Mary's son's familial affections. Furthermore, she uses the confusion as a means of exploring the tensions between public and private versions of genealogical narratives for female royals, caught between dynastic and domestic demands. Adopting Linda Colley's argument that from the eighteenth century to the present day women belonging to royal families have been role models for girls and women across classes, Gilmartin reads Mary as a monarch who was sacrificed to genealogy, her proximity to the succession line of the English throne making her too great a threat to Elizabeth I.

Scrutinizing what she describes as "Victoria's 'creative' interpretation of her family tree" (59), Gilmartin traces Scott's influence on Victoria's revisionism of her own history and the writer's drive to play up the "Scottish blood" of Victoria's uncle, George IV. Victoria's own adoration of Scotland has been well documented, but Gilmartin returns to the issue of Scottish fashion and, following Adrienne Munich, she points to the ways Victoria created a "genealogy through clothes" (65), first adopting Scottish costumes for masquerade balls and then later wearing her trademark Scottish widow's cap. As a figure of national influence, Victoria thus disseminated her assumed Scottish identity across the nation, as widows from all walks of life adopted the cap as part of their attire. Gilmartin continues, in this richly cross-disciplinary section, to provide close readings of paintings and literary representations of Mary, arguing that she became, via Victoria, a "mirror of matriarchy" (101) for nineteenth-century women.

The role of race in Victorian women's writing is central to Susan Meyer's major study *Imperialism at Home* (1996). Meyer offers an in-depth analysis of representations of race and colonial imagery in *The Mill on the Floss* and *Daniel Deronda*, although the bulk of this work deals with the Brontës. Meyer addresses connections between the marginalized Englishwoman and the colonized other. Her study opens with an examination of how nineteenth-century male writers, including Dickens and Trollope, have been complicit in aligning white women with slaves. Meyer then discusses the ways in which race has been adopted as a metaphor to explore gender issues, paying particular attention to the domestic novel which is, according to Meyer, a site where these concerns take a new shape. She comments that ''since the gender positioning of British women writers required them to negotiate an association with 'inferior races,' their feminist impulses to question gender hierarchies often *provoked* an interrogation of race hierarchies.''

Possibly the most interdisciplinary study under consideration here, Jonathan Taylor's *Mastery and Slavery in Victorian Writing* (2003) is a remarkably broad study of Carlylean heroism and the Hegelean master-slave dialectic, which reads works by George Eliot, Wilkie Collins, Carlyle, Dickens, and George Du Maurier alongside theorists including Hegel, Mill, and Alexis de Tocqueville. Incorporating politics and musicology into his analyses, Taylor's study impresses with its sheer intellectualism. His chapter on North American slavery is especially illuminating, with its close readings of Dickens, Frederick Douglass, and Carlyle. However, Taylor perhaps overstates Dickens's involvement with the Eyre Defence League in 1865–1866, leading him to interpret comments from Dickens's second visit to the United States in 1868 in rather too Carlylean a manner and suggesting a political commitment that Dickens no longer felt by the final years of his life. Most useful of all in this complex and challenging work are Taylor's studies of Jewishness and antisemitism, in which he moves from between examinations of marginalized Jewish musicians in texts like *Daniel Deronda* and *Trilby* to consider the outsidedness of real-life musicians and their works, such as Gustav Mahler or the ''opposition between the Germanic and the Semitic'' in the works of Richard Wagner (150).

Equally broad in scope is Patrick Brantlinger's *Dark Vanishings* which charts the nineteenth century's ongoing anxiety concerning the extinction of other races, beginning with Mary Shelley's *The Last Man* (1826) and closing with H. G. Wells's *The War of the Worlds* (1896). Brantlinger considers the reasons and theories behind the decimation of indigenous peoples across the globe through what he terms an ''extinction discourse'' (5), examining a wide selection of literary and scientific figures, including Carlyle, Darwin, Dickens, T. H. Huxley and R. L. Stevenson. The study addresses violence, genocide, warfare, disease, and eugenics alongside a discourse of savagery—encompassing superstition, cannibalism, and human sacrifice—created as a justification for expediting a process of "self extinguishment." Picking up on one of the major concerns of *Rule of Darkness*, Brantlinger returns to his concern with the "Noble Savage," setting this idealized and greatly fetishized figure up against the notion of the self-extinguishing "savage," unable to contend with "civilization." This wide-ranging study lays out the Victorians' paradoxical combination of mourning and nostalgia for almost-extinct races even as they were helped along towards eradication, and draws parallels between indigenous peoples across the globe. Chapters are organized geographically, offering a series of contrasts between the treatment of the other in a sequence of different colonial settings. The work's focus moves from the Irish famine of the 1840s to the much-contested death of the last Tasmanian, purportedly in 1876, closing with an important discussion of the sinister legacy of eugenics in the modern world.

Among the studies of individual authors and their engagement with imperialism, Deborah Thomas's superb *Thackeray and Slavery* stands out as a significant contribution. Having spent his early years in India, surrounded by slavery in all but name, the image of the slave haunted Thackeray's imagination and recurred in his major novels from *Barry Lyndon* to *Henry Esmond*. In her clearly written study, Thomas engages with slavery as a recurrent trope in Thackeray's fiction, equating his fascination with the institution with a yearning for his lost Indian childhood. Curiously, while for Fanny Trollope and Charles Dickens, a visit to the United States clearly defined their respective stances against slavery, for Thackeray experiencing slavery at first hand convinced him that it was not so bad as it seemed. In addition to modifying his stance on slave ownership, Thomas argues, Thackeray's exposure to slavery robbed him of an important motif in his writing and "the image of slavery no longer worked so well in [his] fiction" (195). Thomas offers much more than a consideration of Thackeray's stance on the slave issue, skillfully interlacing biographical material with close readings of the author's major works and detailed examinations of orientalism. In an acute discussion of *Vanity Fair*, Thomas reveals how the novel as a whole is saturated with slave imagery, arguing that Amelia Sedley has to adjust her conduct from a condition of oriental slavishness in her relationship with George Osborne to a more equal, but less fulfilling, partnership with the loyal William Dobbin. Ultimately, Thackeray's overt depictions of slavery in novels like *The Virginians* are, for Thomas, less successful than his earlier orientalist fantasies. *Thackeray and Slavery* provides a detailed map of Thackeray's shifting stance on one of the most divisive issues of the nineteenth century, concluding with the assertion that the author's creative vision falls into line with the ebb and flow of public opinion on the issue.

Although not a figure one would immediately align with the British empire, George Eliot in an imperial context is the subject of two major studies. Nancy

Henry's *George Eliot and the British Empire* looks at the imperial backdrop to Eliot's life and work, considering how the empire operated at the periphery of her characters' lives and, of course, examining the role that it played in offering solutions to domestic penury. Henry explores Eliot and Lewes's responses to the presence of colonial cultures in London, looking at their fascination with the London Zoo and suggesting that this collection of displaced animals constituted an exhibition of imperial manliness. Other metropolitan spectacles included Caldecott's "Zulu Kaffir Exhibition" of 1853, which evoked moral concerns for both Eliot and Lewes about displaying native peoples and about whether colonialism advanced or degenerated the colonizing nation (37). Indeed, so crucial is Lewes to Henry's analysis, that he should really have appeared in the work's title.

Henry's concern with masculinity develops into a discussion of the novels and the more familiar topics of evolution and inherited traits. Given the sparsity of imperial references in Eliot's novels, much of the discussion here deals with Eliot's life; as Henry points out, while Eliot may have resisted the urge to dispatch her characters to colonies of settlement, she persuaded Lewes's sons to migrate to South Africa and attempted to induce her sister to emigrate to Australia. One of the most interesting aspects of this concise study is the attention Henry devotes to fleeting imperial wealth. She offers an especially engrossing section on post-Mutiny India and the issue of Indian debt, as outlined in John Bright's speeches, which Eliot read as part of her preparation for writing *Middlemarch*. Henry also notes "the inseparability of private capital and political reform" in India, arguing that as both an investor and a writer, Eliot was associated with these issues (105). Henry goes on to observe that Eliot, in the later years of her life, as her association with John Cross developed, came to understand more about colonial wealth than the average British investor. With that understanding came a growing consciousness of the imagined imperial community and the need to critique such enterprises that is reflected in Eliot's last works. Alicia Carroll's *Dark Smiles: Race and Desire in George Eliot* offers a much more sustained study of Eliot's major novels than Henry's work, as a result of its emphasis on race, rather than empire. Like Henry, Carroll provides an excellent contextualization of Eliot's understanding of other races, but her subject-matter allows her to move freely between discussions of the empire to consider issues like exoticism and Jewish identity. Carroll's chapter on desire in *Daniel Deronda* is especially strong, unpacking Orientalist and Shakespearean imagery and explaining Eliot's blurring of Eastern cultures. Henry argues that the novel is a series of tales within tales, proposing that George Eliot actually becomes Scheherazade in the process of writing the story, so numerous are the references to *The Thousand and One Nights*. Taken together, these two studies form helpful companion pieces, combining to present deeper discussion of what has, in the past, seemed a marginal concern in Eliot's writing.

The Late Victorians and Imperial Critique

In addition to its marvelously witty title, Anne McClintock's *Imperial Leather* (1995) assembles an impressive body of scholarship spanning over a century. McClintock brings together postcolonialism, psychoanalysis, feminism, and Marxist theory to consider links between mapping, gender politics, and even advertising, looking at the adventure narratives of Rider Haggard and ending with a section on 1990s South Africa. Victorian scholars are likely to find the chapter on the partnership of nineteenth-century barrister Arthur Munby and his housemaid, later wife, Hannah Cullwick to be among the most useful. McClintock provides a helpful overview of the unconventional cross-class relationship, incorporating an interesting and provocative selection of photographs. Drawing on race and gender theories, McClintock considers the master-slave dynamic between Cullwick and Munby, suggesting that Cullwick's adoption of a symbolic "slave band," which she displayed prominently, was, in addition to signifying her servitude, also a paradoxical sign of self-assertion in that it allowed her to "take possession of the symbolic realm" (151). McClintock continues to draw provocative parallels among colonized others, Victorian wives, and domestic servants, considering domestic space as a microcosmic representation of the broader empire. The scope of this lengthy text is wonderfully broad, and the work in its entirety is a compelling read.

Fears of the empire fighting back had begun to crystallize by the end of the century and while for the mid-Victorians home was a place of sanctuary to be preserved from imperial influences, by the century's close it had become a place under constant threat. Joseph Childers's "At Home in the Empire," in the collection *Homes and Homelessness in the Victorian Imagination* moves smoothly from an examination of late nineteenth-century imperial policy towards "others" to an exploration of what happens when the Empire "comes home." Having incisively elucidated some of the pitfalls of postcolonial theory, which can be complicit in marginalizing those it seeks to emancipate, Childers flips his argument back onto the colonizing power to probe the nature of Englishness. This wide-ranging essay goes on to examine English responses to late-Victorian Jewish migrants from Eastern Europe, focusing particularly on the novels of Israel Zangwill and the difficulties of Jewish assimilation. Childers concludes by identifying Zangwill's *Children of the Ghetto* as a text which anticipates a number of contemporary difficulties in discussing essentialism and identity politics, thus neatly tying together his close reading of the novel and his broader critique of postcolonialism.

Benjamin Disraeli famously declared the East to be a career, and Daniel Bivona takes this oft misquoted assertion at face value in *British Imperial Literature, 1870–1940: Writing and the Administration of Empire* (1998).

Bivona's study explores the vertical trajectory of the colonial administrator at a time when the position was becoming increasingly professionalized. The Victorian attitude to bureaucracy was ambivalent to say the least; on the one hand, withering satires like Dickens's Circumlocution Office pointed to an excess of red tape that led only to inertia. On the other, however, many Victorians felt a great respect for what they perceived as the efficiency and dedication of those working in far-flung imperial outposts. Bivona examines a growing national fascination with the power behind the bureaucratic machinery, exploring the connections between the growth of administration and the increased rivalry among European powers struggling to carve up the remaining uncolonized areas of Africa at the end of the nineteenth century. Taking Kafka's short story "In the Penal Colony" as his starting point, Bivona expresses the central premise that the colonial bureaucrat "justifies writing on bodies by submitting his own body to be written upon" (4), viewing the administrator as a kind of tabula rasa upon which any prevalent ideology may be inscribed. While the day-to-day running of a colony was mundane and tedious, Bivona elevates his subjects to almost epic heights, asserting that the imperial service became a form of dramatic "stage" upon which bureaucracy was able to flourish and gain an unprecedented momentum.

This book's main focus is the "Scramble for Africa," but Bivona looks back to the Crimean War and the 1857 Indian Mutiny to examine the reconstruction of British administration overseas in the wake of these two defining national calamities. Indeed, the study begins with an examination of Lord Cromer and his extraordinary impact on the face of colonial administration across the globe—but particularly in Africa—before stepping back to consider Livingstone and Stanley and the role the pair played in paving the way for aggressive colonization. According to Bivona, it was H. M. Stanley's 1878 travelogue, *Through the Dark Continent*, based on his "solo" exploration of the Congo with a supporting army of three hundred and fifty men, that was largely responsible for presenting Africa to Britain as an area in need of colonial intervention. At the heart of colonial management, as with so many aspects of fin-de-siècle British life, lay deep-rooted anxieties that the apparently slick organization was all just an elaborate façade. Rival powers like Germany seemed, comparatively speaking, so much more impressive and efficient in their government of imperial holdings, and the imperial bureaucrat was under constant scrutiny. Bivona's interesting and well-researched study charts the valorization of the paper-pusher and the ways in which he displaced maverick heroes like Cecil Rhodes in the public imagination. With sections on Kipling, Gordon, Conrad, T. E. Lawrence, Orwell, and Joyce Cary, Bivona's book is pleasingly interdisciplinary and covers key transitional phases in the rise and fall of the British colonial venture.

Bivona's efforts to make bureaucracy interesting owe a great deal to Thomas Richards's earlier work, *The Imperial Archive*, in which Richards asks how the Victorians grappled with a deluge of imperial knowledge. Richards examines the shifting nature of knowledge in the nineteenth century, declaring that information became the only means by which the empire could be retained. Dealing with the great age of imperialism in the final third of the century, Richards discusses the Victorian mania for taxonomy and pays attention to the "imperial sciences" like geography and map-making. He draws the important distinction between governing the written word and ruling an empire, observing that it is much easier to unify words on a page than disparate peoples living worlds apart. *The Imperial Archive* considers the role played by the museum (particularly that great imperial repository, the British Museum) in consolidating imperial identity, but also tackles the role of novels in creating a "myth of a unified archive" (6). The work includes extended discussions on the role of information-gathering in Kipling's *Kim* and Bram Stoker's *Dracula*, as well as early twentieth-century texts like Wells's *Tono-Bungay*. Almost mimicking the process he is outlining, Richards adds to the huge range of interpretations of Dracula, reading the Count as an "alienated colonial intellectual" whose crime is to violate Victorian codes of understanding (61). Richards makes a convincing case for considering Dracula as a mutant, devoid of origins, whose existence violates Darwinian theories of development and who therefore threatens to overturn the Victorian knowledge base. Thus, Richards joins the long line of critics, including Stephen D. Arata, who view Dracula as an embodiment of the late Victorian imperial crisis.

At the other end of the spectrum of imperial heroism is Joseph Bristow's now classic work, *Empire Boys*, a study of the more romantic side to the imperial adventure. Bristow considers the role played by imperial adventure narratives in constructing late Victorian masculinity and disseminating an ideal of moral and physical well-being that was frequently at odds with the state of the majority of the British population. The work as a whole constitutes a cultural history of boyhood, adolescence, and the realities of adulthood at the height of British imperial activity. Bristow reads adventure novels alongside articles from periodicals, government reports, and a wealth of additional contextual material to elucidate the ideological role of the growing number of stories for boys at this time. Attention is paid to the role of the public school in forming future rulers of the empire, suggesting that the late nineteenth-century schoolboy was faced with demands, both mental and physical, that were completely unprecedented. Bristow considers the spread of competitive sport and academic competitions and the parts that they played in coaching young men for the demands of civic life. Other chapters address the influence of Defoe's *Robinson Crusoe* in creating what Bristow terms an "island story" and the roles of H. Rider Haggard, G. A. Henty, and Rudyard Kipling. Bristow pays particular attention to the question of why adventure fiction was so bound up with Africa and examines the rise of the myth of the 'dark continent' in the aftermath of the abolition of slavery. According to Bristow, a conspiracy of evangelists, explorers, and anthropologists conspired to present Africa in excessively savage terms, which appealed to a number of late Victorian novelists. Bristow's work examines the often uncomfortable parallels between militarism and the education of young boys in a world where whiteness was equated with masculine power and blackness with both female sexuality and weakness.

David Alderson's more recent study *Mansex Fine* is similarly concerned with issues of masculinity and education, but from more of a religious perspective. Taking its curious title from Gerard Manley Hopkins's "The Bugler's First Communion," Alderson's work focuses on the veneration of the male body in Victorian culture, but commences at the beginning of Victoria's reign to trace a "tradition" of manliness. Alderson aligns the masculine with the dominant Protestant religion, whilst arguing that the marginalized Catholic religion was constructed as its effeminate binary opposite. According to this paradigm, manliness became the desirable attribute of the imperial high-flyer, while Catholicism was equated with anarchy and potential revolution, both in political and gendered terms.

By refusing to focus on the fin de siècle in isolation, Alderson helpfully traces the origins of the stridently imperial late Victorian consciousness, reminding the reader that it did not simply materialize overnight. While the study pays particular attention to Hopkins, it also contains an interesting chapter on Kingsley's Alton Locke and a welcome study of John Henry Newman, along with more familiar analyses of the English public school system and same-sex desire between men. Most useful of all, however, is Alderson's attention to the dynamic of imperial relations between England and Ireland, culminating in a discussion of the ever-problematic Oscar Wilde. Here, Alderson notes that the Anglo-Irish Wilde complicated the neat gender and religious binaries through his refusal to observe conventional boundaries. The undergraduate Wilde, like a number of his peers, gave serious consideration to converting to Catholicism, in his case, Alderson argues, as a retreat from the Protestant work ethic and its underlying moral code. Considering the complexities of the Irish political climate, in which Protestant families like the Wildes could align themselves with home rule without any sense of contradiction, Alderson reads Wilde's drive towards sexual, religious, national, and aesthetic individuality as an attempt to shrug off the constraints of taxonomizing identity.

The Boer War of 1899–1902 signaled a transition between the nineteenth and twentieth centuries, and a movement to different, less gentlemanly rules of engagement, although perhaps this shift can be dated back to the Crimean War, with its grim harbingers of what we would today term weapons of mass destruction. In *Gender, Race, and the Writing of Empire*, Paula M. Krebs considers the last Victorian war and its relation to both New Imperialism and New Journalism. Krebs opens with an examination of Mafeking Night: ostensibly an evening of spontaneous celebration, but in fact a carefully orchestrated spectacle designed to rally national and imperial enthusiasm for a deeply unpopular war. For Krebs, Mafeking Night is more than a celebration in the streets; it is a testament to the growing power of the media and its ability to construct heroes like Baden-Powell. Krebs pays a great deal of attention to the role of the press, offering a much-needed examination of the coverage of British concentration camps. By the end of the war, tens of thousands of people had died in the camps, although it was only the deaths of white victims that were reported. Krebs asserts that the controversy surrounding the camps offers a case study through which to examine the Boer War in its entirety, with especial attention to issues of race and gender and the spread of the imperial celebrity.

Crime and Empire

Policing the empire became an increasingly important concern for the late Victorians, whether it was the policing of the male body, or the broader government of imperial subjects. Upamanyu Pablo Mukherjee's *Crime and Empire* outlines some of the problems faced by those seeking to enforce law and order in the empire. Mukherjee reminds us of the difficulty in transplanting a new and controversial policing system from Britain to India and argues that the rise of the "new police" force in Britain had a significant impact on the administration of India. Mukherjee's work considers a number of crime stories from the 1820s to 1868. He looks at well known texts like Philip Meadows Taylor's work on Thuggee and less mainstream works, including *Pandurang Hari*, by William Hockley.

For Mukherjee, the Indian Mutiny not only complicated British rule in India, but also created a completely new version of criminality that defied the dangerous exoticism of the criminals more traditionally associated with the subcontinent, for instance the Thugs. According to Mukherjee, the uprising exposed a conflict in perceptions of Indians and their relationship to British rule, whereby on the one hand a discourse of progress and reform legitimated the imposition of colonial law, while, on the other, Indians were regarded as "natural criminals" who could only be kept in line through displays of imperial might. The Mutiny notoriously undercut British claims to military prowess, and extreme disciplinary measures, including the blowing of rebels from cannon, incited further violence and certainly did not frighten the Indians into submission. Mukherjee examines what he calls the "transformation of the figure of 'criminal' Indian into that of a victim and, eventually, of the avenger" (129), commenting that this shift in representation has complicated British myths of progress and also the writing of Mutiny histories as crime narratives. This excellent study concludes with a survey of Mutiny novels written in the immediate aftermath, culminating in a section on *The Moonstone* as a text which condemns imperial brutality, suggesting that faulty policing overseas will always result in repercussions back at home.

Joseph McLaughlin's complementary work *Writing the Urban Jungle* is more focused on the imperial center and metropolitan writing by Doyle, General Booth, Jack London, Conrad, and T. S. Eliot. In his socio-geographical study, McLaughlin considers London as a point towards which all imperial detritus gravitated, whether in the form of people or the more usual forms of rubbish. McLaughlin examines late Victorian angst about Britain's place in the world and its future and ponders the paradox of the urban jungle. Acknowledging his debt to predecessors including Rachel Bowlby, Thomas Richards, and Anne McClintock, McLaughlin claims that the growing global commodity culture of fin-de-siècle Britain was a significant factor in changing perceptions of the metropolis. The literary texts considered in this study have all been chosen for the "fresh" perspectives they offer on the city of London and its growing otherness. McLaughlin is especially attentive to the increasing use of colonial metaphors to discuss the dark underbelly of the city as he charts the reconfiguration of urban rhetoric. He presents a particularly thorough examination of the dialogue between General Booth's reformist writings and H. M. Stanley's African anecdotes. *Writing the Urban Jungle* also draws on contemporary events like Imre Kiralfy's Empire of India Exhibition (1895–96) to contemplate how urban imperial spectacles like Kilafy's Indian City formed a backdrop to texts like *The Sign of Four* and informed perceptions of the urban landscape. McLaughlin contends that this replica of an Indian city, complete with Indian people, elephants, and camels, promised "new pleasurable possibilities for the consumption of empire within metropolitan London" (78). The urban jungle is presented here as a space to be tamed or colonized, and while T. S. Eliot—who forms McLaughlin's final case study—was horrified by the anarchic city and its multitudinous foreign influences, for Doyle and Booth it offered endless challenges.

Catherine Wynne's *The Colonial Conan Doyle* moves beyond the Sherlock Holmes stories to offer an important analysis of Ireland's colonial identity and a re-examination of the quintessentially English Conan Doyle. Wynne argues for a slippage between Doyle's more English-than-the-English public persona and his Irish-Catholic and Scottish heritage, complicating previous assessments of the author as a jingoist. McLaughlin takes this position still further, contesting that *A Study in Scarlet* may be read as an historical novel. Wynne considers Doyle's stance on the Irish question, examining a wealth of sources, including the author's many letters to the newspapers and his pamphlets in support of the Boer War. The study traces a tradition of resistance to English hegemony in Doyle's family, citing his uncle, the cartoonist Richard Doyle (who resigned from *Punch* in 1850 over the journal's anti-Catholicism), as a prominent predecessor. Wynne's careful analysis explores how Conan Doyle's very public pro-imperialist stance was reconciled with his sympathies toward Irish nationalists, commenting that his straightforward public pronouncements on the empire were often undercut by more complex fictional negotiations of colonial issues.

Inevitably, Wynne's study turns to the Sherlock Holmes stories, many of which engage with imperial concerns. Her focus ranges from the contamination anxieties of a piece like "The Adventure of the Speckled Band"—which Wynne connects to Doyle's concerns regarding colonial exploits in the Belgian Congo—to a consideration of the evil Professor Moriarty as a colonial criminal. For Wynne, Holmes is symptomatic of a late nineteenth-century climate of imperial crisis and she argues that the detective's popularity stemmed from his ability to reduce everything to hard facts in a climate of degeneration, uncertainty and imperial decline. The most intriguing chapter in this provocative study is a discussion of *The Hound of the Baskervilles*, in which Wynne re-reads the atavistic Devon countryside, arguing that Grimpen Mire is in fact an Irish bog. Some of Wynne's assertions are perhaps a little overstated, in particular her argument that the presence of the Fenian activist Michael Davvitt in Dartmoor Prison in the 1870s would have altered Doyle's perception of the landscape (65). Nevertheless, Wynne offers an important reevaluation of an author frequently represented as an arch-jingoist.

***

The past fifteen years have seen immense progress in the study of the literature of imperialism, and critical enthusiasm for this compelling subject shows no sign of abating. In an increasingly uncertain world of global conglomerates and neo-imperialism, we have much to learn from the Victorians and their confrontations with the other. Through studying nineteenth-century reactions to terror, cultural difference, and national identity, we are able to trace the mapping of the world we know and the colonial origins of a number of present-day conflicts. More work remains to be done on the colonized and their perceptions of the dynamic and industrious Victorians, and efforts to reclaim silenced voices must continue. As Shearer West cautions, we must avoid holding the Victorians responsible for the present state of the world,

but we have much to learn from their imperial ventures and some of the
mistakes that they made.

WORKS CITED

Alderson, David. *Mansex Fine: Religion, Manliness and Imperialism in Nineteenth-
Century British Culture.* Manchester: Manchester UP, 1998.

Archibald, Diana C. *Domesticity, Imperialism and Emigration in the Victorian Novel.*
Columbia, Missouri: U of Missouri P, 2002.

Arata, Stephen D. "The Occidental Tourist: *Dracula* and the Anxiety of Reverse
Colonization" *Victorian Studies* 33, 4 (1990): 621–45.

Barringer, Timothy. "Images of Otherness and the Visual Production of Difference:
Race and Labour in Illustrated Texts, 1850–1865" *The Victorians and Race.* Ed.
Shearer West. Hants: Scolar, 1997. 34–52.

Bar-Yosef, Eitan. " 'An Ocean of Soap and Water': The Domestication of *Dombey
and Son.*" *Dickens Quarterly* 19, 4 (2002): 220–31.

Bivona, Daniel. *British Imperial Literature, 1870–1940: Writing and the Administration of Empire.* Cambridge: Cambridge UP, 1998.

Brantlinger, Patrick. *Dark Vanishings: Discourse on the Extinction of Primitive Races,
1800–1930.* Ithaca: Cornell UP, 2003.

———. *Rule of Darkness: British Literature and Imperialism, 1830–1914.* Ithaca:
Cornell UP, 1988.

Bristow, Joseph. *Empire Boys: Adventures in a Man's World.* London: Harper Collins
Academic, 1991.

Bryden, Inga. "Reinventing Origins: the Victorian Arthur and Racial Myth" *The
Victorians and Race.* Ed. Shearer West. Hants: Scolar, 1997. 141–55.

Buzard, James. " 'Anywhere's Nowhere:' Dickens on the Move" *Dickens, Europe
and the New Worlds.* Ed. Anny Sadrin. Basingstoke: Palgrave, 2001. 113–27.

Carens, Timothy L. "The Civilizing Mission at Home: Empire, Gender, and National
Reform in *Bleak House.*" *Dickens Studies Annual.* 26 (1998): 121–45.

Carroll, Alicia. *Dark Smiles: Race and Desire in George Eliot.* Athens: Ohio UP, 2003.

Chakravarty, Gautam. *The Indian Mutiny and the British Imagination.* Cambridge:
Cambridge UP, 2005.

Cheadle, Brian. "Despatched to the Periphery: the Changing Play of Centre and Periphery in Dickens's Work" *Dickens, Europe and the New Worlds*. Ed. Anny Sadrin. Basingstoke: Palgrave, 2001. 100–112.

Childers, Joseph. "The Empire at Home" *Homes and Homeless in the Victorian Imagination*. Ed. H.M. Daleski and Murray Baumgarten. New York: AMS, 1999.

David, Deirdre. *Rule Britannia: Women, Empire, and Victorian Writing*. Ithaca: Cornell UP, 1996.

Erikson, Charlotte, ed. *Emigration from Europe 1815–1914: Selected Documents*. Documents in Economic History Series. London: Adam and Charles Black, 1976.

Fields, Darin E. " 'Two Spheres of Action and Suffering': Empire and Decadence in *Little Dorrit*." *Dickens Quarterly* 8, 4, (1990): 379–383.

Finkelstein, David and Douglas M. Peers. *Negotiating India in the Nineteenth-Century Media*. Basingstoke: Macmillan, 2000.

Gilmartin, Sophie. *Ancestry and Narrative in Nineteenth-Century British Literature: Blood Relations from Edgeworth to Hardy*. Cambridge: Cambridge UP, 1998.

Grewal, Inderpal. *Home and Harem: Nation, Gender, Empire, and the Cultures of Travel*. Durham: Duke UP, 1996.

Gribble, Jennifer. "Borrioboola-Gha: Dickens, John Jarndyce and the Heart of Darkness" *Dickens, Europe and the New Worlds*. Ed. Anny Sadrin. Basingstoke: Palgrave, 2001. 90–99.

Henry, Nancy. *George Eliot and the British Empire*. Cambridge: Cambridge UP, 2002.

Jacobson, Wendy S., ed. *Dickens and the Children of Empire*. Basingstoke: Palgrave, 2000.

Kestner, Joseph A. "The Colonized in the Colonies: Representations of Celts in Victorian Battle Painting" *The Victorians and Race*. Ed. Shearer West. Hants: Scolar, 1997. 112–27.

Kooiman, Dick. "The Short Career of Walter Dickens in India." *The Dickensian* 998 (Spring 2002): 14–28.

Kranidis, Rita S. *The Victorian Spinster and Colonial Emigration: Contested Subjects*. New York: St. Martin's, 1999.

Krebs, Paula M. *Gender, Race, and the Writing of Empire: Public Discourse and the Boer War*. Cambridge: Cambridge UP, 1999.

Lewis, Reina. "Women and Orientalism: Gendering the Racialized Gaze" *The Victorians and Race*. Ed. Shearer West. Hants: Scolar, 1997. 180–93.

Lindfors, Bernth. "Charles Dickens and the Zulus." *Africans on Stage*. Ed. Bernth Lindfors. Bloomington: Indiana UP, 1999. 62–80.

Litvack, Leon. "Dickens, Australia and Magwitch Part I: The Colonial Context." *The Dickensian* 95 (Spring 1999): 24–50.

———. "Dickens, Australia and Magwitch Part II: The Search for *le cas Magwitch*." *The Dickensian*. 95, (Summer 1999): 101–27.

——— "Dickens, Ireland and the Irish, Part I." *The Dickensian* 99, (Spring 2003): 34–59.

——— "Dickens, Ireland and the Irish, Part II." *The Dickensian* 99, (Summer 2003): 137–152.

Lorentzen, Eric G. " 'Obligations of Home': Colonialism, Contamination and Revolt in *Bleak House*." *Dickens Studies Annual* 34 (2004): 155–84.

Mara, Miriam O'Kane. "Sucking the Empire Dry: Colonial Critique in *The Mystery of Edwin Drood*." *Dickens Studies Annual* 32 (2002): 233–46.

McClintock, Anne. *Imperial Leather: Race, Gender and Sexuality in the Colonial Context*. New York: Routledge, 1995.

McLaughlin, Joseph. *Writing the Urban Jungle: Reading Empire in London from Doyle to Eliot*. Charlottesville: UP of Virginia, 2000.

Meyer, Susan. *Imperialism at Home: Race and Victorian Women's Fiction*. Ithaca: Cornell UP, 1996.

Milligan, Barry. *Pleasures and Pains: Opium and the Orient in Nineteenth-Century British Culture*. Charlottesville: UP of Virginia, 1995.

Moore, Grace. *Dickens and Empire: Discourses of Class, Race and Colonialism in the Works of Charles Dickens*. Aldershot: Ashgate, 2004.

Morgentaler, Goldie. *Dickens and Heredity: When Like Begets Like*. Basingstoke: Macmillan, 2000.

Mukherjee, Upamanyu Pablo. *Crime and Empire: The Colony in Nineteenth-Century Fictions of Crime*. Oxford: Oxford UP, 2003.

Myers, Janet C. "Antipodal England: Emigration, Gender and Portable Domesticity in Victorian Literature and Culture." PhD diss. Rice University, 2000.

Nayder, Lillian. *Unequal Partners: Charles Dickens, Wilkie Collins, and Victorian Authorship*. Ithaca: Cornell UP, 2002.

Nunokawa, Jeff. "For Your Eyes Only: Private Property and the Oriental Body in *Dombey and Son*" *Macropolitics of Nineteenth-Century Literature: Nationalism, Exoticism, Imperialism*. Eds. Jonathan Arac and Harriet Ritvo. Philadelphia: U of Pennsylvania P, 1991. 138–58.

Oddie, William. "Dickens and the Indian Mutiny." *The Dickensian* 68 (January 1972): 3–17.

Park, Hyungi. " 'Going to Wake Up Egypt': Exhibiting Empire in *The Mystery of Edwin Drood.*" *Victorian Literature and Culture* 30:2 (2002): 529–50.

————. "The Story of Our Lives: *The Moonstone* and the Indian Mutiny in *All the Year Round.*" *Negotiating India in the Nineteenth-Century Media.* Eds. David Finkelstein and Douglas M. Peers. Basingstoke: Macmillan, 2000. 84–109.

Paxton, Nancy L. *Writing Under the Raj: Gender, Race and Rape in the British Colonial Imagination, 1830–1947.* New Brunswick: Rutgers UP, 1999.

Perera, Suvendrini. *Reaches of Empire: The English Novel from Edgeworth to Dickens.* New York: Columbia UP, 1991.

Peters, Laura. " 'Double-Dyed Traitors and Infernal Villains': *Illustrated London News, Household Words,* Charles Dickens and the Indian Rebellion." *Negotiating India in the Nineteenth-Century Media.* Eds. David Finkelstein and Douglas M. Peers. Basingstoke: Macmillan, 2000. 110–34.

————. *Orphan Texts: Victorian Orphans, Culture and Empire.* Manchester: Manchester UP, 2000.

————. "Perilous Adventures: Dickens and Popular Orphan Adventure Narratives". *The Dickensian* 94 (Winter 1998): 172–83.

Randall, Don. *Kipling's Imperial Boy: Adolescence and Cultural Hybridity.* Basingstoke: Palgrave, 2000.

Rajan, Rajaswari Sunder. " 'The Shadow of that Expatriated Prince': The Exorbitant 'Native' of *Dombey and Son.*" *Victorian Literature and Culture* 19 (1991): 85–106.

Richards, Thomas. *The Imperial Archive: Knowledge and the Fantasy of Empire.* New York: Verso, 1993.

Sadrin, Anny, ed. *Dickens, Europe and the New Worlds.* 1999. Basingstoke: Palgrave, 2001.

Said, Edward W. *Orientalism: Western Conceptions of the Orient.* Harmondsworth, 1978. Middlesex: Penguin, 1995.

Sharpe, Jenny. *Allegories of Empire: the Figure of Woman in the Colonial Text.* Minneapolis: U of Minnesota P, 1993.

Smith, Grahame. "Suppressing Narratives: Childhood and Empire in *The Uncommercial Traveller* and *Great Expectations.*" *Dickens and the Children of Empire.* Ed. Wendy S. Jacobson. Basingstoke: Palgrave, 2000. 43–53.

Stanley, Joachim. "Opium and Edwin Drood: Fantasy, Reality and What the Doctor Ordered." *Dickens Quarterly* 21:1, (March 2004). 12–27.

Suleri, Sara. *The Rhetoric of English India.* Chicago: U of Chicago P, 1992.

Tambling, Jeremy. "Opium, Wholesale, Resale, and for Export: On Dickens and China" *Dickens Quarterly*. 21 (March 2004): 28–43.

———. "Opium, Wholesale, Resale, and for Export: On Dickens and China" (part two). *Dickens Quarterly* 21 (June 2004): 104–13.

Taylor, Jonathan. *Mastery and Slavery in Victorian Writing*. Basingstoke: Palgrave, 2003.

Thomas, Deborah. *Thackeray and Slavery*. Athens: Ohio UP, 1993.

Thurin, Susan Schoenbauer. "China in Dickens." *Dickens Quarterly* 8 (September 1991): 99–111.

———. *Victorian Travelers and the Opening of China, 1842–1907*. Athens: Ohio UP, 1999.

West, Shearer, ed. *The Victorians and Race*. Hants: Scolar, 1997.

Wynne, Catherine. *The Colonial Conan Doyle: British Imperialism, Irish Nationalism, and the Gothic*. Westport: Greenwood Press, 2002.

Recent Studies in Nineteenth-Century Women Narrative Poets, 1995–2005

Linda K. Hughes

Charles Dickens's inclusion of narrative poems by Adelaide Procter in Household Words *and* All the Year Round *was no aberration. The production of narrative poems by nineteenth-century women poets was steady, rich, and varied. Narrative poems, moreover, reveal women's ethical and epistemological assumptions and register women's repeated interventions in public debates. Yet very little work has been devoted to women's narrative poetry as such despite a general outpouring of scholarship on women poets in the last decade. After considering why this is so, the present essay surveys finding aids for primary sources, foundational scholarship in the mid-1990s, and more recent scholarship devoted to narrative poetry and gender politics, the place of women's poetic narratives in literary histories, international politics, religion, publishing history and commodity culture, and narratology. The essay concludes by outlining questions ripe for further investigation and urging that studies of narratives in fiction and poetry be integrated.*

The relevance of nineteenth-century women narrative poets to readers of *Dickens Studies Annual* is clear from the first Christmas number Dickens assembled in his newly-launched *All the Year Round* in 1859. *The Haunted House*, as the special number was titled, moved with ease and no evident sense of disparity from Dickens's setting of the scene (''The Mortals in the House'') to stories by ''Hesba Stretton'' and George Augustus Sala (''The Ghost in the Clock Room,'' ''The Ghost in the Double Room'') to a narrative

---

poem by Adelaide Anne Procter, "The Ghost in the Picture Room"—better known today as "A Legend of Provence"—before continuing on to stories by Wilkie Collins ("The Ghost in the Cupboard Room"), Elizabeth Gaskell ("The Ghost in the Garden Room," better known as "The Crooked Branch"), and Dickens, who claimed space for two of his own stories ("The Ghost in Master B.'s Room" and "The Ghost in the Corner Room"). On what terms did Dickens and his audience read the poem in relation to the short fiction? Did story *qua* story trump generic differences as readers moved from prose to heroic couplets in which predominantly end-stopped lines emphasized the poem's rhythm and rhyme scheme? Was the concentrated language of poetry considered to elevate the tone and cultural prestige of the Extra Christmas Number, especially since Procter's couplets harked back to the seventeenth and eighteenth centuries and so fostered, like Christmas itself as reinvented by Dickens, an identification with the English past? Or, considering that Procter narrated a tale of a medieval nun who is seduced by the young wounded knight she nurses, leaves the convent, becomes a prostitute, and one day returns to the convent to find that the Virgin Mary has assumed the nun's guise and kept her place until her return, did the verse import a touch of sensationalism to spice the fare on offer in the Christmas number and glance obliquely toward the ongoing serialization of Collins's *The Woman in White*?

Dickens felt no need to theorize his editorial decision to place a woman's narrative poem squarely in the middle of an assortment of short stories. In this he largely anticipated criticism of the twentieth and twenty-first centuries. For the paradox of this essay on recent studies in nineteenth-century women's narrative poems is that it surveys a sub-field that for all practical purposes does not exist. That women wrote a wide array of verse narratives in the nineteenth century is unquestionable, as is the excellence of a considerable body of scholarship devoted to individual works and poets. But studies of nineteenth-century narrative poetry are scant and studies of women narrative poets nil. I want to pause to consider why this is so, and the implications for the approach to the scholarly survey I conduct here, before I turn to the scholarship itself.

Since the nineteenth century, when *Childe Harold, Aurora Leigh, Idylls of the King*, and *The Ring and the Book* commanded attention, narrative poetry has so diminished in prestige that a current poet asks, "Why, in the 21st century, would anyone tell a long story in verse? Not only are you likely to get more readers (and money) if you turn your material into a novel or screenplay, but even in the narrow world of poetry the highest praise usually goes to work that is lyrical, personal and short" (Wiman 25). In the academy lyric has come to be identified with poetry itself, as Jerome McGann comments in *The Poetics of Sensibility*: "twentieth-century pedagogy set the lyric as the model of poetic form'' (6). It can hardly be surprising that much of the distinguished scholarly work devoted to women poets foregrounds lyric rather than narrative verse. In *Victorian Sappho*, for example, Yopie Prins explores the ''textual embodiment'' of lyric (4) that Sappho came to figure as a result of the Ovidian narrative of Sappho's leap to her death, of gender ideology that identified the woman poet with spontaneous effusions unmediated by literary form or convention, and of naïve reading practices that sought an authorial presence behind the effect of lyric voice performed by print culture. In poems that evoked Sappho as a living voice, Prins thus finds an allegory of the lyric condition, a gesturing toward living voice that is merely a textual effect. Given this approach Prins naturally emphasizes the lyrics in *The Improvisatrice*, by Letitia Landon, a first-person narrative of passionate but thwarted love interspersed with inset tales and songs that ends in the woman poet's inevitable death.[1]

Since, moreover, no nineteenth-century woman poet wrote narrative poems to the exclusion of lyrics, study of women's poetry or individual figures typically ends in the subordination of narrative to lyric, the academy's preferred form. Virginia Blain's brief theorizing of women's narrative poetry is thus as welcome and as important as it is rare. Noting that in lyrics women poets can suspend politics and ethics, fashioning utterance that is ''purely ontological,'' Blain contends that as soon as ''poetry narrates action, it joins fiction in becoming ethical; that is, it implies consequences in human behaviours, including the behaviour of pleasure-seeking'' (''Women Poets'' 174). Ontology of course intersects with cultural politics, but Blain's point about the potential apoliticism of lyric and the necessary engagement of narrative with ethics stands as a significant contribution to study of the form. More typically, scholars identify and/or theorize poetic strategies that could operate either in narrative or lyric verse, making it difficult to isolate the distinctive elements of narratives.

Another challenge to the study of narrative poetry by women is the narrow band of it cited in scholarship. *A Companion to Victorian Poetry*, edited by Richard Cronin, Alison Chapman, and Antony H. Harrison, includes essays on epic, domestic and idyllic poems, the dramatic monologue, and the verse novel, all of which involve narrative; but there is no essay on narrative poetry itself, as there is on lyric. *Romantic and Victorian Long Poems: A Guide*, by Adam Roberts, lists a number of women's narrative poems. But since Roberts confines his study to poems one thousand lines or longer, hundreds of narrative poems, including Procter's ''A Legend of Provence,'' are necessarily excluded from his survey. *The Oxford Book of Narrative Verse*, edited by Iona and Peter Opie, is problematical for another reason: it includes only one poem by a woman in almost four hundred pages of verse: ''Goblin Market,'' by Christina Rossetti. "Goblin Market" suggests another problem in representativeness. My survey of scholarship could focus solely on "Goblin Market" and Barrett Browning's *Aurora Leigh* and still exceed readers' patience; doing so would only entrench salient omissions in the scholarly record.

Instead, I emphasize scholarship that helps bring into view an elusive, large, and highly complex archive of narrative poems by women that awaits further theoretical and critical work. Since scholarship devoted to Elizabeth Barrett Browning and Christina Rossetti is chronicled year by year in *Victorian Poetry* (the former by Dorothy Mermin and more recently Marjorie Stone, the latter by Florence S. Boos), my discussion of these poets will be highly selective relative to the rich commentaries they attract. Below I begin with resources for locating women's narrative poetry and foundational scholarship of the mid-1990s. I then survey scholarship devoted to a range of political and religious issues with which women's poetic narratives grappled. I conclude the survey with approaches based on publishing history, commodity culture, and narratology.

I. Databases, Anthologies, and Finding Aids

Much narrative poetry by nineteenth-century women poets remains unrecovered in individual volumes or in the pages of periodicals, gift books, and nineteenth-century anthologies.[2] Fortunately, the excellent electronic archive entitled the Victorian Women Writers Project, edited by Perry Willett and located on the Indiana University website, makes available gratis a wide range of narrative poetry. There one can read or download Mathilde Blind's evolutionary narrative, *The Ascent of Man* (1889); her powerful critique of the Highland clearances, *The Heather on Fire* (1886); and shorter poems like "The Russian Student's Tale" in *Dramas in Miniature* (1891). Other titles on the site include Caroline Norton's "The Creole Girl, or, The Physician's Story" (1840), Augusta Webster's *Lota*, a novel in verse (1867), and E. Nesbit's *The Moat House*, a New Woman narrative (1886).[3]

A series of scholarly anthologies published from 1995 to 2001 has enhanced access to narrative poems in print, although the premium on space in any anthology limits the reprinting of narrative poems, which are often long. Andrew Ashfield, Paula Feldman, and Isobel Armstrong and Joseph Bristow thus print only excerpts from Mary Tighe's mythological narrative, *Psyche* (1805); Armstrong and Bristow and Margaret Higonnet only sample Caroline Bowles Southey's autobiographical narrative, *The Birth-day* (1836); Higonnet presents only the songs from George Eliot's *The Spanish Gypsy* (1868); and Angela Leighton and Margaret Reynolds include only Book V from Emily Hickey's verse novel about English rule in Ireland, *Michael Villiers, Idealist*

(1891). On the other hand, Feldman reprints a generous cluster of Mary Howitt's narrative poems ("The Spider and the Fly," "The Voyage with the Nautilus," "Tibbie Inglis, or the Scholar's Wooing") as well as Elizabeth Trefusis's "Aurora, or the Mad Tale Madly Told." Armstrong and Bristow present in full Amelia Opie's "The Negro Boy's Tale" and "The Warrior's Return," Louisa Stuart Costello's "The Maid of the Cyprus Isle. A Ballad," Letitia Landon's "The Phantom Bride," Jean Ingelow's *Gladys and Her Island (On the Advantages of the Poetical Temperament)*," Procter's "A Tomb in Ghent," and Rosamund Marriott Watson's "The Story of Marpessa (As Heard in Hades)." Higonnet makes available Janet Hamilton's "Leddy Mary—a Ballad" as well as Ingelow's "The High Tide on the Coast of Lincolnshire, 1571" (this last also included by Armstrong and Bristow). Like Feldman, Armstrong and Bristow, and Virginia Blain, Leighton and Reynolds reprint Felicia Hemans's "Casabianca"; they also make available Dora Greenwell's "Christina," May Probyn's "The End of the Journey," and A. Mary F. Robinson's "The Wise-Woman." Blain adds to this mix of narrative poems "The Fight at Rorke's Drift. January 23rd, 1879," by Emily Pfeiffer (recounting an incident in the Zulu Wars), "Tiresias," by Michael Field, and "Wilderspin," by Mary Coleridge. All the anthologies reprint Rossetti's "Goblin Market" and a generous selection from Elizabeth Barrett Browning's poems.

Other resources for locating narrative poems by nineteenth-century women poets are the *Dictionary of Literary Biography* volumes dedicated to *Victorian Women Poets* (*DLB* 199) and *Late Nineteenth- and Early Twentieth-Century Women Poets* (*DLB* 240), both edited by William Thesing. Because the essays are sufficiently long to survey complete careers they often single out narrative poetry, much of which comprised political commentaries. In the first volume we learn from Kathleen McCormack (26) of Isa Blagden's fallen woman narrative, "The Story of Two Lives" (1873); from Marya DeVoto (75) of Frances Browne's *The Vision of Schwartz* (1844), a critique of imperialism embedded in a tale of the twelfth-century monk who discovers gunpowder; and from Florence S. Boos (156) of Janet Hamilton's "Grannie's Tale. A Ballad of Memorie," in which a father who complains of a fifth child born during hungry times must cope with the deaths of his four other children and wife. In the same volume Linda A. Julian examines several Harriet Hamilton King narratives, including "The Execution of Felice Orsini" and "Aspromante" (1869), both inspired by Mazzini's republican campaign, "The Lady's Steps" (1869), about a woman's flight from political assassins who plan the murder of her husband, and a two-hundred-fifty page narrative about the martyred priest who served Garibaldi's troops entitled *Ugo Bassi*, part of *The Disciples*, published in 1873 (194–98). Essays detailing narrative poems written later in the century (in *DLB* 244) include those on novelist-poet Bertha

Leith Adams, by Amanda Jo Pettit; Camilla Toulmin Crosland, author of a poetic domestic chronicle, Camilla Toulmin Crosland, by Kathleen McCormack; Toru Dutt, the Indo-Anglian poet, by Alpana Sharma; religious poet Mary Anne Hearn, by Linda A. Julian; Celtic twilight poet Nora Hopper, by Siobhan Craft Brownson; Mary Catherine Hume-Rothery, author of *The Bridesmaid* (1853) and other narratives, again by Kathleen McCormack; Eliza Keary, best-known for mythic narratives, by Naomi Hetherington; Irish nationalists Alice Milligan, by Eugenie Celeste Martin, and Ellen O'Leary, by Rose Novak; feminist activist Bessie Rayner Parkes, by Constance M. Fulmer; Rossetti, by Mary Arseneau; Catharine Amy Dawson Scott, the feminist founder of PEN whose first publication was the epic *Sappho* (1889), by Tonya L. Wertz-Orbaugh; Irish poets Dora Sigerson Shorter, by Deborah A. Logan, and Katharine Tynan, by Michele Martinez; my own essay on the a fin-de-siècle aesthete and New Woman, Rosamund Marriott Watson; Augusta Webster, by Kathleen Hickok; and Oxonian Margaret Woods, by Martha S. Vogeler.[4] No *DLB* volume exclusively dedicated to Romantic women poets has appeared, a glaring omission. If some careers can be traced in volumes devoted to British Romantic poets (e.g., Hemans and Landon), no *DLB* essay is yet available on the important work of Mary Tighe.

In an oft-cited review of the anthologies published in the mid-1990s, Linda Shires points out that "the influence of women on women in the nineteenth century is half the story. The other half concerns exactly what legacy was left by the male romantics for women poets and how women responded to that legacy and to its survival in male poets" (Shires, "Victorian" 605). Adam Roberts bibliographically situates narrative poems by women alongside those of men in *Romantic and Victorian Long Poems*, though he does not explore their exchanges. Roberts theorizes that the nineteenth-century frequency of long poems in experimental forms (verse-novel, epic, monodrama, monologues) resulted from uncertainty about poetry's function and themes, sentimental readings of Homeric epic (which brought love stories into prominence against the backdrop of heroic action), and a far-flung empire that inspired attempts to encompass multiplicitous complexities within a single narrative. Roberts offers the intriguing insight that Paris functions in *Aurora Leigh* much as the underworld does in Homeric epic, but as a whole he is more receptive to work by men than by women. He regrets, for example, the "feeble pastiche" of Hemans and seems rather surprised that "her longer narrative poems . . . are of considerable competence and interest" (98–99). More seriously, his assertion that long poems "were never serialized" (2) is, quite simply, wrong: Landon's successive "Poetic Sketches" as well as her verse tale, *The Bayadere*, were serialized in the *Literary Gazette* before being gathered into *The Improvisatrice* (Feldman 366; McGann and Riess 395).[5] Still, Roberts's guide is a useful finding list. Among the narrative poems he identifies are *Leonore, A Tale* (1860), by Georgiana, Lady Chatterton, which recounts the sequel to an exchange of identities by a princess and her friend at their double wedding in late-fourteenth-century France, and a cluster of poems that narrate late-medieval rivalries between Christians and Muslims: Hemans's *The Abencerrage* (1819) and Landon's *The Fate of Adelaide: A Swiss Romantic Tale* (1821) and *The Troubadour* (1825). In the two Landon titles, romance plots pit a Muslim against a European woman as rivals for the hero's love. Clearly, then, the dearth of scholarship devoted to narrative poetry by women as a whole has nothing to do with the extent of material available.

II. Foundational Scholarly Studies

Though first published prior to 1995, Isobel Armstrong's chapter on women poets, "'A Music of Thine Own': Women's Poetry—an Expressive Tradition?'' (1993), is cited more often than any other critical work in the scholarship surveyed here. In contrast to earlier work on feminist resistance, subversion, and recovery of voice, Armstrong argues that women's poetry is most radical precisely when it appears most conventional, when poets push supposedly unmediated outpourings to such extremes that they call the conventions of the poetess into question. Among the narrative poems she discusses, Armstrong observes a tendency to move the scene of action to a foreign locale associated with passion, thus opening perspectives on lands outside the ideological confines of Britain. Armstrong asserts of Adelaide Procter, for example, "Her narrative poems, dealing with the movement beyond the boundary, with escape, with ex-patriotism and return, are deeply preoccupied with displacement, and through this with the woman's 'place' or displacement in a culture" (336). In Rossetti's "Goblin Market" Armstrong traces the twin poles of expression and repression, overflowing feeling counterpoised by barriers. Laura and Lizzie seem to represent these binaries but are interdependent and at times almost indistinguishable, a strategy that moves the narrative beyond convention to the insight that expression of feeling is predicated on and made possible by repression—an exposure of the social conditions underlying the nineteenth-century poetess. The chapter ends with an account of mythological or masked narratives that delineate irreducible tensions between classes and ethnicities, as in *Aurora Leigh*, Eliot's *The Spanish Gypsy*, and Blind's *The Heather on Fire*, which Armstrong singles out as a narrative of particular power. Armstrong has been criticized for sequestering female poets in a single chapter rather than integrating them with her discussion of male poets. But her chapter remains an essential starting place for anyone seeking to investigate nineteenth-century women narrative poets.

Essential, too, is the collection of essays that Armstrong co-edits with Virginia Blain, *Women's Poetry, Late Romantic to Late Victorian*, which resulted from a landmark conference devoted to women poets in 1995. Armstrong and Blain organize their volume according to the subtopics of theory, the literary marketplace, lesbian poetics, national identities, cultural discourses, and neglected figures. In the lead essay, "Msrepresentations," [*sic*], Armstrong probes the politics of affect in women's poetry. Here "politics" designates state policies and structural oppressions visited upon workers that were inseparable from the politics of gender. Briefly taking up Hemans's *The Forest Sanctuary*, Landon's *The Troubadour*, and their other bloodthirsty explorations of war, Armstrong astutely touches on the disturbing rift between overt acts of state violence and the expected, obligatory stance of empathy and mourning in women's poetry. The resulting incoherence, Armstrong argues, indicates that women's lyrics and narratives of affect are pathologized: the very excesses of their emotional performances inscribe the acts of violence in which they are complicit and against which they struggle. Among the other essays, Linda Peterson remaps literary genealogies in arguing that Elizabeth Barrett Browning synthesized Landon's *A History of the Lyre* and Wordsworth's *The Prelude* in creating the mature Aurora Leigh, who modulates from the self-fashioning of a Romantic poetess to the autobiographical narration of a woman poet ("Rewriting *A History of the Lyre*"). Kathleen Hickok ("Why is this Woman Still Missing?") also addresses literary genealogies in arguing that Emily Pfeiffer belongs in literary histories of Pre-Raphaelitism because of her chivalric tales preoccupied with sexuality, women's roles, and brilliant coloration; these tales and Pfeiffer's novel in verse, *Margaret; or, The Motherless* (1861), also clarify Pfeiffer's gift for narrative despite her usual association with sonnets. In "Sexual Politics of the (Victorian) Closet," Virginia Blain theorizes that personae for whom gender is unmarked offer opportunities to read queerly and proves the value of doing so in her analysis of Margaret Veley's narrative of flirtation and attempted seduction, "A Japanese Fan." If Blain's essay registers the increasing importance of gender studies in emergent scholarship on women narrative poets, postcolonial studies are central to "Hearing her Own Voice: Defective Acoustics in Colonial India," by Meenakshi Mukherjee. Mukherjee examines Toru Dutt's mythological narratives in *Ancient Ballads and Legends of Hindustan* as well as Sarojini Naidu's lyrics, and complicates assumptions about what writing in English, the colonizer's language, may have signified for Indian women. Dutt's major influences were Bengali, not British, and her traditional tales associated with women's oral tradition feature active women who exercise authority. Both Dutt's and Naidu's poetry, moreover, were inseparable from national(ist) politics. Two other essays in the collection concern religion. In "Mysteries Beyond Angels" Linda E. Marshall analyzes "From House to

Home,'' one of the ''Devotional Pieces'' in Rossetti's *Goblin Market and Other Poems* (1862). In contrast to prior scholarship that reads the poem in terms of an aesthetics of renunciation and privileging of salvation over art, Marshall focuses on the chiastic imitation of Christ embedded in the two-part poem, whereby woman and Christ come to mirror the other—an exercise rather than surrender of female and aesthetic power. Gill Gregory offers a less hopeful appraisal of women's relation to religion in ''Adelaide Procter,'' arguing that ''A Tomb in Ghent''—first published in the 29 December 1855 issue of *Household Words*—critiques Tractarian reserve for too easily appropriating and reifying women's silence. Helen Groth takes up the relation of poetic to scientific discourse, concluding that Blind's *Ascent of Man*, in contrast to earlier work by Barrett Browning, Dora Greenwell and others, ascribes the same brutal, violent struggle for survival to natural and rural settings that was routinely associated with urban scenes. Besides doing much to propel current studies of women's poetry, Armstrong and Blain's collection is important in drawing upon feminist recovery while also setting women's poetry (including narratives) alongside work by men and in dialogue with a range of cultural discourses.

Another foundational text is the gathering of essays by Angela Leighton, *Victorian Women Poets: A Critical Reader*. The collection includes the splendid reading of ''Casabianca'' and other narratives of violent loss and sacrifice in ''Hemans and Home'' by Tricia Lootens, who probes Hemans's searching critique of war's brutal violence as part of a larger exploration of the poet's ''complex range of patriotic positions'' (5). As Lootens demonstrates, reading Hemans in terms of collections of verse rather than poem by poem reveals how consistently sentimental patriotism or heroism in one poem is undercut by skeptical treatment in another. Lootens thus offers a mode of reading as well as analysis of individual titles. Of particular interest to *DSA* readers is Gill Gregory's analysis of Procter's ''A Legend of Provence'' in *All the Year Round*, which Gregory situates in relation to Procter's activist work as a member of the Langham Place circle and Dickens's trivializing of her efforts in his thinly veiled portrait of her in Belinda Bates, who goes in for '' 'everything that is Woman's with a capital W''' and who is beseeched not '' 'to fly at the unfortunate men [. . .] as if they were the natural oppressors of your sex' '' (90). Terence Holt's '' 'Men sell not such in any town': Exchange in 'Goblin Market,''' first published in 1990, is a foundational essay in studies of the poem's relation to gender and commodity culture. His nuanced analysis leaves the issue of female power unresolved; if on one hand the market is figured as the preserve of goblin men, from which women, consigned to home, are excluded, on the other hand Laura appropriates the entire scenario and subordinates it to her own story-telling by the poem's end. Yet she does not erase the binaries within the tale itself, and Holt argues that readers intensify the poem's unsettling politics of the market because they are situated as goblin children, listening to the tale and leering, like goblins, at its eroticized details. Angela Leighton's " 'Because men made the laws' " surveys feminist treatment of fallen women in narrative poems by Barrett Browning (*Aurora Leigh*), Rossetti ("Goblin Market" and "Convent Threshold"), Procter ("A Legend of Provence"), Webster ("A Castaway"), and Levy ("Magdalen"), concluding that the prostitute was an empowering figure to the woman poet precisely because she operated outside the law. My article " 'Fair Hymen holdeth hid a world of woes' " shifts attention to the marriage question late in the century and to the sequence of fin-de-siècle poems ("Ballad of the Bird-Bride," "Procris," "Marpessa") by Graham R. Tomson, later known as Rosamund Marriott Watson, that appropriated myth to construct narrative plots aligning marriage with captivity and cruelty. Because Leighton's volume reprints several landmark essays from the 1980s (including Sandra M. Gilbert on Barrett Browning's *Casa Guidi Windows* and *Aurora Leigh*, Jerome McGann on Rossetti's lyrics, and Dorothy Mermin on "The Damsel, the Knight, and the Victorian Woman Poet") as well as a lengthy excerpt from Armstrong's " 'A Music of Thine Own,' " this volume looks back to readings predicated on resistance and subversion as well as ahead to quickened interest in national politics and materialist analysis.

The special issue of *Victorian Poetry* devoted to women poets (Spring 1995), which I guest-edited, rounds out the mid-1990s scholarship that helped support renewed interest in women's poetry. The sole essay to focus exclusively on a narrative poem, " 'Matters That a Woman Rules': Marginalized Maternity in Jean Ingelow's *A Story of Doom*," by Heidi Johnson, argues that Ingelow's ten-book epic subtly but firmly brings into question the role of maternity within biblical scripture and male-dominated religious experience. Johnson's essay, like those of Linda E. Marshall and Gill Gregory in the Armstrong and Blain collection, exemplifies emergent interest in women's relation to religion, a key area of scholarship in the past decade. Ingelow's Niloiya, Johnson points out, tacitly protests Noah's governance and proffers a revised account of Eve and the fall; if Niloiya ultimately submits to Noah's authority, Ingelow's poem nonetheless challenges more celebratory accounts of motherhood as a source of spiritual authority, as in Barrett Browning's *A Drama in Exile*. Florence S. Boos contributes the first of her important series of essays on working-class women poets to the special issue. "Cauld Engle-Cheek: Working-Class Women Poets in Victorian Scotland" examines the brief autobiographical narrative by Ellen Johnston ("The Factory Girl's Reply to Edith") recounting her father's desertion and suicide; Janet Hamilton's "Grannie's Tale: A Ballad o' Memorie," which vividly narrates the effects of rural famine in 1739–40; and "A Dream," Marion Bernstein's utopian narrative of a world in which women have attained full equality and freedom.[6]

The special issue's closing essay by Dorothy Mermin, " 'The fruitful feud of hers and his': Sameness, Difference, and Gender in Victorian Poetry," addresses but also reverses Linda Shires's emphasis on the importance of women poets' relation to work by men, for Mermin reads a number of male narratives (*The Princess*, " 'Childe Roland to the Dark Tower Came,' " and *Sohrab and Rustum*) in light of the issues and strategies developed by women poets. The special issue thus anticipates three key areas—religion, class, and cross-gender analysis—important to subsequent scholarship on women narrative poets while also featuring an original narrative contributed by A. S. Byatt: a new Christabel LaMotte poem and a scholarly letter from Maud Bailey (scholar-protagonist of *Possession*) to the editor.

III. Gender Politics

So many readings of resistance and feminist subversion in the work of Elizabeth Barrett Browning and Rossetti appeared in the 1990s that little work in this vein was left to do. Scholars who have adapted this approach to other figures, however, make a strong case for its continuing relevance, particularly when coupled with feminist analysis of the literary market, religion, and women's relation to male writers. Harriet Linkin integrates gaze theory, commodity culture, and elegant formalist analysis in "Romantic Aesthetics in Mary Tighe and Letitia Landon: How Women Poets Recuperate the Gaze" to demonstrate ways in which the female poet is empowered rather than oppressed by the gaze. Tighe's best-known narrative, *Psyche*, is as Linkin argues particularly suited to this investigation since Psyche's transgression is the forbidden act of looking upon Cupid. Linkin's key strategy is her rigorous distinction between narrative character and poetic acts of narration. The very act of libidinous gazing punished in Psyche is, Linkin argues, appropriated by Tighe in unfolding the spectable of Cupid's beauteous body. Moreover, ambiguous syntax suggests mutually reciprocal acts of gazing between Cupid and Psyche, as when he shoots the arrow of love at her but is himself pricked by the dart. *The Improvisatrice* works within a different economy of the gaze because Landon for the most part submits to the condition of commodity and feminine spectacle in order to attract buyers of her verse. But Landon creates a liminal space for female narration at the poem's end, after the Improvisatrice dies the overdetermined death of a woman trapped by the male gaze of Lorenzo, who inspires her love, abandons her, and eventually possesses her portrait. The posthumous narrator who relays this last detail is never named, foreclosing the shifting of the public's gaze upon Landon herself.

Jennifer Geer ("Many Worlds More" 2004) urges a more hopeful reading of *Gladys and Her Island*, by mid-Victorian poet Jean Ingelow, than those given in the 1990s by Jennifer Wagner and Isobel Armstrong, to whom this tale of an overworked pupil-teacher transported to an isle by the mother and daughter Imagination and Fancy and then returned to a life of drudgery denotes a politics of containment. Conceding that even on the island Gladys is expelled from the Garden of Eden after being present at the creation, Geer suggests that her access to this momentous vision ratifies the power of imagination, for Gladys is positioned prior to the existence of Eve, perhaps even Adam. Moreover, the biblical scripture on which Ingelow draws insists that anyone unworthy or unprepared to witness sacred sights will incur the penalty of death. Gladys survives her vision, which implies her worthiness to be present, just as the maternal role given to Imagination hints that all women share a capacity for poetic agency just as they do a potentially communal relation to poetry.

Insofar as dramatic monologues convey a plot or story,[7] they too fall into the category of narrative. In " 'My love is a force that will force you to care,' ", James Diedrick positions "Song of the Willi" (1871), by Mathilde Blind, alongside Swinburne's "Anactoria" to argue that Blind's speaker actually achieves what Anactoria only yearns to do: she kills through the very force of her love and passion, since the poem is narrated by a woman buried before her wedding day whose unsated desire will not let her rest in the grave, and whose embrace kills her intended bridegroom. If Blind's poem anticipates representations of female desire and the undead later in the century, her poem, Diedrick argues, critiques male aestheticism and specifically Swinburne's equation in 1866 of "adult" with "virile," hence strictly masculine, poetry.

In "Christina Rossetti in Secrecy," Tomoko Takiguchi argues that Rossetti revises conventions of the literature of sensibility in another dramatic monologue, "The Iniquity of the Fathers Upon the Children." In contrast to Landon's *A History of the Lyre*, whose responsive protagonist absorbs others' perspectives to the point of death, in Rossetti's poem secrecy supports a model of female independence rather than subservience. The speaker is the illegitimate daughter of a Lady and woman of sensibility who has concealed her girlhood seduction and now visits her daughter under the guise of aristocratic patronage. Though the mother never acknowledges her maternity, the sensitive, responsive daughter gleans enough to fathom their relation; rather than judging her, the speaker sympathetically suffers with her, and judgment falls instead on the iniquitous father and society's oppressive hypocrisy. Takiguchi relates the poem to Rossetti's work with Magadalens and, more specifically, to the burden of silence imposed on fallen women, who were forbidden to speak of their pasts. Rather than being disciplined by silence, the daughter finds independence in secrecy, solitary walks, and above all in her determination never to marry.

Virginia Blain makes a case for the continuing relevance of studying female tradition even when women poets do not explicitly acknowledge it ("'Be these his daughters?'"). Her test case is the relation of *Aurora Leigh* to Caroline Bowles's *The Birth-Day*, which also represents the formation of a female poet. Elizabeth Barrett Browning certainly knew *The Birth-Day*, since she referred to it, slightingly, in her correspondence with Mary Russell Mitford. The former concluded that Bowles had displaced Robert Southey's daughter in the elder poet's affections after Southey and Bowles married. *The Birth-Day*, Blain argues, is indeed written as a seduction poem to the father-poet Robert Southey, in relation to whom Bowles positions herself as loving, dutiful daughter. The missing genealogy of the debt owed by *Aurora Leigh* to *The Birth-Day*, Blain argues, suggests Elizabeth Barrett Browning's adept recognition of the father-daughter strand in Bowles's poem and her desire to efface it amidst her own wrenching experience of sundered closeness with her father.

IV. Reinsertions of Women's Poetic Narratives into Histories

Earlier work on feminist recovery has enabled scholars to reinsert women's poetic narratives into literary history and to probe self-aware treatments of women's relation to history. Elizabeth Fay is one of several scholars to remap the medieval revival in terms of women narrative poets. In *Romantic Medievalism* (2002) Fay argues that the poet figure central to Landon's *The Troubadour* infused radical politics into romantic medievalism because the individualism of desire and linguistic play associated with the troubadour destabilized historical continuities and hierarchies and hence conservative idealizations of the knight and chivalry. The chivalric poetry of Hemans and Landon is central to the chapter entitled "Feminizing Romanticism" in *Romantic Victorians*, by Richard Cronin, who notes that Hemans did not become widely popular until she turned to narrative verse. Rather than separating the domestic from the public sphere, Hemans reconfigured the domestic to encompass the world and so (like Landon) reinvented chivalry as a female sphere, allotting to women the roles of motivating chivalry by their need for protection, uttering moral exhortations, and expressing support for warriors they send to battle. More significantly still, in Hemans's and Landon's narratives women appropriate the task of articulating chivalry. According to Cronin, Hemans also blurred the boundaries between men and women, who mutually negotiate their roles in *The Siege of Valencia*. What makes Hemans seem so relentlessly feminine nonetheless, Cronin contends, is her all-enveloping style, which never varies in the regularity and purity of its meter and diction no matter what she writes about, rendering her poetry delicate, predictable, and bounded. In discussing "The Romaunt of the Page," Elizabeth Barrett Browning's intervention in nineteenth-century neomedievalism, Linda Shires focuses on "cross dwelling," the poet's ability to inhabit multiple, potentially contradictory political and cultural positions simultaneously ("Elizabeth Barrett Browning,"). "The Romaunt of the Page" critiques patriarchy insofar as the husband's life is saved by his wife, disguised as a page, at the same time that he rejects any infringement of conventional femininity; yet the page's service upholds the male code of honor, redefining it in female terms rather than subverting it altogether—just as the poet, who published the "Romaunt" in a woman's annual, upholds but modifies the male poetic tradition into which she inserts herself.

Florence Boos recovers what she terms "the only working-class woman poet I know of who expressed open and direct poetic sympathies with abandoned women and prostitutes" ("The 'Homely Muse' in Her Diurnal Setting,"). Fanny Forrester's "Magdalene—A Tale of Christmas Eve" (1871) depicts a prostitute who has returned home and recalls former innocent conversations with other girls where she now stands alone, desolate, at the stile by the village church. Forrester's "In the Workhouse.—A Deserter's Story" (1872) exemplifies the importance of integrating supposedly marginal figures into literary history. "In the Workhouse" tells of a soldier who loved a colonel's daughter, was "broken" for his presumption, and ended his days in a poorhouse.[8] Though she does not make the point, the passage Boos quotes is clearly intertextual: "raving! I am raving! as the wretched ever rave/In the ignominious shadow of the dreaded Union grave;/And the portly master, turning from my white, distorted face,/Prates of 'idle scamps not earning such a decent resting-place' " (Boos 272). Forrester's adaptation of the meter and rants of "Locksley Hall" serves to underscore how privileged Tennyson's soldier-speaker is, and how oppressed he might have been had he suffered the real poverty of Forrester's protagonist. Indebtedness to Tennyson is here a critique of his work.

Susan Brown argues that Mathilde Blind finds a way to put the reproductive female body and act of mothering at the center of history, rather than outside time and politics, in *The Heather on Fire* ("'A still and mute-born vision,'"). The narrative at first seems to depict timeless, universal folkways, the stuff of literary nostalgia, whereas the paratextual preface and notes emphasize historical specificity and injustices. Yet the narrative's opening lines disclose a more complicated intent when they single out a huge boulder "that owned a different birth/From all the rocks on that wild coast, alone" and move directly to the lone maid who stands on them above the "grey heaving ocean," another image of birth and fertility. As she would later do in *The Ascent of Man*, according to Brown, Blind here aligns geological and evolutionary processes with human reproduction. By the last two "duans" of the poem, when the political atrocity of the clearances begins, the dual perspective of paratext and narrative converge and mirror the dual perspective of evolutionary biology, which blends specific attention to morphology and species with larger patterns of survival that, in the realm of human biology, shape development. But in the Highland clearances the fittest—the Scottish agricultural laborers—do not survive because of blighting power relations; following the burning of her cottage the principal female is forced to give birth in a hovel during a horrific storm, and she and the babe die. History, politics, and the maternal body are here inseparable. Brown also usefully situates *Heather on Fire* in the larger context of famine poetry (e.g., by Lady Wilde or "Speranza"), which often turned on the suffering of pregnant or nursing women rendered unable to nurture their children, and to women's political poetry that found inspiration in "the generative female body" (131).

In "The 'minor' poetry of Amy Levy," (1999), Joseph Bristow forcefully explicates Levy's "minor" poetry as a mark, and enactment, of multiform dissidence. In an era when Arnoldian principles of universality dictated the secondariness of poetry grounded in differences of class, atheism, Judaism, ethnicity, sex, and sexuality, Levy affirmed the merits of outsider status. "Xantippe" is an early instance, in which the aspiring intellectual must endure a priori exclusion from philosophical discussion on grounds of sex. "A Minor Poet," the title poem of her 1884 volume, positions Levy in a sequence of suicide poems along with those written by Tennyson ("Lucretius") and Arnold (*Empedocles on Etna*), again with a difference. For the frontispiece of *A Minor Poet and Other Verse* depicts a despairing woman seated by a well, separated from the hilltop church in the distance and hiding her head, an image of sequestered female creativity that is elected rather than imposed, as in "The Lady of Shalott."

V. International Politics

As noted above, Isobel Armstrong argues that foreign locales generated opportunities for women poets to explore scenarios and passions outside national and ideological boundaries. International politics not only provided women narrative poets with opportunities to intervene in public debates but also enabled their advocacy or protest of specific policies: in the international arena women suffered no rhetorical disadvantage relative to men because citizenship and the franchise were irrelevant from the outset. Elizabeth Barrett Browning is a central figure in this cultural work, especially her *Casa Guidi Windows*. In contrast to Sandra Gilbert's well-known reading of the poem ("From *Patria* to *Matria*," in Leighton's *Critical Reader*), more recent work has shifted away from the dismantling of patriarchy to the poem's public impact and its intersection with the cultural discourses of nationhood, citizenship, and Dantean poetics. Matthew Reynolds argues that Part I of *Casa Guidi Windows* can be properly understood only if seen as a mode of prophetic writing in the tradition of Shelley, Mazzini, and Carlyle—a point made clearer by the fact that much of it was written prior to the active phase of the Risorgimento (*Realms of Verse*).[9] If, like others, Reynolds notes Elizabeth Barrett Browning's repudiation of prior depictions of Italy as a vulnerable female, he also contends that her hortatory idealization of Italy serves to predict and effect political action so that Italy can emerge as a Hegelian Idea in the process of being realized. Ultimately, however, Reynolds sees the prophetic mode as something of a dead end, not merely because recalcitrant actuality forced a different tone and muted hope in Part II but also because Barrett Browning herself shifted strategies in *Aurora Leigh*. Her verse novel represents political formations indirectly, through characters: the culminating marriage of Romney and Aurora after their earlier strife enacts the ideal of merging disparate polities into a unified, harmonious modern state.

Gender plays a more prominent role in "From *Mythos* to *Logos*," in which Leigh Coral Harris traces Barrett Browning's reworking of the feminized "*la bella Italia*" in both parts of *Casa Guidi Windows*. In Part I the poet dismisses *la bella Italia* and evokes republicanism through Michaelangelo's recurring attempt to sculpt Brutus, slayer of the ancient republic's enemy, only to be stymied for want of an adequate model (a type that the poet hopes will now arise); in Part II the poet recuperates a potentially relevant female image of Italy in the form of the pregnant Anita Garibaldi, who fights alongside her husband and whose miscarriage and death represent the sacrifices demanded to secure liberty. In asserting the inseparability of politics and aesthetics, moreover, the poem reveals British pleasure in Italian art as the product of a feminized land to be a form of colonization; the poem accordingly effects a shift from a mythic, legendary Italy to a potentially political Italy. Indeed, Harris argues, the poet's ambiguous status (English citizen, Italian patriot; empowered prophet, domestic wife and mother) enacts the liminality that characterizes Italy in its current historical moment.

Richard Cronin also underscores gender and what he contends is the rigorous realism of *Casa Guidi Windows*. Chapter 5 of *Romantic Victorians*, devoted to issues of citizenship, explores the Romantic dichotomy between identification with the state (Burke's approach) and the individual's irreducible freedom and particularity (associated with Shelley). Whereas Tennyson embraced the first and Robert Browning the second, Elizabeth Barrett Browning, Cronin opines, suggests a third way. Both men and women in Italy were feminized because they were shut out from citizenship by foreign oppressors; accordingly, Barrett Browning's model of citizenship is a constant process of negotiation, which *Casa Guidi Windows* enacts through its pivot in content and perspective as it moves from Part I to Part II. The poet adopts a genderless speaker in Part I and sees the best in the pope, the Duke, and the people because (as Reynolds likewise argues) this is a liberatory possibility that can inspire political agency in Italians. In Part II the poet characterizes her initial perception as naïve and that of a woman, yet she also now underscores her gendered status as woman and mother. Her maternal vision is crucial because motherhood entails an astute politics, seeing flaws in the beloved child (and kindred humanity) while never reneging or stinting on love.

If Elizabeth Barrett Browning grappled with Italian politics, she also looked westward to America and the politics of slavery in "Runaway Slave at Pilgrim's Point," a dramatic monologue that narrates the radical oppression of sexual violence imposed on a female slave and her resulting act of infanticide. E. Warwick Slinn and Marjorie Stone adopt divergent but equally illuminating approaches to the poem. Slinn aims in V*ictorian Poetry as Cultural Critique* to demonstrate the continuing relevance of theory's linguistic turn by applying speech-act theory and models of performativity and so grounding critique in material intrinsic to poetry—language and form—rather than positing idealist language or undertaking materialist analysis. His approach works especially well with "Runaway Slave at Pilgrim's Point" since, as he points out, the poem is premised on performative speech acts. The dramatic monologue enables the usually silenced figure of the black slave woman to speak and lay claim to human identity, according her tacit equality with whites. Moreover, the speaker's two principal aims are to curse and to wish (which come to the same thing, since she wishes the wives of white slave-owners descended from pilgrim fathers the same joy in childbirth she has had). Her reiterated verb forms, "I look," "I see," also have the force and status of performatives, Slinn argues, for looking positions her as the subject rather than object of the gaze. The motif of the mark, similarly, underscores not only the site marking Plymouth Rock and the violence visited upon slaves by the pilgrims' descendants but also language as sign.

In "Elizabeth Barrett Browning and the Garrisonians," Marjorie Stone shows that materialist analysis can illuminate rather than skirt linguistic performance. Stone draws on manuscript evidence and the discursive, transatlantic, and political contexts of Elizabeth Barrett Browning's contribution to the *Liberty Bell*, an abolitionist annual, to track the poet's adaptation of abolitionist rhetoric and her radical innovations. The explicit inclusion of rape (rather than concubinage) as a precipitating cause of events in "Runaway Slave" broke with precedent, as did presenting a slave mother as a fugitive and rebel who questions God. Stone forcefully demonstrates the deliberateness of these innovations, since Barrett Browning's first draft featured a male speaker, just as most abolitionist texts presented fugitives as male whereas slave mothers were usually depicted in the throes of grief over children sold away from them. Barrett Browning had received issues of *Liberty Bell* prior to submitting her poem and followed transatlantic exchanges in American periodicals and the work of Harriet Martineau, another contributor to the annual. Though the poem's melodramatic elements have been criticized, they acquire new legibility in Stone's hands as she demonstrates the continuity between Barrett Browning's rhetoric and *Liberty Bell* contributions by William Lloyd Garrison, Frederick Douglass, and others.

Elizabeth Barrett Browning's powerful interventions in international politics were predated by the Irish narrative poet Frances Browne, who, as Thomas McLean demonstrates ("Arms and the Circassion Woman"), appropriated international politics to protest Irish oppression in 1844. Browne's *The Star of Attéghéi* turns on the forced removal of a million Circassians from their homeland by Russians. Her narrative, however, interweaves the plight of three oppressed nations, Circassia, Poland, and Ireland, and thus aligns the Russians and British as allied oppressors. If she adopts the older literary form of Byron's Eastern tales in her poem, she revises his gender roles, for the Star of Attéghéi is Dizila, daughter of the Circassian ruler who has affianced her to a Russian prince. Rather than submit, Dizila cuts her hair and leaves with her lover, a Polish soldier who has good reason to oppose Russians, and fights on behalf of her homeland. The story ends tragically—her Russian fiancé kills Dizila when she steps in front of the Polish soldier to protect him, and her lover then dies heartbroken—but Browne intensifies her tale's political valences by having an Irish minstrel narrate events and refer to Ireland at several points as "'England's Poland'" (310). Browne's poem effects an international alliance among disparate peoples and ethnicities to resist oppressions on multiple fronts, even as Browne displaces the trope of the "fair Circassian woman" with a present-day woman soldier—much as Barrett Browning would later supplant "*la bella Italia*" with Anita Garibaldi in *Casa Guidi Windows*.

VI. Religion

Religious poetry found wide audiences in the nineteenth century, as the best-selling poem of the century, John Keble's *The Christian Year* (1827), indicates. Writing and reading devotional lyrics or hymns could be seen as acts of piety for women; narrative poems were slightly more problematic. Merely recounting religious tales risked repeating what was already familiar in a culture that made sermons into bestsellers, while revising or otherwise intervening in religious tradition carried the risk of presumption, even blasphemy. The opportunities and risks of religiously-based poems are alike examined in recent scholarship that approaches religion as a cultural discourse rather than as a site of struggle between faith and doubt.

The most important recent study is *Women's Poetry and Religion in Victorian England*, by Cynthia Scheinberg. Like Julie Melnyk (whose essay I discuss below), Scheinberg views religion as a discourse receptive to women's questioning and revision of theology despite women's exclusion from official religious roles. The feminizing of Christianity that resulted from increased emphasis on Christ's gentleness and compassion, Scheinberg argues, also helped elevate and popularize women poets such as Adelaide Procter and Jean Ingelow, who sold extremely well. Scheinberg's principal innovation, however, is to read Jewish alongside Christian women poets and to demonstrate the degree to which poetry's close association with Christianity shaped Christian and Jewish women poets' appropriation of Jewish tradition, including the Old Testament. Elizabeth Barrett Browning was unusual in having studied Hebrew as well as Greek, and Scheinberg convincingly argues for the centrality of the Miriam-Moses motif in *Aurora Leigh*. In Book 2 Barrett Browning cites only the first half of Miriam's story, her triumphant singing, suppressing the sequel in which Miriam colludes with Aaron against Moses and is blasted with leprosy until cleansed by God's mercy. Romney at first aligns himself with Moses and so, in typological (and hubristic) terms, with Christ but allots minimal agency to women despite the fact that in Jewish tradition Miriam, Moses's sister, arranged his discovery in the bulrushes and so made his leadership possible. After being blinded, Romney hails Aurora as a fully-empowered Miriam whose authority and inspiration he recognizes and follows. But in Christian typology Jewish tradition acquires meaning only in relation to the New Testament, and the role of Miriam leaves Aurora outside the new covenant and outside marriage. Aurora and Romney accordingly revise their typologies, model Christian conversion predicated on the New Jerusalem, and join themselves in imitation of the mystic union of Christ with the church.

Scheinberg links goblins to Hebraic men based on the echo of Isaiah 55.1 in ''Goblin Market'': ''Everyone who thirsts, come to the waters; and you that have no money, come, buy and eat!'' The biblical passage signifies that the Jewish covenant can be sustained by spiritual commitment alone, but Rossetti, Scheinberg argues, viewed Jewishness as a form of incompleteness predicated on indifference to Christ's redemption—a condition shared by contemporary women who, presuming themselves complete already, pressed for equal rights in this world. Scheinberg thus reads ''Goblin Market'' as a tale of temptations posed by Hebrew scriptures that are overridden when Lizzie enacts the roles of Christian suffering and redemption and makes the wine of communion (hence New Life) available to Laura. If the disappearance of the goblins establishes a tacit alignment of the sister-mothers with Mary and her virgin birth, the undeniable sexuality and commerce associated with the goblin marketers is coded with anti-Semitic allusion to contemporary

Jews and their sexual and religious threats to Christian virgins. Scheinberg's reading of Amy Levy's "Magdalen" is equally bold. Though Scheinberg acknowledges that Levy's narrative is customarily viewed as the tale of a prostitute, she argues that it can be construed as a Jewish, resistant reading of the New Testament's "Noli mi tangere" episode. In a Jewish-centered reading Mary Magdalen refuses typological "completion" by refusing to convert, insisting that she does not acknowledge the lover who has returned in his altered guise. Scheinberg's provocative analysis underscores just how much the positing of universalizing Christian versus multiple religious traditions can affect basic as well as complex matters of interpretation.

Scheinberg's discussion of Jewish poet Grace Aguilar is focused mainly on her lyrics. Daniel A. Harris takes up Aguilar's important early narrative poem, "The Wanderers" (which he reprints in an appendix), in "Hagar in Christian Britain." Aguilar, according to Harris, appropriates the figure of Hagar, a non-Jew, because Hagar so effectively tropes the Jewish experiences of expulsion and exile and addresses the uneasy positions of Jews in Christian England and the Jewish woman poet who faces marginality within and without her religious group. Aguilar revises religious tradition, Harris contends, by drawing a parallel between Hagar and Elijah as recipients of divine colloquies. Hagar's story also parallels the Western European, Christian myth of the Wandering Jew, but the alternative annunciations of Jewish and Christian tradition underscore the contrast between the bearing of the Word by Mary, which leads to spiritual transformation, and Hagar's giving birth to Ishmael, which initiates a process of nation building.

Julie Melnyk connects the increasing feminization of Christ in the nineteenth century to new models of middle-class masculinity that valued sympathy and an Evangelical emphasis on sacrifice over the strengths of the aristocratic hunter-warrior. She then gauges the degree to which this increasingly feminine Christ empowered women ("'Mighty Victims,'"). In narrative poems such as Hemans's "Joan of Arc, in Rheims" and Rossetti's "Goblin Market" (in which woman is both savior and saved), women readily identify with Christ's suffering as a means of redeeming others. Rarely, however, do women identify with Christ's power. The notable exception is *Aurora Leigh*, in which Romney undergoes Christ's suffering while Aurora takes on Christ's earthly agency as teacher and speaker. Together, Romney and Aurora inaugurate the new Christ—though at the poem's end the vision granted to Aurora remains a private rather than publicly shared experience.[10]

Three additional articles indicate the range of religious narratives by women and scholarly approaches to them. Dawn Henwood finds in Rossetti's "The Prince's Progress" the vexed ambiguity and interpretive aporias more commonly associated with Rossetti's "Goblin Market" ("Christian Allegory and Subversive Poetics"). Alluding through its title and situation to Christ as the bridegroom who espouses the church as bride, ''The Prince's Progress'' thwarts identification of either the prince (who cannot stay on task) or the princess (who suffers but does not act) with Christ and so preempts any reference point for or resolution to the allegorical reading it seems to invite. Terence Hoagwood argues that in *A Story of Doom* Jean Ingelow thematizes biblical hermeneutics itself (''Biblical Criticism and Secular Sex''), as when she presents divergent accounts of a soliloquy by Noah and omits to indicate either as authoritative, or when she incorporates quotes within quotes within quotes as well as competing sources in imitation of documentary form. Hoagwood also makes an effective case for the intersection of Ingelow's narrative with the discourses of class (given the association of the deluge with revolution and Noah's call for assistance against injustices and oppressions) and eugenics (in reference to foremothers who breed pygmies as slaves). This last was highly topical, since Francis Galton had founded the eugenics movement only two years before *A Story of Doom* was published. Finally, Charles LaPorte adduces *The Legend of Jubal* to demonstrate how George Eliot positioned herself as a female poet and prophet by reworking key elements of the Higher Criticism and the poetess convention (''George Eliot''). A passage in Genesis merely states that Jubal is the ''father'' of ''all'' who ''handle the harp and organ'' (165) and that his father kills a young man to his sorrow; in Eliot's narrative Lamech accidentally kills Jubal's brother and so effects a link between the founding of poetry and personal grief. By this means Eliot enfolds the performance of ''sentimental grief'' (167) into Higher Criticism's perception that biblical authors themselves appropriated mythological material to create a new communal literature.

VII. Publishing History and Commodity Culture

If narratives addressing history, international politics, and religion make the public role of women narrative poets increasingly clear, women also became public figures merely by inserting their poems into the literary marketplace. The efflorescence of book and publishing history in the last decade has extended to women's poetic narratives, as has the more intensively theorized investigation of commodity culture.

The final chapter of *''Colour'd Shadows,''* by Terence Hoagwood and Kathryn Ledbetter, stages a materialist reading of *Denzil Place: A Story in Verse* (1875), a twelve-book novel in verse by Violet Fane. Fane's narrative revolves around international politics, religion, and power relations in marriage: the female protagonist married to an older man (and reactionary Tory) has an affair with a handsome, progressive social reformer and, after a period of suffering and her husband's death, finds happiness and marries her lover;

but she is granted only two years with him in Italy before she dies in child-birth. Hoagwood and Ledbetter[11] focus on the paratextual apparatus of the central narrative, which is so encased in layers of epigraphs and intercalary lyrics that its principal theme, like its realism, concerns its own textual condi-tion. Because its irreducibly mediated textuality is signaled again and again by shifting perspectives, multiple voices, and self-aware artifice, the novel in verse foregrounds acts of interpretation without offering closure or any discernible moral.

Joseph Bristow, in ''Reassessing Margaret Veley's Poetry,'' contributes to publishing history and transatlantic studies alike. First posing the important question of how the body of women's poetry recuperated in the 1990s should be assessed, Bristow opts to trace patterns of distribution[12] and thereby reveals the importance of transatlantic exchanges for women poets. *Harper's Monthly Magazine* was more receptive than British audiences to Veley's verse, includ-ing her narrative ''A Japanese Fan,'' in part because her progressive politics chimed so well with those of the magazine. Veley's reputation also benefited from the promotional efforts of American critic E. C. Stedman and illustra-tions commissioned by the *Harper's* editorial staff that drew attention to her poems in the magazine.

Illustration is the consistent focus of Lorraine Janzen Kooistra's *Christina Rossetti and Illustration*, which examines twentieth-century as well as Victo-rian illustrations and makes three especially important points. First, Kooistra provides overwhelming evidence that ''Goblin Market'' was never intended as a poem for children, both because its first publication in an illustrated edition positioned it in the adult book market and because no bibliographical record indicates that it was ever included in Victorian books designed for children—a shrewd demonstration of her claim that materialist analysis and publishing histories are vital to understanding the function and significance of a book in its own culture. Second, Kooistra documents how innovative Rossetti's best-known volumes were in their material design, anticipating in the 1860s the total book design associated with William Morris in the 1890s. Her brother D. G. Rossetti executed the frontispiece and title page illustrations for *Goblin Market* (1862) and *The Prince's Progress* (1866), and also de-signed the layout and binding of the former. This was no coincidence, ac-cording to Kooistra, since Rossetti's visual imagination conceived ideas and poetic narratives in terms of striking images, and since Rossetti's Tractarian sympathies led to her conviction that visible signs should be subjected to careful study for spiritual significance. Nor were poems and illustrations merely juxtaposed in the resulting volumes. If the frontispieces depicted the climactic moment of the title poems' plots (the clipping of Laura's lock of hair, the prince's arriving to find the princess dead), the title page illustrations invited considerations of character states and thereby thwarted simple or reductive acts of interpretation. The *Goblin Market* frontispiece, for example, seems to contrast soul and flesh as Lizzie flees from the goblin market while Laura offers up her hair for fruit; but the sisters are virtually identical on the title page. Finally, Kooistra demonstrates that poetry and illustration proceeded interactively with Rossetti's 1866 title poem, since D. G. Rossetti's designs for *The Prince's Progress* began months before the contract was signed or the text complete, and at one point Rossetti even offered to change the wording of a line to accommodate her brother's sketch. One inference from this last is that collaborations between Victorian novelists and their illustrators may on occasion have had counterparts in narrative poems.

"Goblin Market" is also the subject of analysis in *Beauty's Body: Femininity and Representation in British Aestheticism*, by Kathy Alexis Psomiades, an important contribution to studies of poetry and commodity culture. The larger argument of *Beauty's Body* is that femininity played a key role in veiling art's relation to the marketplace. Aestheticism's beautiful female icons helped to associate art with defining traits of femininity, including habitation apart from the busy world of commerce and silent, mysterious surfaces that harbored infinite depths within. Both Swinburne and Christina Rossetti, according to Psomiades, resisted this trend. If "Goblin Market" at first seems to align the female body and aesthetic consumption when Laura buys luscious fruits with a curl clipped from her body, the market is displaced at the poem's end in favor of female domesticity and a mode of art—the tales Laura tells to children—that refuses visibility in terms of the female form.

The point of departure in *The Afterlife of Christina Rossetti*, by Alison Chapman, is one shared with Yopie Prins's *Victorian Sappho*: the necessary erasure and posthumous existence of the female poet in print. Chapman's argument, however, emerges from commodity culture rather than the genealogy of the poetess. Citing Catherine Gallagher on the commodity's dematerialization when exchange value overtakes and subsumes the commodity, Chapman argues for a similar emptying out of the authorial self given the close identification between the poetess and her commodified text. Though Chapman finds multiple forms of consumption in "Goblin Market"—prostitution, tuberculosis (the disease, according to Chapman, from which Jeanie dies and Laura suffers), and the exchange of commodities in the goblins' market—she is more interested in the text's afterlife. Because the poem creates contradictory moral and fairy tale narratives and consequently generates an outpouring of critical discourse seeking definitive origins in Rossetti's imagination on which to ground interpretation, the poem, Chapman suggests, allegorizes its own reception. Rather than Laura or Lizzie as a figure of consumption and reading, Chapman prefers Jeanie, who is dead but haunts the poem and Lizzie's memories. Because of Jeanie's multiple displacements, alignment with the abject, and function as a haunting signifier, remembering

Jeanie aptly tropes the more nuanced, mediated reception of textual afterlives that Chapman advocates.

In "Rossetti's Goblin Marketing: Sweet to Tongue and Sound to Eye," Herbert F. Tucker argues that Rossetti's language probes, critiques, and in part counters the exploitative mystification of language in an age of advertising. Juxtaposing advertising's project of selling consumption itself as the means to satisfy unending desire with the nuanced linguistic play of Rossetti's poem, Tucker notes, for example, that in the line comprising his subtitle the initial words of both phrases might be nouns or adjectives succeeded by either prepositions or infinitives. Rossetti's double signifying exposes the goblins' attempt to sell an experience and encourages readers' critical awakening to highly mediated language in print culture. Rossetti also registers a knowing self-awareness of virtual orality, a medium crucial alike to nineteenth-century poetry and the advertising jingle, in the goblins' iterated invitation to "come buy," a marketing pitch and homophone of social invitation ("come by"). According to Tucker, Lizzie bests the goblins because she refuses their seductive linguistic mystification and, with her penny, exposes the open secret of sales that underlies all advertisement. The poem, moreover, marks the moment of Laura's redemption most saliently in linguistic terms, in the chaste diction and rhythms offset by boldly innovative syntax in the description of the morning after Laura's purgation, when "new buds with new day/Opened of cup-like lilies on the stream." In such lines Rossetti maintains admirable simplicity but calls attention to the constructedness of her language rather than shoring up naïve assumptions about unmediated orality. In the end Rossetti achieves, according to Tucker, "sound taste, the sweet redress of the tongue" (130).

Isobel Armstrong's analysis of *Casa Guidi Windows* suggests that Elizabeth Barrett Browning, too, apprehended the alternative poetic possibilities of intervening in and being manipulated by the urban, political, and aesthetic shows of modernity. While arguing, like Tucker, that poetry can partly evade overdetermination by the market, Armstrong connects poetry, commodity culture, and civic and international politics as part of a larger project on glass. The window, she notes, is a particularly modern phenomenon because it can underscore subjectivity and privacy, sealing off the self from public spaces (as it did for the invalid in Wimpole Street), or can function as a liminal site that opens onto public spaces and enables an exchange with urban spectacle and political events. Processions and demonstrations seen through the window can foster a sense of nationhood shared equally by all citizen spectator-participants or manipulate spectators by eliciting desire through artful presentation. Armstrong traces the means by which the artist-spectator in *Casa Guidi Windows* becomes a participant who neither objectifies the visible nor claims transcendence. Just as she endorses participatory community that displaces power and agency away from hegemonic tyranny, so the artist-spectator understands visuality as a process that positions the viewer within a field of interactive forces that mutually shape perception. Fittingly, then, Elizabeth Barrett Browning concludes by contrasting the Crystal Palace, which represents commodities as embodiments of hope, progress, and nationhood only by occluding perception of the labor that produced them, with the child, who refracts and projects light and suggests the human capacity to create myths and symbols.

VIII. Narratology

In "Productive Convergences, Producing Converts," Monique Morgan urges scholars of Victorian poetry to make increasing use of narratology in their work in order to deepen understanding of poetic form's rhetorical effects and politics and test the claims of narratology against more than the realist novel. As an instance of such work, Morgan cites the discussion of *Aurora Leigh* in *Plotting Women: Gender and Narration in the Eighteenth—and Nineteenth-Century British Novel*, by Alison Case. Aurora, Case argues, diverges from most nineteenth-century female narrators, who lack access to the larger significance of their experiences, which they present as if unmediated by narrative itself. In contrast, *Aurora Leigh* features two irreconcilable narratives: a *Künstlerroman* and a love story. The first four books of the poem unfold as a retrospective account of the artist's development, told by an artist aware and in control of the form her narrative assumes. This narrative is predicated on Aurora's repudiation of Romney's marriage proposal, without which it could not develop. In the present-tense marriage plot of the last five books, given in diary form, the narrative drives toward union with Romney and Aurora's realization that she has loved Romney all along and wrongly rejected marriage. These last books thus feature an unreliable narrator, reinstating the conventional feminine narrator in ignorance of her story's full significance. According to Case, the incommensurability of the two narrative modes, their co-existence rather than closure, underscores according to Case the difficulty of putting together artistic agency with middle-class marriage, love, or female identity in the Victorian era.

Meg Tasker offers a more hopeful reading of the poem that relies on poetic form as such ("*Aurora Leigh*"). According to Tasker, Elizabeth Barrett Browning sought "a flexible form which could deal with contemporary reality, but in the heightened language of poetry rather than the drawing-room prose of the novel" (32). Barrett Browning's adoption of the hybrid, innovative form of the verse novel was in part a response to the rising popularity of the Victorian novel, but it also allowed her to enfold multiple perspectives into her work—an important factor in shaping contrary readings of her poem as a conservative or feminist text. Because the hybrid form of the verse novel retained the peculiar resources of poetry, it also allowed for freer exploration of sexuality than in a conventional novel. In poetry readers expected metaphors and were receptive to tracing out implied meanings. Hence Book 5 could open with a celebration of sexual passion that might have gotten a novel (even a male-authored one) banned from circulating libraries. Above all, Tasker emphasizes that Aurora's struggle to determine the proper relation of poetry to the world plays out in a form—the verse novel—that itself opens onto the world and its multiplicitous totality. Aurora's discovery at the end that poetry alone does not suffice is thus less a capitulation to normative marriage than a critique of Romanticism and the elevation of autonomous art over the claims of the world and human relationships. Aurora instead finds that "art needs life" (38). The poetry she is now likely to write, according to Tasker, will ally social claims and conflicts with poetic imagination, exemplified by the concluding apocalyptic imagery associated with visionary power on one hand and the new dawn of a reformed social order and Chartism on the other.

Both Kirstie Blair and Herbert Tucker adopt elements of narratology to demonstrate why Elizabeth Barrett Browning could win acclaim for *Aurora Leigh* when the long narrative poems by male Spasmodists quickly lost favor. In "Spasmodic Affections," Kirstie Blair traces the long association of "spasm" with the hysteric female body and revolutionary change. To ward off identification as emasculated or feminized poets, male Spasmodists typically displaced spasm from the self onto God and the universe. Barrett Browning, in contrast, appropriated the association of spasm with femininity and boldly reworked it to ground poetry in nature, God, and the female body (cp. the "heaving, double-breasted age" of Book 5). Yet spasm is principally associated in the poem with Aurora's early, merely popular work. By withholding representation of passion coursing along the veins and palpitating the heart of the poet protagonist until Aurora's final, convulsive, revolutionary embrace of Romney, Barrett Browning also associates female poetics with a disciplined subjectivity.

Herbert Tucker examines *Aurora Leigh* and Spasmodism in terms of their shared Romantic heritage, and the counterstrategies developed by Elizabeth Barrett Browning to avoid male Spasmodists' attempt to assert the imagination's epic reach in a market economy ("Glandular Omnism and Beyond". The poem's shift in narrative mode from memoir to diary exposes Aurora's fallibility rather than grandiosity; and tying the account of Aurora's career to print culture demonstrates that even if poetry is indeed instinct with the universe it is also dependent on material, commercial production. Finally, Barrett Browning's thoroughgoing emphasis on gender transforms gender

into a visible dimension of poetic imagination that requires a radical reconfiguration of poetics and, in the process, marks all prior Spasmodism as feminine.

Conclusion

To dwell upon nineteenth-century narrative poetry by women is to recognize
anew how much of it women wrote, and how forcibly the historical record
becomes distorted when the Modernist association of poetry with lyric is
granted full sway. Part of the interest of these narrative poems—women's
disposition to enter into the fray of cultural, gender, and social politics—may
also suggest another reason for their neglect: women's narrative poetry flies in
the face of Modernist insistence on autotelic art and, more recently, lingering
assumptions that poetry is an elitist form distanced from political movements
and ideological debate. In these contexts Joseph Bristow's exploration of
alternative literary histories in ''Whether Victorian Poetry'' is apropos. Were
nineteenth-century poetry configured in terms of the ballad, Bristow suggests,
a literary history quite different from those generated by the problematical
rubrics of ''Romantic'' and ''Victorian'' poetry would emerge. He instances
Elizabeth Barrett Browning, whose ballads hark back to ''Romantic'' texts
such as Thomas Percy's *Reliques of Ancient English Poetry* and *Lyrical Ballads*, and whose career ended before the category of ''Victorian poetry'' was
formulated by the American critic E. C. Stedman. Significantly, the ballad
(as Bristow notes) often registers political and communitarian impulses—and,
I would add, a strong narrative impulse too, as in ''The Romaunt of the
Page.'' The eclipse of the ballad as an organizing presence in nineteenth-
century poetry may thus be symptomatic of the larger eclipse of narrative
poetry as well.

   This survey of work on women's narrative poetry also suggests a number
of questions that might be explored were narrative poetry to attract sustained
attention. Fixing the nomenclature of narrative poetry is problematical in a
poetic era defined by the hybridity of its forms. When is a long narrative
poem simply a long narrative, and when it is it an epic or verse novel? Should
a long but narratively-oriented dramatic monologue always be considered a
narrative? How would such poems be distinguished from dramatic monologues more compellingly read in terms of lyric expression? Should any
ballad that tells a story, however concisely, be considered a narrative poem
as well? Regarding women poets' contributions to historical romance and the
medieval revival, to what degree could they claim and exercise authority to
adjudicate the shape and meaning of history, traditionally a prestigious male
domain? Did women more frequently position themselves as successors to

the poetic narratives of Byron or Sir Walter Scott, or did they look to historical work by women contemporaries such as Anna Jameson for inspiration and legitimacy?

Another question begged by this essay is whether it makes any sense to consider women's narrative poems apart from those of men (as Linda Shires has asked of women's poetry in general). To what degree did gender inform or limit choices of subjects and modes of handling them? As the preceding survey indicates, women poets did not shy away from incorporating the battlefield into their poems—witness "The Romaunt of the Page," Garibaldi's wife in *Casa Guidi Windows*, and Browne's *The Star of Attéghéi*—but did they present its contests in the same grim detail as male contemporaries? Contrast, for example, the narrator of Hemans's *The Forest Sanctuary*, who observes that "a lance met me in that day's career" to describe being cut down in battle (Part I, stz. 29), with Robert Browning's insistence that readers dwell upon the twenty-two stab wounds in Pompilia's body in *The Ring and the Book*. Were women free at once to mourn and ironize loss of life, as Tennyson was in "Charge of the Light Brigade," or to assume that they could attract an interested audience if they celebrated masculine feats as Robert Browning did in " 'How They Brought the Good News from Ghent to Aix' "? What about humorous verse narratives? How many women counterparts were there to Thomas Hood's poems such as "Miss Kilmansegg and Her Precious Leg" or the *Ingoldsby Legends* of the Rev. Richard H. Barham? Might Menella Bute Smedley's "The Irish Fairy" or Constance Naden's "Natural Selection" be considered in this light? Or is it more useful to juxtapose the women narrative poets to the figure of the poetess, who is authorized to weep or extol but denied the liberty to wink or grin?

If narrative poetry is to be better understood, more work is also needed on the relation of nineteenth-century narrative poems by women to the novel and (as in Procter's case) to the periodicals in which poems, serialized fiction, travel narratives, social commentary, history writing, satires, and literary criticism appeared side by side. To what degree did periodical editors select poems to complement or contrast other contents of a given issue? What role did women's narrative poems play in attracting readers? And on what principle did illustrated periodicals select women's poems for illustration? If short stories appeared side by side with novels in periodicals, should shorter ballads or other narrative poems be seen as poetic counterparts to the short story? For example, might Elizabeth Gaskell's "The Old Nurse's Story," a first-person narrative about the mutually destructive rivalry between two aristocratic sisters published in the 1852 Extra Christmas Number of *Household Words*, be read in relation to Elizabeth Barrett Browning's "Bertha in the Lane" as well as Tennyson's two narratives entitled "The Sisters"? What do we learn from reading narrative poetry in relation to the novel and vice versa? Christine Sutphin, for example, usefully situates Augusta Webster's "A Castaway" in relation to Dickens's *Oliver Twist* and Wilkie Collins's *The New Magdalen* to clarify the radical implications of Webster's narration from the prostitute's point of view ("Human Tigresses"). What of novelists' practice of citing poems in their fiction or on title pages or even, in George Eliot's case, to writing verse epigraphs for her own chapters? What can their practices tell us about the importance of poetry to Victorian novelists?

Studies of the literary marketplace have tended to disadvantage poetry relative to the much wider-selling genre of the novel; and discussion of "novelized poetry," which draws upon the theoretical work of M. M. Bakhtin, emphasizes in its very sequence of terms the impact of the novel on poetry. Far less study has been devoted to the influence of poetry on the novel, and Jay Clayton's *Romantic Vision and the Novel*, which assesses the force exerted on fiction by Romantic poetry, is an important exception to the rule. That Victorians writers and readers tended to view the relation between poetry and the novel in rather more equable terms is clear not only from the 1859 Extra Christmas Number of *All the Year Round* but also from a work of literary criticism published the same year, *British Novelists and Their Styles*, by David Masson, compiled from a series of lectures delivered to the Philosophical Institution of Edinburgh in 1858. Lecture 1, "On the Novel as a Form of Literature, And on Early British Prose-Fiction," opened by positioning the novel as part of the general category of poetry, and, more specifically, as a counterpart to narrative poetry:

> If we adopt the common division of Literature, into History, Philosophical Literature, and Poetry or the Literature of Imagination, then the Novel, or Prose-Fiction, as the name itself indicates, belongs to the department of Poetry. It is poetry inasmuch as it consists of matter of imagination; but it differs from what is ordinarily called Poetry, inasmuch as the vehicle is not verse, but prose. [. . . The division of poetry into] the Lyric, the Narrative or Epic, and the Dramatic . . . holds also with respect to the Prose Literature of Imagination. The prose counterpart to Lyric Poetry or Song is Oratory, or, at least, a conceivable species of oratory, which might be called the Prose Ode, or Rhapsody. The prose counterpart to the metrical Drama is, of course, the Drama in prose. There thus remains, as the prose counterpart to Narrative Poetry, the Romance or Novel. The Novel, at its highest, is a prose Epic; and the capabilities of the Novel, as a form of literature, are the capabilities of Narrative Poetry universally, excepting in as far as the use of prose, instead of verse, may involve necessary differences.   (1–2)

Ultimately, Masson differentiated the two forms by allocating to verse narratives the greater likelihood of being reread and of being considered a classic (since the resort to verse itself suggests higher purpose and demands more careful, less rapid composition), whereas prose narratives are better suited to comedy and contemporary debates and achieve their greatest effects through the creation of characters (2–32). The main significance of Masson's opening chapter for this survey is his assumption that the novel, and literary criticism of it, benefit from being seen in relation to poetry. Given the Victorian precedents of Masson and Dickens's 1859 Extra Christmas Number, I argue that Victorian studies today would benefit from more systematic, thoroughgoing exchanges between studies of fiction and studies of poetry. Given, too, that in writing narrative poems women perforce revealed how they thought the world worked—its principles of causality, historical process, justice, human psychology; its relation to divinity; the possibilities and limits of action—narrative poetry offers a particularly useful entrée into Victorian gender, genre, and publishing and reading practices.

NOTES

1. In the final section of *Victorian Sappho* Prins discusses narrative in a fin-de-siècle epic by Catharine Amy Dawson Scott, *Sappho*, but concludes that Dawson Scott's narrative negates the heroic feminist impetus that the poet seeks to construct: "if Sappho is one of the unacknowledged legislators of the world, her prophecy is necessarily predicated on her failure." Hence the "epic ambition of Dawson's epic poem, it would seem, is to create a continuous historical narrative out of the reiteration of Sappho's leap: to project Sappho into (future) history by reading repetition as progress" (241, 242).

2. As an instance of this last, see "Omar and the Persian" by the short-lived Sarah Williams (1841–68), in Stedman 335–36.

3. Additional narrative poems reproduced on the Victorian Women Writers website include the following: Caroline Norton (1808–77), *The Undying One* (1830), "The Faithless Knight" (1830), and "The Dream" (1840); Augusta Webster (as "Cecil Home," 1837–94), "Blanche Lisle" (1860), "Once Lovers" (1860), "The Fisherman's Betrothed" (1860), and *Lilian Gray: A Poem* (1864); Lady Jane Wilde ("Speranza," 1826–96), "King Erick's Faith," "Ignez de Castro. From the Portuguese," "The Waiwode. From the Russian," "The Lady Beatriz," "Undiné. From the Danish," and *Thekla. A Swedish Saga* (all c. 1871); Caroline Clive (1801–73), "The Queen's Ball" (1872); Eliza Keary (c. 1827–1914), "Little Seal-skin," "The Legend of Thora," "Asdisa. An Icelandic Legend," *Snowbell. A Legend of Summer*, and "Agnes" (all 1874); Ada Cambridge (1844–1926), "A Dream of Venice," "A Story at Dusk," "The Last Battle of the Cid," "The Midnight Mass: An Incident of the French Revolution," and "Dead" (all 1875); Amy Levy (1861–89), "Run to Death: A True Incident of Pre-Revolutionary French History" (1881); and Constance Naden (1858–89), "Sir Lancelot's Bride," "The Abbot," "The Lady Doctor," "Love *versus* Learning," and "A Modern Apostle" (all 1894).

4. See the two volumes edited by Thesing in the Works Cited for the inclusive page numbers of each essay.

5. For discussion of other serial poems, all by men, see Hughes and Lund.

6. Of special interest to *DSA* readers, Boos points out that Hamilton's "Contrasted Scenes from Real Life," (a lyric) was directly inspired by an article in Dickens's *Household Words*.

7. As E. Warwick Slinn notes, the dramatic monologue is a hybrid form comprised of lyric, dramatic, and narrative elements ("Dramatic" 80). Longer monologues that expand to relay a complex sequence of events inevitably tilt toward narrative; some balladic monologues, such as Blind's "Song of the Willi," do too.

8. "A Deserter's Story" is also briefly discussed in "Lowly Bards and Incomplete Lyres," (1998) by Susan Zlotnick, along with "A Bitter Task," the tale of a seduced sempstress forced to sew the bridal dress of her former lover's bride.

9. Steve Dillon and Katherine Frank also emphasize Elizabeth Barrett Browning's adoption of a Carlylean prophetic mode ("Defenestrations of the Eye"); like Isobel Armstrong in "*Casa Guidi Windows*" (discussed in section VII), they also focus on issues of transparency. But, unlike more recent commentators, they contend that the poet rarely looks outside the window.

10. Linda M. Lewis reads the same passage, and much of Elizabeth Barrett Browning's narrative poetry, in the context of Swedenborgian theology, especially its doctrine of correspondences that images the union of Christ with the church as a marriage that also effects the union of love with wisdom, goodness with truth (165 and passim).

11. This study alternates between assertions articulated by an "I" and by a "we." Since in the Fane chapter an "I" speaks and references one of Hoagwood's prior publications, his single authorship may be indicated. If the instability of reference is deliberate, I wish the authors had made their rationale—perhaps a critique of the assumption that an individual bears sole responsibility for a text?—more explicit.

12. Another important resource for publishing history and women narrative poets is biography. The best known of these is *Christina Rossetti: A Writer's Life*, by Jan Marsh (1995). Other recent examples include *Letitia Landon: The Woman behind L.E.L.*, by Glennis Stephenson (1995); *Caroline Bowles Southey, 1786–1854: The Making of a Woman Writer*, by Virginia Blain (1998); The Life and Work of Adelaide Procter: Poetry, Feminism and Fathers, by Gill Gregory (1998); *Amy Levy: Her Life and Letters*, by Linda Hunt Beckman (2000); and my own *Graham R.: Rosamund Marriott Watson, Woman of Letters* (2005).

WORKS CITED

Armstrong, Isobel. "*Casa Guidi Windows*: Spectacle and Politics in 1851." *Unfolding the South: Nineteenth-century British Women Writers and Artists in Italy*. Ed. Alison Chapman and Jane Stabler. Manchester: Manchester UP, 2003. 51–69.

———. "Msrepresentation: Codes of Affect and Politics in Nineteenth-Century Women's Poetry." Armstrong and Blain 3–32.

———. " 'A Music of Thine Own': Women's Poetry—an Expressive Tradition?" *Victorian Poetry: Poetry, Poetics and Politics.* London: Routledge, 1993.

———, and Virginia Blain, eds. *Women's Poetry, Late Romantic to Late Victorian: Gender and Genre, 1830–1900.* Basingstoke: Macmillan, 1999.

———, and Joseph Bristow, eds. *Nineteenth-Century Women Poets.* Oxford: Clarendon, 1996.

Ashfield, Andrew, ed. *Romantic Women Poets 1770–1838.* Manchester: Manchester UP, 1995.

Beckman, Linda Hunt. *Amy Levy: Her Life and Letters.* Athens: Ohio UP, 2000.

Blain, Virginia. " 'Be these his daughters?' Caroline Bowles Southey, Elizabeth Barrett Browning and Disruption in a Patriarchal Poetics of Women's Autobiography." Garlick 1–21.

———. *Caroline Bowles Southey, 1786–1854: The Making of a Woman Writer.* Aldershot, Hants: Ashgate, 1998.

———. "Sexual Politics of the (Victorian) Closet; *or,* No Sex Please—We're Poets." Armstrong and Blain 135–63.

———. "Women Poets and the Challenge of Genre." *Women and Literature in Britain 1800–1900.* Ed. Joanne Shattock. Cambridge: Cambridge UP, 2001. 162–88.

———, ed. *Victorian Women Poets: A New Annotated Anthology.* Harlow: Pearson Education Limited, 2001.

Blair, Kirstie. "Spasmodic Affections: Poetry, Pathology, and the Spasmodic Hero." *Victorian Poetry* 42.4 (2004): 473–90.

Boos, Florence S. "Cauld Engle-Cheek: Working-Class Women Poets in Victorian Scotland." *Victorian Poetry* 33.1 (1995): 53–73.

———. "The 'Homely Muse' in Her Diurnal Setting: The Periodical Poems of 'Marie,' Janet Hamilton, and Fanny Forrester." *Victorian Poetry* 39.2 (2001): 255–85.

Bristow, Joseph. " 'All out of tune in this world's instrument': The 'minor' poetry of Amy Levy." *Journal of Victorian Culture* 5 (1999): 76–103.

———. "Reassessing Margaret Veley's Poetry: The Value of *Harper's* Transatlantic Spirit." Chapman, ed. 165–94.

———. "Whether 'Victorian' Poetry: A Genre and Its Period." *Victorian Poetry* 42.1 (2004): 81–109.

Brown, Susan. " 'A still and mute-born vision': Locating Mathilde Blind's Reproductive Poetics." Chapman, ed. 123–44.

Byatt, A. S. (as Maud Michell-Bailey). Letter to the Editor. *Victorian Poetry* 33.1 (1995): 1–3.

Case, Alison. *Plotting Women: Gender and Narration in the Eighteenth- and Nineteenth-Century British Novel.* Charlottesville: UP of Virginia, 1999.

Chapman, Alison. *The Afterlife of Christina Rossetti.* Basingstoke: Macmillan, 2000.

———, ed. *Victorian Women Poets.* English Association, Essays and Studies 2003. Cambridge: D. S. Brewer, 2003.

Clayton, Jay. *Romantic Vision and the Novel.* Cambridge: Cambridge UP, 1987.

Cronin, Richard. *Romantic Victorians: English Literature, 1824–1840.* Basingstoke: Palgrave, 2002.

———, Alison Chapman, and Anthony H. Harrison, eds. *A Companion to Victorian Poetry.* Oxford: Blackwell, 2002.

Diedrick, James. " 'My love is a force that will force you to care': Subversive Sexuality in Mathilde Blind's Dramatic Monologues." *Victorian Poetry* 40.4 (2002): 359–86.

Dillon, Steve, and Katherine Frank. "Defenestrations of the Eye: Flow, Fire and Sacrifice in *Casa Guidi Windows.*" *Victorian Poetry* 35 (1997): 171–92.

Fay, Elizabeth. *Romantic Medievalism: History and the Romantic Literary Ideal.* Basingstoke: Palgrave, 2002.

Feldman, Paula R., ed. *British Women Poets of the Romantic Era: An Anthology.* Baltimore: Johns Hopkins UP, 1997.

Garlick, Barbara, ed. *Tradition and the Poetics of Self in Nineteenth-Century Women's Poetry.* Amsterdam: Rodopi, 2002.

Geer, Jennifer. " 'Many Worlds More': Feminine Imagination in Jean Ingelow's *Gladys and Her Island* and *Mopsa the Fairy.*" *Victorians Institute Journal* 32 (2004): 167–88.

Gilbert, Sandra M. "From *Patria* to *Matria*: Elizabeth Barrett Browning's Risorgimento." Leighton, *Critical Reader* 24–52.

Gregory, Gill. "Adelaide Procter: A Poetics of Reserve and Passion." In Armstrong and Blain 355–72.

———. "Adelaide Procter's 'A Legend of Provence': The Struggle for a Place." Leighton, *Critical Reader* 88–96.

————. *The Life and Work of Adelaide Procter: Poetry, Feminisim and Fathers.* Aldershot: Ashgate; 1998.

Groth, Helen. "Victorian Women Poets and Scientific Narratives." Armstrong and Blain 325–51.

Harris, Daniel A. "Hagar in Christian Britain: Grace Aguilar's 'The Wanderers.' " *Victorian Literature and Culture* 27.1 (1999): 143–69.

Harris, Leigh Coral. "From *Mythos* to *Logos*: Political Aesthetics and Liminal Poetics in Elizabeth Barrett Browning's *Casa Guidi Windows*." *Victorian Literature and Culture* 28 (2000): 109–31.

Henwood, Dawn. "Christian Allegory and Subversive Poetics: Christina Rossetti's *Prince's Progress* Reexamined." *Victorian Poetry* 35.1 (1997): 83–94.

Hickok, Kathleen. "Why is this Woman Still Missing? Emily Pfeiffer, Victorian Poet." Armstrong and Blain 373–89.

Higonnet, Margaret Randolph. *British Women Poets of the 19th Century.* New York: Penguin, 1996.

Hoagwood, Terence Allan. "Biblical Criticism and Secular Sex: Elizabeth Barrett's *A Drama of Exile* and Jean Ingelow's *A Story of Doom*." *Victorian Poetry* 42.2 (2004): 165–80.

————, and Kathryn Ledbetter. *"Colour'd Shadows": Contexts in Publishing, Printing, and Reading Nineteenth-Century British Women Writers.* Basingstoke: Palgrave Macmillan, 2005.

Holt, Terence. " 'Men sell not such in any town': Exchange in *Goblin Market*." Leighton, *Critical Reader* 131–47.

Hughes, Linda K. " 'Fair Hymen holdeth hid a world of woes': Myth and Marriage in Poems by 'Graham R. Tomson' (Rosamund Marriott Watson)." Leighton, *Critical Reader* 162–85.

————. *Graham R.: Rosamund Marriott Watson, Woman of Letters.* Athens: Ohio UP, 2005.

————, and Michael C. Lund. *The Victorian Serial.* Charlottesville: UP of Virginia, 1991.

Johnson, Heidi. " 'Matters That a Woman Rules': Marginalized Maternity in Jean Ingelow's *A Story of Doom*." *Victorian Poetry* 33.1 (1995): 75–88.

Kooistra, Lorraine Janzen. *Christina Rossetti and Illustration: A Publishing History.* Athens: Ohio UP, 2002.

LaPorte, Charles. "George Eliot, The Poetess as Prophet." *Victorian Literature and Culture* 31.1 (2003): 159–79.

Leighton, Angela. " 'Because men made the laws': The Fallen Woman and the Woman Poet." Leighton, *Critical Reader* 215–34.

———, ed. *Victorian Women Poets: A Critical Reader.* Oxford: Blackwell, 1996.

———, and Margaret Reynolds, eds. *Victorian Women Poets: An Anthology.* Oxford: Blackwell, 1995.

Lewis, Linda M. *Elizabeth Barrett Browning's Spiritual Progress: Face to Face with God.* Columbia: U of Missouri P, 1998.

Linkin, Harriet K. "Romantic Aesthetics in Mary Tighe and Letitia Landon: How Women Poets Recuperate the Gaze. *European Romantic Review* 7.2 (1997): 159–88.

Lootens, Tricia. "Hemans and Home: Victorianism, Feminine 'Internal Enemies', and the Domestication of National Identity." Leighton, *Critical Reader* 1–23.

Marsh, Jan. *Christina Rossetti: A Writer's Life.* New York: Viking, 1995.

Marshall, Linda E. "Mysteries Beyond Angels in Christina Rossetti's *From House to Home.*" Armstrong and Blain 313–24.

Masson, David. *British Novelists and Their Styles.* Cambridge: Macmillan, 1859.

McGann, Jerome. "Christina Rossetti's Poems." Leighton, *Critical Reader* 97–113.

———. *The Poetics of Sensibility: A Revolution in Literary Style.* Oxford: Clarendon, 1996.

———, and Daniel Riess, eds. *Letitia Elizabeth Landon: Selected Writings.* Peterborough: Broadview, 1997.

McLean, Thomas. "Arms and the Circassian Woman: Frances Browne's 'The Star of Attéghéi.' " *Victorian Poetry* 41.3 (2003): 295–318.

Melnyk, Julie. " 'Mighty Victims': Women Writers and the Feminization of Christ." *Victorian Literature and Culture* 31 (2003): 131–57.

Mermin, Dorothy. "The Damsel, the Knight, and the Victorian Woman Poet." Leighton, *Critical Reader* 198–214.

———. " 'The fruitful feud of hers and his': Sameness, Difference, and Gender in Victorian Poetry." *Victorian Poetry* 33.1 (1995): 149–68.

Morgan, Monique R. "Productive Convergences, Producing Converts." *Victorian Poetry* 41.4 (2003): 500–04.

Mukherjee, Meenakshi. "Hearing her Own Voice: Defective Acoustics in Colonial India." Armstrong and Blain 207–29.

Opie, Iona, and Peter Opie. *The Oxford Book of Narrative Verse.* 1983. Rpt. Oxford: Oxford UP, 2002.

Peterson, Linda H. ''Rewriting *A History of the Lyre*: Letitia Landon, Elizabeth Barrett Browning and the (Re)Construction of the Nineteenth-Century Woman Poet.'' Armstrong and Blain 115–32.

Prins, Yopie. *Victorian Sappho*. Princeton: Princeton UP, 1999.

Psomiades, Kathy Alexis. *Beauty's Body: Femininity and Representation in British Aestheticism*. Stanford: Stanford UP, 1997.

Reynolds, Matthew. *The Realms of Verse 1830–1870: English Poetry in a Time of Nation-Building*. Oxford: Oxford UP, 2001.

Roberts, Adam. *Romantic and Victorian Long Poems: A Guide*. Aldershot: Ashgate, 1999.

Scheinberg, Cynthia. *Women's Poetry and Religion in Victorian England: Jewish Identity and Christian Culture*. Cambridge: Cambridge UP, 2002.

Shires, Linda. ''Elizabeth Barrett Browning: Cross-Dwelling and the Reworking of Female Poetic Authority.'' *Victorian Literature and Culture* 30 (2002): 327–43.

———. ''Victorian Women's Poetry.'' *Victorian Literature and Culture* 27.2 (1999): 601–09.

Slinn, E. Warwick. ''Dramatic Monologue.'' Cronin, Chapman, and Harrison 80–98.

———. *Victorian Poetry as Cultural Critique: The Politics of Performative Language*. Charlottesville: U of Virginia P, 2003.

Stedman, Edmund Clarence. *A Victorian Anthology: 1837–1895*. Boston: Houghton Mifflin, 1895.

Stephenson, Glennis. *Letitia Landon: The Woman behind L.E.L.* Manchester: Manchester UP, 1995.

Stone, Marjorie. ''Elizabeth Barrett Browning and the Garrisonians: 'The Runaway Slave at Pilgrim's Point,' the Boston Female Anti-Slavery Society, and Abolitionist Discourse in the *Liberty Bell*.'' Chapman, ed. 33–55.

Sutphin, Christine. ''Human Tigresses, Fractious Angels, and Nursery Saints: Augusta Webster's *A Castaway* and Victorian Discourses on Prostitution and Women's Sexuality.'' *Victorian Poetry* 38.4 (2000): 511–31.

Takiguchi, Tomoko. ''Christina Rossetti in Secrecy: Revising the Poetics of Sensibility.'' Garlick 177–92.

Tasker, Meg. ''*Aurora Leigh*: Elizabeth Barrett Browning's Novel Approach to the Woman Poet.'' Garlick 23–41.

Thesing, William B., ed. *Late Nineteenth- and Early Twentieth-Century British Women Poets*. Dictionary of Literary Biography 240. Detroit: Gale Group, 2001.

————. *Victorian Women Poets. Dictionary of Literary Biography* 199. Detroit: Gale Group, 1999.

Tucker, Herbert F. ''Glandular Omnism and Beyond: The Victorian Spasmodic Epic.'' *Victorian Poetry* 42.4 (2004): 429–50.

————. ''Rossetti's Goblin Marketing: Sweet to Tongue and Sound to Eye.'' *Representations* 82.1 (2003): 117–33.

Willett, Perry, ed. Victorian Women Writers Project. http://www.indiana.edu/~letrs/vwwp/

Wiman, Christian. Rev. of *The Sugar Mile*, by Glyn Maxwell. *New York Times Book Review* 4 September 2005: 25.

Zlotnick, Susan. ''Lowly Bards and Incomplete Lyres: Fanny Forrester and the Construction of a Working-Class Woman's Poetic Identity.'' *Victorian Poetry* 36.1 (1998): 17–35.

British Non-Canonical Women
Novelists, 1850–1900: Recent Studies

Talia Schaffer

In this survey I review nine major works published since 2000 in the field of fin-de-siècle fiction. I argue that recovery work occurs under uniquely difficult conditions, producing problems that have haunted a good deal of feminist criticism: partisan advocacy and excessive summary. However, as the field matures, this fan club attitude has been slowly disappearing. What has replaced it is a carefully researched historical and cultural awareness, a willingness to tackle the most difficult subjects (the popular, the politically retrograde), and a strong awareness of the material conditions of the literary marketplace. Economically based criticism and cultural studies approaches are transforming the field, allowing us a much richer view of women writers (and of the late-Victorian era) than when we simply searched for feminist foremothers. I point out that recent critics are focusing on certain writers—Margaret Oliphant, Sarah Grand, Vernon Lee—because these writers embody a particular construction of the late-Victorian era that suits our current critical interests. Reviewing a range of monographs, collections, and biographies, I conclude that we are in a kind of golden age for feminist recovery work, and I forecast what the next decade might bring.

The past five years have been a golden age for feminist recovery work, and this seems like the right time to try to figure out why. There have been

Dickens Studies Annual, Volume 37, Copyright © 2006 by AMS Press, Inc. All rights reserved.

dozens of new critical studies; the British Women Writers Association spon-
sors a major conference on the topic every year; Broadview Press publishes
long-out-of-print work; and scholarship and syllabi are changing drastically
to accommodate these newly available and newly discussed texts. A generation after those pioneering feminist studies, Sandra Gilbert and Susan Gubar's
The Madwoman in the Attic and Elaine Showalter's *A Literature of Their
Own,* work on noncanonical woman writers has become a mature field whose
value is generally accepted except in the most conservative niches of the
academy. The fact that a journal like *Dickens Studies Annual* solicited this
review is itself proof of the field's widespread acceptance, and so is the fact
that my initial list of books I wanted to review included over twenty critical
studies, as well as at least a dozen Broadview imprints. It is not just the fact
that there's been an explosion of new work that makes this field worth reviewing; rather, it is the fact that this new work approaches the subject from
some interesting new perspectives.

In this review essay I hope to explain what I see as the major new trends
in work on late-Victorian women writers, and to think about where feminist
recovery work might be heading in the next decade. In order to do so I have
chosen several books published since 2000 that seem to me to exemplify the
most noteworthy new trends in the field, and I have limited that field to fin-
de-siècle women's fiction, where some of the most dramatic new developments have occurred. Christa Zorn explains:

> As more and more women writers have become visible in the 'gap' between
> George Eliot and Virginia Woolf, a much more differentiated picture of the fin
> de siècle emerges, leading to questions about the ways in which Victorian,
> modern, and even postmodern critics claimed and 'dis-claimed' boundaries.
> The increasingly complex and specific readings of New Women literature are
> testimony that we are now at a point where any singular concept of the New
> Woman in the late nineteenth century does not render sufficient historical accu-
> racy. Eventually, more varied modes of criticism, combining social, political,
> psychological, and cultural approaches, have provided more insight into the
> diversity, transformative force, inventiveness, and even contradictions among
> New Women writers.   (xiii)

Zorn is absolutely correct that New Women criticism has become markedly
more sophisticated in recent years, and that the recovery of heretofore neglected women writers at the end of the century (who wrote in other genres
beside New Women fiction) is prompting us to rethink fundamental categories
of cultural, literary, and intellectual history. The practice of those ''varied
modes of criticism'' Zorn invokes has opened up new texts and new ways
of understanding texts that had always seemed too minor, too popular, or too
conservative. To give just one example (but a major example), because the
fin de siècle saw the development of a modern system of book publishing

and sales, we can now trace readership and publication techniques in various markets and consider how such material issues affected the way texts were constructed and readers received them. To demonstrate this shift, I will discuss examples of each of the following genres: collections, studies of single authors, biographies, and cultural-studies readings. They include: Kay Boardman and Shirley Jones, eds., *Popular Victorian Women Writers* (Manchester UP 2004); Vineta Colby, *Vernon Lee: A Literary Biography* (U of Virginia Press, 2003); Annette Federico, *Idol of Suburbia: Marie Corelli and Late-Victorian Literary Culture* (UP Virginia, 2000); Elaine Hartnell, *Gender, Religion, and Domesticity in the Novels of Rosa Nouchette Carey* (Ashgate 2001); Ann Heilmann, *New Women Strategies: Sarah Grand, Olive Schreiner, Mona Caird* (Manchester UP 2004); Angelique Richardson, *Love and Eugenics in the Late Nineteenth Century: Rational Reproduction and the New Woman* (Oxford UP, 2003); Joanne Shattock ed., *Women and Literature in Britain 1800–1900* (Cambridge UP 2001); Beth Sutton-Ramspeck, *Raising the Dust: The Literary Housekeeping of Mary Ward, Sarah Grand, and Charlotte Perkins Gilman* (Ohio UP, 2004); Christa Zorn, *Vernon Lee: Aesthetics, History, and the Victorian Female Intellectual* (Ohio UP, 2003).

In order to understand the significance of what these critics have done, we need to acknowledge a widely shared but largely unspoken situation: in the past, feminist recovery work received little respect. Such criticism can be all too full of embarrassingly emotional pleas, personal overinvestment and overidentification, and woolly terminology. We have, I daresay, all cringed sympathetically as we hear someone pleading for an author to whom she refers by her first name. More seriously, this kind of advocacy suffers from unexamined assumptions: that all neglected Victorian women writers were subversive feminists who have been neglected because of male misognyny; that Victorian feminism can be easily recognized and correlates to our own; that it's good to be in the canon and that we readers have the power to put someone there.[1]

It is not surprising, really, that recovery work has been particularly marked by moments of such well-meaning naïveté. In this field there are enormous, and, I daresay, unique pressures fighting against the critic's ability to maintain an intelligently critical stance. To begin with, feminist critics have an especially anxious relation with their readers. First, readers need to be convinced that this obscure subject is worth exploring, and so the critic has to justify her choice. Since a critic who has spent years on a deeply unfashionable writer feels a certain urgency to get her subject appreciated, the introductory self-justifying line or two can multiply into a virus of passionate pleading that infects the whole text. Second, readers need to be informed about this subject, and that introductory summary material, too, can metastasize. It takes so much work to find basic information in the first place that the critic often has no energy to spare for *doing* something with the data. Biographical or plot summary is safe. It indubitably gives readers information they did not have, and therefore its value cannot be questioned. It avoids the embarrassing subjective identification of the fan-club approach; it is respectably academic and even admirable when it shows signs of serious archival research; and it can be reused from article to article more easily than critical arguments.

There is, however, a deeper reason that much recovery work has difficulty moving beyond the introductory stages: it can be terrifying to embark on criticism entirely alone. The feminist critic has picked up a dusty book—say, Florence Warden's *The House on the Marsh: A Romance*—that apparently nobody has read since 1887. She has had to decide whether it is worth reading, which scenes deserve attention, and what kind of critical methodology can best parse them. That is a lot of responsibility. Anyone doing recovery work must have dark moments of wondering whether she is completely wrong, or, perhaps more urgently, whether a tenure committee will decide that her research interest is just an idiosyncratic personal obsession. Working on Charles Dickens is much easier; readers pretty much accept that *Our Mutual Friend* is worth discussing (they probably even concur which issues are most worth discussing), and the information one needs is already thoroughly and helpfully parsed in the critical tradition and biographical record. But if you put your career at risk to write about *The House on the Marsh,* you are truly on your own.[2] Is it so surprising that critics frantically plead for approbation or scramble to win respect through research?

Let me add that recovery work in the fin de siècle has a special difficulty: it transgresses the century divide. These authors were born in the mid-nineteenth century but died before World War II. Vineta Colby's description of Vernon Lee could aply to almost all women writers of the period: ''Vernon Lee believed that it was her misfortune to have been born before her time, a Victorian who should have been a modern. . . . In the twentieth century, when she might rightfully have established her claims to authority as a woman of letters, she was a relic of Victorianism'' (335). Not only did this lifespan work against canonization, but it also presents difficulty for the modern critic. Is this novel written with a proto-modernist stylistic experimentation or is it simply an unsuccessful Victorian narrative? How does one read a career, let alone a text, that blends political ideas we have been taught to regard as fundamentally opposed and chronologically distinct? These difficulties obviously demonstrate how insufficient our literary-historical categories really are, but that means that the scholar has to develop, explain, justify, and apply painstaking new criteria whenever doing a reading. And that can get tiring.

The odds are against feminist recovery work, then, and given the difficulty of doing it at all, and the enormous difficulty of doing it well, it is remarkable how good much of the recent work in the field is. What has made the biggest difference in post-2000 writing is, I think, the emergence of a new body of theory. Whether one calls it material culture, economic criticism, or even Marxist theory, work by such critics as N. N. Feltes, Peter Keating, Martha Woodmansee, Regenia Gagnier, Kate Flint, Margaret Beetham, Barbara Onslow, and Laurel Brake have demonstrated how intricately literary reputations in the nineteenth century were tied to the literary marketplace, how changes in royalty systems, advertising, libraries, book and periodical production, and readership patterns shaped what and how and why Victorians read and wrote. Readerly preferences and authorial decisions that we had previously assumed to be aesthetically motivated turn out, in fact, to be economically driven, and the attempt to unpack and understand those forces has enabled some fascinating new readings. Because it regards texts as commodities in a complex economy, the new economic criticism has made it easier to connect fiction with other forms of textual expression, and critics like Kathy Psomiades, Elaine Freedgood, Mary Poovey, and Nancy Armstrong have shown us how to read Victorian fiction in its complex resonances with other Victorian pursuits, ranging from anthropology to the textile trade, from accounting to photography. Much of the best recent work on late-Victorian women writers (including two late-1990s collections, Nicola Diane Thompson's *Victorian Women Writers and the Woman Question* and Barbara Leah Harman and Susan Meyer's *The New Nineteenth Century*) follow this theoretical school, reading noncanonical work as cultural products rather than unjustly neglected masterpieces, and explaining their neglect by focusing on the conditions governing their production, distribution, and publicization, rather than by invoking a vaguely nefarious cabal of canonizers. Moreover, the issue of the subject's feminism is, thankfully, moot in most of these books. The new generation of recovery work recognizes that Victorian feminisms looked different from ours, that to slap a single label on an author is to be far too reductive, and that it is much more useful to tease out the complexities of the author's gender ideas than to decide whether they're worthy or not.[3]

Many of the stars of this new economically-informed criticism have contributed to the outstanding new collection *Women and Literature in Britain 1800–1900*, edited by Joanne Shattock. Its roster includes Shattock, Margaret Beetham, Lyn Pykett, Barbara Caine, Elizabeth Langland, Virginia Blain, and Linda Peterson, and, as one might expect, the result is an exceptionally solid array of articles. Each is a carefully researched, useful, and informative review of its subject. The trade-off here is that these reviews are most useful as authoritative introductions for graduate students, with few unexpected ideas to reward readers who already know the field. The most energizingly critical moments are Barbara Caine's insistence that critics have neglected women's journalism (99–100) and Elizabeth Langland's daring assertion that "it is because George Eliot is so consistently caustic about the emptiness of ladies' domestic lives that she has been hailed for her realism. Her vision coincides so perfectly with patriarchal orthodoxy'' that nobody has challenged it (134). Those occasional sparks of anger illuminate a collection that is otherwise a smoothly reliable and seamless review of the field.

Indeed, the volume is so impressive that it takes a moment to realize that hardly any of these articles discusses the literature in any sense that would have been recognized before 2000. For *Women and Literature* showcases the shift to material criticism in an almost startling way. What I find interesting here is that in the self-avowed task of defining ''women and literature in Britain 1800–1900'' there is absolutely no anxiety about issues of literary quality. The critics manifest a serene conviction that women writers' work was shaped by the conditions of the marketplace: relations with publishers, types of editions, genres, and expectations for women writers, and posthumous biographies. There is very little discussion of the writing itself; instead, writers focus on the conditions that made that writing possible. For instance, in Judith Johnston and Hilary Fraser's fine article on ''the professionalization of women's writing: extending the canon,'' one might expect Johnston and Fraser to plead for extending the canon to accommodate deserving writers, to offer passionate descriptions of the underacknowledged vriutes of such writers' work, and to forecast how our field might benefit from their inclusion. But this sort of advocacy could not be further from their minds. Instead, Johnston and Fraser issue a coolly informative overview of the many genres within which women published: periodical literature, science writing, history writing, biographies, and, of course, the novel. Their aim is to chart how women gradually came to ''be recognized as professional writers'' (246) in the nineteenth century, not necessarily to alter our modern assumptions about them. (Although this review has room only to discuss work on fiction, readers who want to follow up on women's involvement in non-fiction forms of writing would be well advised to consult Barbara Onslow's eye-opening *Women of the Press in 19th Century Britain*.) Personally I found this approach a welcome corrective to the usual sentimental investments, a sign that recovery work no longer needs to apologize for itself, and a pleasant indication of the importance of the new material criticism; but readers with more traditionally literary tastes might be bewildered.

Readers looking for such considerations of literary value would be better advised to turn to another multi-authored collection, Kay Boardman and Shirley Jones, eds., *Popular Victorian Women Writers*. This volume offers a useful review of Victorian women writers, focusing mainly on the middle of the century (Braddon, Wood, Yonge, Howitt, Meteyard) but with some fin-de-siècle subjects (Fothergill, Molesworth, Ewing, Broughton). Most of the articles offer plot summaries, reviews of lives and careers, and assertions that the books are indeed worth reading. In other words, the assumption is that the reader is unfamiliar with these authors and that it is the critics' job to introduce and justify them, a stance that is understandable but perhaps inevitably gives rise to the 'value' issue. Anxiety about worthiness haunts the collection. In the introduction Boardman and Jones write: "But this takes us back to the rather knotty question of interpretation and evaluation . . . . This may not be something the critic aiming at inclusivity wants to confront yet it cannot be avoided; if a tradition of writing is to be fully explored then all avenues must be journeyed and all the material assessed" (10). Yet Boardman and Jones neither journey nor assess, but instead segue into a summary of the articles in the book. Apparently the knotty question *can* be avoided. At the end of the introduction they once again tackle the issue: "If part of the task of extending the canon is to offer up neglected writers for attention and to encourage new perspectives on those who have received attention then surely part of that task is to engage with questions of literary value, of interpretation and evaluation." Perhaps so, but, Boardman and Jones conclude, "no matter what the aesthetic agenda is on literary merit and how it might be redrawn, we believe that all the authors covered are eminently engaging and worthy of our attention" (15). In other words, evaluative issues are important, but no matter how they get decided, we think these authors are good. Correctly insisting on the need to use qualitative criteria—and to rethink those criteria—Boardman and Jones shy away at the last moment, taking refuge in a simple assertion instead of doing the work they appear to have intended. I find Boardman and Jones's treatment of 'quality' a fascinating indication of the state of the field today. 'Quality' exists as a kind of ghostly trace of an earlier recovery-work anxiety, and although Boardman and Jones can't quite bring themselves to dismiss it, they approach it only to find that it no longer has any substance.

Whatever the editors' concerns, the contributors have moved into economic criticism; indeed, the articles in *Popular Victorian Women Writers* are almost as focused on the literary marketplace as in *Women and Literature*. The authors quite briskly review their subjects' careers without much concern about their worthiness; indeed, Helen Debenham rather refreshingly goes so far as to insist that "if [Jessie] Fothergill deserves attention today, it is not as a forgotten genius, but rather as a passionate, perceptive, uneven writer, whose novels, enlivened by a sharply sarcastic wit, provide exceptional insights into some of the moral, social and literary dilemmas of her time, and whose literary career shows the fate of an author whose serious concerns clashed with the demands of the mass market for entertainment and excitement" (68–69). I very much like this description, which provokes interest in Fothergill precisely because of the specificity of her talents and situation instead of making her into a synecdoche for martyred women writers.

These collections reveal whose reputation is rising most dramatically among mid-to-late Victorian women writers: Margaret Oliphant. Oliphant is featured in almost all the articles in Shattock's collection, and both Broadview Press and Penguin have novels of hers in print. Oliphant's opaquely ironic presentation of strong yet guileless women fascinates feminist critics, and Oliphant's interest in financial, political, and marital institutions speaks to our economic criticism today. Her humor and stylistic finesse make her a pleasure to teach. Finally, her career brings up fascinating issues about women writers' ability to maneuver in the literary marketplace. Embodying all our current critical interests, and now available in mass-market paperbacks, Oliphant is clearly the Victorian woman writer for our times, and I suspect that within the next ten or twenty years she will appear more often than Gaskell, and perhaps even as frequently as Eliot, in courses on the Victorian novel.

If Oliphant's complex gender ideas attract scholars of mid-to-late Victorian fiction, her counterpart at the fin-de-siècle is clearly Sarah Grand. Grand figures in almost every book under review here and is the center of three major studies. She was also the subject of an outstanding study by Teresa Mangum that unfortunately appeared a few years too early for this review. Like Oliphant, Grand offers issues in which we are interested: popular fiction, conservative politics mixed with radical work, experimental form, and material that includes domestic, psychological, and degenerative interests.

Grand is one of the key figures in Ann Heilmann's *New Women Strategies: Sarah Grand, Olive Schreiner, Mona Caird*. A theoretically sophisticated study that uses French feminism to read women's writing, Heilmann explicitly sets out to evade the usual simplistic ascription of feminism to New Women writers. This is the sort of substantive work that most fields rely upon, a well-developed and accurate account of central texts. (The remarkably productive Heilmann, who has produced or edited an astonishing five books on New Women since 2000, is as much responsible for the maturation of the field as anyone.) *New Women Strategies* opens by wondering about Grand's multiple, unstable, regressive/progressive positions, warning us about "the dangers of applying monolithic interpretative paradigms to the sexual politics of New Woman writing" (15). Heilmann is framing her book explicitly as an alternative to traditional homogenizing readings of the New Woman movement, and Grand is the ideal subject for complicating this agenda.

Yet *New Women Strategies* takes an unexpected turn. Heilmann resolves the issue of Grand's ideological instability by cautiously asking whether her conservativism was "a deliberately preposterous flaunting," a clever performance aiming to "mobilise the cult of femininity . . . for her feminist purposes" (16, 17). In fact, Heilmann would like very much to believe that Grand's regressive pronouncements were actually strategic feminist ploys. And in spite of the avowed use of French feminism and Bakhtinian theory, the book becomes increasingly enamored not of instability and irresolution, but of the notion of a sophisticated feminism that could explain away Grand's otherwise bafflingly retrograde moments. Moreover, Heilmann yearns towards the idea that Grand's fiction sends us "a poignant message" (74) in clever fictional disguises. For instance, Grand's trilogy, she concludes, "can thus be considered feminist blueprints, framing a warning" (46). Similarly, *The Heavenly Twins* "illustrate[s] the need for women's active and continued resistance to gender-role expectations" (65). While Grand herself described her method this way occasionally, I don't necessarily think it does her (or us) a service to believe it. In general I am suspicious of reducing complex narratives to deliberately encoded messages. Might not Grand's conservative work might indicate a politics that is inchoate, in flux, contradictory? And might not the fiction complicate its avowed message with unconscious ideas that are not always under the author's control? While Heilmann's work on Schreiner and Caird is less concerned to prove them properly feminist, the message-ism occasionally recurs ("Caird's novel offers a fuller programmatic vision than Schreiner's and Grand's fiction," she comments approvingly [196]). In short, although Heilmann sets out with the best intentions of complicating (if not outright dismissing) the old assumption that New Women writers must be 'feminist,' she ends up reinstating it almost in spite of herself.

Like Heilmann, Beth Sutton-Ramspeck has produced a study of three major figures in the movement, including Sarah Grand. *Raising the Dust: The Literary Housekeeping of Mary Ward, Sarah Grand, and Charlotte Perkins Gilman* does fascinating work across fields. Scrupulously careful and deeply useful, *Raising the Dust* offers the chance to read Gilman, Grand, and Ward in the context provided by turn-of-the-century housekeeping theory. This offers unusual insights; for instance, Sutton-Ramspeck links "The Yellow Wallpaper" to decorating manuals, revealing the extent to which Gilman drew on her period's fears about the visual and chemical contamination of the home. Sutton-Ramspeck also provides marvelous readings of soap advertisements drawn by Gilman, along with reproductions of the images. In this sense, *Raising the Dust* is an impressive example of the new material culture criticism. Instead of using domestic labor as mere 'background' or dismissing it as irrelevant to literature, Sutton-Ramspeck demonstrates that the strategies, concerns, and images of home care were intimately associated with these writers' literary and political work. When we read Grand's famous injunction to sweep out the dark corners (in the article usually credited with inventing the term 'New Women'), we must now read it differently, and more richly, thanks to Sutton-Ramspeck.

Indeed, if the book has a problem, it is the typical problem of a pioneering document. Sutton-Ramspeck connects British and American authors, literary and cultural-studies texts, progressive and conservative authors, nineteenth—and twentieth-century texts, and domestic science with fiction. The stress of covering so much material shows here in a strenuous focus on tiny details that sometimes makes it harder to stand back to see the larger picture. Focusing Ward, Grand, and Gilman with fierce concentration, Sutton-Rams-peck works hard to show that they shared a vocabulary and an imagination shaped by the domestic science discourses of their period, and now that she has laid the groundwork, readers can begin to theorize about what this domes-tic-literary nexus might mean for other readings of noncanonical (and canoni-cal) texts.

Another study that combines cultural history with literary work is Angelique Richardson's impressive *Love and Eugenics in the Late Nineteenth Century: Rational Reproduction and the New Woman*. Interestingly, Richard-son immediately critiques feminist emphasis on progressiveness (6–7) and chooses, instead, to focus on a repressive ideology that was very much present in New Women thought. In this respect, Richardson carries on Heilmann's critique of simplistic feminist readings, and, like Heilmann, does so by tack-ling the dark side of Sarah Grand. *Love and Eugenics* is an exemplary study in its thoroughness of research: for instance, Richardson's extensive footnote on Victorian categories of race (24) could have been an encyclopedia entry. But Richardson's book is especially noteworthy for its daring focus on a potentially unpopular topic that links reactionary, even Nazi-associated thought, with feminist pioneers. The carefully documented and historically, politically, and economically rich research of this book make it probably the fundamental study in its field and a model for future writers.

However, as in Heilmann's book, the complex preparations lead to a sur-prisingly simple result. Here, Richardson mobilizes her extensive evidence mainly to say that Grand was a eugenicist. I would have liked to see some close readings, some sense that Grand's eugenic allegiance might be compli-cated by unconscious feelings or contradictory ideas. Richardson's afterword sums up this problem. Whereas one might usually expect to find a restatement of the fundamental issues and a movement towards a resolution of them in the afterword, Richardson begins by flatly stating, ''I have argued that eugenic feminism finds repeated expression in both the journalism and fiction of many New Women writers'' (215). The remainder of the afterword updates the history of eugenics by connecting it to biotechnology and generic engi-neering. In other words, Richardson has set out to show that eugenics played a part in New Women's writing, she has successfully accomplished this mis-sion, and now the book can end. I hope future scholars can build on Richard-son's impressive achievement to show how consideration of eugenics reshapes our understanding of the New Women movement, challenges our assumptions about nineteenth-century politics, and helps us read turn-of-the-century texts differently. Like Sutton-Ramspeck, Richardson seems to find that the enormous effort of cataloguing this vast cultural field and bringing it into alignment with the literature—a heroic effort, admirably achieved—is enough, and this means that other critics can have the luxury of thinking about the big questions now that the spadework is done.

The only fin-de-siècle woman writer whose popularity among today's critics may be said to be on a par with that of Oliphant and Grand is Vernon Lee, though she represents quite a different version of the period. Lee offers a complex and prolific writing life that spans several genres, including considerable achievements in aesthetic philosophy, eighteenth-century history, and psychology, and evokes issues of sexual and intellectual self-definition. In short, to address Lee is to conjure up a fin de siècle marked by serious scholarly work, as opposed to the popular journalistic bestsellers of the New Women.

Christa Zorn's *Vernon Lee: Aesthetics, History, and the Victorian Female Intellectual* is substantial, smart, and sensitive to the manifold complexities of Lee's writing. Zorn offers an admirably detailed analysis that shows how rewarding it can be to read Lee carefully. Zorn sets up her study by asking: ''how then does Vernon Lee's work allow us to test our assumptions about the role of the intellectual woman at the turn of the century? How does she alter the history of aestheticism?'' (xxiii) Although Zorn situates her study of Lee in the rich context of multiple fin-de-siècle cultural movements and the recent critical studies that have begun to appreciate them, Zorn's primary goal is to reconsider the category of the public intellectual or Victorian sage by reexamining Lee's career. It's useful to be reminded of a Victorian woman writer who made her mark in the male-dominated fields of history and aesthetic philosophy as well as in fiction. The problem for those of us looking for a new reading of the period is that this is still a single-author monograph. Like Richardson and Sutton-Ramspeck, Zorn sometimes addresses a more specialist reader than probably exists right now. *Vernon Lee* sometimes subsides into careful, intensive readings of Lee's major work in each of her major genres. This is certainly a useful resource for scholars working on Lee, although personally I would prefer to be reading a book that uses Lee to perform the exciting larger project of rethinking Victorian canonical, literary-historical, sexual, and intellectual assumptions. Yet the fact that Zorn can promise both a historical rethinking and an individual recuperation—and the fact that she does deliver both, more or less, though not necessarily always in the same place—is entirely admirable.

In 2003 Lee scholars were lucky enough to get not only Zorn's critical study but also the definitive new biography of Lee, Vineta Colby's *Vernon Lee: A Literary Biography*. Colby is a pioneer in the field of recovery work, whose *The Singular Anomaly: Women Novelists of the Nineteenth Century* (1970) was a landmark study of underread writers like John Oliver Hobbes and Mary Ward, and whose *The Equivocal Virtue: Mrs. Oliphant and the Victorian Marketplace* (co-authored with Robert A. Colby) began the Oliphant trend. Colby's new biography is exemplary in its meticulous research, thorough reading, and decisive conclusions. At every possible moment, Colby allows her subjects to speak for themselves by quoting their own words from their correspondence, creating a richly documented and authentic narrative. Like Zorn, Colby foregrounds Lee's intellectual status. The first paragraph of the biography explains that "reading Vernon Lee is also a process of discovery, layer by layer, of the complex intellect that informed her work" (xi), and the second paragraph describes "her long and turbulent intellectual life" (xi). Colby is quite fearless about announcing who Lee was and what she felt, whether a "social innocent" (95) or "not an adventurous traveler" (252), nor does she have any problem with announcing that a tale is "a gruesome and rather pointless story" (143) or a novel was "a mistake" (109). While this sort of certainty can be a little surprising for readers accustomed to a more restrained biographical voice, it also enlivens the biography considerably. Taken together, Zorn's and Colby's books solidly establish Lee as a major figure in the period worthy of sustained scholarly attention, and they make that attention possible.

Not every late-Victorian women writer, however, offers the intellectually impressive oeuvre of Vernon Lee, or the politically challenging record of Sarah Grand, and I would like to finish this review by talking about another new trend in feminist recovery work: recuperating the apparently hopelessly popular author. Three new studies go far towards establishing their subjects as significant objects of study. In so doing, they are, again, indebted to economic criticism, which has made us aware of the foolishness of automatically stigmatizing a writer simply because she produced best-sellers, and instead has shown us how (and why) to study the fascinating accommodations that made it possible for women to succeed in the literary marketplace.

Elaine Hartnell undertakes an almost impossible goal in *Gender, Religion, and Domesticity in the Novels of Rosa Nouchette Carey*; she aims to sum up a gigantic oeuvre of forty-one novels produced over almost as many years. Carey specialized in the domestic romance, a traditional form centered on girls finding marital bliss, and if we have swallowed the myth of the inevitable rise of modernism we will find it extremely peculiar that Carey's mid-Victorian-style fiction remained enormously popular through World War I. Hartnell correctly surmises that the vast readership of Carey's novels is worth exploring, and she isolates elements that may make Carey's work useful to contemporary scholars. Hartnell deserves congratulations for the hard work with which she recuperates as much of Carey as humanly possible. Yet in so doing, Hartnell does fall into the advocacy mode. She rather defensively insists that Carey's work champions women, subverts the domestic model, stands up for spinsters, and questions the need for male approval. While I have no doubt that many of Carey's novels do perform this sort of progressive gender work, I also feel fairly sure that many of them adhere to more retrograde notions, and it seems to me that the best way to restore Carey to critical interest is not to strenuously argue that she was a feminist pioneer in disguise but rather, to show that her gender politics were fascinatingly contradictory, and that she attracted so many readers precisely because she mingled a reassuringly traditional message with invigorating hints of a new model. (A similarly advocacy-based work recovering an unusual women writer is Patricia Lorimer Lundberg's *An Inward Necessity: The Writer's Life of Lucas Malet*, although I am not including it in this essay because I have reviewed it elsewhere.)

By contrast, Annette Federico's landmark book on Marie Corelli analyzes this "Queen of the Circulating Libraries" without a hint of partisanship. *Idol of Suburbia: Marie Corelli and Late-Victorian Literary Culture* uses Corelli's myth-making to think about the politics of building a literary reputation, dealing with publishers and critics and readers, and creating a public persona. It is sure not only to set the record straight about Corelli's vexed life but also to inspire new ways of thinking about Corelli. It has been too easy to sneer at Corelli for her naked egotism, her naive fantasizing, and her semi-religious bestselling fictions. It is, therefore, remarkable that Federico analyzes Corelli without an iota of condescending disdain or anxious self-justification. Perfectly convinced that Corelli is an interesting case, Federico is confident enough to write from that perspective without troubling herself about readers' preconceptions, and she therefore convinces the reader better than if she used dozens of pages of strenuous special pleading. Federico also uses Corelli brilliantly to elucidate fascinating aspects of the period, ranging from the suburban middle-class ethos to forms of spiritualism to fears of decadence. In each case she demonstrates the internal conflicts ripping through categories that modern critics might normally dismiss. The suburban mindset is shared by the royal family; anti-decadence involves identifying with absintheurs; religious fervor includes non-Christian theology. My only concern is that Federico may well have written the book on Corelli; it is hard to imagine what is left for anyone else to say.

What we see in these volumes is a rich variety of ways of reading the fin de siècle and an insistence on maintaining that variety instead of reducing it to a simplistic master narrative. Women's difficulty breaking into traditional publishing networks—their efforts to figure out how to approach publishers, use agents, negotiate contracts, and develop advertising—is the focus of a good deal of attention, but scholars like Shattock, Boardman and Jones, and Zorn are also thinking about how late-Victorian women struggled to get respect for their contributions to male-dominated genres like history, or to improve the status of female-dominated ones like children's literature. At the same time, critics are focusing on constructing a much richer understanding of the New Women movement. No longer do we believe that New Women were simply feminist pioneers unjustly maligned by their male peers and neglected by posterity. Thanks to critics like Heilmann, Richardson, and Sutton-Ramspeck, we are now developing a narrative of the New Women that allows for more political complexity and accommodates inconvenient ideas like eugenics, housekeeping, and conservative publications. The central figure of Sarah Grand provides an emblem of the new New Woman, a much more contradictory persona than has previously been recognized. At the same time, scholars are investigating women who wrote outside of the New Women movement, like Vernon Lee, Rosa Nouchette Carey, and Marie Corelli, and rethinking the way we read the period because of it. Instead of assuming that all women writers of the period were New Women, and therefore all feminist activists, we now recognize alternative genres in which women could write—aestheticism, popular fiction, romances, not to mention history, philosophy, and journalism—and we are achieving a fascinating new sense of the period as a result.

What do these books indicate about the future of recovery work? After seventies feminism's urgent search for pioneer foremothers, the second generation of feminist critics has swung the other way, emphasizing Victorian writers' uncomfortable specific historical alterity instead of insisting that they shared our feelings. On the good side, that means that blindly partisan advocacy is being replaced by painstaking analysis of authors' retrograde politics. On the other hand, this historical sensitivity encourages the other problem I mentioned at the beginning of this review, the tendency to turn one's work into data-dumping summary. I don't think this problem will disappear until feminist critics are secure enough with the status of their work that they don't have to prove their research credentials. I am not calling here for a lessening of research—far from it—but for an ability to place the massive amounts of research necessary for working on noncanonical figures in the context of interesting theoretical arguments, instead of letting the transmission of that information become an end in itself.

I predict that the next decade will see a lot more single-author studies. Currently we are seeing the interesting trend of the three-subject book (Sutton-Ramspeck, Richardson, and Heilmann), which may be occurring because none of the three subjects seems famous enough to justify a monograph on her own. But Zorn, Federico, and Mangum have managed to publish monographs on their subjects, and Linda K. Hughes's long-awaited *Graham R.: Rosamund Marriott Watson, Woman of Letters* has just appeared (too late, unfortunately, for this review). These studies are exemplary in their care and thoughtfulness, and I hope that they will serve as models for future full-length studies of other writers. We need a book on Mona Caird. We desperately need one on Ouida. For both of these figures, existing biographical resources are woefully outdated and critical considerations are rare. There has been a good deal of recent work on Olive Schreiner, but it is scattered, and she too deserves a volume of her own, which incidentally would be a good place to introduce more issues of postcolonial and transnational identity into ideas of the New Women movement.

Finally, I hope critics will continue to develop histories of significant cultural and intellectual trends of the late-nineteenth century that can help us inform our readings. Richardson's and Sutton-Ramspeck's studies are good models, and so are two books that appeared too late for review here, Diana Maltz's *British Aestheticism and the Urban Working Classes, 1870–1900: Beauty for the People* and Lise Shapiro Sanders's *Consuming Fantasies: Labor, Leisure, and the London Shopgirl, 1880–1920.* I hope new studies will look into other fields; how were women writers affected by contemporary notions of philanthropy, leisure, sport, hobbies, sanitation, warfare, marriage laws? We also need a better understanding of how the period's writings relate both to mid-Victorian narratives or to nascent modernist and ongoing popular forms of the twentieth century. Some excellent recent work in this field, Jessica Feldman's *Victorian Modernism* and Ann Ardis's *Modernism and Cultural Conflict, 1880–1922,* provides a richer vocabulary for articulating turn-of-the-century writers' styles that we can use to inform in-depth studies.

In short, then, I am hopeful about the future of recovery work, which seems to me to be slowly shedding its problematic habits and becoming a fully established field. In reading all these books, I have learned not just about the women writers, but also something deeper about what makes good feminist criticism. Recovery work is not about recovering authors, but about reconstructing the conditions that make those authors worth recovering. Let us teach our readers, not that Florence Warden deserves to be read, but that by reading Warden we can suddenly make heretofore unseen aspects of this period visible. I think here about *Our Mutual Friend,* a novel that is all about recovery. The villainous Silas Wegg digs through the dust mounds to find a treasure. To some extent older feminist recovery work has been like that; if we work through the vast dustheap we will hopefully find the coveted nugget, a feminist foremother we can display with pride. The feminist critics of this generation, however, work more like Noddy Boffin, the Golden Dustman, who painstakingly sifted all that material to compile the heaps in the first place. So too do the new feminist critics examine the cultural artifacts that previously seemed too unattractive: too popular, too retrograde, too silly. But building up information bit by bit, one can change the landscape.

NOTES

1. It is instructive to compare the conference schedules from an early meeting of the British Women Writers Association (the fourth conference, 1995) with one

ten years later (the thirteenth, 2005). In 1995, speakers were mostly concerned to identify their subjects—talks had titles like "Catherine Macaulay Graham, Historian''—and to justify their work as admirable (one panel was called "Reconceiving Female Heroism"). A typical panel, simply called "The New Woman,'' had a paper entitled "The New Woman Writer—Same Old Story? Mary Cholmondeley's *Red Pottage*.'' Clearly participants wanted to argue that these writers existed and their works were new and different. In the 2005 conference, the emphasis is on complex forms of reading, not basic identification. Both panels and papers lean heavily on words like "constructing," "interpreting," "struggling," "negotiating," "redefining.'' The New Woman panel of 2004 was "Redefining Her World: The New Woman and Victorian Culture'' and it included "What Made Victoria/ns Cross? Femininity and Domesticity Redefined by *Anna Lombard*.'' One sees here the advent of cultural studies, inasmuch as *Anna Lombard* is being read in terms of period attitudes and domestic and gender models, as well as the assumption that *Anna Lombard* does not need to be identified.

2. This is a real novel, and I did pick it up off a dusty shelf in a used-book store several years ago. Although I don't plan to write about it, I think of it as a fairly typical example of the kind of challenge that confronts recovery critics who do want to do intensive work on an unknown text. Nothing about it is certain. It rewrites *Jane Eyre* in more sexually disturbing terms, although whether that is a deliberate critique of Brontë or an inept attempt to emulate Brontë is unclear (and it is the first thing a critic would need to decide). According to library catalogues Warden's name is a pseudonym for F. A. P. James, and in that case we don't even know her gender. Of course, Warden and James might be original and marital names. According to a pencilled date with question mark on the flyleaf, the publication date of 1887 is uncertain. Warden (or James) seems to have written dozens of popular novels, most of which are of course unavailable, and it is impossible to say whether *The House on the Marsh* is a typical example of her (his?) work. In other words, if someone wanted to write on this novel, it would take months of hard sleuthing simply to decide whether it was a viable project.

3. A whole review essay could be done on new directions in studies of fin-de-siècle women's poetry, highlighting important work by Linda K. Hughes, Marion Thain, Ana Parejo-Vadillo, Angela Leighton, Margaret Reynolds, Margaret Randolph Higonnet, and Joseph Bristow, among others.

WORKS CITED

Ardis, Ann. *Modernism and Cultural Conflict, 1880–1922.* New York: Cambridge UP, 2002.

Boardman, Kay and Shirley Jones, eds. *Popular Victorian Women Writers.* New York: Manchester UP 2004.

Colby, Vineta. *Vernon Lee: A Literary Biography.* Charlottesville: U of Virginia P, 2003.

Federico, Annette. *Idol of Suburbia: Marie Corelli and Late-Victorian Literary Culture.* Charlottesville: U of Virginia P, 2000.

Feldman, Jessica. *Victorian Modernism: Pragmatism and the Varieties of Aesthetic Experience.* New York: Cambridge UP, 2002.

Harman, Barbara Leah and Susan Meyer, eds. *The New Nineteenth Century: Feminist Readings of Underread Victorian Novels.* New York: Garland, 1999.

Hartnell, Elaine. *Gender, Religion, and Domesticity in the Novels of Rosa Nouchette Carey.* Burlington, VT: Ashgate, 2001.

Hughes, Linda K. *Graham R.: Rosamund Marriott Watson, Woman of Letters.* Athens, OH: Ohio UP, 2005.

Heilmann, Ann. *New Women Strategies: Sarah Grand, Olive Schreiner, Mona Caird.* New York: Machester UP, 2004.

Mangum, Teresa. *Married, Middlebrow, and Militant: Sarah Grand and the New Woman Novel.* Ann Arbor: U of Michigan P, 1998.

Maltz, Diana. *British Aestheticism and the Urban Working Classes, 1870–1900: Beauty for the People.* New York: Palgrave, 2005.

Onslow, Barbara. *Women of the Press in 19th Century Britain.* New York: Palgrave Macmillan, 2001.

Richardson, Angelique. *Love and Eugenics in the Late Nineteenth Century: Rational Reproduction and the New Woman.* New York: Oxford UP, 2003.

Sanders, Lise Shapiro. *Consuming Fantasies: Labor, Leisure, and the London Shopgirl, 1880-1920.* Columbus: Ohio State UP, 2006.

Schaffer, Talia. "Review: Patricia Lorimer Lundberg, *An Inward Necessity: The Writer's Life of Lucas Malet.*" *ELT* 47:3 (2004): 347-49.

Shattock, Joanne, ed. *Women and Literature in Britain 1800–1900.* New York: Cambridge UP, 2001.

Sutton-Ramspeck, Beth. *Raising the Dust: The Literary Housekeeping of Mary Ward, Sarah Grand, and Charlotte Perkins Gilman.* Athens, OH: Ohio UP, 2004.

Thompson, Nicola Diane. *Victorian Women Writers and the Woman Question.* New York: Cambridge UP, 1999.

Zorn, Christa. *Vernon Lee: Aesthetics, History, and the Victorian Female Intellectual.* Athens, OH: 2003.

Recent Studies in Robert Louis Stevenson: Letters, Reference Works, Texts—1970–2005

Roger G. Swearingen

This essay surveys publications since 1970 on the life and works of Robert Louis Stevenson (1850–1894), excluding biography and literary criticism. It has three parts: Letters, Reference Works, and Texts. A fourth part, Biography, and a fifth part, Criticism, will appear in a future issue of Dickens Studies Annual. Both in my summaries and in my comments and corrections I have been as specific as possible, recognizing that access to inclusive research libraries is far from universal and that having the correct information now may be preferable to waiting until time allows a research visit. Almost all of the publications surveyed are in English, and much good work has been published in other languages. And, since there are valuable works in English that I have not been able to consider or may have overlooked, there is plenty of room for a sequel. Taken as a whole, the publications that I discuss show that serious study of Stevenson is not only possible, it has begun.

[Editors' note: Because of the length and scope of this survey, bibliographical details are included within the essay, rather than in a separate Works Cited section.]

It is a pleasure to survey what has been done during the last 35 years on the life and works of Robert Louis Stevenson (1850–94), above all because so much has been accomplished. In 1970, critical studies of merit could be counted on the fingers of one hand: G. K. Chesterton (1927), Janet Adam Smith (1937), David Daiches (1947), Robert Kiely (1964), and Edwin M. Eigner (1966). Texts of RLS's works, except for Janet Adam Smith's *Collected Poems* (1950; 2nd ed., 1971), derived essentially from the Edinburgh Edition (1894–98) augmented chiefly by the Vailima Edition (26 vols., 1922–23) and the Tusitala Edition (35 vols., 1923–24). Letters, except for Janet Adam Smith's two-sided compilation, *Henry James and Robert Louis Stevenson: A Record*

---

of Friendship and Criticism (1948), and DeLancey Ferguson and Marshall Wain-grow's edition of RLS's letters to Charles Baxter (1956), were available only as edited by Sidney Colvin (1895, 1899; 4 vols., 1911; augmented in collected editions through the Tusitala Edition). Except for local studies such as those by Anne Benson Fisher on RLS in Monterey (1946), Anne Roller Issler on RLS's time in San Francisco, Oakland, and the Napa Valley (1939, 1949), Sister Mary McGaw on Hawaii (1950), and Charles Neider's edition of Fanny's Samoan journals (1955), there were only three biographies worth consulting: by RLS's second cousin Graham Balfour (2 vols., 1901), Rosaline Masson (1923), and J. C. Furnas (1951). Until Furnas's biography, it was not generally known how little support there was for the claims of tell-all controversialists in the line of J. A. Steuart (1924), G. S. Hellman (1925), and Malcolm Elwin (1939, 1950). Bibliography and access to published and unpublished materials had been greatly aided by the completion of George L. McKay's catalogue of the Edwin J. Beinecke Collection at Yale, *A Stevenson Library* (6 vols., 1951–64), adding depth, breadth, and detail to the bibliography by W. F. Prideaux and Flora Livingston (1917). The RLS entry in the *New Cambridge Bibliography of English Literature* had been updated by Bradford A. Booth (1969). But that was pretty much all.

This essay surveys more than 150 publications on RLS between 1970 and 2005, excluding works of biography and literary criticism. A discussion of biographical and critical studies will appear in a future issue of *Dickens Studies Annual*. Many of the scholarly works that I consider here are significant in quality and interest; others are disappointing, promising more than they deliver or offering conclusions that are not supported by fact. Strong and weak, their importance is in the aggregate. The publications in the last 35 years show that serious study of Stevenson's life and literary career is not only possible—it has begun.

My survey includes three main sections—Letters, Reference Works, and Texts—and within each section and sub-section (except for the section on Reference Works) the order follows the chronology of RLS's life and publications, not that of the studies themselves. And while I have done my best to list every contribution of interest or value during the last 35 years, I am keenly aware that I must add: "that I know of and have read." Only a few reviews are cited, for instance, and much good work has appeared in reviews. Only a few works in languages other than English are cited, and much good work has appeared in other languages. And I have surely missed, or have been unable to obtain, or have not yet had time to study, some valuable contributions in English. In a few instances, all of them clearly noted, I have relied on someone else's summary or citation—but only in order to avoid omitting mention altogether of an obviously important work. There is plenty of room for a sequel.

Internet and online-database information presents an additional challenge. It is always subject to change without notice. Pages and data are continually being moved, deleted, added to, corrected, enhanced, and updated. In the present survey, I have simply ignored this electronic information—but only because Richard Dury of the University of Bergamo has for some years maintained a splendid, inclusive, and continually updated RLS website with links and lists of all kinds:

http://dinamico.unibg.it/rls/rls.htm

Dury's lists of studies have been of great assistance in the present survey. He includes items, particularly in languages other than English, that I have been unable to cover;

and, unlike anything printed, his lists are always current. His website is a major scholarly contribution—and it is another sign of how far we have come. Long may it prosper.

In this survey, my goal has been to create as reliable and as inclusive a guide as I could and to make it as useful as possible to scholars and to ordinary readers alike. If literary scholarship is to survive at all in this new century, its results must win their way with readers whose training is other than literary: men and women whose interest in literature is other than professional and whose day jobs are neither academic nor literary. Many of the entries in this survey are, for this reason, much longer than is customary in surveys of this kind. I have tried to present, not only to evaluate or to encode for specialists, what matters in every contribution. When important errors or omissions exist, I have tried to correct the most important deficiencies, at least when it has been possible to do so concisely, rather than simply warn that problems exist and then pass on. Access to all-inclusive academic libraries is not as available as one might think, and a good summary may be all that one needs at the moment. I have not been sparing of technical details, however, especially on reference, textual, and biographical matters when it has seemed to me necessary to show, as sometimes can only be shown in such a way, and in detail, what could have been done but wasn't.

I have also tried to be mindful of the fact that we are all fallible human beings, especially in an undertaking as arduous and difficult as literary scholarship. And I am also aware that my own comments in this survey may not—and probably should not—always win assent. Friedrich Klaeber, quoting 1 Thessalonians 5, 21–22, put all of this especially well at the end of his own welcoming preface to his annotations of *Beowulf* (1922): *Omni probate. Quod bonum est, tenete.* This survey is meant to be useful and helpful. It is not meant to be the last word.

Stevenson's letters are quoted from and are cited by letter number, date, and recipient, in the authoritative edition, *The Letters of Robert Louis Stevenson*, ed. Bradford A. Booth and Ernest J. Mehew (8 vols., New Haven: Yale UP, 1994–95), referred to here as the Yale Letters. References to materials in the Beinecke Rare Book and Manuscript Library, Yale University, are identified as ''Beinecke'' and the item number, if they are listed in the catalogue by George L. McKay, *A Stevenson Library* . . . (6 vols., 1951–64). Other such items are identified simply as ''Yale.'' Items offered in the three-part sale at the Anderson Galleries, New York, 1914–16, are identified as Anderson, followed by the part and item number in the catalogues of this sale. References to Graham Balfour's biography are to the English edition, *The Life of Robert Louis Stevenson*, 2 vols., London: Methuen, 1901. Quotations from Stevenson's published works follow the first book-form edition and are identified by title and date of first publication. Page references are for the most part omitted except in the case of book-length works. RLS's initials are used whenever it has made sense to save space by doing so.

Letters

Booth, Bradford A., and Ernest J. Mehew, eds. *The Letters of Robert Louis Stevenson*. 8 vols. New Haven: Yale UP, 1994–95. Among the most distinguished works of literary scholarship in this or any other generation, this edition was begun in the 1960s by Booth of the University of California—Los Angeles. After Booth's death at the end of 1968, the project over the next 25 years was carried to completion by Mehew in the precious intervals of time that were allowed to him by his job as a career civil servant in London—by him, and by his wife Joyce, whose contributions were at all stages considerable. All of the annotations, final texts, dates, and supplementary and introductory materials are Mehew's, and they are the distillation of a lifetime of engaged, indefatigable, insightful, and profound study that was begun many years before an edition was even in prospect.

The remarkable thing, to me, is how unobtrusively all of this knowledge is placed in the service of the material itself. We are told what we, as readers, want or need regarding the present letter and what it says—no more and never less. When needed, introductory commentary is used. An unvarying standard of excellence is achieved in these eight volumes that inspires gratitude and admiration. Stevenson's letters are now available and accessible to everyone, and with the supporting details that make it possible for all of us to read and understand them as they would have been understood by the original recipients. This is a remarkable and breathtaking literary achievement.

There are in these eight volumes of the Yale edition more than 2,800 letters. The fact that the text of 2,400 of them—more than six out of seven, 85%—comes from the autograph manuscripts bears witness to Mehew's persistence, ingenuity, and vigilance, and to the kind of luck that comes to those who are superbly prepared. Of some two dozen manuscript letters that have turned up in the ten years since the Yale Letters were completed, fewer than half were not previously known in some form and included in this edition. (These strays, although they are discoveries rather than examples of scholarly study as such, are discussed in the next section of this survey.) Additional letters will still come to light, of course, but nearly all of them have now been found, and nearly all of these have now been dated, transcribed, and well annotated. Mehew's introduction to the first volume offers insightful, detailed, and convincing portraits of all of RLS's principal correspondents and much else. Although there is no single, general index, the indexes in the individual volumes are accurate, inclusive, and useful.

Four of the most thoughtful reviews of the Yale Letters offer solid assessments not only of the edition but of RLS among letter-writers of the nineteenth century: Richard Holmes, "On the Enchanted Hill," *New York Review of Books*, 8 June 1995, 14–18, who finds RLS "our greatest nineteenth-century letter-writer after Byron"; Nicholas Rankin, *Literary Review*, November 1995, 36–38; William Maxwell, "Stevenson Revealed," *New Yorker*, 2 January 1995, 134–41; and Barry Menikoff, *Nineteenth Century Literature*, 50 (1996), 541–51.

Mehew, Ernest J., ed. *Selected Letters of Robert Louis Stevenson*. New Haven: Yale UP, 1998. Mehew's selection from the eight-volume Yale Letters consists of 608 pages that give all or part of 317 letters by RLS and one by his wife Fanny selected from the total of more than 3,100 pages and 2,800 letters. It is, in Mehew's own modest and exact words, "a representative group of letters from each period of Stevenson's mature life, giving preference to those that seemed the most characteristic and amusing, those of literary interest and those that throw light on his life, work and personality . . . a generous sample that conveys the flavour of Stevenson as a letter-writer'' (vii). In addition, Mehew has also preserved all of the admirable qualities of detail, annotation, and indexing from the complete edition. But it is also much more. As Nicholas Rankin observes in his review of the *Selected Letters*, ''Mehew has succeeded admirably in giving us two books in one.'' In addition to providing the letters themselves, the volume is divided into fifteen sections, each with it own title, ''[and the] introductions to and the links between those sections, as well as the invaluable footnotes, make up the best and most complete biographical framework of Stevenson's life I have read. Here you have the letters, and the life, in one'' (*Literary Review*, November 1997, 43). This is not a biography, of course. But there is no better self-portrait of RLS than in his letters, and no better guide than Mehew to the factual details.

New Letters

RLS to Sidney Colvin, Sunday, Swanston [probably 24 May 1874]. Yale. ''Morley has accepted that damned thing and I have seen it printed; and I hate it like poison: I can't make out why he took it.'' This short note is similar in tone and content to Letter 274 to Mrs. Sitwell, 23 May 1874. The reference is to RLS's review ''Lord Lytton's *Fables in Song*,'' *Fortnightly Review*, June 1874.

RLS to his mother, Hôtel du Val de Grâce, Rue St.-Jacques 304, Paris, Sunday [30 June or 7 July 1878]. Autograph of Letter 540, previously known only in Colvin's edition. Offered on the Internet by David J. Holmes Autographs, Collingswood, NJ, January 2001. Annotated in pencil in an unknown hand, no doubt RLS's mother's, ''1878'', and docketed on the verso: ''Paris Summer 1878 I think.'' This pencil annotation and the one on ''Madame Adam'' at the very end of the letter are both new: ''Madame Adam—Not Mrs. Adams—is the widow of Monsieur Adam: who he was, I don't know; but he was a political swell.''

RLS to W. E. Henley, [June 1878]. University of South Carolina. This is a brief note in which RLS says that he is sending him the last part of the story ''The Young Man With the Cream Tarts'' (*London*, 8 June–27 July 1878). It is very close in tone and style to RLS to W. E. Henley, June 1878, Letter 553, which probably precedes it by only a couple of days.

RLS to his mother, Cernay-la-Ville, [18 October 1878]. David Magee Collection, Brigham Young University. Autograph of Letter 576, previously known from an excerpt in the Brick Row Book Shop catalogue (1921) omitting the first and last sentences. ''My dear mother,'' RLS begins, ''I am very well and hope you are.'' In the last sentence, he writes: ''My spirits are not so good as they might be, but I suppose they'll come right somehow.'' Except for these two new sentences, the text is the same.

RLS to his mother, 12 November 1878. Syracuse University Library. Autograph of Letter 580, previously known only from the typescript at Yale.

RLS to W. E. Henley, 17 Heriot Row stationery, [May 1879], probably contemporary with Letter 616 to Bob Stevenson. Private collection; brought to my attention by Ernest Mehew. ''My dear Henley, I have been very bad again: deal of pain. Am ordered away for my health, so will likely see you soon. Still somewhat bust, but happy. Weather splendid. Am jaggered. Yours ever, R. L. S.''

RLS to E. W. Gosse, 15 December 1880. Syracuse University Library. Autograph of Letter 762, previously known only from the typescript at Yale.

RLS to his parents, 21 December 1880. Syracuse University Library. Autograph of Letter 763, previously known only from Colvin's galley proofs at the RLS Silverado Museum, St. Helena, California.

RLS to his Parents. Marseille, 18 October 1882. RLS Silverado Museum, St. Helena, California. "I am a mere wreck; but so is Fanny; so I write." This one-page letter on printed stationery of the Terminus Hotel, Marseille, is dated by RLS's mother and is accompanied by a longer letter by Fanny Stevenson probably of the same date. RLS and Fanny were then preparing to take up residence at Campagne Delfli, five miles from Marseille. "We go tomorrow to inventorize. All today we have been buying things; I know bankruptcy's at the door; and we're dead. They are so cheap—and you know what that means." RLS reminds his parents about money: "Please let us have our allowance by the 1st of the month. I forsee we shall be bitterly in want of it." And he is very pleased: "Lovely things, a lovely house, a decently lovely climate, which seems to agree with me.''

Fanny Stevenson to W. E. Henley, [ca. May 1885]. Yale. When this letter was offered at auction by Phillips Auctioneers, London (Books, Atlases, Photographs & Manuscripts, 17 November 2000, lot 455) it was widely publicized as having to do with *Dr. Jekyll and Mr. Hyde.* "RLS's Jekyll and Hyde wife burned classic horror tale" was the headline in the *Scotsman*, Edinburgh, 25 October. "How houseproud wife nearly put paid to Jekyll and Hyde" appeared in *The Times*, London, also on 25 October. But as Ernest Mehew pointed out in an interview with the *Times Literary Supplement*, 3 November 2000, the letter in fact dates from a time five or six months before the writing of *Dr. Jekyll and Mr. Hyde*: "the period mid-April to mid-June 1885, when Henry James was in Bournemouth visiting his invalid sister. He went to the Stevenson household every evening." The manuscript that Stevenson wrote, Fanny said, was "nearly a quire of utter nonsense" and had been written in recent period of delirium: "fortunately he [RLS] has forgotten all about it now, and I shall burn it after I show it to you. He said it was his greatest work." Fanny's main concern was that if RLS were to come up to London for "a change of scene and air" (as Dr. Scott was recommending) Henley would ruin the whole effort by drawing RLS into renewed excited efforts to get a play produced. She agrees with RLS that Henley should "back down reluctantly and gracefully" and accept H. Beerbohm Tree's latest offer.

RLS to "Dear Fellow" [Fanny Stevenson], British Museum stationery, early August 1886, during RLS's stay with Sidney Colvin, at the British Museum. William Andrews Clark Memorial Library, Los Angeles. "I am having a real good time but begin to weary for home and the comforts of a Folleen ['Folly'' was a nickname RLS used for Fanny]. Last night dined with Burne Jones, an enchanting card to meet, far better than his paintings; he offers to come and see us at Bournemouth." Fanny joined RLS in London soon after this letter was written, the decision having by then been made to visit Will H. Low and his wife in Paris. In writing to his mother that he was about to "meet Burne-Jones" at lunch with the painter W. B. Richmond (RLS to his mother, 10 August 1886, Letter 1676) RLS is for reasons unknown forgetting or passing over the earlier meeting mentioned in this letter.

RLS to Chatto and Windus, two letters: [before 28 July 1887], and 21 August 1887. Chatto and Windus Archive, University of Reading. Both letters appear in Andrew Nash, "Two Unpublished Letters of Robert Louis Stevenson," *Notes and Queries* 245 (2000): 334–36. In the first letter, written at the end of July 1887 (Andrew Chatto's reply is dated 28 July), RLS proposes a two-volume collection of *Familiar Essays*, the first volume reprinting *Virginibus Puerisque* (1881), the second volume collecting or, in a couple of instances, publishing for the first time, 15 essays, in the same order and with the same titles as they were eventually published as *Memories and Portraits*. "This will all be ready to go to press in a few days; certainly unless I fall very ill again before the end of the week." RLS would like the same terms as for *The Merry Men*, except without an advance: a royalty of one shilling on the published price of six shillings. He is still doubtful about including the essay on his father, who had died in May of that year, doubts which he seems to have put aside as this is his only reference to them. On 2 August, RLS asked for acknowledgment that copy had been received for both volumes and enclosing an additional essay, "A Gossip on a Novel of Dumas's" to appear third from last (Letter 1861). Chatto replied on 7 August (the firm's outgoing letter-books and other records are also at Reading) accepting RLS's terms but suggesting that to avoid confusion the title *Virginibus Puerisque* be kept and that a title other than *Familiar Essays* be found for the second volume, as it would be "apt to be confused with *Familiar Studies of Men and Books*." Stevenson agreed, and on 16 August the contract was signed for a uniform but otherwise separate edition of the two books, *Memories and Portraits* having by then been adopted for the second. The second letter is dated 21 August, on the eve of RLS's departure for the United States. "The proofs are to hand," he says, and asks that payments be made to Charles Baxter in Edinburgh. For publication in November, 1,000 copies of *Virginibus Puerisque* were sent for binding on 29 September, 2,000 copies of *Memories and Portraits* on 7 October. Nash also notes, probably also from Chatto and Windus records, that an additional 1,000 copies of *Memories and Portraits* were bound on 15 August 1888, bringing RLS's proceeds on that volume alone to about £100 in less than 10 months. The last of the 4,000 copies printed for the first edition were sold shortly after Stevenson's death in December 1894, bringing his lifetime proceeds from the book to about £200.

RLS to Gleeson White, [17 August 1887]. Sold on the Internet via eBay to an undisclosed buyer by Todd Mueller Autographs, The Colony, Texas, 19 January 2003. A short note written by RLS on the back of one of his Savile Club/Bournemouth visiting cards, with the original stamped, addressed envelope postmarked Bournemouth 17 August 1887–in other words, nearly on the eve of his departure for the United States aboard the *Ludgate Hill*: "I do not leave tomorrow. Suppose you called tomorrow about 7 P. M.? R L [S]."

RLS to Thomas Russell Sullivan, three letters: the first postmarked 27 January 1887, the second dated 7 June 1887, and the third written sometime after 8 April 1888. All three letters are in the American Antiquarian Society, Worcester, Massachusetts. The first appears in Katherine Linehan's Norton Critical Edition of *Dr. Jekyll and Mr. Hyde* (2003), 85–86. The others are in her "Two Unpublished Letters From

Robert Louis Stevenson to Thomas Russell Sullivan,'' *Notes and Queries* 50 (2003): 320–23. ''I am not in the least struck by the liberties you have taken,'' RLS writes in late January 1887; ''on the contrary, had I tried to make a play of it, I should have been driven to take more: I should have had Jekyll *married*.'' On 7 June 1887 he congratulates Sullivan on the successful stage premiere in Boston of Sullivan's adaptation of *Dr. Jekyll and Mr. Hyde*, starring Richard Mansfield. ''I was sincerely pleased that you and Mr Mansfield had so considerable a success; sincerely pleased, too, to have a share of my own in what you both have done, and to see my thoughts taking new shape, and my children bringing grandchildren to my knee'' (321). The third was written after 8 April 1888. RLS thanks Sullivan for the present of a bottle of whiskey (Sullivan had visited RLS at Saranac Lake in March) and lets him know that he has responded in the strongest possible terms to Mansfield's agent E. D. Price's unauthorized use of private letters from RLS to promote the Sullivan-Mansfield version, this in an article in the *New York Times*, 8 April 1888. Sullivan himself he holds completely blameless. In all three letters, RLS treats Sullivan with a cordiality and respect that he was soon to withdraw altogether from Mansfield and his agent, no doubt (as Linehan suggests) responding in kind to the respectful courtesy of Russell's own approaches to him.

RLS to Valerian Gribayedoff, Saranac Lake, [October 1887]. Photographic negative together with a photographic negative of the engraving, Yale. ''Dear Sir, I send off today a signed copy of the etching. When I pass again through New York, I shall be pleased, if you should still care, to give you another and longer sitting. The pleasure of your artistry will very properly repay me for the trouble. Yours very truly, Robert Louis Stevenson.'' According to Gertrude Hills, *Robert Louis Stevenson's Handwriting* (New York: privately printed, 1940), 44–45, the etching of RLS to which this letter refers is lost. But it is reproduced and credited to the Mansell Collection in Alanna Knight, *The Robert Louis Stevenson Treasury* (London: Shepheard-Walwyn, 1982), 61. The better-known etching of RLS by Gribayedoff derives from a photograph taken at Sydney in 1893 and was published, although possibly not for the first time, in *The Book Buyer* [New York], 21 (Sept. 1900), 88.

RLS to James Bain, April 1889. RLS Silverado Museum, St. Helena, California. Autograph of Letter 2160, previously known only from the version published by Bain, *A Bookseller Looks Back* (London: Macmillan, 1940), 175–76.

RLS to Harry J. Moors, Apia, [? December 1891]. Offered on the Internet via eBay, by an individual, 17 October 2001 and at other times. Brief undated note on Christmas dinner plans. ''My dear Moors, Proposal: Suppose you and yours dined with me and mine on Christmas at Kai Sam's [possibly: Chez Louis]; and then went and finished the evening at your house? I am willing to listen to amendments and am Yours to command R. L. S.'' In her diary, 25 December 1891, Fanny Stevenson describes a dinner and Christmas celebration at Moors's house, noting that ''[t]here was only one person at dinner outside of our two families,'' although others came later in the evening—in *Our Samoan Adventure*, ed. Charles Neider (1956), 159–60; see also the account by RLS's mother, who remained at Vailima, enjoying the peace and quiet, in her *Letters From Samoa 1891–1895* (London: Methuen, 1905), 116–17.

RLS to the Rev. Arthur E. Claxton, 1 October 1892, Letter 2466. A previously unknown copy of this letter breaking with Claxton when he returned to Samoa is in the London Missionary Society Archives, London, together with a copy of Claxton's reply, both of which RLS transcribed and included in his letter to Sidney Colvin, 8 October 1892, Letter 2463. It is published with a lengthy commentary on the matter in Ann C. Colley, *Robert Louis Stevenson and the Colonial Imagination* (2004), 160–61.

RLS to Lady Jersey, Oxford Hotel, Sydney, 28 February 1893. Private collection; brought to my attention by Ernest Mehew. "We have just arrived and find you leaving tomorrow," RLS begins. "But as one of my chief motives was a wish to have an interview with Lord Jersey, I do hope he may be able to spare me some moments in the day." RLS's concern was undoubtedly with "A Regulation for the Maintenance of Peace and Good Order in Samoa," also known as "The Sedition (Samoa) Regulation," published on 29 December 1892 by John Bates Thurston as British High Commissioner, Western Pacific. RLS first saw it at the beginning of February; he had reason to think that it was wholly or partly directed at him; and Lord Jersey was just ending his service as governor of New South Wales. It is unknown whether the interview that RLS sought occurred, but it seems likely that it did; and Lord Jersey did promise to make RLS's views know when he returned to London. See details and annotations in Letters 2535–2542 and Beinecke 5003 and 5005.

RLS to Elliott and Fry, photographers, 12 July 1893, humorously declining a proposed sitting in London. Listed in *American Book Prices Current*, 1985.

RLS to an unknown correspondent, [? 1894]. RLS Silverado Museum. A one-page letter with no date or place but clearly of the Vailima period, written in response to a fan letter from a young admirer. The recipient is addressed as "Dear Mr [?]," but the surname is illegible, and there is no envelope. The letter seems to have remained in the hands of the recipient's descendants, in Auckland, NZ, for more than a century. "I am glad to have interested you; I will tell you in confidence—I only care to be read by young men; they alone can read," RLS writes in part. "I read now; yes, and with pleasure; but some years ago I read with the greed and gusto of a pig, sucking up some of the very paper (you would think) into my brain. And that is the only kind of reading for which it is worth while to support the pains of writing." Compare RLS's similar comment in a letter to Ernest Rhys, 11 August 1894, Letter 2771: "When I remember my own youth—what heights of admiration I knew, what heats of gratitude—it always seems to me there is only one thing worth writing for—the appreciation of the young."

RLS to S. S. McClure, 7 September 1894. Offered on the Internet by James R. Pepper Rare Books, Santa Barbara, CA, December 2005. On 11 July 1894 Charles Baxter reported to RLS that for the serial publication of *St. Ives* he had provisionally accepted £14 per 1,000 words from the *Pall Mall Budget* and S. S. McClure's offer of £8/10s per 1,000 words for American newspaper syndication: "You will I suppose be the highest paid writer of the day" (Letter 2772, n. 2). On 9 September, referring to this letter to McClure, RLS wrote to Baxter: "I have sent a most unappetising epitome of *St Ives* to McClure according to order. The price seems to me exorbitant. But who am I to complain?" (Letter 2783). In the present letter, written two days earlier, RLS writes in part: "I have the pleasure to send you an epitome of St. Ives. Without doubt it was a task! And I fear it will not increase the interest of any human being, but you must be judge of that, and employ it accordingly or not, as your better wisdom shall suggest." RLS's "epitome" does not appear to have survived, and he died three months later, without completing the novel. With an ending by Arthur Quiller-Couch, it was first published serially in the *Pall Mall Magazine*, London, and *McClure's Magazine*, New York, in 1896–97.

RLS to Harold M. Sewall (addressed as ''My dear Suasese,'' Sewall's Samoan name), Vailima, 7 October 1894. Offered on the Internet by Michael Silverman, bookseller, London, September 2005. Responding apparently to an article or book that Sewall had sent him, RLS comments: ''I prefer your account of your shipwreck to your political speech, as I presume you to have expected. But let difference of opinion—even as to matter of fact—never lessen friendship! You will always be to me the redoubtable Suaese, the hero of the circumnavigation of Tutuila, and I shall always be glad to hear of your welfare and your wife's.'' Sewall (1860–1924) was United States consul in Samoa during much of Stevenson's time there and in April 1891 brought RLS along with his party on a visit to the easternmost of the Samoan islands, Tutuila. RLS's account of the trip appears in Balfour's *Life*, II, 96–101.

Letters by Others

Atkinson, Damian, ed. *The Selected Letters of W. E. Henley*. Aldershot: Ashgate, 2000. Especially during the nearly fifteen years between their first meeting, in Edinburgh in February 1875, and their quarrel beginning in March 1888, Henley and Stevenson were in constant touch by letter. As a result, of the 250 letters in Damian Atkinson's splendid, well-indexed, well-annotated selection there are 38 letters to RLS and 24 to their mutual friend Charles Baxter. Excerpts and complete letters from the time of the quarrel appear in the Yale Letters, which are used here to good effect in the annotations and for context; but it is good to have Henley's letters over the whole course of their friendship, if only to see Henley's other activities and correspondence and to see him in his various roles in relation to RLS: collaborator, editor, business agent, and friend. ''If I'm rude, forgive me,'' Henley writes on 28 March 1885 after yet another lapse in Stevenson's health brought on by overwork:

> I feel strongly, & I can't help my rudeness. For I do anticipate the worst. If you cannot & will not take a decent amount of rest, then I cannot but believe the wretchedest. Learn a language; play patience; read in chronological order the works of Dumas *père* & George Sand; do anything rather than cripple yourself like this. Do you want company? here are any of us at your service. Do you want collaboration? behold me! Shall I borrow you Ruskin? I can & will. Only refrain from being an ass—a noble, honourable, glorious ass; & I am—we are—content.   (141–42)

From this and many other examples it is easy to see what an exasperating mixture of egotism and affection Henley must have presented.

Demoor, Marysa, ed. *Dear Stevenson: Letters from Andrew Lang to Robert Louis Stevenson with Five Letters from Stevenson to Lang*. Leuven: Uitgeverij Peeters, 1990. Andrew Lang was introduced to RLS by Sidney Colvin at Mentone in February 1874, and they became lifelong friends, although more as fellow writers than as intimates. More than 4,500 letters by Lang survive, 102 of them to RLS, but Lang did not keep letters written to him. To the five letters by RLS to Lang published here, the Yale

Letters added only two more complete letters and three fragments quoted in letters by H. Rider Haggard. So we can only guess at RLS's side of their correspondence. Lang's letters are almost always about his own, RLS's, and others' current literary projects—informal and often devoted to business rather than to reflection, and never very long—and one is grateful for Demoor's many careful annotations identifying them. In her introduction she surveys the many points of contact between RLS and Lang: Lang's liking for RLS's early essays, his enthusiasm for *Treasure Island* and other works of adventure, including H. Rider Haggard's, and their shared interests in primitive cultures and Scottish history—this last including RLS's beginning at Lang's suggestion a novel about Prince Charles Edward's time as an exile in France, "The Young Chevalier" (1892).

Demoor, M[arysa], ed. *Friends Over the Ocean: Andrew Lang's American Correspondents 1881–1912*. Gent: Rijksuniversitet Gent, 1989. Lang's correspondence with the American critic J. Brander Matthews has a dozen passing references to Stevenson. Among them are comments on *A Child's Garden of Verses* ("I adore them," 11 March 1885, 63), *Dr. Jekyll and Mr Hyde* ("it is *good*," 2 December 1885, 67), and on stories in *The Merry Men* (1887): "I can't care for Will o'the Mill, or Franchard's treasure, but I think The Merry Men one of R.L.S.'s *best* things. Especially the scenery and the Scotch" (7 March 1887, 79). "We hear Stevenson is a great lion, like Buffalo Bill over here," Lang wrote to Matthews on 5 October 1887 about RLS's reception in America. "We hope it will do him good" (89). RLS's South Seas letters, are not "bounderish" as Kipling's "The Light That Failed" is, but "as they appear in a journal, they are not very good reading. Why, I can't guess. I wish I had a chance at the South-Seas, not for writing but for existing" (27 March 1891; 113). Of the novel that RLS began, later in the year, under the title "The Young Chevalier" Lang writes: "The island outline reminds me that I have to send Stevenson bales of material for a novel I invented; I daresay, if he ever does it, he won't leave much of my invention. But it was so Stevensonian that I could not dream of touching it myself. It is a pity one can't write one's own novels" (8 February 1892; 114). "Henley, as you say, wrote in character on Stevenson," Lang commented on Henley's denunciation of Graham Balfour's biography of RLS. "A more loathesome exhibition I never saw" (28 December 1901; 146). Earlier he had written: "Stevenson has really been very ill; Henley seems to think his illness a romance invented to keep him, Henley, remote! I should not care for W. E. H. about me much, if I were an invalid, more of an invalid, rather" (25 July 1887; 87).

Bicknell, John W., and Mark A. Reger, eds. *Selected Letters of Leslie Stephen. Volume 1: 1864–1882*. Columbus: Ohio State UP, 1996. Includes (137–39) Stephen's long letter to RLS, 15 May 1874 (Beinecke 5549; a facsimile is in the Beinecke Collection catalogue, facing 1590), accepting and discussing details in "Victor Hugo's Romances," RLS's first contribution to the *Cornhill Magazine* (August 1874).

Reference Works

Swearingen, Roger G. "Robert Louis Stevenson 1850–1894." *The Cambridge Bibliography of English Literature: Volume 4 1800–1900*. Ed. Joanne Shattock. 3rd ed.

Cambridge: Cambridge UP, 1999. Columns 1688–1702. Lists of the manuscripts, bibliographies, book-form publications of RLS's works during his lifetime and afterwards, forgeries, film versions, translations, and biographical and critical studies. The volume as a whole is also of great value for the entries on Stevenson's well-known (and lesser-known) contemporaries, nineteenth-century children's books, the book trade, and international influences.

Kiely, Robert. "Robert Louis Stevenson." *Victorian Fiction: A Second Guide to Research.* Ed. George H. Ford. New York: Modern Language Association, 1978. 333–47. Making good the omission of RLS from the first *Guide* (1964), Kiely concisely traces the whole history of RLS's literary reputation through the mid-1970s. He offers shrewd, balanced, telling assessments of the most important works of biography and criticism and a good list of then recent academic contributions.

Swearingen, Roger G. *The Prose Writings of Robert Louis Stevenson: A Guide.* Hamden: Archon, 1980. This chronologically ordered guide to the more than 350 prose works—essays, novels, stories, plays—with which Stevenson was engaged during the course of his short life includes the details of date, publication, and collection; manuscripts and their locations when known; and notes on the composition, revision, and sources of each work, including publication agreements and what Stevenson was paid. Works that were only planned or that were left unfinished in manuscript are also included. It extends to the end of Stevenson's career and supersedes my checklist, "The Prose Writings of Robert Louis Stevenson: An Index and Finding-List, 1850–1881," *Studies in Scottish Literature,* 1974, and the corresponding material on RLS's early career in my Ph.D. dissertation (Yale, 1970), which is decribed later in this section.

In the 25 years since the publication of *The Prose Writings of RLS: A Guide,* no previously unknown prose works by Stevenson have turned up. The record seems to be complete, and it seems to have been complete in 1980. This is a gratifying result, but it is not really surprising. Stevenson died young and suddenly, in mid-career, before there could occur any great dispersal of his manuscripts privately by sale or gift. And his wife kept nearly everything together until she herself died twenty years later, when her daughter Belle sold nearly everything at auction, and all at once, in November 1914 at the Anderson Galleries, New York. As a result, the Anderson catalogue offers a record of almost everything that was in Stevenson's hands at the time of his death, including notebooks from his entire career. The challenge has been in tracing their whereabouts since.

Minor changes and additions in my account are, of course, necessary throughout, chiefly due to the publication of the Yale Letters and the need, as a result, to update references, and to the many works of scholarship that are the subject of the present survey. As to dates, I agree with Kenneth Gelder's suggestion that "The Plague-Cellar" is probably a work of 1865 or 1866 or later, a year or two later than I had placed it on the basis of family testimony. But I still think that "The Enchantress" dates from the *Casco* voyage (June 1888–January 1889), as Lloyd Osbourne says that it does, not from the later voyage on the *Equator,* as William and Linda Hardesty believe. Details appear in my discussion of "The Enchantress" in the section on Texts. In her edition of *Treasure Island* (1998), 211, Wendy Katz notes that the attribution of Johnson's *A General History of the Pyrates* (1724) to Daniel Defoe originated with John Robert Moore in 1932, was accepted by Manuel Schonhorn in his 1972 edition, "but [is] no longer accepted since the publication of *The Canonization of Defoe* by P. N. Furbank and W. R. Owens in 1988." Other adjustments are no doubt needed as well.

The great changes in the last 25 years are two: first, that dozens of manuscripts have moved out of private hands into libraries and museums. 25 years ago, sometimes all one could do was to pass on what was said in an auction catalogue dating from 50 or more years before. The Robert Louis Stevenson Silverado Museum in St. Helena, in the Napa Valley, California, opened in 1969 and continues to grow, with more than ten thousand items by and about Stevenson and of Stevenson interest. Yale has continued adding to the Beinecke Collection through gifts and purchases, and the National Library of Scotland has been active as well. Among the most notable additions to the NLS collection, which was already rich in Stevenson's letters to Baxter and to Mrs. Sitwell, are the complete business and engineering records of the Stevenson family of engineers, an archive covering more than four generations including Stevenson's own. The second change is that serious interest in establishing, tracing the revision history of, and making accessible to readers the best possible versions of Stevenson's texts has at last begun. Details appear in the section titled Texts later in this survey.

Swearingen, Roger G. "The Early Literary Career of Robert Louis Stevenson 1850–1881: A Bibliographical Study." Diss. Yale U, 1970. As noted in the previous entry, the first part of my dissertation (which in any event extended only to 1881) has been assimilated into and superseded by *The Prose Writings of RLS: A Guide* (1980). The second part, "Stevenson's Reading, 1850–1873," is still of use, however. It consists of a detailed descriptive commentary (438–541) and a list (542–619) of all of the works, including the locations of his own copies when known, that Stevenson can be shown to have read, or that were read to him, up until his early twenties, after which time his reading can be followed easily through his publications and letters. The range is extraordinary: from the Bible to J. W. M. Reynolds, Covenanting history and religious biographies to *Cassell's Illustrated Family Paper* and the plays in Skelt's Juvenile Drama. As I observed, Stevenson, as a man and as a writer, was "to a very great extent just what his childhood reading had made him." Somehow piety and romance,

> Skelt and the Bible, color and certainty, could be recombined, into a mature vision, as they had once been combined during his and other men's childhoods; Stevenson's continuing drive as a writer, the source alike of his moral unoriginality and his penchant for the striking, was to devise if he could some way of reuniting the twin strands, symbolized by the Bible and Skelt's Juvenile Drama, which run throughout his earliest reading and which mark "The History of Moses" almost portentously his own.   (451)

Spehner, Norbert. *Jekyll & Hyde Opus 600*. Roberval, Québec, Canada: Ashem, 1997. Spehner lists year by year, from 1886 through 1997, six hundred editions and translations of *Dr. Jekyll and Mr. Hyde*. He gives publication details and format, and the names of translators and the reprint history when known. He also includes a short list of recent studies. As Spehner notes in his Introduction, the number 600 is arbitrary, a limit imposed by what fits into 64 pages, and therefore he has excluded abridgements, adaptations, school texts, and audio, video, and film adaptations.

Bethke, Frederick John. *Three Victorian Travel Writers: An Annotated Bibliography of Criticism on Mrs. Frances Milton Trollope, Samuel Butler, and Robert Louis Stevenson*. Boston: Hall, 1977. This compilation has value chiefly as a checklist of comments from initial publication during Stevenson's lifetime through 1974 on *An Inland Voyage*, *Travels With a Donkey*, *The Amateur Emigrant*, *The Silverado Squatters*, and *The South Seas*. There are many errors and much carelessness in details, and the annotations are generally not very informative.

Wainwright, Alexander D. *Robert Louis Stevenson: A Catalogue of the Henry E. Gerstley Stevenson Collection, the Stevenson Section of the Morris L. Parrish Collection of Victorian Novelists, and Items from Other Collections in the Department of Rare Books and Special Collections in the Princeton University Library*. Princeton: Princeton U Library, 1971. Wainwright wisely uses the same order and arrangement of materials that G. L. McKay used in the Beinecke Collection catalogue, and there are abundant cross-references to make relationships clear. Thanks to the famous collection of M. L. Parrish, variant bindings and pirated editions are especially numerous: seven versions each of *An Inland Voyage* (1878), *Edinburgh: Picturesque Notes* (1878), and *Virginibus Puerisque* (1881); nine of *Treasure Island* (1883); and more than a dozen of *Dr. Jekyll and Mr. Hyde* (1886). All of these were published during Stevenson's lifetime. But there is also one of the three surviving copies of *Penny Whistles*, the trial version of *A Child's Garden of Verses*, this one being William Ernest Henley's copy marked ''No 6'' and bearing his address; a proof of the title page of *Dr. Jekyll and Mr. Hyde* addressed to Stevenson and date-stamped 14 November 1885; 456 leaves of the earlier of the two manuscripts of *St. Ives* (1894); and eighteen books that RLS himself once owned, including his copy of *The Trial of James Stewart . . .* (1753), a key source for *Kidnapped* (1886). All of these are precisely and completely described, with indications whenever a copy is the same as a certain one in Beinecke. Also listed are the contents of nineteen folders in the general correspondence files in the Charles Scribner's Sons Archives that apply directly to Stevenson. There are eleven excellent black-and-white reproductions, including a pastel by Girolamo Nerli and a self-portrait that RLS did of himself.

Updating the printed catalogue is a list of additions to the Stevenson section of the Parrish Collection, 1971–1995, on the Princeton University Library website:

http://libweb2.princeton.edu/rbsc2/parrish/Stevenson.index.pdf

Almost all of the additions are recent publications. Among first editions, another variant copy of *Treasure Island* brings the total to ten. Two more variants of the first edition of *The Silverado Squatters* bring that total to seven. Although manuscript material is not catalogued, it is noted that there have been few such additions, of which two are mentioned: ''the autograph manuscript of 'Hester Noble's Mistake; or a word from Cromwell,' a drama in four acts, on three leaves . . . and a self-portrait of Stevenson in academic garb offering carrots to a donkey, entitled 'Dominie—and I,' in pen and ink, signed.'' The only new association copy is J. Wilson M'Laren, *Scots Poems and Ballants* (1892), inscribed to RLS by the author, sold originally as Anderson II, 300.

Edinburgh City Libraries. *Robert Louis Stevenson: supplementary catalogue of the Stevenson Collection in the Edinburgh Room with a select list of books and manuscripts in Lady Stair's House Museum*. Edinburgh: Edinburgh City Libraries, 1978.

This checklist has some value in listing a few secondary sources and other studies since 1950 not generally listed elsewhere. But the earlier guides, although these, too, are sketchy, give a better picture: *Robert Louis Stevenson 1850–1894: Catalogue of the Stevenson Collection in the Edinburgh Room, Central Public Library, George IV Bridge* (Edinburgh Public Libraries Committee, 1950); and *Lady Stair's House Museum including the Robert Burns, Sir Walter Scott, Robert Louis Stevenson Collections* (Libraries and Museums Committee, Corporation of Edinburgh, 1966). The collection at Lady Stair's House, now the Writers' Museum, is especially strong in photographs, including several large albums of photographs that Lloyd Osbourne took during the Stevensons' several Pacific cruises.

Bowlin, Bruce A. *Robert Louis Stevenson: A Finding List of Stevenson Editions at the University of South Carolina.* Columbia: Department of Special Collections, Thomas Cooper Library, University of South Carolina, 1994. This library has a very good collection of first editions, but the high points are the original *Young Folks* serial versions of *Treasure Island* (1881–82), *The Black Arrow* (1883), and *Kidnapped* (1886).

Cain, Alexander M. *Robert Louis Stevenson: A Catalogue of his Works and Books Relating to Him In the Rare Book Collection State University of New York at Buffalo.* Buffalo: State University of New York, Buffalo, 1972. SUNY-Buffalo's collection of first editions includes "The Pentland Rising" (1866), "The Charity Bazaar" (1875), *Treasure Island* (1883), *Dr. Jekyll and Mr. Hyde* (1886), and "Father Damien" (1890), among many others. But the gems of the printed collection are forty books from Stevenson's library: Scottish history, notably John Hill Burton's *History of Scotland* (2nd ed., 8 vols., 1873); French history, chiefly on the Camisards and the Cévennes; French literature including RLS's copies of Dumas's *Le Bâtard de Mauléon* (1871), *Le Comte de Monte-Cristo* (Nouvelle edition, 6 vols., 1887), and *Le Vicomte de Bragelonne* (6 vols., 1884), De Laclos's *Les Liaisons dangeruses* (1869), Flaubert's *L'Education sentimentale* (1870), George Sand's *Correspondance, 1812–1876* (1882), and other works; three sourcebooks on the life of Wellington; Abraham Fornander's *An Account of the Polynesian Race* (1880); and the *Poetical Works of Geoffrey Chaucer* (5 vols., ed. Robert Bell, London, n. d.).

Not listed in this catalogue are the manuscripts at SUNY-Buffalo, among them a one-page notebook draft, "Prologue: At Monte Carlo," by the look of the handwriting possibly written in early 1874 after RLS's visit there with Sidney Colvin; from the same notebook, a few notes on Hobbes's *Leviathan*; notes from the mid-1870s on medieval French history comprising separate batches on Charles VI and on the Huguenots; the beginning of a novel set in the American West, "The Squaw Men" (1881–82); and a partial or complete list of 20 chapters with titles and page numbers (ch. 20 begins on p. 110), of an otherwise unknown novel seemingly set in the West of Scotland, "The Beacon Bell" (probably 1883).

Maixner, Paul, ed. *Robert Louis Stevenson: The Critical Heritage.* London: Routledge, 1981. "If Stevenson was the victim of his admirers," Maixner comments in his introduction, "he also had the remarkable good fortune to find during his life a sizeable readership capable of a more or less full appreciation of his work and a just and reasoned estimate of his achievement" (4). In this distinguished contribution to a valuable series, Maixner offers more than a hundred well-chosen and well-annotated excerpts from reviews and essays about Stevenson's work published at the time that it appeared. He also includes contemporary comments from private letters and journals, as well as comments by Stevenson and his friends and family. With the help of Ernest Mehew and others, Maixner has also identified the authors of many reviews that were published anonymously. His introduction is lengthy and informative, and he traces, book by book, the contemporary reception of Stevenson's work. There never was unanimity, of praise or of blame. Stevenson's contemporaries were often remarkably insightful, and they saw strengths as well as weaknesses. And the main critical issues were seen and identified. Maixner also comments on RLS's own views of his art and his success: "At times he regarded himself as an artist working without any immediate awareness of the public at all. . . . More often, however, Stevenson thinks of his art as . . . [an] obligation or debt . . . offering entertainment or solace" (4–5). Writing was a job like any other, to be done honestly and well. This is a valuable scholarly contribution.

Terry, R. C., ed. *Robert Louis Stevenson: Interviews and Recollections*. Iowa City: U of Iowa P, 1996. Extending the scrapbook tradition of J. A. Hammerton, ed., *Stevensoniana: An Anecdotal Life and Appreciation of RLS* (2nd ed., 1907), of the *Bookman* Extra Number on RLS (1913), and of Rosaline Masson, ed., *I Can Remember RLS* (1922), Terry reprints 49 short excerpts offering contemporary and posthumously recollected glimpses of RLS by friends and family, journalists and visitors, from his childhood until his death and burial in Samoa in December 1894. The portrait that emerges is of Stevenson the celebrity: a person whom everyone found memorable and about whom everyone wanted to write quotably. There is much good information here, and much also for the student of Stevenson's contemporary and posthumous reputation.

Nollen, Scott Allen. *Robert Louis Stevenson: Life, Literature and the Silver Screen*. Jefferson, NC: McFarland, 1994. This is a well produced and very well illustrated guide (using stills, lobby cards, and advertisements) to the dozens of movie versions of all of RLS's works. Even *The Silverado Squatters*, it turns out, exists in a film version: *Adventures in Silverado*, Columbia, 1948, characterized by Nollen as "[a] B western produced by a minor studio" and unique in the respect that RLS appears as a character (125). Nollen writes at length and with sanity and gusto about each of the films, summarizing and even reviewing them ("Without a doubt, [Orson] Welles's Long John Silver is the worst on film," he writes of an ill-fated 1972 version of *Treasure Island*, 108), as well as giving many details about casts and crews. He also lists other adaptations including radio and television programs, even children's action-figure toys; and he summarizes the books themselves and their background, sources, and publication. Oddly, Nollen's list of radio programs (410–16) is confined to British examples, causing him to miss such programs as Welles's great triumph in the Stevenson line, the Mercury Theater of the Air adaptation of *Treasure Island* in 1938, and the adaptations during the 1940s of "The Body-Snatcher" and "Markheim" in the long-running radio series *Suspense* (1942–62); his list of television programs likewise seems better stocked with British than American examples. Early records are, as Nollen says, incomplete and unclear, but he also seems to have missed the fact that a four-minute 1909 American Mutoscope-Biograph film "The Suicide Club" (1909), which he lists, is said to have been directed by D. W. Griffith and to have starred Herbert Yost and others. Too late for inclusion, of course, are more-recent curiosities such as *Mary Reilly* (1996, starring Julia Roberts and John Malkovich), *Muppet Treasure Island* (also 1996, with Kermit the Frog and Miss Piggy), the cartoon epic *Treasure Planet* (2002), a long-running Broadway musical *Jekyll & Hyde* (1,543 performances, 28 April 1997–7 January 2001), and a number of much-less-fanciful adaptations. As recently as 1995 Francis Ford Coppola was engaged by CBS television to do a version of *Kidnapped* (Los Angeles *Times*, 9 January 1995). This project seems to have languished, but the popularity of Stevenson's works in other media continues unabated. The popular Internet Movie Database lists RLS as the originating author of no fewer than 145 films so far.

Glut, Donald F. "The Dual Horror of Dr. Jekyll." *Classic Movie Monsters.* Metuchen: Scarecrow, 1978. 68–129. Glut offers an inclusive and often very fully annotated list not only of stage, film, radio, and television versions of *Dr. Jekyll and Mr. Hyde* but also audio recordings, comic books, parodies, soap opera and pornographic versions. He says that *Dr. Jekyll and Mr. Hyde* is "[t]he most frequently filmed horror story of all time . . . [and] has probably been adapted to the motion picture screen more often than any other piece of literature of any genre" (68). To Scott Nollen's and other filmographies Glut adds that the earliest film version is said to have been made in 1897, the first confirmed version being the 1908 version by Selig Polyscope Company—also released under the alternate title *The Modern Dr. Jekyll*—to which Nollen also refers.

King, Charles. "*Dr. Jekyll and Mr. Hyde*: A Filmography." *The Journal of Popular Film and Television* 22 (Spring 1997): 9–12. [not seen in this form] Revised by the author for the Norton Critical Edition (2003), ed. Katherine Linehan, 159–63. This is not, as its title suggests, an inventory with production details, but a good general essay about the film versions of *Dr. Jekyll and Mr. Hyde*. It is especially valuable on films of the 1970s through the early 1990s, in which RLS's story becomes not so much the plot as a point of departure or analogy. One compelling addition of this kind, since King's essay, is the film *Fight Club* (1999), based on the novel (1996) by Chuck Palahniuk (b. 1962).

Hammond, J. R. *A Robert Louis Stevenson Companion: A Guide to the Novels, Essays, and Short Stories.* London: Macmillan, 1984. Part of a series to which Hammond has also contributed volumes on Edgar Allan Poe, H. G. Wells, and George Orwell, this is a capable survey and assessment of Stevenson's works arranged by genre. It is augmented by a 14–page biographical sketch; 16 pages on "Stevenson's Literary Achievement"; an alphabetical list of the short stories and essays, unfortunately without dates or the places of original publication, each with a very short summary and a note of the volume in which it was first collected and the volume number in which it appears in the Tusitala Edition; a 26–page list of characters and locations in Stevenson's works; a very brief filmography; and a short annotated list of works about Stevenson. Nine familiar photographs are reproduced, chiefly from the Writers' Museum, Edinburgh.

In the essays that make up most of the book, Hammond is neither daring nor controversial. He wants to make sure that the basics are understood, and as a result his comments are sometimes obvious to the point of platitude. "The vividness of his

[Stevenson's] images," Hammond writes of *Dr. Jekyll and Mr. Hyde*, for example, almost as if this were all there was to say or show, "is such as to etch them indelibly on the imagination and to remain in the memory long after the tale has been completed" (120). Hammond has read Stevenson carefully, alertly, and completely, however—and it is these virtues of thoroughness that enable him to note, for example, similarities between passages in Poe and in *Dr. Jekyll and Mr. Hyde* and *The Master of Ballantrae*, and to observe that the character Northmour in "The Pavilion on the Links" (1880) "could be regarded as a trial sketch of the figure later to be drawn in Long John Silver . . . one of the earliest examples of Stevenson's fascination with moral ambivalence. In his combination of physical courage with unscrupulosity he anticipates such characters as Hoseason in *Kidnapped*, James Durie in *The Master of Ballantrae*, and Attwater in *The Ebb-Tide*" (76). Viewed as a collection of introductions rather than as a study in depth, Hammond's companion has much to offer.

Hammond, J. R. *A Robert Louis Stevenson Chronology*. Basingstoke: Macmillan, 1996. Hammond's chronology is part of a series designed to make it easy "[to] check a point quickly or to obtain a rapid overview of an author's life or career"—and to do so with an exactness not always desirable in biographies (ix). In 81 pages Hammond lists events and publications in RLS's life year by year from his birth in 1850 to 1867, then monthly from February 1870 through his death in December 1894. There is an undeniable appeal in this bones-only approach. Event follows event, publication follows publication follows event, with much of the rough, spiky oddity of life itself. We have the Timetables of History without the history and narrowed to the events in a single person's life. (That the Franco-Prussian war was on RLS's mind at Earraid in 1870, and that he felt as if he heard the guns, is not mentioned here.)

Unfortunately, this is not an inspired handling of the form: it is marred not only by a large number of errors but by troubling omissions. The challenge is to make sure that the story gets told despite the economy of method. There is no mention of the death in 1860 of RLS's maternal grandfather that brought the Colinton Manse era to an end; nor of North Berwick or East Lothian—facts important to readers interested in the personal origins of the scenery in "The Lantern Bearers," "An Old Song," and "The Pavilion on the Links," or in the Bass Rock in *David Balfour*. Mention is made of Baudelaire, but until 1873 none of Whitman, a much greater influence—and nothing at all, anywhere, of Herbert Spencer. There is no mention of the goat ranch or of Oakland: key places in RLS's stay in California in 1879–80. Nor is there any mention of Sargent or St. Gaudens, creators of two of the most familiar images of Stevenson; or of King Kalakaua and his sister Lilioukalani of Hawaii, with whom RLS was friends in 1889 and afterwards. Mention is made of donations to Dr. Barnardo's Homes (1888) and RLS's support for a memorial to the children's author J. M. Ballantyne (1893), but there is nothing on his thoughts for a memorial to Ferguson and Burns linking the two Roberts with a third, himself (RLS to Charles Baxter, 18 May 1894, Letter 2734). Unimportant facts again and again take space that should have been used for important ones. And some things should probably have been left alone. RLS's reading, for example, is too extensive to be covered by scattered notes such as the following from August 1890: "During this month, reads Hall Caine's *The Bondman*."

There are also many errors. Fanny Stevenson's older son Samuel Lloyd Osbourne was not "usually known as Lloyd" but started using his middle rather than his first name in his late teens. RLS first knew him as Sam. RLS's first meeting with Henry James cannot have been on 30 July 1879. This was the day that RLS, in Edinburgh, told his parents that he was "called away on business" and started for America. RLS and Mark Twain spent an afternoon together in New York in the spring of 1888–not 1887. On 27 March 1890, from Sydney, RLS sent out printed copies of his impassioned denunciation, *Father Damien: An Open Letter to the Reverend Doctor Hyde of Honolulu.* In Britain, it was published in the *Scots Observer* in two installments, 3 and 10 May 1890, and by Chatto and Windus on 19 July 1890. Hammond's statements about this work are not accurate as to what occurred, or when it happened; nor do they indicate the importance of the work.

Knight, Alanna. *The Robert Louis Stevenson Treasury.* London: Shepheard-Walwyn, 1982. More than two-thirds of the pages in this compilation (255/359) are devoted to an alphabetical list titled "People, Places and the Printed Word," which purports to provide entries for all of Stevenson's published works; for his friends, relatives, and acquaintances; for places where he lived or only stayed a few nights; and for miscellaneous details in his life, such as the names of ships that he sailed on or the Edinburgh law firm where he worked briefly as a copying clerk in 1872. Also included are dozens of miscellaneous and generally unannotated citations of secondary and other sources. Sixteen of these pages are occupied by selections from Lloyd Osbourne's *An Intimate Portrait of RLS* (1924), seemingly in place of a more straightforward biographical summary. Individual works are sometimes quoted, sometimes summarized, sometimes only identified by place and date of first publication. Biographical entries generally lack dates of birth and death, and often much else. The amount and level of detail is highly variable; how much detail is offered follows no discernible plan; and the information itself is available in other, better sources.

There are, in addition, countless errors. Dr. William Bamford looked after RLS, in Oakland, in 1880, not "when [RLS] arrived in California" at the end of August 1879, in Monterey (10). "By-ways of Book Illustration" (24) was not one essay but the general title of a continuing series of essays in *The Magazine of Art* by various writers. To this series, RLS contributed essays on Bagster's *Pilgrim's Progress* (February 1882) and, under the subtitle "Two Japanese Romances," on two recent renditions of the Japanese tale first published in English in Mitford's *Tales of Old Japan* (1871), "The Forty-Seven Ronins" (November 1882). *New Arabian Nights* was not purchased by the *Century Magazine* (29). It was favorably reviewed there by H. C. Bunner in the February 1883 issue, a fact that makes sense of Fanny's remark, quoted in the entry, telling how proud she was "think[ing] of all the people I know reading about Louis."

No date is given for John Singer Sargent's portrait of Stevenson, nor is there any indication that Sargent actually painted three portraits of RLS, two of which survive, in December 1884, August 1885, and April 1887 (173). No doubt Knight's reference is to "Robert Louis Stevenson and His Wife," the well-known 1885 painting that shows RLS striding across the room, with Fanny seated in Arabian dress in the corner. Bringing Knight's entry up to date, it can be added that Sargent made a gift of the painting to RLS; it is signed on the back "To R. L. Stevenson, his friend John S. Sargent, 1885." After Fanny Stevenson's death, it was sold at the 1914 Anderson sale, for $14,800, and it remained with the original purchaser John Hay Whitney and his descendants for more than eighty-five years. On 19 May 2004 it was sold at Sotheby's, New York, for $8,880,000 (including buyer's commission) to the Las Vegas casino operator Steve Wynn for exhibit in his collection of art works.

The rest of the book consists of lists: of unpublished manuscripts (6 pages), fictional characters and places (13); a partial list of published letters, mostly from the Tusitala Edition, organized by recipient and annotated with a word or two as to the contents (34); titles and first lines of poems (16); musical settings (2); films and BBC television and radio adaptations and programs (12); Stevenson's works sorted by genre and date (6); titles of the volumes in the Tusitala Edition (2); and recommended further readings, especially biographies (3). Most of this information is available with more accuracy and detail elsewhere.

Texts

This section surveys textual contributions of four different kinds: Editions, generally of single works, that are designed to establish and offer a definitive text or to present a text enriched with supplementary materials—or sometimes both; Collections that include works by Stevenson published or reprinted for the first time or that include useful supplementary materials or annotations; Books and Articles that shed light on particular texts as such; and Exhibition Catalogues covering the centenary year of Stevenson's death in 1994 and other displays. Within sections and in each subsection, the order is chronological within Stevenson's career. Collections that are of interest only for their introductions will be covered in the discussion of criticism.

Editions

Swearingen, Roger G., ed. *The New Lighthouse on the Dhu Heartach Rock, Argyllshire.* St. Helena, CA: Robert Louis Stevenson Silverado Museum, 1995. This is the first publication of RLS's 450–word essay drafted in 1872, taken from the manuscript in the Huntington Library and completed by adding the material that RLS included by reference to sources now in the National Library of Scotland and the Silverado Museum. Also included in the Introduction are several previously unpublished sketches that RLS made during his stay nearby on Earraid in August 1870 (Free Library of Philadelphia) and passages from the day-to-day logs of the site foreman Robert Goodwillie (Monterey State Historic Park, CA). These include his brief mention of RLS's two visits to the rock, 8 and 13 August 1870, at least the first visit in company with the painter Sam Bough, and that of RLS's mother and father when they too visited, on 19 August. RLS's mother, then age 41, was "the first woman we have had on the rock," Goodwillie noted. The front cover reproduces, in color, Sam Bough's striking painting of the lighthouse during its construction, based on sketches that he made during his visit there with RLS (private collection).

Prose Poems, 1875. Six of the fifteen or more prose poems that RLS wrote in 1875, three of them previously unpublished, appear as an appendix in vol. 2 of the Yale

Letters, 332–38. RLS writes about them in letters to Mrs. Sitwell and Sidney Colvin in May and June 1875 (Letters 391–96).

Swearingen, Roger G., ed. *An Old Song and Edifying Letters of the Rutherford Family.* Paisley: Wilfion, 1982. ''An Old Song'' is RLS's first published story, unknown until its publication in this edition. It was first published, anonymously, as a feuilleton in *London,* 24 February—17 March 1877, and was never acknowledged or reprinted by RLS although he did once refer to it indirectly and mentioned it, although not by title, in a letter just before it began serial publication. The identification is certain, thanks to the survival of one page of the manuscript (Beinecke 6106), possibly because RLS rewrote that page. In its atmosphere, East Lothian setting, and lonely and tortured characters, ''An Old Song'' looks forward to ''The Pavilion on the Links'' (1880). In its grim depiction of quarreling brothers it looks ahead especially to *The Master of Ballantrae* (1889). ''Edifying Letters of the Rutherford Family'' is an unpublished early work of autobiographical fiction obviously referring to RLS, to his cousin Bob Stevenson (who returned from Cambridge to Edinburgh in 1871), and to the secret society to which they and others belonged during the early 1870s, the L. J. R., the initials standing for Liberty, Justice, Reverence (Beinecke 6185). First notice of my discovery and the attribution of *An Old Song* was in '' 'An Old Song' (1877): Robert Louis Stevenson's First Published Story, A New Discovery in the Yale Libraries,'' *Yale University Library Gazette,* 54 (January 1980), 101–13. This has been assimilated into the introduction of the present volume.

Schiffman, Nancy Blonder. ''A Critical Edition of Robert Louis Stevenson's Unpublished Play Autolycus in Service.'' Diss. U of South Carolina, 1973. The manuscript is in the Folger Shakespeare Library, Washington, DC, and the several versions of this amusing but slight dramatic piece—a project that came and went over almost ten years starting with a short story by RLS in November 1874–are well transcribed and adequately annotated. There is a minor misunderstanding about the number of leaves, leading to a suggestion by Schiffman that pages may be missing. The manuscript is, in fact, complete, Schiffman's count of leaves having included a page added when the manuscript was offered for sale.

Sanger, Andrew, ed. *An Inland Voyage with a Travel Guide to the Route by Andrew Sanger.* Heathfield: Cockbird, 1991. This beautifully produced little book, ideal for the canoeist's or the walker's pocket, divides the text of *An Inland Voyage* into four itineraries. Each begins with a map by Denys Baker. Then follows a substantial installment of RLS's text illuminated with many pen-and-ink sketches and watercolors by Michael Reynolds. Each itinerary ends with half a dozen pages of ''Travel Guide'' in which Sanger comments informatively on the route, towns, and points of interest, then and now, even mentioning good restaurants that he has found along the way. Also included is a small reproduction of Peter Severin Kröyer's portrait sketch of RLS at Cernay-la-Ville, 20 June 1879 (Hirschsprung Collection, Copenhagen); Lloyd Osbourne's account of the time at Grez in *An Intimate Portrait of RLS* (1924), 1–6; and Fanny Stevenson's similar account originally published in the Biographical Edition, 1905.

Golding, Gordon, ed. *The Cevennes Journal: Notes On A Journey Through The French Highlands.* Edinburgh: Mainstream, 1978. Also in French: *Journal de Route en Cevennes,* trans. Jacques Blondel. Toulouse: Edouart Privat for the Club Cévenol,

1978. Golding offers a complete transcription of RLS's journal of his 1878 walking tour in the Cevénnes that resulted in *Travels With a Donkey* (1879). It is carefully transcribed from the manuscript in the Huntington Library, together with valuable historical and topographical annotations. The French translation has in its annotations much additional local and historical detail not in the English version.

Stevenson, Robert Louis. *Travels With a Donkey in the Cevénnes.* London: Cave, 1980. This facsimile reprint of the first edition is part of a series of such reprints. It makes the first edition text readily and correctly accessible, of course. But it also shows that, even at its most ordinary, late-Victorian commercial book design could result in inviting, attractive, readable pages.

Hart, James D., ed. *From Scotland to Silverado.* Cambridge: Belknap/Harvard, 1966. In this first so-called complete publication of *The Amateur Emigrant* (1879–80) passages from RLS's manuscript are awkwardly inserted, as needed, into the version published after Stevenson's death in the Edinburgh Edition (1895). The result is a single uneven text stitching together revised and unrevised material alike, neither wholly a draft nor wholly the final version. Hart also includes, for the first time in book form, RLS's essay on the Carmel Mission, "San Carlos Day" (*Monterey Californian*, 11 November 1879; traced to Stevenson and first published by G. R. Stewart, *Scribner's Magazine*, August 1920); and a previously unpublished fragment on Simoneau's restaurant in Monterey (Beinecke 6589). Also included are RLS's essays on Monterey (*Fraser's Magazine*, November 1880) and San Francisco (*Magazine of Art*, May 1883) and the periodical version of *The Silverado Squatters* (*Century Magazine*, November—December 1883).

Swearingen, Roger G., ed. *The Amateur Emigrant.* 2 vols. Ashland: Lewis Osborne, 1976–77. This edition offers the first complete publication of RLS's manuscript, now at Yale (Beinecke 5956), with introductions on Stevenson's own experiences, the history of the work's composition and publication, and on the galley proofs that contain comments by Sidney Colvin and the publisher C. Kegan Paul and that were returned to Stevenson, who was then still in California, in the early summer of 1880 (Beinecke 65, 7403). Period illustrations, a few explanatory notes, and, in the second volume, reproduction of a United States railway map of the period, were added by the printer and publisher Lewis Osborne, a noted specialist in Western Americana. As he wrote it during 1879 and 1880, Stevenson's account of his journey across ocean and continent from Scotland to California in August 1880 is titled "The Amateur Emigrant, with some first impressions of America." Part I, called "The Emigrant Ship," consists of seven chapters and ends with the chapter titled "Personal Experience and Review." Part II, eight chapters, is titled "America: The Emigrant Train" and begins with the chapter "New York." When *The Amateur Emigrant* was first published as a whole work, in the Edinburgh Edition (1895), after Stevenson's death, the chapter "New York" was made the last chapter in the first part, to preserve as a unit the eight chapters published during his lifetime as "Across the Plains" (July–August 1883; book form, 1892). For the same reason, the two parts were renamed "From the Clyde to Sandy Hook" and "Across the Plains."

Noble, Andrew, ed. *From the Clyde to California: Robert Louis Stevenson's Emigrant Journey.* Aberdeen: Aberdeen UP, 1985. In his title, Andrew Noble is no doubt deliberately echoing the title of James D. Hart's collection, *From Scotland to Silverado*

(1966). In his Acknowledgments, Noble refers to Hart's collection as "both model and extremely erudite source" (ix), and the tables of contents are identical. The only significant difference textually seems to be that Noble follows my edition of the complete manuscript of *The Amateur Emigrant* (1976–77), not Hart's hybrid version—a fact which makes Noble's use of the later section titles (as in Hart and the Edinburgh Edition) oddly inconsistent, all the more so in that Noble restores the chapter "New York" to the beginning of the second part, as it is in the manuscript.

The most noticeable new feature of Andrew Noble's edition is that he includes slightly more than three dozen historical photographs and illustrations, about the trans-Atlantic voyage, Monterey, and San Francisco, as well as about the rail journey. (Of the ten railway pictures in Noble's edition, only three are in common with Jim Murphy's collection, described in the next entry.) Certainly the most valuable of these are the external and internal design drawings of the *Devonia* done expressly for this edition by Fred M. Walker of the National Maritime Museum, Greenwich. These appear as the end-papers, together with a concise technical description of the ship and a summary of its history. (The interior plan does not exactly match Stevenson's own description of where second-cabin passengers like himself were berthed, but this may have been a changeable setup.) In his introduction, Noble also quotes Anchor Lines promotional materials about the *Devonia* (20–21), and in the text he includes an Anchor Lines advertisement (19) and a photograph of the *Devonia* (37). The page layout generally and the quality of some of the photographs (for example, of Jules Simoneau, 109) is less than could be desired, however, and the Notes are more like digressions than notes. We find half a page on Zola annotating a passing mention (280), a page and one-half quoting Henry James's *The American Scene* (282–83) in the annotation of a reference to Castle Garden: such allocations of space in the Notes are excessive, all the more so when other details, such as a quotation from *Marmion* in the chapter "Early Impressions," are passed over in silence.

Murphy, Jim. *Across America on an Emigrant Train*. New York: Houghton Mifflin/ Clarion, 1993. Murphy's account is a not an edition of "Across the Plains," but it could serve as a companion to one, and for this reason I have listed it here. Augmenting his account with 85 well-chosen historical photographs and magazine illustrations, Murphy fills in the background on every aspect of the railroad journey from New York to San Francisco as Stevenson would have experienced it in 1879: from train wrecks to trestles, rolling stock to railroad towns, Native Americans to buffalo, not omitting many evocative pictures of the emigrants themselves in transit. The end-papers have a map of Stevenson's route and the major railroad routes in the United States in 1912.

Randier, Jean, ed. *Treasure Island*. New York: Viking-Penguin, 1996. Illustrations by François Place, notes translated by Wiley Wood. Originally: *Le Île de Tresor*, trans. Jacques Papy. Paris: Gallimard Jeunesse, 1994. Filled with helpful, detailed historical and explanatory illustrations with extended captions, this edition, first published in France, makes *Treasure Island* a virtual encyclopedia of pirate lore and seamanship.

Katz, Wendy R., ed. *Treasure Island*. Edinburgh: Edinburgh UP, 1998. From a textual point of view, *Treasure Island* is straightforward. The manuscript does not survive; there is only one periodical version (*Young Folks*, 1 October 1881–28 January

1882) and according to RLS he went back to his manuscript in revising the text for book-form publication; after the book appeared, on 14 November 1883, the day after his thirty-third birthday, he seems never to have returned to it. "I do desire a book of adventure—a romance—and no man will get or write me one," he wrote to W. E. Henley, probably in June 1884:

> Dumas I have read and re-read too often; Scott, too, and I am short. I want to hear swords clash. I want a book to begin in a good way; a book, I guess, like *Treasure Island*, alas! which I have never read, and cannot though I live to ninety. I would God some one else had written it! By all that I can learn, it is the very book for my complaint. I like the way I hear it opens; and they tell me John Silver is good fun. And to me it is, and must ever be, a dream unrealised, a book unwritten.
>
> (RLS to W. E. Henley, June 1884, Letter 1287)

At some point, RLS wrote "76,000 words" in pencil on the title page of a copy of the first edition (Beinecke 7507), just as he did in writing "25,000 words" on the title page of a copy of the first American edition of *Dr. Jekyll and Mr. Hyde* ("Twenty-Eighth Thousand," paper covers, 1886, RLS Silverado Museum). In his inscription of a copy of the first American edition of *Treasure Island* to Dr. Brandt, at Royat, 13 June 1884 (William Andrews Clark Library, Los Angeles, quoted in Letter 1281, n. 1), RLS noted the mistake of printing all of the map annotations in red, "since Captain Flint, Mr Bones and Jim Hawkins can hardly have used the same ink-bottle"—a detail about which, as Katz notes (241), he had been clear in his instructions to Cassell's (2 September 1883, Letter 1134). In the same inscription he also remarked, without elaboration then or later, that "the text is pretty corrupt"—an odd remark given that the American edition was at some point published from stereotype plates of the English edition that he himself had overseen (RLS to Henley, February 1885, Letter 1393). Later in the same year, 1884, RLS asked that a subscription be entered for him to *Le Temps*, in order to read the French translation that was then appearing as a daily feuilleton, 25 September—8 November 1884 (RLS to Alfred Nutt, 4 October 1884, Letter 1308). He must also have looked at the book again, at least in French, when this same translation appeared in book form in 1885. Of the illustrations he wrote enthusiastically to his father (28 October 1885, Letter 1482) and also in an essay never completed or published during his lifetime but probably intended for the "By-Ways of Book Illustration" series in *The Magazine of Art*, on which see the next entry. During RLS and Fanny's visit to Will and Berthe Low in Paris in August 1886, RLS and Low, not saying who they were, bought a copy of the French translation at the shop of the publishers, Hetzel, mischievously getting the clerk's wholehearted endorsement of it; RLS inscribed this copy to Berthe Low on 18 August 1886 (Beinecke 248; Letter 1677; a facsimile appears with Low's account of the mischief in his *A Chronicle of Friendships*, 1912, 332–34). In September 1892, in Samoa, Stevenson gave a copy of the Cassell's illustrated edition, "Fifteenth Thousand," 1886, to his step-grandson Austin Strong, for success in his schoolboy studies (Beinecke 7510)—again without comment or any indication that he had reread it. In short, there is no reason to disbelieve Stevenson's own comment that after *Treasure Island* was published in book form he never really went back to it, at least not in

English. Hardly any of these informative supporting details, it might be added, appear in Katz's edition, a parsimony that seems to me unduly austere.

For all of the apparent simplicity of the editorial task that is presented by *Treasure Island*, however, reference to the Edinburgh Edition (1895) and to later editions derived from it discloses several important substantive differences from the text in Katz's edition, on neither of which any comment appears. The first is in the Dedication. In Katz's edition, as in the first edition in 1883 and in all editions published during Stevenson's lifetime, Lloyd Osbourne is identified only by his initials. But in June 1894, with the Edinburgh Edition in prospect, Stevenson himself asked that the initials S. L. O. be expanded to Lloyd Osbourne (RLS to Charles Baxter, 18 June 1894, Letter 2745; also in *RLS: Stevenson's Letters to Charles Baxter* [1956], 360). This change was made for the Edinburgh Edition and, of course, it is followed in later editions derived from it. In the sixth paragraph from the end of ch. 24, "The Cruise of the Coracle" (p. 197, line 3 in the first edition), Katz follows the first edition in printing "worse" where the word "worst" should appear. "For some time she [the *Hispaniola*] had been doing the worse thing possible for me—standing still" (146). The reading in *Young Folks* is correct—"worst"—no doubt because this is what appeared in RLS's manuscript; it also fits with RLS's using "worst" a second time later in the same paragraph. The same corrected reading "worst" also appears in the Edinburgh Edition, and it is one of three corrected printing errors to which G. L. McKay calls attention in his supplementary entry of *Treasure Island* in vol. 6 of the Beinecke Collection catalogue (1964; 2256). A fourth error, not mentioned by McKay, was also corrected. In ch. 8, "At the Sign of the 'Spy-Glass,' " (p. 63, lines 5–6 in the first edition), the Edinburgh Edition correctly reads "at a glance" for "at glance" in the first edition.

In Katz's edition, none of these changes are made or even mentioned. These are important lapses, especially in an edition that pretends to authority, accuracy, and fidelity to "the author's final intentions" (243). Moreover, in the light of RLS's own comment to Dr. Brandt that the first edition text was "pretty corrupt"—a remark not mentioned by Katz—collation of the earlier versions against the Edinburgh Edition might also have made sense, even despite its lack of any direct authority except in the Dedication. This is not quite the definitive edition that one might expect.

Katz's account of the composition and publication of *Treasure Island* is, on the whole, accurate, derived as it is chiefly from RLS's own account in "My First Book" (1894) and the Yale Letters, although, as she herself remarks (238), her discussion is split between the "Introduction" (xix–xxiii) and the "History of Composition and Publication" (238–42). This is an unfortunate result of the general policy of the series. Katz also gives a good account of Stevenson's revisions between the *Young Folks* and the book form versions and of RLS's acknowledged sources. There are nevertheless a number of minor errors and omissions, and in my opinion Katz too often seems content simply to pass on, without analysis or extension, what has long been known.

The map that RLS sent to Cassell's along with his corrected manuscript was indeed lost. But there is no reason to think that this was "Lloyd's original map" (241) rather than a version that Stevenson himself prepared for his publishers. Two years had passed, and Lloyd was a boy of thirteen when (according to his own account more than forty years later) he had painted it at Braemar. In "My First Book" (1894),

moreover, RLS himself says that he, not Lloyd, created the original map. Katz credits
this comment too, seemingly unaware of the self-contradiction (238). The replacement
map that was drawn in the Stevenson engineering office and that was used as the
frontispiece in the book-form edition is now in the National Library of Scotland.
Especially given RLS's own comments on the point, it is unfortunate that in this
edition the map appears only in a blurry monochrome reproduction from the first
edition, not in colors as it did in reality. The illustrated edition first published by
Cassell's in 1885 actually contains all but two of the illustrations by George Roux
that RLS admired. Katz writes as if the Cassell's edition used only the four illustrations
by F. T. Merrill in the American edition published by Roberts Brothers earlier in the
year; in fact, both sources were used (xxv).

There is no reason to wonder about the authorship of the shanty "Fifteen men on
the dead man's chest" (xxxiii, 214). Katz mentions RLS's letter to W. E. Henley, 24
August 1881, Letter 843, but she seems to have overlooked his plain statement in
writing to John Paul Bocock, November 1887, Letter 1939: "The shanty in *Treasure
Island* is my own invention entirely; founded on the name of one of the Buccaneer
Islets—the Dead Man's Chest."

In the discussion of sources (xxx–xxxiii) Katz might have mentioned that RLS's
copy of Captain Charles Johnson's *The History of the Lives and Actions of the Most
Famous Highwaymen . . . to which is added A Genuine Account of the Voyages and
Plunders of the Most Noted Pirates* (Edinburgh, 1814) was sold in the Anderson sale,
II, 261. Among RLS's predecessors (and models) in the genre of boys' adventure
stories should be mentioned "that cheerful, ingenious, romantic soul, Mayne Reid"
(" 'Rosa Quo Locorum,' " 1893), upon whose work RLS patterned his own childhood
story "The Adventures of Basil," dictated when he was six, and of whom, in Samoa,
he remarked "I could not but be reminded of old Mayne Reid, as I have been more
than once since I came to the tropics; and I thought, if Reid had been still living, I
would have written to tell him that, for me, *it had come true*" (RLS to Sidney Colvin,
3 November 1890, Letter 2266). Of the adaptation by Lloyd Osbourne and Austin
Strong, *Treasure Island: A Melodrama in Five Acts* (1902), two other copies exist in
addition to the typescript in the United States Library of Congress, the only copy that
Katz mentions (xxviii). Typescripts are at Yale and in the RLS Silverado Museum.
Silverado also has the manuscript and beautiful hand-painted color drawings of each
scene by Austin Strong. This copy, the original, is dated on the title page 18 June 1902.

Stevenson's agreement with Cassell's for the book-form publication of *Treasure
Island* is quoted from the Society of Authors Archive in the British Library (242).
But there is no mention of its importance. As Peter Keating points out in *The Haunted
Study: A Social History of the English Novel 1875–1914* (London: Secker and War-
burg, 1989), this agreement actually made *Treasure Island* among the first British
books to be published on royalties (16). RLS's £100 was an advance, as it would be
today, not an outright purchase, and by 1886 Cassell's had paid £272/10/0 on the
first 12,000 copies. Having quoted the agreement, Katz simply repeats the usual bibliographical data and moves on: "*Treasure Island* appeared on 14 November 1883 and
was reprinted in December 1883 and March 1884. Two thousand copies were printed
for the first edition" (242). William Ernest Henley's comment, in a letter to RLS on
Christmas Day 1883, is much more to the point: "The booksellers are raging for it"

(Beinecke 4774). This comment appears in Katz's edition only in a footnote about the good reviews that *Treasure Island* received (xxix, n. 8).

Katz also does not mention G. L. McKay's account, in his entry of *Treasure Island* (Beinecke 240), of the four binding orders for the first edition. The first was for 750 copies, 250 more were ordered ten days later, another 750 on 3 December, and on 11 December, less than a month after publication, the remaining 250 copies were bound. These details show that *Treasure Island* sold at a remarkable rate, no doubt partly because it was published just before Christmas, and its success continued. In 1884, besides an American edition published in February, there were at least three more printings. The Beinecke catalogue records copies of a "Second Edition" and a "Fourth Edition," both dated 1884. The earlier edition, Beinecke 242, has advertisements dated 5R-12.83 (December 1883), as in some copies of the 1883 first edition, among them Beinecke 7509. In other words, no time was lost in getting out more copies of the book as soon as this could possibly be done. Yale's copy of the so-called fourth edition, 1884, Beinecke 243, has a printer's note 15.884 on page 292, suggesting a press run of 1,500 copies in August 1884. The advertisements are dated 5R-2.85, however, indicating that this batch must have lasted six months, into February 1885.

The English illustrated edition appeared in November 1885, and the first printing, seemingly the 2,000 copies printed in August 1885, with advertisements dated November 1885 (Beinecke 246), was gone by the end of the year. Beinecke 247 is a copy of the second issue of the first English illustrated edition with the printer's note 20.1285 and advertisements dated 5B.1.86–indicating that it was printed in December and bound in January. When the illustrated edition appeared, copies rather than editions were noted on the title page. The "Fifteenth Thousand" appeared within a year, in July 1886, probably in a yet another printing of 2,000 copies (Beinecke 7510, the copy that RLS gave to Austin Strong). There was a "Twenty-Ninth Thousand" in 1889, with a printer's note 25.589 and advertisements in at least one copy (my own) dated 5G.11.89. By 1891, copies of the "Thirty-Eighth Thousand" were in print—signifying publication of more than 15,000 in the previous five years—a number which according to RLS's agreement with Cassell's would have brought his total earnings from royalties alone, over the space of six or seven years, to more than £600–a huge sum by anyone's arithmetic.

No one needs to be presented with all of these details about the authorial and publishing history of *Treasure Island*, of course, although it is hard to say where if not in a scholarly edition they should be recorded. But their meaning should be stated plainly. In book form, *Treasure Island* sold very quickly and very well, and it kept its popularity. Thanks to its publication on royalties, it also paid Stevenson handsomely. Katz leaves all of these details aside—and in so doing deprives her readers of answers to some of the most obvious questions about the book that she is attempting to present.

Katz also greatly limits the value of her edition by describing rather than quoting RLS's own account of the origins and composition of *Treasure Island*, "My First Book" (1894), and his essay on the illustrations (1885), and she says nothing at all about RLS's fable "The Persons of the Tale," in which Captain Smollett and Long John Silver supposedly discuss *Treasure Island* just before RLS began writing the next-to-last chapter. The manuscript of "My First Book" is in the Syracuse University Library and was published in the *Syracuse University Library Associates Courier*, 21 (Fall 1986), 77–88. Page-proofs of the essay, deposited in August 1895 by S. S. McClure to secure American copyright, are in the Library of Congress. The manuscript of the essay on George Roux's illustrations is at Yale (Beinecke 7062), and it was published by Kevin Carpenter in *Notes and Queries*, 1982. "The Persons of the Tale" is of unknown date and was first published with other fables by RLS posthumously in 1895. The exclusion of these works about *Treasure Island* from the volume that contains the text itself makes one wonder what more appropriate place in this collected edition was envisioned for them. Annotated drawings of a typical schooner would have helped with the nautical terms. The Chronology (xv–xvii) repeats many of the errors in the chronology in *Weir of Hermiston* (1995) by the general editor of this series, Catherine Kerrigan.

Carpenter, Kevin. "R. L. Stevenson on the *Treasure Island* Illustrations." *Notes and Queries* 29 (1982): 322–25. As a preface to his publication of RLS's untitled essay on the illustrations by George Roux in the first French translation of *Treasure Island*, Kevin Carpenter traces concisely the book-form publication history of the translation and of the illustrations—all but two of which were used, without credit to Roux and generally with his signature removed, in all versions of the English illustrated edition (1885), the only book-form illustrated edition published during Stevenson's lifetime. The translation, which was first published, anonymously and without illustrations, as a daily feuilleton in *Le Temps*, 25 September–8 November 1884, appeared for the first time in book form early in 1885, with illustrations by Roux and the translation attributed to André Laurie, a pseudonym of Paschal Grousset: iii + 356 pages, 18mo, Paris, "Collection Julius Hetzel," 1885; the British Library copy, Carpenter says, is stamped 2 March 1885. Completely reset in a larger and more expensive format with 22 illustrations, an ornamental title page, a vignette on the first page, and a tail-piece on the last page, it appeared later in the year as *L'Île au Trésor. Traduction par André Laurie. Dessins par George Roux.* J. Hetzel et Cie: Bibliothèque d'Éducation et de Récréation, 1885: ii + 262 pages, 8vo. The British Library copy is stamped 23 December 1885, but RLS had a copy in October, at which time he wrote enthusiastically about the illustrations to his father (28 October 1885, Letter 1482) and also in an essay, never completed or published during his lifetime but probably intended for the "By-Ways of Book Illustration" series in *The Magazine of Art*, to which he had already contributed essays on Bagster's *Pilgrim's Progress* (February 1882) and on "Two Japanese Romances" (November 1882). RLS's essay, now at Yale (Beinecke 7062), consists of five paragraphs and the beginning of a sixth, 1420 words, and Carpenter presents the complete text and many helpful annotations. In her edition of *Treasure Island* (1998), 218, n. 47, Wendy Katz notes that Stevenson, in commenting on Roux's making the *Hispaniola* not a schooner, as the text had described it, but a full-rigged brig, actually wrote that "this very amazing artist is quite right; for in the days of John Silver, there was no such vessel as a schooner known upon the seas." (This is the actual reading of the manuscript. Katz follows Carpenter's misreading of the word "amazing" as "annoying.")

Swearingen, Roger G. "Notes on the Port of St. Francis (1951)," *Quarterly Newsletter, Book Club of California* 69: Spring 2004, 35–41. This essay is an introduction to a remarkable black-and-white non-fiction descriptive film, a little more than twenty minutes long, created, directed, filmed, and edited by Frank Stauffacher in San Francisco in 1951 but never released commercially. Chiefly but not only through the "Art in Cinema" programs that he organized in San Francisco and Berkeley during the late 1940s and early 1950s, Stauffacher did much to awaken and educate interest in Northern California in the then-new idea that film might or could be a form of art. "Notes on the Port of St. Francis" is one of only two or three films that Stauffacher (who died in the mid-1950s) made himself, although he worked as a cinematographer for others on a few other films. It is narrated by Vincent Price and with only one or two exceptions the words are from RLS's essay on San Francisco, "A Modern Cosmopolis" (1883).

Sullivan, John P., and Peter Whigham, eds. *Epigrams of Martial Englished by Divers Hands*. Berkeley: U of California P, 1987. Three of RLS's sixteen translations from Martial appear in this attractive selection, in which the Latin and English versions appear on facing pages: "Look round: You see a little supper room" (II.59, "Mica vocor: quid sim cernis, cenatio parva:," 118–19); "Call me not rebel, though in what I sing" (II.68, "Quod te nomine iam tuo saluto," 120–21); "O Nepos, twice my neighbour, since at home" (VI.27, "Bis vicine Nepos—nam tu quoque proxima Florae," 228–29). In his introduction, "On Translating Martial," Whigham notes that translation of Martial reached a low point during the Victorian period, because of a diminished interest in ordinary life in classical times and a low esteem for the epigram itself as a form (35–38). All 16 of RLS's translations appear in Janet Adam Smith's edition of RLS's *Collected Poems* (2nd ed., 1971), 292–300, without the Latin but with helpful notes quoting RLS's own comments on Martial; she dates these translations from the time of RLS's residence in Hyères, 1883–84 (522–24). RLS's marked copy of a French edition and translation of Martial, *Œuvres Complètes* (2 vols., 1864), is at Yale (Beinecke 2558); a facsimile of one page is in the Beinecke Collection catalogue, facing 779.

Sullivan, J. P., and A. J. Boyle, eds. *Martial in English*. London: Penguin, 1996. All sixteen of RLS's translations are included (255–63), but without the Latin texts or Janet Adam Smith's helpful comments. In his "General Introduction," Sullivan mentions RLS's comments on Martial in "Books Which Have Influenced Me" (1887) and remarks that in his liking for Martial RLS was unusual for his time.

Smith, Janet Adam, ed. *A Child's Garden of Verses . . . With nine poems not published in prior editions*. San Francisco: The Press in Tuscany Alley, 1978. Designed and printed by Adrian Wilson, this edition includes from the Yale copy of *Penny Whistles* (Beinecke 191) the nine poems that appeared in the trial edition but were not published in *A Child's Garden of Verses* (1885). Smith published one of them, "Lesson on the Sea," in the notes to her edition of RLS's *Collected Poems* (2nd ed., 1971), 552–53; the others had previously appeared only in a privately printed edition by L. S. Livingstone (1912) and in the catalogue of the Widener Collection at Harvard (1913).

Lewis, Roger C., ed. *The Collected Poems of Robert Louis Stevenson*. Edinburgh: Edinburgh UP, 2003. RLS published three volumes of poetry during his lifetime: *A Child's Garden of Verses* (1885), *Underwoods* (1887), and *Ballads* (1890). From manuscripts and contents-lists that he sent back to England for that purpose in 1894, a fourth collection, *Songs of Travel*, was published posthumously in the Edinburgh Edition (1895). In November 1914, 20 years after his death, the sale of Stevenson's manuscripts, notebooks, paintings, books, and other possessions by his step-daughter Belle (Isobel Field), after her mother's death earlier that year, made available outside the family the makings of what eventually became a fifth collection of poems. These poems were chiefly in notebooks and in a number of fair-copy collections consisting of from half a dozen to a dozen poems written on folio-size folders, no doubt for private circulation. None of these poems was ever chosen by Stevenson for publication, although he must have looked at some or all of them once, or even several times, in getting together the poems for *Underwoods* and the volume that became *Songs of Travel*, and at other times as well. He also annotated many of them, no doubt some years after they were written, with the place of composition and often derisory comments: "Bon," "Pas mal," "Bien mal," or "Tout à fait intolérable" (examples quoted in Smith, 44).

Poems from these manuscript sources first appeared in two volumes printed in 1916 by the Bibliophile Society, Boston, edited by George S. Hellman: *Poems by Robert Louis Stevenson: Hitherto Unpublished*. A third such volume appeared in 1921. The transcriptions were inaccurate, as were many of the presumed dates of composition, and the biographical and other commentaries that were also supplied have been discredited or superseded. Stevenson's stepson Lloyd Osbourne, always a step behind Hellman, regained some control by publishing the texts from the first two Bibliophile Society volumes, in consecutive order just as he found them but without the commentaries or dates, as *New Poems* (1918). Four years later, after the third Bibliophile Society volume appeared, he published all three volumes together, also without the commentaries or dates but with a few uncollected poems from other sources, in the Vailima Edition, 1922, and then separately as the *Complete Poems* and in the Tusitala Edition, both of these in November 1923.

Stevenson also included poems in his letters and wrote them in dedications, prefaces, and presentation inscriptions. At Davos during 1881 and 1882, he and his stepson Lloyd Osbourne also printed a number of his poems in booklet form for friends and family, efforts that eventually appeared in facsimile in the Edinburgh Edition in 1898 and separately as *A Stevenson Medley* in 1899. At the same time, in Davos he also wrote two collections of satirical poems. He sent one collection—the droll and savage sonnet sequence "Brasheana" about the recently deceased Edinburgh barkeeper Thomas Brash—home to Edinburgh, where his friend Charles Baxter had some of them set in type and had proofs made, from which source they were printed in the *Catalogue* (1912) of the Widener Collection at Harvard.

This is the context of Janet Adam Smith's edition, *Robert Louis Stevenson: Collected Poems* (London: Rupert Hart-Davis, 1950; 2nd ed., 1971), which in 1950 was the first new edition of Stevenson's poems in 25 years. It is a remarkable and engaging achievement. Smith presented complete, carefully transcribed, annotated versions of the poems in the four volumes published or begun during Stevenson's lifetime, and she brought dates, order, annotations, and (whenever manuscripts made this possible) accuracy to the jumble of the posthumous poems. She also reprinted the Davos booklets with the woodcuts in facsimile as illustrations. Of the 243 so-called New Poems in the Tusitala Edition, Smith chose 105, slightly fewer than half, corrected many of the texts, and put them into chronological order in two groups, before and after 1880, and a third group called Light Verse. She also published five of the sonnets on Brash and a score of other poems, dedications, and occasional pieces. Her edition, which was also attractively designed and printed, is a pleasure to read and hold; it defined the Stevenson poetical canon, and it has set the standard for a generation. She also gave a detailed, lucid account of the remarkable (and appalling) history of the dispersal and publication of the manuscripts of Stevenson's poems after 1914.

The first thing that strikes an intending purchaser of *The Collected Poems of Robert Louis Stevenson*, edited by Roger C. Lewis for the Edinburgh University Press (2003), is how different it is from Smith's *Collected Poems*—in particular, how unattractive and heavy it is. Between the covers, the typography and page layout—the book design—at first seem innocuous. But there are many more lines on the page than RLS ever wished to see on a page of verse. The type is too small to hold its own consistently against the white space on pages of such width, and when the matter is prose, as in the Introduction, the lines are too long for easy reading. The pages are thin enough for show-through to be noticeable more than occasionally, especially in the reproductions of the Davos woodcuts. And except in the poems in *Ballads* no line numbers appear, a major nuisance when one tries to associate notes and variants with poems presented many pages away.

The contents are mostly the same as in Janet Adam Smith's edition: the four authorized volumes, the Davos booklets, and 91 of the 243 posthumously published or uncollected poems in New Poems. This last inclusion brings the number of these poems that are now available in other than their original printed form to about sixty percent of the whole (147/243): 56 of them uniquely in Smith, including the translations from Horace and Martial, 41 others uniquely in Lewis, 50 poems in both. Lewis also includes 29 poems from other sources, more than half of them also available in Smith or in Stevenson's letters. The significant new items in Lewis's collection are the remaining poems in "Brasheana" (304–07), the comic glee of which is much diminished, unfortunately, by the absence of RLS's own drawings in his letters or a facsimile of the much grander typography that Baxter obtained; the hitherto unpublished (and much less funny) series "Casparadies," on the merchants of Davos (307–12); 41 more of the poems in New Poems; a thoughtful speculative reconstruction of the process by which "In Memoriam F. A. S." (*Underwoods*, I.xxvii) seems to have evolved (424–27); and five pages of long and short unused verses gleaned from RLS's notebooks for *A Child's Garden of Verses* (346–50). It would have been helpful, especially in understanding these last two pieces, if Lewis had mentioned that facsimiles of more than two-dozen pages of the notebook from which these and other variant readings come (RLS/C, at Yale) are available in the Boston Bibliophile Society volume, *Stevenson's Workshop*, ed. William P. Trent (1921). Inaccurate though the transcriptions and commentaries in them often are, these Bibliophile Society volumes are of great value and interest for their many facsimiles.

The big difference between Lewis's edition and Janet Adam Smith's is in the space given to content other than poems: to introductions, variants, and notes. In Smith's edition, the poems-to-comments ratio is three to one: 73% of her active pages (392/536) contain poems by Stevenson. In Lewis's edition, this ratio falls to near-equality: only 314 of his 611 comparable pages, 51%, contain poems. The other 297 are variants and commentary. Lewis's edition is, of course, more ambitious and inclusive: more scholarly, one might say. The trouble is that, in Lewis, this additional content is at times of limited or no value; it is also, unfortunately often, presented in an inconvenient way.

The Explanatory Notes, a mere ten pages, are all but invisible near the very end of this 641–page book. And none of them is so long that it would have caused harm if all of the notes, Textual and Explanatory alike, had been put into a single list called Notes. Such a consolidation would have helped readers who might not at first have thought to look in the Textual Notes, rather than in the Explanatory Notes, for details such as "Place/date of composition" and "Letters"—information that almost never relates to the text as such. The running heads for this single list of Notes could then have shown the page numbers on which the corresponding poems appear (not even the volume or topic title appears now)—always a convenience when notes and contents are separated.

If the focus had been on delivering facts to the reader rather than on adhering to certain predefined editorial categories, we would also have been spared (for example) such convoluted annotation paths as the following: line 14 of "To Andrew Lang" in *Underwoods* ends with the word "sanhedrin" followed by a comma, as it does in the first edition (82). Lewis's Textual Note more than 300 pages away indicates that in RLS's manuscript the word is spelled "sanhedrim" and is not followed by a comma, and then he adds: "see Explanatory Note, p. 624" (409). Here we are told: "p. 82 *sanhedrin*: RLS wrote 'sanhedrim,' a common misspelling: it was the supreme Jewish court of Jerusalem, responsible for the trial of Christ" (624). How much more pleasant it would have been for readers to have had all of this information in one place.

Another serious problem is that the volume itself seems to have been published without much concern for accuracy or for details. In the Chronology (xxi–xxii), there is no mention of *Travels With a Donkey* (1879), although Lewis later refers to it in his notes; and half a dozen errors are still present from Catherine Kerrigan's edition of *Weir of Hermiston* published eight years before, several of them no more accurate in their rewritten versions than they were originally. Stevenson was not "served with" The Sedition (Samoa) Regulation in 1892, it was merely published. *More New Arabian Nights* and *The Dynamiter* are the title and the sub-title of the same book, not one book "and" another, "both with Fanny." These are lapses in the general editing, but there are other more specific errors.

Half a dozen pages scattered here and there in Lewis's presentation of *A Child's Garden of Verses* are devoted to black-and-white illustrations. Except that, on the back of the title page, credit for these is given to the Beinecke Rare Book and Manuscript Library at Yale, Lewis says nothing at all about these illustrations, not even who drew them: not on the pages themselves, nor in the list of illustrations, nor, I believe, anywhere else. The decision to include illustrations, at all, is itself an odd one, as *A Child's Garden of Verses* never appeared in an illustrated edition during Stevenson's lifetime. In addition, a full stop always mistakenly follows the first name of RLS's friend, the American painter and book illustrator Will H. Low, perpetuating a usage that RLS himself accepted in *Underwoods*, may have wrongly supposed correct—or, more likely, didn't even notice (79–80, viii, 397, 512). Janet Adam Smith simply emends this error. Nor does it build confidence in the editor's knowledge of

Stevenson, or of Scottish geography, to read of RLS's trips to "lighthouse sites near Fife, Anstruther, Wick and Earraid" (552). As RLS's own essays on "The Education of an Engineer" make clear, Fife is a region—an ancient kingdom, in fact, not a town—north across the Firth of Forth from Edinburgh. Anstruther is a harbor town on "The Coast of Fife" (RLS uses this phrase as the subtitle of one of his two essays), and the engineering work there, as it was at Wick, was not on a lighthouse but on a harbor breakwater. Only at Earraid was a lighthouse in question, the islet being used as the shore station for building the Dhu Heartach lighthouse at sea.

The fundamental claim of any edition, no matter how elaborate or humble it may be, is that it puts in front of readers a text that the author would wish us to be reading. The greatest problem with Lewis's edition of Stevenson's poems is that he fails to convince us that this is so. In this edition we find not Stevenson's texts but versions of them that again and again differ, without notice or explanation, not only from the received versions but even from the versions that Lewis himself says that he is following. In addition, the choices of copy-texts and individual readings alike disclose an editorial system that seems mainly based on the editor's intuition. And the presentation of variants, especially when manuscripts exist, is haphazard and uninformative. Not only can we not trust the accuracy or the authority of Lewis's readings; we cannot even discover what the correct readings might be.

In the preface to his Textual Notes, Lewis tells us that "[a] full list of variants is provided"—except that "spelling mistakes, Americanisations, and errors in grammar, syntax, and punctuation have been silently corrected, although RLS's idiomatic punctuation has been retained" (340). Whatever this means—how ordinary punctuation errors, for example, can be distinguished from RLS's "idiomatic" usages, or whether normalizing spelling is a good idea in the case of a writer who learned English in Scotland, or whether it is ever wise, in editing poetry, to correct seeming errors in grammar, syntax, and punctuation—this approach tells us nothing definite about what has been "silently corrected," why, or how much of this silent correction was needed. What Lewis gives us with one hand—an actual list of variants—he takes away with the other, offering an indeterminate list of exceptions.

The differences are not trivial. In *A Child's Garden of Verses*, for example, Lewis passes over—in silence—noticeable differences between his versions and his own copy text, the first edition. In line 20 of "Travel," in the phrase "negro hunters' huts," he changes, without explanation or comment, the first edition "hunters'" (plural) to "hunter's" (singular). Commas present in the first edition at the end of line 1 in "The Land of Counterpane" and at the end of line 44 in "To Minnie" are absent from Lewis's edition—again, without explanation or any apparent need due to "errors in grammar, syntax, and punctuation." It is not mentioned that the title "A Song of the Road," used for the poem in *Underwoods* that, in the manuscript, RLS calls "The Gauger's Flute," is not RLS's title but was supplied by William Ernest Henley when, in what Henley called "a sudden emergency," he had to publish it, without an intended illustration, to fill space in the *Magazine of Art* (Henley to RLS, 18 November 1885, Beinecke 4851). Nor was the poem written at Hyères (397). Even as Lewis prints it, "Forest of Montargis, 1878" appears at the end as the location and date (74), and in his note Lewis makes clear that this information is correct (398). In line 14 of "Ticonderoga," Lewis changes, again without comment or explanation, the word "mist" (singular) to "mists" (plural), even though the singular is used again five lines later and appears in the *Scribner's Magazine* version and in both the American and the English first editions. In line 24, he changes "a man of a score"—a man among twenty—to "a man of score," again without comment or explanation and again in spite of the unanimity of all of the previously published texts. King Kalakaua of Hawaii's name is misspelled, both in the title of the poem dedicated to him and in the table of contents (187, x).

Quotation marks appear before all three stanzas of "Since I am sworn to live my life" (266), first published in Graham Balfour's *Life*, I, 110, and later among the New Poems (Tusitala Edition, LXXVIII, 3), as if the poem were spoken by an imaginary speaker, not the poet. In fact, the quotation marks come not from the poem but from the house style used for quotations in the American edition of Balfour's *Life*, (I, 131), which Lewis, for reasons unknown, follows and always cites instead of the English edition. The English edition has quotation marks only at the beginning and end. The manuscript and the version in New Poems, of course, have nothing. In addition to the manuscripts at Yale on which Lewis relies for "The wind blew shrill and smart" (268–69; New Poems, Tusitala Edition, XC), there is also, among the many RLS items at the State University of New York—Buffalo, a notebook version of the first two stanzas. Additional manuscripts of three of the poems in *Songs of Travel*—"To My Old Familiars," "The tropics vanish, and meseems that I," and "The House of Tembinoka"—are in the Syracuse University Library. These other manuscript versions are not used or even mentioned in Lewis's collations. Again and again, Lewis promises one thing and does much less, and in so doing he undermines the claim of his edition to present Stevenson's poems as he wrote them or as he wished to see them published.

Fair-copy manuscripts by Stevenson exist for most of the poems published posthumously in *Songs of Travel*, and, according to Lewis, Stevenson's friend Sidney Colvin not only was "[in the] habit of ignoring the poet's [RLS's] stated intentions" (483), but also "inflicted on RLS's texts, especially on his letters, . . . bowdlerisations, pedantic 'corrections' and assorted anilities" (478). Given this account of Colvin's supposedly chronic misbehavior in relation to RLS's texts, one would expect that in working with *Songs of Travel* Lewis, as an editor, would often have had to use the manuscripts to rescue RLS's intentions and words from his friend's corruptions. In fact, this is not the case.

In his Textual Notes, Lewis identifies only 26 instances in the slightly more than 1,000 lines of verse that comprise *Songs of Travel* in which his reading differs from what Colvin published in the Edinburgh Edition. And in eleven of these instances the reading that Lewis himself adopts in preference to the Edinburgh Edition is the reading that later appears in the 1896 book-form edition, also prepared by Colvin. The changes are not only few, they are also small. Only two of the 26 differences are in wording. Both of these are changes in a single word, and both are easy to attribute to the difficulty of reading Stevenson's hand: "Bake" for "Bathe" in line 20 of "To My Wife," following the manuscripts (Lewis says nothing about what the other printed versions have); "nuzzle" for "nozzle" in line 10 of "Mater Triumphans," following the manuscripts and the 1896 edition. Another change is that in line 31 of "If This Were Faith," where Lewis prints "forever" as a single word, as in the manuscripts and the Thistle Edition, rather than as two words. But in ''(To the tune of Wandering Willie)'' he does the opposite, following the Edinburgh Edition in giving ''for ever'' as two words and rejecting the single-word variant ''forever'' in the Thistle Edition. All of these changes are made silently and without explanation. The three stanzas in ''I know not how it is with you'' are numbered, following the manuscript but none of the printed versions, again without comment. And there are other such changes, including thirteen in punctuation.

The only other differences between what Colvin has and what Lewis adopts are, first, that Lewis includes two poems—''Ditty (To an air from Bach)'' and ''The Last Sight''—that Colvin did not include in the Edinburgh Edition. Janet Adam Smith included these poems also, and in this she and Lewis both follow the choice that was in fact first made in the Thistle Edition. Second, Lewis prints ''Dark Women'' as a poem of eight eight-line stanzas. Colvin published only the second and third stanzas of this poem, according to Lewis ''suppressing the remainder'' (489). There is nothing in Lewis's confusing presentation of the manuscripts, however, to suggest that any late copy ever had more than six stanzas. He himself says that the stanzas that he prints as the fourth (''Dark as a wayside gypsy'') and fifth (''Tiger and tiger lily'') ''appear only in . . . an early sixty-eight line draft,'' Beinecke 6136 (489–90). Lewis, not Colvin, may be the editor who is ignoring Stevenson's intentions here. He says nothing to explain why the absence of these two stanzas from all of the later manuscripts does not suggest that Stevenson himself rejected them. Nor does he seem interested in the possibility that Colvin's ''suppression'' of four stanzas from the later manuscript versions occurred because Colvin was aware of having added another poem on Fanny, ''To My Wife'' (it is not mentioned in any of RLS's own lists), and therefore decided to include only two stanzas from ''Dark Women,'' which also refers to her, albeit obliquely—or even because Colvin felt that they were not very good.

The truth is that in preparing *Songs of Travel* Colvin followed RLS's manuscripts carefully, and that in preparing the separate book-form edition in 1896 he seems to have been trying to improve even the Edinburgh Edition text. Lewis's harsh words therefore seem undeserved. Not only does Colvin follow the manuscripts, but Lewis himself almost always follows Colvin.

One of the most important tasks of an editor is choosing the copy-text. According to Lewis, however, there is ''no alternative'' to making the 1895 Edinburgh Edition the copy-text of *Songs of Travel*. ''RLS explicitly designated Colvin as the editor of his verses, sending him finished copy and leaving the final ordering up to him'' (482). Even so, readers of a full-dress edition such as this one might wish to learn why, since both are posthumous and both were done by Colvin, an alternative to the 1895 Edinburgh Edition does not exist in Colvin's 1896 separate book-form edition, which incidentally was chosen by Janet Adam Smith for her copy-text—all the more so in light of the fact that in 11 of the 26 instances in which Lewis's own text differs from the 1895 Edinburgh Edition, it is the 1896 book-form edition that he follows instead. We also have final manuscripts of nearly all of these poems, and several possible tables of contents, all sent home by Stevenson with plans for publication. So it is not obvious why one should make either of Colvin's published versions the copy-text—especially if, in Lewis's words, Stevenson's own ''idiomatic punctuation'' matters. One can almost always start with Stevenson's own fair-copy manuscript instead. Unfortunately, Lewis says nothing about any of these questions of copy-text.

Moreover, Lewis's presentation of variants appears haphazard. In the 144-line poem "The Woodman," for example, the Thistle Edition text differs in six places from the version in Lewis's edition. Despite his promise to list all significant variants, Lewis mentions only one such difference, that there is a blank line after line 33. He does not mention that in line 39, where he has "And bade," the Thistle Edition has "And bid." The 1896 book-form edition differs in nine places from his version. Lewis mentions only two, and though he comments that in line 73 the spelling "sylvan" appears in the 1896 version instead of "silvan," he does not remark that in line 62 "Brier" appears instead of "Briar." Lewis's treatment of variants, in this instance, excludes from his edition material that might have linguistic as well as literary interest: Ian McLaren's Kailyard novel *Beside the Bonny Brier Bush* appeared in 1894, and RLS too was a Scot. No mention at all is made of the proofs of "The Woodman" that Edmund Gosse was sent for the Edinburgh Edition, not even to say (if this is the case) that they contain no variants. About the state of the poem in this source we cannot learn anything.

Most important of all, Lewis mentions neither of the differences between his own edition's version of "The Woodman" and his copy-text. In the Edinburgh Edition, as in the Thistle Edition, there is a blank line after line 13. In Lewis's edition, as in the 1896 book-form edition, this line is the last on the page. There is no indication either in the spacing of the next page or in Lewis's notes that there should be a blank line at this point or that the blank line in the Edinburgh and Thistle editions has been omitted editorially by Lewis. (Lewis calls these stanza breaks, but the poem is not stanzaic. The same obliteration of a line break at the foot of a page occurs after the first six lines of "The House Beautiful," 75–76.) For the first two words in line 39, Lewis has "And bade"—as in the 1896 book-form edition. The Edinburgh Edition and the Thistle Edition both begin "And bid."

Lewis's handling of the manuscript evidence is even less illuminating. All manuscripts are treated alike, as mere sources of variants rather than as links in a creative chain from inspiration to publication. At the beginning of his notes for "The Woodman," Lewis lists four manuscripts, all of them at Yale, but he does not describe any of them or suggest a sequence among them. Only from Lewis's lists of variants can we gather, not without effort, that at least three of the manuscripts are partial and that the fourth is probably complete. Lewis's unwillingness merely to describe the manuscripts is distressing. He obscures what ought to be clear.

Elsewhere than in the notes to "The Woodman" Lewis describes a bound volume at Yale (Beinecke 7065) that contains fourteen manuscript poems and proofs of twelve others (460, 480). No doubt, as Lewis suggests, this is the mixed collection that RLS described on 26 November 1890 when he sent this material to Scribner's for possible addition to the volume *Ballads* (Letter 2278). Despite the possible importance of this submission in helping us understand the history of the poem, nowhere in the Textual Notes to "The Woodman" does Lewis mention that "The Woodman" was among these 26 poems sent in November 1890. This fact can be found only in the general "History of Composition and Publication" for *Songs of Travel* as a whole (480). Here too one might brush aside this lapse as a mere inconvenience, an annoying defect of cross-reference or bad arrangement. But it is a major disservice that Lewis also never mentions which of the four manuscript versions of "The Woodman" (from all of which he gives variants) is the one that is in this bound volume—it is the manuscript Beinecke 7181–or that this manuscript has at the top the number VII, no doubt indicating the place that RLS then thought it might have in a sequence. Lewis makes none of these connections, nor does he make it possible for his readers to make them. Instead, he gives only a list of the poems in the bound volume. "The Woodman" is indeed the seventh, but as far as can be told from Lewis's edition, this placement may be due only to the whim of the unknown compiler of the bound volume. The truth is that RLS himself numbered these poems.

In his brief catalogue entry of Beinecke 7181, G. L. McKay observes that this manuscript of "The Woodman" is numbered at the top "VII," that it has 144 lines and thus is complete, and that "the text of this manuscript is recorded almost verbatim in *Songs of Travel*." Although Lewis himself does not report these facts, his list of variants confirms McKay's summary. According to Lewis's own collation, there are only twelve differences between Beinecke 7181 and the Edinburgh Edition text that Lewis follows, and only four of these are other than differences in punctuation or (in one instance) capitalization. Possibly, then, it was this manuscript that was used in preparing "The Woodman" for publication, just as McKay appears to suggest. Even if it was not, RLS thought well enough of it to include it among the manuscripts that he sent to Scribner's in 1890, and by his own numbering to place it seventh in the sequence.

Not only is information tracing the chronological (and creative) chain usually absent in this edition, inaccurate statements are not uncommon. All of the possibly relevant published versions of "The Woodman" appeared posthumously, beginning in January 1895 (before the Edinburgh Edition) with the poem's publication in *The New Review*, of which RLS's friend W. E. Henley was then editor. This published version, Lewis maintains, "deserves attention as copy for it was sent by RLS to Henley" (526). This is an odd comment, as no reference to "The Woodman"—or to any other poems by RLS—occurs in either side of the correspondence between RLS and Henley during the 1890s. Lewis offers no citation or even a date when RLS sent the supposed "copy for it" to Henley, nor does he say where he thinks the "copy" that Henley used might be today: whether it is Beinecke 7181 (seemingly the only complete manuscript version) or a printed copy possibly made by Scribner's—or another manuscript version that has not survived. In fact, the version in *The New Review* almost certainly comes from what must have been a version sent to Henley by Colvin in late 1894, probably a typescript or proof copy that included the dozen changes that Colvin himself had made in preparing the poem for publication in the Edinburgh Edition.

At times, a poorly done edition from a well-known press is mistakenly assumed to be definitive and for a while lessens the possibility of support being given for a truly authoritative work. Unfortunately, in my opinion, Roger Lewis's edition is an example of this. The job of editing Stevenson's poetry needs to be done again—properly and inclusively, and in a manner that enables it to supersede Janet Adam Smith's edition first published more than 50 years ago.

Anobile, Richard J., ed. *Rouben Mamoulian's Dr. Jekyll & Mr. Hyde*. New York: Universe Books, 1975. Anobile's well-produced picture book consists of more than 1,500 individual frames and, with them, the complete dialogue of the influential Paramount film released on 31 December 1931, starring Fredric March, who shared the

Academy Award as best actor for his performance. This presentation makes it easy to see why *Dr. Jekyll and Mr. Hyde* is today so often associated with sexual excess. Not only are women characters added, as they had been in Thomas Russell Sullivan's 1887 stage adaptation for Richard Mansfield during Stevenson's lifetime. The camera lingers on them provocatively. In his introduction, Anobile notes that Metro-Goldwyn-Mayer bought the rights (and the prints) of this version "and condemned it to almost total obscurity"—this in hopes of aiding the success of their 1941 version starring Spencer Tracy and Ingrid Bergman. The 1931 version was not shown publicly again until it was rescued from M-G-M for a 1967 tribute to Mamoulian, and by then two whole scenes had been cut and others edited—seemingly first, before its original release, to get the approval of the National Board of Review, the so-called Hays Office, certifying that it was not indecent, and possibly again, later, to shorten its running time. These cuts have been restored in later versions such as the MGM/UA Home Video videocassette release (1989), which runs 97 minutes including seventeen minutes of "previously censored material"; the Warner Home Video digital video disc release (2004), which includes this restored version, the 1941 M-G-M version and its theatrical trailer, and a seven-minute Bugs Bunny cartoon, *Dr. Jekyll's Hide* (1955). The film itself is discussed, with a plot summary of the cuts, in Virginia Wright Wexman, "Horrors of the Body: Hollywood's Discourse on Beauty and Rouben Mamoulian's *Dr. Jekyll and Mr. Hyde*," *Dr. Jekyll and Mr. Hyde After One Hundred Years*, ed. Veeder and Hirsch (1988), 283–307.

Geduld, Harry M., ed. *The Definitive Dr. Jekyll and Mr. Hyde Companion.* New York: Garland, 1983. To a reprint of the story without annotations or any indication of the source of the text, Geduld adds an eclectic and intriguing range of supplementary materials. Poe's "William Wilson" (1839) is followed by a curious modern story by Thomas Berger (1924–), "Professor Hyde," first published in *Playboy*, December 1961, and collected in *The Fully Automated Love Life of Henry Keanridge and 12 Other stories* (Chicago: Playboy Press, 1971). A long excerpt from Ralph Tymms's excellent study of nineteenth-century psychological theories, *Doubles in Literary Psychology* (Cambridge: Bowes and Bowes, 1949), is followed by four pages from Malcolm Elwin on the composition of the story (1950) and the first account of the manuscript, Eugene Limedorfer's sometimes misleading article, "The Manuscript of *Dr. Jekyll and Mr. Hyde*," *Bookman* [New York] 12 (1900): 52–58. Two paragraphs by W. H. Stevenson on "The Surname Jekyll" consolidate four articles originally in *Notes and Queries*, 18 November and 9 December 1899, and 24 February and 14 April 1900. Versions of the name, in England, are known in documents as early as the Domesday Book (1086). It is of Breton origin, *Judic-hael*, and its roots combine words for "battle" (Indo-Germanic *iudh*) and "generous man" (Celtic *hael*). This is followed by five paragraphs from Masao Miyoshi, *The Divided Self: A Perspective on the Literature of the Victorians* (New York: New York UP, 1969), suggesting that the name brings to mind the idea of "the hidden '*je*' in each of us" and that the story depicts conflict between "[t]he hidden '*Je*' . . . [and] the social 'I' "—a suggestion as to the name that was first made in Joseph J. Egan, "The Relationship of Theme and Art in *The Strange Case of Dr. Jekyll and Mr. Hyde*," *English Literature in Transition*, 9 (1966): 28–32.

Criticism is represented by three selections. The first is a long comment by Theodore Watts-Dunton (who wrote favorable reviews of *Kidnapped* and *David Balfour*) deploring the fact that a noble, almost timeless, idea is in Stevenson's hands degraded into "a hideous tale of murder and Whitechapel mystery" revealing "[a] morbid strain which is so often associated with physical disease." This is quoted without an indication of its source by James Douglas in his memoir, *Theodore Watts-Dunton, Poet, Novelist, Critic* (London: Hodder and Stoughton, 1904), from which source it appears here. The second is Irving S. Saposnik's "The Anatomy of *Dr. Jekyll and Mr. Hyde*," first published in *Studies in English Literature*, 11 (Autumn 1971): 715–31, and reprinted in his *Robert Louis Stevenson* (New York: Twayne, 1974). The third is an essay by Mark Kanzer, M. D., "The Self-Analytic Literature of Robert Louis Stevenson," in George B. Wilbur and Warner Muensterberger, eds., *Psychoanalysis and Culture* (New York: International Universities P, 1951)—a confident psychiatric reading finding in the story "parricidal thoughts," "symptoms of a masturbatory conflict," "phallic-voyeuristic fantasy," and "typical symbols of castration anxiety."

Four out-of-the-way works make up an intriguing section titled "Jeux d'Esprit." The first is a reprinting of "The Untold Sequel of the Strange Case of Dr. Jekyll and Mr. Hyde" (Boston: Pinckney Publishing Company, [*ca.* 1890], attributed in other sources to Francis H. Little; Beinecke 1880 is a version of this published as an advertisement by the John H. White Company, manufacturers of wood-working machinery, Dover, NH, 1890). Skeptical about Jekyll's account of his self-transformations into Hyde, Utterson investigates further and finds Jekyll's murdered body in a secret passageway leading from the house. With it is a manuscript confession by Edward Gorman Hyde, an opium-addicted American who had met Jekyll in New York and had been engaged by him as a kind of caretaker while he made his experiments. Unable to control himself, Hyde had killed Sir Danvers Carew and, later, Jekyll himself. A former actor, Hyde visits Lanyon and pretends to turn himself into Jekyll, thereby concealing the murder, and at Lanyon's request he writes an account of the experiments. His addiction has returned, however, and he does not expect to live much longer. The second piece in this section, "The Stranger Case of Dr. Hide and Mr. Crushall: A Rum-antic Story [by] Robert Bathos Starving Son" (London: Benington & Co., n.d. [1886–87]), is a would-be-humorous account of Mr. Utterduffer, lawyer, Dr. Layiton, M. D., and Dr. Hide, F. R. S., "dear old pals in the Autumn of life." Hide has the misfortune to invent a pair of immensely strong electrical legs, which he embeds in a pair of trousers that by mistake he leaves with a pawnbroker. The trousers are placed on a dummy for display, but the dummy soon gets loose and nothing can prevent its kicking everything in its path, causing havoc all over London. Hide is able to get the contraption home with him, where, overcome by disgrace and failure, he sets fire to the dummy, the trousers, and himself. (The entry of this work the British Library catalogue differs slightly from Geduld's citation in giving the purported author's name as Stavingson and the publisher as Bevington.) The third selection is Munro Leaf's "The Strange Case of Dr. Jekyll and Mr. Hyde By Robert Louis Stevenson, a thrifty Scotsman who made one character do the work of two" (*American Magazine* 121: May 1941, 104) is a trifling, jocular, brief summary of the story offering the moral: "One can't live as cheaply as two." (Leaf's similar condensation of *Treasure Island* appeared in the same magazine in September 1940.)

Robert Bridges's "Jekyll Meets Hyde" (Geduld's title) is an excerpt from Bridges's dialogue, *Overheard in Arcady* (London: J. M. Dent, 1894), in which various Stevenson characters discuss themselves and their creator. It is a thoughtful, short dialogue between Jekyll and Hyde in Jekyll's laboratory eight years after the story was published. Although Bridges cannot have known this, the dialogue is exactly in the manner of Stevenson's own "The Persons of the Tale" in which Captain Smollett and Long John Silver discuss *Treasure Island* just before RLS begins writing the next-to-last chapter. Although written earlier, RLS's dialogue was not published until 1895. To Jekyll's praise of RLS for depicting human beings as mixtures of good and evil, Hyde *"with a satirical smile"* responds: "As a man wholly wicked I approve of that. Nothing will so rapidly lead men my way as these vague distinctions." Stevenson is not a moralist, he continues: "he is a writer of stories for the sake of the story. Don't load him down with subtleties which never entered his head." When morality does appear, says Hyde, laughing, "[it's] pretty bad morality often, I'm glad to say. He has a way of making his wicked men far more attractive than his good ones—which is the way of the world, isn't it, my learned Doctor?" Even Jekyll's own philanthropy has elements from Hyde: a fear of not seeming respectable.

A substantial section titled "Jekyll and Hyde in Theatre and Film" (157–82) includes excerpts from the accounts of the original New York stage adaptation given by Paul Wilstach, *Richard Mansfield: The Man and the Actor* (1908), and by William Winter, *The Life and Art of William Mansfield* (2 vols., 1908); one review each of Mansfield's and Daniel Bandmann's stage versions and of the two film versions in 1920, starring John Barrymore and Sheldon Lewis; and Thomas R. Atkins's interview (*Film Journal*, 2 [January–March 1973]: 36–44) with the director Rouben Mamoulian about the film version starring Fredric March (1931). Appendices list editions, adaptations and parodies, sound recordings, and film, stage, and radio and television versions, including fourteen pages listing film and other variations on motifs in *Dr. Jekyll and Mr. Hyde*—lists that are almost but not quite superseded by the more recent lists by Norbert Spehner (1997) and Scott Nollen (1994), described above in the section on Reference Works.

In his introduction, Geduld emphasizes the late-Victorian scientific context—in particular, theories of multiple consciousness articulated by Pierre Janet in France and the emergence of inoculation and drug therapies for diseases of all kinds during the 1880s. "In 1881, both the germ theory and the principle of immunization were demonstrated, and between 1882 and 1885, the causes of and/or inoculations against tuberculosis, diphtheria, cholera and hydrophobia were discovered. By 1886, any medical advance by serum seemed possible" (8). This, Geduld believes, was enough to make the story "produce an immediate response of mass dread" based on "a collective fear that a Jekyll-Hyde split might really happen" (8). If there was such a response, however, it has never been documented. All one can say is that such concerns were no doubt present in the public mind, as, of course, were very many others. Geduld also offers a taxonomy of thematic elements: "*Dr. Jekyll and Mr. Hyde* is now recognizable as a prototype of innumerable stories and films in which human transformation (or some equally unnatural phenomenon) occur as the result of scientific experiment" (11). He then gives a good account of the remarkable number of variations that have appeared on the themes and sub-themes in the story.

Pinkston, C. Alex, Jr. "The Stage Premiere of *Dr. Jekyll and Mr. Hyde*." *Nineteenth Century Theatre Research* 14 (1986): 21–43. Drawing on a prompt book for the Boston and New York productions in the Mansfield Costume Collection, Smithsonian Institution, Washington, DC, Pinkston describes in detail the action, sets, lighting, entr'acte music, critical reception, and the text of Mansfield's successful adaptation. Illustrations include a billboard advertising the New York production; the well-known double-exposure photograph showing Mansfield as both Jekyll and Hyde; and five sketches of sets, all of them conventionally Victorian. Lighting effects were considerable, Pinkston writes. Jekyll delivers one soliloquy "before the red glow of the fireplace, presumably to suggest Jekyll's Faustian preoccupation with unknown and demonic forces" (27). Hyde's first appearance takes place as Jekyll's fiancee Agnes Carew is playing, at her father's request, an old Indian air that reminds him of her mother. "As Agnes played, green calcium lights overwhelmed the warmer lights, casting a green gloom across the room, and the sinister figure of Hyde emerged through the moonlit doors" (27). For the last twenty minutes, in Act IV, Mansfield held the stage alone with only one brief interruption, again with "haunting sound effects and lighting changes" (37). Pinkston also comments briefly on a version of the text in the Lincoln Center Theatre Collection, New York Public Library, surmising that it is an early draft (23–24). In their edition, *Jekyll and Hyde Dramatized* (2005), however, Martin Danahay and Alex Chisholm suggest, I think correctly, that this material is not part of a Sullivan-Mansfield version but is instead for a version by J. W. Comyns Carr first performed in 1910. The spelling is British, the theatrical agent whose name appears on the first page was not active until after 1900, and Act II, Scene 3, is a late addition to the Mansfield version (191–92).

Veeder, William, and Gordon Hirsch, eds. *Dr. Jekyll and Mr. Hyde after One Hundred Years*. Chicago: U of Chicago P, 1988. Two incomplete manuscript versions of *Dr. Jekyll and Mr. Hyde* exist. The earlier is a notebook draft, 25 leaves at Yale with one leaf in the RLS Silverado Museum; one leaf sold separately as Anderson I, 321, but untraced since then; and, at Princeton, two cancelled leaves on the same paper from what seems to be a somewhat earlier version originally in the same notebook. The other is RLS's final manuscript copy, used for setting type but with deletions, marginal changes, and insertions, 34 leaves at the J. Pierpont Morgan Library, New York, again with one leaf in the RLS Silverado Museum. In an edition of *Dr. Jekyll and Mr. Hyde* (2004) that I discuss below, Richard Dury offers a complete account of these manuscripts and complete, accurate transcriptions of them, including the correction of a number of errors in Veeder's transcription in the present volume (111–62, 167–74). Dury also comments on Veeder's mistaken assessment of the final manuscript due to his using a later, reprint edition in his collations rather than the first edition. In another edition (2003), described below, Katherine Linehan offers a selection of the manuscript readings and of changes at the proofreading stage (69–74).

Veeder's textual contribution in the present volume (3–56) has now been superseded. But his contribution was pioneering, since it was the first publication of the notebook draft, and the first publication of RLS's final manuscript after Eugene Limedorfer's "The Manuscript of *Dr. Jekyll and Mr. Hyde*," *Bookman* [New York] 12 (1900): 52–58. Like Dury, Veeder offers in a single consecutive sequence everything that survives in the two manuscript versions, presenting them side by side in two columns for the part where both versions exist—a presentation that is somewhat easier to follow than Dury's putting them one above the other. Veeder and Hirsch also present a selection of illustrations over the years (95–104)—the book was not illustrated during Stevenson's lifetime—and a fascinating collection of pictures and photographs, some of them rarely or perhaps never previously reproduced, from the stage and film versions (209–19). The rest of the volume is a collection of critical essays, on which I will comment in my section on Criticism.

Dury, Richard. "Stevenson's *Strange Case of Dr Jekyll and Mr Hyde*': Textual Variants." *Notes and Queries* 40 (1993): 490. Dury shows that William Veeder greatly overstates the number of "last-minute corrections" that RLS made between his final manuscript and the first printed edition (Veeder, 1988, 54–56; previous entry). The mistake occurs because Veeder's text for comparison is not the first English edition but a later reprint into which changes not by RLS were introduced, no doubt inadvertently. Veeder also missed four changes that were not picked up or followed in the edition that he used. As noted in my previous entry, correct lists of the changes that RLS made at this late stage appear in the editions by Linehan (2003) and Dury (2004). Dury also notes that the page numbers that Veeder gives (54–56) do not match those of the first edition but rather of the Penguin edition, and that this reprint seems to follow the Tusitala Edition, 1924 (199, n. 5).

Dury, Richard, ed. *The Annotated Dr Jekyll and Mr Hyde*. Milan: Edizioni Angelo Guerini, 1993. 2nd ed. Genova: ECIG, 2005 [2nd ed. not seen]. Dury presents a sketch of Stevenson's life and career and of the composition of *Dr. Jekyll and Mr. Hyde* followed by a detailed analysis and summary, virtually a taxonomy, of the main lines of critical discussion (15–82). This is followed by the English first-edition text with detailed annotations of words and phrases or summaries of what critics have said interpreting various passages (83–178) and a list chiefly of then recent studies (180–87). In his introduction to the criticism, Dury surveys the book's richness, resonance, and multiplicity. These ideas intersect with his analysis of the language in the concept that there is in *Dr. Jekyll and Mr. Hyde* a "pervasive indeterminacy on many levels"—an indeterminacy that can be seen concretely in "the use of obscure words and phrases, in the frequent reference to obscure and uncertain phenomena, in the mixture of positive and negative characteristics in descriptions, and in the frustration of reader expectations of consistency of presentation" (33). Dury documents these suggestions well in his annotations of words and phrases and in the sections on language, names, and motifs in his introduction. The annotations often occupy half the page, however, and especially on points of interpretation they are almost always too long. The reader's own memory and alertness to patterns and repetitions should be trusted more, and there should be fewer flies in amber: "Fink (1990:45) sees the following dialogue in its menace and power as reminiscent of Pinter, or of the dialogue between Gertrude and Hamlet in Gertrude's bedchamber" (104, n. 26). "Nabokov (1980: 182) says, however, that . . . Charyn (1981: 111) agrees . . . Herdman (1990: 136) says tantamount to the same . . . " (162, n. 33).

Much of the material in this annotated edition has quite naturally been assimilated into Dury's recent edition (2004). But the annotated text remains an independent work, with different aims, and it has not been superseded except in the text and the accounts of composition and publication. Of the second edition (2005) Dury writes, in a summary also used by his publisher:

> The second edition corrects some mistakes and includes seventy illustrations and two new Appendixes: an annotated checklist of Jekyll and Hyde Studies 1993–2004 and annotated listings of derivative works: films, stage versions, comic books, prose retellings, songs and video games.

Wolf, Leonard, ed. *The Essential Dr. Jekyll & Mr. Hyde.* New York: Penguin/Plume, 1995. This self-indulgent book consists mostly of the editor's lengthy commentary at the foot of the text pages: "Stevenson had a warm spot in his heart for housemaids" (61); "The Proximity of the words 'mystic' and 'transcendental' . . . raises the possibility that Stevenson, the prankster, is remembering the lines in Gilbert and Sullivan's *Patience*: [ten lines quoted]" (116); "Though I have stressed that women have little or no effective part in this story, it is worth noting that thin though it is, there *is* a thread of femininity woven into this fiction. As the story comes to an end, we can count a minimum of six females in it" (132). These comments could have been attached as easily to any one of a number of other passages. Better still, they should have been consolidated into points that were then made and defended, as such, in the introduction. Strewn about almost at random, supposedly as notes to the text, they often seem digressive.

Nor is the text itself well handled. The chapters are numbered, as they were not by Stevenson, and RLS's chapter titles are demoted typographically to something resembling headings. The title itself has the definite article added, as if Stevenson wrote of *The* Strange Case of Dr. Jekyll and Mr. Hyde; the source of the text is not indicated; and nothing is said about manuscript versions. A sketch of Davos appears on the fifth page of the text (35), as well as a re-touched photo of RLS's house at Bournemouth in the fourth chapter (65): the story was written at Bournemouth, but the connection with Davos, where RLS spent the winters of 1880–81 and 1881–82, is unexplained—if there is one. Three movie stills also illustrate the text, two of them quite incongruously, as the first shows Hyde attacking his Soho mistress Ivy Pierson, in the 1931 version (49), and the second shows a beautifully dressed Ingrid Bergman, in the 1941 version, in the same female role but now renamed Ivy Peterson, conversing with another beautifully-dressed young woman (120). These scenes and characters are not in the book at all, only in the movie versions. Between the chapters appear, one per chapter, full-page general comments, these being (according to the back cover, where alone this information appears) contributions by "leading contemporary horror writers including Brian Aldiss, Karl Edward Wagner, Joyce Carol Oates, and many more." Wolf's ten-page afterword follows the text itself directly, without an intervening page or even a typographical cue that it is not another chapter by RLS. Stevenson text is continually crowded aside by digressive material and by editorial and miscellaneous comment.

The introduction and the other choices of illustrations are no better; most of the supplementary texts are readily available elsewhere; and there are many errors. Wolf includes a photograph of the RLS Silverado Museum and mentions a scale model there of the bunkhouse where RLS and Fanny took up residence after their marriage in 1880; but he also gets the date, place, and the title of the presiding minister at the marriage wrong (20–21). The relevance of the bunkhouse (or of a picture of the Silverado Museum) in an edition of *Dr. Jekyll and Mr. Hyde* is not obvious; but what is most unfortunate is that during his visit there Wolf seems to have missed the fact that Silverado also has one leaf from each of the surviving manuscript versions of *Dr. Jekyll and Mr. Hyde*. Even if they were not discussed in detail—Wolf says nothing at all about the manuscripts—either of these manuscript pages would have made a much better illustration of Stevenson's handwriting than the blurry photo identified no more precisely than as "A letter from Stevenson to Henry James" (5). The letter to James in the photograph (20 November 1887, Letter 1945), written almost two years after *Dr. Jekyll and Mr. Hyde* was published, is not mentioned elsewhere in this edition, and it has nothing to do with *Dr. Jekyll and Mr. Hyde*.

Almost one-third of this edition is given to reprinting four other Stevenson stories, with no nearby indication of their dates, or that three of the four are from the summer of 1881: "Thrawn Janet," "The Body Snatcher," "Markheim," and "The Merry Men." The earlier stories are briefly mentioned in the introduction (21), but "Markheim" is discussed only in Wolf's running commentary. Except in omitting RLS's letter to J. P. Bocock (mid-November 1887, Letter 1939), the contemporary reviews (257–81) exactly duplicate the selection in Paul Maixner, ed. *Robert Louis Stevenson: The Critical Heritage* (London: Routledge, 1981) 199–231, but without Maixner's helpful commentary nor any acknowledgement of Maixner as the source. Of some interest are inferred architectural renderings of Jekyll's house by Glen Montag (249–51), and an inferred calendar of the events in the story (253–56). Also included are Wolff's own translation of Théophile Gautier's "Le Chevalier Double" (1840; 239–47), some new artwork by Michael Lark, a brief list of film and television versions by Nancy C. Hanger (283–89), and a short secondary bibliography of secondary materials (291–95).

Danahay, Martin A., ed. *The Strange Case of Dr. Jekyll and Mr Hyde*. Peterborough, Canada: Broadview, 1999. Danahay says that his edition is "a reproduction of the first edition . . . published by Longmans in January 1886" (28). But it is certainly not a reproduction in the sense that a photographic facsimile might be. It is only a lightly annotated reprint, and neither Longmans nor Scribner's ever called it "The" *Strange Case of Dr. Jekyll and Mr. Hyde*. To the story itself Danahay adds the texts of "A Chapter on Dreams" (1888), "Markheim" (1885), and Brodie's soliloquy "Rogues all, rogues all," from Act I, Scene ix, in RLS and Henley's *Deacon Brodie* (1880, 1888)—all of them welcome but all of them taken from a 1921 reprint of the Thistle Edition (27 vols., New York: Scribner's, 1895–1912) rather than any more direct sources. A selection of letters is included, among them RLS's long reply to John Addington Symonds's letter of 3 March 1886, but these come from Sidney Colvin's versions even though the Yale Letters were complete in 1995 and by 1998 were even available as the *Selected Letters*. The main cost of this is the omission of a pungent sentence of continuation after the words "but why should we be honoured?" in RLS's letter to Edmund Gosse, 2 January 1886, Letter 170: "We are whores, some of us pretty whores, some of us not, but all of us whores: whores of the mind, selling to the public the amusements of our fireside as the whore sells the pleasures of her bed."

Other background materials include excerpts from reviews, comments, and a parody in *Punch*, all of these taken from and credited to Paul Maixner, ed. *Robert Louis*

Stevenson: The Critical Heritage (London: Routledge, 1981). Considerable space (160–96) is given to excerpts on "Degeneration and Crime" (Darwin, Lombroso, Nordau), "London in the 1880s" (G. A. Sala, Arthur Ransome, William Booth, and others), and "Jack the Ripper" (newspaper accounts, three long serious poems from *Punch*, and a doctor's reminiscences). Published for the first time are excerpts from an annotated prompt copy now in the Smithsonian Institution, Washington, DC, of the first version of the Sullivan/Mansfield adaptation, which had its premiere in Boston on 9 May 1887 (147–59). The complete text is now available with many related items in Danahay and Alex Chisholm, eds., *Jekyll and Hyde Dramatized* (2005), described below. Film versions are not described, nor are there excerpts from recent criticism. Both of these choices reinforce the effect of the items that have been chosen, anchoring *Dr. Jekyll and Mr. Hyde* firmly in a gloomy, anxious, dark, late-Victorian context.

A major disappointment, especially in a book that seems intended for students, are the many errors in Danahay's biographical sketch at the beginning of his introduction (11–14). During the early 1870s, the contention between RLS and his father was not over what profession he would pursue but over religion. The L. J. R. was not "a socialist club at the university" but a secret society created in the early 1870s by RLS, his cousin Bob, and a very few other friends devoted to "Liberty, Justice, Reverence." In 1876, at Grez, Fanny and RLS met in September, not July. The cause of RLS's going to America seems to have been a sudden illness of Fanny's, not the fact that her husband had "left her," as he had not. "Across the Plains" is the second part of *The Amateur Emigrant*, not a separate work. There are no "Silverado Hills" in California. "The scene of this little book is on a high mountain," RLS himself begins *The Silverado Squatters* (1883). Mt. St. Helena is the mountain, while Silverado is the name of the abandoned mining town. At Bournemouth, in 1884, RLS and Fanny spent almost three months in various hotels and lodgings before they rented the house known as Bonallie Tower (RLS usually calls it Bonallie Towers) in early November. It was John Singer Sargent, not Whistler, who painted RLS's portrait during this Bournemouth period—more than once, in fact. RLS's father died in May 1887, not May 1886, a fact that is given correctly in the chronology a few pages later. The scheme of a South Seas cruise developed gradually over the winter of 1887–88: RLS, his mother, and Lloyd Osbourne may have "abruptly decamped" when Fanny found the yacht *Casco* for hire, but not because of a sudden change of plan. Fanny had gone ahead to San Francisco on purpose to find a yacht for the cruise. *The Master of Ballantrae* was not "written" at Saranac Lake, only begun there, and it is odd to find it the very last work of Stevenson's mentioned except in the chronology a few pages later—as if his years in the Pacific were unproductive.

Linehan, Katherine, ed. *Dr. Jekyll and Mr. Hyde*. New York: Norton, 2003. In a distinguished contribution to this well-known series—the first appearance of any work by Stevenson in a Norton Critical Edition—Katherine Linehan presents the first-edition Longmans text with good annotations and selected variants among RLS's notebook drafts, his final manuscript, and the first edition. Her presentation of the evolution of the text is especially good. She gives the complete text of both of the cancelled notebook leaves at Princeton, probably the earliest bits of manuscript that we have, and of interest also for the appearance in one of them of a young man called

Lemsome who does not appear in any later version. She then presents 23 passages, of various lengths, in which the continuous notebook draft at Yale differs notably from the final version; and then a separate list of three dozen differences between the final manuscript and the published text (63–74). Linehan publishes for the first time a letter from RLS to Thomas Russell Sullivan, postmarked 27 January 1887, commenting on Sullivan's dramatic version, this being a discovery of her own at the American Antiquarian Society, Worcester, Massachusetts; and she includes, among other excerpts from the Yale Letters, the familiar paragraph from RLS's letter to J. P. Bocock remarking, among other things, that Hyde was "not, Great Gods! a mere voluptuary" (mid-November 1887, Letter 1939; 85–86).

These are helpful inclusions, but more than a page is spent summarizing the zealous commentary by F. W. H. Myers (23 February, 1 March 1886, Letters 1559, 1567), and giving RLS's responses; Myers's commentary, itself, is in Paul Maixner, ed. *Robert Louis Stevenson: The Critical Heritage* (London: Routledge, 1981), 212–22. Myers is an interesting and not unique example of a reader treating the story as if it all actually happened, but in my opinion this space would have been much better spent on RLS's own long and brooding reply to the letter that he received from John Addington Symonds, 3 March 1886 (Letter 1571), represented now only by a two-sentence snippet (85)—all the more so as an excerpt from Symonds's letter is actually included here (98–99). This would have brought into the discussion RLS's comment in his reply to Symonds, "*Raskolnikoff* is the greatest book I have read easily in ten years," and permitted at least a note on RLS's comments about other works of Dostoevsky in a letter to Henley shortly after the writing of *Dr. Jekyll and Mr. Hyde*, a letter first published in the Yale Letters: "Dostoieffsky is of course simply immense: it is not reading a book, it is having a brain fever" (early November 1885, Letter 1487).

The choice of the Myers letters over the reply to Symonds reflects what I think is the one important defect in Linehan's edition. The literary context of *Dr. Jekyll and Mr. Hyde* is very slightly considered, and never really treated as such. It is revealing that the section titled "Literary Contexts" is subtitled "Doubles, Devils, and Monsters," as if this were all the context there is. References to Poe's "William Wilson" (1839) and Théophile Gautier's "Le Chevalier Double" (1840) appear, but elsewhere than in this literary contexts section, and then only in connection with a letter to Andrew Lang, who had asked RLS about them (Letter 1498; 81). Hogg's *The Private Memoirs and Confessions of a Justified Sinner* (1824) is briefly described and RLS's great interest in it duly noted, but only in two widely separated footnotes (49, n. 6; 125, n. 4). Dostoevsky appears only in a passing reference to his novella *The Double* (1840) in an essay by Karl Miller (125, n. 4). Three paragraphs by Jenni Calder are quoted, supposedly to fill in the Scottish background (122–28), but no historical events or persons or specific works are mentioned or quoted by her, and the segment looks mostly like a chance to mention and summarize "Thrawn Janet" and "The Body Snatcher" (126–28). Deacon Brodie and the play that RLS and Henley wrote about him are mentioned, but not in the excerpt by Calder, and then only in a footnote to "A Chapter on Dreams" (90, n. 5).

The Gothic tradition is discussed in terms of what it signifies—"The monster's body, indeed, is a machine that, in its Gothic mode, produces meaning and can represent any horrible trait that the reader feeds into the narrative"—not by giving details or samples of specific works that might have been known to Stevenson, all of this in excerpts from Judith Halberstam's *Skin Shows: Gothic Horror and the Technology of Monsters* (Durham, NC: Duke UP, 1995) 129–31. Biblical allusions are annotated but nowhere discussed.

The text of RLS's Dostoevskian story "Markheim" (1885) is included. But nothing is said anywhere about *Crime and Punishment* (1866), and "Markheim" itself is presented as exemplifying "the Victorian Market for Sensation Fiction" (103). There is some truth in this designation, but not much. The tradition (or market) of "Markheim" is actually an upscale and highly literary branch of the much larger tradition of sensation fiction. It is a genteel branch that includes Dickens's Christmas stories and Henry James's *The Turn of the Screw* (1899), but it is very far removed from the branch that RLS writes about in "Popular Authors" (1888), one paragraph of which is included here (122). Richard Dury comments on the genteel tradition in the textual notes in his 2004 edition, discussed below (187, n. 13). Unlike the psychological emphasis that one finds in "Markheim" and *Dr. Jekyll and Mr. Hyde*, however, works in the truly popular sensational tradition specialize in bold narrative strokes such as "The Discovery of the Dead Body in the Blue Marl Pit" or "Dr. Vargas Removing the Senseless Body of Fair Lilias," to quote two of RLS's own examples, and it is clearly to this other sensational tradition that one reviewer referred by condemning *Dr. Jekyll and Mr. Hyde* as "a mere bit of catch-penny sensationalism" (94). Works like G. W. M. Reynolds's *Mysteries of the Court of London* (begun 1847) offer the sort of thing that this reviewer has in mind—and, indeed, in the "Monster Man" chapters in that work (London: John Dicks, 1850; chs. 161, 167–68, 175, 184, 220), Reynolds offers a remarkable anticipation of RLS's story. "[T]here are times when I fancy that I have two minds—two minds, separate and distinct—one urging me in this direction, and the other in that," Reynolds's hero James Melmoth explains. A "species of madness" had overtaken him, he penitently reports later, "imbuing me with appalling tendencies, but not depriving me of the faculty of deploring them . . . and heaven knows the thoughts, the instincts, and the impulses which waged their tremendous warfare in my soul." High or low, Dostoevsky, Hogg, or Reynolds, the actual literary works and traditions that shape *Dr. Jekyll and Mr. Hyde*—and to which it also contributes—are all but invisible in this edition, alike in the discussion and in the examples. This absence is, of course, mostly due to space limitations. But the allocation of space also suggests that cultural, political, psychosexual, and other concerns are now very much more the lingua franca of academic and classroom discussion than are literary-historical ones.

Linehan's presentation of these other concerns is good, although here too it is limited by the extreme shortness of the selections. As in *Alice in Wonderland,* we are always being hurried along before we quite understand where we are or what we are being shown. Linehan's own critical essay, at the very end, turns out to be the longest piece in the collection except for the texts by Stevenson—and it is a mere nine pages. Not mentioned in the political section is a 22–page booklet by Arthur Law, *Strange Case of the Prime Minister and Mr. Muldoon. (With Apologies to Mr. R. L. Stevenson)* (London: Empire Printing and Publishing Company, 1886). In his entry of this item (Beinecke 1858) in the catalogue of the Beinecke Collection, G. L. McKay describes it as a "parody" in which Gladstone acquires the "power to assume the personality of a 'brutish' Irishman.'' Linehan makes a good selection from the contemporary reviews and other comments (93–104). In her rather lengthy section on stage and film versions (150–80) she rightly emphasizes the Sullivan/Mansfield play and the 1931 film; this section also includes a good collection of photographs and a useful checklist summarizing each of the main adaptations. The chronology of Stevenson's life and career is excellent, and there is a good bibliography. One curious point is that although there are pictures of the cover of the first English edition (in wrappers, 1886 altered by hand from 1885) and of an 1885 map of central London (2–3), there is no example of Stevenson's own handwriting even though many pages survive from the manuscript versions.

Dury, Richard, ed. *Strange Case of Dr Jekyll and Mr Hyde*. Edinburgh: Edinburgh UP, 2004. Richard Dury's splendid edition of *Dr. Jekyll and Mr. Hyde* consolidates and extends his own and others' work over many years on the manuscripts, the published versions, the history of composition and revision, and on the language, literary and historical contexts, and the critical interpretation of the story. He even offers fresh work of his own on publication details, quantities, and royalties, from the Longman Archive at the University of Reading (183–84), on translations of the story through 1935 and on reprint editions (163–66), even on what might have been the paper on ''subconsciousness'' that Fanny Stevenson says ''deeply impressed'' RLS when he read it ''in a French scientific journal'' (188, n. 16). This is a wonderfully thorough and successful piece of work, and it is made all the stronger by Dury's meticulous accuracy, careful footnoting, and clear, exact explanations why he offers the conclusions that he does.

Dury follows the first English edition, published by Longman's on 9 January 1886, emending it only in seven small details, all duly noted, where it seems clear that printers' mistakes were made in the punctuation (193–98). RLS, as Dury says, ''was a meticulous proofreader,'' and within two weeks of his handing over the manuscript to Longman's, as he did at the end of October 1885, he was reading proofs, thereafter making 37 small substantive changes as he did so (182, 191). As to the punctuation, between RLS's final manuscript and the first edition there is, Dury says, ''no indication at all of the MS punctuation being substituted by that of the compositors.'' The ten changes of compounds and hyphens ''could well be a house-style change that was merely accepted by Stevenson.'' But the 32 changes in punctuation ''do not represent a general substitution of one system by another'' but only scattered changes that often are not made in other instances of a similar kind; indeed, says Dury, many of them ''seem to be typical of RLS's own pointing'' (192). All of these changes are here for us to evaluate, clearly labeled and set out, as are the complete texts of all of the manuscript pages that precede publication, on which see my remarks on the edition by Veeder and Hirsch (1988), above. In his introduction, Dury comments briefly but insightfully on trends in the manuscript changes (xxii–xxiii) and traces the critical reception of the story. But most of his introduction extends his earlier annotated edition (1993) by offering a useful descriptive classification and review of dozens of critical essays, chiefly academic criticism during the last twenty years.

Dury's annotations are mostly accurate and useful. But, as in his earlier edition (1993), too often they drift from annotation into commentary and sometimes into the pursuit of a word or a phrase for its own sake. For example, annotating the phrase "a stranger in my own house" at the end of the fifth paragraph of "Henry Jekyll's Full Statement of the Case," Dury appropriately tells us that this is "a phrase which seems to have originated with Stevenson" (105, n. 61). It would have been more helpful to say what I think is meant: that although the phrase sounds biblical, and is perhaps meant to echo Moses's description of himself as "a stranger in a strange land" (Exodus 2:22), it seems to be RLS's own. There is, however, no benefit in continuing, as Dury does, to cite a somewhat similar locution in a 1917 essay, no doubt actually written in German, by Sigmund Freud, or its recent use in song titles and lyrics by music groups including "Cattle Company 1994" and "The Slugs 2000." (Dury seems to have missed other such occurrences, in songs by Foreigner, 1987, and Tower of Power, 2003.) These later occurrences are completely extrinsic to the text being annotated and matter, if they matter at all, only insofar as they can be added to other such occurrences to make a general case for the continuing influence of RLS's phrasings—a case which is, of course, not the subject here. In the same way, Dury's further remark in this same annotation that in his essay "The Foreigner at Home" (1882) RLS "portrays the Scot in England as in a similar ill-at-ease position as Hyde in Jekyll's house" highlights a similarity that has neither verbal resemblance nor relevance as an allusion.

Danahay, Martin A., and Alex Chisholm, eds. *Jekyll and Hyde Dramatized: The 1887 Richard Mansfield Script and the Evolution of the Story on Stage*. Jefferson, NC: McFarland, 2005. From the copy licensed by the Lord Chamberlain's office, 27 July 1888, in the British Library, Danahay and Chisholm present a complete script of Thomas Russell Sullivan's popular stage adaptation of *Dr. Jekyll and Mr. Hyde* for the actor Richard Mansfield. It was in this form that it was performed at the Lyceum Theatre, London, mostly in August and September 1888, a year after RLS left Britain. With this version they compare, in their notes, the two earlier versions of the Sullivan-Mansfield adaptation: a prompt copy of the first version, which had its premiere in Boston on 9 May 1887, this from a typewritten and annotated prompt copy now in the Smithsonian Institution, Washington, DC; and the revised version that was first performed at the Madison Square Theater in New York, on 12 September 1887, with RLS's wife and mother in attendance (RLS had already gone on to Newport), this as published by the American Play Company, from a copy now in the New York Public Library. Anderson 1914 has program from the performance. Excerpts from the prompt copy itself, as such rather than only as annotations, appear in Danahay's edition of *Dr. Jekyll and Mr. Hyde* (1999), 147–59, discussed above.

With this text, which occupies only 32 of the 230 pages in their edition, Danahay and Chisholm present a cornucopia of additional materials, all of them valuable and all of them helping us to see how, within little more than a year after its publication, *Dr. Jekyll and Mr. Hyde* had acquired a new, separate life of its own in Mansfield's version. These materials include biographical notes on RLS, on the playwright Thomas Russell Sullivan (1849–1916), and biographical and performance details on Mansfield (1854–1907) and his relations with RLS. The details on Mansfield come in summaries by the editors and in lengthy excerpts from Mansfield's biographers, press interviews, and reviews. Of the performance that RLS's wife Fanny and his mother saw, for example, the reviewer for the New York *Herald* had this to say, among other comments:

The play of "Dr. Jekyll and Mr Hyde" is a clever and scholarly semi-perverted amplifi-
cation in substance, of the English author's presentation in realistic mental and bodily
yet supernal shape of a spiritual dualism in man. It is interesting, fascinating, and yet at
times rather wearisome . . . . The introduction of the female element, which the original
lacks, is happy for stage purposes, but the almost entire lack of comedy is strongly felt.
(115; New York *Herald*, 13 September 1887)

Among the interviews is a lengthy written response by Mansfield (New York *Sun*, 1
January 1888; 100–102) inspired by RLS's comments then just published in "A
Chapter in Dreams" (*Scribner's Magazine*, December 1887) and in an interview with
George Iles (29 October 1887, Letter 1928, published in the Toronto *Globe*, 27 December 1887, and no doubt elsewhere). Mansfield emphasizes that even though it is
derivative, his is an original creation, different from RLS's: "A man may dream a
dream, and, telling it, another may be so powerfully impressed that he may also dream
a dream of his own, founded, however, upon the dream that has been related to him."
At the end, Mansfield's Jekyll is, in Mansfield's words,

an unhappy and a most wretched man . . . bowed down with remorse at the thought of
the monster he has conjured up betwixt himself and the beautiful woman to whom he is
engaged. . . . To me the last act is immensely touching. . . . I wish I could act it as well
as I feel it.   (100)

Although this fact is not noted here, RLS was quite at ease with these differences,
remarking in a letter to Sullivan in late January 1887, "I am not in the least struck
by the liberties you have taken; on the contrary, had I tried to make a play of it, I
should have been driven to take more: I should have had *Jekyll married*" (in Linehan,
ed., *Dr. Jekyll and Mr. Hyde*, 2003, 85).

Thirty-four pages are also given to the complete text of the actor Daniel E. Bandmann's rival adaptation, first produced at Niblo's Garden, New York, on 12 March
1888 and in London licensed by the Lord Chamberlain's office on 23 July 1888, four
days before Mansfield's version, this from a typescript now in the British Library. (If
other copies exist, none are mentioned here.) In addition to contemporary reviews
("At the Opera Comique . . . Mr. Bandmann contrived to make the whole thing out-
rageously ridiculous. His Jekyll was as nauseous as Mr. Mansfield's is maudlin, but
there any possible comparison ends."—*Times* [London], 12 August 1888; 165), the
editors also present and quote at length from the press coverage of the war of words
and litigation in London that Mansfield ultimately won. Bandmann was forced to
make do with the two performances that he was able to mount in early August 1888.

Also presented is still another stage version: the adaptation by J. W. Comyns Carr
performed by H. B. Irving at the Queen's Theatre, London, in 1910 (191–225). Irving's
father, Henry Irving, had acquired from Longman's the exclusive rights to perform
adaptations of *Dr. Jekyll and Mr. Hyde* in the United Kingdom, but he himself never
appeared in it. The Comyns Carr text is from a complete typescript in the British
Library licensed by the Lord Chamberlain's office on 31 January 1910, and the editors
believe that it is to this adaptation that the drafts in the New York Public Library
discussed by C. Alex Pinkston, Jr. (1986) are related—not to any version of the
Sullivan-Mansfield version, as Pinkston suggests.

Materials on the "Jack the Ripper" murders in Whitechapel that began in September 1888 occupy 24 pages. These include a (previously unpublished?) facsimile and transcript of a four-page letter to the City of London Police, 5 October 1888. It is signed only with the initials "M. P.," and in it the writer asserts that "when I went to see Mr Mansfield Take the Part of Dr Jekel & Mr Hyde I felt at once that he was the Man Wanted & I have not been able to get this Feeling out of my Head" (180). To judge by the excerpts from press comments and letters to the press in this collection, it was not unknown for an affinity to be seen between the Whitechapel murders and Stevenson's story, to which the play was then giving renewed celebrity. (The first of the murder victims was discovered on 7 August 1888, three days after Mansfield's opening at the Lyceum.) No doubt this contributed, in turn, to the still sometimes heard assertion that *Dr. Jekyll and Mr. Hyde*, written at the end of 1885, was "based on" the murders of Jack the Ripper, which actually occurred almost three years later, in 1888. Uses of the Jekyll-and-Hyde notion to criticize contemporary politicians in the months contemporary with the play's London run to are cited, with a reproduction of John Tenniel's drawing commenting on the darker side of Irish Home Rule, "Dr. M'Jekyll and Mr. O'Hyde" in *Punch* 95 [18 August 1888]: 167–69. Tenniel's drawing also appears in Linehan, ed. (2003), 145. Also included is an interesting—but to RLS, *Dr. Jekyll and Mr. Hyde*, and Mansfield, irrelevant—letter to the *Star*, 24 September 1888, on tenements and the Whitechapel murders, by George Bernard Shaw (who was then 32, a novelist, and a Fabian Society speaker).

From the biographical excerpts in this edition, we can piece together the details that Mansfield's run in Boston was for a week, 9–13 May 1887; that the New York run began on 12 September 1887 and was very successful; and that the London run in 1888 began on 4 August, was an expensive failure so that by the end of September Mansfield had to replace it with another play, and was followed only by a one-night benefit performance in London on 10 December (82–87). A concise, complete history of performances—not only of Mansfield's but of other versions—would have been a helpful addition, both for its exactness and especially in conveying a sense of the great spread and popularity of the stage versions. Scott Allen Nollen, *Robert Louis Stevenson: Life, Literature and the Silver Screen* (1994), 163–64, discussed above in the section on Reference Works, fills in one gap: after three weeks in New York, 12 September–1 October, Mansfield took his production on an extended tour in the United States, 3 October 1887–25 June 1888. One disappointing note is the repetition (23–25) of the error-filled sketch of RLS's life and career that first appeared in Danahay's edition of *Dr. Jekyll and Mr. Hyde* (1999).

Menikoff, Barry, ed. *Robert Louis Stevenson's Kidnapped, or the Lad with the Silver Button: The Original Text.* San Marino, CA: Huntington Library P, 1999. In this beautifully produced and illustrated volume, Barry Menikoff publishes for the first time, from RLS's own fair-copy manuscript now in the Huntington Library, the manuscript of *Kidnapped* (all but the last three chapters, which are unknown except in published form) more or less exactly as RLS submitted it in 1886 for serial publication in the children's weekly *Young Folks*. *Kidnapped* was the last of RLS's three contributions to *Young Folks*—which by then was known as *Young Folks Paper*—after *Treasure Island* (1881–82) and *The Black Arrow* (1883). It appeared serially in fourteen weekly installments from 1 May through 31 July 1886 and was published in book form by Cassell and Company on 14 July 1886–before, but not long before, the serial publication came to an end.

The manuscript of *Kidnapped*, Menikoff says, demonstrates "heavy use of the holograph during the production of the book," this being apparent in "editorial queries in the margins that sent the pages back to Stevenson for response" (lx). Menikoff does not reveal, and possibly it cannot be determined, at what stage these "editorial queries" were made: whether they came from *Young Folks*, or from Cassell's during the preparation of the first edition, or from both. Nor does he quote any of these comments or trace what might have been the results of them. Menikoff refers to the behavior of the compositors in the same way, without differentiation, remarking only that "At times, individual compositors for the periodical *Young Folks* and the first English edition punctiliously followed Stevenson's text; but in the main they altered and regularized the punctuation" (lxii). Nor does he indicate whether he thinks that the Cassell edition represents a fresh start from the manuscript, as was the case with *Treasure Island*, and may well have been the case here also, or whether the published version in *Young Folks* was the starting point for, or even the only source of, all later versions.

None of this greatly matters, however, because according to Menikoff the published versions of *Kidnapped*—in *Young Folks*, in the first edition, and beyond—are all defective, indeed so unfaithful to Stevenson's actual achievement as to make the manuscript the one version that we ought to read. About the language in the published versions, for example, Menikoff remarks:

> There is not room enough here to analyze the linguistic differences between Stevenson's manuscript and the serial and first book editions, but they are substantial and significant. Words on the holograph were deleted or altered, and others not there were added. From simple misreadings to deliberate revisions, from small changes in vocabulary to the elimination or recasting of sentences, the printed editions represent major departures from Stevenson's handwritten text. The changes bore particularly on his deliberate and pervasive use of Scots. . . . Stevenson's English was corrected as well . . . [acting to] plane the contours and coarsen the surfaces of Stevenson's style.			(lxiii–lxv)

Menikoff gives examples, but these serve mainly to clarify rather than to demonstrate his claims. Nor is one person's definition of "substantial and significant" necessarily another's, any more than there is a simple rule by which to tell when changes, singly or together, finally do amount to "major departures." We need to see and judge for ourselves on the basis of a complete comparison of (at least) the manuscript text and the first edition. Menikoff does not provide such a comparison, and rightly so. His version of *Kidnapped* is for readers rather than textual scholars. But he has made such a comparison possible. And the comparison has in fact begun—albeit with some harm to Menikoff's own rather sweeping claims.

In a series of articles published online during 2000 and 2001 in the now defunct web magazine *Capital Letters*, sponsored by the Edinburgh bookseller James Thin, the historian Owen Dudley Edwards tells the story of his own detailed comparison of the manuscript version published by Menikoff against the 1886 versions in *Young Folks* and the first edition. By his count, Edwards says, there are "at least two hundred points of difference'' between the manuscript and one or more of the published versions. The differences are slighter, and they matter much less than the changes between the serial and the book-form versions of *Treasure Island*, he remarks, suggesting that this is so because RLS was by then at ease with the form and with his publisher and typesetters.

Edwards then discusses from a literary point of view twenty or so of the passages in which the manuscript version differs from the version in *Young Folks* or the first edition, or both. He attaches great literary importance to them, but the changes in themselves are really very slight. For example, in the 35th paragraph of ch. 3 in the manuscript, David comments about his uncle Ebenezer's parsimony: "I made the best of my own way back to the kitchen, where he had lit the fire (for he kindled it afresh for every meal, to save a penny's worth of fuel in a month) and was now making the porridge'' (Menikoff, 28). In the published versions, the words in parentheses are omitted. Two paragraphs later, the paragraph ends: "if my uncle was certainly a miser, he was one of that thorough breed that make the vice respectable'' (29). In the published versions, the phrase "that make the vice respectable'' is changed to "that goes to make the vice respectable''—hardly a major change or one that merits the exegesis that Edwards devotes to it. In the eighth paragraph from the end of ch. 4 another parenthesized comment is dropped from the published versions. In the manuscript, David refers to "my uncle (or rather, what I now saw him to be, my enemy)'' (40). In the published versions, he is simply "my uncle.'' In the first paragraph of ch. 7, the complicated, long third sentence, beginning "The whole world now heaved giddily up,'' is in the manuscript divided into two sentences with a paragraph break between them (57). This might be a mere printer's error, Edwards suggests; but it also seems to me possible that RLS himself is trying to render by means of the more difficult sentence David's own confusion of mind. Nine paragraphs later, the manuscript reading "haunt the pillow of fever'' (59) is changed to "haunt the bed of fever''—a change, as Edwards notes, that is "entirely to the text's advantage: pillows were far from poor David at that point and if Stevenson did not make the change he had no need to disown it.''

Although Edwards provides other examples of minor changes, the most notable feature of his comparison is what is absent. There is not one instance in which changes to clarify or get rid of Scottish words or spellings seemed to Edwards worthy of discussion; and, as he notes, sometimes the change is in the opposite direction: "from time to time the MS 'you' is changed to 'ye.' '' Although the typesetters of both versions were in London and presumably English, they showed themselves perfectly capable of respecting and setting Scots. In his introduction, Menikoff quotes the following appeal by Alan Breck, from the manuscript version of the thirteenth paragraph from the end of ch. 26, rightly noting Stevenson's "use of a vigorous Scots vocabulary''—a usage that seems to me further enhanced by RLS's employing a great many English words (e.g., boat, shillings, world, go, do, warm, bed) that are pronounced differently in Scotland.

"If we lack that boat, we have but three shillings left in this wide world; and where to go, and how to do, and what other place there is for us except the chains of a gibbet—I give you my naked word, I kenna! Shall we go wanting, lassie? Are ye to lie in your warm bed and think upon us, when the wind gowls in the chimney and the rain tirls on the roof? Are ye to eat your meat by the cheeks of a red fire, and think upon this poor sick lad of mine, biting his finger ends on a blae muir for cauld and hunger? Sick or sound, he must aye be moving; with the death grapple at his throat he must aye be trailing in the rain on the lang roads; and when he gants his last on a rickle of cauld stones, there will be nae friends near him but only me and God.''

If there is a trend in the published versions to reduce what Menikoff calls (with some exaggeration, I think) RLS's "deliberate and pervasive use of Scots" in *Kidnapped* (lxiii), it is certainly not apparent here. The manuscript is followed exactly in the first edition: not even a comma is different. Nor was this passage changed (except to hyphenate "death-grapple") even in the Edinburgh Edition edited by Sidney Colvin (1895)—a version that is based at one remove on a marked copy of *Kidnapped* that RLS sent home in December 1893, a copy discussed in my next entry. Here, at least, the manuscript reading, with all its Scots, has been looked after punctiliously—and through no less than four separate groups of compositors, editors, and settings of type. It may not be house style, or individual compositors' style, but Stevenson's own evolving style, that we are seeing in the successive revisions of *Kidnapped*.

The great contribution of Menikoff's edition is that discussions like these are now possible. My own collations of the first edition here and there against the manuscript as it appears in Menikoff's edition confirm Edwards's general observations and also suggest that as to Scottish words and phrases *Kidnapped* was written with considerable restraint. *Kidnapped* is not a dialect story in the manner of "Thrawn Janet" (1881). What we find in *Kidnapped*, and at all stages from the manuscript forward, are "Scotticisms used deliberately"—to use RLS's own phrase in writing of *Kidnapped* to Marcel Schwob some years later when a French translation was in prospect (3 January 1891, Letter 2290). Even in dialogue, the language is not really Scots. It is English "tipped with Scots"—to use a phrase that William K. Wimsatt, Jr., once used of Burns in a graduate seminar at Yale University. RLS may have found, as Burns surely had found a century earlier, that in matters of dialect less is sometimes more.

At the very outset of RLS's writing of *Kidnapped* the editor of *Young Folks* James Henderson cautioned him against having "much broad Scotch in it . . . a little of that goes a long way with our English readers" (James Henderson to RLS, 17 March 1885, Beinecke 4356). In the manuscript, and in the successive published versions, I think we may actually be seeing the result of RLS's own discoveries (begun at the manuscript stage and continued into the published versions) that Henderson was right. Creating a strong regional flavor does not require making the text as a whole much more difficult than standard English prose. Used deliberately and, when needed, in denser concentrations at high dramatic moments such as in the paragraph just quoted, Scots words and phrases could be used in such a way as did not compromise readability or literary effect. That there are fewer Scottish words in the published versions than appear in the manuscript may actually be the result of RLS's finding that he could do without them.

In addition to the text itself, Menikoff reproduces thirteen illustrations from the original drawings by William Boucher for the *Young Folks* version, these now being in the Writers' Museum, Edinburgh; three pages from the manuscript; RLS's presentation inscription and one annotated page from Henry James's copy of *Kidnapped*, now at Harvard, the annotations being page numbers for his essay on RLS written in 1887; the title-pages of the first edition and the copyright edition; and the front cover of the first American edition. The frontispiece reproduces an etching of RLS by William H. W. Bicknell, now at Harvard, not otherwise identified but possibly done posthumously from a photograph. Two etchings by Paul Sandby are also included, from originals in the Huntington Library: here too there is no indication of who Sandby was, or when he lived, or what might be the connection with *Kidnapped*. Only part of the fold-out map that appeared in the first edition is used. It is splendidly enlarged as end-papers but the result is that the map is now decorative rather than, as RLS intended, useful. Menikoff's explanatory notes are excellent, and he includes both a glossary and gazetteer. Menikoff's long critical introduction (xi–xlvii) looks forward in many excellent ways to his breathtaking and splendid *Narrating Scotland: The Imagination of Robert Louis Stevenson* (2005)—on both of which I will defer comment until the section on Criticism.

Menikoff, Barry, ed. *Kidnapped: Or, the Lad with the Silver Button.* New York: Random House, 2001. This Modern Library edition combines the text, illustrations, and the gazetteer of Menikoff's transcription of the Huntington Library manuscript, as well as a new critical introduction by Margot Livesey. While it is good to have the manuscript text available cheaply, and in paperback, readers other than specialists are likely to think that this new version is a definitive or final text of *Kidnapped*—all the more so in the absence of Menikoff's own introduction. In fact, it is just the opposite, merely the first of at least four versions of the text with which Stevenson can be shown to have had direct personal involvement over the space of seven years. Especially in an edition intended for a large audience of nonspecialist readers, it seems to me irresponsible to present this manuscript version—the final draft—as if it were the version of his book that Stevenson would have wished most, or even very many, of his readers a century later to be reading.

In December 1893, having just finished marking a copy of *Kidnapped* for a planned two-volume edition bringing *Kidnapped* and *Catriona* together for the first time as two parts of the same story, RLS sent the marked copy to Harriet Baker, a Braille writer in London who was then preparing an edition for the blind and who had written to him asking about possible changes. RLS asked Mrs. Baker to note the changes and then to pass the book along to Cassell's for publication. He also told Cassell's of the plan and asked them to send her a copy of *Catriona* (RLS to Harriet Baker, RLS to Cassell and Company, both 5 December 1893, Letters 2661–62).

No doubt owing to the decision to launch the Edinburgh Edition and to RLS's death at the end of 1894, this edition in two volumes—RLS's title for it was *The Adventures of David Balfour*—was not published until April 1895. In the text of *Kidnapped* there are more than 150 differences between the first edition and the 1895 Cassell edition. They occur throughout the book, from the Dedication to the very last page, and they are of all kinds: deletions, changes, and additions in wording; changes in punctuation, the hyphenation of compound words, capitalization, and spelling; and the correction of typographical errors. David's age is changed from sixteen to seventeen and the year of his birth correspondingly from 1734 to 1733. In the twenty-first paragraph of ch. 2, instead of letting the paragraph end with the words "comforted my heart," the

first edition and the manuscript both continue: "comforted my heart wonderfully—more, I feel sure, than a whole flask of the lily of the valley water that Mrs.
Campbell set so great a store by." The opening words of ch. 22 are changed from
"More than eleven hours of incessant, hard travelling" to the more reasonable "Some
seven hours' incessant, hard travelling"—and these changes are typical. Stevenson's
marked copy does not survive, so it cannot be determined which changes are his and
which are due to the compositors or others who would have seen this version through
the press. All or most of the deletions, changes, and additions, the alterations of "oh"
to "O" in exclamations, and the three additional glosses of words, are almost certainly
his. Some or possibly all of the changes in punctuation, hyphenation, capitalization,
and spelling may also be his, for there is in them no clear pattern as there would be
in the imposition of a house style, and as there clearly is, no doubt for this very
reason, in the Edinburgh Edition published later in 1895 and derived from the Cassell
edition. In the Cassell edition, these changes seem more like corrections than changes
to impose consistency or conform to a style. On the other hand, in most instances,
especially in the punctuation, the usages that are being changed are instances in which
the first edition follows RLS's manuscript. He may have changed his mind, of course,
but this might suggest that some or all of these emendations may not be his. We
simply cannot tell.

In his transcriptions of the manuscript versions of "The Beach of Falesá" (1984)
and *Kidnapped* (1999), Menikoff urges the superiority of the manuscript versions
over anything printed, and it is true that both manuscripts sometimes capture emphases
and nuances of speech and dialect that are conveyed by Stevenson's own punctuation
and spelling but are lost in standardized print. Stevenson also accepted from his
friends, editors, and printers changes from the words and spellings that he himself
used, of which the change in the marriage certificate in "The Beach of Falesá" is
only the best known. Even though he himself never undid these changes, it is also
arguable that RLS never really had a chance or the stamina to do so; and also that it
is only in the manuscripts that we have access to Stevenson's intentions alone and
purely, unmerged with an indeterminate number of unknown additional changes by
others. Against all of this, of course, is the undeniable fact that—especially in *Kidnapped*—intentions that belong to Stevenson do exist in versions later than the manuscripts. The history of *Kidnapped*, once it reaches print, is not only one of decline,
nor only one of the imposition by others onto Stevenson's creative intentions (represented by his manuscript) of their ideas of what should be given to the public. Even
before marking a copy of the book in 1893, Stevenson mentioned in his letters changes
that he himself wanted to see; and even earlier he had had a chance to give tangible
form to his own intentions as he corrected the proofs both of the *Young Folks* version,
published serially, and the first book-form edition—and no doubt he did so, in both
iterations. And many passages in which one might expect to see changes remain the
same, among them the eloquent speech by Alan Breck on which I have commented
in the previous entry.

Stevenson's work marking a copy of *Kidnapped* in 1893, seven years after the first
edition was published, is significant because it shows that when finally he had written
and published the always-intended sequel he lost no time preparing the earlier book for
publication jointly with the later one, as two parts of the same whole. For *Kidnapped* as

Stevenson left it, with the sequel at last in place, rather than as he had first written it, seven years earlier, we must look to the 1895 Cassell edition. It is true that—as in all versions of the book later than the manuscript—the work of persons other than Stevenson is present, and at all levels from the spelling of words such as ''niether'' correctly, all the way up to changing them. But Stevenson's intentions are present also: as the author, making changes of his own, and as a privileged collaborator in the production of the book, interacting with, and no doubt at times undoing, the work of others as he corrected proofs and then, later, marked a copy of the book for a new edition that, as it happened, he never lived to see. Whatever may be our own opinion of them, in the Cassell edition of 1895 are embodied many of Stevenson's own wishes as to the text that he hoped that a century later we would read. This cannot be said of the manuscript that he handed over to *Young Folks* in the early summer of 1886.

Parfect, Ralph. ''Robert Louis Stevenson's 'The Clockmaker' and 'The Scientific Ape': Two Unpublished Fables.'' *English Literature in Transition* 48 (2005): 387–403. Rpt. as '' 'God Bless My Tail!': Two Unknown Fables by Robert Louis Stevenson,'' *Times Literary Supplement* (20 Jan. 2006): 11–13. ''The Clockmaker'' appears separately, without Parfect's comments or ''The Scientific Ape,'' in *Harper's Magazine* 312 (Apr. 2006): 26–29. In a follow-up letter to the *TLS* (10 Feb. 2006): 17, Parfect notes on the authority of Jean-Pierre Naugrette that the two fables were actually first published in French, as *Fables* trans. Pierre-Alain Gendre (Paris: Corti, 1985), rpt. in *Intégrale des nouvelles* ed. Michel LeBris (Paris: Phébus, 2001).

RLS wrote fables at intervals over his whole career, and in 1888–89 he seems to have had in mind publishing a collection. But it was not until 1895 that a selection of 20 of his fables was first published, posthumously, by Sidney Colvin. The manuscripts of the fables that Colvin published were sold after Fanny Stevenson's death as Anderson I, 376, and are now in the British Library, London, MS. Add. 39173. According to the catalog description, this collection consists of 49 pages, folio and quarto, in ink and in pencil. The first page is headed ''Æsop in the Fog'' over a cancelled heading ''The Fabulist,'' and this heading is followed by a list of 16 titles, ''six of which differ from the printed work, as does the order.''

The manuscripts of the two fables published here were sold as a separate, single lot in the same sale (Anderson II, 393) and are now at Yale. ''The Clockmaker'' (Beinecke 6102) is numbered VI and is written on pages numbered 15–19. ''The Scientific Ape'' (Beinecke 6831) is numbered VIII and is on pages 22–25. Both end with a heading ''Moral,'' but in neither is a moral present. The paper is the same in each, as is the handwriting. The back of the last page of ''The Clockmaker'' is blank, and the page number on which ''The Scientific Ape'' begins has been altered from 20 to 22, as if at one time there was a short fable numbered ''VII'' between the two but RLS deleted it, forgetting to correct the page and item numbering when he did so. All of this suggests that at some point, and possibly more than once, as he did with his poems, RLS created his own selection and arrangement of his fables—with, or without, these two. Parts of two other fables were offered in the same sale: a one-page fragment of ''Faith, Half-Faith, and No Faith at All'' (I, 362), and part of another fable not identified by title (I, 350).

In the introduction to his transcriptions, Ralph Parfect does not mention the manuscripts in the British Library, nor does he comment on the physical details of the two fables that he presents here, except to say that the numbering of the pages suggests that they were meant to be "part of a series" (388). He assumes that Colvin, when he made his selection, had all of the fables in hand, including these two, and thus that the decision not to publish them was Colvin's. But the manuscript evidence and other details may show that the choosing hand was RLS's. Neither of these fables seems to be unfinished. Morals appear only sometimes at the end of RLS's fables, so the absence of morals here is not decisive. But both of these fables are inconclusive, as if RLS could not find a telling point or paradox that the narratives embody; he himself may have set them aside in creating the collection from which Colvin eventually chose. Parfect suggests a date of the mid–1880s, but I think Claire Harman is probably correct in suggesting, in a letter to the *TLS*, 3 Feb. 2006: 15, that these two fables owe something to RLS's acquaintance with Dr. Trudeau's tuberculosis laboratory at Saranac Lake, New York, and thus date from 1887–88 or later. If so, they may have been part of a collection that RLS made in the late 1880s toward the fulfillment of a contract for a book of fables that he had signed with a representative of Longmans in New York on 31 May 1888 but still had not completed by the following year (RLS to Charles Longman, 6 March 1889, Letter 2139). The collection from which Colvin chose may have been a different, later one from which RLS himself had already omitted both of these fables.

The two fables presented here are slight but interesting. "The Clockmaker" tells the story of the elaborate philosophical theories that microbes living and multiplying in a vase of water that goes unchanged for a month develop in making sense of the surroundings that they observe, including a pendulum clock and two differently-facing windows. Their story (and existence) ends when a man finally comes in to wind the clock and drinks the vase of water. He himself is made ill by this, and the public water supply in the district is, as a result, "completely overhauled" (400). "The Scientific Ape" tells of an ape who has lately escaped from a vivisectionist's laboratory and who suggests to his fellow apes that they turn the tables. "By vivisecting men, we find out how apes are made, and so we advance. . . . Say that they do suffer. Well, they suffer in the interest of a lower race, which requires help: there can be nothing fairer than that" (402). Because grown men are strong and have guns, however, the apes steal a baby—whom they must immediately return, on the orders of the chief of the apes. "'Great cocoanuts,' cried he, 'is this a nightmare? Can apes descend to such barbarity? Take back that baby where it came from'" (403).

Mann, David D., and Susan Garland Mann, eds. "The Enchantress." *Georgia Review* 43 (Fall 1989): 550–68. As was noted in my entry of "The Enchantress" in *The Prose Writings of RLS* (1980), 198–99, this story was known from its appearance as Anderson II, 387, in a small quarto notebook that also contained the beginning of RLS's unfinished "Story of a Recluse" and an early outline of *The Master of Ballantrae*, which RLS began at Saranac Lake in late 1887; and it came up for sale again, separately, with a facsimile of the first page in the catalogue, at the American Art Galleries, 18 April 1923. Acquired by Yale in 1983 from a private collector, the manuscript is published for the first time here, unfortunately with many errors of transcription and a misleading and at times fanciful introduction. The story, according to these editors, was written not on a "yacht" (as RLS's stepson Lloyd Osbourne said that it was, referring to the *Casco* voyage that ended in Honolulu in January

1889) but on the trading schooner *Equator*, on a voyage that was memorable chiefly for the Stevenson party's stay in the Gilbert Islands while the *Equator* was away trading elsewhere. "The Enchantress," the Manns maintain, was "denigrated" by RLS's stepson Lloyd Osbourne, who also "blocked . . . [e]fforts to publish the story" during the 1920s (552). Lloyd's suppression of the story occurred possibly because it was "too biographical" and might have been construed as an unflattering portrait of Fanny, or because RLS's depiction in it of "a strong woman who succeeds despite the social and legal restrictions then placed on women" raised "questions . . . about social classes and gender roles" that might have made the story, in Osbourne's eyes, "unmarketable or uncharacteristic of Stevenson's fiction" (552).

No reasons are given for thinking that Lloyd was mistaken in associating the story with the *Casco* voyage, and in my opinion Lloyd's association still fits well with his calling the vessel a "yacht," as the *Casco* was, not a schooner or a trading schooner, as the *Equator* was; with his further recollection that the story was written as one of a group of tales, "a la Boccacio" (Lloyd's spelling), that each of the passengers on the *Casco* (one of whom was RLS's mother) wrote and read aloud to pass the time, as could have been done easily in the luxurious cabins on the *Casco*; with Captain Otis's recollection that stories were told on board; and possibly with the absence from the notebook as it existed originally of anything that can be dated later than the end of 1887 or early 1888, this being an early outline of *The Master of Ballantrae*. As was noted by one of the crew members on the *Equator*, Thomson Murray MacCallum, in his account of that later voyage, RLS was busy then on *The Wrecker*, and the shipboard entertainment consisted of fishing for sharks, inventing schemes to start a trading company, and even making fun of Captain Reid ("Reminiscences of Robert Louis Stevenson," *Adrift in the South Seas* [1934], 232–46).

Nor are any details given about who tried to publish "The Enchantress," or when, still less about Lloyd's having "blocked" their efforts, or, if he did so, having had any motives other than the fact that the story was a trifle that Stevenson himself never saw fit to publish. According to Lloyd, "RLS never attached the slightest importance to it" (photostat of an undated note from Lloyd Osbourne to Benjamin H. Stern, Bancroft Library, University of California—Berkeley; quoted in *The Prose Writings of RLS* [1980], 199, but omitted here). If the story itself reflects unfavorably on Fanny, RLS must have been very tactless (or brave) to write it, and to read it aloud, in an undertaking in which Fanny too was participating. For all of these reasons, I still think that my original suggestion, that the story was written aboard the *Casco*, is correct.

Publication of "The Enchantress" was discussed by Herbert Mitgang, in *The New York Times*, 1 November 1989, and reported from this source in *The Times* (London) on 2 November. In a letter to *The Times* published on 13 November, Ernest Mehew characterized the editors' account of the supposed suppression of the story as "a piece of high-flown nonsense" and corrected a number of other errors and misstatements in the *The New York Times* account of 2 November:

> The story is a slight and trifling anecdote which Stevenson himself evidently considered unworthy of publication. . . . There is nothing in it which reflects the circumstances of Stevenson's own marriage, and the heroine bears not the slightest resemblance to his wife.

"The Enchantress" was reprinted, with a shorter version of the introduction, in the London *Telegraph Weekend Magazine*, 4 August 1990, 20–22, 49–53. It also appeared in a bilingual edition of 3,000 copies with Italian and English on facing pages and a "Publisher's Note" taken from the introduction and, in one detail, from *The New York Times* article, this giving the auction price in 1923 as $232.50.

Mehew, Ernest J., ed. *The Wrong Box: The Authentic Text Published From Stevenson's Manuscript and Corrected Proofs*. London: Nonesuch, 1989. *The Wrong Box* was first published by Charles Scribner's Sons in New York in June 1889, but due to a misunderstanding the publication had proceeded without the benefit of RLS's corrections from the twelfth chapter through the end. These changes, in proofs that reached Scribner's after the novel had been published and that were retained by them, were substantial: to create a new chapter by dividing ch. 14 into two chapters and the addition, for the newly-created chapter, of five new pages in manuscript amending two passages that must have seemed to RLS on second thought unduly complicated. RLS also passed for publication, in the first eleven chapters as well as in these later proofs, many misreadings of his own handwriting present in the typescript copy and then in the proofs that Scribner's had sent him—in part because his manuscript was not returned.

All of these errors, large and small, were not corrected in any subsequent edition, including the Edinburgh Edition. Graham Greene saw the corrected proofs at Scribner's Rare Book Department in New York not long after World War II, but nothing came of his urging, then, or in a letter to the *Times Literary Supplement*, 30 October 1970, that a correct version of *The Wrong Box* be published. Not until 1989–the centenary of its first publication—did the novel finally appear as RLS had corrected it, in this exemplary, definitive edition by Ernest Mehew from the proofs and the manuscript, both now at Yale. In addition to a detailed, clear discussion of the complicated history of the text, including the real-life originals of many of the characters, and of the relative contributions of RLS and his stepson Lloyd Osbourne—*The Wrong Box* was the first of their three collaborations, each of them different—Mehew also provides explanatory annotations of the story and of changes made in the text as it evolved. Pages from Lloyd's original typescript remain and they confirm, as Mehew says, "what could surely not be doubted by anyone familiar with Stevenson's work, that the form and manner of the final version is almost entirely his. Although he was able to incorporate some of Lloyd's typed pages into the manuscript, these have usually been heavily revised and amended, and the style improved." Lloyd's contributions were considerable, but mostly in the ingenuity of the plot and the characters rather than in the final text (xx).

Rennie, Neil, ed. *In the South Seas*. London: Penguin, 1998. Rennie reprints the four-part, 35–chapter version of RLS's account first put together by Sidney Colvin and published in the Edinburgh Edition (1896). But he has collated the text against the manuscripts in the Huntington Library, San Marino, California, and the versions published at irregular intervals in *Black and White*, 1891–92, and the Auckland *Star*, 1891. As Rennie notes, his is not a full or definitive collation, and because Colvin's edition may embody changes attributable to Stevenson he has emended the text "only when it seemed obviously in error" (xxxvi). Nevertheless, from his sources he offers 27 plausible emendations of words and spellings, none of them more than a word or two (283–84). In his introduction Rennie gives a good account of the process of composition, noting that *In the South Seas* is still very much a work in progress in which chronological narration is mixed rather than integrated with other materials. "[I]n rewriting the journals for publication, Stevenson was forming thematic and aesthetic patterns, sometimes incorporating material from later voyages and making later inter-island comparisons, all at the expense of the consecutive narrative of events" (xxvi). Rennie also offers explanatory notes, all of them useful, accurate, and to the point.

Jolly, Roslyn, ed. *The Cruise of the Janet Nichol among the South Sea Islands.* Sydney: U of New South Wales P, 2004. Roslyn Jolly reprints from the first edition published in 1914, shortly after Fanny Stevenson's death, Fanny's account of the three-and-one-half-month cruise that she, RLS, and her son Lloyd Osbourne took on the trading schooner *Janet Nichol* from 11 April to late July 1890, while the first house was being built at Vailima in Samoa. Fanny's original day-to-day account, written in a Letts Australasian Diary and Almanac for 1890, is in the RLS Silverado Museum and was incorporated almost in its entirety into the published account, which also contains much additional material and commentary. As Jolly notes in a substantial introduction, Fanny's account is of interest not only as a record of what RLS saw and did and learned. Details and people from the *Janet Nichol* cruise turn up again and again in RLS's nonfictional South Seas writings, as well as in "The Beach of Falesá," *The Wrecker*, and *The Ebb-Tide*. Fanny's account is also of interest, in its own right, for glimpses of the so-called labor trade in which, for years, natives had been in various ways forced into service on plantations often far from home, and into the social interactions of trade—in short, of "life in some of the last independent Pacific kingdoms and societies just passing under colonial rule" (43). To a selection of 13 of the 24 photographs in the first edition, Jolly has added 13 more, previously unpublished, from the original photo albums in the Writers' Museum, Edinburgh. Although attribution is difficult, almost all of the photographs, in both versions, were probably taken by Lloyd Osbourne and intended as illustrations for RLS's big book on the South Seas.

Menikoff, Barry. *Robert Louis Stevenson and 'The Beach of Falesá': A Study in Victorian Publishing.* Stanford: Stanford UP, 1984. The received text of RLS's 30,000–word story "The Beach of Falesá" is the version that was published by Cassell and Company as the first of three stories in the volume *Island Nights' Entertainments* in early April 1893. It derives ultimately from a complete fair-copy manuscript, now in the Huntington Library, intended for publication and sent by RLS to Charles Baxter on 14 October 1891, a printed version of which RLS read, corrected, and returned to Cassell's for book-form publication a little more than a year later, in late 1892 or early 1893. In the first paragraph, however, three of the six sentences differ from what RLS's manuscript contains, and this pattern and level of difference continues throughout.

The story is told in the first person by the English trader Wiltshire. "I saw that island first when it was neither night nor morning," Wiltshire begins. The first sentences are the same. But in the published version, we find some changes in punctuation and spelling. A comma is added to the second sentence, a comma is added and the spelling of a word is changed in the fourth sentence, and a colon is substituted for a semicolon in the sixth sentence. These are the changes:

> 2nd sentence, MS. The moon was to the west, setting but still broad and bright./1893. The moon was to the west, setting, but still broad and bright. [comma added]
>
>   4th sentence, MS. The land breeze blew in our faces and smellt strong of lime and vanilla:/1893. The land breeze blew in our faces, and smelt strong of lime and vanilla: [comma added, spelling changed]
>
>   6th sentence, MS. Here was a fresh experience; even the tongue would be quite strange to me; and the look of these woods and mountains, and the rare smell of them, renewed my blood./1893. Here was a fresh experience: even the tongue would be quite strange to me; and the look of these woods and mountains, and the rare smell of them, renewed my blood. [colon replaces semicolon]

These changes are typical, and with many others of their kind—and a few larger ones—they are the principal subject of a 100–page essay with which Menikoff precedes his transcription of RLS's fair-copy manuscript.

Menikoff's argument is aesthetic. The changes—whoever made or missed or accepted them, when, or for what reasons—almost without exception result, in his opinion, in an inferior work of art. And this is true in two distinct respects: representational and thematic. Stevenson's manuscript version, Menikoff argues—and by means of his careful transcription of the manuscript he gives us the means of deciding for ourselves—is greatly superior in rendering the atmosphere and characters. Far better than does the published version, the manuscript vindicates RLS's own belief that he had written "the first realistic South Sea story; I mean with real South Sea character and details of life; everybody else who has tried, that I have seen, got carried away by the romance and ended in a kind of sugar candy sham epic, and the whole effect was lost" (RLS to Sidney Colvin, 28 September 1891, Letter 2351). The manuscript version is also very much more successful in advancing the story's main themes, which according to Menikoff include "the abuse of men and the exploitation of women" (57), "widely held prejudices about the superiority of white European civilization" (59), "an exposure of white racism" (71), and "an attack on the entire class system, economic and political" (81)—all this in an effort to "disquiet the Victorian reader (or rather the late Victorian editor) by disturbing his most profound prejudices: race, miscegenation, and colonialism" (89). RLS's aim, says Menikoff, is to embody the view, which he had already expressed outside of his fiction, that, as Menikoff puts it, "the responsibility for the destruction of the brown cultures rested with a white civilization whose presumed racial and cultural superiority was nothing more than a cover for European expansionism" (98).

The changes in the first paragraph of "The Beach of Falesá" show clearly the truth of Dale Kramer's observation that the supposed difference between substantives and accidentals (substantives affect meaning, accidentals do not) is chimerical—true, if it is true at all, only at the remotest extremes of the continuum. Punctuation, too, is meaning, all the more so in dialogue and in first-person narration. ("The Compositor as Copy-Text." Rev. of George Eliot, *Romola*, ed. Andrew Brown. 1993. *Text* 9 [1996]: 369–88). In the first paragraph of "The Beach of Falesá," the changes of punctuation clearly do change Wiltshire's rendering of his experiences. "The moon was to the west, setting but still broad and bright." Adding a comma after the word "setting" puts much more emphasis on that word, as if what mattered most was the setting of the moon, not the less-easily-grasped idea of its breadth and brightness even as it was also setting. Such an idea might have been intended by RLS to continue and add to Wiltshire's saying in the first sentence that it was "neither night nor morning" when he first saw the island. "The land breeze blew in our faces and smellt strong of lime and vanilla." Adding a comma after the word "faces" has a similar effect: breaking into to two separate details an experience that is being presented as one experience with multiple aspects. "Here was a fresh experience; even the tongue would be quite strange to me; and the look of these woods and mountains, and the rare smell of them, renewed my blood." Changing RLS's semicolon to a colon after the word "experience" puts more emphasis on the opening clause and makes the details in the rest of the sentence subordinate, mere explanatory illustrations of what was "fresh" about the experience, not additional, equally important, aspects of the experience itself.

Spelling also matters—all the more so when an effort is being made, as here, to give a spoken quality to the text and to capture idiosyncrasies of outlook and voice. Mark Twain discussed the importance of dialect unforgettably in his explanatory note prefacing *Huckleberry Finn* (1884), a book that RLS read immediately when it came out and greatly admired, and there is a similar attentiveness in RLS. In the sentence "The land breeze blew in our faces and smellt strong of lime and vanilla," changing RLS's spelling of the word from "smellt" to "smelt" might have been intended to correct a slip of the pen while still preserving Wiltshire's choice of the variant instead of the normal preterite "smelled"—a conjecture that might also be supported by the fact that the adverb "strong," which follows, is not changed to "strongly." But the change of spelling to "smelt" nonetheless suppresses what might have been an effort to mimic pronunciation, and it certainly lessens the emphasis that Wiltshire's choice of this word instead of "smelled" would have received if it had been underscored by the unusual spelling.

These changes also have a thematic effect. The more conventionally exotic Wiltshire's experiences of the sights, sounds, and people of the South Seas are—the clearer and the easier they are to imagine—the less his story becomes, as in Melville's *Typee* (1846) and Conrad's *Heart of Darkness* (1899), a journey of self-confrontation and self-discovery. By its greater straightforwardness and clarity, the story is moved in the direction of idyll, and away from nightmare, difficulty, ambiguity, and disorientation. In the same way, the less different from ourselves Wiltshire is in views, speech, and spelling, the easier it is to see him sentimentally: as a rough diamond saved in spite of himself (and his prejudices) by the love of a good woman.

In his long prefatory essay, Menikoff presents dozens of examples of much the same kind. The experience itself, in the published version, is presented as somewhat less complicated and somewhat more conventional, and Wiltshire as not quite as rough and unlettered a fellow as he seems in the manuscript. There is a limit to how much undoing of an author's intentions can be accomplished with commas, colons, and spelling, however; and at the very end of his essay Menikoff also concedes that at least some readers of the received version have managed to admire and understand the story much as he does, despite having never laid eyes on the manuscript text (98).

This is an extremely damaging concession, however. For it shows that if, in addition to changes, there was also a conspiracy—a conscious, unconscious, individual, self-inflicted, or cultural effort to subvert and alter the meaning that Stevenson expressed in his manuscript—such an effort was wholly or partly a failure. That there was such a conspiracy is a major additional claim of Menikoff's, and I have purposely not mentioned it until now, to do justice to the excellence, relevance, and value of his presentation of the manuscript text. According to Menikoff, the manuscript not only differs from the published version, and in fairly consistent ways such as those we have seen in the first paragraph. It also contains, and is in fact the only true source of, a story that Stevenson tried to tell—wished to tell—but was somehow prevented from telling. Menikoff's lengthy and detailed presentation of the differences is made all the longer by a single-minded and often tedious effort to show, in every case, that the manuscript reading, whatever it may be, is superior to the published version—efforts that at least one later commentator has suggested "occasionally may reveal more about his own [Menikoff's] textual ingenuity than about the bad faith of the Victorian publishing world" (William Gray, *Robert Louis Stevenson: A Literary Life* [Basingstoke: Palgrave Macmillan, 2004] 146). Not only this: Menikoff also insists that the supposedly inferior readings of the published version were chosen in some manner on purpose to diminish and emasculate the story. "There was no simple way a compositor, proofreader, editor, or publisher could contravene the meaning of the story, short of destroying it altogether," Menikoff writes in one such passage, assuming what one might expect to see proved: that there was a desire to "contravene the meaning of the story" (59).

> The most reasonable procedure was therefore to manipulate the language, which was systematically gutted through additions, deletions, and substitutions. Although in each case there is a clear reason for the alteration, the overall effect is to contain Stevenson's criticism of imperialism and to domesticate, as far as possible, the violence and vulgarity of the narrative. These intentions were not, of course, at the front of each compositor's or proofreader's mind. But a pattern was operative, and the result was a tamer book.
>
> (59)

"[A] comparison of the manuscript with the printed texts," Menikoff writes, "enables us to see precisely how a finished and artistically sophisticated novel was reduced to a vulgar and meretricious shadow of itself" (32–33).

In my opinion, neither of these claims can be sustained even for the changes in the first paragraph. The manuscript is not everywhere superior, and Stevenson, or his meaning, was not conspired against, "systematically" or otherwise. The claim of superiority is refuted by the fact that there are not very many instances in which an intelligible aesthetic case cannot be made as easily against as for the reading in either version—and that the case for superiority depends very much on what one supposes Stevenson was trying to do. Menikoff simply assumes that RLS's intentions never changed after their first realization in the manuscript. Yet he concedes of the changes that "in each case there is a clear reason for the alteration," and elsewhere he writes that, except for one lengthy omission, "there were not many alterations made on a scale larger than a phrase or two or three words" (76). The published version does not seem to me consistently better or worse than the manuscript version. They simply differ, and in the same fairly consistent ways that we have seen in the first paragraph. As to Menikoff's second point, changes in themselves offer no proof of a conspiracy, of a deliberate or even an unwitting aim to subvert rather than, for example, to give effect to changes in Stevenson's own intentions, or his acceptance of changes made by others, or the bad result of good intentions, or of muddle, or even of an effort to achieve an author's ends within the limits of a highly conventionalized medium such as print and readers in the habit of interpreting what they read with reference to those conventions. Printing "smelt strong" rather than "smelled strongly" (or the manuscript's "smellt strong") may in fact be a brilliant solution to a difficult problem—a better one than Stevenson's own, in the manuscript—not an unfeeling or cynical act of suppression. The only possibility that Menikoff ever allows, however, is that everything we see was the result of a conspiracy.

Nor does the external evidence support his claim. Menikoff provides an invaluable and detailed account of the lengthy multi-sided correspondence among Stevenson, Charles Baxter, Colvin, the brothers McClure, Scribner's and their London agent Lemuel Bangs, Cassell's, and Clement Shorter, editor of the *Illustrated London News*. There were problems at every turn. The story was much shorter than RLS had estimated it to be. It was also too short for publication as a separate volume, but it was not in RLS's opinion well suited to appear with "The Bottle Imp"—or vice versa. Neither Scribner's nor Shorter nor Cassell's wanted to, or did, publish the cynical and callous marriage certificate as Stevenson had written it, and Shorter simply omitted it: that Uma was "illegally married to *Mr. John Wiltshire* for one night, and Mr. John Wiltshire is at liberty to send her to hell the next morning" (124). Other passages were also of the sort (in Charles Scribner's words to Lemuel Bangs on 19 February 1892) that made the story "one that we could not publish without modification" (qtd. 17); and this was an opinion that had already led Robert McClure, independently, to send Stevenson one of the typewritten copies "asking him to modify or rewrite it" (Bangs to Scribner, 24 February 1894, qtd. 18). As Bangs reported to Scribner, however, Stevenson's reply was "that he would not change it in any way" (4 April 1892, qtd. 19), and not long afterwards RLS put Scribner's and Baxter in more or less complete charge of the remaining business details and Colvin in charge of the text—at least for the *Illustrated London News* version, which commenced publication on 2 July 1892.

Notwithstanding RLS's explicit refusal to make changes, the marriage certificate was simply omitted, an action that Shorter himself later acknowledged was "ruthless vandalism" although Stevenson "bore it very well" in silence (*Letters to an Editor*, 1914, iv). Also omitted was a short passage at the end of the fourth paragraph in the second chapter telling of two Samoan boys slipping out of their sheets (lava-lavas) "mother-naked," on which Stevenson commented to J. M. Barrie: "The celestial idiots cut it out. I wish we could afford to do without serial publication altogether. It is odd that Hardy's adventure with the barrow and mine of the little children should happen in the same year with the publication and success of *Tess*. Surely these editor people are wrong" (1 November 1892, Letter 2479; the reference is to ch. 23 in *Tess of the D'Urbervilles*, as published in *The Graphic*: instead of carrying the milkmaids across a stream in his arms, Angel Clare must carry them in a wheelbarrow). Both of these omissions were restored in the 1893 Cassell's edition, although not exactly as they had stood in the manuscript. Deleted at the stage of galley proofs was a 10–line passage, about 200 words, in the first chapter showing (in RLS's words criticizing the omission as unwise) "how far men go, and Case has gone, to get copra" (RLS to Colvin, 29 August 1892, Letter 2452). This was never restored, by Stevenson or anyone else, and it appears for the first time in Menikoff's edition.

To Menikoff, the story of the book's production is the same as is revealed in the textual details. "We must recognize," he insists, "that from start to finish there was nothing in *Falesá* that could truly please the people who were responsible for the production of Stevenson's books and for the promotion of his reputation. They could not do anything about his chosen story, his *donnée*, but they could, and they did, eviscerate it" (75). This story is rendered all the more sad and deplorable, Menikoff says, by the fact that it is also

> a story of what happens to a work of art when it is converted into a commodity to satisfy the taste and prejudices of the period—a story of stylistic abuse by printers and proofreaders, of literary abuse by publishers, editors, and friends, and finally the abuse of art by Stevenson himself in sanctioning the publication of a corrupt text.   (5)

If the story really is one of abuse, however, it seems to me surely one of abuse accomplished with no evident intent to cause harm or any placing of personal gain or other interested motives ahead of what were believed to be Stevenson's own best interests. Stevenson was, moreover, involved in the publication process, correcting proofs at two different stages; and as Menikoff himself notes, "when Stevenson himself explicitly aimed at restoring an excised passage, the restoration was made" (83). As with his handling of the internal evidence, Menikoff seems to me unduly fond of righteous indignation, even, or especially, when the evidence itself admits of more benign or less clear-cut interpretations. There is little room in his account for good intentions or unintended consequences: it is all black or white and intensely dramatic.

Although the claim of a conspiracy is dubious, Menikoff's case against the published version is convincing. RLS prepared the fair copy with great care, and from past experience he knew that his luck with printers was bad. Even as early as 1880 he had remarked to William Dean Howells about a poem of his that had been accepted for the *Atlantic Monthly*: "May I hope for proofs? I am one who never was yet correctly printed, even under the synod of intelligent friends. My mind is not sympathetic with that of the Average Printer" (August/September 1880, Letter 716; qtd. 33). Except to refuse to make changes himself and except to comment later on misprints in the periodical version and on the three passages that were omitted there, RLS never said a word about, or against, the published text of "The Beach of Falesá," and he was also directly involved in preparing it. Menikoff's preference for drama and conspiracy thus leaves him with no alternative but to blame Stevenson, or Stevenson's supposedly deep ambivalence about commercial success, for "the abuse of art by Stevenson himself in sanctioning the publication of a corrupt text." But it seems to me that there is another possibility, one to which we have access thanks to Menikoff's deep and thorough scholarship.

As is true of *The Amateur Emigrant*, there are perhaps two versions of "The Beach of Falesá": an almost bitterly candid, even abrasive, first version pushing the limits of taste and propriety in the pursuit of a heightened realism meant to reveal as well as depict; and another more literary, polished—but not eviscerated—second version later. In the manuscript and published versions alike, as Menikoff himself remarks of "The Beach of Falesá," there are "two distinct voices, each in conflict with the other: the one easy, idiomatic, and oral, the other formal, conventional, and written" (51). Stevenson's intentions, in both works, change with time: the versions are different because the intentions are different. In "The Beach of Falesá," an alert, meticulous, impressionistic realism of rendering—of voices, sights and sounds, experiences, personalities, and outlooks—is joined with a sentimentality of plot and a fondness for melodramatic scenes and incidents, and this is true of the manuscript and published versions alike. What changes is the balance between these, as Stevenson tries other ways of achieving what remains, in essence and overall effect though not in every detail, the same flexibly defined work of art. With both works, we may prefer the earlier versions, but the later ones are also Stevenson's own.

Meleisea, Malama, ed. *A Footnote to History: Eight Years of Trouble in Samoa.* Auckland: Pasifika, 1996. In this attractive edition, the Samoan historian Malama Meleisea offers a concise and intelligible sketch of Samoan history, politics, and social institutions during the nineteenth century, providing a context for RLS's history of the years just before he arrived in Samoa at the end of 1889. Of special interest are maps showing locations mentioned in the text and the traditional political districts in Samoa and seventeen illustrations chiefly from historical photographs in the Alexander W. Turnbull Library, Wellington. These include a panorama of Apia, pictures of Mata'afa, Tamasese, and Malietoa, Samoan fortifications and warriors, and the British consulate. An index has also been added.

French, William Fuller Kirkpatrick, ed. *Plain John Wiltshire on the Situation.* Midland, TX: Privately printed, 1989. This is the first publication of a mock letter by RLS on the 1893 "Regulation . . . for the Maintenance of Peace and Good Order in Samoa," about which RLS himself complained in a letter published in *The Times* (London), 4 April 1893 (Letter 2537; RLS includes the text of the Regulation in his letter, and it is also summarized and quoted in Graham Balfour's *Life*, II, 205–06). In this edition there is no facsimile of any part of the manuscript, which is of unknown origin; but even from the printed version it is clear that it has been transcribed inaccurately or itself has errors. Nor has reference been made to an original typescript copy by Lloyd Osbourne, at Yale, or a carbon copy of this in the Huntington Library. The Yale typescript even includes postscripts by Wilshire (so spelled) and Uma, neither of which appear in this edition. Nor is anything said in the introduction about the historical context—an omission which, as Ernest Mehew observes, causes the point of the joke to be lost (Letter 2539, n. 3). For additional details on this edition see my review in *Fine Print*, 16 (Summer 1990), 92–93.

Croft, P. J., ed. *Autograph Poetry in the English Language.* 2 vols. Oxford: Oxford UP, 1973. II, 145. In this inclusive reference collection of manuscript facsimiles of nearly 200 poems by 146 poets from the fourteenth to the twentieth centuries, with typeset transcriptions, Croft chooses from RLS a draft of "Bright is the ring of words" (Beinecke 6051), a poem first published in *Songs of Travel* (1896). As Croft notes, the manuscript shows RLS focused, in the manner of Horace and Pope, on "the varying expression of a single 'commonplace' idea." An amusing sidelight is a smear in the upper left-hand corner that RLS himself identifies as a bug that he has squashed: "A yellow beasts guts. . . . The Bard!"

Hinchcliffe, Peter, and Catherine Kerrigan, eds. *The Ebb-Tide: A Trio and Quartette*. Edinburgh UP, 1995. On 5 June 1893, having written this date also at the end of his manuscript, RLS finished and sent the first ten chapters of *The Ebb-Tide* to Sidney Colvin in London (Letter 2577). He sent the last two chapters by the next mail, on 18 June (also Letter 2577), and Colvin had the complete manuscript by 21 July 1893, remarking on that date to Charles Baxter that contrary to his dislike of the earlier chapters he found the final ones "done with astonishing genius" (Beinecke 4256). After serial publication in the first thirteen weekly issues of Jerome K. Jerome's new magazine *To-day*, 11 November 1893–3 February 1894, and in the United States in six monthly installments in *McClure's Magazine*, February—July 1894, *The Ebb-Tide* was published in book form about a year after RLS had sent off his manuscript: on 15 July 1894, by Stone and Kimball in Chicago, and on 15 September by William Heinemann in London, this being the date of publication that appears in the publication history in Heinemann's reprints of the first edition.

Hinchcliffe and Kerrigan have chosen the Stone and Kimball book-form edition as the copy-text for their edition, because, they say confidently, "it represents the author's final intentions" (159). This confidence seems to me entirely misplaced. All four of the versions of *The Ebb-Tide* that were published in the year after RLS sent his manuscript to Colvin—two each, in serial and in book form, on either side of the Atlantic—are deeply compromised. Each is made up of a jumble of intentions in which Stevenson's own text is merged with substantial and often untraceable interventions (and errors) by others, including typists, compositors, and editors. *The Ebb-Tide* seems at first to offer great challenges editorially. But the history of the text, although it is complicated, turns out to be not at all difficult to understand or to act upon. The complications begin early. On 23 June 1893, letting Charles Baxter know that he had received the first ten chapters, Colvin urged that "a copy ought to be set up in type or typewriting *at once*, both because of the risk of loss and in order that I may revise it before it is printed, even in serial form." The difficulty of RLS's handwriting was also a concern: "they make such awful hash of his copy" (Beinecke 4252). Four days later, Colvin reiterated: "please don't let it go to press for serial or other publication without my revision" (27 June 1893, Beinecke 4253). Two typescript copies were duly made, and to all appearances the manuscript was never again looked at, by Colvin, RLS, or anyone else. The typescripts in effect became the manuscript—or, rather, the manuscripts.

When the serial publication in *To-day* came to an end in February 1894, Colvin sent to RLS a complete set of clippings of *The Ebb-Tide* as it had appeared in this form. RLS was very pleased and surprised with the book, these serial clippings being the first rendering of it in print that he had seen. "I retired with The Ebb-Tide, and read it all before I slept," he told Colvin. "I did not dream it was near so good; I am afraid I think it excellent" (RLS to Colvin, 26 February 1894, Letter 2705). Colvin received RLS's corrections on 22 May 1894, and he used them in correcting proofs of the Stone and Kimball edition published in July. The clippings themselves do not survive. But there are differences between the Stone and Kimball book-form edition and the version in *To-day* that cannot be traced simply to the fact that the Stone and Kimball edition was set independently: from the *McClure's Magazine* version, which itself derives ultimately from a different typewritten copy from the one used for the *To-day* version. Among these differences are surely some or all of the corrections that RLS himself made on the clippings from *To-day*. An indeterminate number of them may be due to others, however, including Colvin himself.

My own collations, and independent investigations by other scholars who have been kind enough to share their results with me over the years, show that the *To-day* version that was sent to RLS has a great many errors of transcription from the manuscript, as Colvin predicted that it would. Not all of these errors were corrected, and the text itself was further emended by Colvin in many places, on the typewritten copy or at some later stage in the production of the *To-day* version, or both. These are not Stevenson's corrections, whatever he may have thought or done about them later, but a mixture of printers' errors and of changes that Colvin wished to make. That RLS saw and made corrections on the *To-day* version after it was published—and in so doing overlooked or accepted dozens of departures from his manuscript, which probably was not returned to him—signifies, in my opinion, not a desire or intention to promulgate this particular version (which in any case is not followed in the present edition) but only his passive and possibly unknowing acceptance of the changes that Colvin and others had made getting it into print. Only in the case of his own corrections on this version, insofar as these can be inferred, are we looking at RLS's own active choice of readings other than those in the manuscript.

None of this particularly matters as to the present edition, however, because the Stone and Kimball book-form edition has a different history. This edition was set from the *McClure's Magazine* version that was running in the United States as the book itself was being set in type. The *McClure's Magazine* version was not set from RLS's manuscript, nor was it set from any state of the *To-day* version, corrected or uncorrected. It comes, directly or ultimately, from the other typewritten copy of the manuscript that was made in the beginning. It has neither the benefit, nor the harm, of Colvin's corrections and changes, and it has, or at least it began with, all of the errors that the typists made. It has other changes, too, including corrections that were made by S. S. McClure on his copy of the typescript or by him or others in the course of production for the magazine. Still further changes were made by Stone and Kimball in setting the book from the *McClure's Magazine* version.

Stevenson seems never to have seen the Stone and Kimball version of *The Ebb-Tide*, before or after it was published. His only reference to any book-form edition is to an error of his own that he noticed on page 225 of the Heinemann edition, there being no such page in the Stone and Kimball edition, this in a letter to Colvin, 6 November 1894, Letter 2797. He did see the *McClure's Magazine* version from which it was derived, but his only comment on that version was to deplore the "cursed illustrations" there by Alfred Brennan (RLS to Charles Baxter, 20 April 1894, Letter 2721). Having just corrected the English version in *To-day*, he probably paid little or no attention to the text in this American version. Nor had he seen either of the typewritten copies, before or after their correction by Colvin. The version that RLS saw and corrected was the *To-day* version. So it is hard to find in the Stone and Kimball version, set from *McClure's Magazine*, very many of Stevenson's intentions, if there are any at all, except in his own corrections added by Sidney Colvin in reading the proofs.

The Heinemann version has its own troubled history. It was meant to have had the benefit of RLS's corrections on the clippings from the *To-day* version, but these pages somehow became lost after Colvin had corrected the Stone and Kimball version, with the result that Colvin told Heinemann to use the *McClure's Magazine* version and to bring into the edition the corrections that he had made in the Stone and Kimball edition (Colvin to Baxter, 23 May, 6 July 1894, Beinecke 4293, 4303). According to the present editors, who do not mention the source of their conclusion, Heinemann did not do this, reverting instead to the typewritten version used in the setting of *To-day* (158).

Hinchcliffe and Kerrigan never say why, given all this, they did not adopt the manuscript, now at Yale, as their copy-text—as Ernest Mehew did in his edition of *The Wrong Box*, for instance—only that the Stone and Kimball edition represents RLS's "final intentions." By this they must mean that no published version before it contains the changes that RLS made in the *To-day* version, and this is true. But the Stone and Kimball edition also contains very much that is not Stevenson's, including errors that go back to the typewritten versions. RLS had nothing to do with these, or with the publication of the *To-day* version, or with the *McClure's Magazine* version, or with the Stone and Kimball edition before or after it was corrected. This was all looked after by Colvin and S. S. McClure. And it is not as if RLS's corrections would be lost to us if we did not adopt the Stone and Kimball edition as the copy-text. His corrections are recoverable and, more important, separable from other changes—not to a certainty, of course, as the clippings that he marked do not survive, but to a practical and reasonable likelihood—by inference, comparison, and common sense. If RLS's manuscript had been adopted as the copy-text for this edition, many more of his intentions would be present in the book that we would be reading now, and there would be many fewer of the intentions (and mere errors) of others trailing in their wake.

For example, in the thirty-third paragraph from the end of ch. 6, RLS wrote that Herrick found himself conscious of "a pleasant glow, a pleasing excitement." The Stone and Kimball version, followed here, replaces this with "a pleasant glow, an agreeable excitement" (63), but not because RLS asked for this change. It was made before he saw any version of the printed text—in the version of *To-day* that was prepared from one of the typewritten copies and supervised by Sidney Colvin. Other such unasked-for changes are at the end of the second paragraph of ch. 1, where "*purao* tree" replaces "purao" (3); in the eleventh paragraph of ch. 1, where "Not long before a ship from Peru had brought an influenza," replaces RLS's "A ship from Peru had brought not long before an influenza" (7); in the forty-fifth paragraph from the end of ch. 10, where "Look for your cigar then, you swine!" replaces RLS's version of Davis's exclamation as he flings Huish forward on his face at the end of the pier, "Look for your cigar there, you swine!" (106); and in the thirty-second paragraph from the end of ch. 11, where "perilous" replaces RLS's "forlorn" in his description of Huish's wading toward Attwater: "it seemed no less forlorn an enterprise . . . than for a whelp to besiege a citadel" (125). Both of these last two changes are probably not even changes but simply uncorrected misreadings of Stevenson's hand, probably by the original typists.

There are dozens of instances like these, and they suggest that choosing the manuscript as the copy-text makes sense not only on circumstantial and logical but also on aesthetic grounds. Too much of RLS's own work is being left out of Hinchcliffe and Kerrigan's edition, and his 1894 corrections are not unrecoverable. Indeed, it is an ironic and no doubt unintended tribute to the manuscript that in this edition 44 of the manuscript readings were adopted as emendations, mostly to correct errors in the printed version or versions (162–63), and that more than 70 others were adopted because they seemed to have the authority of changes made for the Stone and Kimball version or, in the opinion of the editors, were simply better (164–72). In fact, the Stone and Kimball changes also derive from the manuscript, through the typewritten copy on which the *McClure's Magazine* version was based.

Whatever one thinks of the text itself, the presentation of variants in this edition is extremely inconvenient and in some places seriously in error. Variants appear in four separate lists, each of which must be consulted to get the whole picture of a given adopted reading and among which the same word or expression may appear in more than one list. For example, the manuscript reading "memories" that is used in the next-to-last sentence of the first paragraph instead of the word "memoirs" in the printed texts is listed under "Substantive Emendations From MS" and then again under "Substantive Variant Readings." This is inconvenient, but there are also serious defects in the lists and in what is said about the variants. There is no direct or inferential evidence known to me that the Stone and Kimball version "restores from *MS*" anything whatever, and it is misleading to suggest that it does (159). There is no evidence that the manuscript was ever consulted, by anyone, after the typewritten copies were made; and the readings in the Stone and Kimball version that agree with the manuscript, almost without exception, are actually survivors from the *McClure's Magazine* version upon which it is based—a fact that goes unrecognized in the list of variants here and seems to be unknown to these editors. Everything is presented here as if it were a correction made in 1894 (159–61). Worst of all, there are two sizeable gaps in the list of differences: no entries at all for any pages between 78 and 95 or between pages 108 and 114, and no chapter heading later than chapter VII (161). It is astonishing that such an error in typesetting could have gone unnoticed by printers and editors alike. There are also unexplained differences between the two lists of substantive variants and between these lists and the text itself.

The Introduction and the Explanatory Notes also contain errors and misconceptions; and the Chronology is taken, virtually unchanged, from the flawed one that appeared earlier in Kerrigan's edition of *Weir of Hermiston* (1995), discussed in the next entry. Lloyd Osbourne's role as collaborator is belittled and minimized, as if RLS ought to have been ashamed of him, as he was not; the accounting of who wrote what and when is confused and in error; and there is no evidence that Lloyd ever "believed that the collaboration was a mistake" or that he "harbored some resentment over *The Ebb-Tide*," expressing this obliquely in his own novel *The Adventurer*, published in 1907 (xvii–xix). No mention is made of the fact that *The Ebb-Tide* was from the very outset meant to be a collaboration or that during the early stages, when it was known as *The Pearl-Fisher*, it was intended for Robert Bonner's sensational New York *Ledger*.

Bonner and S. S. McClure visited Saranac Lake together in March 1888, at which time RLS accepted Bonner's offer of £1,000 for a book to be serialized. *The Pearl-Fisher* was one of several works that RLS and Lloyd at one time or another considered for this commission, but in the end nothing came of the plan. In the Explanatory Notes, words and phrases—"sight of crammers," "broach the beer," "footpads," "hot coppers," and other expressions—are explained without any reference to the *OED* for their possible meaning and with highly fanciful derivations as a result. RLS's personal associations with the song "Adelaide" ("Einst O Wunder!") and elsewhere with Heine and Virgil, are overlooked. Fakarava is not "part of Paumotu" (141) but one of the islands in the group called the Paumotus; and it might have been mentioned that RLS, Lloyd, and the rest of their party spent just over a fortnight there, 9–25 September 1888, on their way from the Marquesas to Tahiti during the *Casco* voyage. More might have been said about Findlay's *Directory* (144), if only to add that it was a favorite at Saranac Lake when the first South Seas trip was being planned and that the *Casco* copy, with some short diary-like entries by Lloyd, is now in the Stevenson House Collection, Monterey State Historic Park, California. Why a map has been created showing the route of the schooner *Farallone* from Tahiti to Attwater's island and placed opposite the General Introduction (ix) is nowhere explained, but it creates the highly misleading impression that *The Ebb-Tide*, like *Treasure Island* and *Kidnapped*, was published with a map, which it was not. In this as in so many other ways, the present edition is a disappointment and should be redone.

Kerrigan, Catherine, ed. *Weir of Hermiston*. Edinburgh: Edinburgh UP, 1995. After making a substantial start on the novel in late 1892 and early 1893–enough of a start for Colvin and Baxter to begin negotiating serial rights as early as March 1893 (Beinecke 4235–36, 4240, 4498–99)—Stevenson put *Weir of Hermiston* aside for nearly a year before returning to it in the spring of 1894, and again at the end of September. (He was still at work on it on the day he died, 3 December 1894.) In this second effort, with his stepdaughter Isobel Strong now his amanuensis, Stevenson dictated the whole novel again from the beginning, using his own earlier drafts and new notes as he went farther. The result is a complete working manuscript copy of the still-unfinished novel as it stood at the time of Stevenson's death: 217 pages in Belle's legible hand, occasionally corrected by RLS, in the Beinecke Collection at Yale; and slightly more than 100 miscellaneous pages of early and late drafts, outlines of chapter-titles, and genealogical notes, most but not all of these in the J. Pierpont Morgan Library, New York.

In this first volume of the so-called Centenary Edition from Edinburgh University Press, Catherine Kerrigan does as Sidney Colvin did in preparing *Weir of Hermiston* for publication in 1896. She follows the final working manuscript whenever possible, and emends it in the dozen and a half places where, to Colvin at least, emendation seemed necessary to correct errors or to keep the chronology correct. Thus we lose, again, RLS's own phrase about Archie's stirring the maidens of the county "with the charm of Byronism before Byron" in favor of Colvin's fussy emendation "with the charm of Byronism when Byronism was new"—an emendation traceable to the fact that the first three cantos of *Childe Harold's* Pilgrimage appeared in 1812, when

Archie would have been nineteen (50, 163). Owing to the policy of presenting "clear texts, free from any editorial signals" (x), there is no more indication in the text of this edition than there was in Colvin's edition when a substitution or an addition has been made, even when, as in the enumeration of Sundays in 29th paragraph from the end of ch. 7, Kerrigan, following Colvin's emendation, adds a whole sentence: "On the two following, Frank had himself been absent on some of his excursions among the neighbouring families" (100, 164). Kerrigan does at least tell us in her Textual Notes what has been changed, but, especially in an edition that lays claim to "accuracy, authority and authenticity" (ix), emendations that alter rather than merely try to undo lapses in what the author wrote seem at least gratuitous, all the more so in a work known to have been unfinished when the author died.

The most important contribution made by this edition is the presentation, from manuscripts earlier than the final working copy, of six paragraphs and a few words completing ch. 4 (45–46, 164) and six sentences and 20 additional paragraphs, mostly of dialogue, at the end of ch. 9, beyond the end of the working manuscript as it stands (116–17, 165). These additions are presented in the main text itself, not in the notes, and, as with the emendations, there is no indication in the text that they come not from the final working manuscript but from the earlier one—as if RLS meant to include them but somehow did not. This, too, seems to me unwise, especially as a great many shorter passages from the 1892 version are not promoted to the main text but presented only in the list of Substantive Variants (165–78). Kerrigan does, however, use the final working manuscript to restore or undo two dozen small deletions or changes that Colvin made, usually, but not always, for clarity. For example, in ch. 6, when the young Kirstie is at church, it is not only without hurry but also "with perfect haughty unconsciousness" that she allows her eyes to move "in the direction of the Hermiston pew" (70). Later in the same chapter, the state of her mind "still in the turmoil of a glad confusion" is elaborated by the additional phrases "the most beautiful of her sex by her victories at the kirk—the gayest by her more recent triumphs in the bosom of her own family" (77).

Kerrigan also presents, as appendices (141–54), a genealogical chart that RLS drew up of the dates and relationships of the Elliotts and the Rutherfords; two earlier versions of the "Introductory" and the opening of ch. 1, in one of which first-person narration is used briefly, as well as the three versions of a portion of ch. 1 that Graham Balfour published in 1901; half a dozen short passages of dialogue seemingly from scenes that were never written; and four draft lists of chapter titles. (A fifth list, of three titles in the hand of Isobel Strong, Beinecke 7107, is mentioned in a general comment on manuscripts, 159, but is not included.) As Kerrigan notes about these lists of titles, all four "develop the plot up to a projected trial of Archie by his father, but only the third and fourth drafts contain references to the murder of Frank Innes . . . . None of the drafts include the escape from prison and flight to America described by IS [Isobel Strong] as the projected ending of the novel" (143). Under the heading Substantive Variants (165–78) Kerrigan also presents from two of the manuscripts of the earlier version now in the Morgan Library (MA 993, MA 1419) a selection of more than sixty long and short passages that affect "plot, character, structure and meaning," a full collation being impractical owing to the frequent illegibility and the amount of revision in these earlier manuscripts (165). Unaccountably missing is Colvin's lengthy and informative "Editorial Note," which not only shows how the book was presented originally but also contains much valuable information (most of it not in the present edition) about personal and literary sources of the book.

Kerrigan's treatment of manuscript versions other than the manuscripts in the Morgan Library and the final working version at Yale is much less successful; and from the absence of references in her list of Substantive Variants other than to these main sources, it seems possible that she did not even consult them. For example, Kerrigan does mention, in commenting not on the text but on the chapter outlines, that Frank Innes's first name at one time was Pete or Peter and that this usage appears in the manuscripts (143). She also observes that Frank is called "Patrick Innes" in RLS's first letter about the book, to Sidney Colvin, 29 October 1892, Letter 2477 (159–60). But nowhere does she note that the title of ch. 7, "Enter Mephistopheles," in which Innes first appears, was not the first title that RLS used for this chapter. In a draft of the end of the sixth and the beginning of the seventh chapters at Yale, Beinecke 7122, the second of these chapters is titled "Pete enters" and it begins: "Two days later a gig from Crossmichael deposited Peter Innes at the doors of Hermiston." In the final working version, as G. L. McKay notes in his description of this later version, Beinecke 7116, the chapter-title appears as "The idyl and the serpent" but this has been crossed out, with the final title inserted in pencil below it in an unknown hand. That "Enter Mephistopheles" is the third of at least three versions of the chapter-title, and a very late one, is not discoverable from this edition.

Kerrigan's account of the manuscripts in California is confused and erroneous, and this, too, compromises both the completeness and the accuracy of her edition. There are actually two manuscripts in California, not one, and Kerrigan's description of these is inaccurate. Moreover, nowhere in her collations or notes does she refer to or quote from either of the two manuscripts. The one that she describes as being in the "F. W. Heron Collection, Silverado Museum, California, MS 642D" (159) is not at Silverado but in the Stevenson House Collection, Monterey State Historic Park. This single manuscript page does not consist of "notes" for ch. 7, as Kerrigan reports, but of finished text, in RLS's hand, corresponding to pages 225–37 in the first English edition, pages 98–102 in this edition. It never belonged to Charles Warren Stoddard (who died in 1909) but is inscribed "I Field to Frank Unger 1910." Unger was an old friend of Belle's (and RLS's) from San Francisco.

The other manuscript, not described by Kerrigan at all, is in the Robert Louis Stevenson Silverado Museum, St. Helena, California, although not in a Heron Collection (there is no such collection at Silverado) and not under the number that Kerrigan gives. It too is in RLS's hand, and it consists of 139 words (including deletions) comprising the end of the twentieth paragraph from the end of ch. 6 (p. 85 in this edition). It ends a sentence with the words "to abound in his humour whatever that might be," and it continues to the end of the paragraph. It differs from the final version only in lacking a comma after the word "humour," in the inadvertent omission of the indefinite article "a" before the words "subdued twilight" owing to a deletion, and in beginning a new sentence with the phrase "and chance had served her well." The deletions show that RLS's sentence about "The dramatic artist, that lies dormant or only half awake in most human beings" was not present in his first version of the passage, and that before settling on the phrasing that the younger Kirstie looked at

Archie "with a subdued twilight look," RLS had tried "a sort of luminous seriousness" and "a kind of divine seriousness, that became her beyond all expression,"
as well as "a subdued twilight expression." These are substantive variants of genuine
interest, and they are nowhere mentioned in this edition. This manuscript fragment
also has written on it, in Stoddard's hand: "Autograph notes written by Robert Louis
Stevenson of Vailima, Samoa was the very last thing he wrote. Sent to me by Belle
Strong. Charles Warren Stoddard." Not only has she included nothing from either
manuscript, Kerrigan has somehow merged bits of two different descriptions into one.

Kerrigan's account of the so-called Copyright and Preparatory issues printed by
Stone and Kimball in Chicago (161) is wrong in suggesting that there is any difference
between these versions except in the trimming of the edges and the binding of all
three parts together in boards, with the top edges gilt, rather than in wrappers; in the
omission of the separate title pages of the second and third parts; and (according to
Prideaux only) in the omission of the printer's note by R. R. Donnelley and Sons on
the back of the last page. G. L. McKay points all of this out in his entry of Yale's
copy of the version in three parts as Beinecke 628. The other supposed omissions to
which Kerrigan refers are in fact common to both versions. In a pencil note in the
copy of the first part in the Widener Collection at Harvard, H. I. Kimball says that
this was "one of about six copies printed (in three parts) and issued from January to
March 1896. The regular edition did not appear until May 20th." Kerrigan does give
these dates, but the order of the sentences in her account creates the erroneous impression that these Stone and Kimball versions were made in response to Robert Mc-
Clure's sending final corrected copy to them on 7 April 1896, with instructions how
it was to be set in type (161). In fact, the printing in parts was finished at least a
month before then.

Kerrigan does not mention or seem to draw upon Sidney Kramer's detailed account
of the financial arrangements, copyright publication, and then the transfer of the book-
form publication from Stone and Kimball to Scribner's when the partnership was
dissolved in March/April 1896–all of this in his *A History of Stone and Kimball . . . -
with a Bibliography of Their Publications 1893–1905* (Chicago: Norman W. Forgue,
1940), 81–84. Kramer says that Fanny Stevenson, in a very unwise venture into
negotiating publication details, asked Graham Balfour to place the book, and that in
1895 Balfour sold it to Scribner's for a 20% royalty and an advance of £500, not
knowing, of course, that at the very same time Charles Baxter was also selling the
book, through Robert McClure in London, to Stone and Kimball (Robert McClure to
Herbert Stone, 7 September 1895, Beinecke 5180). When the partnership was dissolved, Kimball turned over the rights to *St. Ives* as well as *Weir of Hermiston* to
Scribner's and notified Charles Baxter to this effect on 7 May 1896. Kerrigan has not
pursued Kramer's possibly mistaken note that three more parts of the copyright edition
were received by the Library of Congress: the fourth part on 4 April 1896, the fifth
and sixth parts on 7 April 1896 (Kramer, 360). Nor has she anything to say about six
proof-sheets, now in the Newberry Library, Chicago, of what would appear to have
been intended for a Stone and Kimball edition of *Weir of Hermiston*. Numbered 73–78
in blue pencil, with corrections in the margins by Sidney Colvin, they contain parts
of chs. 7 and 8.

As a textual editor, Kerrigan seems to me much less in command than she ought to be of the material itself—extant manuscripts and publication details especially. And, unfortunately, this lack of command extends into the areas of explanation and information as well. The Chronology in particular shows a disturbing vagueness about Stevenson's life and publications, as well as carelessness in details. In 1873 RLS went alone, not "with his cousins the Balfours," to Cockfield Rectory in Suffolk. He met Fanny Osbourne at Grez, not Fontainebleau, in September 1876, not 1875, after the canoe trip with Sir Walter Simpson that occurred in Belgium as well as in Northern France. He published nothing in the *Cornhill Magazine* in 1875, and only one essay there before May 1876, "Victor Hugo's Romances" (May 1874). The *Devonia* was a passenger liner, not a "merchant ship." During the seven weeks that he spent at Braemar in August and September 1881, RLS did much more on *Treasure Island* than "develop the plot." He also wrote a dozen and a half chapters, and at Davos soon afterwards he finished the book. At Bournemouth, the Stevensons did not acquire or move into the house that they named Skerryvore until April 1885, after nine months in lodgings and other rented accommodations there. The play *Admiral Guinea* was never called *Austin Guinea*, and in 1885 there was published only one collection of stories, not two, namely *More New Arabian Nights: The Dynamiter*. There is no definite article in the title of *Strange Case of Dr. Jekyll and Mr. Hyde*, nor is there an indefinite article before the title of RLS's *Memoir of Fleeming Jenkin*. It was not Scribner's but S. S. McClure who in 1888 commissioned RLS's letters from the South Seas. Although in 1888 *The Black Arrow* was indeed serialized by McClure and was first published in book form by Scribner's, the novel was in fact written in 1883, when it was published serially in *Young Folks*. RLS lived the last five years of his life at Vailima, on the island of Upolu, which is not in the Gilbert Islands but in Samoa.

Unfortunately, this same chronology is used almost verbatim in the Edinburgh University Press editions of *The Ebb-Tide* (1995) and *Treasure Island* (1998), and errors from it persist even in the edition of RLS's *Collected Poems* (2003).

There are various mistakes throughout Kerrigan's Introduction and Explanatory Notes as well, even typographical errors such as "RSL" for "RLS" and "Grequory" for "Gregory." The essay in which RLS refers to the attraction of great writers is in fact "A Note on Realism" (1883) and what he actually said about changes was that one finds "sweeping alterations in the manner of their art"—not their "style" (xix). Raeburn's portrait of Lord Braxfield did not appear in Henry Cockburn's *Memorials of his Time* (1856), at least not until a new edition (Edinburgh: T. N. Foulis, 1909) was published fifteen years after Stevenson's death (xx). *The Hanging Judge* (1886–87) exists not only in the typescript at Yale (Beinecke 6273–not 627, as given here) but was privately printed and later published in the Vailima and the Tusitala editions; and it has to do with a husband and his wife, not a father and his son (xxxiv-v, n. 3). RLS's brief study, *The Pentland Rising: A Page in History 1666* (1866), is also readily accessible, and, as its title reminds us, it is not "a history of the Covenanters" but a short commemorative study of a single incident (xxxiv-v, n. 3).

Kerrigan notes that a number of errors in the English and American book-form editions "were subsequently corrected by Colvin in the Edinburgh Edition" (161). But for reasons unknown she has not brought these into her edition. In the first sentence of ch. 3, for example, "Judiciary Court" still appears, wrongly, in place of

"Justiciary Court" (25). Whether the word "hawse" (not "hawes" as it appears in the Glossary, 123) was a mistake is not a "long-standing crux" as Kerrigan describes it (163, 136). It was a speculation by M. R. Ridley in a letter to the *Times Literary Supplement*, 28 August 1959 (not 28 September, as given here), and in the next several weeks Ridley's suggestion was immediately and thoroughly refuted. RLS's choice of word is correct and his usage exact. It was not RLS's Edinburgh friend Charles Baxter, but the modern editor of their letters, DeLancey Ferguson, who said that "[to] the very end, Colvin still had to be assured that Scots idioms were not misprints" (*RLS: Stevenson's Letters to Charles Baxter* [1956], viii). Furthermore, the remark is quite unfair: Colvin really did try to get the Scottish details right.

Minutiae like these may not greatly matter, but there are many larger errors, of fact and of interpretation. One example among many is that it is simply wrong to say that Henry James was "always fulsome in his praise of RLS" (xvii) or that in their "eulogies" on the book when it was first published James and Colvin alike "protected *Weir* from adverse criticism" by suggesting that "attacks on the work would have been like defiling the very grave" (xviii). This is a colorful assertion, but the remarks that Kerrigan quotes from James cannot have had, or even contributed to, such an effect even if it had existed: they were published almost four years later. And, although in a letter to Colvin, 5 July 1895, Beinecke 4910, quoted by Kerrigan only in her Textual Notes (160), James praised the novel highly and urged Colvin to proceed at once with its publication, he did not review it. In fact, James made no comment at all in print on *Weir of Hermiston* until he made a brief mention of it in his review in January 1900 of Colvin's edition of *RLS's Letters . . . to His Family and Friends*. And as Janet Adam Smith, Kenneth Graham, and George Dekker, among others, have noted, James was in general surprisingly measured in his published comments on RLS.

In his "Editorial Note" Colvin was indeed lavish in his praise, but this too hardly had the chilling effect on criticism that Kerrigan claims that it did. On the contrary, as Paul Maixner remarks in his introduction to the Critical Heritage volume (1981), "[t]hose who reviewed the book when it appeared . . . even those sympathetic to Stevenson, were surprisingly unenthusiastic" (40). In his review in the *Speaker*, 6 June 1896, Arthur Quiller-Couch even took Colvin to task for attaching such enthusiastic remarks to the book, lest doing so rouse "a mild and wondering resentment among those . . . who have not yet enjoyed a course of critical instruction at Mr. Colvin's feet," a resentment that he feared might even extend "to the book itself" (in Maixner, 469). The contemporary reception of *Weir of Hermiston*, in short, was neither uncritical nor highly enthusiastic, and its tone was neither set nor even much influenced by what Colvin and James had to say publicly or privately.

In the Explanatory Notes, we find numerous errors. The history of the Covenanters that is given here (129) pertains to an earlier period: the "Killing Time" was in 1689. The Roman jurist contemporary with Papinian in the third century B. C. was not the Christian apostle Paul (132–33) but Julius Paulus. There is no Supreme Court of Scotland (130), but rather the Court of Session for civil matters and the Court of Justiciary for criminal ones. And the following is surely not the description that RLS—or d'Artagnan, a native of the French region of Gascony but never a musketeer nor ever named Gascon—would have accepted for one of his own favorite books or of Athos, Porthos, and Aramis: "*The Three Musketeers*: Alexandre Dumas's romance about Gascon, a poor gentleman who goes to Paris and meets up with two friends to become the trio who seek their fortunes in heroic adventures'' (135).

Calder, Jenni, ed. *St. Ives: The Adventures of a French Prisoner in England.* Glasgow: Drew, 1990. On 24 January 1893 RLS wrote to Sidney Colvin that he had begun ''a new story'' and that he was also trying a new method of composition: ''I am writing by dictation, and really think it is an art I can manage to acquire.'' Finishing the same letter on 30 January, RLS wrote out the titles of 29 chapters of *St. Ives* (''I don't know where to stop,'' he remarked), the last three of which were ''XXVII. The Aeronaut. XXVIII. *The True Blooded Yankee*. XXIX. In France'' (Letter 2514). *St. Ives* was still unfinished at the time of Stevenson's death at the end of 1894, however, and in writing five chapters in 1897 to complete the story Arthur Quiller-Couch could find nothing to explain the title ''The True Blooded Yankee'' or any evidence that American privateers were in British waters during the War of 1812, when the novel takes place. The result, as Ernest Mehew notes, was that Quiller-Couch ''was forced to invent a convoluted story to explain what happened'' (Letter 2514, n. 13).

In a detailed foreword to the present edition, R. J. Storey shows that there really was an American privateer called the *True Blooded Yankee* active off the west coast of Scotland at that time, and he suggests from the list of chapters that RLS probably intended to have his hero make his escape from Edinburgh in a balloon and be rescued and taken home to France by the ship. Jenni Calder writes up all of this in a sprightly and entertaining new ending in this edition. But at the time that Calder and Storey wrote, it remained unknown where RLS could have learned the story.

Annotating Stevenson's chapter-title, ''The True Blooded Yankee,'' Ernest Mehew supplied the answer: Wellington's *Dispatches*, which RLS would have read in 1885 while planning a never-completed contribution to the English Worthies series that he had contracted with Longman's to write. And the books themselves remained with him in his library in Samoa. ''When he was British ambassador in Paris in 1814,'' Mehew writes, ''Wellington complained to the French authorities about American privateers using French ports: in a letter of 8 October 1814 he referred specifically to the fact that the 'American privateer called the *True Blooded Yankee* has been completely fitted for sea at Brest, and manned with a crew of 200 men' (*Dispatches*, ed. Gurwood, 1838, XII, 143)'' (Letter 2514, n. 13).

Shaffer, Ellen, ed. *Prayers Written at Vailima.* Atlanta: Tudor Press, n. d. [? 1973] Fourteen of the prayers that RLS wrote for family worship at Vailima were first published in vol. 21 (1896) of the Edinburgh Edition. Two more draft prayers were printed, with facsimiles, from a notebook now at Yale (Beinecke 8348, 6738) in the Boston Bibliophile Society volume, *Hitherto Unpublished Prose Writings* (1921), 191–95. Four others were published in vol. 26 (1923) of the Vailima Edition, three of them from RLS's notebook for *Travels With A Donkey* (1879), now in the Huntington Library; these three also appear in Gordon Golding's edition of the notebook, *The Cevennes Journal* (1978), 69. All 20 of these prayers appeared in vol. 21 (1924) of the Tusitala Edition, and these are the twenty that appear in the present handsomely printed paperbound volume. RLS's prose, however, is printed as if it were verse—an oddity that shows how deeply-cadenced albeit in prose these prayers are. Also included is Fanny Stevenson's account of RLS's prayers, first published in the Biographical Edition (1905) and as a ''Prefatory Note'' in the Tusitala Edition. Variants of two of the Cévennes prayers are at Yale (Beinecke 6736, 8349); at least one other prayer, unpublished and written during the war in Samoa in 1893 and including an optional passage referring to Malietoa Laupepa, is among the uncatalogued manuscripts at Yale.

Collections

Gelder, Kenneth, ed. *Robert Louis Stevenson: The Scottish Stories and Essays*. Edinburgh: Edinburgh UP, 1989. In addition to the well-known stories and essays, Gelder includes two works written when RLS was still in his teens: a story called "The Plague-Cellar" (1864, possibly 1866) that had not been available before except in my Ph.D. dissertation (Yale, 1970) and as published by Gelder in the *Weekend Scotsman*, 25 August 1985; and the privately-printed pamphlet *The Pentland Rising: A Page in History 1666* (1866), which is generally treated as RLS's first actual publication and is included in all of the collected editions beginning with the Edinburgh Edition. RLS had nothing good to say about either work, but they are among the earliest examples in a lifetime of engagements with his Scottish heritage. Another welcome rarity, published here for the first time since its appearance in *Scribner's Magazine*, October 1893, is RLS's "Note" introducing his grandfather's account of Sir Walter Scott's voyage on the annual inspection tour of the Scottish lighthouses in 1814, in which Scott participated officially as sheriff of Selkirk. It would have been fitting to have included Stevenson's grandfather's account as well. Scott's own journal of the six-week cruise, which was begun three weeks after *Waverley* was published, appeared in Lockhart's *Life* (1837–38). It has been reprinted with period illustrations as *The Voyage of the* Pharos: *Walter Scott's Cruise Around Scotland in 1814*, ed. Brian D. Osborne (Motherwell: Scottish Library Association, 1998).

Gelder's introduction and notes are insightful and informative, especially on the key role of Covenanting histories in the shaping of Stevenson's imagination, offering as they do narratives of confrontation, betrayal, and nemesis, as well as narrators who are often partisan to the point of fanaticism. "The Pavilion on the Links" and "The Merry Men," are, on the other hand, in "the line of Scott." These stories share Scott's ambivalence about a rougher, more colorful Scottish past that no longer seems within the reach of their Anglicised heroes (10–11). In RLS's essays of Scottish recollection and description, however, and in his two stories in Scots dialect, "Thrawn Janet" and "The Tale of Tod Lapraik," he manages to fuse history and description and turn those " 'old doings' into a 'leevin' experience." (13). A glance at the longer works, even though they were not included, would have rounded out this fine introduction. The novels, finished and unfinished, the longer stories such as *An Old Song* (1877) and, especially, *Dr. Jekyll and Mr. Hyde* (1886), and the descriptive essays in *Edinburgh: Picturesque Notes* (1878) all embody themes, attitudes, and techniques that Gelder finds in the shorter works as well.

Hubbard, Tom, and Duncan Glen, eds. *Stevenson's Scotland*. Edinburgh: Mercat, 2003. This inclusive, well-annotated collection of excerpts from Stevenson's essays, poems, fiction, and letters shows how widely he ranged all over Scotland, from Carrick and Galloway to Orkney and Shetland. *Edinburgh: Picturesque Notes* (1878) is reprinted in its entirety. The collection also includes two previously unpublished pieces, from manuscripts now at Yale. The first is an untitled fragment of 350 words beginning an essay on the Water of Leith (Beinecke 6506). It was probably written in 1890 or 1891, possibly for a new series of essays meant for *Scribner's Magazine*. In the fourth sentence from the end, however, the correct reading is "the Black Avon of Forth, the wild Highlandman's bridle" (not "hurdle"). To a note from Neil Macara Brown, 11 November 1994, I also owe the observation that the reference comes from "a now not too well known saying" referring to the headwaters of the river, "Forth bridles the wild Highlandman," found, for example, in Scott's *Rob Roy*, ch. 28, paragraph 6. RLS himself uses it in the second paragraph of ch. 26 of *Kidnapped* (1886).

The other new piece by RLS is "The Antiquities of Midlothian" (Beinecke 5970), 875 words about Craigmillar Castle and Corstorphine Church dictated by RLS to his mother in February or March 1861, when he was ten. Except for a French translation in Michel LeBris, *A travers l'Ecosse* (1992), "The Antiquities of Midlothian" had appeared before only in my Ph.D. dissertation (Yale, 1970). In his account of Craigmillar Castle, RLS refers to the well-known illustrated account by Robert William Billings, *The Baronial and Ecclesiastical Antiquities of Scotland illustrated by Robert William Billings Architect 1845–52*. 4 vols. Edinburgh and London: William Blackwood and Sons, [1852]. Arranged alphabetically, the first volume has engravings and brief accounts of Craigmillar Castle and Corstorphine Church. RLS's copy, ultimately from the Stevenson family home at 17 Heriot Row, is now in the Robert Louis Stevenson Silverado Museum, St. Helena, California. These volumes are also important in that, as RLS himself remarked (RLS to E. L. Burlingame, 6 January 1888, Letter 1994), he based his description of Durrisdeer in *The Master of Ballantrae* in part on Billings's account and on five engravings of Cragievar Castle, Aberdeenshire, as well as on Pinkie House in Musselburgh, near Edinburgh.

Treglown, Jeremy, ed. *The Lantern Bearers and other essays*. London: Chatto and Windus, 1988. Both in his substantial introduction and in his excellent selection of essays, Treglown has taken RLS seriously as an essayist. "Between the high rigour of Carlyle and Macaulay and the brilliant but ultimately arid playfulness of Wilde," he writes, "a unique voice is heard in Stevenson, both moral and irreverent, subjective and socially aware, keen to draw conclusions yet always aware of relativism and the unreliability of dogma; and, in all this, light in tone and vividly concrete" (viii). RLS wrote and published more than a hundred essays of many kinds, from Hazlitt-like personal revelations, impressionistic travel and sketches, to literary criticism, first for the *Cornhill Magazine*, which was edited by Leslie Stephen when RLS began there, and later in *Longman's* and *Scribner's*. Treglown offers examples of all of the many types of essays that RLS wrote—31 essays in all—beginning with "The Philosophy of Umbrellas" (*Edinburgh University Magazine*, Feb. 1871) and including for the first time in book form two of RLS's Parisian sketches published under the heading "In the Latin Quarter" in the short-lived weekly *London*: "A Ball at Mr Elsinare's" and "A Studio of Ladies" (10 and 17 Feb. 1877). Other appealing rarities are "The Misgivings of Convalescence" (*Pall Mall Gazette*, 17 March 1881), an essay that was not included with RLS's other "Swiss Notes" when these were reprinted for the first time in *Essays and Criticisms*, 1903; "Confessions of a Unionist" (1888; written and carried to the stage of galley proofs for *Scribner's Magazine* in 1888 but never published; it was privately printed in 1921 from the galley proofs at Harvard); and the essay on payment and accounting practices, "Authors and Publishers" (1890–91; MS. Yale), published by Treglown for the first time, with a useful commentary, in "R. L. Stevenson and the Authors-Publishers Debate," *Times Literary Supplement*, 15–21 January 1988, 58–59. These lesser-known pieces are welcome, and they complement the more familiar essays such as those on John Knox, Whitman, Burns, and Pepys, "A Gossip on Romance" and "A Humble Remonstrance," "Forest Notes," "The Old Pacific Capital," "An Apology for Idlers," "Father Damien," and others. Treglown has also taken some care with the texts, mainly using the first book-form editions, which RLS generally supervised attentively, rather than either the periodical versions or any of the collected editions.

Menikoff, Barry, ed. *Tales from the Prince of Storytellers*. Evanston: Northwestern UP, 1993. The great strength of this edition is Menikoff's long critical introduction, but because the entire contents—introduction, texts, glossary, and notes—appear again, with *Dr. Jekyll and Mr. Hyde* and ten additional stories, in Menikoff's Modern Library edition of the *Complete Short Stories* (New York, 2002), this later edition effectively supersedes the earlier one. Menikoff here publishes, for the first time, the final manuscript version of "Markheim" (1885, Harvard) and the only manuscript version of "The Isle of Voices" (1893, Rosenbach Collection and Museum, Philadelphia). In both stories, as Menikoff notes, the differences between the printer's manuscript and the printed versions are "numerous" (386). But nearly all of the differences in "Markheim" are in punctuation, not always to the advantage of the manuscript; and the half-dozen substantive differences are slight, chiefly the undoing of misreadings or emendations. In "The Isle of Voices" the changes are mostly the division of a number of long paragraphs in the manuscript into multiple paragraphs. For example, the first three paragraphs in previously published versions, including the first edition, are in Menikoff's edition presented in one long paragraph, as in the manuscript (357). The seven paragraphs toward the end of the story beginning "It was all bare in the strong sun" and ending "he forgot the island and all his sorrows" are a single paragraph in the manuscript (372). Although it is perhaps true that Stevenson preferred "large units of prose, both for aesthetic as well as narrative reasons" (386), in neither of the present instances is it evident what might be the effects Stevenson had in mind by keeping things together or that they are not outweighed by the clarity and ease of understanding achieved by breaking things up. Menikoff's annotations are adequate but slight. For example, he does not comment on the earlier manuscript of "Markheim," also at Harvard. This was cut into printer's takes for publication in the *Pall Mall Gazette* at Christmas 1884 but was withdrawn in favor of "The Body-Snatcher," and it has a number of important earlier thoughts. In "The Isle of Voices," although in a note, quoting Stevenson, Menikoff gives the correct spelling of the surname of François Donat-Rimarau, in the text he perpetuates the misspelling of that name. Donat-Rimaru was acting vice-resident of Fakarava, in the Paumotus, with whom RLS became friends in September 1888 and to whom he owed much of the background for the story [see Ernest Mehew's note on RLS to Donat, 10 September 1888, Letter 2108]. The glossary of Scottish words is very helpful, especially in reading "Thrawn Janet" (1881).

Norquay, Glenda, ed. *Robert Louis Stevenson on Fiction: An Anthology of Literary and Critical Essays*. Edinburgh: Edinburgh UP, 1999. Norquay presents 14 of RLS's essays, from "Child's Play" (1878) to "Letter to a Young Gentleman Who Proposes to Embrace the Career of Art" (1888), all of which, she remarks in her introduction, "explore fiction-making: what makes for a good or bad book; the ways in which writers, including [RLS] himself, work; the nature of literary realism; the influence of childhood reading on the adult mind; and the importance of imagination for both writers and readers" (1). These are among the many themes in these essays, and Norquay does her best to relate RLS's sometimes elusive statements of literary theory to his own practice and to his essays on particular authors, although she does not cover RLS's observations in his letters and in various interviews with the press. Norquay's annotations are helpful and detailed, and they have the unexpected side benefit of showing the remarkable breadth and variety of Stevenson's reading. She also calls attention to a few differences between the periodical and later versions of these essays—for example, restoring RLS's paragraph on the individual illustrations in " 'A Penny Plain and Twopence Coloured' " (*Magazine of Art*, April 1884). At the end of the second paragraph of "A Chapter on Dreams," however, "hell gasped for him" is an obvious later error. The *Scribner's Magazine* version is obviously correct, since hell is a hole or pit into which one might fall at any moment: "hell gaped for him."

Day, A. Grove, ed. *Robert Louis Stevenson: Travels in Hawaii*. UP of Hawaii, 1973. From the 20–page original in the Huntington Library (part of HM 2412), Day publishes for the first time RLS's day-to-day working notes on the Kona Coast of Hawaii, 28 April-2 May 1889, intended for the newspaper series and as a quarry for his big book on the South Seas (183–205). This appears without annotations but with a brief statement observing that the Bingham of whom RLS writes with mixed admiration and disapproval in several passages is the missionary Hiram Bingham, writing in his *A Residence of Twenty-One Years in the Sandwich Islands* (1847). RLS omitted these remarks from the published versions.

After their appearance in seven weekly installments in the New York *Sun*, 31 May–12 July 1891, RLS never revised the accounts that he eventually wrote, from notes such as these, of visiting the Hawaiian islands of Molokai (22–31 May 1889) and Hawaii (26 April–3 May 1889). Nor did his accounts of Hawaii appear again during his lifetime, or in the Edinburgh Edition after his death, possibly on the grounds that, unlike the South Seas material that was chosen for reprinting, RLS never revised this material after its newspaper publication. With a new division of the first three installments into five chapters, and some minor revisions, the material on the island of Hawaii was first reprinted as Part III, "The Eight Islands," of *In the South Seas* in Volume 18 of the Swanston Edition (25 vols., London: William Heinemann and Longmans Green, 1911–12). The same year, all of this Hawaii material was also reprinted, no doubt from the original newspaper sources, in nine chapters in an unauthorized collected edition called the "Vailima Edition" published by Peter Fenelon Collier (9 vols. New York, 1912). This is not the same "Vailima Edition" that was published under Lloyd Osbourne's supervision in the 1920s (26 vols., London: William Heinemann and others, 1922–23).

This is Day's source in the present volume. Why he chose this derivative source rather than use the original publication in the New York *Sun* or the photostats of RLS's contributions at Yale (Beinecke 1082) is not explained. In the 1920s, the material on Molokai eventually found its way into the authorized Vailima and Tusitala editions, but never, as in the present edition, in the same place with the material on the island of Hawaii. As a tenth chapter, using his own title ''Another Molokai'' in place of RLS's own subtitle ''Leprosy at Penrhyn,'' Day rather strangely includes the second half of RLS's account of visiting the island of Penrhyn, first published in the New York *Sun*, 24 May 1891, and collected in the Vailima and Tusitala editions. Penrhyn is not one of the Hawaiian islands, and RLS's visit there took place a year after he visited Molokai, on 9–10 May 1890 during the cruise of the *Janet Nichol*. The only connection with the material on Hawaii is the appearance in Penrhyn of leprosy brought from Hawaii and RLS's discussion of the problem in general. These accounts are annotated, here and there, within the text, generally to supply names. Detailed annotations would have been much more useful, especially coming from as knowledgeable an expert on Hawaii as Professor Day.

In his introduction, Day summarizes RLS's two stays in Hawaii concisely, concretely, and well, chiefly drawing on Sister Mary Martha McGaw's *Stevenson in Hawaii* (Honolulu: U of Hawaii P, 1950). This is also the source of the well-reproduced maps. There are also 19 photographs, familiar and lesser-known. Day includes, from the versions published by Sidney Colvin, two dozen of RLS's letters written in Hawaii during his visits in 1889 and 1893, as well as RLS's ''Open Letter'' on Father Damien written in Sydney early in 1890. The letters have now been superseded by the versions in the Yale Letters, but it is handy to have them as part of the collection. ''The Bottle Imp'' (first published in 1891) is not included, despite its affinity, in landscape and many other respects, with Ho'okena on the island of Hawaii and the possibility that it was inspired or even first drafted there. Day also includes seven poems, including three of the four short poems first published in Arthur Johnstone's *Recollections of RLS in the Pacific* (London: Chatto and Windus, 1905) 305–08.

Jolly, Roslyn, ed. *South Sea Tales*. Oxford: Oxford UP, 1996. World's Classics series. To the three stories in *Island Nights' Entertainments* (1893) and the novel *The Ebb-Tide* (1894), Jolly adds two short fables first published in 1895 after Stevenson's death: ''The Cart-Horses and the Saddle-Horse'' and ''Something in It.'' The explanatory notes are generous and helpful, and in a substantial introduction Jolly brings out the ways in which RLS's Pacific fiction not only breaks new ground in realism but also commands attention for its modernism and ''insights into the emergence of twentieth-century global culture'' within and largely in spite of the dominant but waning imperial ideal (xxii). ''The Beach of Falesá,'' she remarks,

> displays a modernist's interest in the '' 'subjective' adventure'' (to use Henry James's term) and the limited narrator, while *The Ebb-Tide* shows how Stevenson preceded Conrad in working out a narrative mode that overlaid extreme realism with symbolism and a kind of dreamlike imagistic excess to explore the nightmare of imperialism. (xxxii-iii)

Jolly follows the first English book-form editions for all of these works, emending here and there, and, in her notes, includes from Barry Menikoff's edition (1984) some of the more notable readings in the manuscript version of ''The Beach of Falesá.'' She explains her choice of the book-form editions as copy-text (manuscripts also exist for ''The Isle of Voices'' and *The Ebb-Tide*) on the plausible but possibly questionable grounds that these are the texts that RLS "finally passed for publication" and that all of the changes in the published versions, whoever might have made them, "were accepted by the author" (xxxv). Stevenson paid great attention to style, even down to the level of punctuation. Writing about "The Beach of Falesá" to Sidney Colvin on 28 September 1891 RLS remarked that after having written and rewritten it

> I've got to overhaul it once again to my sorrow; I was all yesterday revising and found a lot of slacknesses and (what is worse in this kind of thing) some literaryisms. . . . [T]he beginning remains about a quarter tone out (in places); but I have rather decided to let it stay so."
> (Letter 2351)

Because of the many practical difficulties imposed by his remoteness from England, editorial preference for the published versions may sometimes be unwise, especially since we often have access to the manuscripts that Stevenson sent home. As Dale Kramer has remarked, the doctrine of "passive authorial acceptance" may in practice have the effect of "elevating a printing-house stylesheet administered by the printer's editor and a group of compositors over [the] author":

> the contours of the pacing of the words by different types of punctuation—commas, semicolons, dashes, and the like—were embedded within the words themselves by the author her/himself, at that time of creative attention arguably more acute than at times of subsequent reconsideration.

As Kramer notes, this is not an aesthetic but a practical argument, and it must be decided case by case. ("The Compositor as Copy-Text." Rev. of George Eliot, *Romola*, ed. Andrew Brown. 1993. *Text* 9 [1996]: 369–88.) In editing Stevenson's later works, given both his concern for style and his remoteness, one might need to be brave enough to use the manuscript, including its punctuation, as copy-text, just as the original printers did. Later readings would be accepted conservatively, and only when they could be shown to be the result of RLS's active correction, not (as in this edition) his presumed acquiescence. Emendation would be used as Menikoff uses it, chiefly to get rid of needless distractions such as clearly misspelled words, unclosed parentheses, unintended omissions during revision or copying, and inconsistent spellings of proper names.

Robinson, Roger, ed. *Robert Louis Stevenson: His Best Pacific Writings*. Honolulu: Bess, 2003. Robinson offers an engaging selection of letters, stories, poems, and nonfiction by RLS, even an excerpt from *The Ebb-Tide* (1894), and a generous selection of photographs and original illustrations, many of them not at all well known. All of these materials are intended to convey a sense of what Stevenson's life was like in the South Seas, and what he made of that environment. Particularly welcome is an excerpt from "The Feast of Famine" (*Ballads*, 1890), which, as Robinson observes, is striking for its "direct and unvarnished . . . rendering of Marquesan custom, lore, war, psychology and even sex" and for RLS's attempt to find a vehicle that could embody the "despondency" that he found in the Marquesas (302). In a brief foreword, the Samoan novelist Albert Wendt describes the great influence that Stevenson continues to have on his own work.

Kucich, John, ed. *Fictions of Empire: Complete Texts with Introduction, Historical Contexts, Critical Essays*. Boston: Houghton Mifflin, 2003. New Riverside Editions series. [not seen] According to the publisher's description, this collection includes complete texts of Conrad's *Heart of Darkness* (1899), Kipling's *The Man Who Would Be King* (1888), and RLS's "The Beach of Falesá" (1892), and a range of excerpts under headings such as "Historical Contexts," "Biographical Contexts," Fictions of Empire," "Ancillary Texts," and "Critical Responses." Historical and other background texts range from Darwin, William Ellis, and Melville to King Leopold II of the Belgians, Chinua Achebe, and Patrick Brantlinger. Stevenson is covered biographically by Roslyn Jolly, in her essay "Robert Louis Stevenson and Samoan History: Crossing the Roman Wall" (1996), and critically by Katherine Linehan, "Taking Up With Kanakas: Stevenson's Complex Social Criticism in 'The Beach of Falesá' " (1990).

Menikoff, Barry, ed. *The Complete Short Stories of Robert Louis Stevenson:* Strange Case of Dr. Jekyll and Mr. Hyde *and Nineteen Other Tales*. New York: Random House, 2002. Adding as it does *Dr. Jekyll and Mr. Hyde* and ten other stories, this Modern Library edition augments and thereby supersedes Menikoff's earlier collection, *Tales from the Prince of Storytellers* (1993), from which the glossary and notes are also borrowed. Menikoff's first-rate critical introduction is also kept, with a few small changes. An odd but welcome bonus is "Stevenson in the *OED*" (811–18), a list of some 200 words in the first or second edition of the *Oxford English Dictionary* for which a quotation from one of RLS's short stories is used as an illustration, sometimes as the only one.

The texts are generally from the first English book-form editions, and they are presented—unfortunately without dates or details of their original publication—in the order that the collections appeared and then in the order that the stories appeared within the collections. This leads to spectacular anomalies such as the appearance of "Will o' the Mill" (*Cornhill Magazine*, Jan. 1878) just before both "Markheim" (*The Broken Shaft*, Christmas 1885) and "Olalla" (*Court and Society Review*, Christmas 1885), all three of these immediately after *Dr. Jekyll and Mr. Hyde* (1886), which was written and published later; and the appearance of all of the "Latter-Day Arabian Nights" stories (as they were called in their first publication, serially in *London*, from June to October 1878) and "The Pavilion on the Links" (*Cornhill Magazine*, Sept.—Oct. 1880) before "A Lodging for the Night" (*Temple Bar*, Oct. 1877) and "The Sire de Malétroits's Door" (*Temple Bar*, Jan. 1878). "An Old Song" is among the last four stories in the volume, all of which are placed there only because they were not published in volume form during Stevenson's lifetime. But it was Stevenson's first published short story, appearing anonymously in four weekly installments in *London* in February and March 1877. A chronological arrangement would have been much more helpful to readers anxious to follow the evolution of Stevenson's themes and techniques, as would have been giving the date of each story somewhere; information on each volume of collected stories could have appeared in the notes.

Exceptions to the general rule of following the first book-form edition are that the manuscript versions of "Markheim," "The Beach of Falesá," and "The Isle of Voices" are used in preference to any published version; and that instead of the versions of "The Story of a Lie," "The Body-Snatcher," and "The Misadventures of John Nicholson'' that were published during Stevenson's lifetime, a 1912 reprint collection of them is for some unknown reason used instead. ''An Old Song'' comes from my own edition (1982), from the original and only publication in the weekly periodical *London*. The story, by the way, was not found ''in the files'' of *London* (784) but was actually published there anonymously. ''The Plague Cellar,'' ''When the Devil Was Well,'' ''The Enchantress,'' and ''The Waif Woman'' are all omitted, no doubt on the plausible grounds that Stevenson never chose to publish any of them. Dorothy Sayers seems to have admired the self-contained tale that, in ch. 9 of *The Master of Ballantrae* (1889), James Durie tells Mackellar during the voyage of the *Nonesuch*, and she includes it as a separate short story under the title ''Was It Murder?'' in her Everyman's Library collection, *Tales of Detection* (London: J. M. Dent, 1936) 49–52. She comments: ''The excerpt from Stevenson's *The Master of Ballantrae* is an excellent example of the 'perfect murder' that seeks to baffle justice by escaping beyond the range of legal and material proof'' (xiii). In his splendid critical study, *Narrating Scotland: The Imagination of Robert Louis Stevenson* (San Marino, CA: Huntington Library P, 1999), 183–201, Menikoff himself has many good things to say about ''Black Andie's Tale of Tod Lapraik,'' ch. 15 in *David Balfour* (1893), another self-contained, embedded tale that is often treated as a short story. There is no harm omitting these other works, but it would have helped readers interested in Stevenson's efforts in short fiction to be reminded of them somewhere. There is no excuse, however, for passing over in complete silence the fourth collection of short stories that Stevenson published during his lifetime: *More New Arabian Nights: The Dynamiter* (1885). It is true that this collection is a collaboration, but ''Zero's Tale of the Explosive Bomb'' is generally accepted as Stevenson's alone, and all but two of the remaining stories are the result of his close collaboration with his wife. Readers of Stevenson are bound to stumble across these stories eventually, and they have an important place in his development.

  Bell, Ian, ed. *Robert Louis Stevenson: The Complete Short Stories*. 2 vols. Edinburgh: Mainstream, 1993. To the well-known stories this collection adds ''The Plague Cellar,'' ''When the Devil Was Well,'' ''Edifying Letters of the Rutherford Family'' (which despite its interest is not really a short story), ''An Old Song,'' ''Diogenes'' (also doubtful as a short story), ''The Enchantress,'' and ''The Waif Woman''—none of these with any acknowledgement of their prior publication, still less of the details. There is only a brief general introduction; there are no notes or comments on the individual stories; and no trouble whatever has been taken over the texts. These come from such sources as a 1912 Chatto and Windus reprint of *New Arabian Nights*; an undated reprint of *The Merry Men* published by Eveleigh and Grayson; and, for ''When the Devil Was Well,'' vol. 3 of an edition of RLS's works unknown to me published in 1924 by the Waverley Book Company. This recension was favored over the story's first appearance, in a volume printed by the Bibliophile Society (Boston, 1922) or the manuscript at Yale.

Books and Articles

Scally, John. ''Writing Around the World.'' *The Robert Louis Stevenson Club 150th Birthday Anniversary Book*. Ed. Karen Steele. Edinburgh: Robert Louis Stevenson

Club, 2000. 31–34. This was published earlier as "Unravelled Travel," *Scottish Book Collector*, 5 (1998) 12, 26–27. Scally describes copies of *Virginibus Puerisque* (1881) and *Underwoods* (1887) annotated by RLS for his parents with the places where each of the essays or poems was written. Both are now in the National Library of Scotland, and Scally provides the complete lists for both collections. As he notes, some of the annotations for the essays were included, from an auction catalogue description, in my guide to RLS's prose writings (1980). New information indicates that "Ordered South" (1874) is dated "Davos. 81."—the reference being to the note that Stevenson added at the end when the essay was reprinted in *Virginibus Puerisque* (1881). "Walking Tours," "Some Portraits by Raeburn," and "The English Admirals" are annotated "Edinburgh." "Æs Triplex" is designated "Gretz-London," "El Dorado" as "Swanston (?)," "Pan's Pipes" and "A Plea for Gas Lamps" are both annotated "London," and "Child's Play" as "Swanston." Most of RLS's annotations in *Underwoods* confirm identifications of place already made from other sources in Janet Adam Smith's notes in her edition of RLS's *Collected Poems* (2nd ed., 1971). All of them are included, often with additional details or greater precision, in Roger C. Lewis's edition of RLS's *Collected Poems* (2003).

Hardesty, William H., and David D. Mann. "Robert Louis Stevenson's Art of Revision: 'The Pavilion on the Links' as Rehearsal for *Treasure Island*." *Papers of the Bibliographical Society of America* 82 (1988): 271–86. Hardesty and Mann discuss the many changes that were made between the first appearance of "The Pavilion on the Links" in the *Cornhill Magazine*, September—October 1880, and its publication in book form in the second volume of *New Arabian Nights* (2 vols., 1882). In this, as they acknowledge, they cover in detail ground first broken by Arthur Conan Doyle, "Mr. Stevenson's Methods in Fiction" (*National Review*, January 1890; rpt. in his *Through the Magic Door*, 1907), and G. F. McCleary, "Stevenson's Early Writings," *Fortnightly Review*, n.s. 162 (1950). The most important changes are the dropping of the first paragraph, in which the story was originally framed as being told by the narrator Frank Cassilis to his children about himself and their mother; and the condensation of five paragraphs down to one (from about 400 words down to 42) in what is now the 31st paragraph of the sixth chapter, greatly moderating the description of Clara's father, the defaulting banker Huddelstone. "The omitted passage," Hardesty and Mann write,

> depicts Huddlestone not just as a defaulting banker who has ruined others, but as a religious fanatic; surrounded by devotional books (436), he prays unctuously and tries to get Cassilis to sing a hymn with him (this last provoking Northmour to angry sarcasm) (437). The new paragraph presents a different view of him; he is ill, weary, and frightened.
>
> (279)

The other changes sharpen and improve the characterizations and clarify motivations. In the magazine version, Cassilis is sentimental and priggish and cannot say enough to his children about their mother, "the dear angel of my life": most of this is eliminated in the revision. Clara is made much more decisive, her father less repellent, and Northmour is made even more taciturn and enigmatic. And there are two dozen changes of a word or two, to correct misreadings of RLS's handwriting or to improve clarity or precision. The connections that Hardesty and Mann perceive with *Treasure Island*, which RLS was writing at about the same time as he was revising this story and which, in turn, he began revising not long after the revised version of the story appeared, consist not only of similarities of events, characters, and themes (unexpected danger from without, treasure, siege, isolation, the escape of "the antagonist/rival/ double" without punishment, and "ambiguity in the interpretation of events"). In revising "The Pavilion on the Links" Stevenson was also discovering ways, at the level of individual words and sentences, as well as generally, to make first-person narration more precise, more immediate, and faster moving, using these discoveries to good effect in the clean, efficient narrative style of *Treasure Island.*

Gelder, Kenneth. "Robert Louis Stevenson's Revisions to 'The Merry Men'." *Studies in Scottish Literature* 21 (1986): 262–87. RLS finished a complete draft of "The Merry Men" at Pitlochry in mid-July 1881 (RLS to W. E. Henley, mid-July 1881, Letter 828), and he made at least some revisions to it at Davos that winter, before its first publication in two installments in the *Cornhill Magazine*, June—July 1882. He revised it again for the collection *The Merry Men and Other Tales* (London: Chatto and Windus, 1887). Gelder presents a complete collation of the two published versions: no manuscripts survive. The collation shows that misprints were corrected, and, assuming that all of the differences are due to RLS rather than to the compositors, that RLS also made many changes in details such as punctuation. For example, in the book version, hyphens always appear in compound words, and there are consistent changes in the rendering of Scottish pronunciations: *couldnae* becomes *couldna*, *neednae* becomes *needna*, and so on. "Most of the substantial changes," Gelder writes, "affect those passages presenting dialogue between Charles Darnaway and Mary Ellen (in chs. 2 and 4) and those passages concerning the negro or 'black man' (in ch. 5)." In the *Cornhill Magazine* version, Charles proposes marriage to Mary, who accepts without hesitation. In the book version, Charles cannot put his proposal into so many words and Mary, preoccupied with her father, seeks a delay: "Let me be a while: let me be the way I am; it'll not be you that loses by the waiting!" Their relations, later in the story, are also made more tentative.

The shipwreck survivor is made mysterious rather than comical. In the *Cornhill Magazine* version, he is generally called the "negro," is smiling, talkative, child-like, and subservient. Describing their first encounter, Charles Darnaway explicitly recalls Crusoe's man Friday: "It was plain that we should have to rely upon the language of looks and gestures; and I was reminded of a book I had read, *Robinson Crusoe*, where, upon an island in a far part of the world, another Englishman relates difficulties of the same nature with another negro." "For all his height, which was almost gigantic, and his strength and activity, which seemed truly formidable, he appealed to me rather as a child than as a full-grown man." In the book-form version, published five years later, the survivor is consistently called the "black." The reference to *Robinson Crusoe* is gone, and the survivor now conducts himself "with a grave obeisance like a fallen king." RLS also removed details underscoring his uncle Gordon Darnaway's religious background, thereby making Charles's role in his death harder to assess. A whole paragraph in the *Cornhill Magazine* version describes the uncle's drunken dance as a ship is wrecked and his singing, among other tunes, "old Scottish psalms and verses of the Psalms of David." Young Rorie, it is noted later, "had not been fed, in youth, like my uncle among the Cameronians, on tales of the devil appearing in the similitude of a black man, and, with cozening words and specious pretexts, luring men to ruin.'' Both of these passages were omitted from the book version.

James Payn published "The Merry Men" in the *Cornhill Magazine* without the benefit of RLS's proof corrections. Most of the mistakes were in the June installment, among them (as Ernest Mehew notes in the Yale Letters) "gorgie" for "girzie," "Ben Ryan" for "Ben Kyaw," "brean" for "ocean," and the ch. 3 heading "Lad and Leo in Sandag Bay" for "Land and Sea in Sandag Bay." There are fewer mistakes in the July 1882 installment, but RLS made changes in these last two chapters for the book publication (1887)—see Letter 1027, n. 2, and Letter 1765. The error in the June 1882 installment ("horror of the charnel brean" for "horror of the charnel ocean") led to a question from James A. H. Murray, then at work on the *New English Dictionary*, inquiring what the word meant. See RLS to Murray, 21 February 1887, Letter 1765.

Pierce, Jason A. "The Belle Lettrist and the People's Publisher; or, The Context of *Treasure Island*'s First-Form Publication." *Victorian Periodicals Review* 31 (Winter 1998): 356–68. Drawing upon original issues of *Young Folks* and the *Times* obituary (26 Feb. 1906) of its editor and publisher James Henderson, Jason Pierce provides an informative account of the weekly children's paper in which *Treasure Island* first appeared. He even reproduces (presumably from *Young Folks*; no source is given) a portrait of Henderson. Among the most successful of its kind, *Young Folks* was one of more than seventy children's magazines founded in Britain between 1865 and 1875, and, in lasting 26$\frac{1}{2}$ years, until 1897, it was among the longest-lived. Although chiefly aimed at boys, *Young Folks* always included at least one domestic story for girls, as often as not by a woman author. As Pierce notes, its full title at the time that *Treasure Island* was serialized was *Young Folks: A Boys' and Girls' Paper of Instructive and Entertaining Literature*. In addition to *Young Folks*, Henderson also published the successful provincial newspaper, the *Weekly Budget: A Family Newspaper for the People*, the weekly *South London Press*, and at least two other successful weekly penny magazines, *Scraps* and *Funny Folks*.

Pierce's account of the reception of *Treasure Island* by the original readers of *Young Folks* is not quite correct, however. As Pierce says, *Treasure Island* was not at first very well-liked. But he is wrong in saying that the response that he quotes from "Our Letter-Box," 19 November 1881, by an assistant editor named Clinton, was Clinton's first defense of the story. It was his second, a fact which suggests that the disapproval was of some duration. Clinton's first defense had appeared the previous week; RLS refers to it with amusement, especially for the style, in a letter to Edmund Gosse, 9 November 1881, Letter 866; and it was in exactly the patronizing tone that Pierce says was not adopted. In the 12 November issue Clinton had assured a young correspondent: "That which you condemn is really the best story now appearing in our paper, and the impress of an able writer is stamped on every paragraph of *The Treasure Island*. You will probably share this opinion when you have read a little more of it" (qtd. in Letter 866, n. 6). The following week, in the reply quoted by Pierce, Clinton was simply being more emphatic: "We cannot speak too highly in praise of the story . . . [and] can only believe that they who fail to discover marked merit in it are deficient in power to recognize what is really good." Whether as a result of these editorial defenses or for other reasons, letters about *Treasure Island* from its first readers seem to have become somewhat more positive toward the end of the run.

Pierce is also, I think, mistaken in the account that he gives of the change of title from *The Sea-Cook* to *Treasure Island*. Quoting, for reasons unknown, J. A. Steuart rather than the original publication, Pierce says that in the 24 September 1881 issue of *Young Folks* there appeared an announcement that in the next week's issue, 1 October 1881, would commence *"Treasure Island . . .* a deeply interesting romance of sailors in the olden style." Professor A. H. Japp was the link between RLS and the publisher James Henderson in London. In the account of his role that he gave many years later, Japp said that "the numbers of *Young Folks* were printed about a fortnight in advance of the date that they bear under the title." From this remark, Pierce concludes that the 24 September issue announcing the title *Treasure Island* "must have been set in type sometime around September 10"—two or three weeks before Stevenson and the editor and publisher of *Young Folks* James Henderson "met or had any direct contact with one another." Therefore, Pierce reasons, both Henderson and RLS must have been mistaken in saying, as each did in separate accounts, that it was not until RLS visited Henderson in London, in late September 1881, that RLS's own title *The Sea-Cook* was discarded, supposedly in accord with Henderson's suggestion, inspired by the fact that Treasure Island was the title on RLS's map. Pierce thinks that, on the contrary, "the story's published title was not suggested by the publisher and agreed to by the author but instead was created by the publisher and perforce accepted by the author. Though the story of *Treasure Island* was Stevenson's, the title was Henderson's" (361). The same is probably true, Pierce continues, of the attribution "By Captain George North," which, by Pierce's arithmetic, again using Japp's two-week estimate, would have been printed by 17 September, also before Stevenson's arrival in London. This too, says Pierce, was probably created by Henderson or an associate "as a marketing ploy" and, like the title, it was also presented to Stevenson in late September as a fait accompli. The first installment had already been printed. To think otherwise, Pierce continues, "would be to ignore the dynamic relationship between a powerful publisher and a relatively inexperienced fiction-writer."

Japp did not work for or with Henderson, however. In fact, until he brought him the manuscript, Japp says, he and Henderson were not even acquainted, so that the intimacy Japp suggests he had with Henderson's printing practices is at least questionable. As Ernest Mehew notes in the Yale Letters, inferring this from the fact that RLS, then in Davos, commented on the 12 November issue in letters to Gosse and Henderson written before that issue date, copies of *Young Folks* appeared a week before the nominal issue date (Letter 866, n. 2). Thus, the issue announcing the title as *Treasure Island* would have appeared on or about 17 September. Using Japp's figure of two weeks, this would push back the supposed date of printing to 3 September—three days before RLS, in Scotland, wrote to Japp accepting Henderson's offer to publish and conveying through Japp his hope that he would receive proofs or his manuscript to use as he continued the story (RLS to A. H. Japp, 6 September 1881, Letters 846, 847). Henderson must have been very bold indeed to go to press with the announcement of a story for the following week that he had only just made an offer on. Japp also says that the numbers were ''printed'' two weeks before the nominal issue date. If this were true, Henderson would have had to store all of the printed copies of each issue somewhere for a week or ten days until it was time to distribute them. Pierce does not explain why he accepts Japp's claim of a two-week lead time but backs away from this second assertion. He says that ''the new title was set in type sometime around September 10'' (361), but not that it was printed. If so, the text was obviously not then final. What is set in type can be altered in type, and at no great effort or expense. So the notion of two weeks also falls to the ground. There is simply no good reason to think that the installments of *Young Folks*, like most periodicals then and now, were not printed in the day or two before the day of publication—up to which time (and even afterwards) changes could still be made easily.

Treasure Island was the title under which Henderson chose to announce the book in the issue dated 24 September, published on or about 17 September. In this he was following the name on the map, and he may have done so without consulting RLS. But by then author and publisher had been in touch, through Japp and no doubt directly, for almost a fortnight; it was only an announcement; and Stevenson would be in London returning corrected proofs of the first installment before a final decision was necessary on the title and on the choice of authorial pseudonym if one were to be adopted. Neither RLS nor Henderson ever mentioned the announcement or who thought up the name Captain George North. Nor was it ever hinted by anyone in a position to know that what led to the change of title and the choice of pseudonym was the fact that the first installment had already been printed, not only set in type, by 17 September (it is not clear whether Pierce himself believes this) or that Henderson then took advantage of this fact and of his supposed standing as ''a powerful publisher'' to impose his wishes on RLS.

At the end of September RLS was returning proofs of the first installment, so it must have still been in type, not yet printed, and he was hardly the ''relatively inexperienced fiction-writer'' that Pierce paints him as being. He had been publishing stories for nearly five years, and in magazines considerably more prestigious than *Young Folks*. He and Henderson both emphasize the cordiality of their relationship, in fact, and in both of their accounts it sounds more like a friendly collaboration between colleagues than anything else. Japp's comments about the fortnight's lead time make some sense if they are taken to refer to galley proofs of the text, all the more so given that on many pages the text had to flow artfully around one or several illustrations and that such a practice would gain time for this. The pages themselves no doubt could and did remain open for corrections almost until the day of publication. If so, the stories told both by Henderson and RLS fit perfectly with the 1 October nominal publication date of the first installment. RLS's letter formally agreeing to publication is dated 24 September and despite its Edinburgh address was probably handed by RLS to Henderson personally in London (Letter 853). There is, in short, no good reason to disbelieve the received version told by both of the principals. In the issue dated 24 September Henderson went no further than to announce a title, *Treasure Island*, that he thought his author would approve. When they met personally, a week later, proof changes in the actual text had yet to be made, leaving RLS free to approve or disapprove the change of title (and perhaps the pseudonym) that his publisher had suggested. He was pleased with the change and let it stand.

Hardesty, Patricia Whaley, William H. Hardesty, III, and David Mann. "Doctoring the Doctor: How Stevenson Altered the Second Narrator of *Treasure Island*." *Studies in Scottish Literature* 21 (1986): 1–22. Not long after the serial version of *Treasure Island* had completed its run, RLS (who may have begun rewriting already) wrote to Sidney Colvin that Fanny was now pleased with the beginning and the end and that "only some six chapters situate about the fork, midst or privates of the tale [need] to be rewritten" (RLS to Colvin, 13 February 1882, Letter 910). RLS made many changes throughout the book, these authors write, but those that he made in the characterization of Dr. Livesey are "the most extensive that Stevenson did in the novel" (2). Hardesty and her associates present and discuss all of the changes that affect Livesey, and they offer a complete collation of the three chapters in which Livesey takes over the narration, comparing the version in *Young Folks* with chs. 16–18 in book form. In these chapters, and before and after them, RLS "carefully rewrote the doctor's narrative to make him less stuffy, less moralistic, less rhetorical, and less didactic . . . to reduce the doctor's satiric or foolish elements . . . [and to make him] less garrulous and more a mentor to Jim" (6, 10, 11). These changes differentiate Livesey, in the book, much better from the comical Captain Smollett, and they enhance the impression of forthright, intelligent reasonableness made by his clearer, less pompous narration. Many of the changes that RLS made simply to improve and clarify the narration also serve these ends.

Mann, David D. and William H. Hardesty, III. "Stevenson's Revisions of *Treasure Island*: 'Writing Down the Whole Particulars.' " *Text* 3 (1987): 377–92. Hardesty and Mann discuss slightly more than a dozen passages in which Stevenson greatly improved the periodical version in revising it for the first book-form edition. Deletions keep the focus on the action—for example, at the beginning of ch. 24, "The Cruise of the Coracle," where RLS deletes from the end of the fourth paragraph an unnecessary sentence describing the sea lions wrestling and dropping into the water, and deletes after the end of the ninth paragraph three additional paragraphs in which Jim tells how the gulls followed his boat, that he had a biscuit for breakfast, taking care that it was dry, not soaked in sea-water, and that the sun rose as he was finishing. Additions make the characters more complex, odder, and less stereotypical, and in Jim's narration they make his experiences more vivid by presenting what he dreamed and imagined, not only what he did and thought. For example, following (but not to the letter) a suggestion made by his father, RLS added to the passage beginning with the 20th paragraph in ch. 15 slightly more than 100 words (after the words "to hear of") in which Ben Gunn recalls his mother and his own curious adventures with piety. In the *Young Folks* version, the passage reads simply: " 'Jim, Jim,' says he, quite pleased apparently. 'Well, now, Jim, I've lived that rough as you'd be ashamed to hear of. But it were Providence that put me here. I've thought it all out. You don't catch me tasting rum so much." In the first chapter of the book version, RLS also more than doubled the length of the eighth paragraph, which originally had consisted only of the first two sentences. He has Jim go on to tell some of the actual ways in which he imagined "the seafaring man with one leg" might look:

Now the leg would be cut off at the knee, now at the hip; now he was a monstrous kind of a creature who had never had but the one leg, and that in the middle of his body. To see him leap and run and pursue me over hedge and ditch was the worst of nightmares. And altogether I paid pretty dearly for my monthly fourpenny, in the shape of these abominable fancies.

The only thing more chilling than reading this passage is to hear Orson Welles's reading of it in the broadcast adaptation for the Mercury Theatre on the Air, 18 July 1938. The hour-long script consists almost solely of Stevenson's own words. *Treasure Island* was the second broadcast in this series (*Dracula* was the first), which is now best known for the Halloween-night adaptation of *War of the Worlds* later in the same year.

Angus, David. "Youth on the Prow: The First Publication of *Treasure Island*." *Studies in Scottish Literature* 25 (1990): 82–99. Between the version of *Treasure Island* serialized in *Young Folks* and the first book-form edition there are "about 250 alterations to the original printed text, of varying degrees of importance" (84). These are now available in the Textual Notes of the edition by Wendy Katz (Edinburgh UP, 1998) and most of the changes have been discussed in the articles by William H. Hardesty and David Mann. But it is convenient to have a list and general discussion of them here as well.

Menikoff, Barry. "Toward the Production of a Text: Time, Space, and *David Balfour*." *Studies in the Novel* 27 (1995): 351–62. Drawing chiefly on letters and other records in the Charles Scribner's Sons Archives at Princeton and in the Beinecke Collection at Yale, Menikoff describes "the byzantine nature of the publication process . . . the labyrinth of negotiations and correspondence that swirled around" each of Stevenson's later books as, and usually long before, each became ready. His focus is on the novel that Stevenson called *David Balfour*, published in book form on 1 September 1893, which, of course, Cassell's insisted on calling *Catriona*, as it is called to this day in Britain—a change that Charles Scribner for the very same reason (to avoid confusion) just as emphatically insisted would be

> *very very* unwise; it would seriously cripple the book here. David Balfour is the name of the hero well-known in "Kidnapped" and at once associates the new book with perhaps Stevenson's best—whereas the new title suggested has no advantages and would greatly complicate matters owing to the previous serial publication under another name.
> (Charles Scribner to Lemuel Bangs, 21 May 1893, Princeton; qtd. 353)

Stevenson finished *David Balfour* on 26 September 1892, remarking to Sidney Colvin on the 30th: "*David Balfour* done, and its author along with it, or nearly so" (Letter 2463; the date of completion comes from RLS's mother's diary). But by then S. S. McClure had been begging RLS and others for more than two months to send him at least the beginning of the story, in manuscript, so as not to hold up newspaper serialization in Washington, New York, San Francisco, and seemingly also in Australia, Britain, and the West Indies, and magazine publication in the girls' magazine *Atalanta* beginning in December, a starting date later revised to November (McClure to RLS, 21 July 1892, Beinecke 5199; qtd. 355). "If I fail to receive copy of the opening chapters of David Balfour by next post, I shall have to postpone publication,'' McClure wrote to RLS in desperation on 10 September, following this letter with another on 4 October complaining that the terms he was now being offered by Baxter were ''galling and humiliating'' and explaining his lengthy syndication and publication process in detail (Beinecke 5202, 5203; qtd. 355–56). As Menikoff remarks, whatever might have been McClure's usual practice, in this instance he made arrangements before he had copy. McClure ''gambled that Stevenson would finish the novel in time to provide him with copy for his client newspapers. But it got just a little tight at the end'' (358).

The process for creating the book-form edition from the text that was published serially in *Atalanta* was equally complicated and equally driven by time, with Colvin acting as a general go-between linking the author, in Samoa, with his publishers on two continents on both sides of the Atlantic. As they became available, Colvin sent galley-proofs of the Cassell edition annotated with his own comments to RLS, then conveyed RLS's final corrections to the two publishers as he received the corrections back. Not until 22 July 1893 did Colvin have the last of RLS's corrections, remarking to Baxter with some vexation that there were many fewer than had been expected, ''so that for all the alterations he [RLS] has made, the book might as well have been out two months ago'' (Beinecke 4256; qtd. 360). Chaotic, time-driven, and at times acrimonious though the process was—Menikoff remarks rightly that it even had its ''Chaplinesque'' moments (361)—it is notable how important it was, to all concerned, to do right by Stevenson's words. As Charles Scribner wrote to his London agent Lemuel Bangs in two letters a month apart: ''You have sent us the *Cassell* proofs and three copies [corrected issues] of *Atalanta* but we must of course wait for Stevenson's final corrections before publishing''—and, a month later: ''We shall simply await the final corrected proofs of text & map and hurry the work as much as possible after their receipt'' (16 June, 13 July 1893, Princeton; qtd. 361).

Exhibition Catalogues

Scally, John. *Pictures of the Mind: The Illustrated Robert Louis Stevenson*. Edinburgh: Canongate/National Library of Scotland, 1994. In this beautifully produced and designed collection of full-color and black-and-white reproductions, Scally presents more than 125 illustrations, frontispieces, and book covers published during Stevenson's lifetime and throughout the twentieth century, from the first editions of *An Inland Voyage* (1878), *Travels With a Donkey* (1879), and *The Silverado Squatters* (1883), the *Young Folks* and first illustrated editions of *Treasure Island* and *Kidnapped*—all the way to Ralph Steadman's *Treasure Island* (1985) and Barry Moser's *Dr. Jekyll and Mr. Hyde* (1990). Also included are five of RLS's own drawings, regrettably none of them in color. These include his childish sketch, done and colored at age six, of the Israelites going out of Egypt (''The History of Moses,'' National Library of Scotland), the front cover of the first issue of ''The Sunbeam Magazine'' (age 15, Yale), one of his sketches in the Cévennes (Yale), and two of the woodcuts that he did at Davos. The wonderful picture of Jim Hawkins in the rigging of the

Hispaniola ready to fire his pistols down at Israel Hands, drawn by the French illustra-tor George Roux and used in the first illustrated edition of *Treasure Island*, is repro-duced to good effect at twice its original size, although it is incorrectly attributed to the engraver rather than to the illustrator, whose signatures in the French edition were removed in the English edition (28). Roux also did the illustrated title page, which is also included but without attribution (27).

Giroud, Vincent. *R.L.S.: A Centenary Exhibition at the Beinecke Rare Book & Manuscript Library Commemorating the Death of Robert Louis Stevenson.* New Ha-ven: Yale University, 1994. This is a well-produced catalogue of an exhibition of more than one hundred high points from the finest collection of Stevenson materials in the world. Twenty-four pages are devoted to black-and-white and photographic illustrations, and these include manuscript pages, notably a leaf from RLS's notebook draft of *Dr. Jekyll and Mr Hyde*; book covers both in paper and cloth; the front pages of both *Kidnapped* and *The Black* Arrow as they first appeared serially in *Young Folks*; sketches done by RLS in the Cévennes and the Marquesas; and a charcoal sketch of RLS by John Singer Sargent probably done in 1885 and previously repro-duced only as the frontispiece to Volume III of the Beinecke Collection Catalogue (1956). There is also a generous selection from the many photographs and other images of RLS at Beinecke, all of which are still uncatalogued except in general terms. Especially notable are the reproductions, for the first time, of RLS's mother's leather accordion folder, pictures in place, holding the twelve photographs known since they were first published in the Edinburgh Edition by the tooled label on the cover, ''From Baby to Bar,'' and four of the earliest photographs in it; and the original glass plate of the photograph of RLS looking up from his writing-desk at Bournemouth, a snapshot taken by his stepson Lloyd Osbourne at Bournemouth, here reproduced next to what appears to be a cabinet print of the same image. One error among the captions is that the two photographs facing page 50 are not ''Scenes from life at Vailima'' but of life at the house that RLS rented at Waikiki, Honolulu, in 1889. Both are reproduced, from other sources, cropped and greatly inferior in detail, in McGaw, *Stevenson in Hawaii* (Honolulu: U of Hawaii P, 1950) 48–49, and else-where. Apart from this catalogue, the only considerable use of the many photographs and other images in the Beinecke Collection is in Edward Rice, *Journey to Upolu: Robert Louis Stevenson, Victorian Rebel* (New York: Dodd, Mead, 1974) to be dis-cussed in the section on biographies.

On the front cover, in color, appears Beinecke's copy of the portrait of RLS by Count Girolamo Nerli, well and dramatically cropped to show only RLS's head and shoulders. This was not, however, ''painted from life in Samoa in 1892''—there are five versions of this portrait, only one of which, now in the Scottish National Portrait Gallery, Edinburgh, was done from life—but is a copy that Nerli made in Melbourne, sometime between 1902 and 1904. See the discussions of Nerli and this portrait by Roger Neill (1997) and Peter Entwisle, et al. (1988) in my forthcoming section on biographies. The fold-out end-papers/cover depict, also in color, a large tapa that every RLS scholar who has worked at the Beinecke Library knows and loves, as it has been there since the building opened in 1964 and hangs, now as always, on the long wall just outside of the reading room. My own research in the last year, however, suggests that it is not (as we have always thought and as is stated in the caption in the catalogue and on the wall) a ceremonial tapa presented to RLS in 1890, when he had only recently arrived in Samoa. The tapa that fits this description is in the Monterey State Historic Park Collection, California, and it may even have been a souvenir from Niue, acquired or commissioned during the *Janet Nichol* voyage in 1890. The Beinecke tapa appears to be of Fijian origin and may have been given to RLS by a visitor in 1894. Whatever its origins may prove to be, it is an old and lovely friend nevertheless and is beautifully reproduced.

Calder, Jenni, ed. *Treasure Islands: A Robert Louis Stevenson Centenary Anthology.* Edinburgh: National Museums of Scotland, 1994. This is the color catalogue of a surprising, thoughtful, and wide-ranging centenary exhibition that Jenni Calder created for the National Museums of Scotland in 1994. The catalogue is beautifully produced, and the images are remarkable and splendid. Calder weaves together short passages from RLS's letters and works with historical images—some of them long before Stevenson's own time, others from contemporaries whom he never knew, such as Gauguin, others familiar from more conventional Stevenson contexts, and juxtaposes them with striking contemporary photographs and paintings, all of this to remind us in his own words of the breathtaking scope and meticulous detail of Stevenson's achievement. The common thread is islands, in Stevenson's stories, novels, essays, and letters, and Calder rightly hopes that the excerpts and pictures ''will tempt the reader to ask for more, and go to the books from which the extracts come'' (13). The pictures come from a wide range of sources, not only from collections in Scotland.

Mesenhöller, Peter, and Alison Devine Nordström, eds. *Picturing Paradise: Colonial Photography of Samoa, 1875 to 1925.* Daytona Beach: Daytona Beach Community College, 1995. More than fifty beautifully-reproduced photographs from an exhibition of more than 150 items are accompanied by substantial and informative essays by the editors and others and a complete checklist. Commercial photography was well established in Apia by the time RLS arrived at the end of 1889. John Davis came first, setting up business there in the 1870s, and he did well enough to hire an assistant, Alfred John Tattersall, from New Zealand in 1886. Davis died around 1893, and Tattersall continued the business until 1949. The stock of his photographs and Davis's was destroyed by a hurricane in 1966, but a great many of them survive in other collections. Thomas Andrew, also a New Zealander, arrived in 1891 and remained in Apia until his death in 1939. After about 1916, however, Andrew seems to have relinquished photography for business. RLS, of course, was a popular subject, and most of the well-known photographs of Vailima, RLS, and the household are by Davis. One of them is reproduced here (101) and a small section of the exhibition was devoted to RLS. Also included are two fine photographs by Joe Strong, from an exhibition of 19 of his Samoan photographs originally at the Bishop Museum, Honolulu, in 1893 (25, 77). As the editors point out, these photographs of Samoa are both a record and a revelation of attitudes. They show much about RLS's physical environment and the view publicly taken of Samoans during the 1890s as well as in the years before and after.

INDEX

(Page numbers in italics represent illustrations)